**Federal Document
Depository Item
DO NOT DISCARD**

345

Combat Operations

TAKING THE OFFENSIVE
October 1966 to October 1967

NORTH VIETNAM

DEMARCATION LINE

QUANG TRI

L A O S

THUA THIEN ● Hue   I CTZ

SOUTH CHINA SEA

● Da Nang

T H A I L A N D

QUANG NAM

QUANG TIN

QUANG NGAI

KONTUM

S O U T H
V I E T N A M

BINH DINH

PLEIKU

C A M B O D I A

PHU BON

PHU YEN

*Tonle
Sap*

DARLAC

II CTZ

*KHANH
HOA*

QUANG DUC   *TUYEN DUC*

● Da Lat

*NINH
THUAN*   ● Cam Ranh

*BINH
LONG*   *PHUOC
LONG*

TAY NINH   III CTZ   *LAM DONG*

*BINH
DUONG*   *LONG
KHANH*   *BINH THUAN*

*HAU
NGHIA*   *BIEN
HOA*   *BINH
TUY*

✪ SAIGON   *SOUTH
CHINA SEA*

*CHAU
DOC*   *KIEN PHONG*   *KIEN TUONG*   *LONG AN*   *GIA
DINH*   *PHUOC TUY*

*AN
GIANG*   *SA
DEC*   *DINH TUONG*   *GO CONG* ● Vung Tau

KIEN GIANG   *VINH LONG*   *KIEN HOA*

*PHONG
DINH*   *VINH BINH*

*GULF OF
THAILAND*   IV CTZ   *CHUONG
THIEN*   *BA XUYEN*

BAC LIEU

AN XUYEN

SOUTH VIETNAM
1966–1967

———— Corps Tactical Zone Boundary

·········· Administrative Boundary

Hue   Autonomous Municipality

0   150 Miles

0   150 Kilometers

United States Army in Vietnam

Combat Operations

TAKING THE OFFENSIVE
October 1966 to October 1967

by

George L. MacGarrigle

MILITARY INSTRVCTION

Center of Military History
United States Army
Washington, D.C., 1998

Library of Congress Cataloging-in-Publication Data

MacGarrigle, George L. , 1930–
     Combat operations : taking the offensive, October 1966 to October
1967 / George L. MacGarrigle.
          p.   cm. — (United States Army in Vietnam)
     Includes bibliographical references (p.   ) and index.
     1. Vietnamese Conflict, 1961–1975—United States.   2. Vietnamese
Conflict, 1961–1975—Campaigns.   3. United States Army—History—
Vietnamese Conflict, 1961–1975.   I. Title.   II. Series.
DS558.M3   1998
  959.704'3373—DC21   98–9975
                                                                          CIP

CMH Pub 91–4

First Printing

For sale by the U.S. Government Printing Office
Superintendent of Documents, Mail Stop: SSOP, Washington, DC 20402-9328
ISBN 0-16-049540-7

United States Army in Vietnam

Jeffrey J. Clarke, General Editor

Advisory Committee
(As of September 1997)

. . . to Those Who Served

Foreword

Well before the end of the American involvement in the Vietnam War, the Center of Military History committed itself to the production of a comprehensive historical series documenting the U.S. Army's role in that conflict. This volume is the seventh of those works to appear and the first of the combat histories. Still to come are additional battle histories, a study examining the war from the perspective of the headquarters that oversaw field operations, a work that discusses logistics, another that examines the engineer effort, and a final study that tells the story of U.S. advice and support to the South Vietnamese between 1960 and 1965.

Covering combat operations during the critical year that began in October 1966, this volume tells the story of how one of the best armies the United States has ever fielded took on both the enemy's guerrilla units and his main forces and time and again drove them from the battlefield. It also shows, however, that the enemy retained the initiative, fighting only when it suited his purposes and retreating with impunity across South Vietnam's borders into Laos and Cambodia, where his sanctuaries were inviolable to American forces.

It is a story that goes to the very essence of the Vietnam War, filled with the triumphs that Americans have always expected of their soldiers, but also with a measure of the inevitable bitterness and frustration inherent in an irresolute conflict. I believe there is much here for both soldier and civilian to learn. I commend the book to all who seek answers about the war, and especially to those who find themselves engaged in military operations that place great demands on their initiative, skill, and devotion. This first combat volume is dedicated to the memory of those who sacrificed so much.

Washington, D.C.
24 April 1998

JOHN W. MOUNTCASTLE
Brigadier General, USA
Chief of Military History

The Author

George L. MacGarrigle graduated from the United States Military
Academy and received an M.A. in history from Pennsylvania State
University. Commissioned as a second lieutenant in 1952, he served with
the 1st Cavalry Division in Korea as a rifle company commander and
again with the 1st Cavalry Division during the Vietnam War as an infantry
battalion commander. He directed the military history program while
assigned to the ROTC at Pennsylvania State University and has taught
American history at the University of Virginia, Arlington County. He
served as a civilian historian with the Center of Military History, where he
coauthored *Black Soldier/White Army: The 24th Infantry Regiment in Korea.*
Among his other works, MacGarrigle has written two narratives entitled
Aleutians and *Central Burma* for the Center's series The U.S. Army
Campaigns of World War II. He retired from the Center in 1997.

Preface

This book describes a single year in a long war. By October 1966 the American troop buildup in Vietnam, which had begun eighteen months earlier, had reached a point where the war effort could move beyond simply defending South Vietnam. For the first time, General William C. Westmoreland had enough arms and men to take the initiative from the enemy. He believed that the next twelve months would show significant progress on all fronts. There would be no quick victory, however. Westmoreland understood that he faced a prolonged war of attrition, one that would test the Army's abilities and America's staying power.

Well aware of American intentions, North Vietnam stepped up the infiltration of its own troops into the South, aiming to wage its own war of attrition to force the United States out of the conflict. While the insurgency in the South remained the cornerstone of Communist strategy, it was increasingly overshadowed by main force military operations. These circumstances set the stage for intensified combat. How well both sides fared during this year is the subject of this volume.

In the course of my research and writing, I have received the generous support of many individuals. The late Charles B. MacDonald, former chief of the Current History Branch, laid the foundations for the U.S. Army's Vietnam series and provided valuable advice and assistance early in this project. His successors, Drs. Stanley L. Falk, John Schlight, and Jeffrey J. Clarke, also made important contributions to this volume. But my last chief, Dr. Joel D. Meyerson, deserves special credit for bestowing final shape to the project. Taking time off from his own Vietnam volume, he moved the manuscript through its late-stage revisions and the innumerable steps toward publication.

There are many others to whom I owe a debt of gratitude. The successive chiefs of the Histories Division at the Center of Military History—Cols. John E. Jessup, James F. Ransone, and James W. Dunn; Lt. Col. Richard O. Perry; and Cols. Robert H. Sholly, William T. Bowers, and Clyde L. Jonas—provided important support throughout. So did successive Chiefs of Military History—Brig. Gens. James L. Collins, William A. Stofft, Douglas Kinnard, Harold W. Nelson, and the present chief, John W. Mountcastle. My thanks extend to my colleagues in the Histories Division who were always willing to share their research and knowledge: Charles R. Anderson, Lt. Col. John D. Bergen, Dr. John M. Carland, Vincent H. Demma, Dr. William M. Hammond, Dr. David W. Hogan, Dr. Richard A. Hunt, Jefferson L. Powell, Dr. Edgar F. Raines, Dr. Ronald H. Spector, and Lt. Col. Adrian G. Traas. Special thanks go to Drs. Andrew J. Birtle and Clayton D. Laurie, and especially to Dale Andrade, for their work late in the project.

Those most helpful outside the Center include Richard L. Boylan, National Archives and Records Administration; Dr. Richard J. Sommers, U.S. Army Military History Institute; Col. Ray L. Bowers, Office of Air Force History; Dr. Jack Shulimson, History and Museums Division of the U.S. Marine Corps; and Glen E. Helms, U.S. Naval Historical Center.

The study also benefited from the advice of the official U.S. Army review panel chaired by Dr. Jeffrey J. Clarke, Chief Historian, and including General William B. Rosson; Lt. Gen. Edward M. Flanagan; Brig. Gen. Frank H. Akers; Drs. Eric M. Bergerud, Jack Shulimson, Graham A. Cosmas, and Joel D. Meyerson; John W. Elsberg; and Thomas W. Collier.

Gustenia B. Scott and Gabrielle S. Patrick of the Histories Division typed several drafts of the manuscript. John W. Elsberg, Editor in Chief, provided guidelines on style and format. I give special credit to my editors, Diane Sedore Arms and Diane M. Donovan, for their valuable work under very heavy time pressure; to my cartographer, S. L. Dowdy, whose maps are essential to this study; and to my book designer, John Birmingham, who brought talent and good cheer to the layout. Thanks also go to Catherine A. Heerin, chief of the Editorial Branch; Arthur S. Hardyman, chief of the Graphics Branch; Beth MacKenzie; Frank R. Shirer; and indexer Susan Carroll.

Finally, my wife, Lois, deserves special mention for enduring a husband who at times seemed more attentive to his manuscript than to her.

The author alone is responsible for the interpretations and conclusions in this volume, as well as for any errors that may appear. The views expressed herein do not necessarily reflect the official policy or position of the Departments of the Army and Defense or the U.S. government.

Washington, D.C.   GEORGE L. MacGARRIGLE
24 April 1998

Contents

PART ONE

Toward the Offensive

PART TWO

Out From Saigon

PART THREE

Farther North

PART FOUR

Looking for Momentum in I Corps

PART FIVE

Trouble in Mid-Country

PART SIX

Protracted War in III Corps

PART SEVEN

Winding Up

Table

Maps

Illustrations

Illustrations courtesy of the following sources: pp. 18, 161, 323, Vietnam Center, Texas Tech University, Lubbock, Texas; 26, 218, Lyndon Baines Johnson Library, Austin, Texas; 42, U.S. Army Museum of Hawaii, Schofield Barracks, Hawaii; 129, 371, 380, *The 25th Infantry Division: "Tropic Lightning" in Vietnam, 1966–1967*; 166, U.S. Army Military History Institute; 207, National Infantry Museum, Fort Benning, Georgia; 211, *1st Air Cavalry Division: Memoirs of the First Team, Vietnam, August 1965–December 1969*; 222, Robert W. Komer; and 334, Sharp and Westmoreland, *Report on the War in Vietnam (As of 30 June 1968)*. All other illustrations from the files of Department of Defense.

PART ONE

Toward the Offensive

1

An Expanding War

In the fall of 1966 General William C. Westmoreland, commander of the U.S. Military Assistance Command, Vietnam (MACV), had reason to be optimistic about the Vietnam War. Because of the rapid buildup of American troops that had begun eighteen months earlier, North Vietnamese and Viet Cong main force units no longer threatened Saigon with imminent collapse. South Vietnam's faltering army was back on its feet, and American units were taking the offensive. Westmoreland believed that the buildup had succeeded in "disrupt[ing] the enemy's efforts to prepare his battlefield [and had] thrown his plans off balance." But it was during the following year, 1967, that he expected significant results. "During the period 1 November 1966 to 1 May 1967," he told his superiors at Pacific Command headquarters in Honolulu, Hawaii, "we will maintain and increase the momentum of our operations. Our strategy will be one of a general offensive." In October 1966, for the first time since the spring of 1965, when the American phase of the Vietnam War began in earnest, Westmoreland felt he had sufficient troops to strike at the enemy, pin him down, and inflict heavy casualties.[1]

Westmoreland's optimism was not wholly shared on the American home front, however, because the nature of the war was not clearly understood. As the conflict raged, it was difficult for the general public to observe any achievements according to the traditional military bench marks of progress—cities and towns taken, rivers crossed, and territories won. Instead, because Vietnam's hot climate, swampy coast, and mountainous interior militated against the modern technology of an army organized, equipped, and trained to fight a conventional, mechanized conflict, American combat units had been forced to fight a grueling war of attrition.

At the same time, successfully dealing with their military opponents, a mix of light infantry forces and full- and part-time guerrillas, had also proved difficult. Yet, American ground forces, Army and

---

[1] Msg, Commander, U.S. Military Assistance Command, Vietnam (COMUSMACV), to Commander in Chief, Pacific (CINCPAC), 26 Aug 66, sub: Concept of Military Operations in SVN, Historians files, U.S. Army Center of Military History (CMH), Washington, D.C.

General Westmoreland

Marine Corps alike, had managed to prevail on the battlefield, generally punishing the enemy severely in almost every encounter. American casualties had been high—some 5,700 killed and 26,800 wounded by October 1966.[2] Nevertheless, the balance was clearly swinging to the side of the allies—that loose coalition of South Vietnamese, American, South Korean, Australian, and New Zealand military forces now defending the Republic of Vietnam. And as more allied troops arrived every month, the prognosis for allied military success seemed increasingly favorable.

Westmoreland had cemented his views on the coming "year of the offensive" at an August 1966 meeting with officials in Honolulu and during a later discussion in Washington with President Lyndon B. Johnson. Publicly, the MACV commander described the conflict as a "total war" centering on a political struggle with sociological, economic, and psychological—as well as military—aspects. From a purely military standpoint, North Vietnam's open invasion of the South was, he believed, transforming the revolutionary struggle into a war of attrition, with the enemy seeking to break American morale by inflicting heavy casualties on the battlefield. These actions, he maintained, had failed and would continue to fail. Instead, MACV was "making progress on all fronts," destroying the enemy's main force conventional units and supporting Saigon's pacification campaign. Ultimate success, however, would depend on American "endurance," both in South Vietnam and at home.[3]

To his own field commanders and staffs, Westmoreland repeated these themes. During the previous spring American spoiling attacks in the northernmost part of the country and in the mountainous Central Highlands had made it impossible for the enemy to take advantage of South Vietnamese political turmoil earlier in the year. Elsewhere, the security campaign in the Vietnamese countryside was making slow but

---

[2] Defense Intelligence Agency (DIA), Southeast Asia Military Fact Book, Jan 68, p. A–95 (hereafter cited as SEA Mil Fact Bk), Historians files, CMH.

[3] Address, Gen William C. Westmoreland at Honolulu Press Club, 12 Aug 66, Westmoreland History files, no. 8, tab C, Incls 3 (8–C–3) and 4, CMH.

undeniable gains. Although the conflict would continue to be a war of attrition, American ground forces were now prepared to take the initiative on a major scale.[4]

Westmoreland wanted to launch a sustained offensive between November 1966 and May 1967 because it offered the best weather in the southern half of South Vietnam. During these months the southern dry season would favor U.S. air and ground operations, providing greatly improved flying weather and improved trafficability for armored vehicles and supply convoys. The season that previously had been characterized by major enemy initiatives on the battlefield would now belong to the Americans. To the north the situation would be somewhat reversed. The powerful northeastern monsoon pushing out of the Pacific would bring heavy rains and high winds to the coastal lowlands, compelling allied forces to adopt a less aggressive posture in the northern half of the country. There, and throughout much of North Vietnam, the adverse weather would also dampen enemy operations, although the Annamite mountain chain and its many spurs would allow the insurgents' north-south supply networks to remain relatively dry. Nevertheless, the revolutionary forces in the far south, especially around Saigon, would now bear the brunt of the American attack.

To fuel the American offensive, Westmoreland expected heavy reinforcements during the second half of 1966 and the first month of 1967, nine U.S. Army brigades and regiments, which would give him a total of twenty-seven Army and Marine brigade-size forces in South Vietnam. Of the arriving forces, Westmoreland slated four brigades and a regiment for the III Corps area around Saigon, one brigade for the Mekong Delta south of Saigon, and the remainder for II Corps in the Central Highlands and coastal lowlands. The additions, he believed, would give him a "well-balanced" expeditionary force that could "be sustained indefinitely . . . [to] see this war through without calling up the Reserves."[5]

Of course, the South Vietnamese would play a role in the coming offensive, though they would mostly secure the countryside, with the government's regular and territorial units overseeing pacification and freeing American troops to chase the enemy. In turn, Westmoreland hoped that this would allow improved local recruitment, training, and desertion control on the part of the South Vietnamese forces throughout the nation.

He had little control over how Saigon managed its forces, however. In April 1965 Westmoreland had put forth the idea of placing the South Vietnamese military under his command, but the Saigon government was opposed. Fearful of being accused of colonialism, MACV backed off the idea, and the issue was never raised again. By keeping American forces

---

[4] Westmoreland Jnl, 17 Aug 66 and 1 Sep 66, Westmoreland History files, 8–C and D, CMH.

[5] Westmoreland Jnl, 17 Sep 66, Westmoreland History files, 8–E, CMH; Admiral U. S. G. Sharp and General William C. Westmoreland, *Report on the War in Vietnam (As of 30 June 1968)* (Washington, D.C.: Government Printing Office, 1968), app. J.

separate but equal, Westmoreland evaded charges that Saigon was subordinate to the United States. This meant, however, that he sometimes had to cajole South Vietnamese commanders to cooperate.

Like any major conflict, the war effort in Vietnam fell under the authority of diverse, yet interrelated, elements. All U.S. military forces in South Vietnam were technically under the operational control of MACV headquarters, which Westmoreland had commanded since June 1964. In addition, he headed a subordinate Army component command, the U.S. Army, Vietnam (USARV), and served as chief American military adviser to the South Vietnamese Joint General Staff. American Ambassador Henry Cabot Lodge also was responsible for many aspects of the American war effort, including various police, propaganda, and intelligence programs. Within MACV headquarters, the Studies and Observations Group staff section, which was involved in cross-border raiding, intelligence, and rescue programs, reported to the Joint Chiefs of Staff in Washington.

Admiral Ulysses S. G. Sharp, heading the U.S. Pacific Command in Hawaii, controlled the air campaign in North Vietnam except for the southernmost portion, which Westmoreland controlled as an extension of the South Vietnamese battlefield. In the Laotian panhandle, Westmoreland conducted an air interdiction campaign against the enemy supply network, or Ho Chi Minh Trail, subject to rules of engagement prescribed by the U.S. ambassador in Vientiane, Laos.

Admiral Sharp, Westmoreland's immediate superior, answered directly to the secretary of defense, Robert S. McNamara, and the chairman of the Joint Chiefs of Staff, General Earle G. Wheeler, U.S. Army. In practice, however, Westmoreland often dealt directly with McNamara, Wheeler, and even President Johnson, and for more technical matters with the three service chiefs, especially the Army chief of staff, General Harold K. Johnson. On political matters Westmoreland and his staff worked closely with Ambassador Lodge and the representatives of the U.S. civilian agencies included in Lodge's "mission," or staff. Most important were the U.S. Agency for International Development, the U.S. Information Service, and the Central Intelligence Agency. Locally, Westmoreland was responsible for coordinating U.S. military operations with both the South Vietnamese and the other allies, the South Koreans and Australians.

To coordinate their separate military operations, MACV headquarters and the South Vietnamese Joint General Staff were in the process of revising their current combined campaign plan. Although not formally published until November 1966, it would reflect the division of labor already in effect.[6] The plan divided South Vietnam into three mission-oriented areas. Critical were those designated as "National Priority Areas" and "Areas of Priority for Military Offensive Operations." The remainder constituted a

[6] See JGS (Joint General Staff)/MACV (Military Assistance Command, Vietnam) Combined Campaign Plan for Military Operations in the Republic of Vietnam, 1967 [7 Nov 66], AB 142, an. A (hereafter cited as CCP 1967), Historians files, CMH.

6

mix of sparsely inhabited regions of less military consequence or areas where weather, terrain, or troop strength limited allied effectiveness, such as those opposite the Demilitarized Zone dividing North and South Vietnam or along the Laotian border. The two priority categories comprised about half of South Vietnam and included about 77 percent of its population, 85 percent of its food production, and 75 percent of its roads. According to MACV headquarters, these areas also contained 77 percent of the enemy's conventional units and 43 percent of his bases.[7] (*Map 1*)

Ostensibly, South Vietnamese forces would have primary responsibility for providing security in the National Priority Areas—heavily populated zones with reasonably good road and water networks. For this mission, all South Vietnamese regular infantry battalions were to receive special revolutionary development, or pacification, training during 1966 and 1967, and at least half were to be assigned direct pacification support or security missions as soon as possible. Meanwhile, the more mobile American forces would take the fight to the enemy in the less accessible Areas of Priority for Military Offensive Operations. Only in the IV Corps zone were both securing and offensive missions given to South Vietnamese commanders.

The published combined campaign plan stated that "there will be no clear cut division of responsibility" between the different allied national components. However, the plan clearly formalized the existence of two different types of war, each with its own strategy, or formula for success. While the South Vietnamese would pursue a strategy of pacification, U.S. forces would follow one of attrition. Although the two would overlap in many areas, they were essentially distinct from one another. Yet, if either was to succeed, both the Americans and South Vietnamese would have to retain sizable forces outside of the so-called priority areas—blocking the Demilitarized Zone, for example, or defending the vital highland plateau and the outlying province and district seats. In the end American forces would have to attack the enemy whenever and wherever he chose to mass his forces within the borders of South Vietnam.[8]

Locating Viet Cong and North Vietnamese forces, or at least large concentrations of them, was Westmoreland's primary operational concern in 1966. To do this, MACV had been pushing away from the populated areas and establishing bases out of which U.S. troops could operate. Each of these bases housed forward supply points, tactical support units, and small airfields capable of receiving Air Force cargo planes. These forward base camps, which were generally home to a brigade, were placed in a checkerboard pattern throughout South Vietnam so that none was more than seventy kilometers from another. By September 1966 engineers had completed fifty-three forward base camps, and within another twelve months fifteen more would become operational.

---

[7] MACV Briefing Book for Secretary of Defense, 10–14 Oct 66 (hereafter cited as MACV Briefing Bk for Sec Def), J–3 Briefing, tab 4, Historians files, CMH.

[8] CCP 1967, pp. 1–8.

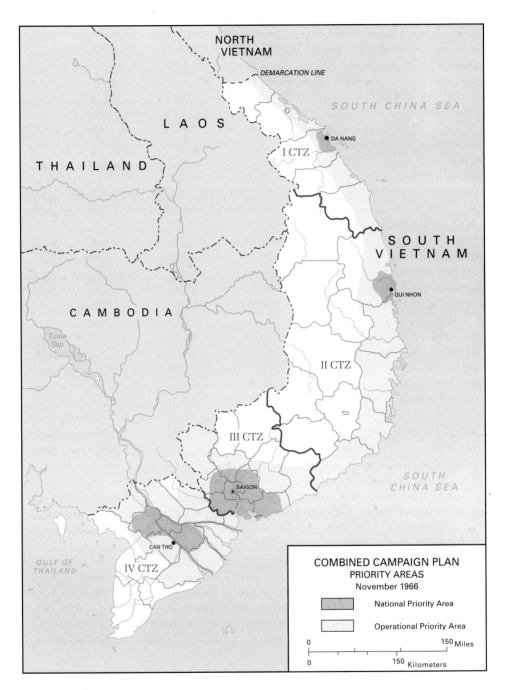

NORTH VIETNAM

DEMARCATION LINE

SOUTH CHINA SEA

LAOS

THAILAND

● DA NANG

I CTZ

SOUTH
VIETNAM

● QUI NHON

CAMBODIA

Tonle
Sap

II CTZ

III CTZ

SOUTH
CHINA SEA

SAIGON

CAN THO ●

GULF OF
THAILAND

IV CTZ

COMBINED CAMPAIGN PLAN
PRIORITY AREAS
November 1966

National Priority Area

Operational Priority Area

0   150 Miles

0   150 Kilometers

MAP 1

The fire support base, or firebase, had evolved over the past year into a vital part of the American method of waging war in South Vietnam. Considerably smaller than the forward base camp, the firebase contained one or more artillery batteries and normally the command post of an infantry battalion. Often situated in enemy-dominated territory, the bases provided artillery support within range of the infantry scouring the countryside. Theoretically for temporary occupation only, firebases were hastily built and dismantled on short notice.

So far at least, firebases had been placed no more than ten thousand meters apart, the maximum effective range of the 105-mm. howitzer, so that when attacked they had been able to count on artillery support from adjacent bases. Additional fire support had been provided by heavier artillery from the forward base camps and by helicopter gunships. Forward base camps housed the vital forward air controllers and airborne forward artillery observers needed to coordinate the entire fire support effort.[9]

Another ingredient in the American tactical formula was airmobility, the use of helicopters to transport and resupply tactical units in the field. Given the limited road network in South Vietnam, the rough terrain, and the guerrilla nature of the war, helicopters had been dictating the tempo of American operations. Their use allowed commanders to "air-assault" troops into one area of the battlefield, only to "extract" them with equal ease in a matter of minutes for insertion elsewhere. On the other hand, though helicopters were giving U.S. infantry commanders operational mobility around the battle area, their contribution to tactical mobility had often been illusory, as they could do little for the troops once on the ground operating in heavily forested terrain. There, American tactical flexibility was often greatly reduced by the jungle and by the need to spread out ground units on exhausting reconnaissance missions throughout the countryside. Commanders who remained in the air had been finding it difficult to lead troops on the ground, while those on the ground often could not provide much direction beyond the limits of their physical presence. Yet the absence of helicopters would have made the decentralized operations of the past year impossible, or at least exceedingly risky, and the Americans, Westmoreland later commented, would have repeatedly forfeited the initiative.[10]

During the summer of 1966, which corresponded to the dry season in the northern half of South Vietnam and the wet season in the southern portion, the MACV commander had focused on the enemy buildup opposite the Demilitarized Zone and the security of his northernmost U.S. Army Special Forces camps opposite the Laotian border. The fall of the A Shau Valley camp in March only underscored the vulnerability of a similarly

---

[9] Maj. Gen. David E. Ott, *Field Artillery, 1954–1973*, Vietnam Studies (Washington, D.C.: Department of the Army, 1975), p. 69.

[10] Interv, CMH historians with Gen William C. Westmoreland, Comdr, MACV, 6 Dec 89, Historians files, CMH. See also Lt. Gen. John J. Tolson, *Airmobility, 1961–1971*, Vietnam Studies (Washington, D.C.: Department of the Army, 1973).

exposed outpost at Khe Sanh in the northwestern corner of I Corps. But a major offensive in the north had never come, and the specific intentions of the North Vietnamese commanders remained opaque.

Throughout 1966, in fact, both Viet Cong and North Vietnamese units had become increasingly elusive, and Westmoreland's field commanders fretted over their inability to locate the enemy. Time and again American units had swept through portions of the countryside, which MACV intelligence analysts had believed to be prime enemy operating areas, only to come up empty-handed. If the expanded American search and destroy effort was to have any chance of success, this situation would have to change dramatically.[11]

At a 28 August commanders' meeting in Nha Trang, Westmoreland and his principal staff officers thrashed through these and related matters with the leading U.S. field commanders. The conferees duly noted statistical advances in the official "measurements of progress," which included an estimated enemy attrition rate of 7,000 per month, but had no evidence to indicate a decline in overall enemy strength or capabilities. More B–52 heavy bomber, or ARC LIGHT, strikes would help the attrition campaign, they believed, but the specific effects of such attacks were difficult to evaluate, and they saw no way of reducing the ten-hour mission-to-target response time or of interfering with the Soviet trawlers that appeared to be tracking the large aircraft. Instead, MACV's hope for more productive air and land operations lay in improved intelligence capabilities.

Under the leadership of Maj. Gen. Joseph A. McChristian, Westmoreland's J–2, or intelligence chief, the American military intelligence apparatus in South Vietnam had grown steadily since 1965 and was beginning to produce concrete results. Through the laborious process of collating all reports of enemy activity and analyzing local topographic and demographic data, the MACV intelligence staff had identified some eighty-six enemy base areas. Although the tabulation was the result of only the first round of what would become a regular intelligence cycle, McChristian believed that the results were accurate enough for the immediate future and was confident "that the enemy is based in these . . . areas, is dependent on these bases, generally moves between these bases, and will be found in or near each base the greater part of the time." Westmoreland agreed, noting that both Viet Cong and North Vietnamese commanders were "creatures of habit, who do the same things over and over; . . . use the same ambush sites, [the] same tactics, [and the] same infiltration routes—which are certainly no mystery to us now." To take advantage of the situation, the conferees recommended targeting each American combat brigade on a specific base area for an extended period, allowing each to become familiar with the local terrain and reducing the

[11] For example, see Westmoreland Jnl, 24 Jul 66 and 10 Aug 66, 8–A and B, and Mission Council Action Memo 125, 27 Sep 66, sub: Minutes of the Mission Council Meeting, September 26, 1966, 9–B–1. All in Westmoreland History files, CMH.

often confusing and always expensive practice of moving units back and forth across the country.[12]

Evolving Strategy

During 1966, if not earlier, the war had slowly begun to evolve into a more conventional conflict, something Westmoreland felt well equipped to fight. Although the broad insurgency and counterinsurgency organizations of the belligerents remained in place, their activities were increasingly overshadowed by the purely military operations of each side. Nevertheless, the overall war strategies of the opponents remained unchanged. Both expected to wage a long war of attrition that would test both the military abilities and the political staying power of the other. There would be no climactic battles or quick victories; the Americans were too strong and the insurgents too elusive. The struggle between the U.S. 1st Cavalry Division (Airmobile) and several North Vietnamese regiments during late 1965 in the Ia Drang Valley had made that situation clear. Although the Americans could bring massive firepower to bear on the Southern battlefields, their desire to avoid expanding the conflict had restricted the ground fighting to the South. It was this constraint that had helped fuel the growing network of enemy military bases in Laos and Cambodia just outside South Vietnamese territory. With main force units from these cross-border sanctuaries harassing the Americans up and down Vietnam's western boundaries, the Communist leaders appeared confident that they could prevail in the more critical but less visible struggle within the heavily populated coastal regions where the indigenous insurgency had first begun.

General Westmoreland intended to end the war expeditiously, either by destroying the enemy or by convincing him that he could not win and should seek negotiations. To accomplish this goal, in July 1965 he had outlined a three-phase campaign using American, South Vietnamese, and other allied military forces. During the first phase, he would halt the "losing trend" by conducting spoiling attacks against the enemy's most threatening units. He had originally envisioned accomplishing this by December 1965 with about fifteen allied combat brigades and regiments, mostly American troops, and a few of Saigon's better units. These forces would then move into a decisive second phase during the first six to nine months of 1966, mounting a sustained offensive to drive the enemy from the populated areas. Spearheaded by about twenty American and allied combat brigades, this campaign would create an environment within which the

---

[12] Quotes from Memorandum for the Record (MFR), 3 Oct 66, sub: MACV Commanders' Conference, 28 August 1966, Westmoreland History files, 8–D–4, CMH. See Maj. Gen. Joseph A. McChristian, *The Role of Military Intelligence, 1965–1967*, Vietnam Studies (Washington, D.C.: Department of the Army, 1974) for McChristian's efforts to enhance MACV's intelligence capability.

larger pacification program could proceed. Westmoreland believed that by April 1967 enemy losses would exceed replacements through infiltration and recruitment. If attained, the result would mark at least a statistical turning point in the war if not actual light at the end of the tunnel. But in case the enemy persisted, the allies might need a third phase lasting twelve to eighteen months to eliminate the surviving insurgent forces. Westmoreland's strategy assumed that the highly mobile American units could bring the ragtag enemy forces to battle and defeat them with superior firepower. The United States could then turn the defense of the nation over to a rejuvenated South Vietnamese Army, and the withdrawal of American and other foreign troops could begin by the end of 1967.[13]

All this depended on the pace at which American military forces could be brought to Southeast Asia. In March 1965 the United States had begun deploying ground combat units to South Vietnam, generally in brigade-size increments. The limited American support base in Southeast Asia and President Johnson's decision against mobilizing the reserves all dictated a slow, measured buildup of a primarily conscript expeditionary force. By the beginning of January 1966 Westmoreland had some thirteen U.S. combat brigades and regiments in Vietnam, representing part of a military buildup that in one year had increased the number of uniformed American troops there from all the services from about 24,000 to 185,000. At that time, a pause in the deployment of further combat forces had been necessary while the services raised and trained additional troops in the absence of mobilization and while Army, Navy, Air Force, and contract engineers and logisticians constructed the support base necessary to sustain the existing forces and those projected for 1966 and 1967.

Between January and October 1966 Army and Navy logisticians, assisted by a variety of service engineer commands and massive civilian construction organizations, fashioned an island logistical system based on a series of coastal support commands, each with its own port, depot, communications, and transportation facilities, including air bases. From north to south these islands, or logistical enclaves, included Da Nang for the Navy and Marine Corps and, for the Army, Qui Nhon, Cam Ranh Bay, and a number of complexes in the greater Saigon area to the south. Much, however, still needed to be done to expand South Vietnam's limited port facilities, get the depots running smoothly, and improve the coastal road network, not to mention push air and road supply lines into the less hospitable interior.

The increased American presence in South Vietnam also demanded a new command structure. By mid-1966 Westmoreland had established his

---

[13] See Westmoreland Briefing Notes for Sec McNamara Visit, 10–13 Oct 66, sub: MACV Policies Governing Force Development and Prosecution of the War, 9–D–6; and Westmoreland Notes for Discussion with Amb Lodge, 13 Oct 66, sub: COMUSMACV Policy Points, 9–D–7. Both in Westmoreland History files, CMH. MACV History 1965, pp. 141–42, CMH. In Sharp and Westmoreland, *Report*, pp. 99–100, Westmoreland does not schedule the third phase.

own intermediate field commands which generally paralleled the South Vietnamese corps headquarters. Each one of the American corps-level field commands—called a field force so as not to confuse them with the local South Vietnamese corps headquarters—controlled a variable number of U.S. ground combat units. In the I Corps Tactical Zone, the III Marine Amphibious Force, headed by Lt. Gen. Lewis W. Walt, U.S. Marine Corps, directed American operations in South Vietnam's five northern provinces: Quang Tri, Thua Thien, Quang Nam, Quang Tin, and Quang Ngai. To the south, in the II and III Corps zones, similar U.S. Army corps-level headquarters supervised American military operations. Based in Nha Trang, I Field Force, Vietnam, commanded by Lt. Gen. Stanley R. Larsen, controlled all American ground forces in II Corps, an area with two distinct geographical regions: the Central Highlands in the west and the coastal lowlands to the east. In the III Corps area, II Field Force, Vietnam, headed by Lt. Gen. Jonathan O. Seaman, directed American efforts around and especially north and northwest of Saigon. From his headquarters at Long Binh, some thirty kilometers northeast of the capital, Seaman also had the tasks of ensuring the safety of the largest allied base complexes in Southeast Asia and of protecting Saigon itself. Between them, these three field force commanders controlled almost all American ground forces in Vietnam. At the time, no large American units had entered the heavily populated but marshy deltas of the IV Corps zone in the far south of the country. Nevertheless, U.S. Army and Air Force aviation units had long supported South Vietnamese forces there from a network of smaller bases under the supervision of the local senior American adviser, Brig. Gen. William R. Desobry.[14]

With the exception of IV Corps, Westmoreland's field force commanders also served as senior advisers to the respective South Vietnamese corps commanders, supervising the U.S. combat advisory teams as well as those assigned to provinces and districts and the Special Forces teams running local border security programs. These advisory tasks meant that like Westmoreland they had both military and nonmilitary responsibilities, although the latter were still ill defined. In addition, all the field force commanders, Army and Marine Corps alike, had aviation, artillery, engineer, and other direct combat-support units in their immediate control. In the case of the Army, however, the U.S. logistical apparatus in II and III Corps, as well as the majority of nondivisional Army aviation, engineer, communications, medical, and intelligence units stationed there belonged to parent units in the Saigon area working directly for U.S. Army, Vietnam, at Long Binh.[15]

With the logistical pipeline and the command structure needed to direct the incoming troops in place, the buildup proceeded, but it was nei-

---

[14] Sharp and Westmoreland, *Report*, apps. J, K; Maj. Gen. George S. Eckhardt, *Command and Control, 1950–1969,* Vietnam Studies (Washington, D.C.: Department of the Army, 1974), pp. 47–84.
[15] Sharp and Westmoreland, *Report*, pp. 146–47, app. G.

Troops of the 4th Infantry Division come ashore.

ther as fast nor as large as Westmoreland would have liked. After a lull from February to July 1966, when only five infantry battalions arrived, the flow resumed in late July and August, with three battalions of the 4th Infantry Division for the Central Highlands, plus two independent units—the 196th Light Infantry Brigade and the 11th Armored Cavalry Regiment—for the Saigon area by the end of September. The 5th Battalion, 7th Cavalry (Airmobile), the ninth and final battalion of the 1st Cavalry Division, deployed in August. Also during that time frame the 4th Battalion, 503d Infantry (Airborne), a third battalion but not the last for the 173d Airborne Brigade, deployed to Bien Hoa. In October MACV received the rest of the 4th Division, followed in December by the 199th Light Infantry Brigade, and in December and January by the 9th Infantry Division. Between July 1966 and January 1967, Westmoreland received twenty-eight U.S. Army maneuver battalions, nearly doubling the forces he had available for offensive operations.

In III Corps, one of the new brigades, the 3d of the 4th Infantry Division, would go to the 25th Infantry Division rather than to its parent unit in the Central Highlands, as would the new 196th Light Infantry Brigade. Rounding out the 25th Division, the reinforcing brigades placed around the capital two complete infantry divisions, the 1st and the 25th, the former with three combat brigades, the latter with four. In addition,

14

the arrival of the separate 11th Armored Cavalry Regiment would bolster the regional reserves, then consisting only of the 173d Airborne Brigade. Westmoreland expected the two new brigades and the regiment to be ready for action by October. December and January would see the arrival of two brigades of the 9th Infantry Division, allowing MACV to place strong American forces both east and west of Saigon. With the arrival in January of the riverine force (the 2d Brigade, 9th Division) in the Mekong Delta, a force concentration of twelve brigades and a cavalry regiment would form the basis of MACV's dry season offensive in III and IV Corps.

In II Corps, the Republic of Korea (ROK) 9th Infantry Division had in September joined its sister, the Capital Division, along the coast. The newly arrived U.S. 4th Infantry Division, less its 3d Brigade, was scheduled to take over responsibility for the western highlands, employing two organic brigades, the 1st and 2d, and the 3d Brigade of the 25th Infantry Division.[16] The new arrivals would allow General Larsen's I Field Force greater flexibility in employing its reserves, the helicopter-mobile 1st Cavalry Division and the 1st Brigade of the 101st Airborne Division, and give him a total of seven American brigades with which to work.

In the far north, the I Corps zone, Westmoreland wanted General Walt's III Marine Amphibious Force, with its two U.S. Marine Corps divisions, to conduct a holding action until the reversal of Vietnam's monsoon seasons in mid-1967, when he intended to reinforce the Marine command with Army units.

These soldiers and marines were as well equipped as any who had marched to war throughout America's history. In 1965 most came to Vietnam armed with the M14 rifle, the latest evolution of the World War II M1 Garand. But by early 1967 most M14s were replaced by the new M16 assault rifle. A complete departure from older military rifles, the M16 weighed about seven pounds—almost two pounds lighter than the M14—and fired a 5.56-mm. round, also smaller and lighter than the M14's 7.62-mm. cartridge. When set on automatic, it was deadly at close range. Soldiers could carry about 1,000 rounds of M16 ammunition in their rucksacks, along with more than a dozen fragmentation grenades, a few smoke grenades, and two claymore antipersonnel mines. The stronger men also packed 100 to 200 rounds of 7.62-mm. ammunition in belts for the squad's M60 machine gun, while at least one soldier in each squad carried an M79 grenade launcher, a 40-mm. single-shot weapon that could accurately fire an explosive round about 350 meters. Although all this made for a heavy load, there was still room for the soldier's personal gear.[17]

---

[16] These mission assumptions would leave the U.S. 25th Division controlling the 4th Division's 3d Brigade in the III Corps zone and the 4th Division controlling the 25th Division's 3d Brigade in the II Corps zone, an anomaly ended in August 1967 by redesignation of the two orphan brigades.

[17] Edward C. Ezell, *Small Arms of the World* (Harrisburg, Pa.: Stackpole Books, 1983), pp. 751–52; Edward F. Murphy, *Dak To* (Novato, Calif.: Presidio Press, 1993), pp. 47–48.

American infantry weapons were among the best in the world, but artillery was the staff of life for soldiers in the field. And as the number of U.S. troops arriving in Vietnam climbed, so too did the number of guns. During the lull from February to July, when the influx of infantry units was light, artillery deployments were also thin. Only four U.S. Army battalions reached Vietnam. All that changed in August. In the surge between August 1966 and February 1967, eighteen battalions arrived, with three more battalions arriving in March. This included 8-inch and 175-mm. battalions as well as 105-mm. and 155-mm. tubes. By March 1967 Westmoreland had forty-one U.S. Army artillery battalions in South Vietnam: twenty-six were 105-mm. howitzer units; the rest were heavier.

Air support was also slow in coming. The manpower buildup of 1965 had outstripped the deployment of aircraft, a problem not remedied until late 1966. At the beginning of 1966, the U.S. Air Force had 509 aircraft based in South Vietnam, 144 of them F–4 Phantom and F–100 Super Sabre fighter-bombers. By the end of the year the number had climbed to 338 fighter-bombers out of a total of 834 aircraft. One of the major problems inhibiting deployment was a lack of airfields and munitions. During the summer of 1966 rockets were in short supply, particularly the 2.75-inch rocket used by forward air controllers to mark targets on the ground. In April the Air Force borrowed 15,000 rockets from the Army, barely enough to do the job. Air controllers tried to use smoke grenades thrown from the windows of their airplanes, but that expedient did not work well. Bombs were also in short supply. By April stocks of 250- and 500-pound bombs, the workhorse of close air support, were dwindling, and it was not until the end of the year that the Pentagon acted, releasing munitions reserves from Korea and the United States for use in Vietnam.

Airfield construction also showed improvement during 1966. Before the construction of a new 10,000-foot runway at Phan Rang on the coast south of Cam Ranh Bay in October 1966, F–4s flying air support missions were forced to take off from temporary aluminum plank runways. Bad weather affected operations, with the runways becoming flooded or hot temperatures preventing the crews from conducting repairs until after dark. By the end of October, construction had caught up with demand, resulting in a total of 116 fully operational airfields for the C–123 Provider cargo plane. The heavier C–130 Hercules could land on sixty-six of them. At the same time, eight major airfields were in place, housing thirty-six squadrons of fixed-wing bombers and fighter-bombers. From bases in Thailand and from others as far away as Guam and as near as the U.S. Navy's aircraft carriers in the South China Sea, MACV could count on additional assistance by the diversion of those aircraft supporting interdiction campaigns in southern Laos and southern North Vietnam.[18]

[18] John Schlight, *The War in South Vietnam: The Years of the Offensive, 1965–1968*, The United States Air Force in Southeast Asia (Washington, D.C.: Government Printing Office, 1988), pp. 154–55; MACV Briefing Bk for Sec Def, J–3 Briefing, tab 4, chart 31. The breakdown of fighter-bomber squadrons in Vietnam was 20 U.S. Air Force, 10 U.S. Marine Corps, and 6 Republic of Vietnam Air Force.

But if the supply of airplanes and airfields showed improvement during 1966, that of helicopters did not. These aerial war horses, especially the UH–1 Iroquois, or Huey, had proved their worth at the battle of the Ia Drang and other skirmishes in 1965 and 1966, and demand far outstripped production and pilot training. During the first half of 1966, eleven Army helicopter companies deployed to Vietnam, followed by a mere three during the latter half of the year. During the autumn, as Westmoreland gathered the bulk of his ground troop strength, he had 1,374 Hueys and 137 CH–47 Chinook cargo helicopters, not enough to make his units sufficiently airmobile. Not until early 1967 did the number increase, with sixteen companies sent from the United States between January and June and an additional twenty-three during the latter half of the year. By October 1967 Westmoreland would have 2,039 Hueys and 249 Chinooks, plus 391 heavy-lift and light observation helicopters.[19]

The Enemy

The heavy fighting of 1965 and 1966 also prompted changes in the enemy camp, reigniting old arguments about the correct strategy for the war in the South. After initial uncertainty in the face of the U.S. troop buildup—something they had not anticipated—North Vietnamese and Viet Cong leaders decided to intensify their own main force war, sending new troops to the South and gearing up to face the Americans. But the decision to emphasize big unit warfare did not come easily. General Nguyen Chi Thanh, the field commander in South Vietnam and a long-time advocate of conventional war, saw the increasing strength of his enemies as a vindication of his beliefs. Lt. Gen. Tran Van Tra, one of Thanh's deputies, recounted the trepidation among his officers over facing the Americans head-on. "Should we disperse our main force so that we can wage a protracted guerrilla war in order to defeat the enemy?" he recalled his officers asking. "I emphatically said no. . . . There was absolutely no question of changing the strategic line."[20]

Actually, there was a debate at the highest levels over what form Hanoi's strategy should take. General Vo Nguyen Giap, the hero of Dien Bien Phu, had long argued with Thanh over his big unit tactics. Giap considered them suicidal and ultimately unnecessary, pointing out that Hanoi had already made substantial gains using guerrilla tactics. Although Giap was North Vietnam's minister of defense, he was apparently unable to convince the Politburo that he was right; beginning in 1965 and running through 1966, North Vietnamese forces waged a big

[19] Office of the Chief of Staff, Army Buildup Progress Rpt, 17 Jul 68, p. 8, CMH.

[20] Col. Gen. Tran Van Tra, *Vietnam: History of the Bulwark B2 Theater*, vol. 5, *Concluding the 30-Years War*, trans. Foreign Broadcast Information Service, Joint Publications Research Service 82783, Southeast Asia Report 1247 (Ho Chi Minh City: Van Nghe Publishing House, March 1982), pp. 59–60, copy in CMH.

General Thanh

unit war against the Americans, trying to entice U.S. troops into remote border areas in an attempt to defeat them decisively.[21]

By May 1966 Hanoi had lost the initiative to Westmoreland's search and destroy operations, and arguments over strategy flared again. For the first time since the U.S. intervention, factions within the Politburo, led by Giap, began to question Thanh's leadership. Thanh fought back loudly and in public; in a July 1966 article in *Hoc Tap*, a Communist periodical, he called those who advocated guerrilla warfare "old-fashioned." Although he did not name Giap in the article, he was clearly attacking the venerable general, accusing him of "mechanically copying one's past experiences or the experiences of foreign countries . . . in accordance with a dogmatic tendency."[22]

By the fall of 1966 it was clear that Thanh had again won the debate and that North Vietnamese strategy would continue as before. He had convinced Hanoi that, with the Americans propping up the Saigon regime, the only way to defeat it was to keep the cost high for Washington. International pressure, he believed, and an increasingly vocal American antiwar movement would combine to drive the United States out of the war and thus doom South Vietnam. Giap disliked relying on these nebulous outside forces to ensure victory, preferring instead to use what he knew best—guerrilla warfare. But he would have to wait more than a year before his viewpoint would triumph over Thanh's. In the meantime, North Vietnamese forces continued to seek out big battles, and they reorganized their command structure accordingly.

In a mirror image of Westmoreland's strategy, the enemy also resorted to attrition. Realizing they could not defeat U.S. forces outright, they instead sought every opportunity to inflict casualties on the Americans, even at the cost of heavy casualties to their own forces. Hanoi believed

[21] Phillip B. Davidson, *Vietnam at War: The History, 1946–1975* (Novato, Calif.: Presidio Press, 1988), p. 417.

[22] Nguyen Chi Thanh, "Ideological Tasks of the Army and People in the South," *Hoc Tap* (July 1966).

18

that steady losses would weaken the will of the American people to continue the war. Seeking to retain the military initiative against superior American mobility and firepower, during 1966 the enemy organized its regular units to achieve what MACV called strategic mobility. By concentrating large numbers of battalions at several different points, the enemy compelled the allies to disperse their own forces, creating opportunities to choose the time and place for an engagement. The North Vietnamese repeatedly sent units through the Demilitarized Zone into northern I Corps to force the marines to shift troops away from Da Nang and Hue. In the area around Saigon, the North Vietnamese periodically concentrated forces in their sanctuaries in Cambodia, pushing into South Vietnam whenever they felt they held the advantage.

In the late spring of 1966 Hanoi reorganized its military and political commands in the South to reflect this strategy. *Region 5*, the northern half of South Vietnam, formerly two jurisdictions, was split into four major commands: the *B1 Front* in the six coastal "middle" provinces, the *B3 Front* in the Central Highlands, the new *B4 Front* in Quang Tri and Thua Thien Provinces south of Highway 9, and the new *B5 Front* in Quang Tri Province north of Highway 9. The other major command, the *B2 Front*, answered to the Southern branch of the Communist Lao Dong Party, better known as the *Central Office for South Vietnam* (*COSVN*), which controlled the war in the southern half of the country. *COSVN* constituted the most critical command and control apparatus of the revolutionary movement. Its geographical area of responsibility included the heavily populated Mekong Delta region and all the important urban areas in and around Saigon. (*Map 2*)

Tactically, allied information on the strength and general location of the major Viet Cong and North Vietnamese forces was fairly accurate by the middle of 1966. In October MACV intelligence analysts assessed the overall enemy strength in South Vietnam at 283,000 men. They divided these into three broad categories: conventional forces (131,000, or 46 percent); militia (113,000, or 40 percent); and political cadre (39,000, or 14 percent). Enemy conventional units included seven division and thirty-two regimental headquarters. Five of the division commands and nineteen of the regiments were from the *People's Army of Vietnam* (*PAVN*, or North Vietnamese army units), and the remainder belonged to the *People's Liberation Armed Forces* (*PLAF*, or Viet Cong). Subordinate to these headquarters or working separately were 178 battalions, of which eighty-two were North Vietnamese formations. In addition, MACV headquarters identified 197 separate Viet Cong companies, which generally worked directly for insurgent regional, provincial, or district headquarters.[23]

MACV classified all enemy conventional divisions and regiments and a few of the better independent battalions as main force units. Such formations were directly assigned to a higher military headquarters such as the *B3 Front*. Although not bound by strict organizational struc-

---

[23] MACV Briefing Bk for Sec Def, J–2 Fact Sheet, tab 3A.

NORTH
VIETNAM

DEMARCATION LINE

SOUTH CHINA SEA

B5 FRONT *QUANG TRI*

B4 FRONT

• *Hue*

THUA THIEN

• *Da Nang*

L A O S

QUANG NAM

REGION 5

QUANG NGAI

T H A I L A N D

KONTUM

B1 FRONT

BINH DINH

GIA LAI

B3 FRONT

PHU YEN

C A M B O D I A

Tonle Sap

DAC LAC

KHANH HOA

QUANG DUC *TUYEN DUC*

MR 10

• *Da Lat*

NINH THUAN

PHUOC LONG

B2 FRONT

BINH LONG

LAM DONG

MR 6

TAY NINH

MR 4 *THU DAU MOT*

COSVN

MR 1

BINH THUAN

GIA DINH

BIEN HOA *LONG KHANH*

KIEN TUONG *LONG AN*

KIEN PHONG

SAIGON

SOUTH CHINA SEA

AN GIANG

MR 2

BA RIA

MY THO

RUNG SAT SPECIAL ZONE

VINH LONG *BEN TRE*

CAN THO *TRA VINH*

GULF OF THAILAND

RACH GIA

MR 3

SOC TRANG

CA MAU

SOUTH VIETNAM
COMMUNIST ADMINISTRATIVE AREAS
1966–1967

—————— Front Boundary

– – – – – Military Region Boundary

———— Administrative Boundary

0   150 Miles

0   150 Kilometers

MAP 2

tures, the enemy divisions operating in South Vietnam normally contained three infantry regiments and a small support base. A regiment fielded three infantry battalions and a heavy weapons "artillery" battalion containing mortars, recoilless rifles, and antiaircraft machine guns. Assorted direct-support units, including engineer, signal, transportation, and medical units, rounded out these elements but had little heavy or sophisticated equipment.

The manpower strength of these light units varied greatly. MACV estimated that the operating strength of a full North Vietnamese infantry division was roughly 9,000 men and a similar Viet Cong division 7,350; that for divisional and independent infantry regiments was 2,175 North Vietnamese and 1,750 Viet Cong soldiers; while their infantry battalions, their basic fighting units, were 450 and 350 men, respectively. In contrast, U.S. and South Vietnamese infantry divisions were larger, with about 15,000 and 10,000 men, respectively, but rarely would their infantry battalions put more than 340 or 250 soldiers in the field at one time. Such numerical comparisons between the two forces were misleading, however, since the lack of adequate support elements made it difficult for the enemy's units to sustain combat more than a day or so.[24]

Local militia-like forces, all Viet Cong, consisted of battalions and separate companies subordinate to province or district committees. Seldom did these units operate outside their home provinces and districts. Authorized strength for a local force battalion was approximately 425 men, with normal operating strength at 300; that of a separate company, about 100, with normal operating strength at 70. Their major opponents were South Vietnam's Regional Forces companies and Popular Forces platoons—the territorial forces—as well as regular allied combat units assigned securing missions.[25]

Of the 178 battalions that MACV identified in South Vietnam, 149 were infantry battalions, and only 29 were support units—artillery, antiaircraft, engineer, transportation, medical, and signal formations. But both components were steadily growing, and American intelligence estimated that by mid-1967 the combined enemy army would have 199 combat and 103 support battalions operating in South Vietnam, for an overall total of 302 battalions. Most of these troops were well armed, carrying Soviet- or Chinese-made infantry weapons, such as AK47 assault rifles and RPG2 rocket-propelled grenades, as well as an array of mortars and machine guns that were just as good as those carried by American and South Vietnamese soldiers. Nevertheless, MACV did not believe that the increasing number of support units would greatly add to the overall combat capabilities of the enemy.[26]

---

[24] Ibid.; Periodic Intel Rpt, MACV, Oct 66, 20 Nov 66, p. ix, Historians files, CMH. *PAVN* units in South Vietnam fielded about 75 percent of their authorized strength, while *PLAF* main force units fielded about 70 percent. The authorized strength of a *PAVN* division was 12,100 men, a *PLAF* division, 10,500.

[25] MACV Briefing Bk for Sec Def, J–2 Fact Sheet, tab 3A.

[26] Ibid.; CCP 1967.

The most important source of support to the conventional North Vietnamese and Viet Cong forces was the militia, or guerrilla units, and the insurgent political underground, which provided a continuous flow of intelligence, foodstuffs, guides, and laborers. MACV's order of battle holdings regarding the strength of these groups were hazy. MACV recognized three types of militia units: guerrillas, self-defense forces, and secret self-defense forces. Each subdivision, MACV arbitrarily estimated, contained a third of the total militia strength. MACV intelligence identified guerrillas as full-time soldiers organized into platoons and squads that operated under Communist Party committees at the village and hamlet level; although many were skilled soldiers with long experience, others were teenage recruits with none. American analysts regarded the other two subdivisions as paramilitary forces at best. When not tilling their fields, members of the self-defense force worked for village and hamlet Party committees in insurgent-dominated areas, performing such duties as constructing fortifications and serving as trail watchers; normally, they were unarmed and had little military training. Secret self-defense forces consisted of individuals who operated covertly in government-secured areas, leading a legal existence during the day and joining together only for operations at night. Their missions often involved intelligence collection as well as propaganda and sabotage activities for the insurgent political organization.

Of the three major categories of enemy strength, MACV knew the least about the political cadre. U.S. intelligence efforts against nonmilitary aspects of the insurgency had been minimal, and given the small size of the advisory detachments at the province and district levels, MACV had understandably left this difficult task to South Vietnamese and U.S. civilian agencies who had primary responsibility for it. But the capabilities of these agencies were also weak. A South Vietnamese study conducted in 1965 had concluded that there were 39,000 Communist political cadre operating in South Vietnam but offered few specifics. Lacking anything better, MACV analysts accepted the general figure and incorporated it into their own official estimates. Since MACV's primary concern was the enemy's conventional combat units, the matter seemed of little importance at the time.[27]

Also difficult to determine was the enemy's ability to replenish his losses by infiltration from the North or by in-country local recruitment. For example, MACV later estimated that overall enemy losses during the first nine months of 1966 exceeded 67,000 men; yet their estimates of overall enemy strength in South Vietnam during this period increased by 20 percent.[28] The precise origin of the replacements was a puzzle that was

---

[27] Monthly Order of Battle Summary, Combined Intelligence Center, Vietnam, Oct 66, pp. 2–3 (hereafter cited as Monthly OB Sum, CICV), U.S. Army Military History Institute (MHI), Carlisle Barracks, Pa.; SEA Mil Fact Bk, p. A–78.

[28] MACV Force Requirements FY 1968, 5 Apr 67, app. A, an. F, Historians files, CMH; MACV Briefing Bk for Sec Def, J–2 Briefing, tab 3A. MACV computed enemy losses using a two-stage process which, first, totaled enemy reported killed in action, captured, and

further muddled by a continuous internal debate over the initial strength figures and the accuracy of the casualty estimates.[29]

Based again on compromises and rough "guesstimates," MACV believed that infiltration from North Vietnam would increase insurgent conventional strength in the South from 131,000 to 202,000 by the end of 1967. The 202,000 figure was especially disconcerting, because MACV based the estimate on the assumption that allied forces, including American and South Korean units scheduled to arrive during the next fourteen months, would eliminate 115,000 of the enemy during that period. With local insurgent recruiting also continuing at a high level, some at MACV wondered if the attrition of enemy forces would ever be greater than the enemy's ability to replace them. Westmoreland's staff could only conclude blandly that the "enemy intends to increase his strength . . . and [to] continue to wage a protracted war of attrition while seeking psychological and political advantages."[30] American leaders in Saigon thus believed that for the immediate future Hanoi would continue its commitment to the struggle in the South.

Hanoi was willing to pay whatever price to see the war through, a resolve that Washington did not share. American political and military leaders had provided Westmoreland with little operational or strategic guidance and had produced no strategic plan to integrate the American political, economic, social, psychological, and military efforts. Instead, while seeking a military solution to an essentially political problem, they hastened to announce a negative "strategy" to prevent the war from expanding into a conflict with the People's Republic of China or the Soviet Union. The United States "at present" had no intention of invading North Vietnam and would respect the neutrality of Cambodia and Laos, thus limiting the ground war to South Vietnam. These policies in turn kept Westmoreland on the strategic defensive, contending with an enemy who was constructing a network of supplementary bases and supply lines across the South Vietnamese border. Washington also placed stringent controls on the slowly escalating and indecisive air war against North Vietnam to minimize the possibility of Chinese intervention. But despite these voluntary restraints and the well-known opposition of many field commanders to them, American leaders at the national level continued to believe that a gradual escalation of the war would prevent it from turning into a larger conflict. This would force Hanoi out of the struggle once its leaders realized that a military victory was

---

defected, and, second, added to that sum the number expected to either die of wounds or survive disabled. The last number was believed to be 29 percent of reported enemy killed; it was raised to 35 percent in 1967.

[29] For background on the enemy strength controversy and its reverberation in the United States, see Bob Brewin and Sydney Shaw, *Vietnam on Trial: Westmoreland vs. CBS* (New York: Atheneum, 1987), and Sam Adams, *War of Numbers: An Intelligence Memoir* (South Royalton, Vt.: Steerforth Press, 1994).

[30] MACV Briefing Bk for Sec Def, J–2 Briefing, tab 3A.

impossible and that the cost of continuing the war indefinitely would be catastrophically high.[31]

Measuring Success

The specific approach of Washington's leaders to the struggle in Vietnam emphasized statistical results and the efficient management of military resources in attaining those results. Under the influence of Secretary of Defense McNamara, the use of raw statistics to gauge the progress of the war had become, according to General Westmoreland, an "engraved methodology well prior to the arrival of American ground troops."[32] At a MACV commanders' conference in July 1966 Westmoreland noted that President Johnson himself had "emphasized quite firmly" his desire to have "a system set up to measure progress" by the field commanders so that in the future he "would be able to count some coonskins on the wall."[33] The result was the MACV system for measuring progress, which for calendar year 1966 had established somewhat arbitrarily the following goals: increasing the number of base areas "denied" to the insurgents from 10 percent to about 50 percent; raising enemy casualties (attrition) to their current level of recruitment; increasing the number of open roads and rail lines from 30 to 50 percent; expanding the "secure population" from 50 to 60 percent; and completely "pacifying" four geographical "priority areas."

At the time—in fact throughout the war—American military commanders puzzled over the precise meaning of all these terms. How could the necessary statistical measurements be produced, and what, if any, was their ultimate significance? How, for example, could jungle base areas be declared "denied"? ("Through frequent entry or by stationing forces in and adjacent to them," was Westmoreland's immediate answer.) How could a commander judge that a village, hamlet, or district was completely pacified or that a road was totally secure? Were the percentages to be computed by the number of villages and hamlets or by their estimated population? Were the roads secured to be measured by their size, length, trafficability, or some other criterion? Equally difficult was ascertaining

---

[31] George C. Herring, "The Vietnam War," in *Modern American Diplomacy*, eds. John M. Carroll and George C. Herring (Wilmington, Del.: Scholarly Resources, Inc., 1986), pp. 161–81. See also Larry Berman, *Planning a Tragedy: The Americanization of the War in Vietnam* (New York: W. W. Norton & Co., 1982), and Bernard B. Fall, *The Two Vietnams: A Political and Military Analysis*, 2d ed. (New York: Frederick A. Praeger, 1963).

[32] Interv, CMH historians with Westmoreland, 6 Dec 89.

[33] Quotes from MFR, 17 Aug 66, sub: MACV Commanders' Conference, 24 July 1966, Westmoreland History files, 8–B–1, CMH. Westmoreland was referring to his meeting with President Johnson in Honolulu in February 1966. Extensive discussion of Defense Department statistical guidelines is in Thomas C. Thayer, "How To Analyze a War Without Fronts: Vietnam 1965–72," *Journal of Defense Research, Series B: Tactical Warfare, Analysis of Vietnam Data* 7B (Fall 1975): 767–943.

enemy casualties with any degree of certainty or attempting to measure local insurgent recruitment rates or their infiltration rate from North Vietnam. Nevertheless, with minimal foot dragging, American field commanders agreed to adopt these strategic guidelines and gear their own operations and, as best they could, those of the South Vietnamese, to achieve the desired statistical results.

Using statistical measurements, American leaders in Washington believed that the basic attrition strategy was succeeding. According to MACV estimates, the enemy had lost 35,000 men during 1965 and nearly twice that number during the first nine months of 1966, while during those same periods allied losses (killed in action only) totaled roughly 12,600 and 11,600, respectively. The trends on the battlefield were unmistakable. Whatever the validity of the "body count," the momentum of the insurgency appeared to have been halted. Only the massive infusion of North Vietnamese troops and units into the South had made the final outcome less than certain. In addition, further American reinforcements, requested by Westmoreland and approved by McNamara in December 1965, would soon be forthcoming, all of which could be expected to generate even more favorable statistical measurements of progress.[34]

But McNamara's enthusiasm for statistics led him to the eventual conclusion that Westmoreland's strategy of attrition did not work—no matter what standard he used to judge it. Although he had encouraged the numbers game in the first place, by the fall of 1966 he was making his doubts known to the president. "[Hanoi] knows we can't achieve our goals," he informed Johnson in October. McNamara pointed out that although U.S. and South Vietnamese operations over the past twelve months had blunted enemy offensives, Hanoi's willingness to continue fighting remained strong. "Any military victory the Viet Cong may have had in mind 18 months ago has been thwarted by our emergency deployments and actions," concluded the secretary of defense. "My concern continues, however, in other respects. This is because I see no reasonable way to bring the war to an end soon. Enemy morale has not broken—he apparently has adjusted to our stopping his drive for military victory and has adopted a strategy of keeping us busy and waiting us out." In other words, Hanoi had its own strategy of attrition, one which McNamara liked to call "attriting our national will."[35]

But U.S. strategy was too well ingrained to be changed in midstream, and besides, given the administration's unwillingness to widen the war, there seemed to be no other choice. This was reflected in the opinions of other policy makers. Presidential assistant Robert W. Komer pointed out

---

[34] MACV Briefing Bk for Sec Def, J–2 Briefing, tab 3A, attchmt D, estimates enemy losses through 30 September 1966 as 69,200. Allied killed-in-action totals are in SEA Mil Fact Bk, p. A–95.

[35] *The Senator Gravel Edition of the Pentagon Papers: The Defense Department History of United States Decisionmaking on Vietnam*, 4 vols. (Boston: Beacon Press, 1971), 4:348; Larry Berman, *Lyndon Johnson's War* (New York: W. W. Norton & Co., 1989), p. 13.

Secretary McNamara (left) *briefs President Johnson. Looking on* (from the left)
*Army Chief of Staff General Harold K. Johnson and Air Force Chief of Staff
General John P. McConnell.*

in November 1966, "I suspect that we have reached the point where we are killing, defecting, or otherwise attriting more VC/NVA strength than the enemy can build up." This was not just the opinion of the civilian leadership. Col. Robert N. Ginsburgh, the National Security Council's liaison with the Joint Chiefs of Staff, wrote the following month to National Security Adviser Walt W. Rostow that "our figures [indicate] the beginning of a gradual erosion in communist strength. These latest figures indicate that the communists by now ought to be in really serious trouble."[36]

McNamara wondered just what "serious trouble" meant, and he visited South Vietnam between 10 and 13 October for preliminary talks with Westmoreland before a larger defense conference scheduled to convene in Hawaii on the thirteenth. Westmoreland reiterated his view that time and more troops were the basic ingredients for victory. The United States was in for "a long war and we should gear ourselves for it." Westmoreland had been making this point since 1965, though few in the civilian leadership seemed to be paying attention. To see it through, the MACV commander recommended raising American ground strength to between 480,000 and 500,000 troops, a force which he believed "could be supported indefinitely by our manpower and industrial base." But even this

---

[36] Berman, *Lyndon Johnson's War*, pp. 20–21.

force, he cautioned, "will not permit us to do all things at one time" and at best "will provide the flexibility to shift troops as required by the enemy situation and forces that present themselves." He further warned that "if this level-off force is inadequate, I see no choice but to go to full mobilization and bring whatever troops are required to do the job. Only time will tell."[37]

Westmoreland believed that a war like that in Vietnam could be won only over the long haul. He repeated this contention like a mantra, to civilian and military officials alike. What Westmoreland failed to realize, however, was that for this undeclared war at least an unlimited time frame was an unaffordable luxury. With American soldiers dying in combat in a faraway land for hazy goals, the American people started asking why. Attrition was not an explanation they could long accept. But Westmoreland thought it was enough to warn the leadership in Washington that they must be ready for a long war.

President Johnson traveled to Manila on 23 October for a seven-nation summit meeting of Asian allies. Vietnam dominated the agenda. During a private meeting with Westmoreland, the president asked for a frank assessment of the military situation. According to notes of the meeting, the MACV commander reported, "By every index, things were improving." He cited the usual indicators: casualty figures, defections, and captured weapons. "Above all, an optimistic spirit was now unmistakable in Vietnam." Johnson was concerned that the enemy might launch another large-scale attack sometime during the fall, a possibility Westmoreland acknowledged but discounted as having no chance of success. American military operations over the past year had taken the punch out of the North Vietnamese and Viet Cong. "The enemy is relying on his greater staying power," concluded Westmoreland. "It is only his will and resolve that are sustaining him now, and his faith that his will is stronger than ours."[38]

Uncertainty Prevails

For all his bravado, the MACV commander harbored reservations about the coming dry season offensive in the South that he had not shared with his field commanders. At the weekly mission council meeting of 17 September with Ambassador Lodge and his staff, he voiced outright discouragement. In nearby Long An Province, he observed that some 8,600 South Vietnamese troops had done next to nothing against an estimated 3,200 Viet Cong soldiers who actually controlled most of the area. Maj. Gen. Frederick C. Weyand's 25th Division had been busy trying to plug up the many north-south infiltration routes into Saigon, with little

---

[37] Westmoreland Jnl, 17 Oct 66, Westmoreland History files, 9–D, CMH.
[38] Berman, *Lyndon Johnson's War*, pp. 18–19.

time to lend a hand in Long An or anywhere else.[39] Later, while confiding to Admiral Sharp, he discounted General Desobry's optimistic assessment of the situation in the Mekong Delta, where he believed that South Vietnamese forces had achieved only "limited success" and that "meaningful progress" would eventually require American ground combat forces.[40] Meeting with his own staff, he worried about MACV's inability to halt enemy supplies from reaching II, III, and IV Corps via Cambodia during the dry season. Later, in November, he would even ask his officers to draw up plans for the seizure of Sihanoukville, Cambodia's principal port, and for the interdiction of the Mekong and Bassac Rivers, which flowed between the two countries.[41] Nevertheless, in September he also ordered MACV's contingency plans for the northern I Corps area updated in case the North Vietnamese chose to launch a major offensive there under the cover of the winter-spring monsoon. At the time he had just returned from visiting Da Nang, where he had warned General Walt that "the enemy may be hoping that by massing troops in the north, he can suck our forces from the rest of the country."[42] Finally, any major enemy operation against such border outposts as Khe Sanh, Duc Co, or Loc Ninh, he told Admiral Sharp several days later, would also severely upset his own offensive plans.[43]

A conventional North Vietnamese thrust across the Demilitarized Zone continued to weigh on the mind of the MACV commander. At a mission council meeting on 26 September Westmoreland suggested the "strong possibility" that "the enemy appears to be seeking a Dien Bien Phu in Quang Tri," and went over several measures that he had recently taken to alleviate that concern: one U.S. Army 175-mm. battery would soon displace from the Saigon area to the Demilitarized Zone, and scarce AM–2 aluminum matting had been diverted from II Field Force to airfields in the north at Dong Ha and Khe Sanh, increasing their all-weather

[39] Mission Council Action Memo 122, 20 Sep 66, sub: Minutes of the Special Mission Council Meeting, September 17, 1966, Westmoreland History files, 8–E–3, CMH.

[40] Msg, Gen William C. Westmoreland, COMUSMACV, MAC 8212 to Adm Ulysses S. G. Sharp, CINCPAC, 20 Sep 66, sub: Containment of Enemy Forces in Sanctuaries, Westmoreland History files, 9–A–2, CMH.

[41] For the September staff meeting, see MFR, 17 Sep 66, sub: Current Intelligence Indication Center (CIIC) Meeting 17 September 1966, 8–E–6. For the November meeting, see MFR, 12 Nov 66, sub: CIIC Meeting 11 November 1966, 11–B–4. For Cambodian resupply, see MACV J–2 Intelligence Study, 30 Sep 66, sub: The Role of Cambodia in the NVA–VC War Effort, 9–B–3. All in Westmoreland History files, CMH. See also Msgs, Westmoreland MAC 8213 to Sharp and Gen Earle G. Wheeler, Chairman, Joint Chiefs of Staff (CJCS), 20 Sep 66, 9–A–1, and Westmoreland MAC 8212 to Sharp, 20 Sep 66, sub: Containment of Enemy Forces in Sanctuaries, 9–A–2, both in Westmoreland History files, CMH.

[42] MFR, Brig Gen William K. Jones (U.S. Marine Corps [USMC]), Director, MACV Combat Operations Center, 18 Sep 66, sub: COMUSMACV's Visit to III MAF (Marine Amphibious Force), 16 Sep 66, Westmoreland History files, 9–A–5, CMH.

[43] Msg, Westmoreland MAC 8212 to Sharp, 20 Sep 66, sub: Containment of Enemy Forces in Sanctuaries.

capabilities.[44] Shortly afterward he also dispatched to I Corps two newly arrived Army artillery battalions, one 175-mm. and one 105-mm. self-propelled, placed one infantry battalion from the 173d Airborne Brigade at the disposal of III Marine Amphibious Force, and approved sending Army Special Forces–led mobile guerrilla force units into the A Shau Valley just west of Hue, and into western Pleiku Province.[45] Finally, on 9 October he had his staff begin preliminary studies with visiting Department of Defense officials on the possibility of establishing some sort of anti-infiltration ground barrier immediately south of the Demilitarized Zone.[46] Perhaps American technology could somehow make up for the vulnerabilities that Westmoreland perceived along the Demilitarized Zone and the western borders.

Westmoreland's basic concern in the north centered on his uneasiness with his Marine Corps subordinates at III Marine Amphibious Force. While regarding the marines as "professional and excellent fighters," both "cheerful and cooperative" in their dealings with MACV headquarters, he worried that "their self-confidence makes them hesitant to plan ahead in anticipation of enemy initiatives" and "reluctant to ask for assistance or reinforcements."[47] In this respect, Washington's prohibition against naval gunfire north of the Demilitarized Zone was lamentable, since it allowed North Vietnamese troops to mass at their leisure and placed Walt's marines in constant danger.[48] A conventional enemy thrust across the Demilitarized Zone could never be ruled out.

Worries about the northern front were the exception, not the rule, and during the fall of 1966 offense, not defense, was in the forefront of Westmoreland's mind. For the first time since the beginning of the U.S. troop buildup some eighteen months earlier, the MACV commander finally had the troops and the logistics to take the offensive, and he looked forward to it. "We now have three consecutive large scale operations planned starting after the first of the year," he asserted confidently. "This is the first time I have had enough troops to engage in such an ambitious program."[49]

---

[44] Mission Council Action Memo 125, 27 Sep 66, sub: Minutes of the Mission Council Meeting, September 26, 1966.

[45] Westmoreland Jnl, 8 Oct 66, Westmoreland History files, 9–B and C, CMH.

[46] Ibid.

[47] Westmoreland Jnl, 17 Oct 66, Westmoreland History files, 9–D, CMH.

[48] See Mission Council Action Memo 125, 27 Sep 66, sub: Minutes of the Mission Council Meeting, September 26, 1966.

[49] Westmoreland Jnl, 13 Dec 66, Westmoreland History files, 11, CMH.

2

ATTLEBORO: The Coming Storm in III Corps

The year of the offensive began sooner than Westmoreland had expected. He had planned to delay the start of his operations until the new year, allowing the ground to dry out in November and December 1966 and giving his reinforcements time to become acclimatized to Vietnam. The enemy, however, was not inclined to wait and made ready to launch a "winter-spring" campaign as soon as the weather improved slightly.

Most threatened was III Corps, where the terrain favored combat. Gently rolling hills or flat, jungled plains dominated; it was a transition zone from the low-lying and swampy Mekong Delta to the south and the southern foothills of the Annamite Mountains of the Central Highlands to the north. Elevations ranged from sea level in the south to some seven hundred meters above sea level along the northeastern boundary. The southwestern provinces of Hau Nghia and Long An were typical of the northern delta, low and wet. The western and central provinces of Tay Ninh, Binh Long, Binh Duong, Bien Hoa, and Phuoc Tuy featured undulating terrain rarely rising more than two hundred meters above sea level. In the far northeast, Phuoc Long, Long Khanh, and Binh Tuy Provinces formed the sometimes rugged foothills of the Annamites. Nestled among the hills of central and western Binh Tuy lay a large, low basin known as the rice bowl, one of the most fertile areas of South Vietnam outside of the Mekong Delta.

The importance of III Corps to the enemy could not be underestimated. Not only did the region include the nation's capital, it was easily accessible to enemy troops just over the border in Cambodia. (*Map 3*) And as MACV intelligence was beginning to realize, Prince Norodom Sihanouk, Cambodia's mercurial ruler, tacitly allowed the enemy buildup along his border and the flow of materiel from the port of Sihanoukville to the Communist bases. This confluence of logistical pipelines made III Corps a natural target for the North Vietnamese, and their command structure and order of battle reflected this. Saigon was the ultimate objective, and *COSVN* established some of its key base areas on the fringes just inside Cambodia. Within III Corps itself, in the northern part of the territory, the North Vietnamese occupied War Zones C and D, which for the past two years had been launching pads for several enemy offensives. In late 1966 nothing had changed: the North Vietnamese still planned to keep Saigon under siege and to pin down South Vietnamese units so they

III CORPS TACTICAL ZONE
December 1966

MAP 3

could not be shifted to thwart attacks elsewhere in the country. To accomplish this, the enemy placed three regular divisions—the *5th PLAF, 7th PAVN,* and *9th PLAF*—under direct *COSVN* control in outlying jungle bases. Closer to Saigon, some 24,000 local forces and perhaps as many as 9,000 guerrillas lurked, although as elsewhere in the country no one in the allied camp was sure of the numbers.[1]

Westmoreland made certain the approaches to Saigon were well guarded, giving General Seaman's II Field Force headquarters control over eight U.S. Army brigades plus a regiment in III Corps. Three brigades (numbered 1 through 3) belonged to the 1st Infantry Division

[1] MACV Briefing Bk for Sec Def, J–3 Briefing, tabs 4A and 13; Monthly OB Sum, CICV, Oct 66, p. I–1.

General Seaman

("The Big Red One"). The 25th Infantry Division ("Tropic Lightning") controlled four brigades: its own 1st and 2d, the 3d of the 4th Infantry Division, and the 196th Light Infantry. The last brigade, the 173d Airborne, was an independent unit, as was the 11th Armored Cavalry Regiment. Seaman also had an advisory group to help coordinate his activities with those of the local South Vietnamese forces, which included the 5th, 18th, and 25th Army of the Republic of Vietnam (ARVN) Divisions, plus five ranger battalions, three armored cavalry squadrons, several general reserve (airborne and marine) battalions, and more territorials than in the two northern corps zones. However, due to their proximity to the capital, most of these units were heavily politicized and in the eyes of American commanders had little to recommend them. On the other hand, the one allied brigade-size unit in III Corps, the combined Australian–New Zealand Task Force, did have potential.

November in III Corps found six brigades of the U.S. 1st and 25th Infantry Divisions patrolling the southern borders of War Zones C and D. East of the capital the Australians covered Binh Tuy Province, while the 173d Airborne Brigade, the MACV reserve, was based near Saigon at Bien Hoa. Also east, the 11th Armored Cavalry had established an additional base camp, but the mechanized unit normally reinforced the infantry units operating around Saigon. Originally, Seaman had positioned one of his new brigades, the 3d of the 4th Division, at Bearcat, a vacated 1st Division camp also east of Saigon, where he hoped it could be rapidly broken in with routine security and patrolling missions. Within a month the brigade had joined the 25th Division northwest of Saigon.

During the U.S. troop buildup over the previous year, many of the largest operations were aimed at keeping the enemy off balance in his traditional base areas. In April 1966 MACV launched ABILENE, a spoiling operation to prevent an enemy move toward Saigon from the east. That same month the 1st Division began Operation BIRMINGHAM, which succeeded in capturing enemy supplies near the Cambodian border. In June and July the 1st Division linked up with the South Vietnamese 5th

Men of the 1st Infantry Division in the Saigon River corridor

Division in a series of thrusts on the eastern flank of War Zone C, opening Highway 13 from Saigon to the rubber plantations in the north. American and South Vietnamese units caught the *9th Division* massing near An Loc, a provincial capital; the allies inflicted heavy losses and forced the remnants back into their Cambodian sanctuaries.

In the fall of 1966 interdiction remained a high priority, and, until the dry season began in earnest, Westmoreland's primary concern remained blocking the three infiltration corridors into Saigon proper. One went east from Cambodia's Svay Rieng Province; a second began in War Zone C and wound its way south along the Saigon River; and a third originated in the northeast, in War Zone D, and followed the Song Be River south.

Opening Gambit

Senior Col. Hoang Cam, commander of the *9th Division*, had his orders: "destroy a 'vital' element of the enemy, support the local [revolutionary] movement, oppose enemy pacification and expansion effort, break the oppressive government control, widen friendly liberated areas, and provide security and protection for storage facilities and base areas of Dung Minh Chau [War Zone C]."[2] This was standard operating procedure

[2] Periodic Intel Rpt 34, II Field Force, Vietnam (IIFFV), 7 Nov 66, pp. 2–3 and an. B. Quote from Rpt, MACV J–2 Log 03–3331–67, 6 Apr 67, sub: TRANSLATION RPT; Title:

for a dry season offensive, but in the fall of 1966 the *9th Division* was weakened by heavy losses that the previous summer's combat had inflicted. Despite this, General Nguyen Chi Thanh, the *COSVN* commander, decided to use that unit, his most reliable and experienced, for a November offensive in Tay Ninh Province. His guidance to Colonel Cam was to direct his "main effort" on the inexperienced 196th Brigade, just settling in at Tay Ninh, and local territorial and CIDG (Civilian Irregular Defense Group) units, small teams that U.S. Army Special Forces advised.

Cam planned to open the offensive on 3 November with three regiment-size attacks. First, he assigned the *271st PLAF Regiment*, a unit of about 1,500 men, to strike the 196th's base at Tay Ninh West and attempt to lure and annihilate any of the brigade's reaction forces. His *272d PLAF Regiment* with two battalions was to move south across the Saigon River and join the *14th PLAF Local Force Battalion*, the provincial Viet Cong unit for Tay Ninh Province, to attack South Vietnamese territorial outposts at Suoi Cao, thirty kilometers southeast of Tay Ninh City. The remaining battalion of the *272d* was to join the *101st PAVN Regiment*, a unit of the *7th Division* on loan to Cam, for the third and main effort, the destruction of a Special Forces camp at Suoi Da, fifteen kilometers northeast of Tay Ninh City. For this mission Cam provided to the *101st* an antiaircraft and a mortar company from his own division. In all, the reinforced regiment would have about 3,000 troops. Cam himself intended to accompany the *101st Regiment*, a unit that had seen little combat and was unfamiliar with the terrain of War Zone C, to its forward assembly areas near Suoi Da and then to depart to occupy a central position from which to coordinate all three assaults.[3]

Of course, the Americans knew none of this. Cam's main target, the 196th Brigade, a relatively green unit, had arrived in Vietnam less than two months earlier, on 14 August 1966. Disembarking at Vung Tau, the brigade deployed immediately to Tay Ninh, coming under the operational control of General Weyand's 25th Division. Shortly after the brigade commander, Col. Francis S. Conaty, reported his unit to General Seaman, he was replaced by Brig. Gen. Edward H. de Saussure. General Westmoreland had a policy that each separate brigade have a general officer as commander. Colonel Conaty was to remain as General de Saussure's deputy until another command became available for him.[4]

After Action Report, Tay Ninh Campaign (3 Nov–30 Dec 66), Military Affairs Committee (*Group 129*), SVN Liberation Army, no. 23/N1, 1 Feb 67, p. 5 (hereafter cited as Tay Ninh Campaign). See also "Tay Ninh Battle," an. to *South Vietnam: Initial Failure of the U.S. "Limited War"* (Hanoi: Foreign Languages Publishing House, 1967), pp. 45–54. All in Historians files, CMH.

[3] Tay Ninh Campaign, pp. 4–6. See also *Su Doan 9* [*The 9th Division*] (Hanoi: People's Army Publishing House, 1990), pp. 76–78 (hereafter cited as *9th Division*), copy in CMH. The *9th Division*'s third regiment, the *273d PLAF*, had moved to War Zone D and would take no part in the offensive.

[4] William C. Westmoreland, *A Soldier Reports* (Garden City: Doubleday, 1976), p. 275; Interv, author with Col Francis S. Conaty, Comdr, 196th Light Inf Bde, and Comdr, 1st Bde, 25th Inf Div, 24 Sep 75, Historians files, CMH.

General de Saussure (left) and Lt. Gen. Chae Myung Shin, commander of South Korean forces in Vietnam

Although pleased to have a command, de Saussure wished it had been under other circumstances. Considered by many a superb staff officer and an authority on missiles, he had no experience commanding infantry. But he did have proven ability with artillery units and before joining the 196th had served fifteen months as the assistant division commander for support in the 25th Division, four months of that time in Vietnam. Although Conaty's presence made the situation awkward, his knowledge of the brigade that he had organized and trained, de Saussure hoped, would assist him in the early stages of his assignment.[5]

Wasting no time getting into the field, on 14 September the 196th Brigade began a series of battalion-size probes around Tay Ninh, code-named Operation ATTLEBORO. While one battalion was in the field the other two remained behind to finish construction of the base camp. These initial sweeps proved unproductive, and by October the unit was looking for a new mission. So, when troops of the 25th Division uncovered a large rice cache in the Saigon River corridor about thirty kilometers southeast of Tay Ninh City, Weyand sent some of de Saussure's forces farther east in search of other stockpiles.[6]

On 19 October de Saussure moved one of his battalions to Dau Tieng, a district seat on the northern edge of the corridor, and had it begin to scour the area, which varied from low, flat terrain and cultivated fields to scrub brush and thick jungle. On the fifth day, 23 October, operating north of the town, the unit stumbled on a long row of sheds covered with black plastic and filled with tons of rice. In the days that followed, the Americans uncovered other large caches. Elated, de Saussure asked permission to move his command post to Dau Tieng

---

[5] Interv, author with Conaty, 24 Sep 75.

[6] After Action Rpt (AAR), Opn ATTLEBORO, 196th Light Inf Bde, 15 Dec 66, an. A, p. 11, Historians files, and MFR, 19 Dec 66, sub: MACV Commanders' Conference, 20 November 1966, p. 44, Westmoreland History files, 11–C–3, both in CMH.

and bring another battalion into the vicinity of the cache site as soon as possible. Brig. Gen. George G. O'Connor, commanding the 25th Division while Weyand was serving as temporary commander of II Field Force, agreed. On 30 October ATTLEBORO became a full-fledged brigade operation.[7]

Evacuation of the rice posed a problem. Located well away from the Saigon River and any road, it had to be lifted out by Chinook helicopters, then in short supply, and it also had to be bagged beforehand, a time-consuming process for the two infantry battalions. Although 843 tons of rice had so far been uncovered, over the next three days the brigade removed only 120 tons.[8]

Also, de Saussure was running out of time. One of his units patrolling along an oxcart trail that led north from the enemy rice depot discovered a document from the *82d Rear Service Group*, the *COSVN* element responsible for supply in War Zone C. The document revealed that there were other supply bases to the north and that the Viet Cong were in the process of organizing an area defense.[9]

Anxious to seize all the depots before the enemy could react in force, on 1 November O'Connor instructed de Saussure to spend only one more day evacuating the rice, to destroy what was left, and then to move north toward the Ba Hao, a stream emptying into the Saigon River seven kilometers northwest of Dau Tieng. In the interim he gave him the 1st Battalion, 27th Infantry, from his 2d Brigade, to begin the probe, which it did using "eagle flights."[10] On 2 November the battalion conducted several such flights along the fringe of the objective area and spotted several trails. It found no caches and met no opposition.

The Battle Begins

On the morning of 3 November, in a complicated maneuver, de Saussure sent two of his own battalions, the 2d Battalion, 1st Infantry, and the 4th Battalion, 31st Infantry, north from the cache site over four separate jungle routes toward the Ba Hao. At the same time he air-assaulted two companies of the 1st of the 27th Infantry into widely divergent blocking positions just south of the stream, one to the west of the attacking columns, the other to the east. The third company of the 1st of the 27th

[7] AAR, Opn ATTLEBORO, 196th Light Inf Bde, pp. 10–11; AAR, Opn ATTLEBORO, 25th Inf Div, n.d., pp. 6, 10–12, Historians files, CMH.

[8] AAR, Opn ATTLEBORO, 196th Light Inf Bde, pp. 10–11; AAR, Opn ATTLEBORO, 25th Inf Div, p. 12.

[9] AAR, Opn ATTLEBORO, 196th Light Inf Bde, an. A, pp. 15–19.

[10] During eagle flights, an infantry platoon orbited suspected enemy areas via helicopter. Periodically, soldiers landed, rushed into the brush for a brief search, and then flew elsewhere to repeat the process. If they made contact with the enemy, a battalion would reinforce them.

remained at Dau Tieng, and the 196th's 3d Battalion, 21st Infantry, remained at Tay Ninh West, both serving as reserves.

The operation went badly from the start. With no linkup plan, little appreciation of the enemy and terrain, and command and control difficult, the two blocking and four attacking forces quickly became separated from one another, lost in the dense jungle. Shortly before noon an enemy force of unknown size attacked the western blocking company in tall elephant grass, killing the company commander and inflicting heavy casualties. The arrival of two reserve companies from Dau Tieng and Tay Ninh West and two companies from the westernmost attacking column failed to turn the tide. Mines, booby traps, and snipers were a constant hazard. Flying overhead, de Saussure spent the rest of the afternoon assisting his battalion commanders as they regrouped their units, evacuated casualties, and brought in extra ammunition, rations, and especially water. The humidity and heat had taken a lot out of the men.[11]

Nightfall found the Americans in two laagers. On the west, where the fight had taken place, Maj. Guy S. Meloy, commander of the 1st Battalion, 27th Infantry (he had arrived during the battle), had five companies: his western blocking company, the two reserve companies, and the two companies from the attack column. De Saussure ordered the rest of the committed units, the four remaining attack companies and the eastern blocking company, to assemble and form a perimeter several kilometers to the east. Placing the senior lieutenant colonel, Hugh H. Lynch, commanding officer of the 4th Battalion, 31st Infantry, in command, de Saussure began to plan how he would unscramble his units on the following day.

Meanwhile, unknown to the Americans, the U.S. foray had caused the *9th Division* commander to change his attack plans. Informed of the American movements, Colonel Cam reduced the planned attacks against Tay Ninh West and Suoi Cao to diversions, and scrapped the assault on the Suoi Da Special Forces camp. He would direct his main effort against those elements of the 196th operating northwest of Dau Tieng.

The following day, 4 November, the fight intensified all across the battlefront. (*Map 4*) Cam's diversionary efforts—a carefully planned mortar attack against de Saussure's Tay Ninh base camp to the west and a series of determined assaults against Suoi Cao to the south—were both executed during the early hours, further confusing the Americans. Suoi Cao was saved only by the ineptitude of the attacking *272d Regiment*, heavy U.S. air and artillery fire, and a staunch South Vietnamese defense. The enemy left 53 dead on the battlefield. Tay Ninh was spared a ground attack, but damage to the 196th's communications system was extensive, prompting de Saussure himself to make an emergency trip to his home base camp.[12]

---

[11] Sitrep, 196th Light Inf Bde, 2–3 Nov 66, Historians files, CMH, and the excellent account in Maj. Gen. Guy S. Meloy, "Operation Attleboro: The Wolfhounds' Brave Stand," *Vietnam* 10 (October 1997): 39–44.

[12] Tay Ninh Campaign, pp. 17–18; Periodic Intel Rpt 34, IIFFV, 7 Nov 66, p. 2; Intel Sum 235, IIFFV, 4 Nov 66, pp. 2–3, and Sitrep, 196th Light Inf Bde, 3–4 Nov 66, both in

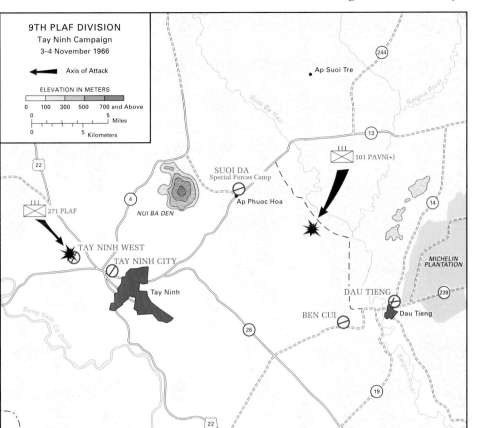

MAP 4

But it was northwest of Dau Tieng, in the heavy woods near the Ba Hao, that Cam set out to produce a victory. His division had established its forward command post within a fortified stronghold less than five hundred meters northeast of Meloy. Having already rushed the division's security platoon and reconnaissance company to block Meloy's advance, Cam reinforced with the *3d Battalion* of the *101st Regiment*, ordering it across the Ba Hao into prepared positions. His instructions to the battalion were clear: let the Americans enter the woods, then attack. He did not have long to wait.[13]

Historians files, CMH.

[13] Tay Ninh Campaign, pp. 8, 20.

The two field positions under Meloy and Lynch had remained secure throughout the night except for minor probes of Meloy. After the morning fog lifted the men were resupplied and their commanders given the order of the day: disentangle their units and resume the sweep north. There seemed no rush to get started, since the brigade's mission appeared attainable within a few hours. But the maneuvers that de Saussure and his staff had worked out were no improvement over those of the previous day. Two of the companies that had spent the night with Meloy, those from the 2d of the 1st Infantry, were to trek east about three kilometers and resume their original attack north. Meloy was to attack northeast to an arbitrary spot south of the stream on Route 19, an old French logging road, and link up with his eastern blocking company, which would attack west from its night laager with Lynch. To avoid friendly fire problems, Meloy gave the companies of the 2d of the 1st Infantry an hour's head start. Then he moved out to the northeast.

Lying in wait a short distance away were the North Vietnamese in mutually supporting bunkers. Some of the bunkers were made of concrete, and all had thick overhead log coverings and bristled with machine-gun emplacements and camouflaged fighting positions. Interconnecting tunnels and trails hidden from the air provided access for rapid reinforcement.[14]

The disciplined North Vietnamese regulars held their fire until the lead U.S. unit walked into a series of concealed fire lanes extending from the bunkers. "One minute it was quiet," Meloy recalled later, "and the next instant it was like a Fort Benning 'Mad Minute.'"[15] Returning fire, the Americans tried without success to flank the enemy. Although Meloy called in artillery, it had no appreciable effect on the volume of hostile fire. Over the next hour he committed his other two companies on either flank, but North Vietnamese fire pinned both to the ground. Unable to advance or withdraw and taking casualties, including everyone in his battalion command group except a radio operator, Meloy radioed for reinforcements.

First to respond were the two companies that had left him that morning. Less than a kilometer away, they halted at the sound of gunfire and wheeled north, taking several casualties before reaching Meloy in the afternoon. Meanwhile, the eastern blocking company, led by Capt. Robert B. Garrett, advanced from its laager with Lynch and ambushed a North Vietnamese platoon moving to Meloy's front. But for reasons not clear then or later, de Saussure ordered it to turn around

---

[14] Daily Jnl, 1st Bn, 27th Inf, 4 Nov 66, Historians files, CMH; AAR, Opn ATTLEBORO, 196th Light Inf Bde, pp. 12–14; Periodic Intel Rpt 34, IIFFV, 7 Nov 66, an. I.

[15] *The 25th Infantry Division: "Tropic Lightning" in Vietnam, 1966–1967* (Doraville, Ga.: Albert Love Enterprises, 1967), p. 8, copy in CMH. A "Mad Minute" was a training demonstration of firepower during which all of a unit's weapons were fired continuously for one minute to familiarize troops with the total impact of their armament.

and rendezvous with the rest of the Lynch elements well east of the fight. These units would not rejoin the battle until the next morning.[16]

Also reinforcing was Company C from Meloy's sister battalion, the 2d of the 27th Infantry. O'Connor had sent the company and battalion headquarters over to Dau Tieng the night before, promising de Saussure a second company the next morning and a third on order. Four hours after the firefight started, and after three enemy human-wave assaults that nearly carried the Meloy position, the company from the 2d of the 27th, accompanied by the battalion commander, Lt. Col. Willlam C. Barrott, landed just to the west, soon ran into an enemy position, and came under fire. Casualties from the first bursts were heavy, including the company commander, who was killed. A half hour later, while trying to find a way to Meloy's perimeter, Colonel Barrott was also killed.

Because of the short distance separating the company from Meloy, it was impossible to bring artillery fire on the enemy between them. Nor could Meloy provide supporting fire for fear of hitting the company's survivors. Twice during the night he tried to relieve them in place and bring them out, attacking through apparent gaps in the enemy lines. The first attack ran into a line of bunkers and was repulsed, sustaining five dead and eight wounded. The second attack, toward dawn, triggered a big firefight and also failed to break through. Seven Americans died in that action.[17]

Meanwhile, throughout the fourth de Saussure's superiors had continually monitored the battle, becoming increasingly unhappy with his performance. Early in the day, while de Saussure was back at the brigade base at Tay Ninh surveying the damage from the mortar attack, Maj. Gen. William E. DePuy, the 1st Division commander, and one of his assistant commanders, Brig. Gen. James R. Hollingsworth, arrived at the command post at Dau Tieng. Upon learning of the brigade's complicated plan for the day and the reported locations of its scattered units, DePuy sensed a disaster in the making. Even more shocking was the absence of the brigade commander at what DePuy considered a critical time. He ordered de Saussure to return to Dau Tieng at once.

When de Saussure arrived he briefed the visiting generals using his personal map. The locations of his units as he plotted them were different from those of his staff, and DePuy felt the maneuver plan was illogical and confusing. Convinced that de Saussure might lose control of the situation, DePuy offered some pointed advice and then left with Hollingsworth.[18]

[16] Daily Jnl, 1st Bn, 27th Inf, 4 Nov 66; Lt. Col. Guy S. Meloy comments on S. L. A. Marshall, *Ambush* (New York: Cowles Book Co., 1969), concerning the 1st Battalion, 27th Infantry, during ATTLEBORO, p. 9 (hereafter cited as Meloy Comments), Historians files, CMH.

[17] Meloy Comments, p. 10; Daily Jnl, 1st Bn, 27th Inf, 5 Nov 66, Historians files, CMH; AAR, Opn ATTLEBORO, 196th Light Inf Bde, pp. 14–16.

[18] Ltr, Lt Gen James R. Hollingsworth to Col William E. LeGro, 22 Jan 76, sub: Answers to Written Questions Submitted by Author; Interv, author with Gen William E. DePuy, CG, 1st Inf Div, 3 Oct 77. Both in Historians files, CMH.

A wounded Major Meloy (left) *directs the battle.*

In the afternoon Lt. Gen. John A. Heintges, the MACV deputy commander, also landed at de Saussure's command post for a briefing. He too disliked what he saw, and from his helicopter he asked General Weyand to meet him at Bien Hoa Air Base. There, Heintges urged Weyand to have DePuy take over ATTLEBORO, since the 1st Division had more experience fighting the large main force units that the 196th had apparently run up against. Weyand agreed.[19]

That evening planes started landing at Dau Tieng with a battalion of the 1st Division, followed by DePuy and his headquarters. DePuy immediately placed his 3d Brigade command post at Suoi Da and ordered his supporting artillery and cavalry to move by road throughout the night to join the brigade, which he intended to commit to battle on the fifth. Turning to the 196th, he told de Saussure to break contact the next day, assemble all his units in a clearing south of Meloy, and unscramble the companies and return each to its parent organization. In the meantime, he put Meloy, who had been cool under fire, in charge of the battle.[20]

[19] Daily Jnl, G–3, 25th Inf Div, 4 Nov 66, Historians files, CMH; Interv, author with DePuy, 3 Oct 77; AAR, Opn ATTLEBORO, 1st Inf Div, 6 Apr 67, p. 8, Historians files, CMH.

[20] AAR, Opn ATTLEBORO, 1st Inf Div, p. 8; AAR, Opn ATTLEBORO, 196th Light Inf Bde, an. C, app., and Fragmentary Order (FRAGO) 17. DePuy placed Brig. Gen. John R. Deane, another assistant commander of the 1st Division, in an "overwatch" capacity with instructions that should de Saussure fail to follow DePuy's instructions, Deane was to relieve him in DePuy's name and take command of the 196th Brigade. See Interv, author with Gen

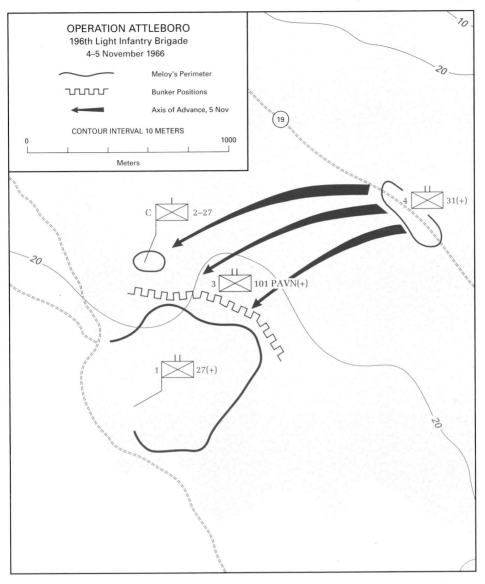

OPERATION ATTLEBORO
196th Light Infantry Brigade
4–5 November 1966

Meloy's Perimeter

Bunker Positions

Axis of Advance, 5 Nov

CONTOUR INTERVAL 10 METERS

0   1000

Meters

C ⊠ 2–27

4 ⊠ 31(+)

3 ⊠ 101 PAVN(+)

1 ⊠ 27(+)

MAP 5

Cool or not, Meloy had his work cut out for him: a tattered company to rescue and a fighting withdrawal to effect. It took him most of 5 November. Succor came from the rest of the 2d of the 27th, which airassaulted piecemeal into his perimeter, and three companies that had spent the night with Colonel Lynch, with Captain Garrett in the lead.

John R. Deane, Asst Div Comdr, 1st Inf Div, and CG, 173d Abn Bde, 5 Jan 78, Historians files, CMH.

Those three companies brought to eleven the number under Meloy's command, a remarkable moment for a fairly young major on the promotion list who had spent the last six months as an adviser to the South Vietnamese Airborne Division. But it was Garrett who made the breakthrough. By noon, after coordinating with Meloy and the artillery, Garrett attacked south and finally reached the trapped company, which had just repelled a determined North Vietnamese assault. (*See Map 5.*) Four hours later Garrett and the Barrott survivors found Meloy and relative safety after circling well to the west around the enemy bunkers. Then came disengagement, another two hours, with Meloy breaking contact company by company, leapfrogging them to the rear under covering artillery, and then extraction by helicopter to bases at Dau Tieng and Tay Ninh West. The next day, 6 November, the *101st Regiment* having pulled out, elements of the 196th returned to the battlefield to retrieve the remaining dead.[21]

The three-day engagement was at best a standoff, although the enemy apparently had been hurt the most, suffering upwards of 200 dead. Only later would the Americans learn the full extent of the damage they had done. According to the *9th Division* after action report, one of the companies from the *3d Battalion, 101st Regiment*, had been mauled on the fifth and had fled without orders. The other survivors of the battalion took six days to reassemble north of the Ba Hao, and for the remainder of ATTLEBORO the *3d Battalion* never regained its fighting effectiveness. But American losses were also heavy. While the North Vietnamese boasted 600 Americans killed, actual losses were substantial enough—60 dead and 159 wounded, most of them in the two battalions of the 27th Infantry. The 25th Division had paid the price for de Saussure's mistakes.[22]

The three-day battle marked the first time in III Corps that the North Vietnamese had sustained prolonged combat with a large U.S. force. It proved to be a harbinger of battles to come, as Colonel Cam ordered all three of his regiments to pull back into War Zone C to continue the fight.[23]

[21] Meloy Comments, p. 14; AAR, Opn ATTLEBORO, 1st Bn, 27th Inf, p. 4; AAR, Opn ATTLEBORO, 196th Light Inf Bde, pp. 15–17; Daily Jnl, 1st Bn, 27th Inf, 5 Nov 66.

[22] AAR, Opn ATTLEBORO, 196th Light Inf Bde, pp. 15–17; Tay Ninh Campaign, pp. 8–9, 16; Meloy, "Operation Attleboro," p. 44.

[23] AAR, Opn ATTLEBORO, 196th Light Inf Bde, pp. 1–15; Interv, author with DePuy, 3 Oct 77.

3

ATTLEBORO: The Battle Widens

From 4 to 25 November ATTLEBORO became a large-scale search and destroy operation as II Field Force threw battalion after battalion into the jungle northwest of Saigon. When General DePuy took control of the operation on 4 November, he had only his 1st Division command post and a battalion, which he airlifted to Dau Tieng from his base camp at Di An that night. Over the next two days two of his brigades, the 2d and 3d, joined him on the battlefield in rapid succession. Both flew to Dau Tieng, but the 3d moved forward to Suoi Da. While DePuy made certain of his supply lines, both brigades started after the *9th Division* early on the sixth.[1]

Rather than conduct a multi-unit sweep that would take time to develop and would allow the *9th Division* to slip into Cambodia, DePuy decided to insert his forces quickly at a point close to the suspected enemy bases in hopes of generating a hasty and unplanned response. Only as a last resort would he "jungle bash" as de Saussure had, using large units on long, often fruitless, but sometimes costly, searches for the enemy.

Since taking command of the 1st Division in March, DePuy had concluded that the trick to jungle fighting was to find the enemy with the fewest possible men and destroy him with the maximum amount of firepower. So far, most operations in Vietnam had consisted of hundreds of hours of patrolling punctuated by a few minutes of intense, close-quarters combat, which, more often than not, the Viet Cong had initiated. Experiences during the summer of 1966, most notably the War Zone C battles at Srok Dong and the Minh Thanh Road, in which 1st Division forces had destroyed enemy ambushes with storms of fire, had confirmed for DePuy the wisdom of this approach.

To find the enemy during ATTLEBORO, DePuy intended to have his troops sweep forward in a series of methodical tactical maneuvers called cloverleafing, employed when enemy contact appeared imminent. Typically, the unit would move forward on an assigned azimuth and then

---

[1] MFR, 19 Dec 66, sub: MACV Commanders' Conference, 20 November 1966, p. 41; AAR, Opn BATTLE CREEK, 2d Bde, 1st Inf Div, 13 Dec 66, p. 1, Historians files, CMH. DePuy chose a new name—BATTLE CREEK—for his operation against the *9th Division*. On 15 November, to end the confusion, General Weyand directed a return to the name ATTLEBORO. Contemporary 1st Division records, however, retain the code name BATTLE CREEK.

General DePuy (right) *on the day he took control of* ATTLEBORO

stop to set up an "overwatch" position, whereupon one squad would advance fifty to one hundred meters, depending on the density of the jungle, while another squad moved a like distance to one flank. The trace of each route taken would be an arc resembling a cloverleaf. If the patrols made no contact they returned, and the unit moved forward to establish a second overwatch position and repeat the process, with the check to the flank made in the opposite direction. Although time-consuming, the maneuver allowed an infantry unit to search an area thoroughly while at the same time reducing its vulnerability to ambush.[2]

Upon locating the enemy, DePuy planned to destroy him in a deluge of firepower. In addition to the artillery in the divisions, ATTLEBORO was supported by the rapidly growing resources of II Field Force—two new battalions and an artillery group had arrived in October—plus a large arsenal of bombers and fighter-bombers from Bien Hoa and Phan Rang. Orchestrating this symphony of power, especially air power, was no easy matter. Air Force personnel were integrated into every aspect of ATTLEBORO, beginning with the 3d Direct Air Support Center at Bien Hoa, which coordinated aerial operations over the III Corps area. At the division level, both

[2] Intervs, author with DePuy, 3 Oct 77; with Col William E. LeGro, G–2, 1st Inf Div, 15 Jan 76, Historians files, CMH; Ltr, Col Jack G. Whitted to author, 14 Jan 76, sub: Clover Leaf Techniques, Historians files, CMH.

the 1st and 25th had a division air liaison officer, while each brigade in ATTLEBORO had an Air Force control party consisting of a brigade air liaison officer, his assistant, and three forward air controllers flying the venerable O–1 Bird Dog. As ATTLEBORO escalated into a showdown with the *9th Division*, the Air Force tactical role would climb sharply.[3]

Early on the sixth, believing time was of the essence, DePuy launched his offensive. One battalion helicoptered to the area that the 196th Brigade had just vacated, while two more landed ten kilometers farther north. There, a Special Forces mobile strike force battalion of Nungs (ethnic Chinese) had bumped into the *101st Regiment* and had been roughly handled.[4] From then on, a heavy barrage would precede each air assault. Although two of DePuy's battalions made early contact with the enemy, the shelling apparently prevented interference with the landings. As night approached, all three U.S. units reported firm contact, although no decisive engagement developed.

Just before dark a seven-man ambush patrol from the 3d Brigade observed 150 Viet Cong, armed with carbines and carrying packs, slipping south along a trail toward Route 13. The patrol quickly called for artillery and mortar fire against the entire length of the enemy column. As the rear element passed the patrol's position, the Americans set off a claymore mine, firing a wall of lethal pellets into the column. Moments later artillery hit the rest of the column. The following morning patrols found 70 enemy bodies on the trail.

Throughout the night of 6 November artillery and Air Force fighter-bombers pounded suspected enemy locations around the perimeters of the three battalions. Moving out soon after daybreak, each unit found a number of shattered enemy fortifications and counted an additional 100 dead. Losses during the 1st Division's opening day of ATTLEBORO combat totaled 1 killed and 23 wounded, compared to 170 enemy dead.[5]

ATTLEBORO Upgraded to a Field Force Operation

Convinced that the 1st Division had struck the heart of the enemy *9th*, General Weyand turned ATTLEBORO into a field force operation. On the seventh he instructed General O'Connor, still acting in his stead as commander of the 25th Division, to deploy the 2d Brigade headquarters and a battalion to Tay Ninh West, there to establish a forward command post for the 25th Division. That accomplished, Weyand returned to O'Connor

[3] MFR, 19 Dec 66, sub: MACV Commanders' Conference, 20 November 1966, pp. 44–45; Ott, *Field Artillery*, pp. 47–48; Schlight, *Years of the Offensive*, pp. 213–14.

[4] For mobile strike force operations during ATTLEBORO, see Periodic Intel Rpt 35, IIFFV, 14 Nov 66, an. F, and Ltr, Hollingsworth to LeGro, 22 Jan 76, sub: Answers to Written Questions Submitted by Author, both in Historians files, CMH.

[5] AAR, Opn BATTLE CREEK, 3d Bde, 1st Inf Div, 15 Dec 66, pp. 3–4, Historians files, CMH; AAR, Opn BATTLE CREEK, 2d Bde, 1st Inf Div, p. 6.

the three battalions of the 25th under control of the 1st Division so O'Connor's 2d Brigade, now reconstituted, could sweep north with the 1st Division, using Route 4 as an axis of advance. Weyand wanted O'Connor to complete the realignment as soon as possible.[6]

Meanwhile, DePuy sent two additional battalions into the region northeast of Suoi Da, but neither those nor the three already committed were able to regain contact with the enemy. That evening, as the eastern-most battalion, the 1st of the 28th Infantry, commanded by Lt. Col. Jack G. Whitted, bivouacked in a savanna grass clearing, word came that the unit would be extracted by helicopter the next morning for commitment elsewhere.

Early in the morning the battalion's listening posts reported move-ment to their front. Just before first light, Whitted pulled in the outposts and told all his companies to conduct a reconnaissance by fire with mor-tars and small arms. As the firing moved around the northern edge of the perimeter, two trip flares ignited, and hidden enemy troops opened fire.

Twenty minutes later a company from the *101st Regiment* launched a frontal attack against Whitted's northern defenses. Because the battalion's claymore mines, laid in two concentric circles outside the perimeter, were still in place, the attack was doomed to failure. By detonating the outer bank of claymores the defenders broke the assault, and the North Vietnamese fell back.

Whitted requested air strikes and artillery fire, but the battery sup-porting his unit had started to displace. For twenty minutes the howitzers were silent, forcing Whitted to rely on his mortars.[7] (*Map 6*)

When the enemy attempted a second assault, the howitzers were ready to fire. Storming in again from the northwest, that attack broke down when the defenders fired their inner bank of claymores, and the artillery began dropping shells along the northwest edge of Whitted's position. When the requested Air Force support arrived overhead, Whitted shifted the artillery to the west and southwest so the fighter-bombers could begin their runs. The forward air controller who put in the air strikes later recalled:

> We put the bombs out 200 feet in the jungle, although that was within the envelope of hitting the friendlies. But they were landing in the jungle [and] the fragmentation wasn't going to get the troops. We put napalm in a little closer, and CBU [cluster bomb units] a little closer than that, and the 20-mm. right on the tree line.[8]

[6] AAR, Opn ATTLEBORO, 25th Inf Div, p. 17; AAR, Opn ATTLEBORO, 173d Abn Bde, 30 Dec 66, pp. 4–5, Historians files, CMH. The three 25th Division battalions returned from the 1st Division were the 1st and 2d Battalions, 27th Infantry, and the 1st Battalion, 5th Infantry (Mechanized). Since 5 November, the latter had patrolled the road between Tay Ninh West and Dau Tieng.

[7] AAR, Opn BATTLE CREEK, 3d Bde, 1st Inf Div, pp. 4–8; Interv, author with Col Jack G. Whitted, Comdr, 1st Bn, 28th Inf, 1st Inf Div, 19 Jan 76, Historians files, CMH.

[8] Contemporary Historical Examination of Current Operations (CHECO) Rpt, Opn ATTLEBORO, Pacific Air Force (PACAF), 14 Apr 67, p. 26, Historians files, CMH.

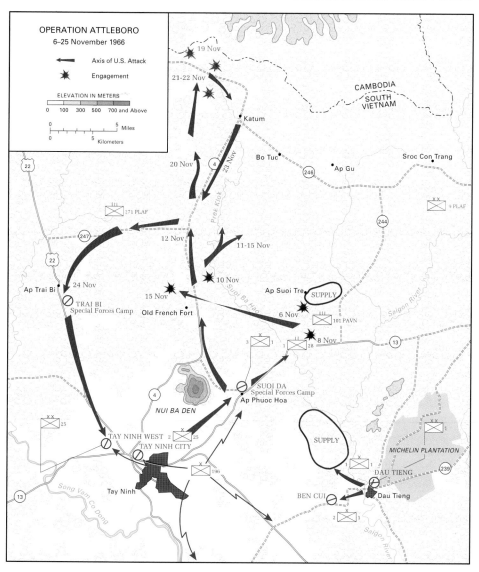

MAP 6

Despite heavy losses, the *101st* sent a second battalion into the fight at sunrise. Committing its units piecemeal at five-minute intervals, that battalion hurled its men against Whitted's west and southwest flanks. To use the enemy's own description of what happened, the attackers "missed a chance to destroy the enemy in the pocket of resistance because of lack of determination."[9]

[9] Tay Ninh Campaign, p. 9. This force was believed to include elements of the *2d Battalion, 101st Regiment*, and the *2d Battalion, 272d Regiment*.

While daylight made it easier for the fighter-bombers to find their targets, it also revealed the location of Whitted's men, particularly his company commanders close by their radio antennas. All three were soon hit, but Whitted, although bleeding from a wound himself, arranged to replace them.

At a climactic moment in the fight, one of those replacements, Capt. Euripides Rubio, realized that a smoke grenade intended to mark the enemy's position for an incoming air strike had landed perilously close to his own men. As he ran forward to scoop up the grenade and throw it into the enemy ranks, he made a ready target and was quickly wounded. Undaunted, he continued forward, the burning grenade in his bare hands, until he had worked to within twenty meters of the enemy. As he threw the grenade, enemy fire cut him down. Captain Rubio was posthumously awarded the Medal of Honor.[10]

The air strike that Rubio had marked and others that followed hit the enemy force regrouping for another attack. Colonel Whitted had by that time reinforced the threatened sector with the last of his reconnaissance platoon, which he had maintained as a reserve, and the men were able to hold without further help. The enemy soon began to disengage his shattered units, and at 1130, as the Americans downed the last of a number of snipers hidden in trees to cover the retreat, the action came to an end. Although DePuy tried to cut off escape routes, using the 3d Brigade under Col. Sidney M. Marks, the North Vietnamese made good their withdrawal.

Enemy analysts later claimed that "one [U.S.] company was completely destroyed [and] another . . . suffered heavy losses (over two hundred men)." The enemy had actually killed 19 Americans. Enemy dead totaled 305; the next day another 85 bodies would be found stuffed in a tunnel. The subsequent discovery, just north of Whitted, of a huge supply complex containing tons of grenades, explosives, mines, food, and clothing, made clear why the *101st* had attacked.[11]

After Whitted's fight on the eighth, DePuy was certain that the enemy force northeast of Suoi Da was still large and threatening, so he sought to have his 1st Brigade join him in Attleboro. Weyand agreed. DePuy could have asked to keep the 196th, but since his meeting with de Saussure on the fourth, he had lost confidence in that brigade.

So had General Westmoreland. After examining General de Saussure's performance from 3 to 5 November, Westmoreland concluded that the 196th needed fresh leadership. De Saussure, Westmoreland noted, had committed his units piecemeal and had lost control of parts of his command in the brigade's first significant action, albeit a "rough one." "Perhaps no one under the circumstances," General Westmoreland wrote later, "could have done better," and Westmoreland blamed himself

---

[10] U.S. Congress, Senate, Committee on Veterans' Affairs, *Medal of Honor Recipients, 1863–1973*, 93d Cong., 1st sess., 1973, p. 920.

[11] AAR, Opn Battle Creek, 3d Bde, 1st Inf Div, p. 4; Interv, author with Whitted, 19 Jan 76. Quote from Tay Ninh Campaign, p. 9.

for giving command of an infantry brigade to an officer "lacking in tactical infantry experience."[12]

So DePuy got his 1st Brigade, not the 196th. Yet, until he could gain a clearer picture of the *9th Division*'s whereabouts, he felt compelled to reserve judgment on his dispositions. Accordingly, when the 1st Brigade arrived, he gave its commander, Col. Sidney B. Berry, the mission to guard the division's forward base at Dau Tieng and to replace the 196th. By the morning of the tenth DePuy had under his immediate command eight of the 1st Division's nine battalions, while the remaining battalion and a task force composed of rear-service units protected the division's bases nearer Saigon.[13]

Marks' 3d Brigade continued to find hastily abandoned camps and ammunition stores but failed, as did the 2d Brigade, to regain contact with the *101st*. On the eleventh, therefore, DePuy shifted the 2d Brigade under Lt. Col. Sam S. Walker to search for a "700-man Viet Cong force" reported near the Ben Cui Plantation. Finding no trace of the unit, Walker went on to conduct a cordon and search operation at Ben Cui II, a hamlet inside the plantation, which agents had reported as a major Viet Cong supply point.[14]

Operations of that sort, which would be used again and again throughout the war, had three objectives: first, to gather intelligence and root out the Viet Cong underground; second, to help the Saigon government show concern for the welfare of the people; and third, to search a populated area for weapons and other items of military value.[15]

Late on the evening of the twelfth Walker's men encircled Ben Cui II, completing the seal just before daylight. South Vietnamese officials followed, assembling the inhabitants for questioning by a National Police team. Most were elderly people or children. After the police segregated all men between the ages of fifteen and forty-five for further interrogation, government officials organized a hamlet festival, known to the Americans as a county fair. The officials made speeches about the need for the people to support the Saigon government, distributed safe-conduct passes and how-to-surrender leaflets, provided a meal, and generally attempted to befriend the people of the hamlet. Meanwhile, a U.S. Medical Civic Action Program (MEDCAP) team consisting of a doctor and medical assistants treated 190 villagers who had minor illnesses.

All the while, the 2d Brigade searched the hamlet. Although the troops found few weapons and military stores, the joint U.S.–South Vietnamese effort resulted in the capture of twenty-seven Viet Cong and the discovery that Ben Cui II was a requisition processing point for *COSVN's 82d Rear Service Group*. Enemy units would send carrying parties to the hamlet with

---

[12] Westmoreland, *A Soldier Reports*, p. 276.

[13] AAR, Opn BATTLE CREEK, 1st Bde, 1st Inf Div, 10 Jan 67, p. 2, Historians files, CMH.

[14] AAR, Opn BATTLE CREEK, 2d Bde, 1st Inf Div, pp. 3, 7.

[15] Lt. Gen. John H. Hay, Jr., *Tactical and Materiel Innovations*, Vietnam Studies (Washington, D.C.: Department of the Army, 1974), pp. 137–38.

money for the inhabitants to purchase food and supplies in Dau Tieng and Tay Ninh City. The villagers in turn brought the requested commodities to the waiting Viet Cong, who used them to replenish their jungle depots. Yet the 1st Brigade, not the 2d, would reap the benefit of that information. Soon after moving into the region, Colonel Berry's men found six caches, which contained over 1,300 tons of rice.[16]

As the 1st Division continued its search for the enemy *9th*, General Weyand brought the 25th Division into ATTLEBORO. He instructed O'Connor to enter War Zone C on the 1st Division's west flank but not to proceed beyond the 80 east-west grid line, thirty kilometers north of Tay Ninh City. Weyand wanted that area searched carefully before risking a more daring sweep farther north.

The 2d Brigade of the 25th Division established a firebase on 10 November at Bau Co, an old French fort located on Route 4, ten kilometers north of Nui Ba Den, the dominant hill mass overlooking War Zone C. The brigade then deployed its forces to the northeast, where intelligence had traced the *271st Regiment*. To conserve helicopters for resupply missions, O'Connor ordered the 196th Brigade, upon return to his control on the twelfth, to open the ground route between Tay Ninh and Bau Co.[17]

Meanwhile, the *9th Division* commander, Colonel Cam, was rapidly losing control of his fighting force. He had instructed his *101st Regiment* to protect the *82d Rear Service Group*'s ammunition stores and to fight a delaying action; but the *101st*, battling Whitted at Suoi Da on unfamiliar ground, was in full retreat by the afternoon of the eighth. Retreat turned into panic when the rear service troops joined the fleeing regiment rather than facing American firepower alone. When the *9th Division* ordered supplies for its maneuver units, nobody was left to deliver them.[18]

Desperate, the division commander sought to regain the initiative, ordering two regiments, the *271st* and *272d*, to attack ATTLEBORO's two main supply bases. In response, the *271st* sent two units toward Tay Ninh West. During the night of the eleventh, one force fired seventy mortar rounds into the camp of the 196th, killing three Americans and wounding thirty-two. The other force shelled a Special Forces camp at Trang Sup, four kilometers to the north, and overran a territorial outpost. That same night, a contingent of the *272d* fired seventy mortar rounds into the 1st Division's forward base at Dau Tieng. Fourteen Americans were wounded.[19]

---

[16] AAR, Opn BATTLE CREEK, 2d Bde, 1st Inf Div, pp. 3, 8–9; AAR, Opn BATTLE CREEK, 1st Bde, 1st Inf Div, pp. 5–6. The *9th Division* also received supplies from sanctuaries in Cambodia, as indicated by sightings of motor convoys of fifty to sixty vehicles moving eastward on Highway 1 on the nights of 5 and 6 November. See CHECO Rpt, Opn ATTLEBORO, PACAF, p. 19.

[17] AAR, Opn ATTLEBORO, 25th Inf Div, p. 1; Critique, Opn ATTLEBORO, 25th Inf Div, 13 Dec 66, p. 2, Historians files, CMH.

[18] Tay Ninh Campaign, p. 16.

[19] Periodic Intel Rpt 35, IIFFV, 14 Nov 66, p. 2, and Intel Sum 243, IIFFV, 12 Nov 66, p. 2, both in Historians files, CMH.

As the *9th Division* struggled to influence the battle, General Westmoreland met with General Weyand on 14 November. Pleased with the performance of the 1st Division, Westmoreland felt that DePuy should continue searching west of the Saigon River for another week but told Weyand that he should begin planning to return the division to its original operational area north of Saigon. Once the division had left, Westmoreland said, he intended to station the 3d Brigade, 4th Division, newly arrived in Vietnam in October, at Dau Tieng under the control of the 25th.

Turning to the 25th Division, Westmoreland suggested that it make a rapid thrust north with its 2d Brigade along Route 4 toward the Cambodian border in an attempt to spark an enemy reaction. As an objective, Westmoreland had in mind *COSVN* headquarters, reported to be situated near Katum. If *COSVN* remained elusive, the 2d Brigade could turn west and drive toward Lo Go, a border village thirty-five kilometers northwest of Tay Ninh City that seemed to be a major supply base for War Zone C. In so doing the brigade would pass through a region where electronic intelligence reports had located various sections of *COSVN* headquarters. If the move to Lo Go came up empty, Weyand was to end ATTLEBORO and wait for new intelligence before reinitiating operations in War Zone C.[20]

While the two commanders discussed the last phase of ATTLEBORO, the 2d Brigade of the 25th was searching for the *271st Regiment* east of Route 4 and north of the French fort. When the change of orders from II Field Force arrived on the fourteenth, General O'Connor instructed the brigade's commander, Col. Thomas M. Tarpley, to terminate that operation and move north to find *COSVN*.

The following day, 15 November, Tarpley's brigade began its advance, spearheaded by two mechanized battalions. Within a day it had established a firebase eight kilometers north of its starting point and had pushed reconnaissance elements north and west. Tarpley relocated his command post to the newly established firebase, but his units found few signs of the enemy until the nineteenth. That morning one of the mechanized companies came upon an entrenched Viet Cong platoon northwest of Katum. The company's armored personnel carriers overran the position with little difficulty, killing eleven Viet Cong. Most of the enemy unit involved, a battalion from the *70th Guard Regiment*, stayed hidden nearby, apparently unwilling to risk a fight against armor.

Later that day a second mechanized company bumped into another entrenched enemy force, an antiaircraft company attached to *COSVN*, armed with 12.7-mm. machine guns. That unit, and a second from the *271st* that arrived posthaste, held the Americans at bay for several hours, despite heavy U.S. air and artillery support. They withdrew after dark, having killed one and wounded twenty-three of Tarpley's troops. Analyzing what

---

[20] Westmoreland Jnl, 25 Nov 66, Westmoreland History files, 11–C, CMH; MFR, 19 Dec 66, sub: MACV Commanders' Conference, 20 November 1966, p. 44; Critique, Opn ATTLEBORO, 25th Inf Div, p. 3, and Daily Jnl, MACV Combat Operations Center (COC), 10 Nov 66, both in Historians files, CMH.

B–52 Stratofortresses

had happened, enemy commanders concluded: "We lacked coordination between the *1st Battalion, 271st Regiment* and the anti-aircraft unit, and the *2d Battalion, 271st Regiment* did not join in the battle. If we had coordinated, the killed enemy would have been more and more numerous."[21]

Documents taken from enemy dead after the fights and information from a prisoner confirmed the presence of a major enemy force—possibly a full regiment. With that in mind, Tarpley brought all of his battalions forward but failed to make further contact. Even so, the enemy remained nearby, for on the night of 21 November forty mortar rounds fell on the 2d Brigade's command post, wounding a man. ATTLEBORO ended shortly after that. On the twenty-second Tarpley closed down his firebases and began conducting feints to the east and northwest of Katum to cover the withdrawal. His last unit reached Tay Ninh on the twenty-fifth, the final day of the multidivision operation.[22]

In the meantime, having assumed the 25th Division's original mission to search the woods northwest of the French fort, DePuy's 1st Division had stirred up a fight. On 15 November, following an intensive bombardment, Marks' 3d Brigade moved a battalion by air into the southeastern corner of the woods. Once that battalion was safely inside, Marks ordered a second battalion into a smaller clearing four kilometers to the northwest.

---

[21] AAR, Opn ATTLEBORO, 25th Inf Div, p. 8; AAR, Opn ATTLEBORO, 2d Bde, 25th Inf Div, 10 Dec 66, p. 4, Historians files, CMH. Quote from Tay Ninh Campaign, pp. 11, 20.

[22] AAR, Opn ATTLEBORO, 2d Bde, 25th Inf Div, p. 4.

Landing in groups of five helicopters at a time, the men began to secure the clearing. As helicopters of the third lift deposited their loads, took off from the site, and turned south over the trees, they flew into a hail of enemy bullets. Three Hueys went down, their crews subsequently rescued. The rest of the battalion skirted the danger zone and continued to land.

Having encountered a major enemy unit, Colonel Marks ordered both battalions to execute cloverleaf patrols into the jungle. Once they made contact with the enemy, he called for all available firepower. The air strikes blew away a portion of the overgrowth, revealing a large enemy base camp.

Sporadic firing continued throughout the night. The next morning, reinforced by a third battalion, Marks' men entered the base camp. There they found a number of enemy bodies, shattered emplacements, and at one location a small camp still occupied by Viet Cong. Rather than assault the fortified position, Marks pulled his men back and again called for heavy fire support.

The fight was still in progress when General DePuy received an electronic intelligence report locating the *273d Regiment* a few kilometers northwest of Marks' battalions. Although the enemy unit was actually the *101st*, the specific identification made little difference. When Marks reported that the enemy facing him was trying to withdraw in that direction, DePuy requested B–52s. Since it would take twenty hours to bring in the big bombers, DePuy sought to pin the enemy in place with artillery and air strikes. Between bomb and shell bursts that continued throughout the night, Colonel Marks' men could hear enemy movement within the strike zone. Then came the big bombs, and all was quiet.

When patrols reached the target area, they found only a few bodies and several collapsed bunkers; the bulk of the enemy had escaped. The next day the men discovered a large but vacated hospital complex nearby containing over thirty structures. The largest building, 120 feet long, was a combination training center and mess hall with a stage and seating for 150 men. After examining several medical booklets and reports, intelligence analysts concluded that the 3d Brigade had found the Viet Cong medical center for War Zone C.[23]

An Assessment

Conceived as a series of battalion-size sweeps to search for caches west of the Saigon River, ATTLEBORO soon mushroomed into a major operation. All totaled, over 22,000 American and South Vietnamese soldiers participated in the offensive, including 18 U.S. and 3 South Vietnamese infantry battalions and 24 batteries of artillery. The 196th Brigade's incursions north-

---

[23] AAR, Opn BATTLE CREEK, 3d Bde, 1st Inf Div, p. 7; AAR, Opn ATTLEBORO, 1st Inf Div, p. 13; Periodic Intel Rpt 36, IIFFV, 21 Nov 66, p. 9, Historians files, CMH.

west of Dau Tieng had compelled the *9th Division* to abandon its planned attack on Suoi Da, forcing it instead to defend its own supply depots. A more determined effort south of War Zone C at Suoi Cao might have lured the Americans away from these jungle bases and afforded the reinforced *101st Regiment* more time to deal with the inexperienced 196th. But the *272d Regiment*, which American commanders considered the *9th Division*'s most reliable, failed to take Suoi Cao and for the remainder of ATTLEBORO inexplicably avoided combat. With this failure, the enemy division lost the battlefield initiative.[24]

After 6 November strong logistical and fire support gave the Americans a clear edge. During the operation, Air Force cargo planes flew 3,300 sorties to Tay Ninh West and Dau Tieng, transporting 11,500 passengers and 8,900 tons of supplies, 30 percent of the total tonnage moved during ATTLEBORO. During the early stages of the buildup at Dau Tieng, C–123s were landing every seven minutes.[25]

With that kind of logistical backup and with so few civilians in the area, American commanders were free to use their firepower. During the last three weeks of ATTLEBORO, a daily average of 88 artillery pieces fired a total of over 100,000 rounds for the 1st Division alone. On 8 November, the day of the division's heaviest fighting, the artillery expended over 14,000 rounds.[26]

Fire support from above was equally impressive. American airmen in B–57s, F–4s, and F–100s flew over 1,600 sorties and used 12,000 tons of bombs, rockets, napalm, and 20-mm. cannon shells. Only a third of those sorties were "immediate" missions—flights in response to emergency requests for air support against identifiable targets. The remainder, including 225 sorties by B–52s delivering 4,000 tons of bombs, were "preplanned" missions targeted well beforehand against suspected enemy locations and lines of communication.

Such strikes destroyed or damaged many installations but seldom added new numbers to the total count of enemy killed. Only when ground units conducted post-strike reconnaissance or when air observers could substantiate beyond a reasonable doubt that casualties had occurred were such results tallied. For these reasons American commanders believed that enemy losses were much higher than the official results.[27]

---

[24] Tay Ninh Campaign, p. 16. According to a document captured later, two *9th Division* regiments—the *101st* and the *271st*—received awards for their conduct in the winter-spring offensive. The *272d Regiment* received no award, probably because of poor performance in the Suoi Cao attack. See Periodic Intel Rpt 8, IIFFV, 28 Feb 67, p. 8, Historians files, CMH. In *9th Division*, pp. 75–78, ATTLEBORO is described as a "resounding victory." See also Operational Summary (Op Sum), 1966, MACV History Backup Material, Opn ATTLEBORO, 14 Sep–25 Nov 66, CEDAR FALLS Collection, Historians files, CMH.

[25] Ray L. Bowers, *Tactical Airlift*, The United States Air Force in Southeast Asia (Washington, D.C.: Government Printing Office, 1983), p. 270.

[26] AAR, Opn ATTLEBORO, 1st Inf Div, an. D, p. 8.

[27] CHECO Rpt, Opn ATTLEBORO, PACAF, pp. 32–33; AAR, Opn ATTLEBORO, 1st Inf Div, p. 15 and an. D, p. 8. Immediate missions generally comprised one-quarter of all com-

Although seemingly rigid, the rules for counting enemy dead were open to error. Air observers usually chose to report "possible" kills rather than chance running into enemy fire while flying at treetop level to make an actual count. Despite the Air Force's continual requests for ground searches, especially to justify the cost-effectiveness of the B–52s, ground commanders were rarely able to comply. Most preplanned missions struck remote locations, and ground commanders were little inclined to risk their men in areas they could not readily reinforce.

As was the general practice following a firefight in Vietnam, ground units determined the number of casualties by counting enemy bodies left behind, the so-called body count. The accepted tally for ATTLEBORO was 1,016 enemy dead. Yet, as was almost always the case, that figure represented more of an educated guess than a precise tabulation. The enemy, for example, admitted losing half that number, while an unconfirmed agent report indicated that enemy losses were twice as much as the final American count.[28]

The fact that both sides tended to exaggerate enemy casualties throughout the Vietnam War is undeniable, and probably commonplace in all military contests. Since American commanders had few opportunities to canvas the battle area thoroughly, and with the growing emphasis on statistical results, few had qualms about adding estimates of enemy dead to the actual counts. The basic problem with the body count was that soldiers under combat conditions had neither the time nor the inclination to make minute tallies of enemy dead. Nor were higher headquarters generally interested in questioning the accuracy of the figures they received. Besides, most military leaders recognized that even a careful visual count could seldom be exact. Many bodies went undiscovered, since the Viet Cong and the North Vietnamese carried their dead from the field whenever possible, while others simply lay hidden and undiscovered where they fell.

Not included in counts or estimates, except for planning purposes at MACV headquarters, were those enemy soldiers who died of wounds or were permanently disabled. Nor did the allies make any attempt to include enemy losses from disease in the official totals. Those losses could be considerable: an enemy document captured after ATTLEBORO revealed that at the start of the operation 652 men of the *9th Division*—10 percent of the division's strength—had malaria.[29]

---

bat sorties flown. See Thomas C. Thayer, ed., *A Systems Analysis View of the Vietnam War: 1965–1972*, vol. 5, *The Air War* (Arlington, Va.: Defense Documentation Center, Defense Logistics Agency, c. 1975), pp. 109–28, Historians files, CMH.

[28] Sitrep 328–66, MACV, 26 Nov 66, Historians files, CMH; Tay Ninh Campaign, pp. 12–13; Agent Rpt 6–026–1943–66, 149th Military Intel Group, Dec 66, Historians files, CMH. The last source puts enemy losses during ATTLEBORO at 2,130 killed and over 200 missing or captured.

[29] Westmoreland, *A Soldier Reports*, p. 273; McChristian, *Military Intelligence*, p. 128; Sitrep 328–66, MACV, 26 Nov 66.

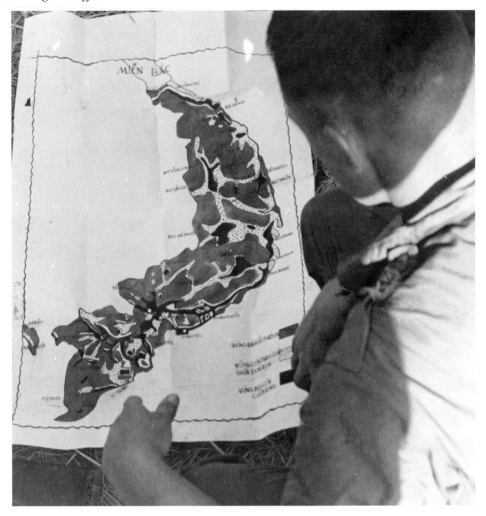

A Viet Cong map, showing U.S. bases, captured during ATTLEBORO

Whatever the precise figure for enemy casualties, the vast quantities of supplies that *COSVN's 82d Rear Service Group* abandoned are more verifiable. Within a three-week period the Americans had seized 2,400 tons of rice; had captured large ammunition caches with over 24,000 grenades, 600 mines, and 2,000 pounds of explosives; and had destroyed some 68 enemy base camps. Unanswered was what percentage of the enemy's existing supplies and bases in War Zone C had been lost or how quickly they could be replaced.[30]

[30] Intel Estimate 2 of Situation in III Corps, IIFFV, 20 Nov 66, p. 18, Historians files, CMH; MFR, 19 Dec 66, sub: MACV Commanders' Conference, 20 November 1966, p. 43; Periodic Intel Rpts 36, IIFFV, 21 Nov 66, p. 14, and 37, IIFFV, 28 Nov 66, an. D, both in Historians files, CMH.

General DePuy saw ATTLEBORO as a serious setback for the enemy. He believed that the *9th Division's 272d Regiment* was rendered ineffective and that the *101st* and *273d Regiments* were "badly hurt." But captured documents later revealed that only the *101st* had taken heavy losses, while the *272d* had suffered moderate casualties, and the *273d* had escaped unscathed. The *271st's* losses also were slight.

DePuy, a strong advocate of the main force war, had recommended that II Field Force conduct a vigorous pursuit of the enemy during the last week of ATTLEBORO in the belief that it could completely destroy the *9th Division*. General Weyand viewed the situation differently. Although never one to shun a fight, he questioned the utility of undertaking another massive maneuver without sufficient intelligence as to the enemy's whereabouts. Rather than chance finding nothing, Weyand instead chose to return his units to their original operational areas in the provinces surrounding Saigon, where they could reestablish their support for the South Vietnamese government's pacification effort. Weyand's own division, the 25th, had been performing that role since its arrival in Vietnam, and he had become convinced that despite the importance of operations against the enemy's big units, it was also important to destroy the guerrillas and the omnipresent Viet Cong underground. While he realized that operations in populated areas were generally unspectacular and produced low body counts and little recognition for the units involved, they still had to be conducted if Saigon and its surrounding provinces were to be made secure.

When General Seaman resumed command of II Field Force on 29 November, he fully supported Weyand's rationale for ending ATTLEBORO, as did Westmoreland.[31] But ATTLEBORO was obviously the forerunner of the large-scale offensives that General Westmoreland planned for the coming year. And if the Americans were to make full use of their technological edge, DePuy's tactics would serve as the model for the battles to come. Trying to "comb" the jungles with rifles, as de Saussure had attempted, was just too expensive.

---

[31] Interv, author with Lt Gen Jonathan O. Seaman, CG, IIFFV, and Dep CG, USARV, 25 May 76, Historians files, CMH.

4

West Toward the Border

If defending III Corps and Saigon were Westmoreland's immediate goals in the fall of 1966, the Central Highlands were his biggest long-term worry. In the early months of the buildup he simply did not have enough men to deploy to such underpopulated battlegrounds as the II Corps plateau; instead, he had relied on the 1st Cavalry Division at An Khe to meet enemy threats as they developed. Until the division arrived, responsibility for the highlands had fallen to nine widely separated Special Forces camps, which had provided a slight measure of security along the border. Two South Vietnamese regiments, plus rangers and territorial forces, had rounded out the highlands defenses.

Holding the highlands was complicated by the fact that Westmoreland had to fight on the populated coast as well, an area much different from the plateau. In the lowlands he could count on more troops. Eight allied brigades, three from the 1st Cavalry Division and four from the South Korean Capital Division and marines (soon to be reinforced by the South Korean 9th Division) were working the foothills immediately outside the villages and towns. Between the two divisions, the 1st Brigade, 101st Airborne Division, was providing an aggressive American presence in Phu Yen Province. Behind this shield, two South Vietnamese infantry divisions were performing security and pacification support missions from Binh Dinh to Binh Thuan. It was a mark of the extreme unit dispersion in the sector that while the commander of II Corps, Lt. Gen. Vinh Loc, had his headquarters on the far plateau at Pleiku City, General Larsen's I Field Force command post overseeing the Americans was over two hundred kilometers away on the coast at Nha Trang.[1]

The logistical effort was as dispersed as the troops it supported. The key allied support complexes in II Corps were located at the ports of Qui Nhon and Cam Ranh Bay. Qui Nhon was the more important operationally, however, because of its proximity to the scene of the fighting, both inland and on the coast. From Qui Nhon, the main overland line of communication, Highway 19, climbed westerly through the base at An Khe to Pleiku City, a 130-kilometer supply avenue to the highlands,

---

[1] MACV Briefing Bk for Sec Def, J–3 Briefing, tab 4.

which the North Vietnamese and Viet Cong interdicted whenever they could. The upland airfields at Pleiku and Kontum were thus of special tactical importance to the American war.

If Westmoreland saw the Central Highlands as a problem, the North Vietnamese regarded them as an opportunity. Hanoi recognized the Central Highlands as crucial to one of its strategies: cutting South Vietnam in two from the mountains to the coast. Geography lent itself to such a plan. Rugged terrain butting up against the enemy bases in Cambodia made it difficult for the Americans to operate along the border, while a well-defined insurgency in the coastal provinces prevented the allies from placing all their forces in the mountains. In 1965 Hanoi had planned its *Dong Xuan* ("winter-spring") campaign with the aim of seizing the highlands and precipitating a collapse of allied defenses along the coast.

This would not be easy. Varied terrain in II Corps made operations there difficult for both sides. Stretching from Ban Me Thuot in Darlac Province north to the southern border of I Corps, this area consisted of two distinct and very different territories. Seven of II Corps' twelve provinces comprised the Central Highlands; the other five formed the coastal plain. The entire region encompassed 78,780 square kilometers—about 46 percent of South Vietnam's land mass—with the Central Highlands making up almost two-thirds of that. Most of II Corps' 2.5 million people lived in fertile enclaves along the coast, leaving the highlands sparsely populated, with only a handful of towns of any size. Many of the highlands' inhabitants were seminomadic tribesmen, called Montagnards (highlanders) by the French. Ethnically and culturally different from the Vietnamese, they were often referred to as *moi* ("savages") by the rest of the population.

As the name implies, mountains dominate the Central Highlands. The Annamite Mountains, 1,650 kilometers in length, formed the backbone of the territory, running from the Demilitarized Zone in the north to the northern border of III Corps in the south. The Central Highlands are actually the southern foothills of the Annamites, a high plateau about 200 kilometers wide by 400 kilometers in length, rising from about 200 meters to over 1,000 meters.

The climate of this plateau is the most varied in the country. Rugged mountains along the Cambodian border are cloaked with jungle and, during much of the year, low-lying clouds. Because of its mass, the mountain chain determines the region's weather. From May to October the water-filled clouds of the southwest monsoon blow northeast from the Gulf of Thailand into the highlands, where they burst open in a deluge. Runoff from the storms runs into the steep-walled valleys and ravines, washing out roads and bridges and making travel difficult. The damage is often severe, but seldom does the flooding reach the coastal plains. In November the winds shift, blowing in the northeast monsoon. Rain falls on the lowlands, but the mountains are dry. Rivers slow and streams dry up, leaving ready-made trails into the jungle-choked valleys. But soldiers could not stray far from these streams, nor from the

An O–1 Bird Dog spotter plane assesses air strike damage in the Central Highlands.

few roads leading into the mountains; thick underbrush and double-canopy jungle made cross-country travel almost impossible.

Despite the Central Highland's sparse population and rugged landscape, it was a crucial battleground from the earliest days of the war. Beginning in 1962 U.S. Army Special Forces organized Montagnard tribesmen into Civilian Irregular Defense Groups as a screen against North Vietnamese border infiltration into the South. When U.S. ground forces began taking over the war in 1965, some of their earliest combat occurred in the highlands. In July a Viet Cong regiment attacked a Special Forces camp at Duc Co in Pleiku Province near the Cambodian border. When the enemy threatened to overrun the Green Berets, Westmoreland ordered the 173d Airborne Brigade, the first U.S. Army ground combat unit to enter Vietnam, from its base at Bien Hoa to the outskirts of the beleaguered camp. Its presence broke the siege.

From that point on, Westmoreland kept one eye on the Central Highlands at all times. In October 1965 MACV intelligence noticed the arrival of three new North Vietnamese infantry regiments onto the plateau, which Westmoreland feared might be the prelude to an attempt to overrun the border camps, capture Pleiku, then rush down Highway 19 to An Khe and on to Qui Nhon by the sea. If successful, the enemy would slice the Republic of Vietnam in two.

To preempt this blitzkrieg, Westmoreland relied on the mobility of the 1st Cavalry Division, commanded by Maj. Gen. Harry W. O. Kinnard. Tailor-made for the terrain of the western highlands, the new airmobile division used its helicopters to leapfrog over the mountains into the heart of the enemy before he could attack. On 23 October, reacting to assaults on the Special Forces camp at Plei Me, the division flew one battalion and its artillery over the North Vietnamese and landed in their rear, overwhelming the *33d PAVN Regiment* and sending it fleeing for Cambodia. As many as one-third of the estimated 3,000 North Vietnamese soldiers attacking Plei Me were killed or wounded during the battle. This was airmobility at its best: neutralizing the terrain and keeping the enemy at bay.

A Special Forces–trained Montagnard strike force

The North Vietnamese tried again in November, gathering their forces in the Ia Drang Valley. Aware of the buildup, Westmoreland decided that this time he would not allow the enemy to choose the time and place for a fight. The 1st Cavalry Division flew up and down the Chu Pong Massif looking for the North Vietnamese, and on 14 November it found them. Over the next four days, in the war's bloodiest combat thus far, the enemy was again driven away with the better part of another regiment rendered ineffective, although American casualties were also high. North Vietnamese units lay low for the remainder of the year, but MACV head-quarters knew that fighting would begin anew with the next dry season.

As U.S. units entered South Vietnam in 1966, Westmoreland was able to beef up his troop presence in the highlands without undermining his defense of the coast. Beginning in January the 3d Brigade, 25th Infantry Division, deployed to Pleiku, followed by a battalion of the 2d Brigade, 4th Infantry Division, in July. The rest of the 4th Division, commanded by Maj. Gen. Arthur S. Collins, came to II Corps in August and October, except for the 3d Brigade and its armor component, which went to III Corps to reinforce the other two brigades of the 25th Division. (*Map 7*) To make up for the armor shortfall, in May MACV sent the 1st Battalion, 69th Armor, to the highlands, where it would spend the duration of the war attached to the 4th Division. Equipped with fifty-four medium battle tanks, all M48A3 Pattons, its mission was to keep the main roads open, mostly in Pleiku Province.[2]

[2] General Donn A. Starry, *Mounted Combat in Vietnam*, Vietnam Studies (Washington, D.C.: Department of the Army, 1978), pp. 63–64.

MAP 7

General Larsen (left) *and Secretary of the Army Stanley R. Resor*

The highlands also received new artillery units to supplement the two battalions already there. In June 1966 the 52d Artillery Group came to Pleiku, followed by three battalions attached to the 4th Division, some of which arrived in August, the rest in October. Two other artillery battalions were attached to I Field Force, though the last of those did not deploy until March 1967.

Even before the new troops were in place, I Field Force launched several operations in 1966 aimed at keeping the North Vietnamese off balance in western II Corps. In May the 3d Brigade, 25th Division, opened Operation PAUL REVERE to engage North Vietnamese units around the Chu Pong. The following month, the 1st Brigade, 101st Airborne Division, attacked the *24th PAVN Regiment* in Kontum Province, an operation dubbed HAWTHORNE. The paratroopers stopped the enemy just north of Dak To and sent them reeling into Cambodia.

By the autumn of 1966 General Larsen had six infantry battalions, a tank battalion, and a divisional armored cavalry squadron—slightly less than a division—in the Central Highlands, not much of a force to deal with the better part of two North Vietnamese divisions. The coastal lowlands and Saigon received the lion's share of command attention. Westmoreland's order to divert the 3d Brigade, 4th Division, to III Corps and Larsen's decision to have the division's 1st Brigade help protect the rice harvest in Phu Yen sorely disappointed Collins. He was absolutely certain that holding an area as large as the highlands with less than a full division was only asking for trouble. But the plan was in place; he would do the job with what he had.[3]

For the most part, campaigning in this vast inland plateau took place west of Highway 14, a road sixty kilometers east of and parallel to the Laotian-Cambodian border. Larsen's guidance to Collins was simple: "hit the enemy early" and keep him off balance by launching spoiling attacks. "If you ever let him get set," Larsen cautioned, "you're going to pay hell getting him out." This approach, he believed, "kept the enemy at home [in Cambodia.]"[4]

The enemy indeed had a special interest in the area, both as a potential political base and for the corridors it provided to the rest of South Vietnam. In 1964 Hanoi had activated a distinctive "battle" command for the sector, and the *B3 Front*, under Maj. Gen. Chu Huy Man, became the largest North Vietnamese headquarters outside the North.

The front counted six maneuver regiments under the *1st* and *10th PAVN Divisions*, plus numerous logistical installations. Included among the latter were several large depot complexes called *binh trams*, each containing hospitals, storage sites, rest centers, and rice farms. The largest of these complexes was Military Station North (Base Area 609), located in the tri-border area where South Vietnam, Cambodia, and Laos joined. It was responsible for the main north-south infiltration corridor from the North and for two arterial corridors that extended eastward to the coast. Seventy kilometers to the south, Military Station Central (Base Area 702) served as a training base and headquarters of the *B3 Front*. And still another fifty kilometers south, Military Station South (Base Area 701) was the starting point for two supply routes supporting the *5th PAVN Division* in Phu Yen and Khanh Hoa. For the most part these supply routes followed South Vietnamese provincial or district boundaries, where government forces seldom operated. Allied fire coordination was complicated in these areas by having to obtain clearance from at least two government headquarters.

Opening Moves

In October 1966 Man received orders to attack the U.S. units defending Pleiku, the heart of the allied support system on the plateau, in the hope that

---

[3] AAR, Opn PAUL REVERE IV, 4th Inf Div, 28 Jan 67, pp. 1–6, box 4, 67A/5216, RG 334, National Archives and Records Administration (NARA), Washington, D.C.; Operational Report–Lessons Learned (ORLL), 1 Aug–31 Oct 66, 4th Inf Div, 22 Dec 66, pp. 15–18, 33–34, Historians files, CMH; Msg, Lt Gen Stanley R. Larsen, Commanding General (CG), IFFV, 237 to Westmoreland, 4 Sep 66, sub: Visit of COMUSMACV 4 Sep 66, box 2, 69A/703, RG 334, NARA; Interv, author with Lt Gen Arthur S. Collins, CG, 4th Inf Div, 28 Feb 75, Historians files, CMH.

[4] Interv, Lt Col Robert S. Holmes with Lt Gen Stanley R. Larsen, CG, IFFV, Academic Year 1967, Senior Officer Debriefing Program, MHI.

General Collins
(Photograph taken in 1974.)

the campaign would bring relief to the divisions on the coast. For the last year, starting in the Ia Drang Valley, the 1st Cavalry Division with its fleet of helicopters had thwarted all North Vietnamese efforts to stay in the highlands. General Man may have expected an easier time this autumn with the straight-leg infantry battalions of the 4th Division.[5]

Man moved in early October, targeting two Special Forces camps along the border: Plei Djereng, about forty kilometers west of Pleiku City, and Duc Co, some twenty kilometers farther south. Plei Djereng lay east of the Plei Trap Valley this side of Cambodia. Both were linked by roads to Highway 14.

The dry season had almost arrived in the highlands when Collins received ominous reports of movement in the Plei Trap. He knew the valley was a key infiltration point into the South, a relatively flat, jungle-covered river basin some twenty kilometers wide, marked on the west by the Nam Sathay River and Cambodia, and by the Se San River on the east. Although troop movements and camps were difficult to detect in the valley, the sighting of rafts along the Se San not far from Plei Djereng convinced Collins that he would soon have a fight on his hands.

Subsequent events confirmed Collins' suspicions. On 4 October the morning muster at the Plei Djereng Special Forces camp found that forty Montagnard recruits had deserted, either to the enemy or to avoid the coming battle. Ten days later came a surer sign of trouble, when a Montagnard company on reconnaissance near the camp was battered in a three-day battle with North Vietnamese regulars.[6] The only indicator to the contrary was a somewhat tenuous report of a large enemy buildup

---

[5] AAR, Opn PAUL REVERE IV, 4th Inf Div, pp. 14–26; *Luc Luong Vu Trang Nhan Dan Tay Nguyen Trong Khang Chien Chong My Cuu Nuoc* [*The People's Armed Forces of the Western Highlands During the War of National Salvation Against the Americans*] (Hanoi: People's Army Publishing House, 1980), pp. 42, 43, 50–55 (hereafter cited as *Western Highlands*), copy in CMH.

[6] AAR, Opn PAUL REVERE IV, 4th Inf Div, p. 15; ORLL, 1 Nov 66–31 Jan 67, 5th Special Forces (SF) Group, 1st SF, 15 Feb 67, Incl 10, and AAR, Task Force (TF) PRONG, 5th SF Group, 1st SF, 11 Jan 67, pp. 1–2 (hereafter cited as AAR, TF PRONG), both in Historians files, CMH.

Artillery and airlift at 3 TANGO, as PAUL REVERE IV begins

threatening Duc Co. Collins, however, suspected a feint and made ready at Pleiku to launch toward Plei Djereng on the eighteenth.

He would fight well equipped. Besides his two brigades, eight artillery battalions—five from I Field Force (two of which had just arrived in country)—would provide the steel for the offensive. Hueys would come from a longtime tenant at Pleiku, the 52d Aviation Battalion. Engineers would keep open his high-speed supply line to Plei Djereng, Route 509.

With all in place, Collins made his move. First to attack was the 3d Brigade, 25th Division, under Col. James G. Shanahan. By 21 October the men, moving west, had found several recently used trails and had fought with platoon-size enemy units north of Plei Djereng. From prisoners Shanahan learned that he was up against the *95B PAVN Regiment* of the *10th Division* and that nearby were two other North Vietnamese regiments, the *32d* and *33d* of the *1st Division.*[7]

The following day Col. Judson F. Miller's 2d Brigade, 4th Division, arrived at Plei Djereng and sent forces into the jungles southwest of Shanahan. Collins established his command post at an airstrip called 3 TANGO, just south of Plei Djereng. PAUL REVERE IV had begun.[8]

[7] AAR, Opn PAUL REVERE IV, 4th Inf Div, pp. 5–6, 11–12, 36; Interv, author with Collins, 28 Feb 75; Msg, Larsen A–1500 to Westmoreland, 1 Nov 66, sub: PAUL REVERE IV, box 6, 69A/703, RG 319, NARA.

[8] Intervs, author with Collins, 28 Feb 75; with Lt Gen Glenn D. Walker, Asst Div Comdr, 4th Inf Div, 3 Apr 79; and with Brig Gen James G. Shanahan, Comdr, 3d Bde, 25th Inf Div, 13 Aug 81, 4 Sep 81; AAR, Opn PAUL REVERE IV, 3d Bde, 25th Inf Div, 17 Jan 67, pp. 4–5, 14. Last three in Historians files, CMH.

As both brigades fanned out from the Special Forces camp, they found hastily abandoned enemy base camps but did not face a major enemy force until the twenty-seventh. During the next three days, however, three companies of the 2d Brigade each repelled spirited night attacks, as did a company of the 3d Brigade. In the first twelve days of the operation, 138 enemy died. American losses were 22 dead and 114 wounded.[9]

Having located three enemy regiments, Collins made his decision: he would fight between the water obstacles, the Se San and the Nam Sathay. Miller's brigade would drive to the Nam Sathay and pivot north. Shanahan's brigade would follow Miller's, but would not go as far. Then both brigades would launch up the Plei Trap between the two watercourses.

His only worry was a possible enemy assault at Duc Co in his rear, to which he would not be able to respond from his perch in the Plei Trap. He asked General Larsen for a strong force to screen to his south. The 2d Brigade, 1st Cavalry Division, under Col. George W. Casey, started arriving at OASIS near Duc Co on the thirtieth.[10]

His rear secure and his brigades on line, Collins launched the second phase of PAUL REVERE IV on 5 November. As shells and bombs rained down on the jungle canopy, six battalions started into the rugged Plei Trap, two brigades roughly on line. For the next week the advance was methodical and sure, through predetermined phase lines and checkpoints, the way along the jungle trails paved with artillery and air strikes. It was jungle action in the Pacific all over again, where Collins had commanded a regiment during World War II. And the North Vietnamese, expecting a phalanx of helicopters, not this slow and grinding march, were forced in that first week to give ground and abandon supplies.[11] (*Map 8*)

Collins' march did have one flaw. As his brigades moved up the Plei Trap parallel to the border, their west flank along the Nam Sathay became exposed, giving the enemy a chance to slip by and strike at Plei Djereng. But Collins was willing to risk that; in fact, he welcomed the prospect, hoping the North Vietnamese would cross, mass their units, and start a major fight. As long as he had some warning of their approach, he was sure he could carry the day.[12]

Warning would come from the Special Forces, which had small bases strung along the border in a long trip wire. Their commander at Kontum, Lt. Col. Eleazer Parmly, sent three companies of irregulars, Task Force PRONG, to screen on the west. Another battalion, Task Force NORTH,

[9] AAR, Opn PAUL REVERE IV, 4th Inf Div, p. 36.

[10] Ibid., pp. 16, 36–37; AAR, Opn PAUL REVERE IV, 2d Bde, 1st Cav Div, 25 Jan 67, pp. 4, 7–8, Historians files, CMH; Interv, author with Collins, 28 Feb 75.

[11] FRAGO 20–66, Opn PAUL REVERE IV, 4th Inf Div, 1 Nov 66, Historians files, CMH; AAR, Opn PAUL REVERE IV, 4th Inf Div, pp. 16, 36–40; AAR, Opn PAUL REVERE IV, 3d Bde, 25th Inf Div, pp. 6, 17–19; Intervs, author with Shanahan, 13 and 21 Aug 81; with Brig Gen James E. Moore, S–3, 3d Bde, 25th Inf Div, and Comdr, 1st Bn, 35th Inf, 3d Bde, 25th Inf Div, 4 Aug 81, Historians files, CMH; with Collins, 28 Feb 75.

[12] Interv, author with Collins, 28 Feb 75.

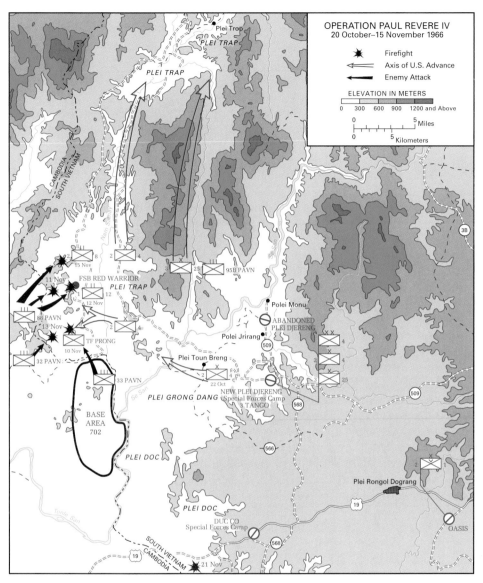

MAP 8

would provide surveillance along the northern limit of Collins' attack.

Collins liked the plan, and he was glad to have the additional troops—roughly 850 men. Yet he wanted to avoid a major fight west of the Nam Sathay, only eight kilometers from Cambodia. He cautioned Parmly to reconnoiter and not to seek combat.[13]

[13] Ibid.; AAR, Opn Paul Revere IV, 4th Inf Div, pp. 7, 48; AAR, TF Prong, pp. 10–1, 10–2.

Collision in the Plei Trap

Both task forces deployed into the Plei Trap Valley on 8 November. Operations in the northern edge of the basin proved unproductive; the difficult terrain had few trails and there was no sign that the enemy intended to move through the area.

West of the Nam Sathay it was another matter. In the southern Plei Trap the river flowed through a jungle plateau crisscrossed with well-used trails and clearings, particularly near the Cambodian border. As a precaution, Collins sent three U.S. rifle companies across the Nam Sathay to secure a clearing into which PRONG could deploy. By nightfall Parmly's force of about four hundred men had made five small contacts with the enemy and split into three company-size groups to perform its screening mission along the border.

The following morning the southernmost group, personally led by Parmly, ambushed a North Vietnamese reconnaissance element. When Parmly pursued, he bounded head-long into a trap. As his men tried to back into a nearby clearing to evacuate wounded, he found his route blocked and called for help.

The center Special Forces company immediately moved south to reinforce but failed to join the stricken unit until late afternoon. In the meantime, close air support and artillery fire prevented Parmly from being overrun. Eventually, Parmly secured the clearing, allowing Collins to land a reserve rifle company the following morning, 10 November.

Out of danger for the moment, Parmly retraced his steps to the ambush of the previous day. He sent the reserve rifle company around one side in an envelopment. But before the two units could come together, a battalion of the *88th PAVN Regiment* attacked the task force and hit it hard.

For the first time in PAUL REVERE IV, allied troops had come very close to Base Area 702, the North Vietnamese enclave over the border. The fact that they were Special Forces–led paramilitary soldiers, lightly armed and dispersed to screen for the 4th Division, made them an even easier target. When the attack came, Collins either had to reinforce or see the task force destroyed. He air-assaulted the remainder of his reserve into the clearing Parmly had vacated that morning. He completed the linkup with the Special Forces commander after midnight.

While the battle progressed, the northernmost element of Task Force PRONG ambushed a company from the *88th* within a kilometer of Cambodia. That evening the PRONG commander risked splitting his strike force to man two ambush sites along a heavily used trail paralleling a dry lake bed. It was a mistake, for at 0600 the following day the enemy attacked and routed both groups. After falling back three times to new positions, the company was able to hold, but not before taking heavy casualties.[14]

[14] AAR, TF PRONG, pp. 10–2, 10–3.

*Men from the 3d Brigade, 25th Infantry
Division, cross an enemy log bridge
in the Plei Trap.*

That morning Collins reassessed the situation. What had begun as a small reinforcement the previous day was turning into a full-scale rescue as the North Vietnamese threatened to chew up everything west of the Nam Sathay. He sent another battalion to aid the Special Forces company, although by doing this he reduced his forces pushing up the valley.

Collins knew that the *95B* and *32d* were still in the Plei Trap. He also knew that the *B3 Front*'s two uncommitted regiments, the *66th PAVN* and *101C PAVN*, were in Base Area 702 in Cambodia, less than a day's march away from the Nam Sathay. It was obvious, therefore, that the closer Collins came to Cambodia, the more dangerous the game became. Nevertheless, he decided on 11 November to move in strength across the Nam Sathay with his entire 2d Brigade, rescue the survivors of Task Force PRONG, and have the 3d of the 25th continue north, but at a slower pace until he determined the enemy's response west of the river.[15]

To rescue the besieged strike force, Miller's 2d Brigade sent its 1st Battalion, 12th Infantry, by helicopter into the battle. One company was able to set down right inside the perimeter, while the rest of the battalion landed to the northeast. As the Hueys hovered, machine guns opened fire from well-prepared positions. One ship burst into flames and crashed. When a second helicopter turned to investigate, it too was shot down.

A forward air controller watched it all from above. Dropping down for a closer look, he spotted six enemy antiaircraft guns ringing a nearby clearing. Had the Americans chosen to land there, they would have taken even heavier losses. Air strikes finished off the enemy guns.[16]

Reinforced by an artillery battery, the men of the 1st of the 12th Infantry spent the rest of the day and all of the next building a firebase and patrolling the immediate area. To the southwest, air and artillery fire seemed to have halted enemy pressure against the strike force and its rescuers, and it again appeared that the enemy would withdraw during the night. The new firebase, christened RED WARRIOR, was less than three kilometers from Cambodia.

[15] Interv, author with Collins, 28 Feb 75.

[16] AAR, Opn PAUL REVERE IV, 4th Inf Div, pp. 40–51; CHECO Rpt, Opn PAUL REVERE/SAM HOUSTON, PACAF, 27 Jul 67, pp. 48–51, Historians files, CMH.

RED WARRIOR

Mortar rounds began dropping onto the base on the evening of 12 November. The day's last patrols were just coming out of the jungle when the barrage began, and they sprinted through the outer perimeter as the shells rained down.

In the sky above, two Air Force A–1E Skyraiders, propeller-driven fighter-bombers, came to the aid of RED WARRIOR. While they circled looking for targets, the enemy's 12.7-mm. machine guns opened fire. As the Skyraiders prepared to dive on the emplacements, two North Vietnamese battalions launched human-wave assaults from the north and west. The fight for RED WARRIOR had begun.

During the next hour the enemy fired over five hundred mortar rounds into the position, the largest concentration of indirect fire that an American unit had yet experienced in Vietnam. Fires burning within the perimeter set off explosions among artillery rounds strewn about the base.

Above, with the explosions and perimeter flares outlining the firebase, the two Skyraiders went to work. Diving without lights to minimize their chances of being hit, the fighters took turns dropping napalm and cluster bombs. After completing a pass, each plane turned on its lights to draw fire as the other made its run. Repeating this tactic, the planes made about forty-five passes during the next thirty minutes, until their ammunition ran out. When no replacement fighters came, the aircraft made dry runs, hoping to distract the enemy.[17]

Another flight of A–1Es finally arrived, joined shortly by other aircraft. Then the base was swallowed up by clouds and rain, and for about two hours air support was impossible. Artillery fire continued into the night, however, catching the attacking troops in the open and doing serious damage. Around midnight the enemy withdrew.[18]

By daybreak on 13 November the battle had cost RED WARRIOR's defenders 5 dead and 41 wounded. The battalion reported 76 enemy dead within sight of the base but made no attempt to comb the undergrowth for more. Collins agreed with the decision; body counts might indicate the outcome of a battle, but they did not greatly concern him. Later that day a helicopter pilot flying low over the landscape counted 400 bodies among the trees and foliage. Despite the victory, more battles were inevitable. Refusing to risk another fight so close to Cambodia, Collins ordered RED WARRIOR abandoned.[19]

While the battalion at RED WARRIOR moved east to establish a new firebase, the remainder of the rescue companies pushed on, fighting small but bitter skirmishes in sight of the Cambodian border. On 18 November

---

[17] CHECO Rpt, Opn PAUL REVERE/SAM HOUSTON, PACAF, p. 57.

[18] Ibid.; AAR, Opn PAUL REVERE IV, 4th Inf Div, pp. 50–51.

[19] AAR, Opn PAUL REVERE IV, 4th Inf Div, pp. 49–51; MFR, 19 Dec 66, sub: MACV Commanders' Conference, 20 November 1966, p. 27; Interv, author with Collins, 28 Feb 75.

2d Brigade units discovered two huge base camps hidden in the southern Plei Trap. The following day Collins assigned three companies, including irregulars, to destroy the bunkers in the larger of the complexes. Shortly after noon elements of the *33d Regiment* ambushed the companies, striking them from three directions. Over the next few hours the defenders held firm, and by nightfall they had established a tight perimeter. Enemy snipers firing from trees plagued the allies through the night, but the North Vietnamese had lost heavily, over 165 men, most from artillery and air strikes, and had no wish to lose more in a risky frontal assault. By morning the allied force had fought the *33d* to a standstill, but at a cost of 19 killed and 53 wounded, most of them Americans. That day, 20 November, having his fill of fighting on enemy terms close to the border, Collins ordered the 4th Division out of the southern Plei Trap.[20]

Another Border Fight

Meanwhile, to the south, the 2d Brigade of the 1st Cavalry Division continued to find little, prompting General Larsen to return one of its battalions to the coast. Nevertheless, Colonel Casey, the brigade commander, continued to send company-size patrols close to the border to follow up sightings. On 21 November his practice ended in disaster, when one patrol ran into a battalion of the *101C Regiment*. One platoon, straying from its company, was completely overrun. When it was over, Casey's losses were 32 dead, many of whom had been captured and executed before artillery, gunships, and air strikes had dispersed the Communists. Strewn about the area the American survivors found 145 enemy bodies, many charred beyond recognition by napalm.[21]

Between 20 and 30 November, after pulling his men out of the Plei Trap, Collins saturated the valley with B–52 strikes. At the same time, he turned both his infantry brigades north in one final attempt to find and fix the two North Vietnamese infantry regiments, the *32d* and *95B*, still reported east of the Nam Sathay. As usual, the advance was methodical, Collins leading with artillery fire and air strikes.

But by this time his troops were spent. After six weeks of grueling combat in inhospitable terrain, the 4th Division had suffered over 100 dead and 500 wounded. Its tired soldiers, most facing the enemy for the first time, were also becoming casualties to malaria, which ultimately did more damage to the ranks than North Vietnamese fire.[22]

Still, the sweep north continued. Rather than end the operation, General Larsen decided to reinforce, and on 9 December he airlifted the

[20] AAR, Opn PAUL REVERE IV, 4th Inf Div, pp. 53–55.
[21] AAR, Opn PAUL REVERE IV, 2d Bde, 1st Cav Div, pp. 23–26.
[22] Monthly Command Health Rpt, 4th Inf Div, Oct 66–Jan 67, Historians files, CMH; AAR, Opn PAUL REVERE IV, 4th Inf Div, pp. 82–83; Interv, author with Moore, 4 Aug 81.

1st Brigade of the 101st Airborne Division from Phu Yen Province into the northern Plei Trap. The following day Larsen upgraded PAUL REVERE IV to a corps-size operation, much as Weyand had done in ATTLEBORO, by establishing an I Field Force forward command post at Pleiku. In its dying moments the operation was now maneuvering on the border with four brigades—Collins' two, and those of the 1st Cavalry and 101st Airborne Divisions. Vinh Loc, the corps commander, added battalions of his own. But by then the North Vietnamese had vanished into Cambodia.

By mid-December Larsen was ready to end the effort. On the twenty-seventh an enemy offensive on the coast led him to withdraw the cavalry brigade, and a week later he pulled the 3d Brigade, 25th Division, out of the highlands. The airborne brigade, under I Field Force control, remained in Kontum Province until late January. For the time being, however, the struggle for the Plei Trap was over.

Like ATTLEBORO, PAUL REVERE IV ended without certainty. Both sides could claim victory of a sort, but neither had achieved decisive results. Since it was Collins' first operation in the Central Highlands, he fought the way those before him had fought: by attempting to meet the enemy at the border. According to the American count, the enemy lost some 1,200 men killed and captured, while the U.S. killed, including Task Force PRONG, approached 300. Intelligence later reported that the *33d* and *95B Regiments* had suffered serious losses. The *33d* remained ineffective for more than a year, and the *95B* never again fought as a unit. That winter the *B3 Front* downgraded the *101C Regiment* to an independent battalion and sprinkled its men into the *32d* and *88th Regiments*.[23]

So, from Collins' perspective, there was reason for cautious optimism. The enemy had been forced onto the defensive. And, although effective border operations had required heavy firepower, the 4th Division had shown some staying power. More opportunities in the highlands were bound to follow.

---

[23] AAR, Opn PAUL REVERE IV, 4th Inf Div, pp. 71–74; AAR, TF PRONG, p. 10–5; AAR, Opn PAUL REVERE IV, 2d Bde, 1st Cav Div, pp. 55–56. The *B3 Front* headquarters claimed its units killed 2,400 allied troops, including more than 2,000 Americans, in a victorious campaign. See *Western Highlands*, p. 54.

5

The Developing Campaign on the Coast

While the U.S. 4th Infantry Division waged war on the western plateau, other American and allied forces sought to sweep clean the II Corps coast. Geography and history ensured that both sides would fight hard for this strategic terrain. Extending along the South China Sea in a narrow strip of some forty kilometers, the lowlands run for 700 kilometers southward from Da Nang to the Mekong Delta. Most of South Vietnam's population north of Saigon lived here, fishing in the teeming ocean and tilling the land. Rich soil and predictable rains made for good farming—so good that the plain stretching between Da Nang and Nha Trang yielded two rice crops annually.

The lowlands also contained most of the U.S. and South Vietnamese logistical bases and airfields serving the allied military establishment outside III Corps. Although the old colonial road, Highway 1, passed through most of these population centers, it was coastal shipping that tied them permanently together. The new deep-water ports at Da Nang, Qui Nhon, and Cam Ranh Bay underscored the role of water transport in uniting a region with communities long separated by enemy-controlled terrain, particularly in Phu Yen and Binh Dinh Provinces.

The combined campaign plan for 1966–1967 had given all coastal provinces "priority" for the new offensive but had declared only the regions around Da Nang and Qui Nhon "national priority areas," since the South Vietnamese military was too weak to accomplish more.[1] In fact, the three units responsible for this key region, the South Vietnamese 2d Division in Quang Tin and Quang Ngai Provinces, the 22d Division still farther south in Binh Dinh and Phu Yen, and elements of the 23d Division down in Ninh Thuan and Binh Thuan Provinces, were spread so thin that they barely had enough men to garrison the main bases and towns. To make matters worse, they were among the poorest units in the South Vietnamese Army. For these reasons Westmoreland had found it necessary to keep at least one U.S. Marine regiment south of Da Nang and to buttress the area with South Korean Army and Marine units as they arrived in country.

[1] See Special Joint Rpt on Revolutionary Development (hereafter cited as RD Rpt), Quang Nam Province, Oct 66, 1 Nov 66, Historians files, CMH.

The integration of the Korean expeditionary forces into the war effort had posed something of a dilemma. Technically, they belonged neither to MACV nor to the South Vietnamese Joint General Staff. Neither Westmoreland nor his field force commanders, General Larsen in II Corps and General Walt in I Corps, nor the two South Vietnamese corps commanders exercised operational control over Korean units. But that force, now a significant contingent, numbered about 45,000 troops in two full divisions, a marine brigade, and its own logistical support groups. For this reason the American and Vietnamese commanders adopted the practice of assigning to the Koreans carefully defined operational zones along the coast, where their activities would be easy to coordinate with the rest of the offensive. Initially, the Korean Capital Division had assumed responsibility for the area around Qui Nhon, while the Korean 2d Marine Brigade operated around the port of Cam Ranh, farther south. In September 1966 the entire Korean 9th Division began replacing the marine brigade; it shifted north to Quang Ngai in southern I Corps.[2]

The Koreans were clearly a boon to the coastal defense, but it was the Americans who went on the offensive. The deployment of the 1st Cavalry Division from the highlands to the coast as recently as August, together with the 1st Brigade, 101st Airborne Division, and, when it arrived in October, the 1st Brigade, 4th Infantry Division, finally allowed Westmoreland to begin aggressive operations in the II Corps lowlands, at first between Qui Nhon and Phan Thiet, the southern extent of the II Corps plain, then gradually expanding.

As in the Central Highlands, artillery made up for any shortfall in manpower. In mid-1966 there were ten artillery battalions in the lowlands: four with the 1st Cavalry Division, two with the airborne brigade, and four organic to I Field Force. In October of that year another battalion deployed to Qui Nhon, adding its 105-mm. tubes to the battlefront. The following March an additional two battalions deployed to Qui Nhon and Tuy Hoa as part of the I Field Force arsenal. Added to the South Vietnamese and Korean guns, artillery support was rarely in short supply.

Westmoreland's prime targets were the marauding big units—the *5th PAVN Division* in Phu Yen and Khanh Hoa Provinces and the *3d PAVN "Yellow Star" Division* up in Binh Dinh—plus any local force guerrillas and operatives swept up in the bargain. As far as "nation building" was concerned, if he could protect the big coastal rice harvest due in October, so much the better for the government.

Here, as elsewhere, Westmoreland was getting the troops and firepower he had been promised. But more than that, the 1st Cavalry Division and the airborne brigade were the most experienced American

---

[2] Sharp and Westmoreland, *Report*, pp. 223–24; Intervs, Charles B. MacDonald and Charles V. P. von Luttichau with Lt Gen Stanley R. Larsen, 6 Dec 68, 11 Mar 70, Historians files, CMH.

units fighting in II Corps—reason enough to be optimistic, if cautiously so, that the balance at last could be righted in this segment of the country.

Westmoreland's optimism was bolstered by operations launched throughout 1966. The mere presence of American troops in the lowlands meant that the enemy no longer had unfettered access to the population. For the *5th Division* in particular, this was bad news. Never strong, the division constantly fell victim to long supply lines and poor recruitment. At the tail end of supply trails coming from both North Vietnam and Cambodia, soldiers often had little to eat and little ammunition. As a result, the division could not maintain more than two regiments, which were divided between Phu Yen and Khanh Hoa. To make matters worse, during 1966 the 1st of the 101st Airborne Division had kept up a drumbeat of operations against the *5th Division*, pushing it back from the villages and slowly bleeding away its hard-to-replace manpower. Early in the year Operations HARRISON, VAN BUREN, and FILLMORE had kept the enemy on the run around Tuy Hoa in Phu Yen Province. During the summer, before moving to Binh Dinh Province, the 1st Cavalry Division had joined forces with the airborne brigade in Operation NATHAN HALE. Later that summer the 1st of the 101st launched Operation JOHN PAUL JONES and in early autumn Operation SEWARD. None were decisive, but from General Westmoreland's perspective this marked the first time that American forces were on the offensive in coastal II Corps.

To the north, in Binh Dinh Province, the *3d PAVN Division* was in much better shape. A constant threat to pacification in this traditionally Communist-sympathetic province, the division was kept fairly well supplied from the Ho Chi Minh Trail. However, the addition of the 4th Infantry Division to the Central Highlands order of battle allowed Westmoreland to aim the 1st Cavalry Division at the North Vietnamese in coastal Binh Dinh. During 1966 operations there had altered the tactical picture, forcing the *3d Division* out of the lowlands and into the mountains west of the An Lao and Kim Son Valleys. As the year came to an end I Field Force maintained the pressure, hoping to keep the North Vietnamese away from the plains.

GERONIMO

Between 31 October and 4 December, with other units working the coast, the 1st Brigade, 101st Airborne Division, took off after the *5th Division* in the interior of Phu Yen. At the time U.S. intelligence believed that the *5th Division*'s two regiments, the *95th PAVN* and *18B PAVN*, had taken heavy casualties the previous summer, were woefully under-strength, and would refuse to give battle.[3] Although some replacements

---

[3] MACV listed a third regiment, the *3d PLAF*, consisting of the *30th* and *32d Infantry Battalions* and the *403d Artillery Battalion*, as part of the *5th PAVN Division*. In May 1966 MACV dropped the *3d Regiment* from its order of battle, carrying only the *30th Battalion*. See Monthly OB Sum, CICV, Mar 66 and May 66.

General Pearson

had arrived from the North, most of the acquisitions had been dragooned by the Viet Cong and were in need of military training. In addition, jungle-associated diseases, particularly malaria, had reportedly decimated the division's remaining ranks. Medical equipment and drugs were scarce, and even food had begun to run out. So, although the monsoon was approaching, the 1st Brigade commander, Brig. Gen. Willard Pearson, decided it was time to finish off the enemy division.[4]

Relying on intelligence that placed the *18B Regiment* in a jungle base about fifty kilometers southwest of Tuy Hoa and twenty kilometers inland from the coast, Pearson assembled his three battalions at the Tuy Hoa South airfield in late October. Using Route 7B, an interior east-west road that paralleled the Da Rang River north of the objective, he intended to move one of his units, the 1st Battalion, 327th Infantry (Airborne), along the road to an area west of the suspected location of the *18B*, while a second unit, the 2d Battalion, 327th Infantry (Airborne), launched an air assault to the south. To conceal the operation, both would move under cover of darkness. At daybreak the South Vietnamese 47th Regiment, 22d Division, would screen Route 7B in the north, and units of the South Korean 28th Regiment, 9th Division, would perform the same task along Highway 1 in the east. Pearson's two battalions would then sweep east through the enemy base; his remaining unit, the 2d Battalion, 502d Infantry (Airborne), would remain in reserve at Tuy Hoa, able to be airlifted anywhere it might be needed. The plan was complex and risky. Night movements were dangerous, and initially his forces would be out of artillery range. But Pearson was counting on the weakness of his enemy. (*Map 9*)

On the evening of 31 October both airborne battalions successfully completed their movements; the only problem occurred the next morning when Chinook helicopters had to ferry the northern battalion across the Da Rang. Despite the effort, Operation GERONIMO I turned up almost nothing. The battalions drove forward to the coast more or less on schedule, but they found no more than a few surprised Viet Cong, a small amount of weapons and equipment, and some leftover rice. The *18B*

[4] MFR, 19 Dec 66, sub: MACV Commanders' Conference, 20 November 1966. See also AAR, Opn JOHN PAUL JONES, 1st Bde, 101st Abn Div, 28 Sep 66, pp. 3–4, Incls 1, 2, and AAR, Opn SEWARD, 1st Bde, 101 Abn Div, 6 Nov 66, pp. 2–4, Incls 1, 2, both in Historians files, CMH.

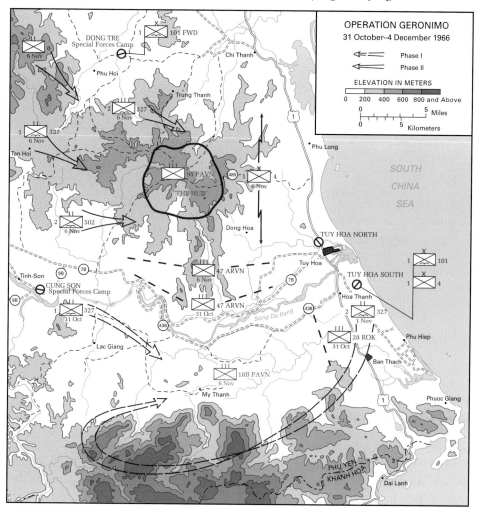

MAP 9

Regiment had moved out a month earlier. Poor intelligence had once more compromised a well-conceived plan.[5]

Undaunted, Pearson learned that the *95th Regiment*, the *5th Division's* other major formation, had moved east from the mountains into the "Hub," a larger base area northwest of Tuy Hoa. The target area actually covered about eighty square kilometers of double-canopied, forested hills interlaced with trails that the insurgents had used for over twenty years. Itching for a fight, Pearson decided to launch a combined allied force of nine battalions to encircle the regiment. While the 1st Brigade of the 4th Division blocked

---

[5] AAR, Opn GERONIMO I, 1st Bde, 101st Abn Div, 3 Jan 67, p. 3, Historians files, CMH.

81

Survivors of the decimated 5th Battalion, 95th PAVN Regiment

the area east of the Hub and the South Vietnamese 47th Regiment deployed along the southern flank (again, Route 7B), the full airborne brigade would land northwest of the enemy force and again sweep eastward, driving it into the waiting 1st Brigade, commanded by Brig. Gen. David O. Byars. Pearson planned to use the traditional "hammer and anvil" tactic to trap and destroy his opponent.[6]

GERONIMO II began at daybreak on the morning of 6 November, soon after a dense fog had lifted. Pearson's forces again conducted air assaults into their initial objectives without difficulty and pushed forward against only token enemy resistance. Weather, terrain, and the sheer size of the operational area made progress slow. On the eighth Larsen gave Pearson operational control over one of Byars' battalions, increasing the size of the "hammer" to four battalions. But only upon nearing the western fringe of the Hub on 10 November did one of the airborne battalions finally meet a large enemy force, later identified as part of the *5th Battalion, 95th Regiment,* entrenched in a base camp. The fight continued sporadically through the night and into the next day, when the Americans finally surrounded the enemy position. At that point, a three-man Army psychological warfare team came forward and convinced thirty-five enemy soldiers to surrender. When no more would leave, the paratroopers overran the camp.[7]

Meanwhile, other American units continued to advance, sweeping through the Hub but finding little aside from some hastily hidden med-

[6] Ibid., pp. 2–3, Incl 1.
[7] Ibid., tab B, Incl 7; MFR, 19 Dec 66, sub: MACV Commanders' Conference, 20 November 1966.

82

ical caches and documents. On 24 November American electronic intelligence indicated that the *95th* had fled west. With heavy rains and high winds limiting the amount of airlift available to him, Pearson decided against expanding the operation.

The coastal operations of the airborne brigade came to an end on 4 December. With the border battle in the western highlands, PAUL REVERE IV, undecided, Larsen ordered Pearson's brigade to Kontum to assist the 4th Division. Five weeks of campaigning in Phu Yen Province had netted the airborne brigade 150 enemy dead, 76 prisoners, and 111 weapons, at a cost of 16 Americans killed and another 78 wounded. Though the *5th Division* remained intact, it was in no better than marginal shape.[8]

From Phu Yen to Binh Dinh

With the departure of the 1st of the 101st for the Central Highlands, operations in Phu Yen and Khanh Hoa Provinces were uneventful for the remainder of the year. While the South Korean 9th Division secured the coast around Nha Trang and Cam Ranh Bay, it also constructed a new base camp at Ninh Hoa and patrolled north as far as Tuy Hoa.

For the area north of Tuy Hoa, Larsen persuaded Vinh Loc, the II Corps commander, to have the 47th Regiment clear the coast up to Song Cao, a small fishing village halfway to Qui Nhon. Sometime early in 1967 he expected the South Korean Capital Division, still protecting Qui Nhon and southern Binh Dinh, to clear the remainder of the coast south to the limit of the 47th's northward advance. To ensure that these clearing actions in Phu Yen went unmolested, he sent the bulk of the 1st Brigade, 4th Division, into Dong Tre, about fifty kilometers south of Qui Nhon, where it would be in a position to halt any aggressive moves eastward by a possibly rejuvenated *5th Division*.

The net result of these clearing and patrolling operations was encouraging. Between early November 1966 and the end of January 1967, the 4th Division's 1st Brigade reported killing 261 enemy, capturing 153, and seizing 126 weapons, while suffering 25 dead and 187 wounded. Korean and South Vietnamese statistics were similar. At the same time, Highway 1 was open to traffic during daylight hours from Song Cao south to the Khanh Hoa–Ninh Thuan provincial border, and the interior roads were declared secure up to twenty kilometers into the mountains. South Vietnamese forces had established checkpoints along the roads, and territorial units and revolutionary development teams had followed the combat units into the villages and hamlets as they were cleared.[9]

---

[8] AAR, Opn GERONIMO I, 1st Bde, 101st Abn Div, p. 4; ORLL, 1 Nov 66–31 Jan 67, IFFV, 6 Mar 67, pp. 16–18, Historians files, CMH.

[9] ORLL, 1 Nov 66–31 Jan 67, IFFV, p. 17. For details, see AAR, Opn ADAMS, 1st Bde, 4th Inf Div, 18 May 67, Historians files, CMH.

Heliport and airstrip, Camp Radcliff

Vinh Loc's staff believed that little of the rice harvest had found its way into the enemy base camps, a judgment which intelligence reports affirmed. Indeed, many enemy prisoners complained that they had to eat less desirable foods such as manioc, a starchy edible root, to survive. In November and December a large number of local Viet Cong, disillusioned by a lack of support from the *5th Division* and nearing starvation, defected to the Saigon government under the *Chieu Hoi* ("open arms") program. In the spring a secret Communist report would state that control of the Phu Yen population had dropped precipitously to 20,000, about 6 percent of the provincial population.[10]

North of Phu Yen and Qui Nhon, Binh Dinh Province was proving a tougher nut to crack. There, the *3d PAVN Division*, with three strong regiments—the *18th PAVN*, the *22d PAVN*, and the locally recruited *2d PLAF*—had long dominated the South Vietnamese 22d Division. The enemy local and guerrilla forces were as strong as the political underground. Binh Dinh, with a population of some 900,000, belonged to the revolution.

In late August 1966 the 1st Cavalry Division left the central plateau and reassembled its three brigades and almost all its combat battalions at Camp Radcliff, a large sprawling base camp near An Khe along Highway 19, about midway between Qui Nhon and Pleiku. Radcliff was one of the few camps that could accommodate the airmobile division's 450 or so

[10] ORLL, 1 Nov 66–31 Jan 67, IFFV, p. 17.

helicopters, five times those of a normal infantry division. Although the cavalry unit was essentially an infantry division, with three brigades of nine infantry battalions, there were significant differences. First, instead of an aviation battalion, the division had an entire aviation group consisting of a general support company; two assault helicopter battalions with UH–1B and UH–1D Hueys, each assault battalion capable of lifting an entire infantry battalion at one time; and an assault support helicopter battalion with CH–47 Chinooks, to move artillery and to maintain aerial resupply. Second, in place of armor and armored cavalry elements, an air cavalry squadron had a mix of scout, Huey gunship, and troop helicopters, the last permanently assigned to carry three rifle platoons. Finally, the division had its heavy 155-mm./8-inch artillery battalion replaced by an "aerial rocket" battalion of thirty-nine UH–1B gunships armed with machine guns and 2.75-inch rockets. In addition, its three direct-support 105-mm. artillery battalions were equipped with lightweight M102 howitzers capable of being lifted not just by Chinooks but by the UH–1D as well. The other support units were also lightened or reduced in size so that, if necessary, the entire force could move by air.[11]

Keeping one of its brigade headquarters and at least one battalion at Camp Radcliff for security, the bulk of the division had begun operations in central Binh Dinh on 13 September and its efforts would continue throughout the rainy season. The division's primary missions were to engage and destroy the *3d Division* and simultaneously to clear the Binh Dinh coast of other large enemy units so that South Vietnamese territorial, police, and administrative officials could move in to reestablish Saigon's authority. The commander, Maj. Gen. John Norton, designated the division objective the "Thayer Area of Operation" and his initial effort Thayer I.

At first glance the Thayer area, an upright rectangle some forty by seventy kilometers, looked more hospitable than the high mountain jungles of the interior. The lower altitude at sea level meant greater air density and a significant improvement in helicopter lift. (*Map 10*) Lying between blue-green mountains and white, palm-fringed beaches, Thayer's coastal region was easily traversable, especially in the dry season. Farther inland, three valleys, the An Lao, Kim Son, and Suoi Ca, reached clawlike into the Annamite Mountains, where canopied slopes combined with steep valley walls and mountain ridges to make ground operations difficult. Along the coast, however, the only natural obstacles were two mountain outcroppings, the Cay Giep and Nui Mieu ridges, and the unfordable Lai Giang River, which ran east and divided Thayer in two. Both the Bong Son Plain north of the river and the Phu My Plain to its south were easy to maneuver upon, particularly for a unit with a lot of helicopters.[12]

---

[11] Shelby L. Stanton, *Anatomy of a Division: The 1st Cav in Vietnam* (Novato, Calif.: Presidio Press, 1987), ch. 10, apps. 1, 2.

[12] Provincial Briefing Folder 7, U.S. Agency for International Development (USAID) Region II, Binh Dinh Province, Nov 66, Historians files, CMH; Intervs, MacDonald and von Luttichau with Larsen, 6 Dec 68, 11 Mar 70.

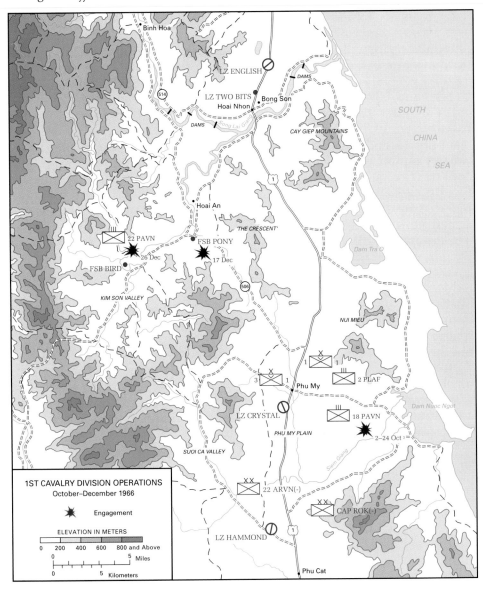

MAP 10

During Operation THAYER I, from 13 September to 1 October, Norton put two cavalry brigades and ultimately seven battalions onto the Phu My Plain, between the Lai Giang and Siem Giang Rivers, while Korean units worked just south of the Siem Giang. Concentrating first on the Kim Son Valley, the cavalry units ended up chasing the *18th Regiment* all around the countryside, finally forcing it to break down into small, company-size units to avoid the aggressive Americans. Then, on 2 October

Soldiers of the 1st Cavalry Division search a village on the Phu My Plain.

THAYER I melded into Operation IRVING, which saw the cavalry drive south, pivoting on HAMMOND, their main forward supply base at the entrance to the Suoi Ca Valley. Simultaneously, the Koreans moved north to the Siem Giang, while a South Vietnamese four-battalion task force pushed directly east from HAMMOND in an attempt to clear the Siem Giang River delta. During these combined operations, lasting some six weeks to 24 October, the three participating allied components claimed to have killed or captured 3,500 enemy soldiers; however, many in the *2d* and *18th Regiments* managed to avoid the trap, and no one could determine the accuracy of the body count.[13]

THAYER II began on 25 October as a continuation of THAYER I. But with the northeastern monsoon beginning, Norton found his efforts hampered by early morning fog, rain, and high winds. Overcast skies obscured the upper ridges of the surrounding mountains, restricting helicopters to the lowlands, where stifling humidity choked soldiers by day and chilled them by night. American offensive operations were limited largely to B–52 strikes against suspected or known enemy base camps, but post-

[13] ORLL, 1 Aug–31 Oct 66, 1st Cav Div, 22 Nov 66, pp. 11–12, 18–20, Historians files, CMH.

strike ground reconnaissance found no evidence of a major enemy force. Norton's combat power was further reduced on 29 October, when Larsen ordered him to send one brigade—Norton chose the 2d at Camp Radcliff—to reinforce Collins in the highlands, obliging him to move the 1st Brigade up to Radcliff, leaving only Col. Charles D. Daniel's 3d Brigade to continue THAYER II with four battalions.

During November and December Norton had Colonel Daniel assign each of his battalions separate operational sectors south of the Lai Giang, breaking them down into company- and platoon-size patrols to cover a larger area. The practice seemed to work, for almost every week one of Daniel's units managed to catch a few hundred enemy regulars, mostly from understrength battalions of the *2d* and *18th Regiments*, as well as several of their smaller rice-gathering parties. In most instances the enemy was forced to leave many dead on the battlefield, escaping only under cover of darkness or thundershowers.

Norton later learned that his opposite, Col. Le Truc, who commanded the *3d Division*, had moved the *2d Regiment* north to Quang Ngai Province in early November due to its high desertion rate. The *18th* seemed no better off. A captured officer later related that the unit had lost the equivalent of two battalions during September and October and that its recent replacements were quickly deserting. Overall strength of each company was but fifty men, many suffering from malaria, while the monsoon rains often washed away the *18th*'s underground base camps.[14]

On the American side the weather also continued to spell trouble. Sixteen inches of rain fell between 24 and 28 November, turning the lowlands into a huge lake. Floodwaters crested at STUART, an American firebase in the Kim Son Valley, to a depth of five and one-half feet, forcing its evacuation and the temporary abandonment of two of its 155-mm. howitzers.

Early in December South Vietnamese officials decided simply to clear the valley of its population, level the hamlets, destroy the crops, and then declare it a "free fire zone." The "area denial" operation, called ROVER, began on 8 December, continued for a week, and displaced eleven hundred civilians. During that period Norton replaced the 3d Brigade with the 1st, which had recently been taken over by a new commander, Col. James S. Smith. Continuing to pursue ROVER—actually a part of THAYER II—Smith's forces worked the Kim Son Valley, locating small pockets of noncombatants who had ignored the government's orders and had hidden in the jungle. Some were dedicated revolutionaries, but others were

---

[14] AAR, Opn THAYER II, 1st Cav Div, 25 Jun 67, pp. 11–12, 15, Historians files, CMH; Intel Sums 256, IFFV, 25 Nov 66, and 272, IFFV, 11 Dec 66, both in Historians files, CMH. See *Su Doan Sao Vang (Su Doan 3) Binh Doan Chi Lang Quang Khu 1; Ky Su [Yellow Star Division (3d Division), Chi Lang Military Group, Military Region 1; Memoir]* (Hanoi: People's Army Publishing House, 1984) (hereafter cited as *3d Division*), pp. 58–61, copy in CMH. See also Special Rpt 1647, Combined Military Interrogation Center (CMIC), 10 Oct 67, sub: OB on the 3d NVA Division, Historians files, CMH.

not. Emotionally tied to ancestral lands, they preferred to brave the battle-field rather than abandon all they held dear.

Sometime in mid-December the *18th Regiment's* *7th* and *9th Battalions* ran out of food. In desperation both moved east of the Kim Son Valley to obtain rice from the inhabitants, and when discovered by the Americans on 17 December the North Vietnamese stood and fought. By nightfall six cavalry rifle companies had entered a fiercely contested battle in which three of their supporting helicopters were shot down. Although the enemy lost nearly 100 men, the rest escaped. American losses were also high, some 34 dead and 81 wounded, and replacements were scarce; because of the approaching Christmas holidays, few were arriving from the United States.[15]

Firebase BIRD

Casualties in the 1st Cavalry Division would soon rise higher. Christmas found one company of the 1st Battalion, 12th Cavalry (Airmobile), and two batteries of artillery securing BIRD, a Kim Son Valley firebase that had been set up hurriedly to replace the washed out STUART. Because of the holiday replacement problem, BIRD's artillery units had less than half their authorized manpower, and BIRD's fixed defenses were still inadequate. No protective wire entanglement enclosed the base; no fields of fire had been cleared in front of the bunkers that formed its perimeter; and no listening posts had been placed forward of the bunker line at night to give early warning of an enemy approach. BIRD presented an easy target to the *3d Division* commander, Colonel Truc. On 16 December Truc ordered the *22d Regiment*, then in the An Lao Valley, to displace south and seize BIRD. The action would reestablish the revolutionary presence in the Kim Son Valley and ease the pressure the Americans had been putting on the *18th Regiment* through mid-December.[16]

Prior to the Christmas truce American intelligence indicated that the *22d Regiment* was in fact moving south, either to replace the *18th Regiment* or to assist in its withdrawal. The 1st Cavalry Division's intelligence offi-cer, Lt. Col. William B. Ray, predicted that the *22d* would strike one of the cavalry's firebases "hard" between the Christmas and New Year's truces.

[15] Intel Sum 278, IFFV, 17 Dec 66, Historians files, CMH; AAR, Opn THAYER II, 1st Cav Div, pp. 11–12, 28–29; Unit Historical Rpt 15, Office of Information and History, 1st Cav Div, n.d., "506 Valley," Historians files, CMH. The *18th Regiment* claimed to have inflicted 700 casualties on the cavalry units while incurring losses of 21 killed and 18 wounded. See Combined Document Exploitation Center (CDEC), no. 06–3300–67, 12 Nov 67, sub: TRANSLATION REPORT; Title: Report on 1966/67 Winter-Spring Campaign, Historians files, CMH.

[16] Intel Sums 284, IFFV, 23 Dec 66; 290, IFFV, 31 Dec 66; 2, IFFV, 2 Jan 67; 3, IFFV, 3 Jan 67; 4, IFFV, 4 Jan 67; and 7, IFFV, 7 Jan 67. All in Historians files, CMH. AAR, Opn THAYER II, 1st Cav Div, pp. 12, 30–32.

By Christmas Eve he concluded that the elusive regiment was concentrating four to five kilometers southeast of BIRD, but he was unsure of its precise objective. Unknown to Ray, the regiment had been prepared to attack BIRD prior to the holidays, but torrential rains and the unit's unfamiliarity with the area had forced a temporary postponement. At 0700 on the twenty-sixth, with the end of the Christmas truce, five batteries of American artillery fired for thirty minutes upon the suspected location, but the enemy was elsewhere.

General Norton, meanwhile, sought the return of his 2d Brigade from the western highlands to increase the division's strength in and around the Kim Son Valley. Larsen agreed but declared that the brigade was unavailable for redeployment until 27 December. Believing that the enemy could surprise his 1st Brigade at several places, Norton reinforced it on the twenty-sixth by airlifting a battalion from Camp Radcliff to HAMMOND to beef up the local reserves. Although Norton felt that BIRD was probably the most logical enemy objective, he was unaware of the base's flawed defenses.[17] (*Map 11*)

Shortly after dark on 26 December the *22d Regiment*'s *8th Battalion* moved unobserved into its final assault positions within twelve meters of BIRD's bunker line, while the regiment's *9th Battalion* occupied a wooded area a few hundred meters east of the base. At 0100, just after mortar and recoilless rifle fire began exploding upon BIRD, a two-battalion ground assault began. Spoiling for a victory, the *8th Battalion* charged forward on line while the *9th Battalion*, farther away and not nearly as bold, moved toward the perimeter more dispersed. Although the 1st Brigade commander had called an alert, the defenders were caught by surprise. The battle quickly came down to a bitter, close-quarters infantry fight. Despite fierce individual defense, organized American resistance quickly crumbled, particularly in front of the *8th Battalion*.

The 1st Brigade learned of the attack soon after the first rounds exploded, but then all communications with BIRD ceased for the next thirty minutes. By the time radio contact was restored, BIRD's northeast sector was in enemy hands and the southeast portion gravely threatened. All appeared lost until 1st Lt. John D. Piper, the executive officer of BIRD's 105-mm. howitzer unit (Battery B, 2d Battalion, 19th Artillery) lowered an artillery tube and fired two "beehive" rounds, each containing 8,500 flechettes—small, razor-sharp metal arrows—point-blank into the *8th Battalion*, then regrouping for its final assault. In the 30-degree cone of fire made by the blast, no man remained standing; the *8th Battalion*, paralyzed and demoralized, faltered. Minutes later Huey gunships, with the aid of illumination flares, began pouring fire on both North Vietnamese battalions; ultimately 424 rockets would be expended. Stunned by the display of firepower, the *22d Regiment* commander ordered a withdrawal.

---

[17] AAR, Opn THAYER II, 1st Cav Div, p. 30; Intervs, author with Lt Gen John Norton, CG, 1st Cav Div, 1–2 Sep 83, 2 Dec 83, Historians files, CMH.

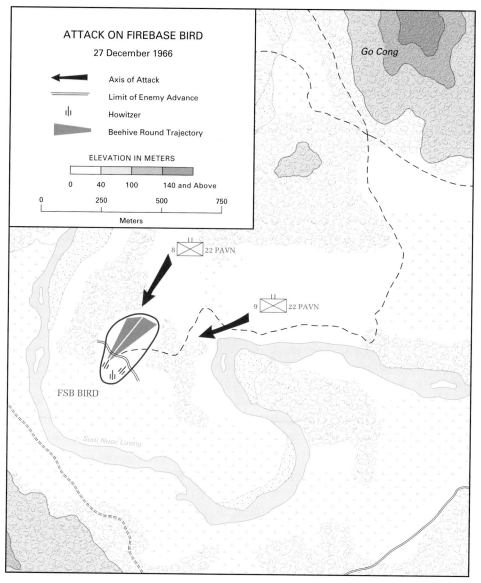

ATTACK ON FIREBASE BIRD
27 December 1966

Axis of Attack

Limit of Enemy Advance

Howitzer

Beehive Round Trajectory

ELEVATION IN METERS

0   40   100   140 and Above

0   250   500   750

Meters

Go Cong

8 ⊠ 22 PAVN

9 ⊠ 22 PAVN

FSB BIRD

Suoi Nuoc Luong

MAP 11

Ostensibly, he had accomplished his mission, claiming to have "spiked" 8 artillery pieces and killed "hundreds" of Americans. Actually, 1 gun had been destroyed, 27 defenders killed, and 67 wounded, but that still represented about 60 percent of the force at BIRD.

Almost immediately, Norton launched vigorous countermeasures, directing over eight hundred rounds into areas north and east of the base and sending the reserve battalion at HAMMOND into landing zones to the east. Shortly afterward he brought the 2d Brigade back from the high-lands to spearhead a general pursuit. The chase ended four days later, at the start of the New Year's truce, and by then the cavalrymen had claimed 267 enemy dead.[18]

As usual, evaluating either the accuracy or the significance of the body counts is difficult. Clearly, the enemy was proving a determined opponent, willing to take severe risks to maintain his hold on the Kim Son Valley. But the Americans were equally persistent. Following the New Year's truce, Shanahan's 3d Brigade, 25th Division, also arrived from the highlands, taking over the THAYER II operational area south of the Lai Giang, while the cavalry division prepared to move north of the river to execute Operation PERSHING in northeastern Binh Dinh.[19]

Although none of the operations in the fall of 1966 was decisive, cumulatively they changed the tactical picture in the coastal lowlands. In previous years the enemy had operated there with virtual impunity, using main force units to cement gains made by the Viet Cong and the political underground. By the end of the year operations launched by newly arrived U.S. units took away that initiative, forcing the enemy out of the populated areas and making large-scale military operations extremely risky for insurgent forces. In their wake, Saigon officials had an opportunity to begin providing security for their administrators and controlling the local population. Whether they could take full advantage of that opportunity remained to be seen.

---

[18] AAR, Opn THAYER II, 1st Cav Div, pp. 30–31. See also S. L. A. Marshall, *Bird: The Christmastide Battle* (Nashville, Tenn.: Battery Press, 1968). For the enemy's account of the fight, see *3d Division*, pp. 61–65.

[19] ORLL, 1 Nov 66–31 Jan 67, 1st Cav Div, 6 Mar 67, p. 6, Historians files, CMH, lists losses of the *22d Regiment* at BIRD as 212 killed and lists (on p. 16) cumulative enemy losses during the quarter for THAYER II as 1,529 killed, 1,012 captured, with allied losses during the same period as 184 killed, 747 wounded, and 2 missing in action.

PART TWO

Out From Saigon

6

Into the Triangle

Certain moments in war define the possibilities of victory. Six weeks
after ATTLEBORO ended, with good weather settling in, Westmoreland
launched the great III Corps offensives, which he hoped would usher in a
new security era all around Saigon. He had been awaiting this opportunity to strike for more than a year and had predicated a major portion of his
request for reinforcements on just this priority objective—the reduction of
the enemy superbases lurking between the capital and Cambodia. Since
his brief forays against the bases in 1965, Westmoreland knew his work
would be cut out for him, for unless these redoubts could be occupied or
rendered unlivable to the enemy, his troops would be obliged to return to
them again and again in search of targets until one side or the other ran
out of steam. Even now, his planners were committing to paper their
ideas for next year's dry season offensive on the doorstep of Saigon,
when there would be even more troops and firepower available, in case
this year's campaign had failed to do the job.

For the campaign just starting, Westmoreland's original primary target was War Zone C, the vast forested piedmont north of Dau Tieng that
U.S. forces had briefly penetrated during ATTLEBORO. But just weeks
before its scheduled onset, advice from General McChristian, his intelligence chief, led to a change in plans. Almost a year earlier, McChristian
had initiated Project RENDEZVOUS, an intensive intelligence collection program aimed specifically at *Military Region 4*, the enemy command that
included Saigon. By early December 1966 McChristian's intelligence spe-
cialists using pattern activity analysis had located several enemy installations thirty kilometers northwest of Saigon, clustered in and around the
Iron Triangle.[1] On maps, the 300-square-kilometer parcel of jungle resembled an inverted triangle with its sides bounded by the Saigon and Thi
Tinh Rivers and its inverted base cutting through the Thanh Dien Forest
on the north. McChristian believed that the insurgents were preparing an
offensive from this fortress against Saigon.

[1] The area was so named because of its similarity to an area on the Korean peninsula
given the same name during the Korean War. See AAR, Opn NIAGARA/CEDAR FALLS, 173d
Abn Bde, 25 Feb 67, p. 1, Historians files, CMH.

General McChristian

Three incidents in December corroborated his fears. On the fourth *Military Region 4's 6th Battalion* attacked South Vietnam's largest and most important air base at Tan Son Nhut on the western edge of Saigon, damaging eighteen aircraft. That evening a large satchel charge exploded on the roof of a building in a U.S. compound inside the city, wounding several Americans. Five days later, on 9 December, the Viet Cong unsuccessfully attempted to destroy the Binh Loi Bridge, a vital link to Saigon.[2]

On 12 December McChristian advised Westmoreland to delay the scheduled operation against War Zone C in favor of an immediate sweep into the Iron Triangle. Westmoreland was noncommittal, deferring the decision to General Seaman at II Field Force, but indicated that he had no objection to a postponement.[3] McChristian briefed Seaman the following day and convinced him to move against the Iron Triangle immediately. It made no sense, Seaman believed, to attack War Zone C with the proverbial fox still active in the Saigon chicken coop. Besides, neutralizing the triangle would take only a few weeks at most, during which time the bulk of the 9th Infantry Division, arriving from the United States, would join II Field Force, freeing other, more seasoned units for the attack on the larger war zone. From every aspect, destroying the Iron Triangle would serve as a suitable prelude for the offensive to come.[4]

American Planning

Seaman decided to launch CEDAR FALLS, the code name for the reduction of the Iron Triangle, in early January 1967 with a massive "hammer and anvil" encirclement of the fortress. To minimize civilian casualties and separate friend from opponent, Seaman planned to remove all civilians

---

[2] Periodic Intel Rpt 39, IIFFV, 12 Dec 66, pp. 2–3, 6–7; McChristian, *Military Intelligence*, p. 117.

[3] Westmoreland Jnl, 13 Dec 66, Westmoreland History files, 11–D, CMH.

[4] Intervs, John Albright with Lt Gen Jonathan O. Seaman, 10 Sep 70, Historians files, CMH; author with Seaman, 25 May 76.

from the triangle, including the village of Ben Suc and several other hamlets along the east bank of the Saigon River. Once evacuated, the region would be declared a specified strike zone, meaning that anyone subsequently found in the triangle would be considered an enemy combatant.[5]

The scope of the operation had many drawbacks. With nearly two-thirds of U.S. combat forces in III Corps participating, CEDAR FALLS required a major troop and supply buildup that might give the offensive away before it began. To achieve surprise, Seaman imposed strict security measures. Believing that the insurgents had penetrated the government and its armed forces, he confined knowledge of the operation to Americans, and even then briefed only certain senior commanders. Outside his immediate circle, he coordinated with the director of the Office of Civil Operations for III Corps, John Paul Vann, the Agency for International Development civilian charged with assisting South Vietnamese refugee efforts. He cautioned Vann to say nothing to his Vietnamese counterparts and their American advisers until after the operation had begun. Since helicopters needed about six hours of maintenance for every hour of flight, he directed his commanders to reduce helicopter operations to a minimum during the second half of December to assure their availability for the operation. He let his subordinates assume that the helicopters were being husbanded for the long-anticipated offensive into War Zone C. For similar security reasons, Seaman decided against stockpiling supplies at the Phu Cuong reception center for the refugees whom CEDAR FALLS was expected to generate.[6] (*Map 12*)

Seaman's troop deployments were also elaborate. To start with, he intended to ring the triangle with six brigades. Two brigades, controlled by Weyand's 25th Division, would take the Saigon River side, while the remaining four, directed by DePuy's 1st Division, would be responsible for the northern (Thanh Dien Forest) and eastern (Thi Tinh River) edges. The latter forces would conduct most of the clearing operations once the cordon was in place. South Vietnamese forces, as available, would be brought in after the operation had begun.[7]

Seaman would have preferred to air-assault his forces all at once, but because he lacked enough helicopters he was obliged to resort to deception. In this, he was aided by the fact that the objective was already bracketed by forward support bases. Cu Chi base camp, twenty kilometers south of Rach Bap (a hamlet near the center of the triangle), served the 25th Division, while elements of the 1st Division were based at Lai Khe, only fifteen kilometers to the east. Ben Cat, on the northeastern corner of the triangle, and Phu Cuong, twenty kilometers southeast of Rach Bap,

---

[5] AAR, Opn CEDAR FALLS, IIFFV, n.d., pp. 11–12, Historians files, CMH. See Lt. Gen. Bernard W. Rogers, *CEDAR FALLS–JUNCTION CITY: A Turning Point*, Vietnam Studies (Washington, D.C.: Department of the Army, 1974), pp. 25–79.

[6] AAR, Opn CEDAR FALLS, IIFFV, p. 13; Interv, Col Clyde H. Patterson with Lt Gen Jonathan O. Seaman, 18 Mar 71, Historians files, CMH.

[7] AAR, Opn CEDAR FALLS, IIFFV, p. 13; Interv, Patterson with Seaman, 18 Mar 71.

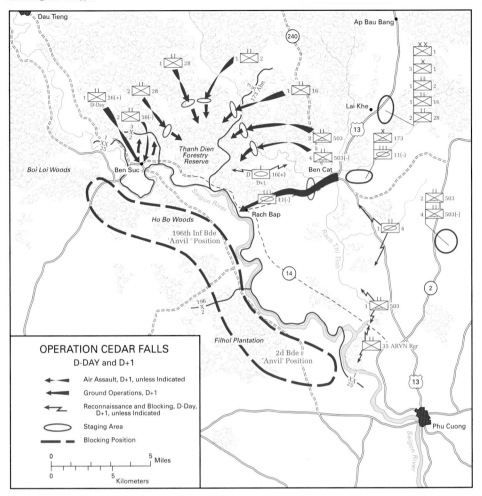

MAP 12

held units of the South Vietnamese 5th Division. A buildup of U.S. forces and supplies in these areas would not be especially unusual.

Prior to the attack, II Field Force directed Weyand to sweep the Ho Bo Woods north of Cu Chi with two battalions of the 196th and two mechanized battalions and to assemble the 2d Brigade, with two infantry and one tank battalion (the 2d of the 34th Armor), at Cu Chi itself. When CEDAR FALLS began, all seven battalions would move to north-south blocking positions along the Saigon River, stretching about twenty-five kilometers from the southern edge of the Boi Loi Woods, south through the Ho Bo Woods and the Filhol Rubber Plantation, and on to the juncture with the Thi Tinh River.

Seaman gave DePuy's 1st Division, with the 173d Airborne Brigade and the 11th Armored Cavalry attached, the most important tasks. DePuy was to ready his 2d Brigade at Dau Tieng, twenty kilometers west of Rach Bap, with three infantry battalions and his 3d Brigade at Lai Khe with another three. If the enemy detected the buildup, it would appear as if the allies intended another foray into War Zone C. At the same time, Seaman wanted one battalion of the 173d and a lone South Vietnamese ranger battalion to conduct limited sweeps south of the triangle, in the area of the Cau Dinh jungle and the confluence of the Saigon and Thi Tinh Rivers, with the 1st Division's cavalry squadron lightly outposting Highway 13 between there and Ben Cat. The remainder of the airborne brigade and one squadron of the 11th Armored Cavalry would remain at Ben Cat.

On D-day, which Westmoreland set for 8 January, units of the 1st Division's 3d Brigade and the attached 173d would air-assault into the northern side of the triangle in the Thanh Dien Forest, while units of the division's 2d Brigade would occupy Ben Suc Village in the triangle's northwestern corner. Simultaneously, the bulk of the 11th Armored Cavalry would make a rapid road march from its base camp east of Saigon to secure the relatively open Thi Tinh River–Highway 13 eastern side of the objective. Only after the Americans completed these deployments would they ask the South Vietnamese to participate, to assist in population evacuation, and to take over portions of the triangle's seal. Meanwhile, American units under 1st Division control would begin sweeping south from the Thanh Dien Forest and into the heart of the triangle.[8]

Preliminary Operations Begin

The preparatory phase began on 5 January 1967, with the 25th Division battalions (Operation PITTSBURGH) and the small 173d Airborne Brigade task force (Operation NIAGARA FALLS) deployed to opposite ends of the triangle but still outside it. There was almost no opposition. Meanwhile, Seaman began a series of air strikes against the one known main force unit in the area, the *272d PLAF Regiment*, believed to be in the Long Nguyen Secret Zone, some twenty-five kilometers north of the triangle. The air attacks drove the unit even farther north, keeping it away from the upcoming offensive.[9]

Just before D-day the Combined Intelligence Center, Vietnam, provided Weyand and DePuy with a final automated printout, the "Viet Cong Installations List," which gave map coordinates of suspected enemy facilities both in the Iron Triangle and in the areas where the blocking forces would operate. The tabulation included the headquarters of *Military Region 4* and the location of various committees of the headquarters, each

---

[8] Operations Plan (OPLAN) 58–66, Opn CEDAR FALLS, IIFFV, 12 Dec 66, Historians files, CMH.

[9] Daily Jnl, G–2, 1st Inf Div, 4, 6, 8 Jan 67, Historians files, CMH; Periodic Intel Rpt 9, IIFFV, 6 Mar 67, p. 1; Monthly Evaluation Rpt, IIFFV, Jan 67, 16 Feb 67, Historians files, CMH.

at different sites, as well as the location of one provincial committee, two district committees, and a *COSVN* logistical organization, the *83d Rear Service Group*.[10]

Once the *272d Regiment* had begun drifting north, intelligence officers at II Field Force saw little chance of encountering large enemy forces during the operation. Although three local force battalions and three separate local force companies were known to frequent the target area, American forces were more likely to meet rear service and guerrilla units using mines, booby traps, and sniper fire. If an organized defense developed, intelligence analysts concluded that it would be directed from the region's center, the village of Ben Suc, long an insurgent stronghold. For this reason General DePuy wanted the village seized even before encirclement of the Iron Triangle was complete. Its rapid neutralization would reduce any initial resistance, and the sooner its civilians could be evacuated, the sooner U.S. forces could freely employ their firepower. It was also possible that an early seal of the village would lead to the capture of senior Viet Cong leaders.[11]

Seizing the Iron Triangle

Just before first light on 8 January troop-carrying UH–1 Hueys began landing at the Dau Tieng airstrip, the staging area for the assault on Ben Suc. Shortly after sunrise men of the lead 1st Division unit, the 1st Battalion, 26th Infantry, led by Lt. Col. Alexander M. Haig, boarded the waiting craft. Ten minutes later sixty helicopters took off, circled Dau Tieng to gain altitude, and formed two "vee" formations, each with three flights of ten helicopters. After flying directly south from Dau Tieng to give the impression that some place other than Ben Suc was the objective, the helicopters, at a point twelve kilometers west of Ben Suc, dropped to treetop level for a final approach eastward into three landing sites west, north, and east of the village. In a further attempt to gain surprise, no artillery preparation or air strikes preceded the operation.

Traveling at 100 miles per hour, the helicopters crossed the Saigon River and precisely at H-hour, 0800, began to land. Within ninety seconds all six flights had cleared the landing zones and were on their way back to Dau Tieng. Thirty minutes later some of them returned to deposit a company south of Ben Suc, completing the encirclement of the village.

Except for an occasional burst of small-arms fire from the nearby jungle, there was no resistance. Once the noisy air armada departed, there

---

[10] AAR, Opn CEDAR FALLS, IIFFV, p. 5. See OPLAN 58–66, Opn CEDAR FALLS, IIFFV, an. A, app. 3.

[11] Interv, author with DePuy, 7 Oct 77; Ltr, Lt Col Robert L. Schweitzer, G–5, 1st Inf Div, to Brig Gen Bernard W. Rogers, Asst Div Comdr, 1st Inf Div, 26 Oct 67, attchmt: Comments Relating to the 15 July 1967 *New Yorker* Article "The Village of Ben Suc," by Jonathan Schell, Historians files, CMH; Rogers, CEDAR FALLS–JUNCTION CITY, pp. 31–34.

was only silence; tactical surprise had been achieved. Minutes later a lone helicopter passed over Ben Suc while a South Vietnamese soldier aboard announced over a loudspeaker that the villagers were to stay in their homes and await further instructions; should they attempt to run, they would be shot.[12]

Shortly afterward artillery shells, rockets from Huey gunships, and Air Force ordnance began exploding in the jungle north of the village to dissuade the inhabitants from escaping. A warm breeze from the north carried smoke from the explosions into the town, partially obscuring a bright blue sky and making the heat and humidity of a typical dry season day that much more uncomfortable.

As the explosions became less frequent and more distant, the airborne loudspeaker returned, announcing that the village was to be evacuated and the people were to assemble immediately with their belongings at the village school. Within an hour about a thousand of the inhabitants had arrived at the designated assembly point.

During that hour additional helicopters airlifted the 1st Division's revolutionary development task force to the site. The group, a small provisional organization under control of the 2d Brigade, was to coordinate the refugee collection effort. Accompanying the task force were three South Vietnamese National Police field platoons and an infantry battalion from the South Vietnamese 5th Division. Only after arriving at Ben Suc did the South Vietnamese learn of their mission. While the police questioned the people and culled out all males between the ages of fifteen and forty-five, the South Vietnamese battalion began searching the large, sprawling village.

By early afternoon the crowd at the school had grown to over 3,500 people. All were fed a warm meal, and those in need received medical treatment. Unfriendly but not openly hostile, the villagers sat and waited stoically in the hot sun. Exploding shells and bombs north of Ben Suc and occasional bursts of small-arms fire punctuated the drowsy calm. Loudspeakers overhead made *Chieu Hoi* appeals, while propaganda leaflets and safe-conduct passes dropped from the sky.[13]

Late in the afternoon helicopters arrived to take the men of the village to the provincial capital of Phu Cuong for questioning. But boats to evacuate the bulk of the population, mostly women, children, and the elderly, never arrived. The delay sprang from the security restrictions imposed on the operation. Although Seaman on 6 January had asked the South Vietnamese III Corps commander, Lt. Gen. Le Nguyen Khang, for riverine craft to evacuate the Ben Suc residents, for reasons of security Khang had waited until the Americans had taken the village before alerting the units involved. By then it was too late. Rather than leave the people in the open overnight, Maj. Robert L. Schweitzer, the commander of the 1st Division

---

[12] AAR, Opn CEDAR FALLS, 2d Bde, 1st Inf Div, 14 Feb 67, p. 4, Historians files, CMH.

[13] Ibid., pp. 3, 5; AAR, Opn CEDAR FALLS, 1st Inf Div, 13 Mar 67, p. 3, Historians files, CMH.

revolutionary development task force, directed them to return to their homes until told to reassemble. Two days passed before the evacuation down the Saigon River began.[14]

Meanwhile, the tactical portion of CEDAR FALLS proceeded as planned. By nightfall on the first day 2d Brigade units operating near Ben Suc had killed forty Viet Cong, uncovered a multitude of tunnels and caches, and destroyed an assortment of mines and booby traps, all without loss of a man. That night U.S. artillery fired illuminating rounds above the village and over a thousand high-explosive rounds on preplanned targets just to the north.[15]

Elsewhere, other American units completed the seal around the Iron Triangle. On D-day, after a 100-kilometer road march that took until midnight, the rest of the 11th Armored Cavalry joined the squadron already at Ben Cat. Stretched out along Highway 13 and the east bank of the Thi Tinh, the cavalry held the east side of the triangle.

The 25th Division, having positioned the 196th on the west bank of the Saigon River near the triangle's northern edge, sent its 2d Brigade up to the river near the southern end. In the process one battalion air-assaulted into a suspected enemy camp and bumped into a Viet Cong battalion. The ensuing series of small firefights lasted through the day before the enemy fled in early darkness. The American battalion suffered 39 casualties, including 6 men killed, while the enemy lost more than 100.[16]

The tactical maneuvers for the second day, 9 January, centered on the Thanh Dien Forest on the northern side of the triangle. Seaman had made the area an additional objective early in the planning, when intelligence indicated that the forest contained major enemy supply installations. Initially, DePuy had planned to have 2d Brigade forces sweep the area while two battalions of the 173d sealed the eastern edge and units of the 3d Brigade remained in reserve. The situation at Ben Suc, however, and reports of increased enemy activity in the forest led him to alter the roles of the two brigades and send the 3d Brigade in at once.[17]

Following B–52 strikes against the forest, at 0735 on 9 January, fourteen batteries of artillery began a sustained preparatory barrage against the first of seven battalion-size landing zones northeast of Ben Suc. After about thirty minutes the artillery shifted to the second landing zone,

---

[14] AAR, Opn CEDAR FALLS, 1st Inf Div, p. 3; Memo, John P. Vann, Dir, Office of Civil Operations (OCO), III Corps Tactical Zone, 14 Jan 67, sub: Complaints of Major General William DePuy to OCO/GVN Performance on Handling Refugees During Operation CEDAR FALLS, p. 3 (hereafter cited as Vann Memorandum), Historians files, CMH; Ltr, Schweitzer to Rogers, 26 Oct 67.

[15] AAR, Opn CEDAR FALLS, 2d Bde, 1st Inf Div, pp. 4–5; AAR, Opn CEDAR FALLS, IIFFV, p. 15; AAR, Opn CEDAR FALLS, 1st Inf Div Arty, 20 Feb 67, p. 5, Historians files, CMH.

[16] AAR, Opn CEDAR FALLS, 1st Bn, 27th Inf, 8 Feb 67, pp. 4–5; AAR, Opn CEDAR FALLS, 2d Bde, 25th Inf Div, 16 Feb 67, p. 4, both in Historians files, CMH; Interv, Patterson with Seaman, 18 Mar 71.

[17] AAR, Opn CEDAR FALLS, 3d Bde, 1st Inf Div, 10 Feb 67, p. 2, Historians files, CMH; AAR, Opn CEDAR FALLS, 2d Bde, 1st Inf Div, p. 4.

Men of the 11th Armored Cavalry Regiment advance in the Iron Triangle.

while helicopter gunships led sixty troop-filled Hueys onto the first. Within five minutes an entire battalion was on the ground, and by early afternoon similar air assaults on five more of the landing zones had put six U.S. infantry battalions on the fringes of the Thanh Dien Forest, four under 3d Brigade's control and two under the 173d. None of the units met organized resistance. With no apparent need to have a reaction force at Dau Tieng, DePuy gave the remaining battalion there to the 3d Brigade commander, Colonel Marks, for an air assault on the seventh and last of the landing zones. But the final landing area proved to be mined, forcing Marks to abort and land the battalion at Ben Suc; the next morning the unit moved by foot to its objective.

While Marks' battalions were sealing the triangle's northern end, other American units penetrated the base itself. The initial sweeping force consisted of two squadrons of the 11th Armored Cavalry, operating as part of Task Force DEANE under the new commander of the 173d Airborne Brigade, Brig. Gen. John R. Deane. After first light on 9 January these units crossed two bridges over the Thi Tinh River at Ben Cat, then proceeded along the trace of a dirt road southwestward across the triangle toward the Saigon River. While one squadron progressively dropped off detachments to form a screen along the road, the other aimed for an enemy headquarters reported to be at the small village of Rach Bap on the river. By midmorning they had seized their objectives against only slight resistance. Engineers with bulldozers accompanied the troopers to help as needed and to repair the road.[18]

As tanks and armored cavalry assault vehicles reached Rach Bap, a helicopter equipped with a loudspeaker directed the inhabitants to gather their belongings in preparation for evacuation but to remain in their homes until told to do otherwise. Shortly before noon, however, some American soldiers inexplicably began evicting people and setting fire to the houses. Frightened, many of the civilians fled east in the direction of Ben Cat, and other farmers living along the river soon joined the flight. By midafternoon over a thousand civilians had crossed the bridges over the Thi Tinh, there to be assembled in a hastily established holding area south of Ben Cat. Few of the refugees had brought any possessions with them.[19]

Ordering a halt to the destruction of the homes at Rach Bap, General DePuy directed that the refugees be returned to the village to collect their belongings. Although the 1st Division had planned to evacuate other hamlets along the Saigon River after the evacuation of Ben Suc was under way, the destruction in Rach Bap prompted DePuy to alter his plans again.[20]

Refugee Evacuation

Before CEDAR FALLS had begun, DePuy suggested that the 1st Division establish and initially operate the camp at Phu Cuong for the expected influx of civilians. Seaman, however, believed that South Vietnamese officials were best qualified to deal with their own people and vetoed the proposal. Although John Vann had agreed to prepare plans for the camp and to provide the South Vietnamese with materials and supplies, the need for security prevented him from informing the Binh Duong province chief of the requirement until after CEDAR FALLS was under way. Not surprisingly, the South Vietnamese bureaucracy responded slowly to the unanticipated relocation effort.[21]

As 9 January came to a close, the seal around the Iron Triangle was complete, but little of a constructive nature had been done regarding the evacuation or resettlement of the area's inhabitants. By then the South Vietnamese 5th Division had committed a second battalion to CEDAR FALLS and promised to provide four more battalions on 10 January, bringing to twenty-six the total number of battalion-size units in the operation.[22] Two of

---

[18] AAR, Opn CEDAR FALLS, 11th Armd Cav Rgt, n.d., pp. 5–6, Historians files, CMH.

[19] AAR, Opn CEDAR FALLS, 1st Inf Div, p. 3; Vann Memorandum, pp. 3–4.

[20] AAR, Opn CEDAR FALLS, 1st Inf Div, p. 3; Interv, author with DePuy, 7 Oct 77.

[21] Intervs, author with DePuy, 7 Oct 77; with Seaman, 25 May 76; Vann Memorandum, pp. 1–3.

[22] The 26 units were grouped as follows: 6 infantry and 3 airborne battalions, 2 armored cavalry squadrons, and 1 cavalry squadron under 1st Division control; 1 tank, 2 mechanized infantry, and 4 infantry battalions under the 25th Division; 1 ranger, 4 infantry, and 2 airborne battalions under the South Vietnamese 5th Division.

American and South Vietnamese troops evacuate villagers along the Saigon River.

the additional South Vietnamese battalions would deploy into the southern portion of the blocking position east of the Thi Tinh River, relieving the lone battalion of the 173d still in the Cau Dinh jungle; the other reinforcements, a South Vietnamese task force with two airborne battalions, were to travel up the Saigon River by boat, assume control of the South Vietnamese battalion at Ben Suc, and assist in the civilian evacuation there.[23]

Anxious to relocate the civilians as soon as possible, General DePuy sent trucks on the morning of the tenth to bring out the residents of Rach Bap and those who lived nearby. By midafternoon those vehicles had delivered 600 refugees with their possessions to the camp at Phu Cuong. An additional 200 refugees followed over the next two days.[24] Meanwhile, between 11 and 13 January, South Vietnamese soldiers evacuated 2,800 refugees by river, road, and air along with over 400 cows and water buffalo and several oxcarts.[25] The evacuation was a helter-skelter affair, thoroughly mixing up the Vietnamese evacuees and their belongings.

[23] AAR, Opn CEDAR FALLS, 1st Inf Div, p. 5.

[24] Ibid., p. 3; Vann Memorandum, p. 5.

[25] AAR, Opn CEDAR FALLS, 2d Bde, 1st Inf Div, pp. 3, 7–10; AAR, Opn CEDAR FALLS, IIFFV, p. 17; AAR, Opn CEDAR FALLS, 1st Engr Bn, 2 Mar 67, p. 8, Historians files, CMH.

On 11 January, at the peak of the relocation effort, General DePuy made a personal inspection of the refugee camp at Phu Cuong and found conditions abysmal. Cooking and sleeping facilities were minimal, shelter insufficient and inadequate, and sanitation facilities poor. He requested that the 1st Division take charge of the camp by the following morning.[26]

Arriving at Phu Cuong later that day, Vann learned of DePuy's complaints. Discussing the situation with General Seaman that evening, Vann admitted there were problems but felt that conditions were hardly as bleak as DePuy had depicted. While there were indeed 3,400 refugees—more than double the number the Office of Civil Operations had been prepared to accept by 11 January—that, he explained, was the result of DePuy's accelerated evacuation. Despite the large influx of people, nobody had missed a meal, and everybody would have shelter and some kind of mat or blanket by midnight. The basic problem, Vann concluded, was the unwillingness of South Vietnamese officials to waste energy or supplies on people they considered an integral part of the enemy's political organization.[27]

After speaking with Seaman, Vann called DePuy to hear his observations firsthand. DePuy angrily repeated what he had said to Seaman. "Just as I told you two weeks ago, Vann," he charged, "your lousy organization has fallen flat on its face and I am going to move in and do the job, as usual."[28] When Vann reported the interchange to Seaman, the II Field Force commander agreed to visit Phu Cuong with the civilian coordinator the following morning to see for himself.

Touring the refugee camp on the twelfth, Seaman concluded that, in view of how little time the South Vietnamese had had to prepare, they were making satisfactory progress. After complimenting the province chief, Lt. Col. Ly Tong Ba, he told the 1st Division's chief of staff, Col. Edward B. Kitchens, to provide Colonel Ba whatever help he could and to let Seaman's staff know if II Field Force could furnish additional support.[29]

While operation of the camp remained Colonel Ba's responsibility, that afternoon trucks from the 1st Division began hauling in tentage, additional water, and other supplies. Although another throng of refugees arrived during the day, cooperation between the Americans and South Vietnamese slowly improved, as did conditions in the camp. When the evacuation ended, the camp contained over 6,000 people, mostly women and children, and what possessions and animals they could find.

It would take five long months to transfer most of the refugees to a permanent government resettlement area ten kilometers to the south.

[26] Intervs, author with DePuy, 7 Oct 77; with Seaman, 25 May 76; Vann Memorandum, p. 6.

[27] Vann Memorandum, p. 6; Interv, author with Seaman, 25 May 76.

[28] Quote from Vann Memorandum, p. 6. Interv, author with DePuy, 7 Oct 77.

[29] Interv, author with Seaman, 25 May 76; Vann Memorandum, p. 7.

There, they lived in cement-block houses with tin roofs, which they themselves constructed.[30] Although their new living quarters were identical to those provided to Vietnamese military dependents, the refugees could hardly have been satisfied with their new surroundings. Nevertheless, few if any returned to their homes in the Iron Triangle, which already had been greatly altered.

Leveling the Triangle

As the first boatload of refugees left Ben Suc on 11 January, the Vietnamese airborne task force assumed the mission of securing the town. From the beginning of the operation it was evident that the village had served as a major logistical center for *Military Region 4*. On the first day of CEDAR FALLS, a captured Viet Cong platoon leader from the *83d Rear Service Group* revealed that four companies of his group operated out of the village. Once South Vietnamese soldiers and police began probing the area, the prisoner's testimony was confirmed. On the surface, Ben Suc appeared no different from any other South Vietnamese village: various thatched huts and masonry houses were in moderate disrepair and streets partially overgrown with weeds. But beneath the ground, hidden from view, was another village, one of underground chambers for storing supplies, maintaining records, providing medical treatment, and manufacturing uniforms, mines, and booby traps. Connecting the chambers was one of the most extensive tunnel complexes to be found during the course of the operation.[31]

On 13 January, following the departure of the last refugees, the destruction of both the surface and underground facilities began. A systematic survey of the entire complex had already been deemed too dangerous. But as bulldozers leveled the structures above ground, their blades uncovered huge quantities of rice, fifty tons of which South Vietnamese troops eventually bagged and evacuated, and additional entrances and exits. In several cases, 1st Division engineers pumped acetylene gas into these apertures and detonated them with electronic igniters. The explosions collapsed tunnels less than seven feet below the surface, while, for deeper passages, up to twenty feet below ground, the engineers used conventional explosives to serve as booster charges for the gas. The effort marked the first extensive use of acetylene gas in destroying tunnels in South Vietnam.[32]

---

[30] Vann Memorandum, p. 7; MFR, Lt Col Edward J. Huycke, Comdr, 1st Med Bn, 10 Oct 67, attchmt: Comments Concerning Article by Jonathan Schell in the 15 July 1967 Issue of *The New Yorker*, Title "A Reporter at Large, The Village of Ben Suc," Historians files, CMH.

[31] AAR, Opn CEDAR FALLS, 2d Bde, 1st Inf Div, pp. 2–6; AAR, Opn CEDAR FALLS, 1st Inf Div, p. 2.

[32] AAR, Opn CEDAR FALLS, 1st Engr Bn, pp. 11–13, 21. See also Rogers, CEDAR FALLS–JUNCTION CITY, p. 69.

A 1st Division soldier enters a tunnel in the Thanh Dien Forest.

On 16 and 17 January, as the destruction of Ben Suc neared completion, South Vietnamese troops left by boat for Phu Cuong. But before their final departure, the engineers made a last effort to destroy all vestiges of the enemy's underground installation. In the center of the village, bulldozers dug a pit thirty feet deep into which engineers placed five tons of explosives—mostly enemy munitions captured in the Thanh Dien Forest—and a half-ton of napalm. Bulldozers then backfilled the hole with ten feet of dirt to confine the explosion as much as possible below ground. After setting a 2½-hour delay fuze, the last engineers departed. Ten minutes after dark the explosion erupted. All that remained of Ben Suc was a large crater.[33]

While Ben Suc was being leveled, the remainder of the 1st Division's task forces scoured the northern side and the interior of the triangle. DePuy assigned the 2d Brigade, with two battalions, the area north of Ben Suc; the 3d Brigade, with four battalions, the Thanh Dien Forest; the 173d Airborne Brigade and 11th Armored Cavalry Regiment the central and southern triangle area; and five Vietnamese units blocking positions on the eastern, Thi Tinh River–Highway 13, side.

Between 11 and 28 January the searching American infantrymen located hundreds of hidden enemy bases, storage areas, and cache sites. Those that DePuy's 2d and 3d Brigades uncovered in the jungles north and east of Ben Suc proved the most lucrative. The finds, which MACV intelligence analysts had previously pinpointed, included the headquarters for the insurgent province of Thu Dau Mot just north of Ben Suc and a nearby storage area with over 750 tons of rice stored in 300-pound bags on tin-roofed platforms. To the east, in the Thanh Dien Forest, units of the 3d Brigade found similar caches containing twice that tonnage. Because the sites were inaccessible, less than 450 tons was hauled out. Chemical and engineer teams destroyed the rest with diesel fuel, flamethrowers, explosives, and bulldozers, or simply by watering it down.

Elsewhere the searchers found not only rice, weapons, and munitions, but also *Military Region* 4's signal and cryptological center containing communication directives, operating instructions, and code books. They also uncovered an underground 100-bed hospital and medical depot,

---

[33] AAR, Opn CEDAR FALLS, 1st Inf Div, pp. 6–7; AAR, Opn CEDAR FALLS, 1st Engr Bn, p. 13; Interv, author with DePuy, 7 Oct 77.

later determined to be the main source of medical supplies for enemy forces operating in III Corps.[34]

As at Ben Suc, searching these underground tunnels and bunker systems proved difficult, especially for the larger ones such as the provincial headquarters, which included an elaborate concrete bunker with three levels of interconnecting tunnels.[35] The dangerous task of exploring and mapping these mazes was undertaken by "tunnel rats," volunteer infantrymen who were either extremely brave or extremely foolish. Normally slight in stature because the passages they would traverse were almost always extremely small, the typical "rat" had to have quick reactions and no trace of claustrophobia. Waiting around a bend might be an armed enemy soldier or, less dangerous, a snake or scorpion. Carrying a pistol, with a silencer when available, a telephone, and a flashlight, he would enter the tunnel, take an azimuth (direction) with his compass, and move forward slowly, using a probe to detect booby traps and trailing his phone line behind him. As he reached each bend and twist of the tunnel, he would stop, estimate the distance traveled, and shoot a new azimuth, reporting that information by telephone to his comrades above ground, who would record it. If he lost contact with the monitor or needed assistance, another soldier would use the telephone wire to find him.

The enemy's defensive arrangements within the tunnels were often quite elaborate. In one case, a tunnel rat mapping a second-level complex found that the narrow passageway he was exploring came to an apparent end. Probing about, however, he discovered a trap door which led down into another tunnel at a third level, only to rise vertically two or three meters to the second level. In the earth, constituting the apparent dead end, were two small holes through which a man might observe and fire. He found a similar arrangement several meters farther. But this time, as he was lifting the trap door to drop down to the third level, he was shot at through one of the peep holes. The shot missed, and the intrepid soldier snapped off his flashlight and, using the telephone wire as a guide, inched his way in total darkness back to safety. In this particular case the exploration was not renewed, and engineers ultimately collapsed the tunnels with explosives, marking the location of several concrete bunkers for later destruction by air strikes.[36]

As the 2d Brigade's role in CEDAR FALLS came to an end, the 3d Brigade also began evacuating its forces from the Thanh Dien Forest, completing the withdrawal on 18 January. On the following morning B–52s struck the remaining concrete bunkers in the Thu Dau Mot provincial headquarters. In response to reports that the enemy had returned to the Ben Suc–Thanh

[34] AAR, Opn CEDAR FALLS, 3d Bde, 1st Inf Div, pp. 4, 17; AAR, Opn CEDAR FALLS, 1st Inf Div, pp. 6, 31; McChristian, *Military Intelligence*, p. 115; MFR, 9 Feb 67, sub: MACV Commanders' Conference, 22 January 1967, Westmoreland History files, 12–D–11, CMH.

[35] AAR, Opn CEDAR FALLS, 2d Bde, 1st Inf Div, pp. 8–9 and an. 1.

[36] Ibid., p. 9 and an. 1.

Members of the 173d Airborne Brigade guard Viet Cong prisoners near Rach Bap.

Dien Forest area, the 3d Brigade conducted company-size air assaults into the region a week later but found only a few Viet Cong stragglers.[37]

To the south, Task Force DEANE also had been busy. By 11 January it had deployed two squadrons of the 11th Armored Cavalry and the entire 173d Airborne Brigade into the Iron Triangle. While retaining screening elements along the Rach Bap–Ben Cat road, the bulk of the task force swept south into a landscape of bamboo jungle, abandoned rubber plantations, and extensive rice paddies. Afforded two full weeks to search the area carefully, the Americans found 1,300 tons of rice, most locally grown, several weapons caches, and many tunnel complexes.

As the operation progressed, Viet Cong soldiers caught in the tunnels chose to surrender in ever-increasing numbers. When one prisoner led an American patrol to a tunnel complex he had helped construct, tunnel rats found a large collection of documents belonging to the intelligence section of *Military Region 4*, which described in detail operations in the area since 1962. Other documents included lists of American and South Vietnamese

[37] AAR, Opn CEDAR FALLS, 3d Bde, 1st Inf Div, p. 5.

110

radio call signs and frequencies, approximately two hundred personal history statements of Communist cadre members, and a notebook containing the names of South Vietnamese officers whom the insurgents could count on to provide information and American ammunition.[38]

The two brigades under 25th Division control on the west bank of the Saigon River had not been idle either. On the eleventh one unit found enemy documents marked "secret" belonging to the *Postal, Communications, and Transportation Section* of *Military Region 4* and revealing the detailed organization of the enemy headquarters and its subordinate military and political arms. Other classified documents indicated that enemy rear service units were buying American weapons and ammunition with South Vietnamese piasters on the local economy. Attached was a price guide to ensure that buyers were not cheated by American, Korean, or South Vietnamese black-marketeers.

A week later another unit discovered a large tunnel complex that appeared to be the operations headquarters of *Military Region 4*. Documents taken from the complex included an outline plan and general objectives for the insurgents' 1966–1967 campaign, as well as after action reports and maps of routes leading from the Iron Triangle into the Saigon metropolitan region.[39]

Assessment

When CEDAR FALLS ended on 26 January, the combined American and South Vietnamese force had found and destroyed all major headquarters installations of *Military Region 4*, including over 1,100 bunkers, 400 tunnels, and 500 other structures. They had captured over 600 weapons along with large quantities of ammunition, mines, and booby traps and had seized over 3,700 tons of rice. The entire civilian population within the Iron Triangle had been resettled elsewhere, and the area made a free-fire zone. Since the allies had drained the civilian "sea" in which the guerrilla "fish" could swim, acts of sabotage, assassination, and harassment dropped precipitously throughout the region. American engineers further reduced the suitability of the area as a base camp by stripping nearly eleven square kilometers of jungle away, eliminating hideouts, and increasing the security of thoroughfares from ambush.

Although the main goal of the operation had been to deny the enemy the use of a major base near Saigon, CEDAR FALLS also succeeded in killing over 700 insurgents and seizing 200 prisoners and 500 ralliers, making it the first operation in III Corps during which the number of enemy who

---

[38] AAR, Opn CEDAR FALLS, 1st Engr Bn, p. 3; Interv, author with LeGro, 15 Jan 76; Periodic Intel Rpt 6, IIFFV, 14 Feb 67, p. 14, Historians files, CMH; McChristian, *Military Intelligence*, p. 124.

[39] AAR, Opn CEDAR FALLS, 196th Light Inf Bde, an. A, pp. 2–4, Historians files, CMH; Periodic Intel Rpt 6, IIFFV, 14 Feb 67, p. 14.

surrendered equaled the number killed. Although almost all prisoners and ralliers were from local force, rear service, and guerrilla units, there were also twelve important Viet Cong officers and political officials. One was a major in charge of military operations in *Military Region 4*. Two others were Russian-speaking North Vietnamese who specialized in recruiting and propaganda. Since there had been only one significant engagement with a cohesive enemy unit, American and South Vietnamese losses were relatively light: 72 dead and 337 wounded Americans; and 11 killed and 8 wounded South Vietnamese.[40]

The Americans had caught the enemy by surprise, though prisoner interrogations revealed that in mid-December *Military Region 4* had warned all units in and near the Iron Triangle to expect an American offensive. Leaves and passes had been restricted and local commanders had even been given a second alert three days after Christmas. But the defenders had taken few if any special precautions. Perhaps the number of alerts, false and otherwise, had eroded any sense of immediacy.[41]

The intelligence windfall from CEDAR FALLS was even greater than anticipated. Of 491,553 pages of enemy documents captured, 52,797 (11 percent) were either summarized or fully translated by the Combined Document Exploitation Center in Saigon. Those documents containing perishable intelligence—information which required immediate action if it was to have value—received the highest priority. In many instances the capturing unit received information for exploitation within twenty-four hours after the center had received the document. Perhaps more important, the captured documents gave MACV analysts a solid base of data concerning the enemy in and around Saigon from which they could plan long-range security campaigns against the insurgent underground. Information gleaned from captured documents and prisoner interrogations also led to the arrest of several enemy agents operating in the city of Saigon and in the neighboring provinces of Gia Dinh and Binh Duong.[42]

CEDAR FALLS proved the value of pattern activity analysis as a means of locating fixed enemy installations. In the operational area of the 11th Armored Cavalry, for example, 177 suspected enemy facilities had been charted by means of that technique. One hundred fifty-eight (89 percent) of these were found within five hundred meters of their reported locations, with an average distance of two hundred meters. Whether the high correlation could be repeated in a less confined area was soon to be tested in War Zone C.[43]

[40] Periodic Intel Rpt 5, IIFFV, 7 Feb 67, an. I, Historians files, CMH; McChristian, *Military Intelligence*, p. 124; Interv, author with DePuy, 7 Oct 77; AAR, Opn CEDAR FALLS, IIFFV, p. 20.

[41] Intel Sums 47, IIFFV, 16 Feb 67, p. 13, and 57, IIFFV, 26 Feb 67, p. 15, both in Historians files, CMH. See also Monthly Evaluation Rpt, IIFFV, Jan 67, 16 Feb 67, pp. 2–3, 5–6.

[42] AAR, Opn CEDAR FALLS, IIFFV, p. 24; McChristian, *Military Intelligence*, p. 125.

[43] Periodic Intel Rpt 4, IIFFV, 31 Jan 67, p. 14, Historians files, CMH; AAR, Opn CEDAR FALLS, IIFFV, p. 8; McChristian, *Military Intelligence*, pp. 34–36, 115.

7

Junction City: The Horseshoe

Buoyed by the results of CEDAR FALLS, in February 1967 Westmoreland turned his attention to War Zone C, home to *COSVN* and the *9th Division*. Code-named JUNCTION CITY, the operation was to be the centerpiece of the III Corps offensive and the largest American operation of the war to date. It would involve two division headquarters, each controlling four brigades for a period of two months. Even with these forces, however, achieving a decisive outcome would be difficult given the ruggedness of the landscape, the depth of the enemy's presence, and the existence of inviolate sanctuaries in neighboring Cambodia. But the stakes were high: a victory here would be a coup for Westmoreland. He had an opportunity to destroy a major part of the enemy's forces in northern III Corps, hobbling their plans there and providing U.S. troops with enough breathing room to begin pacifying the countryside. With the enemy pushed out, moreover, the allies could construct new bases in War Zone C, allowing follow-on operations should the Communists try to return.

For planning purposes, II Field Force divided War Zone C into three tactical sectors using two north-south roads. The farthest west lay between Highway 22 and the Cambodian border, with the upper portion often referred to as the "Elephant's Ear" or the "Dog's Head" due to the outline of the border when viewed on a map. A central region, between Highway 22 and Route 4, was suspected to contain *COSVN* and other major enemy headquarters and support installations. A third section stretched east of Route 4 to the Saigon River and then on to Highway 13, the major north-south artery linking Saigon to northern III Corps.

According to MACV intelligence, the *9th Division* was recovering from ATTLEBORO and dispersed around northern III Corps, with one regiment in extreme western War Zone C, another east of the Saigon River in the Long Nguyen Secret Zone, and a third in southern War Zone D. Operating east of Saigon in Phuoc Tuy Province, the *5th PLAF Division*, with only two regiments, remained inactive, and was too distant to provide timely assistance to *COSVN*. North of War Zone D, the *7th PAVN Division* had two regiments in Phuoc Long Province and since December had regained control of the *101st PAVN Regiment*, which was regrouping in the Fishhook, a sanctuary inside Cambodia north of Tay Ninh and west of Binh Long

Province. So, for the immediate defense of War Zone C, *COSVN* could count on only four regiments: two of the *9th Division*, the *271st* and *272d*; the *101st* in the Fishhook; and *COSVN*'s own security unit, the *70th Guard*, about which MACV headquarters had little information.[1]

Deception Operations

If the Americans were to have a chance at catching the enemy, secrecy was essential. As in CEDAR FALLS, consequently, Seaman chose not to inform the South Vietnamese of the approaching offensive. He also conducted a series of deception operations. Early in February Seaman directed DePuy's 1st Division to move against the Long Nguyen Secret Zone and the *272d Regiment*, while Weyand's 25th Division engaged the *271st Regiment* in Base Area 354, or western War Zone C. The 25th Division effort, code-named GADSDEN, would begin on 2 February and continue right up to the initiation of JUNCTION CITY on the twenty-second. The 1st Division's venture, code-named TUCSON, would be briefer, 14–18 February. Rather than lead enemy units away from the target area as in CEDAR FALLS, Seaman hoped these preliminary affairs would drive them into it.[2]

The 25th Division moved first. Keeping his two organic brigades in Hau Nghia Province, Weyand sent his two attached brigades, the 196th and the 3d of the 4th Division, each reinforced by an additional battalion, into western War Zone C on 2 February. Preceded by B–52 strikes against suspected bases of the *271st*, the eight infantry battalions seized two abandoned border villages, Lo Go and Xom Giua, which served as enemy supply conduits from Cambodia. The operation had the added advantage of interdicting the supply routes during the Tet holidays, 8–12 February, denying their use to the Communists during the truce.

Subsequent sweeps confirmed the presence of the *271st*, *70th Guard*, and *680th Training Regiments* in the Lo Go area, although they failed to bring these forces to battle. When GADSDEN ended on 21 February, the 196th returned to its base at Tay Ninh West, while the 3d Brigade deployed to blocking positions along Highway 22 for JUNCTION CITY. During GADSDEN, U.S. forces seized nearly 300 tons of rice and smaller quantities of assorted military equipment, but accounted for only 160 enemy dead at a cost of 29 American lives.[3]

Seventy kilometers east of GADSDEN, the 1st Division's Operation TUCSON did little better. Beginning on 14 February, Maj. Gen. John H. Hay,

---

[1] Interv, author with Seaman, 25 May 76; Rogers, CEDAR FALLS–JUNCTION CITY, pp. 83–90; Monthly OB Sum, CICV, Jan 67; Periodic Intel Rpt 4, IIFFV, 31 Jan 67, an. B. See also Periodic Intel Rpt 15, IIFFV, 18 Apr 67, par. 2k, Historians files, CMH.

[2] AAR, Opn JUNCTION CITY, IIFFV, pp. 7, 16, and OPLAN 3–67, Opn JUNCTION CITY, IIFFV, 8 Feb 67, an. A, both in Historians files, CMH.

[3] AAR, Opn GADSDEN, 25th Inf Div, 22 Mar 67, pp. 3–8; Periodic Intel Rpts 6, IIFFV, 14 Feb 67, pp. 7–8, and 7, IIFFV, 21 Feb 67, pp. 3–4. All in Historians files, CMH.

General Hay

who had just replaced DePuy as division commander, deployed two brigades into the Long Nguyen Secret Zone in Binh Long Province. In addition to being the main base area for the *272d Regiment*, the redoubt also served as a vital troop and supply link between War Zones C and D. The brief operation uncovered over 1,700 tons of rice, but as in GADSDEN the Americans met only a few Viet Cong support troops.[4]

On 19 February Hay moved his forces out of the secret zone and rearranged them, sending the 3d Brigade to Suoi Da and the 1st Brigade, along with the division's forward command post, to Minh Thanh. Although neither GADSDEN nor TUCSON appeared to have influenced the disposition of the enemy regiments, whose precise location remained hazy, the operations had at least brought strong American forces to the edges of War Zone C with no apparent Communist response.

While Hay repositioned his brigades, he also received control of the 173d Airborne Brigade and immediately began a third deception deployment. Keeping the brigade headquarters and one battalion at Bien Hoa, he ordered the rest of the 173d to a staging area at Quan Loi, somewhat east of War Zone C. The movement coincided with a sharp fight between South Vietnamese irregulars and a North Vietnamese battalion in the area, which enemy commanders might have interpreted as a buildup due north of Saigon. Time would tell if *COSVN* had been put off the scent.[5]

JUNCTION CITY: The Plan

The strength of Seaman's plan lay in its boldness. On D-day, 22 February, three brigades, nine battalions strong, were to come in by air to form a northern arch-like blocking position, generally along Route 246, a dirt road paralleling the Cambodian border between Highway 22 on the west and Route 4 on the east. Eight of the battalions would conduct helicopter assaults, while the ninth would parachute from C–130s. Simultaneously, two other brigades were to move overland, one along

---

[4] AAR, Opn TUCSON, 1st Inf Div, 26 Mar 67, pp. 1–7, Historians files, CMH.

[5] AAR, Opn JUNCTION CITY, IIFFV, p. 16; Intel Sum 51, 1st Inf Div, 20 Feb 67; AAR, Opn JUNCTION CITY, 11th Armd Cav Rgt, 9 Jun 67, pp. 15–17; Interv, author with Deane, 5 Jan 78. All in Historians files, CMH.

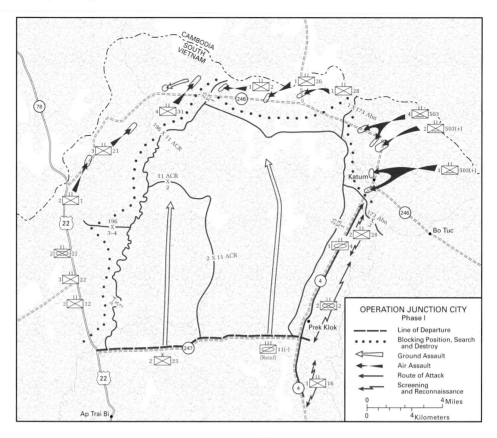

MAP 13

Highway 22, the other along Route 4, to establish blocking positions that would extend each end of the arch southward so the final position would take the form of an inverted "U," or horseshoe. At the open end of the horseshoe, the 11th Armored Cavalry, since marched to Tay Ninh, and an infantry brigade were to screen along Route 247 on D-day and the following morning attack north into the horseshoe in search of COSVN.[6] (*Map 13*)

Initially, the assaulting forces would consist of twenty-two combat battalions. Seaman's plans gave responsibility for the northern, northeastern, and eastern portions of the gigantic seal to the 1st Division, and the northwestern and western rims to the 25th Division. The 25th would also direct the movement of the southern forces into the horseshoe itself. Clockwise, starting in the west, the blocking forces included the three infantry battalions of the 3d Brigade, 4th Division, moving out of Operation TUCSON along Highway 22; the 196th Brigade air-assaulting its three battalions from Tay Ninh to the northwest corner of the block, both brigades under 25th

[6] OPLAN 3–67, Opn JUNCTION CITY, IIFFV, pp. 2–4.

116

Division control; and, under 1st Division control, the three infantry battalions of the 1st Brigade helicoptering into the horseshoe's northern edge; the three battalions of the 173d inserted into the block's northeastern corner, two by helicopter and one by parachute; and the 1st Division's 3d Brigade with some four battalion equivalents moving up from Suoi Da along Route 4, the target's eastern boundary. In the south, in the open end of the horseshoe, the attacking forces would consist of the 11th Armored Cavalry on the right with two organic squadrons and a mechanized infantry battalion, and the 25th Division's 2d Brigade attacking with three battalions. In addition to the twenty-two battalions in the assault force, the newly arrived 1st Brigade, 9th Infantry Division, based near Saigon, was to serve as the corps reserve.

Logistical support for Junction City was to come primarily from Saigon Support Command's large complex at Tay Ninh West. Supplies would move overland to forward installations at Trai Bi, Suoi Da, and, ten kilometers north of the latter, at "Plentitude," the abandoned French fort (for the 25th Division) and at Suoi Da and Minh Thanh (for the 1st Division). Aerial delivery was to be provided by C–130s and C–123s that had already pre-positioned supplies at Quan Loi. Once the operation got under way, the cargo planes were to conduct airdrops to the three northernmost brigades.[7] In addition, engineers were to build a Special Forces camp at Prek Klok astride Route 4, ten kilometers north of the French fort, and an airstrip capable of receiving C–130s at Katum, at the junction of Routes 4 and 246, all to improve logistics.

For Seaman the rapid positioning of his northernmost brigades to keep the enemy penned in was critical. Needing more helicopters than he had in his 12th Aviation Group, he turned to Westmoreland for help. Drawing from the 17th Aviation Group in II Corps and the 13th Aviation Battalion in the Mekong Delta, Westmoreland transferred one helicopter assault battalion and two helicopter assault companies to Seaman's control. On the eve of the operation, Seaman could count on 249 helicopters, making Junction City the largest air assault in the history of U.S. Army aviation.[8]

Junction City was to be a massive conventional encirclement that required timely deployments and tightly controlled movements to isolate and reduce the enemy pocket. Coordinating so many ground assets would not be easy. To improve control of the offensive, Seaman established a forward command post at Dau Tieng to work directly with Hay's temporary headquarters at Minh Thanh and Weyand's at Tay Ninh West. The arrangement marked the first time that an American corps-level headquarters had taken to the field in Vietnam to direct operations.

Fire support for Junction City would be provided by seventeen artillery battalions and over 4,000 Air Force sorties. Because of the extra-

---

[7] Critique 7–67, Opn Junction City I, 1st Logistical Command, 30 Jun 67, pp. 1–3, and AAR, Opn Junction City I, 25th Inf Div Support Command, 6 Apr 67, pp. 1–6, both in Historians files, CMH.

[8] AAR, Opn Junction City, IIFFV, p. 5; Interv, author with Seaman, 25 May 76.

ordinary level of artillery and aircraft activity during the operation, the allies took special care in the use of airspace, including the establishment of artillery warning control centers at the artillery battalion level to provide timely and accurate advisories to aircraft. Even with this measure, ground commanders would still have trouble obtaining air and artillery support simultaneously during JUNCTION CITY. All too often artillery fire had to cease to accommodate the presence of aircraft. Nevertheless, on the whole the fire support system handled an exceedingly complex problem well, and combined air and artillery strikes would play a crucial role in some of the campaign's larger battles.[9]

The Horseshoe Is Pitched

Just before sunrise on 22 February 1967, B–52 bombers struck suspected *COSVN* locations as troops of the 1st Division boarded seventy helicopters at Minh Thanh. After liftoff the UH–1s, carrying the entire 1st Battalion, 28th Infantry, of the 1st Brigade, flew northwest to make an air assault into a meadow eight kilometers northwest of Katum, less than two kilometers from the Cambodian border. Preceded by tactical air and helicopter gunship strikes, the first wave of helicopters landed unopposed at 0724. The helicopters then returned to Minh Thanh twice more to shuttle two more battalions to locations five and eleven kilometers, respectively, west of the first landing zone. A fourth battalion remained behind at Minh Thanh to secure headquarters facilities and to act as the division's reserve.[10]

While the 1st Brigade conducted its air assaults, helicopters lifted a battalion of the 196th Brigade from Tay Ninh and a firebase along Highway 22 to a landing zone near the junction of Highway 22 and Route 246. The rest of the brigade moved by truck to Trai Bi, twenty kilometers to the north, to shorten the turnaround time of the scarce helicopters. Staging out of Trai Bi, a second battalion was then airlifted four kilometers northeast of the first objective, while the brigade's remaining battalion landed six kilometers northeast of the second. The deployment of the entire brigade was complete by early afternoon. The infantrymen of all three battalions spent the remaining afternoon preparing defensive positions, dispatching patrols, and establishing ambushes along the many trails in the region. Occasional sniper fire and fleeting contacts with small enemy forces characterized combat for the day.[11]

While the early air assaults were taking place, the 173d Airborne Brigade undertook what would be the sole American parachute assault of the Vietnam War. Officially carried out to reduce the drain on helicopters,

---

[9] Ott, *Field Artillery*, pp. 112, 116–17.

[10] AAR, Opn JUNCTION CITY, IIFFV, p. 17; Rogers, *CEDAR FALLS–JUNCTION CITY*, p. 101.

[11] AAR, Opn JUNCTION CITY, 196th Light Inf Bde, 4 May 67, pp. 11–14, Historians files, CMH.

Self-propelled 155-mm. howitzers open fire from blocking positions on the eastern edge of the horseshoe.

it also fulfilled the desires of the commander of the 173d, General Deane, and the MACV commander, General Westmoreland, himself a former paratrooper. Although risky, it was the quickest way to put a large number of men on the ground, thus increasing the chance of surprise.[12]

The American tactical commanders had kept the proposed drop zone a closely guarded secret. Having had a previous airborne operation canceled because of a possible compromise, Seaman and Deane officially designated a false, or "notional" drop zone twenty-five kilometers east of Katum at Sroc Con Trang in the heart of eastern War Zone C. Not until 21 February, the day before the jump, after all who were to participate had been sealed in a marshaling area at Bien Hoa Air Base, did Deane reveal that the parachute assault was to be made on a large savanna four kilometers north of Katum. Although Deane had notified MACV headquarters the previous night of the true drop site, Westmoreland's aide did not get the message, and he guided the MACV commander to the decoy area instead. Westmoreland, who had led the only airborne regimental combat team in the Korean War, saw only the last of the jumpers landing.[13]

---

[12] AAR, Opn JUNCTION CITY I and II, 173d Abn Bde, 15 Jun 67, p. 1 and Incl 1, Historians files, CMH; Interv, author with Deane, 5 Jan 78.
[13] Ibid.

C–130s on the Bien Hoa flight line prepare to fly the paratroopers to the drop zone.

Troops of the 25th Division take cover during a firefight in the horseshoe.

After an hour and forty minutes of preparation by fighter-bombers and gunships, thirteen C–130s arrived over the drop zone. As the planes made the first of two passes at 0900, paratroopers began jumping in fifteen-man sticks (thirty men per pass for each plane). Deane was the first to jump, his pearl-handled pistols at his side. Within ten minutes, all 845 men of the 2d Battalion, 503d Infantry (Airborne), and Battery A, 3d Battalion, 319th Artillery (Airborne), were on the ground. Fifteen minutes later the Air Force began dropping supplies and equipment—180 tons by day's end. The airborne soldiers quickly secured the drop zone with only eleven minor, jump-related injuries and one man wounded from sporadic enemy small-arms fire.[14] Many of the supplies were damaged, however.

Loaded and waiting at Quan Loi, fifty kilometers to the east, were seventy helicopters with another battalion of the 173d poised to reinforce immediately should the parachute assault meet serious opposition. When none developed, the battalion helicoptered to landing sites elsewhere near Katum, while in the afternoon General Deane's remaining battalion landed in two clearings just northwest of the drop zone. The entire 173d Airborne Brigade completed its deployment by 1800, all done with little evidence of enemy activity.[15]

As the 173d and the other brigades moved into blocking positions along the arch of the horseshoe, the 3d Brigade, 1st Division, attacked north from Suoi Da over Route 4. Although enemy mines damaged ten vehicles and caused some delay, the brigade's leading contingent linked up with 173d elements south of Katum late that afternoon. Already in position east of Highway 22, the 3d Brigade, 4th Division, continued to secure II Field Force's western flank, encountering only slight resistance.[16]

To complete the encirclement of the objective, the 2d Brigade of the 25th Division deployed two battalions by C–130 from the Cu Chi base camp to Trai Bi, where a mechanized battalion joined the infantrymen to help screen the western portion of Route 247. To cover the eastern part of the road, the 11th Armored Cavalry had moved north from Tay Ninh West.

On the morning of the second day, 23 February, while five brigades assumed blocking positions, the 2d Brigade of the 25th Division and the 11th Armored Cavalry attacked north into the open end of the horseshoe. Hampered more by terrain than by enemy resistance, the assault progressed slowly. By nightfall only one unit, a squadron of the 11th, had reached its assigned objective.[17]

[14] AAR, Opn JUNCTION CITY I and II, 173d Abn Bde, pp. 16–17 and Incl 1. Successful combat jumps usually require at least 700 feet of altitude. To give an extra margin of safety, MACV required a minimum altitude of 1,000 feet for this operation. See Interv, author with Deane, 5 Jan 78.

[15] AAR, Opn JUNCTION CITY I and II, 173d Abn Bde, pp. 16–17.

[16] AAR, Opn JUNCTION CITY, 3d Bde, 1st Inf Div, 25 Apr 67, pp. 2–3, and AAR, Opn JUNCTION CITY, 3d Bde, 4th Inf Div, 12 May 67, pp. 14–15, both in Historians files, CMH.

[17] AAR, Opn JUNCTION CITY, 2d Bde, 25th Inf Div, 10 May 67, p. 4, Historians files, CMH; AAR, Opn JUNCTION CITY, 11th Armd Cav Rgt, pp. 15–18.

That evening, in an effort to accelerate the advance, General Weyand decided to reduce the northern boundary of his 2d Brigade so the 11th Cavalry, which had been making better progress, could turn west. He then flew a two-battalion force of South Vietnamese marines known as Task Force ALPHA into a landing zone secured by the 196th Brigade. The force worked first with the 196th and then with the 11th Cavalry and constituted the only South Vietnamese unit employed in an offensive role during the first phase of JUNCTION CITY.[18]

Between 22 and 27 February the allied units, including some 35,000 Americans, did their best to scour all of central War Zone C. The results were unimpressive. After five days of campaigning, II Field Force appeared to have conducted the largest non-battle of the war. Despite tactical surprise, U.S. forces had failed to prevent the main *COSVN* headquarters from escaping into Cambodia—if in fact it had been located in War Zone C at all. Despite the huge American commitment of men and firepower, known enemy losses totaled 54, against 28 American dead. The allies had pitched the horseshoe quickly and accurately, but the target stake had proved elusive.

The Americans did find enemy base camps aplenty. Most showed signs of recent use, and nearly all contained booby traps, many inert due to the failure of their constructors to connect the activating wires. Perhaps the enemy had departed too hastily, or perhaps he had not deemed the bases necessary. Almost all sites contained well-constructed bunkers with substantial overhead protection, yet few were strongly fortified, an indication that their builders had no intention of defending them.

In one of these bases north of Katum, troops of the 173d Airborne Brigade came upon a steel-roofed underground bunker that had served as a photographic laboratory for a *COSVN* public affairs unit. Inside were several processed rolls of motion picture film and hundreds of still photographs. Intelligence analysts would later learn from the material the identity of many ranking South Vietnamese revolutionaries, some of whom previously had been thought to be loyal to the South Vietnamese government, and also of the presence of several high-level North Vietnamese officials not previously known to have been in South Vietnam.[19]

Reaction and Counteraction

In the end *COSVN* did not take the invasion of its base area lightly. After determining that Route 4 served as a main American supply artery, the enemy high command ordered the *101st Regiment* from the

---

[18] AAR, Opn JUNCTION CITY, 25th Inf Div, 19 Jun 67, p. 11, and AAR, Opn JUNCTION CITY, U.S. Marine Corps Adviser to TF ALPHA, 29 Mar 67, pp. 1–11, both in Historians files, CMH. The South Vietnamese task force operated in coordination with, but not under the command of, the U.S. 25th Division.

[19] AAR, Opn JUNCTION CITY I and II, 173d Abn Bde, p. 21; Interv, author with Deane, 5 Jan 78; AAR, Opn JUNCTION CITY, IIFFV, p. 22.

Fishhook to ambush American convoys en route. *COSVN* also gave the *272d Regiment* of the *9th Division*, which apparently had also been refitting in the Fishhook, the same mission, while directing the *273d* to begin moving west from War Zone D against American convoys on Highway 13. Hit-and-run missions against the U.S. supply lines made the best use of the enemy's light infantry, promised at least some hope of local, tactical success, and might just divert American energies from their main operational objective.[20]

On 28 February, in the first important battle of JUNCTION CITY, a battalion of the *101st* ambushed a company from the 3d Brigade, 1st Division, patrolling fifteen kilometers north of Suoi Da. Hastily forming a defensive perimeter, the Americans threw back successive assaults but took heavy casualties, 25 killed and 28 wounded in four hours of close combat. Assisted by air strikes, the defenders finally forced the enemy to withdraw, leaving behind 167 dead and 40 weapons.[21]

Meanwhile, Seaman, somewhat frustrated, decided to abandon his northern positions opposite Cambodia. On 1 March he directed his 1st Division commander, General Hay, to move against the *101st Regiment* as well as *COSVN*'s military intelligence bureau, both thought to be southeast of Katum and east of Route 4. At the same time he ordered General Weyand to send at least half of his forces into the Elephant's Ear west of Highway 22, searching for the *271st Regiment* and any trace of *COSVN* there.

Hay, in the east, chose to leave his 3d Brigade along Route 4, while the 173d pushed east and then south of Katum, hoping to force the elusive enemy up against Route 4 and the new Special Forces camp at Prek Klok. At the same time, he dispersed his 1st Brigade, sending the headquarters with one battalion to Quan Loi to prepare for the second phase of JUNCTION CITY, while a second battalion secured the airstrip at Katum and the remaining battalion joined the division's reserve at Minh Thanh.[22]

In the west, Weyand directed a similar deployment, returning two of his brigades, the 25th Division's 2d and the 196th, to their respective base camps at Cu Chi and Tay Ninh West. The 3d Brigade, 4th Division, remained along Highway 22, while the 11th Armored Cavalry made a counterclockwise sweep of western War Zone C.

---

[20] Periodic Intel Rpt 9, IIFFV, 6 Mar 67, p. 1; Intel Sums 60, 1st Inf Div, 1 Mar 67; 61, 1st Inf Div, 2 Mar 67; 62, 1st Inf Div, 3 Mar 67; 63, 1st Inf Div, 4 Mar 67; and 64, 1st Inf Div, 5 Mar 67; Periodic Intel Rpt 14, IIFFV, 11 Apr 67, pp. 1, 4. All in Historians files, CMH.

[21] AAR, Opn JUNCTION CITY, 3d Bde, 1st Inf Div, p. 4; Intel Sums 62, IIFFV, 3 Mar 67, and 63, IIFFV, 4 Mar 67. The North Vietnamese claimed to have killed or wounded "nearly 200" Americans. See *9th Division*, p. 84. See also Rogers, CEDAR FALLS–JUNCTION CITY, pp. 112–17.

[22] AAR, Opn JUNCTION CITY, 1st Inf Div, 6 Apr 67, p. 4, Historians files, CMH; Interv, author with Seaman, 25 May 76; Ltr, Rogers to Michael D. Rogers, 4 Mar 67, Historians files, CMH.

The 1st Division Sector

As the redeployment of the 1st Brigade began on 3 March, General Deane moved his 173d command post south to Suoi Da to coordinate the movement of his forces. Slowly, the tempo of combat began to rise. That afternoon a battalion of the *70th Guard Regiment* ambushed one of Deane's companies northeast of Katum near the Cambodian border. In a sharp half-hour fight, the American unit lost 20 men killed and wounded before pulling back to allow air and artillery fire to be placed upon the entrenched Viet Cong. A check of the site the next morning revealed 39 enemy bodies. Meanwhile, fifteen kilometers to the south, a long-range reconnaissance patrol of the 173d had fought another Communist force, killing 8. Documents taken from one of the bodies revealed that the soldier was a member of the *272d Regiment*, giving Americans their first indication that this unit had joined the battle.[23] The following day, 4 March, B–52s flew twenty-one sorties against suspected *COSVN* elements northeast of Prek Klok. Recent electronic signal intercepts had indicated that *COSVN's* military intelligence bureau was still at work there. The strike represented an unprecedented ARC LIGHT concentration against a single target.

Two days later the 173d began its assault southeast of Katum. While the brigade's three battalions were ferried by helicopter into landing zones east of the town, Company D, 16th Armor, moved eastward from Katum along Route 246 to Bo Tuc, an abandoned hamlet, and then turned south. For the next four days the brigade met only scattered resistance.[24]

Immediately west of the 173d's sector, the 3d Brigade continued to guard Route 4 and to man three firebases, Suoi Da, Prek Klok, and Katum, some ten kilometers apart. The strongest of the three was in the middle at the partially completed Prek Klok Special Forces camp. The garrison included the 168th Engineer Battalion (Combat) working on the facility, two batteries of artillery, and the 2d Battalion, 2d Infantry (Mechanized), less one company—some nine hundred men under the command of Lt. Col. Edward J. Collins. Unknown to the Americans, on 2 March *COSVN* had directed the *272d Regiment* to launch an attack in the Prek Klok area as a diversion, enabling members of *COSVN's* military affairs section to escape.[25]

On 7 March units of the 3d Brigade patrolling near Prek Klok began to encounter small enemy forces, alerting the base to the possibility of imminent attack. Collins immediately augmented his nighttime defenses by positioning his armored personnel carriers and attached twin 40-mm. and

---

[23] AAR, Opn JUNCTION CITY I and II, 173d Abn Bde, pp. 23–24.

[24] CHECO Rpt, Opn JUNCTION CITY, PACAF, 17 Nov 67, p. 3, Historians files, CMH; AAR, Opn JUNCTION CITY I and II, 173d Abn Bde, pp. 26–29; AAR, Opn JUNCTION CITY, 1st Inf Div, pp. 4–5, 15.

[25] AAR, Opn JUNCTION CITY, 1st Inf Div, pp. 4–5, 15; Interv, 26th Military History Detachment (MHD) with Maj John D. Simpson, S–3, 168th Engr Bn, 8 Jul 67, Vietnam Interview Tape (VNIT) 48, pp. 15–19, CMH; CHECO Rpt, Opn JUNCTION CITY, PACAF, p. 8.

quad .50-caliber self-propelled guns in dug-in emplacements around the perimeter every evening. Nothing happened for two days, but on the night of 10 March one of his listening posts reported large enemy forces approaching. The defenses braced for an assault.

Shortly after 2200 the enemy hit the base with over 150 rounds of mortar fire, some of it 120-mm., the first ever fired in III Corps. As the shelling subsided, the *272d* launched a company-size diversionary attack against the southwestern periphery of the base while striking with an entire battalion against the eastern face. The adjacent firebases of Katum and Suoi Da, whose artillery would be expected to support the Prek Klok defenders, were also brought under harassing fire. But the assault never had a chance. The attacks against Katum and Suoi Da proved ineffective, and artillery at both bases immediately placed preregistered protective fires around Prek Klok. Flares illuminated the battlefield. With the arrival of close air support, the enemy crumbled, and within an hour of the start of the attack the *272d* withdrew. Although fire from tree lines around the perimeter continued for a time, there seemed little likelihood that the regiment would make a second try.

The following morning, 11 March, the Americans counted nearly 200 enemy dead and captured 5 wounded Viet Cong soldiers. While large quantities of enemy equipment littered the area, the Americans found only 12 weapons. The *272d* had maintained its discipline in retreat but had also wasted the better part of the battalion to kill 3 American soldiers.[26]

Elsewhere west of Route 4 opportunities for combat were scarce, although units of both the 3d Brigade and the 173d uncovered several abandoned and partially destroyed enemy bases within a few miles of Katum containing extensive tunnel systems. In two tunnels American soldiers found large caches of signal equipment, including radios, antennae, generators, and code books belonging to *COSVN*'s military affairs section. The American troops had apparently stumbled upon parts of *COSVN*'s operations center and its military intelligence bureau, the target of the heavy B–52 strikes of 4 March. The staffs of those facilities were long gone.[27]

The last significant action by the 1st Division during Phase I of JUNCTION CITY began on 11 March, ten kilometers east of Prek Klok, when a unit of the *101st Regiment* launched a weak assault against a battalion of the 173d moving south. Within an hour the North Vietnamese were in full retreat with the Americans in pursuit. When the chase ended three days later, the enemy had lost over 50 men; the Americans suffered 14 wounded.[28]

---

[26] AAR, Opn JUNCTION CITY, 3d Bde, 1st Inf Div, p. 7; Interv, 26th MHD with Simpson, 8 Jul 67, VNIT 48, pp. 12–19; Intel Sum 70, IIFFV, 10 Mar 67, p. 9, Historians files, CMH. See also Rogers, CEDAR FALLS–JUNCTION CITY, pp. 117–21.

[27] Daily Jnl, G–2, 1st Inf Div, 9–11 Mar 67, and Periodic Intel Rpt 10, IIFFV, 14 Mar 67, an. D, both in Historians files, CMH; AAR, Opn JUNCTION CITY I and II, 173d Abn Bde, pp. 36–38; Interv, author with Deane, 5 Jan 78.

[28] AAR, Opn JUNCTION CITY I and II, 173d Abn Bde, pp. 10, 29–30.

The 25th Division Sector

While Deane's 173d Airborne Brigade searched east of Route 4, Weyand directed the 11th Armored Cavalry Regiment, led by Col. William W. Cobb, to sweep west of central War Zone C. Mirroring the airborne, the armored cavalry, then at the top of the Elephant's Ear, was to wheel counterclockwise to force any enemy units back against blocking positions manned by the 3d Brigade, 4th Division. Again, Weyand's primary objective was to bring the *271st Regiment* to battle or, at the very least, force it back into Cambodia.[29]

Preceded by B–52 strikes, the sweep began on 7 March, meeting only slight resistance. On 10 March Colonel Cobb's 3d Squadron came upon a large, recently abandoned, regiment-size base camp containing extensive tunnels, reinforced concrete bunkers, and other above-ground facilities. His 1st Squadron discovered a radio transmitter facility, recently stripped of its equipment, which had served as the broadcasting site for the National Liberation Front. One day later Cobb's forces discovered an occupied enemy base alongside a stream marking the border between South Vietnam and Cambodia. While the armor cordoned off the South Vietnamese side, fighter-bombers struck the camp throughout the night. When Americans entered the next morning, they found it deserted, but discovered twenty-eight enemy bodies, a like number of weapons, and, in concrete bunkers, two large electrically operated printing presses that *COSVN's* propaganda and cultural indoctrination section had used.[30]

Although searches continued for another few days, U.S. forces failed to uncover other bases or to find any trace of the elusive *271st*. On 15 March the 3d Brigade, 4th Division, returned to Dau Tieng. The 11th Armored Cavalry traveled back to its bases east of Saigon, ending its participation in Junction City.[31]

At the time the principal American commanders were disappointed that the gains had been so meager. However, the results of the secondary sweeps to the west and east offered hope that persistence might yet be rewarded. Phase II of Junction City was to begin almost immediately.

[29] AAR, Opn Junction City, 25th Inf Div, pp. 8, 12; AAR, Opn Junction City, 196th Light Inf Bde, p. 21; Intervs, author with Maj Gen William W. Cobb, Comdr, 11th Armd Cav Rgt, 26 May 76, Historians files, CMH; with Seaman, 25 May 76.

[30] AAR, Opn Junction City, 11th Armd Cav Rgt, pp. 31–33; Intervs, author with Cobb, 26 May 76; Patterson with Seaman, 18 Mar 71.

[31] AAR, Opn Junction City, 25th Inf Div, p. 12. For the enemy account from 22 February to 18 March 1967, see *9th Division*, pp. 83–85.

8

JUNCTION CITY: The Battle Continues

For Phase II of JUNCTION CITY General Seaman shifted the bulk of his forces east of the original horseshoe to an area roughly bounded by Route 4 to the west, Route 246 to the north, and Highway 13 to the east. Partly because he failed during Phase I to seal central War Zone C and partly because he believed enemy planners were alerted to his intentions, Seaman changed tactics. He established a loose cordon along the three principal roads bordering the new area of operations, with the 196th Brigade assuming blocking positions along Route 4, the 1st Brigade, 1st Division, patrolling Route 246, and the 1st Brigade, 9th Division, holding Highway 13. Within this three-sided box, Seaman deployed three additional brigades—the 3d of the 4th Division, the 2d of the 1st Division, and the 173d Airborne—to scour the area for enemy units and installations.

Although II Field Force continued to coordinate the offensive, Seaman permitted his two principal subordinates, General Hay of the 1st Division and the newly assigned commander of the 25th Division, Maj. Gen. John C. F. Tillson, to operate independently. Tillson controlled the western portion of the tactical area, including the 196th Brigade and 3d Brigade, 4th Division, while Hay commanded the units in the eastern sector. On 12 March Seaman closed his forward command post at Dau Tieng and returned to his headquarters at Long Binh, leaving Hay and Tillson with twenty-four battalions but with little idea of what they might encounter.[1] (*Map 14*)

Suoi Tre (Firebase GOLD)

Phase II of JUNCTION CITY began on 18 March 1967, when the commander of the 3d Brigade, 4th Division, Col. Marshall B. Garth, sent a mechanized battalion to seize a clearing designated Landing Zone SILVER, twenty-five kilometers north of Dau Tieng. The following morning he intended to airlift the remainder of his brigade, one artillery and two infantry

---

[1] General Tillson, formerly MACV J–3, or operations officer, assumed command on 6 March 1967. AAR, Opn JUNCTION CITY, IIFFV, p. 8 and Incl 7; Interv, author with Seaman, 25 May 76.

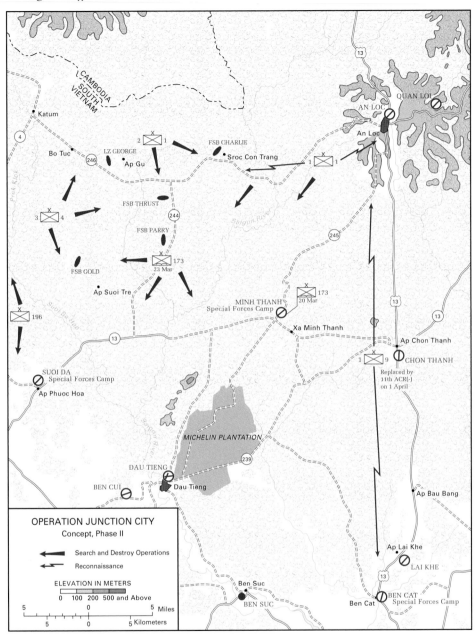

MAP 14

battalions, into the clearing to establish a large firebase there, and then to sweep west toward Route 4. The operation did not go as planned. Slowed by mines and fire from RPG2s, the mechanized force came upon an uncharted stream with banks so steep that the armored personnel carriers

128

General Tillson

were unable to cross. Rather than delay his main effort until the stream was forded, Garth directed the remainder of the brigade to an alternate landing zone on the morning of the nineteenth without the armored security.[2]

After a thirty-minute artillery preparation, his first group of helicopters set down without incident. But when the second lift came in, a mine exploded among the Hueys before the troops disembarked, and two more detonated as the next company landed. The explosions destroyed three troop carriers and damaged others, killing seven helicopter crewmen and ten infantrymen. Believing he already had too many men on the ground to call off the assault, Garth ordered the rest of his troops to follow, but a later search of the landing zone revealed twenty-one unexploded shells, most wired for detonation from nearby hiding places. Clearly, the Americans had been expected. But despite evidence of enemy preparation, Garth decided to build his base on the landing zone.[3] (*Map 15*)

By the evening of 20 March the clearing, known as Firebase GOLD, contained a full artillery battalion and an infantry battalion. The 2d of the 77th Artillery (105-mm. towed) was commanded that day by the deputy commander, 25th Division Artillery, Lt. Col. John W. Vessey. The 3d of the 22d Infantry, less one company, was under the command of Lt. Col. John A. Bender. In all, about four hundred fifty men defended GOLD.

Meanwhile, Garth's other infantry battalion, the 2d of the 12th Infantry, had moved from the firebase to establish a night defensive position a few kilometers to the northwest. And still to the west of GOLD, separated from the base by the stream, was the mechanized unit, the 2d Battalion, 22d Infantry, under Lt. Col. Ralph W. Julian, which by that time had gotten M48s from the 2d Battalion, 34th Armor, provided by II Field Force. Plans for the next day called for battalion sweeps to the north and

[2] AAR, Opn JUNCTION CITY, 3d Bde, 4th Inf Div, pp. 7–8, 25–29, an. D; Intervs, author with Maj Gen Marshall B. Garth, Comdr, 3d Bde, 4th Inf Div, 26 May 76, and with Col Ralph W. Julian, Comdr, 2d Bn, 22d Inf (Mech), 25th Inf Div, 15 Feb 96, both in Historians files, CMH.

[3] AAR, Opn JUNCTION CITY, 3d Bde, 4th Inf Div, pp. 25–26; CHECO Rpt, Opn JUNCTION CITY, PACAF, pp. 19–20; Interv, author with Garth, 26 May 76.

129

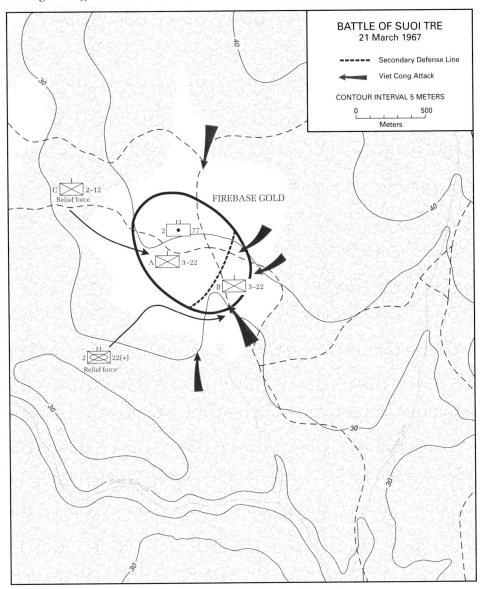

BATTLE OF SUOI TRE
21 March 1967

- - - - - - Secondary Defense Line

◄───── Viet Cong Attack

CONTOUR INTERVAL 5 METERS

0 _____ 500

Meters

FIREBASE GOLD

C 2–12
Relief force

2 • 77

A 3–22

B 3–22

2 22(+)
Relief force

MAP 15

west to locate a thirty- to forty-man enemy force which Garth had seen from his helicopter on the afternoon of the twentieth.[4]

During the night of 20–21 March Bender's listening posts reported heavy movement on GOLD's perimeter, but no assault followed. Dawn

[4] AAR, Opn JUNCTION CITY, 3d Bde, 4th Inf Div, p. 26; Intel Sum 79, IIFFV, 20 Mar 67, p. 3, Historians files, CMH; Interv, author with Julian, 15 Feb 96.

brought a sense of relief, for the enemy seldom attacked a fortified position during daylight. The feeling was premature. At 0631 the area
exploded as mortar shells rained down on the startled defenders. Five
minutes later two battalions of the *272d Regiment* burst from the jungle
and surged toward the camp, firing machine guns, RPG2s, and assault
rifles. Bender's infantrymen scrambled into their holes while the base
howitzers placed high-angle fire on the suspected mortar sites. Artillery
at two nearby firebases chimed in as well, laying down protective bar-
rages all around GOLD.

Notified by Bender that he was under attack, at 0655 Garth ordered
the rest of his force to GOLD. The decision was timely, for only a few
minutes later Viet Cong penetrated the defense line. While a reaction
force of artillerymen contained the breakthrough, a flight of F–5
Freedom Fighters came in, slowing the advance. Other air strikes hit the
eastern wood line, but the air attacks ceased when enemy fire shot
down the forward air controller.

Despite heavy counterfire, the assault gained momentum. Shortly
before 0800, waves of Viet Cong broke through on the southeast, converging on the artillery pieces. Lowering their tubes, Vessey's gunners fired
beehive rounds with fuzes set at muzzle action, stopping the enemy
instantaneously. But within minutes, another group of Viet Cong entered
on the northeast. Bender ordered the men there to fall back and make a
last stand in front of the artillery. Just then, another forward air controller
arrived with several F–100 Super Sabres in tow. Air Force liaison officer
Maj. Bobby J. Meyer recalled the result: "There must have been 500 of
them coming at me, and this guy laid napalm right on top of them and
then I didn't see them anymore."[5] Together with direct fire from the howitzers, air power had halted the second threat.

Yet a third crisis emerged twenty minutes later, when Bender's northern sector began to crumble. Onrushing Viet Cong overran a quad .50-cal-
iber machine gun and attempted to turn it against the defenders. An alert
artillery crew spotted the threat and with a single high-explosive round
destroyed the weapon. By 0840, despite a troubling ammunition shortage,
the American defense, though contracted, was still intact. The momentum
of the Viet Cong assault was slowing, and American reinforcements were
about to arrive.

From the northwest, a company of the 2d Battalion, 12th Infantry,
braved enemy mortar fire and the risk of ambushes and hacked its way
through 1,500 meters of thick bamboo to reach the beleaguered camp at
0840. It charged into the base under covering fire from GOLD's defenders
and assumed responsibility for the southwestern perimeter. Meanwhile,
the mechanized infantry and armor had been frantically searching for a
way to cross the stream that barred them from the firebase. When they
found a place where the stream "disappeared" underground, they turned

---

[5] Schlight, *Years of the Offensive*, p. 254.

toward GOLD with the armored personnel carriers breaking trail.[6] At 0912 the armored column burst from the jungle southwest of the base and rammed into the flank of the enemy infantry just then pulling back. With machine guns blazing and 90-mm. tank guns belching clouds of canister, the armor routed the Viet Cong, crushing many beneath their tracks. The fight was over.

Known as the Battle of Suoi Tre, after a small abandoned hamlet nearby, the four-hour struggle, coupled with the fight three weeks before at Prek Klok, devastated the *272d*. Sweeps of GOLD and the nearby countryside turned up 647 enemy bodies, 94 individual and 65 crew-served weapons (50 of which were RPG2s), and 7 prisoners. The Viet Cong had abandoned nearly 600 RPG2 rounds, 1,900 grenades, and some 28,000 rounds for small arms. The finds suggested that the *272d* had prepared the battle area well in advance. U.S. losses were 31 killed and 109 wounded. That the combatants had fought at close quarters was apparent from the fact that all but one of the U.S. artillery pieces had sustained damage.[7]

Bau Bang (Firebase 14)

While the *272d* was targeting GOLD, its sister regiment, the *273d*, moved from War Zone D to attack the American supply line on Highway 13. At the time one battalion of the 1st Brigade, 9th Division, and the divisional 3d Squadron, 5th Cavalry, were patrolling the highway between Lai Khe and Quan Loi, while the 1st Brigade, 1st Division, had started pushing west on Route 246 into War Zone C. To support the operation, the 9th Division brigade had established a series of firebases along Highway 13, dispatching men each morning to clear either side of the highway out to a distance of two kilometers. At dark the Americans pulled in their patrols and closed the road to traffic.

One of the smaller laagers, known only as Firebase 14, was located about eight kilometers north of Lai Khe near the hamlet of Bau Bang. On the night of 19–20 March it contained Battery B of the 7th Battalion, 9th Artillery (105-mm. towed), protected by Troop A, 3d Squadron, 5th Cavalry. One platoon assumed an ambush position 1,500 meters north of the base, while the remaining two platoons formed around the battery. All together, twenty armored personnel carriers, six tanks, three 4.2-inch mortar carriers, and 129 men—a small but lethal force—guarded the battery and its crew.[8]

---

[6] Interv, author with Julian, 15 Feb 96.

[7] AAR, Opn JUNCTION CITY, 3d Bde, 4th Inf Div, pp. 26–28; Intervs, author with Garth, 26 May 76; and with Julian, 15 Feb 96; *U.S. Biggest Operation Foiled* (Hanoi: Foreign Languages Publishing House, 1967), p. 22, copy in CMH. *9th Division*, pp. 89–90, indicates that both the *101st PAVN* and *272d PLAF Regiments* took part in the attack against Firebase GOLD. See also Starry, *Mounted Combat in Vietnam*, pp. 100–102. The 3d Brigade, 4th Division, received the Presidential Unit Citation for the Battle of Suoi Tre.

[8] ORLL, 1 Feb–30 Apr 67, 1st Inf Div, p. 5, Historians files, CMH.

Following an initial probe spearheaded by a herd of fifteen cattle, shortly after midnight the *273d Regiment* and local guerrillas hit the base with a barrage of mortar, rifle grenade, and recoilless rifle fire. (*Map 16*) Twenty minutes later a battalion of Viet Cong dressed in black pajamas charged through the darkness toward the southern and southwestern perimeters. Flares and tank searchlights illuminated the black-clad soldiers, enabling the troopers and artillerymen to do their gruesome work. But still the enemy came on. "They are swarming all over my track. Dust me with canister," radioed the commander of one of the M113s. Several rounds from a tank swept the enemy off. The Americans had to repeat this procedure throughout the night.[9]

The arrival of air support and three cavalry platoons—Troop A's ambush platoon and two from other elements of the 5th Cavalry—held the enemy in check. For a while it seemed the battle was over, but at 0500 a second battalion attacked. The artillery shifted its fire to the west, while flares and searchlights guided in a pair of F–100s, catching the Viet Cong in the open with napalm and cluster bombs. Fifteen additional F–100s and two F–4s piled on, and the attackers were routed. Twenty-nine tons of air-delivered ordnance, 3,000 artillery rounds, and large quantities of tank and automatic-weapons fire had proved too much for the Viet Cong.[10]

When the cavalrymen searched the area after dawn, they counted 227 enemy bodies, captured 3 wounded Viet Cong soldiers, but found only 11 enemy weapons. American losses were 3 killed, 63 wounded, 2 armored personnel carriers destroyed, and 5 tanks and 11 personnel carriers damaged. The battered *273d* made no further attempts against the supply route.[11]

Meanwhile, north of Bau Bang and west of An Loc, the 1st Division had uncovered few signs of the enemy. The preparatory western push of the 1st Brigade on Route 246 had gone unopposed. So had its construction of a bridge over the Saigon River, a new Special Forces camp there, and an airfield just west of the bridge site. On 20 March the 2d Brigade under Col. James A. Grimsley sent the 1st Battalion, 26th Infantry, overland from the Special Forces camp (now named Tong Le Chon) to erect Firebase CHARLIE some eight kilometers to the northwest near the abandoned village of Sroc Con Trang. General Hay insisted on a ground advance, believing correctly that the clearings around Sroc Con Trang were heavily mined. But the area was undefended, and that night the 2d Brigade, assisted by a South Vietnamese ranger battalion, established its initial base in War Zone C.[12]

---

[9] Rogers, CEDAR FALLS–JUNCTION CITY, p. 132.

[10] Rpt, 17th MHD, 1 May 67, sub: Battle of Ap Bau Bang, 20 March 1967; Rpt, U.S. Army, Vietnam (USARV), 5 Feb 70, sub: History of the 273d VC Regiment July 1964–December 1969, pp. 12–13, both in Historians files, CMH. See also Starry, *Mounted Combat in Vietnam*, pp. 97–100.

[11] ORLL, 1 Feb–30 Apr 67, 1st Inf Div, pp. 5–6; *U.S. Biggest Operation Foiled*, p. 23.

[12] ORLL, 1 Feb–30 Apr 67, 2d Bde, 1st Inf Div, 6 May 67, pp. 1, 5–6, 14–16, Historians

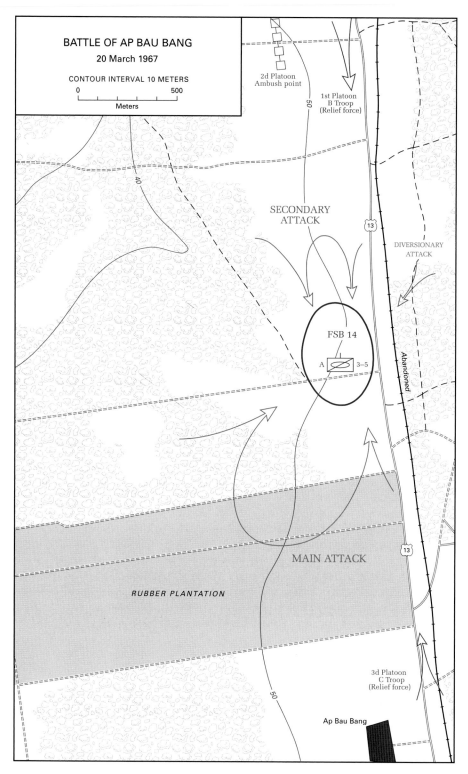

BATTLE OF AP BAU BANG
20 March 1967

CONTOUR INTERVAL 10 METERS

0 _____ 500

Meters

2d Platoon
Ambush point

1st Platoon
B Troop
(Relief force)

SECONDARY
ATTACK

DIVERSIONARY
ATTACK

FSB 14

A ⬭ 3–5

Abandoned

MAIN ATTACK

RUBBER PLANTATION

3d Platoon
C Troop
(Relief force)

Ap Bau Bang

MAP 16

The following morning, 21 March, Grimsley conducted air assaults with the 1st Battalion, 2d Infantry, and the 2d Battalion, 18th Infantry, into landing zones no more than two kilometers from the Cambodian border. Their mission was to sweep south toward Route 246. Recent prisoner interrogations and captured maps had indicated that the area might contain *COSVN's* main headquarters, so the Americans were ready for a fight. But, as before, there was little opposition. During the next week, the troops found camps containing command bunkers with concrete overhead protection, extensive tunnel complexes, and underground assembly rooms with tables and chairs. Most were defended by small caretaker forces, but no larger enemy units were evident.[13]

A C–130 airdrops supplies to the 196th Light Infantry Brigade.

South of Route 246, the results were equally unimpressive. On 20 March a squadron of the 11th Armored Cavalry had begun a two-day push west from Tong Le Chon for fifteen kilometers to secure a clearing along Route 244, which the 173d Airborne Brigade turned into Firebase PARRY. With his artillery and one battalion securing PARRY, General Deane of the 173d sent his remaining battalions into a landing zone eight kilometers south of the base on 23 March, instructing them to sweep northwest. But the force found only small enemy elements and several abandoned base camps. The enemy had apparently vanished.[14]

To the west the 25th Division likewise had few contacts. After GOLD the 3d Brigade, 4th Division, found several base camps, many containing supply caches but all abandoned. The division's other participant, the 196th, remained in blocking positions along Route 4, conducting patrols. Both brigades took casualties, primarily from mines, booby traps, and occasional sniper fire. Once again, however, the Viet Cong seemed able to control the tempo of action.

---

files, CMH; Daily Jnl, G–2, 1st Inf Div, 21–30 Mar 67, Historians files, CMH; AAR, Opn JUNCTION CITY, 1st Inf Div, p. 19; Interv, author with LeGro, 15 Jan 76. See also Rogers, *CEDAR FALLS–JUNCTION CITY*, p. 137.

[13] AAR, Opn JUNCTION CITY, 2d Bde, 1st Inf Div, 13 May 67, pp. 1–4, Historians files, CMH; Daily Jnl, G–2, 1st Inf Div, 21–30 Mar 67.

[14] AAR, Opn JUNCTION CITY I and II, 173d Abn Bde, pp. 4, 13–15.

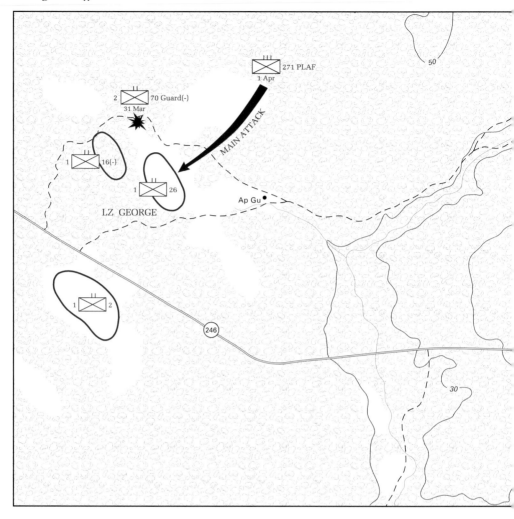

MAP 17

Ap Gu (Landing Zone GEORGE)

On 24 March Lt. Gen. Bruce Palmer took command of II Field Force. Palmer was about to give up what he regarded as a fruitless search of southeastern War Zone C, when fresh intelligence revealed that the *271st Regiment* was moving rapidly west through the area toward Katum. He immediately ordered the 196th north to intercept.[15]

American intelligence rated the *271st* as the enemy's most capable main force unit in the III Corps area. Although the regiment had taken losses

---

[15] AAR, Opn JUNCTION CITY, 3d Bde, 4th Inf Div, pp. 28–37; FRAGO 8, Opn JUNCTION CITY, 196th Light Inf Bde, 27 Mar 67, Historians files, CMH.

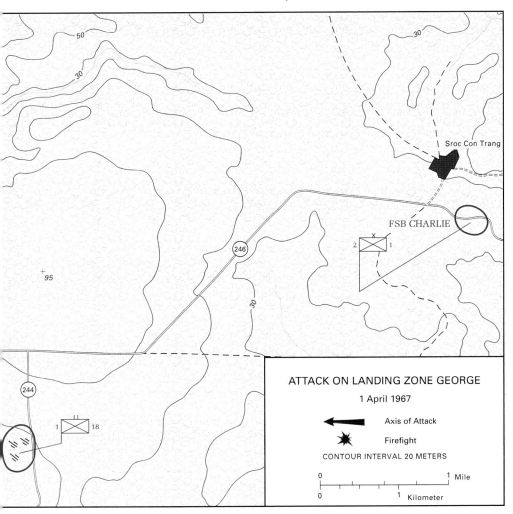

Sroc Con Trang

FSB CHARLIE

246

95

244

1   18

ATTACK ON LANDING ZONE GEORGE

1 April 1967

Axis of Attack

Firefight

CONTOUR INTERVAL 20 METERS

0   1 Mile

0   1 Kilometer

from B–52 strikes and from limited engagements with American troops in February and March, replacements had arrived, probably enough to bring the regiment up to full strength. Located north of the Elephant's Ear near the Cambodian border, the unit received orders on 23 March to move at once to the Fishhook, where the *9th Division* was organizing a defense with the depleted *101st Regiment* and the shattered *272d*. The *271st* made the fifty-kilometer march so swiftly that when the 196th arrived at Katum on the twenty-eighth, the Viet Cong were already far to the east. Soon after reaching the Fishhook, the *271st* was ordered to attack the American firebase at Sroc Con Trang, five kilometers to the south.[16]

---

[16] Daily Jnl, G–2, 1st Inf Div, 30 Mar 67, and Intel Sum 91, 1st Inf Div, 1 Apr 67, both in

Although alerted to the eastward movement of the regiment, Colonel Grimsley, commanding the 2d Brigade at Firebase CHARLIE, continued to search west. On 29 March he had the 1st Battalion, 18th Infantry, establish Firebase THRUST near the junction of Routes 244 and 246, about seven kilometers west of CHARLIE. In the next two days he put two more battalions into Landing Zone GEORGE, a large, dried-up marshy area seven kilometers farther west near the hamlet of Ap Gu. The 1st Battalion, 26th Infantry, under Colonel Haig, landed at GEORGE on 30 March; the 1st Battalion, 2d Infantry, commanded by Lt. Col. William C. Simpson, followed one day later. Both units could count on supporting artillery from CHARLIE and THRUST.[17]

That afternoon Simpson's troops moved south, while Haig's unit probed the wood lines around GEORGE. Eight hundred meters north of the base, his reconnaissance platoon bumped into elements of the *70th Guard Regiment* and had difficulty pulling away. (*See Map 17.*) Soon enough, Haig was ensnared in a major fight, unable to break loose until the afternoon, when the Viet Cong fled north into the jungle. In the meantime, Grimsley had reinforced Haig with another battalion Hay had passed to him. As Haig's men reoccupied their bunkers, the new unit, the 1st Battalion, 16th Infantry, under Lt. Col. Rufus C. Lazzell, quickly set up in brush a few hundred yards to the northwest. During the afternoon firefight, Haig lost 7 soldiers killed and another 38 wounded but had more than 450 men still on hand.

Unknown to the Americans, *COSVN* had canceled the attack against Firebase CHARLIE, perhaps believing it was too heavily defended, and was now concentrating on Landing Zone GEORGE. While the *271st* and the *70th Guard Regiment* planned to hit GEORGE that night from the northeast, other Viet Cong forces were ready to neutralize the artillery at CHARLIE.[18]

The plan was tactically sound except for its failure to take into account the three batteries at Firebase THRUST. Perhaps *COSVN* was unaware of them. But those batteries were well within supporting range of GEORGE and in fact ideally positioned to deal with any threat from the northeast.

Shortly after midnight Haig's listening posts reported movement to the north, east, and south. When a single mortar round exploded outside the perimeter some hours later, he knew that it was registration preliminary to an assault. He immediately ordered an alert.

Haig's position was very strong. Following standard practice in the 1st Division, both battalions, his and the one to the northwest, had prepared earthenwork defenses featuring "DePuy bunkers" with low silhouettes, full overhead cover, and sleeping quarters dug in directly behind.

Historians files, CMH; *9th Division*, p. 91; Interv, author with Gen Paul F. Gorman, G–3, 1st Inf Div, 22 Jun 95, Historians files, CMH.

[17] Interv, Capt George E. Creighton, 17th MHD, with Capt George A. Joulwan, Operations Officer, 1st Bn, 26th Inf, 3 Apr 67, Vietnam Interview (VNI) 122, CMH.

[18] AAR, Opn JUNCTION CITY, 2d Bde, 1st Inf Div, p. 6; AAR, Opn JUNCTION CITY, 1st Inf Div, an. B.

Each normally had a frontal berm to deflect rounds from direct-fire weapons and, an unusual feature, firing embrasures, or openings, at the front corners, to provide interlocking fire with nearby bunkers. As such, they presented more difficult targets to an advancing attacker.

At 0500 on 1 April, about five minutes after the lone mortar round had detonated, a drumbeat of enemy fire began. In the next fifteen minutes some five hundred mortar rounds fell on both battalions. Firebase CHARLIE was also shelled and was able to provide only minimal support to GEORGE. Fortunately, the dug-in Americans at CHARLIE took few casualties. One of the exceptions was Colonel Grimsley, the 2d Brigade commander, who was wounded.

The Viet Cong directed their main assault against GEORGE's northeastern perimeter. Unchallenged and ready for trouble, the artillerymen at THRUST broke up the initial attack. But the insurgents persisted and gradually fought their way into Haig's bunkers. The bunker design apparently confused them, because they were accustomed to emplacements with firing ports at the front. Although they achieved a sizable penetration, surviving defenders fighting at close quarters formed a new line seventy-five meters behind the perimeter. Determined resistance slowly contained the penetration.

As the Viet Cong massed at sunrise to exploit their success, air support arrived just in time. With a deadly chorus of rockets, bombs, and napalm—some dropped within a stone's throw of the bunker line—the jets stopped and routed the attack. As the attackers pulled back, Viet Cong reserves opened fire to cover the withdrawal. When the forward air controller reported green smoke in that direction (green was normally used to mark American positions) Haig told him it was a trick. Guiding on the smoke, fighter-bombers silenced the fire and brought the fight to an end.

While air and artillery struck at likely escape routes, Haig's soldiers rested and nursed their wounds. Chosen to command the 2d Brigade following Grimsley's evacuation, Haig sent Simpson's battalion in pursuit along with Lazzell's. He halted the chase in the afternoon to allow B–52s to strike enemy base camps near Cambodia likely to provide refuge for the attackers.[19]

Sweeps conducted on 1 April in the immediate vicinity of GEORGE revealed nearly 500 enemy dead and 5 wounded, who surrendered; another 100 bodies were found in the nearby jungle. In addition to the small-arms ammunition the defenders expended, sixty-two F–100, six B–57, five F–5, and four F–4 sorties had dropped more than 300 tons of ordnance during the battle, while Army artillery had weighed in with 15,000 rounds of its own. Total American casualties were 17 killed and 102 wounded.[20]

---

[19] AAR, Opn JUNCTION CITY, 2d Bde, 1st Inf Div, pp. 6, 11–13; Intel Sum 91, 1st Inf Div, 1 Apr 67; Daily Jnl, G–2, 1st Inf Div, 1 Apr 67, Historians files, CMH.

[20] ORLL, 1 Feb–30 Apr 67, 1st Inf Div, Incl 10; AAR, Opn JUNCTION CITY, IIFFV, pp. 26–27; AAR, Opn JUNCTION CITY, 1st Inf Div, p. 14; Periodic Intel Rpt 13, IIFFV, 4 Apr 67, p. 1, Historians files, CMH; CHECO Rpt, Opn JUNCTION CITY, PACAF, pp. 34–36; Schlight, *Years of the Offensive*, pp. 254–55.

Troops of the 196th Brigade prepare to be air-assaulted southeast of Katum.

With the end of the battle at GEORGE, activity in the 1st Division's sector fell off sharply. Although enemy forces persisted in mortaring U.S. positions over the next two weeks, they avoided major ground combat. When Phase II of JUNCTION CITY ended on 15 April, all of the 1st Division units had already departed from War Zone C.

To the west, the 25th Division had also completed its part in the operation. After missing the *271st Regiment* near Katum, the 196th Brigade had swept across central War Zone C to Trai Bi and returned to its base at Tay Ninh West to prepare for a move north to I Corps. The 3d Brigade, 4th Division, had swept south toward Dau Tieng, arriving there on 8 April. As the 196th departed, the 3d Brigade, 4th Division, assumed responsibility for defending Tay Ninh West while at the same time preparing to launch a month-long addendum to JUNCTION CITY. This would incorporate Westmoreland's concept of a "floating brigade," which would reenter the enemy redoubt from time to time to investigate new reports of Viet Cong activity. The addendum to JUNCTION CITY turned up little.[21]

---

[21] AAR, Opn JUNCTION CITY, 1st Inf Div, p. 13; AAR, Opn JUNCTION CITY, 25th Inf Div, p. 14.

Piled high on armored personnel carriers, captured rice is evacuated north of Lai Khe.

Assessment

During JUNCTION CITY American troops had destroyed 5,000 enemy structures, captured 850 tons of food and approximately a half-million pages of documents, and killed 2,728 enemy soldiers, dealing the *9th Division* a serious blow. Having remained in War Zone C for nearly two months, the Americans by their very presence had demanded a Communist response. Not only had the operation sharply depleted the enemy's main forces in northern III Corps, but it had forced *COSVN* to relocate many of its training sites and agencies farther from the population. True, the approaching monsoons and troop shortages would limit U.S. reentry into the war zone, shortages exacerbated by the 196th's departure for southern I Corps. Still, the assortment of Special Forces camps in the area—Prek Klok, Tong Le Chon, Trai Bi, Katum, Minh Thanh, and Suoi Da—continued to provide MACV with a U.S. presence, as well as the occasion for some supply-line interdiction and tactical intelligence gathering.

Shortly after the operation ended American troops captured an enemy overlay entitled, "Counter-Offensive Against Operation JUNCTION CITY, 21 February to 15 April," in which *COSVN* headquarters maintained that its

141

forces had killed 13,500 Americans. The actual figure was 282. In reality, senior Communist defectors revealed that *COSVN* considered JUNCTION CITY a major setback. Other captured enemy documents showed that several battalion commanders and political officers were relieved because of their poor performance during the operation, and in May the *9th Division* withdrew from South Vietnam altogether for rebuilding in Cambodia.[22]

Yet for the Americans JUNCTION CITY had not proved to be the victory that Westmoreland had wanted. True, the *9th Division* had been severely handled, but every major action had been the result of enemy initiative. Similarly, although 40 percent of enemy facilities discovered during JUNCTION CITY were within 500 meters of U.S. intelligence predictions, their proximity to the Cambodian border and the area's rugged, heavily tunneled terrain had allowed *COSVN* to escape. General Seaman would later concede that even if he had been able to double the number of forces available for the operation, the main *COSVN* staff still could have slipped between his units to flee undetected into Cambodia. His replacement, General Palmer, agreed. And had the *9th Division* and other enemy units chosen to avoid battle, they too might have escaped with equal ease.[23]

Equally ambivalent were the political results of the battle. Heavy losses in men and materiel had begun to erode the air of inevitable victory that the Communists had always cultivated and that had been one of their strengths. Highly sensitive to the slightest change in the winds of fortune, war-weary peasants were becoming increasingly reluctant to sacrifice their lives and possessions for what seemed less than a sure bet. Yet the Saigon government was no more popular than before, and neutrality, rather than a strong affinity for either party, was becoming the norm in the III Corps countryside. Indeed, 102 hours of aerial loudspeaker appeals, 9,768,000 leaflets, nearly 60,000 free medical exams, 300,000 pounds of donated food and clothing, and a number of other civic action programs had netted only 139 ralliers during JUNCTION CITY. Despite the demonstration of U.S. power, the Viet Cong, while injured, remained elusive, resilient, and defiant.

The enemy command did not fail to notice the lessons of JUNCTION CITY. Stung by American firepower at Suoi Tre, Bau Bang, and Ap Gu, *COSVN* directed its units over the next six months to avoid regiment-size attacks and instead to target objectives that might be gained with smaller units. In practice, hit-and-run attacks by fire rather than ground assaults would characterize enemy initiatives during the upcoming rainy season. Most of these assaults would be against large U.S. installations that made tempting targets for mortars and sappers. The enemy high command also ordered a greater effort against allied convoys by interdicting roads with

---

[22] AAR, Opn JUNCTION CITY, IIFFV, pp. 28–29; *U.S. Biggest Operation Foiled*, p. 27; Periodic Intel Rpt 18, IIFFV, 8 May 67, p. 1, Historians files, CMH.

[23] Intervs, author with Seaman, 25 May 76, and with Gen Bruce Palmer, CG, IIFFV, and Dep CG, USARV, 2 Mar 77, 2 May 78, Historians files, CMH.

mines and conducting small ambushes with antitank weapons. But large-unit operations and mass assaults against fortified American positions were generally suspended.

The enemy's reversion to smaller units, although frustrating for American soldiers, was in fact a positive sign. If the trend continued, the allies themselves could operate small units with greater safety, thus allowing them to cover more of the Vietnamese countryside, essential to pacification. This is exactly what began to happen. Despite the increases in troop strength, the U.S. command in III Corps conducted 40 percent fewer large unit operations (battalion size or larger) in 1967 than during the previous year. On the other hand, small unit operations in III Corps increased 25 percent during the same period, reflecting a growing American willingness and ability to operate small and dispersed.

Although the threat of the enemy's main forces would continue to command attention, the enemy's shift in tactics and the difficulty of bringing *COSVN* to battle during JUNCTION CITY opened the door to greater U.S. participation in rural security. In fact, in 1967 Westmoreland dedicated a steadily rising proportion of his forces in III Corps to population security in the provinces closest to Saigon.[24] As the year wore on, the U.S. and South Vietnamese security drive around the capital would seriously test the two nations' ability to work together to restore order to the countryside.

[24] Office of Assistant Secretary of Defense (Systems Analysis), Southeast Asia Analysis Rpt, Control no. 6–808, Sep 67, pp. 10–12, and Ibid., Control no. 6–810, Nov 67, pp. 54–56, both in CMH.

9

Defending Saigon

Every military campaign needs achievable objectives. When JUNCTION CITY ended in April, the allies had six infantry divisions in III Corps, plus assorted territorials and pacification teams, to go after the insurgent forces in the shadow of the capital and to ensure that the nerve center of the nation remained safe during the war. Both corps commanders, Generals Seaman and Khang, were committed to coordinating the activities of their forces and achieving the balance between conventional, security, and political operations that successfully defending Saigon would require. Neither man underestimated the job ahead. All around the city lay dangerous territory: to the west, Hau Nghia, Tay Ninh, and Long An Provinces; to the north, Binh Long and Binh Duong; and to the east, Bien Hoa, Phuoc Tuy, and Long Khanh. All these provinces had a significant Viet Cong presence, served as safe havens for enemy logistics, and counted scores of villages that were indifferent or historically hostile to the central government. Whatever the gains so far in the big unit war, American commanders would now have to allocate their forces among three sometimes competing missions: protecting U.S. installations, fighting the enemy main forces, and helping provide security for the population against the local forces and the long-entrenched underground. General Seaman would soon face difficult choices in deploying his units in the defense of Saigon.

North and East of Saigon

The most favorable trends in security lay north and east of the capital city. Although the South Vietnamese 5th Division to the north had made little headway against the main forces or the underground, the destruction wrought by CEDAR FALLS and JUNCTION CITY and the enemy's failure to exploit War Zone D had created several months of breathing room for allied forces, allowing pacification to rise in priority. Through the winter and spring of 1967, the thickening network of allied bases in Binh Long and Binh Duong and the 1st Division's counterinsurgency during lulls in the conventional war had continued to make life difficult for the Viet

The Saigon waterfront

Cong, although Generals DePuy and Hay, advocates of heavy firepower, were not comfortable with village operations.[1] One II Field Force operation, a multidivision sweep in the Saigon River corridor starting in late April, tightened the security seal even more. Though fewer than 200 enemy soldiers were reported killed during the three weeks of MANHATTAN, heavy destruction of Viet Cong supply depots near the Iron Triangle put local guerrillas at heightened risk, as did interdiction of infiltration routes from Cambodia supplying many bases north and west of Saigon.[2]

The news east of Saigon was also encouraging, though the fighting there turned out to be much harder. The insurgency had always been questionable in Bien Hoa and Long Khanh, in part because Catholics from the North had resettled there and in part because the resident

[1] Intervs, author with LeGro, 15, 20 Jan 76; with Lt Gen John H. Hay, CG, 1st Inf Div, 29 Apr 80, Historians files, CMH; and with DePuy, 3, 7 Oct 77; ORLL, 1 Nov 66–31 Jan 67, 1st Inf Div, n.d., pp. 4–16; RD Rpts, Binh Duong Province, May 67, 1 Jun 67, and Binh Long Province, May 67, n.d., both in Historians files, CMH.
[2] AAR, Opn MANHATTAN, IIFFV, 20 Aug 67, pp. 3–15; AAR, Opn MANHATTAN, 1st Inf Div, 12 Jun 67, pp. 2–7; AAR, Opn MANHATTAN, 25th Inf Div, 4 Jul 67, pp. 1–10, all in Historians files, CMH.

Chinese rifles captured during MANHATTAN

enemy unit, the *5th PLAF Division,* was far from *COSVN* supply depots in Cambodia and the Mekong Delta. Even so, the *5th* was a formidable unit, and the South Vietnamese Army had never seriously threatened the division's redoubts—the Hat Dich Secret Zone, a densely jungled area some forty kilometers east of Saigon, and May Tao Mountain, another forty kilometers farther east. In fact, the government's nearest unit, the 18th Division, had been notorious for halfheartedly seeking battle.[3]

Into this sector came the 11th Armored Cavalry Regiment in October 1966. Trained and equipped to escort convoys and counter ambushes, the 11th soon found itself bloodily ensnared with the *5th Division.*[4] November

[3] Periodic Intel Rpts 35, IIFFV, 14 Nov 66, an. H; 36, IIFFV, 21 Nov 66, pp. 2, 14; and 38, IIFFV, 5 Dec 66, p. 13, Historians files, CMH.

[4] The 11th Armored Cavalry Regiment's three squadrons each contained a 105-mm. self-propelled howitzer battery (later upgraded to 155-mm.), a company of seventeen M48A3 tanks, and three cavalry troops, each with nine armored cavalry assault vehicles (ACAVs). New to the Vietnam War, the ACAV was a modified M113 armored personnel carrier with two 7.62-mm. machine guns and a .50-caliber machine gun mounted on top of the vehicle. All had armored gun shields. Because it was lighter than a main battle tank, the ACAV could ford streams and keep pace with truck convoys.

was a time of testing for the armored cavalry, as it secured its base near Xuan Loc, extended its coverage outward, and started patrolling Highways 1 and 20, as well as secondary routes. Though an enemy ambush late in the month went badly for the 11th Cavalry, its tanks and armored cavalry assault vehicles soon had use of the main roads to the II Corps border. From that point on, the cavalry's road-running and cordon and search operations helped improve village security as far east as Binh Tuy Province. When elements of the U.S. 9th Division settled near Long Binh in December, the added strength made pursuit operations possible, forcing the *5th Division*'s regiments to disperse. By late winter prisoners reported that their comrades were short of food, badly demoralized, and expecting an American attack on division headquarters in the May Tho stronghold. Not only were recruits from Long Khanh and Binh Tuy harder to acquire than before, but the *COSVN* commander, General Thanh, worried that the *5th Division* might soon go under.[5]

West and South of Saigon

On Saigon's remaining flanks to the west and south, the situation was reversed. These were traditionally Viet Cong strongholds, bolstered by a supportive population, a large network of base areas, and a virtually secure logistical line. To the west, enemy operations were supported by the proximity of the Parrot's Beak, a salient along the Cambodian border penetrating South Vietnam to within sixty kilometers of the capital. Off limits to American troops, the Parrot's Beak was a well-traveled path for enemy forces moving onto the plains west of Saigon. Westmoreland had to stem the infiltration if there was to be any hope of providing security for the South Vietnamese capital.

Much of the task fell to General Weyand's 25th Division. With its base camp and headquarters at Cu Chi in Hau Nghia Province, and operating with four brigades, the division was uniquely positioned west of the capital. Its tactical area contained numerous territorial forces and Special Forces camps that screened the northern approaches to Tay Ninh City. Other camps, astride the Vam Co Dong River corridor, guarded the western approaches from Cambodia. The division maintained a forward base at Tay Ninh West, which protected the airfield west of Tay Ninh City, and one at Dau Tieng.

Like the 1st Division, the 25th had a weak South Vietnamese division in its sector, in this case Brig. Gen. Phan Trang Chinh's 25th Infantry, widely regarded as Saigon's poorest. Two years in III Corps notwithstanding, Chinh's division had failed to gain the loyalty of the popula-

---

[5] AAR, Opn ATLANTA, 11th Armd Cav Rgt, ans. A–C; Interv, author with 1st Lt John Albright, S–1, 1st Sqdn, 11th Armd Cav Rgt, 25 Mar 76; RD Rpt, Binh Tuy Province, Dec 66, 1 Jan 67, pp. 1–5; Periodic Intel Rpt 17, IIFFV, 2 May 67, p. 12. All in Historians files, CMH.

General Weyand (left) *and Lt. Gen. Nguyen Van Thieu, the South Vietnamese chief of state.*

tion. Accusations of bribery, robbery, and black-marketeering were common, and the desertion rate was high. Poor relations between officers and enlisted men poisoned morale, and the Americans considered the leadership at all levels abysmal.[6] Chinh was a political general. A personal friend of Air Vice Marshal Nguyen Cao Ky, Chinh provided the military muscle to ensure Ky's political survival as prime minister. Chinh stationed two regiments just south of Saigon in Long An Province and the third between the Saigon and Vam Co Dong Rivers in western Hau Nghia. All three could march swiftly on the capital in case of a coup.

When it came to providing local security, the South Vietnamese division proved ineffective. In early December a battalion of *Military Region 2's Dong Thap II Regiment* moved into Duc Hoa District, which at that time was the sole responsibility of General Chinh's 49th Regiment. Over a nine-day period the enemy battalion ambushed a Regional Forces company, attacked a South Vietnamese Army battalion at the provincial capital, and assaulted the headquarters compound of the South Vietnamese 25th Division. South Vietnamese losses were heavy, and several civilians were wounded. The attacks occurred in heavily populated areas, but the civilians provided no warning.[7]

During 1966 Weyand deployed three battalions of the 2d Brigade to three of Hau Nghia's districts (Cu Chi, Trang Bang, and Duc Hoa), intending to keep them in place until pacification was complete or until the South Vietnamese regiment charged with the province's security could do the job alone. Weyand's mission was necessary and challenging, because Hau Nghia was one of the least secure provinces in South

---

[6] Staff Study, MACV J–5, 19 Apr 66, sub: Effectiveness of 5th and 25th ARVN Divisions, Historians files, CMH; MACV History 1966, pp. 460–65; Msg, State A–23 to Saigon, 6 Feb 73, sub: Command Histories and Historical Sketches of RVNAF Divisions, Part II, pp. 33–34, Historians files, CMH; RD Rpt, Hau Nghia Province, Oct 66, 1 Nov 66, p. 1, Historians files, CMH; Interv, author with Seaman, 25 May 76.

[7] Intel Sums 270, IIFFV, 9 Dec 66; 272, IIFFV, 11 Dec 66; and 279, IIFFV, 18 Dec 66; RD Rpt, Hau Nghia Province, Dec 66, 1 Jan 67. All in Historians files, CMH.

Vietnam. A hotbed of Communist activity since the 1930s, it supplied much of the rice to nearby Viet Cong troops. Enemy supply routes from Cambodia also cut through the province.

Weyand's agenda included an ambitious civic action program to provide clothing, tools, and other commodities, as well as to repair roads, dig wells, and construct public buildings. But the press of other responsibilities brought the 25th Division's pacification efforts to a virtual halt. With ATTLEBORO rapidly expanding, on 1 November the 2d Brigade deployed two battalions to reinforce the 196th in Tay Ninh Province. The single combat battalion remaining in Hau Nghia could do little more than protect the division's base at Cu Chi from the *272d Regiment*. The 25th Division returned within three weeks, but Weyand believed that the inhabitants never again cooperated with the Americans with the same enthusiasm as before the brief hiatus.

The 25th Division's pacification campaign in Hau Nghia Province enjoyed mixed success. Search and destroy missions may have prevented enemy main forces from operating freely, but Weyand's troops failed to destroy those units or to clear out the Viet Cong bases. Cu Chi and Trang Bang remained within striking distance of enemy strongholds in the Ho Bo and Boi Loi Woods. Despite an impressive number of weapons captured and fortifications destroyed, the Viet Cong maintained their access to manpower in the villages.[8]

South of Saigon, in Long An, the story was the same. Just south of Hau Nghia, Long An's fertile terrain resembled the flat, alluvial plain of the Mekong Delta and was laced with a network of waterways. The province's farmers produced a rice surplus and shipped part of it to Saigon. Two major highways from the rice-growing regions of the upper delta to Saigon passed through Long An Province.

Like Hau Nghia, Long An had the unfortunate combination of a potent insurgent political structure and poorly performing South Vietnamese units. (*Map 18*) An estimated 3,000 armed Viet Cong operated under the general direction of *Military Region 2*. These locally recruited, lightly armed troops concentrated on South Vietnamese Army and territorial forces and avoided confronting the Americans.[9] Two marginal regiments of the South Vietnamese 25th Division focused on holding Highway 4 and Route 5A, the main roads for moving rice to Saigon, and seldom risked operations in Viet Cong areas. Although the government's 8,000-man force (regulars, territorials, and police) outnumbered the Viet Cong in the province, it provided little security for the population.[10]

---

[8] Eric M. Bergerud, *The Dynamics of Defeat: The Vietnam War in Hau Nghia Province* (Boulder, Colo.: Westview Press, 1991), pp. 137–38.

[9] Monthly OB Sum, CICV, Dec 66, 31 Dec 66, p. II–3. Part-time guerrillas and political cadre brought the total enemy strength in Long An to some 6,600.

[10] Richard A. Hunt, *Pacification: The American Struggle for Vietnam's Hearts and Minds* (Boulder, Colo.: Westview Press, 1995), p. 51.

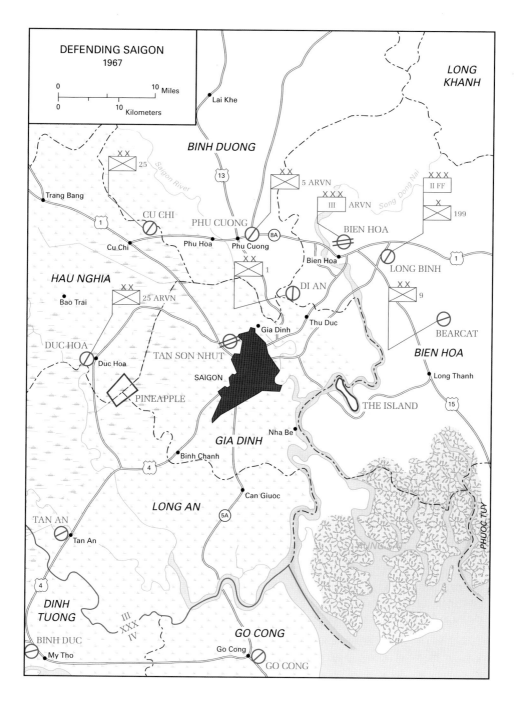

MAP 18

Concerned about Long An's situation, in June 1966 General Westmoreland proposed sending in a battalion of his 25th Division to test how Americans would fight in a heavily populated area. Westmoreland believed that U.S. forces would boost Vietnamese morale and through attrition could break the Viet Cong underground. Ambassador Lodge objected, fearing that American operations would alienate the population, relegate South Vietnamese forces to an ancillary role, and overshadow programs of political and economic development. Before Westmoreland shifted the battalion to Long An, he had General Weyand assure the ambassador that he would subordinate military operations to the goals of pacification. Lodge asked Weyand to include cadre teams in his plans so they could move quickly into the villages cleared by the American unit. With Lodge's consent, Westmoreland deployed a battalion from Weyand's 1st Brigade to Long An in September.[11]

Early in November Weyand committed a second battalion to the province, but not for long. Pressed for manpower, he was forced to redeploy one battalion on 1 December, rotate the second two weeks later, and end operations in Long An early in January. At the time the 25th pulled out, it was having little impact on the life of the province. Rather than challenge the U.S. battalions, as Westmoreland had hoped, the enemy had avoided contact. MACV estimated that the government controlled about 25 percent of the population and less than 10 percent of the hamlets and villages. Less than a tenth of the provincial population voted in local elections.[12] The diversion of units from Long An to crises elsewhere made it clear that the division did not have enough battalions for its combat missions and pacification.[13]

For their part, U.S. civilians felt the experience vindicated their belief that military force by itself would not bring security to the countryside. Lodge saw the need for a consolidated civilian and military effort and in November assigned U.S. Army Col. Samuel V. Wilson as the provisional leader, or single manager, of the entire American advisory team in Long An. The ambassador expected civilian and military advisers to defer to Wilson and battalion commanders to consult with him on combat operations.

As province team leader, Wilson carried out a widely publicized pacification campaign in the Communist-controlled village of Long Huu in Can Duoc District.[14] The Communists used Long Huu, which was located on an island, as a logistical base for units operating in the Rung Sat swamp. The island supplied fish, rice, taxes, and recruits for the enemy. Wilson believed that the Americans could easily take Long Huu by sur-

---

[11] Ibid., pp. 51–52.

[12] Westmoreland, *A Soldier Reports*, p. 208; RD Rpts, Long An Province, Apr 67, n.d., and May 67, n.d., both in Historians files, CMH; ORLL, 1 May–31 Jul 67, 9th Inf Div, 7 Nov 67, p. 27, Historians files, CMH; Intervs, author with Conaty, 24 Sep 75 and 29 Jun 76.

[13] Westmoreland, *A Soldier Reports*, p. 208; AAR, Opn LANIKAI, 25th Inf Div, 19 Mar 67, pp. 1–4, Historians files, CMH; Interv, author with Conaty, 30 Jun 76.

[14] This account of the Long Huu operation is taken from Hunt, *Pacification*, pp. 53–55.

rounding it with overwhelming force and inducing the Communists to defect rather than fight. Wilson wanted to avoid angering the peasants by the needless destruction of civilian crops and homes and to integrate the operation with the efforts of government cadre. On 7 March the 199th Brigade's 2d Battalion, 3d Infantry, and the South Vietnamese 2d Battalion, 46th Infantry, 25th Division, landed on the island and captured it without a fight. Protected by the occupying battalions, workers from various Saigon ministries arrived shortly afterward to start programs to help the villagers and win their loyalty.

Despite the operation's promising start, the Viet Cong regained control. The 199th stayed for only a short time, leaving the island's defense in the hands of the South Vietnamese—three companies of regulars and territorials. The government forces were unable to provide security, and their thefts of produce and poultry alienated the villagers. Government cadre carried out their programs indifferently, and many officials moved out of Long Huu. Viet Cong cadre who had left the island before the operation soon returned to tax and recruit. The operation achieved no lasting change.

Although the single-manager concept in Long An was short-lived and made no breakthroughs, it impressed many U.S. officials. They saw it as demonstrating the need for closer coordination of military and civilian resources and for continued support of pacification by American forces.

Units of the 25th Division continued to be diverted in 1967. In January the 1st Brigade had to cover Hau Nghia and Long An Provinces, because Weyand had committed the 2d Brigade and the 196th to CEDAR FALLS. At the end of January the 2d Brigade went to Binh Duong to help the South Vietnamese 5th Division reestablish a government presence in Phu Hoa, a district long under Viet Cong domination. The 2d left on 22 February to participate in JUNCTION CITY, giving the 1st Brigade responsibility for security south of the Iron Triangle, including Phu Hoa District.

Organized resistance in the district during the next two months declined sharply after a Viet Cong battalion unsuccessfully attempted to overrun an American company in the Filhol Plantation. Engineers reopened Route 8A through Phu Hoa and rebuilt a bridge over the Saigon River. The bridge allowed U.S. forces to move supplies directly from Long Binh to Cu Chi, bypassing congested Saigon. The newly secured road also facilitated the movement of farm goods to market. The presence of the 1st Brigade improved security, but occasional attacks on U.S. forces near Tay Ninh and Dau Tieng diverted American attention from the populated areas to the south.[15]

In mid-March the 25th Division turned its attention to the "Pineapple," an enemy base located amid some abandoned pineapple fields. A mere fifteen kilometers west of Saigon, it was the Viet Cong

---

[15] AAR, Opn CEDAR FALLS, 2d Bde, 25th Inf Div, pp. 11, 23; Periodic Intel Rpt 9, IIFFV, 6 Mar 67, pp. 1–2; Interv, author with Conaty, 30 Jun 76; ORLL, 1 Feb–30 Apr 67, 196th Light Inf Bde, 14 May 67, p. 19, Historians files, CMH.

camp closest to the capital. South Vietnamese forces ordinarily avoided the Pineapple, but in January 1967 two South Vietnamese airborne battalions, supported by U.S. fighter-bombers, launched a well-executed air assault and supposedly trapped a large enemy force there.[16] Then, with the end of the first phase of JUNCTION CITY, General Tillson, Weyand's successor, sent five infantry battalions into the Pineapple, while units of the South Vietnamese 25th Division manned blocking positions. Tillson hoped that the combined effort, code-named MAKALAPA, might accomplish as much as CEDAR FALLS had, but the operation's first three weeks disappointed him. Searchers found little except abandoned bunkers and small caches of ammunition and food. The largest find was 74 weapons hidden in 55-gallon drums and metal boxes.[17]

Meanwhile, Westmoreland turned again to Long An. Some American commanders felt the 25th had been too cautious there. "The 'body count' figure tended to make us look under-productive," the 1st Brigade commander, Col. Francis S. Conaty, later recalled, but he defended his methods:

What we did was to get the people to begin trusting us. We got the RF/PF [Regional Forces/Popular Forces] out of their compounds and back into the field. We opened roads. Many of the people began to stay overnight in these rural homes by their rice paddies, where before they would only work in the fields during the day and live in protected villages at night.[18]

Conaty believed that Westmoreland did not appreciate his prediction that it "would take six months with my entire brigade to show any lasting progress."[19] Westmoreland and Weyand felt that the 25th Division had improved security in Long An, but others disagreed. Deputy Ambassador William Porter, who managed American support of pacification, doubted that the presence of U.S. forces had made a difference there.[20] Westmoreland and the embassy had differing perspectives on how to pacify this province.

In March Westmoreland decided to move the 3d Brigade of the recently arrived 9th Division to Long An. The brigade established its command post at Tan An, the provincial capital, and deployed one battalion each to Binh Phuoc, Tan Tru, and Rach Kien Districts. Some 14,000 South Vietnamese soldiers worked alongside the Americans.

Maj. Gen. George S. Eckhardt, the division commander, instructed the brigade commander, Col. Charles P. Murray, to operate aggressively, to use firepower more freely, and to eradicate the Viet Cong quickly. His

[16] Periodic Intel Rpt 3, IIFFV, 24 Jan 67, p. 2; AAR, Opn MAKALAPA, 25th Inf Div, 26 May 67, pp. 2–3; AAR, Opn MAKALAPA, 1st Bde, 25th Inf Div, 18 May 67, pp. 3–5. All in Historians files, CMH.
[17] AAR, Opn MAKALAPA, 25th Inf Div, pp. 5–6; AAR, Opn MAKALAPA II, 2d Bn, 14th Inf, 12 May 67, p. 19, Historians files, CMH.
[18] AAR, Opn LANIKAI, 1st Bde, 25th Inf Div, 19 Mar 67, pp. 3, 43, Historians files, CMH. Quote from Interv, author with Conaty, 24 Sep 75.
[19] Quote from Interv, author with Conaty, 24 Sep 75.
[20] Hunt, *Pacification*, p. 52.

guidance produced numerical results. Despite the Viet Cong's legendary elusiveness, Murray's battalions fought a multitude of small unit engagements in March and April and claimed to have killed over 800 Viet Cong and to have captured 140 tons of rice. The Americans suffered 74 fatalities. The increased activity may have affected the number of persons defecting under the government's *Chieu Hoi* program, although the rise could not be attributed fully to the 9th's operations. The number of defectors increased from 227 in February to 362 in March, the first full month that Murray's brigade operated in Long An, but the increase had been even more dramatic before the 9th arrived, having jumped fivefold, from 45 in January to 227 in February.[21] Although the 9th operated more aggressively than the 25th had, its operations were not decisive. Intelligence analysts rated both enemy battalions operating in the province as marginally combat effective, but conceded the Viet Cong could replenish their losses quickly through local recruiting. The numerous small unit engagements did not target the underground, which continued to function. The struggle for control of Long An would go on.[22]

Operation FAIRFAX

Even Gia Dinh, the small administrative province surrounding Saigon, was seriously threatened by the insurgency. There, the uprising was controlled by *Military Region 4*, which received instructions from *COSVN*. In October 1966 General McChristian estimated that *Military Region 4* fielded eight battalions, known collectively as the *165A "Capital Liberation" Regiment*. Each battalion had two to three hundred members, most of whom possessed valid South Vietnamese government identification papers that concealed their Communist affiliation and allowed them to function as "legal" citizens.[23]

In late 1966 the Viet Cong presence in two districts, Thu Duc and Binh Chanh—both within fifteen kilometers of the city—was especially strong. In Binh Chanh, they had overrun a police station and threatened the district headquarters. Communist forces had repeatedly approached Saigon from Binh Chanh, cutting roads from Long An to Gia Dinh. Understrength territorial forces and disorganized cadre teams had done little to protect district residents from Viet Cong power.[24] Alarmed by

---

[21] ORLL, 1 Feb–30 Apr 67, 9th Inf Div, pp. 8–9, 11, Historians files, CMH.

[22] Ibid., pp. 9, 12; AAR, Opn ENTERPRISE, 3d Bde, 9th Inf Div, 21 Apr 67, pp. 3–22, Historians files, CMH.

[23] Msgs, COMUSMACV 7503 to CINCPAC, 30 Aug 66, sub: Special Estimate—The Threat to Saigon, and COMUSMACV 02728 to CINCPAC, 23 Jan 67, sub: Appraisal of the HOP TAC Operation, both in Westmoreland Message files, CMH; Westmoreland, *A Soldier Reports*, pp. 82–85; Monthly OB Sum, CICV, Dec 66; Intel Estimate, MACV J–2, 10 Dec 66, Historians files, CMH; ORLL, 1 Nov 66–31 Jan 67, IIFFV, p. 10, Historians files, CMH.

[24] Hunt, *Pacification*, p. 55.

Men of the 199th Light Infantry Brigade and a South Vietnamese ranger during a sweep of Binh Chanh District

deteriorating security so near the capital, Westmoreland wanted to insert American battalions into the province. The murder of six civilians by the Viet Cong and the wounding of forty-nine others during the National Day parade in Saigon in November gave him the pretext to raise the issue with the South Vietnamese. He proposed to the chief of the Joint General Staff, General Cao Van Vien, an operation in Gia Dinh with three U.S. battalions and three from Vien's elite general reserve of highly motivated volunteers stationed in the Saigon area. Vien agreed. This marked the birth of Operation FAIRFAX, the first long-term combined American–South Vietnamese ground operation of the war.[25]

FAIRFAX paired American and South Vietnamese battalions in Binh Chanh, Nha Be, and Thu Duc Districts, which abutted Saigon. According to the plan, the South Vietnamese would work alongside the Americans and

[25] Msg, Wheeler 6339 to Westmoreland, 17 Oct 66, Westmoreland Message files, CMH; CCP 1967, pp. 4, 19; Westmoreland Jnl, 6 Nov 66, Westmoreland History files, 11–A, CMH.

156

conduct clearing operations. The paired units, which varied in size from a squad to a battalion, would operate mostly at night. Thus, they would disrupt community life as little as possible and attack the Viet Cong when they were most active. The military would set up population control checkpoints in coordination with the National Police and establish a security coordination center in each district, consisting of police and military intelligence cadre, to centralize the collection of intelligence. Westmoreland hoped American commanders and advisers would lead by example. As conditions improved, he expected American forces to withdraw gradually so the South Vietnamese could assume full responsibility.[26]

Westmoreland agreed with Seaman's recommendation that II Field Force take charge of FAIRFAX, believing that direction from this level would emphasize American concern for rural security. Seaman selected three battalions with experience in village warfare, one from the 1st Division and two from the 25th. Parent units handled administrative and logistical support. Participating South Vietnamese battalions came under III Corps commander General Khang.[27]

At first the operations seemed effective. During December American and South Vietnamese forces reopened roads, rebuilt bridges, and reestablished outposts. Each day they entered hamlets long under Viet Cong influence and assisted the police in arresting suspected insurgents, draft dodgers, and deserters. The number of enemy in the province fell an estimated 10 percent, with 235 Viet Cong killed or captured, an impressive figure compared to the 15 killed or captured the preceding month. But the statistics—admittedly American tallies—were not all favorable. Viet Cong incidents increased substantially in December. Ambushes by small Viet Cong teams using claymore mines accounted for most U.S. and South Vietnamese casualties.[28]

To American soldiers, combat in Gia Dinh had a surrealistic air. A firefight might break out within a few kilometers of homes, shops, or schools. Inhabitants often appeared oblivious to the clashes, which often included artillery and helicopter gunship fire. The small, intensive struggles failed to disrupt commercial traffic on nearby roads and waterways, sales at local markets, or airplanes taking off and landing at what was then the world's busiest airport, Tan Son Nhut.[29]

As 1966 ended, FAIRFAX made some headway in improving security and in forcing Viet Cong military units to disperse or pull out of the region. Although the enemy still controlled a lot of territory, U.S. commanders believed that government officials had a reasonable chance of

---

[26] ORLL, 1 Nov 66–31 Jan 67, IIFFV, p. 6; Msg, Westmoreland MAC 9974 to Wheeler, 15 Nov 66, Westmoreland Message files, CMH.

[27] ORLL, 1 Nov 66–31 Jan 67, IIFFV, p. 6; Interv, author with Seaman, 25 May 76; Ltr, Seaman to author, 13 Sep 76, Historians files, CMH.

[28] RD Rpt, Gia Dinh Province, Dec 66, 1 Jan 67, pp. 3–5, Historians files, CMH.

[29] Interv, author with Maj Gen James G. Boatner, Comdr, 4th Bn, 12th Inf, 199th Light Inf Bde, 22 May 80, Historians files, CMH.

making additional security gains by attacking the enemy underground and carrying out the reforms at the core of the pacification campaign. Westmoreland and Lodge pressed South Vietnamese officials to do just that, which the White House also encouraged. Saigon's response was sluggish at best, and Westmoreland concluded in late December that if FAIRFAX was to succeed, American forces would have to stay beyond the planned February 1967 withdrawal. He was unsure if South Vietnamese officials would seize the opportunity.

In January 1967 Westmoreland decided to end the somewhat awkward arrangement of using battalions from different divisions and made a single unit, the 199th Brigade under Brig. Gen. Charles W. Ryder, responsible for FAIRFAX, a move that simplified coordination. Also at that time the South Vietnamese high command agreed to the permanent assignment to FAIRFAX of a marine and two ranger battalions, abandoning the practice of rotating units in and out of the province every few weeks.[30]

By improving continuity, those changes energized the operation. In February enemy losses—killed, prisoners, and ralliers—totaled nearly three hundred, equaling the number for the previous two months. American and South Vietnamese forces, employing the "double force," or "buddy," concept, conducted daytime patrols together and manned checkpoints along the roads. These steps helped restrict enemy activity mainly to sniper fire and planting mines. After curfew allied units saturated the operational area with ambushes, but fewer than 10 percent of the ambushes made contact, and only a small percentage resulted in confirmed enemy dead.[31] Officials hoped that the long-established curfew would minimize civilian casualties, but the chance of tragedy was not completely avoidable despite precautions and good intentions. During night ambushes it was often impossible to distinguish between Viet Cong soldiers, civilians impressed into the insurgent supply system, black-marketeers, and noncombatants.[32]

In March Westmoreland made additional changes. He assigned General Ryder as assistant commander of the 4th Division and appointed his special assistant and MACV training director, Brig. Gen. John F. Freund, to command the 199th Brigade. In light of Freund's experience in Vietnam, Westmoreland made a sound choice. Freund had served in the theater since 1964 and had completed a number of sensitive advisory assignments. He enjoyed a close, personal relationship with the armed forces chief, General Vien, and the chief of the South Vietnamese National

---

[30] ORLL, 1 Nov 66–31 Jan 67, 199th Light Inf Bde, 15 Feb 67, p. 1, Historians files, CMH; Interv, author with Boatner, 22 May 80.

[31] AAR, Opn FAIRFAX, 199th Light Inf Bde, 3 Jan 68, an. F, and ORLL, 1 Feb–30 Apr 67, 199th Light Inf Bde, 15 May 67, p. 3, both in Historians files, CMH; ORLL, 1 Nov 66–31 Jan 67, 199th Light Inf Bde, p. 13. See also James G. Boatner, *American Tactical Units in Revolutionary Development Operations,* Air University Rpt 3570 (Maxwell Air Force Base, Ala.: Air War College, August 1968), pp. 29–40.

[32] ORLL, 1 Feb–30 Apr 67, 199th Light Inf Bde, Incl 5.

Police, Brig. Gen. Nguyen Ngoc Loan. Freund knew the strengths and weaknesses of the Vietnamese military leadership, including their family and political connections and economic interests. Freund was also fluent in French, the second language of many high-ranking government officials. He was well qualified for an assignment that had a significant political dimension.

During March and April security in Gia Dinh again seemed to improve, but in May the province senior adviser, Lt. Col. Charles L. Brindel, took the contrary view. He reported that all elements of South Vietnam's revolutionary development program—other than security, which American forces helped to improve—were months behind schedule, a finding similar to the one Westmoreland had expressed in January. Although American forces had reduced the level of enemy violence, government officials had yet to introduce reforms, and their reputation in the eyes of the people remained poor.[33] Officials were slow to exploit the better conditions. Not until late March did they begin the agricultural, public health, and public works projects scheduled for 1967, and then only perfunctorily. Voters were apathetic. Less than half of Gia Dinh's electorate cast ballots in village elections in April. The turnout in May was better, but still well below the national average.

The insurgent shadow government remained strong, notably in the villages and hamlets outside the towns. Despite five separate South Vietnamese intelligence organizations in the province, the campaign to rid Gia Dinh of Communist cadre was producing meager results, partly because the various intelligence agencies often worked at cross purposes. Aware that government officials had so far failed to weaken the enemy underground, General Freund prodded them constantly but with few tangible results. His recommendations to consolidate the intelligence effort, for example, were politely received, but nothing changed. Police units were badly deployed, and their blacklists of suspected members of the underground contained vague and outdated information. The numerous American and South Vietnamese intelligence efforts remained separate and sovereign entities.[34] Even though 70 percent of Gia Dinh's inhabitants lived in hamlets officially rated secure in May, an increase of 10 percent since the start of the year, security had not improved to the point where U.S. forces could leave. Hoping that a continued American presence would eventually promote improvement, in May Freund recommended postponing the withdrawal of U.S. forces from Gia Dinh for a second time.[35]

[33] RD Rpts, Gia Dinh Province, Apr 67, 4 May 67, and May 67, 3 Jun 67, both in Historians files, CMH.

[34] Hunt, *Pacification*, p. 56.

[35] Southeast Asia Hamlet Evaluation System (HES) Data Book for 1967, Office of Assistant Secretary of Defense, Systems Analysis (OASD SA), p. II–31, Historians files, CMH; RD Rpt, Gia Dinh Province, May 67, 3 Jun 67; Memo, Saigon for Amb Robert W. Komer, Deputy Commander for Civil Operations and Revolutionary Development Support (DEPCORDS), 24 May 67, sub: Binh Chanh, Historians files, CMH.

With the passage of time, Westmoreland became convinced that South Vietnamese units working directly with the brigade had developed "a tendency to let the Americans do the job alone." He believed that the 199th could be used more productively elsewhere and that it was "better for South Vietnamese and American units to operate side by side in cooperation than to integrate."[36] The reasons related to the obvious disparity in capabilities. Although American and South Vietnamese commanders had equal authority and reached decisions collectively during FAIRFAX, the South Vietnamese depended on the Americans for helicopter, artillery, and tactical air support. The 199th provided rations to its counterparts, allowing the South Vietnamese soldiers, who normally purchased food on the local market, to put extra piasters in their pockets. These well-intentioned measures engendered a South Vietnamese reliance on the Americans that could not continue indefinitely.[37]

In June Westmoreland notified Vien that by the end of 1967 he would remove the 199th from Gia Dinh Province. Vien agreed, telling Westmoreland that South Vietnamese leaders were embarrassed that American troops had stayed so long in their nation's capital. Until its departure, the brigade undertook an extensive program to train regular and territorial units in the FAIRFAX area.[38] The Vietnamese armed forces chief assigned specific ranger battalions on a permanent basis to work directly with the Americans in each FAIRFAX district. He also instructed the III Corps commander, General Khang, to prepare the 5th Ranger Group headquarters to assume full responsibility for FAIRFAX and to send a liaison team to join Freund as soon as possible. Vien also decided to give the new M16 assault rifles first to his general reserve units and then to the 5th Ranger Group, measures Westmoreland had long advocated.[39]

Beginning in May Freund's units worked directly with the territorials. During the day the integrated forces assisted the police at checkpoints along roads and waterways and conducted cordon and search operations in villages and hamlets. At night they established ambushes in remote areas. By the end of July these patrols were setting up over seventy-five ambushes nightly, double the number three months before. The units also established permanent patrol bases in two Viet Cong base areas, the Pineapple and the "Island," the latter a way station for moving supplies across the Dong Nai River between Gia Dinh and Bien Hoa Provinces. Helicopter gunships patrolled around the clock to intercept enemy sampans entering southern Gia Dinh from

[36] Westmoreland, *A Soldier Reports*, p. 207.

[37] Boatner, *American Units in Revolutionary Development*, pp. 31–32; Interv, author with Boatner, 20 Aug 80; MFR, 12 Oct 67, sub: MACV Commanders' Conference, 24 September 1967, Westmoreland History files, 22–12, CMH; General Cao Van Vien and Lt. Gen. Dong Van Khuyen, *Reflections on the Vietnam War*, Indochina Monographs (Washington, D.C.: U.S. Army Center of Military History, 1980), p. 53.

[38] Westmoreland Jnl, 13 Jun 67, Westmoreland History files, 18, CMH.

[39] Ibid.; AAR, Opn FAIRFAX, 199th Light Inf Bde, p. 5.

A government official explains the Chieu Hoi *amnesty program to families of Viet Cong guerrillas.*

Bien Hoa. Before FAIRFAX ended, gunship and ground fire sank nearly seven hundred enemy sampans.

The success of FAIRFAX depended on small, integrated units employing guerrilla tactics saturating the contested areas outside the capital. These measures proved especially effective in inducing Viet Cong traveling through the region to defect under the *Chieu Hoi* program. Of 155 defectors in Gia Dinh in July, over 75 percent originally came from outside the province. Many were lost and had no ties with the local people. They deserted rather than risking death.[40]

Yet, despite the defectors and the interception of an impressive number of sampans, security in Gia Dinh by most measurements remained unchanged during the May-November period. The government had little success in eliminating the revolutionary underground, and cordon and search operations were rarely productive. During one series of operations, government officials screened 25,000 civilians and identified a single Viet Cong cadre. Such operations also had adverse effects. Misbehavior, accidents, and firefights often alienated villagers from the military and police forces. Even if handled well, these operations often disrupted civilian work routines with few apparent benefits. Worse, absentee landlords occasionally

[40] AAR, Opn FAIRFAX, 199th Light Inf Bde, pp. 14–18; ORLL, 1 May–31 Jul 67, IIFFV, 7 Nov 67, p. 24, Historians files, CMH; RD Rpts, Gia Dinh Province, Jul 67, 3 Aug 67, and Aug 67, 5 Sep 67, both in Historians files, CMH.

accompanied the troops to collect back rent. The South Vietnamese appreciated American medical and economic assistance but knew that when the U.S. troops left, the Viet Cong would return. Under the circumstances, few were inclined to side openly with the government.[41]

During an operation in August Freund was wounded, and the II Field Force chief of staff, Brig. Gen. Robert C. Forbes, succeeded him. Forbes also realized that the South Vietnamese, especially the rangers, had become too reliant on American support. Yet, because they lacked the means to be self-sufficient, there was little he could do but continue to sustain them.[42] So, with Westmoreland's backing, he arranged for the rangers to obtain modern communications equipment and placed American advisers with a South Vietnamese artillery battalion and an expanded logistical organization, which would be formed before the 199th departed.[43]

On 24 September the buddy practice was discontinued, and Americans and South Vietnamese began operating independently in separate sectors. Although they occasionally conducted combined operations, they no longer acted as an integrated force.[44] To facilitate the transition, Forbes helped the 5th Ranger Group headquarters administer a series of training exercises to evaluate the performance of the FAIRFAX ranger battalions. He hoped that improved weapons, communications, and artillery support and the experience they had chalked up with the 199th would keep the rangers a proficient fighting force.

FAIRFAX ended on 15 December, when the last battalion of the 199th left Gia Dinh Province. The eleven-month campaign had focused almost entirely on population security and resources control. Captured documents and prisoner interrogations led the Americans to conclude that FAIRFAX had reduced enemy combat strength in the targeted districts by 60 percent, while the Viet Cong had suffered over 1,200 killed or captured. But though the long-term presence of American units in Gia Dinh helped improve security, it also engendered the outcome Lodge had feared—the tendency of the South Vietnamese to let the Americans take charge. Westmoreland remained convinced that the operation's successes outweighed its weaknesses but also concluded that the extended integration of American and South Vietnamese units was counterproductive, reducing the Vietnamese elements to combat auxiliaries. It was the sort of dilemma that typified the Vietnam experience.[45]

---

[41] AAR, Opn FAIRFAX, 199th Light Inf Bde, ans. D, F; MFR, 24 Jun 67, sub: MACV Commanders' Conference, 11 June 1967, Westmoreland History files, 18–11, CMH; RD Rpts, Gia Dinh Province, Jul 67, 3 Aug 67, and Aug 67, 5 Sep 67; Interv, author with Boatner, 20 Aug 80.

[42] Interv, author with Boatner, 20 Aug 80; Westmoreland, *A Soldier Reports*, p. 207.

[43] Sharp and Westmoreland, *Report*, pp. 140–41; AAR, Opn FAIRFAX, 199th Light Inf Bde, pp. 17–18; Westmoreland, *A Soldier Reports*, p. 207.

[44] AAR, Opn FAIRFAX, 199th Light Inf Bde, p. 16, and an. A.

[45] Westmoreland, *A Soldier Reports*, p. 207; Boatner, *American Units in Revolutionary Development*, pp. 38–41, 55–62.

PART THREE
Farther North

10

New Border Battles

Seeking enemy big units remained General Westmoreland's first priority, and they were nowhere more numerous than in the Central Highlands of II Corps. General Larsen's forces continued to scour the forested hills and valleys, seeking battle wherever they could find North Vietnamese. His marching orders had come straight from the MACV commander, who believed more than ever that control of the highlands remained one of Hanoi's principal objectives, roughly equal to its goals in the lowlands or along the Demilitarized Zone. Summing up his thoughts on the matter in February 1967, the MACV commander emphasized the importance of the isolated plateau, where an enemy victory against the allies might be followed by political initiatives—the open establishment of a provisional government, for example—that could have ramifications for U.S. and international public opinion. For Larsen, the task in the highlands was thus clear. He had to engage North Vietnamese regulars when they crossed over the border, before they had time to establish themselves and threaten the roadnets and base complexes that were central to allied combat power in western II Corps.[1]

Preliminaries

At the beginning of 1967 most of the enemy main forces were still in Cambodia, regrouping after PAUL REVERE IV. During the lull, Larsen reduced his border guard to an absolute minimum, concentrating his infantry brigades around the coastal population. Consequently, when Maj. Gen. William R. Peers assumed command of the 4th Division on 3 January, he had only the 2d Brigade headquarters, four infantry battalions, the division's armored cavalry squadron, and the attached tanks of the 1st Battalion of the 69th Armor to screen the frontier. The mission, a continuation of the PAUL REVERE series, was to sound the alarm if the enemy launched in strength out of Cambodia.[2]

---

[1] Msg, COMUSMACV to JCS, 23 Feb 67, sub: Assessment of Enemy Situation, Westmoreland Message files, CMH.

[2] AAR, Opn SAM HOUSTON, 4th Inf Div, 16 May 67, p. 16, Incl 3, box 5, 68A/4975, RG

General Peers

Peers' predecessor, General Collins, had advised him that the *B3 Front* was attempting to create a "fortified redoubt" in the Plei Trap. The only response, according to Collins, was to build landing zones and firebases, and perhaps even an airstrip for C–130s, before the seasonal rains began.[3] Peers did not need persuading. One of his first acts was to instruct his 2d Brigade to reopen Route 509 to the Se San, bridge the river, and extend the road west to a newly opened firebase. This move marked the start of PAUL REVERE V. The enemy allowed the bridgehead to stand.[4]

But if the enemy main forces were quiescent, the local Viet Cong were not. On 7 January elements of the *H15 Local Force Battalion* and the *407th Sapper Battalion* attacked Camp Holloway, a large airfield near Pleiku that also served as Qui Nhon Support Command's chief supply facility for the western highlands. During the assault, an enemy soldier speaking fluent English made several telephone calls over the base's wire net to sow confusion. Following a twenty-minute mortar attack, sappers breached the perimeter, rushed the runway, and began destroying aircraft and supplies. Their short attack left 6 Americans dead, 61 wounded, and 23 aircraft lying damaged on the tarmac. Enemy losses were unknown.[5]

As the senior U.S. officer in the area, Peers immediately tightened security around his installations and sent 4th Division troops to search neighboring villages. He complemented those sweeps with support for pacification. Soon American soldiers were visiting hamlets and villages, providing medical treatment and materials to construct schools and other

---

319, NARA. The division's 1st Brigade was in Phu Yen Province under I Field Force control, while the 3d of the 25th Division was working with the 1st Cavalry Division in Binh Dinh.

[3] Intervs, author with Collins, 28 Feb 75, and with Lt Gen William R. Peers, CG, 4th Inf Div, 21 Oct 75, Historians files, CMH.

[4] AAR, Opn SAM HOUSTON, 4th Inf Div, pp. 15–17, Incl 10.

[5] Daily Jnl, G–2, 4th Inf Div, 7 Jan 67, Historians files, CMH; Periodic Intel Rpt 1, IFFV, 10 Jan 67, p. 3, box 1, 70A/499, RG 338, NARA.

facilities. More than an outreach program, those missions gathered intelligence, especially in the outlying communities. One such venture was FAMOUS FRIEND, an idea Peers adopted from the 1st Cavalry Division, in which scout helicopters regularly reconnoitered isolated villages. If the village was flying the South Vietnamese flag, then all was well; the absence of the colors meant something was amiss—perhaps Viet Cong were close. Enemy cadre tried to confiscate the flags, but the Americans always brought more. Although the guerrillas continued to exploit these villages for supplies, they could not remain long in any one area, and by the end of January the 4th Division's security and pacification measures had helped to drive the Viet Cong deeper into the mountains and away from the population.[6]

West Toward Cambodia

Although the guerrilla threat had abated, the main forces were back in business. Aerial and ground reconnaissance confirmed that the enemy was in the Plei Trap. Heavy trail usage and sightings of fortified positions under construction prompted two B–52 strikes early in February.[7]

It was all the news Peers needed, and he made ready to respond in force. He sent two battalions (one of which, from his 1st Brigade, Larsen returned to him from the coast) to Duc Co, to check out the Ia Drang Valley and screen to the south. His armor he kept running the roads of Pleiku Province. And his spearhead, the 2d Brigade, he poised at 3 TANGO, midway between Pleiku and the Plei Trap. This would be his launch point—west over the Nam Sathay into the Plei Trap Valley on 15 February. Artillery fires would be amply available—from 3 TANGO, the New Plei Djereng Special Forces camp, and from the new firebase on Route 509—elements of seven battalions in all before it was over, including three battalions from the reinforcing 52d Artillery Group, among which were heavy 8-inch howitzers and 175-mm. guns. His own division forward command post and that of the 2d Brigade would go to 3 TANGO, where supplies were being amassed.[8]

He took the offensive sooner than he planned. The Tet holiday truce began on 8 February, and that very day the *1st PAVN Division* was spotted in the Plei Trap, with the *10th PAVN Division* presumed close. Concerned that the enemy would dig in and be tough to dislodge, Peers and Larsen pushed D-day three days forward. Operation SAM HOUSTON launched on 12 February.[9] (*Map 19*)

---

[6] ORLL, 1 Nov 66–31 Jan 67, IFFV, 6 Mar 67, p. 7; ORLL, 1 Nov 66–31 Jan 67, 4th Inf Div, 20 Mar 67, p. 23; Intel Sums 87–67–C, 4th Inf Div, 9 Jan 67; 124–67–C, 4th Inf Div, 13 Jan 67; and 154–67–C, 4th Inf Div, 16 Jan 67. All in Historians files, CMH.

[7] AAR, Opn SAM HOUSTON, 4th Inf Div, p. 10 and Incl 4.

[8] Ibid., pp. 16–17; Interv, author with Peers, 21 Oct 75.

[9] ORLL, 1 Nov 66–31 Jan 67, IFFV, p. 7.

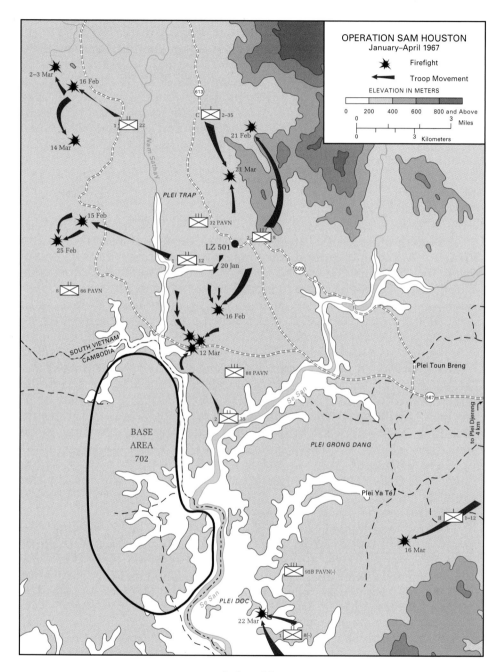

OPERATION SAM HOUSTON
January–April 1967

Firefight

Troop Movement

ELEVATION IN METERS

0   200   400   600   800 and Above

0   3
                  Miles

0   3
                  Kilometers

2–3 Mar

16 Feb

14 Mar

1 ▨ 22

613

C ▨ 2–35

21 Feb

21 Mar

PLEI TRAP

32 PAVN

2 ▨ 8

509

15 Feb

25 Feb

8 ▨ 66 PAVN

LZ 501

1 ▨ 12

20 Jan

16 Feb

SOUTH VIETNAM

CAMBODIA

12 Mar

88 PAVN

Plei Toun Breng

Se San

567

BASE
AREA
702

2 ▨ 35

PLEI GRONG DANG

to Plei Djereng
4 km

Plei Ya Té

B ▨ 1–12

16 Mar

95B PAVN(-)

Se San

PLEI DOC

22 Mar

1 ▨ 8(-)

MAP 19

Memories of PAUL REVERE IV were strong in the division, so the 2d Brigade, assaulting with two battalions, advanced slowly at first, sending a company from each across the Nam Sathay to lock up two landing zones in the valley. On the right, the attack of the 1st Battalion, 22d Infantry, went without incident. On the left, the 1st Battalion, 12th Infantry, found trouble soon enough. After a quiet forty-eight hours, its scouting element (Company C) reported that the wood line surrounding the proposed landing zone, 501–NORTH, contained recently built but unoccupied bunkers. The night of the fourteenth passed uneventfully, but when Company C began exploring nearby hills the following morning, it bumped into North Vietnamese. Within the hour the company was fighting off attempts to overrun the landing zone. Air and artillery support blunted the enemy assault, but enemy intentions were still unknown when the main body of the battalion landed at midmorning on the fifteenth.

Hoping to deceive the enemy, the new 2d Brigade commander, Col. James B. Adamson, ordered a decoy air and artillery preparation on another clearing two kilometers south. Later, around 1330, he attempted to insert the remainder of his unit into 501–NORTH. But the enemy was not fooled. As the first group of troop-carrying helicopters touched down, a reinforced company of the *8th Battalion, 66th PAVN Regiment*, opened fire from the hills. Eight Hueys were damaged, but all landed their troops before limping away.

By early evening the rest of the battalion was on the ground. Throughout the night, under the dull glare of flares dropped by an AC–47 "Spooky" gunship from the 4th Air Commando Squadron, the soldiers carved out an enlarged perimeter. By morning the enemy had vanished. The fight at Landing Zone 501–NORTH proved to be the only occasion during SAM HOUSTON on which the enemy launched a ground assault against a prepared American position.[10]

While the two battalions were moving into the Plei Trap, the 2d Brigade's third battalion, the 2d of the 8th Infantry, was protecting a firebase and patrolling Route 509 east of the Nam Sathay. On the morning of 16 February one of its rifle platoons was ambushed while maneuvering through jungle a few kilometers beyond the firebase. Dense vegetation and the din of rifle fire and exploding grenades prevented the platoon leader from adjusting artillery fire by sight or sound, and he had to talk helicopter gunships into position. Eventually, the platoon's parent company was able to push through mortar and sniper fire to form a corridor, allowing the platoon to withdraw and evacuate its many wounded. A battalion of the *32d Regiment* followed, hoping to renew the struggle, but when darkness fell it withdrew.

A company from the 22d Infantry, the first unit to land west of the Nam Sathay, was also in trouble. Chasing several North Vietnamese sol-

[10] AAR, Opn SAM HOUSTON, 4th Inf Div, Incl 10. A sweep of the area south of 501–NORTH on 16 February discovered 116 enemy dead. The fight at the landing zone left 12 Americans dead and 32 wounded.

diers through the jungle, the unit stumbled into an ambush, and in the firefight snipers nearly annihilated the lead platoon. Although reinforcements arrived in the evening, sniper fire continued through the night, covering the North Vietnamese withdrawal.[11]

In the space of three days the 2d Brigade had fought three sharp engagements with elements of at least two regiments of the *1st Division*. Prisoner interrogations revealed that the *88th PAVN Regiment* was also in the Plei Trap, having replaced the *33d*. Enemy losses according to the Americans' body count totaled nearly 300, while estimated additional kills from air and artillery were twice that number. But U.S. losses were also heavy: 55 dead and 74 wounded.[12]

SAM HOUSTON—Phase Two

Anxious to avoid further high casualties, Peers instructed Adamson to keep his units near their firebases for the next five days. Massive air and artillery strikes followed, including nine B–52 missions.

Peers also asked Larsen for the 1st Brigade, and I Field Force agreed, dispatching all but a battalion to the highlands. Initially, Peers gave Col. Charles A. Jackson, the 1st Brigade commander, control of three battalions, and the 2d Brigade commander, Colonel Adamson, control of two. A sixth battalion, the 3d of the 8th Infantry, would remain in reserve at 3 TANGO. Jackson would be responsible for the battle between the Se San and the Nam Sathay, while Adamson would run the operation to the west, between the Nam Sathay and the Cambodian border. Division armor would attend to the roads, no longer a routine assignment.[13]

Keeping the roads open west of Pleiku became increasingly difficult during the second phase of SAM HOUSTON. Mines hampered operations, and daily mine sweeps became a necessity. "There was a time when we could run our tanks and APCs down the road and take our losses," said one of Peers' assistant division commanders, but now the number of mines made that too dangerous. During SAM HOUSTON fifty-three vehicles were damaged by mines with over 90 percent of the incidents occurring after 14 February.[14]

High infantry casualties continued as well. On 21 February a company on its way to investigate the results of a B–52 strike was ambushed by a North Vietnamese battalion east of the Nam Sathay. The Americans dug

---

[11] CHECO Rpt, Opn PAUL REVERE/SAM HOUSTON, PACAF, pp. 73–78; AAR, Opn SAM HOUSTON, 4th Inf Div, Incl 10; Interv, author with Peers, 21 Oct 75.

[12] Intel Sums 2–170–67–C, 4th Inf Div, 16 Feb 67, and 2–235–67–C, 4th Inf Div, 21 Feb 67, both in Historians files, CMH; AAR, Opn SAM HOUSTON, 4th Inf Div, pp. 5–6; Critique, Opn SAM HOUSTON, 4th Inf Div, 27 Apr 67, pp. 2–3, and Ltr, CG, 4th Inf Div, sub: Operation SAM HOUSTON, 20 Jun 67, pp. 1–3, both in Historians files, CMH.

[13] AAR, Opn SAM HOUSTON, 4th Inf Div, Incl 3.

[14] Ibid.; Critique, Opn SAM HOUSTON, 4th Inf Div, p. 44.

A xenon searchlight on an M48A3 tank picks out targets on a road west of Pleiku.

in furiously, and throughout the night lay anxiously under the flying bullets. With bayonets fixed, they awaited the enemy assault, but none came. By daybreak American losses were 8 killed and 61 wounded.

The 1st Brigade reacted to the ambush by air-assaulting a battalion to the north and west and sending another battalion overland to the south. But, aside from 5 bodies near the ambush, the enemy had vanished. Although Peers thought that high enemy losses had forced the unit back into Cambodia, the Americans were still having no luck bringing the elusive North Vietnamese Army to decisive battle.[15]

Meanwhile, Adamson's 2d Brigade continued company-size sweeps west of the Nam Sathay. Closer to the border the danger of ambush was even higher, and the Americans moved with great care. Caution paid off on 25 February, when one rifle company detected an enemy force quietly waiting. Reacting quickly, the unit coiled and called in artillery and air strikes. The surprised North Vietnamese regulars attacked and then fled. With no opportunity to recover casualties, they left 48 dead and 3 wounded soldiers on the battlefield. One American died in the action.[16]

Supplementing company-size operations, the 4th Division dispatched a daily average of seven long-range reconnaissance patrols throughout SAM HOUSTON. These special units, composed of six to eight men, monitored enemy movement along trails, ambushed small patrols, located possible landing sites, and assessed bomb damage from B–52 strikes—all dangerous work.[17]

On 27 February a helicopter inserted one of these teams to check the results of a B–52 attack east of the Nam Sathay, in an area where the river formed the South Vietnamese–Cambodian border. Apparently disoriented, the pilot set the men down west of the river inside Cambodia. An hour later the team surprised 2 enemy soldiers, killed 1, and then asked to

[15] Msgs, Maj Gen William R. Peers, CG, 4th Inf Div, PKU 157 to Larsen, 22 Feb 67, sub: Action: B/2/8—21–22 Feb 67, and Peers PKU 161 to Larsen, 24 Feb 67, both in Westmoreland Message files, CMH. The 4th Division set enemy losses for 21 February 1967 at 11 observed killed, 32 observed wounded, and added estimates of 30 killed or wounded by ground action and 75 to 100 probably killed or wounded by air and artillery. See AAR, Opn SAM HOUSTON, 4th Inf Div, Incl 10.

[16] AAR, Opn SAM HOUSTON, 4th Inf Div, Incl 10; Critique, Opn SAM HOUSTON, 4th Inf Div, p. 4.

[17] AAR, Opn SAM HOUSTON, 4th Inf Div, p. 41.

be extracted, having compromised its position. Only then did U.S. commanders realize that the soldiers were on the wrong side of the border. Shortly afterward a large North Vietnamese force spotted the patrol but failed to react, apparently equally surprised at seeing Americans. Before enemy commanders could gather their wits, helicopters whisked the team away. This was neither the first nor the last time that Americans would accidentally cross the border.

Peers wanted to relieve the offending commander on the spot for what he called an "almost unbelievable error." In keeping with explicit instructions from MACV headquarters against incursions, the 4th Division had scrupulously avoided the border. Yet, everyone knew that even if the maps showed the border clearly, actually finding it among the mountains and trees of the highlands was a daunting task. Peers relented. After all, good commanders were hard to find.[18]

Peers had concerns more important than petty border violations. His troops had not closed with any sizable North Vietnamese units. Being among an enemy and seeing only his shadow was perplexing, but they did what they could. After the 2d Brigade had a brief encounter near the border, soldiers identified the enemy force there as the *32d Regiment*, which was apparently no longer east of the Nam Sathay and was possibly in the process of leaving the Plei Trap altogether. Shortly afterward nine B–52s struck the area with unknown results.

Even if the *32d* had left the Plei Trap, the *88th Regiment* remained, entrenched in bunkers near the point where the Nam Sathay followed the border. On the morning of 12 March, while moving through heavy jungle, a company of the 1st Brigade's 2d Battalion, 35th Infantry, ran into rifle fire from bunkers along the trail. The Americans stormed the fortifications, but when the commander realized what he was up against, he backed off. Sending small teams to make their way into the complex for a look around, he found that the North Vietnamese were picking off his men one by one.

Realizing that artillery fire and air strikes would probably not suffice to drive out the enemy, the battalion commander, Lt. Col. Clinton E. Granger, reinforced with two companies delivered by air, one south and the other east of the firefight. But the rescuers themselves were soon pinned down, and by dark all three of Granger's companies were mired in battle, their vision limited by the heavy jungle.

Later that night mortar fire from the Cambodian side of the border struck Granger's units. Calling for fire support and illumination, the Americans were stunned when in the glow of the flares they saw a mass of North Vietnamese soldiers wading the Se San toward Cambodia. Huey gunships raced in to kill as many as they could before the soldiers reached the safety of the border.

[18] Interv, author with Col Clinton E. Granger, Comdr, 2d Bn, 35th Inf, 3d Bde, 25th Inf Div, 15 Nov 85, Historians files, CMH. Quote from Msg, Peers PKU 168 to Larsen, 27 Feb 67, sub: Border Incident, 27 Feb 67. Msg, Peers PKU 172 to Larsen, 28 Feb 67, sub: Border Incident. Both in Westmoreland Message files, CMH.

The next morning Peers provided two additional battalions in an attempt to trap any of these soldiers remaining in the South, but it was too late. The enemy had fled, leaving behind 51 dead. Peers believed an additional 200 North Vietnamese soldiers had been killed by gunships and artillery. American casualties were 14 killed and 46 wounded.[19]

Elsewhere in the Plei Trap, American units concentrated on constructing firebases amid occasional hit-and-run mortar attacks. The worst barrage came on 13 March and lasted 36 hours, with over 800 mortar rounds striking several American positions. Hit hardest, with over 300 rounds, was the command and supply complex at 3 TANGO. The base was so jammed with munitions, equipment, and soldiers that almost any round landing inside was bound to hit something. Together the attacks cost 1 dead, 87 wounded, and 25 vehicles destroyed or damaged.[20]

The Plei Doc

The third phase of SAM HOUSTON began on 16 March, when the 2d Brigade launched into an area called the Plei Doc, fifteen kilometers southwest of 3 TANGO and an equal distance northwest of Duc Co. A month earlier Montagnard trail-watchers and American long-range reconnaissance patrols reported that the North Vietnamese were moving supplies forward and possibly preparing for an offensive once the rainy season arrived in April. At the time the U.S. commitment in the Plei Trap made a march into the Plei Doc impossible, but now SAM HOUSTON would move south.[21]

The first American thrust provoked a reaction. Landing on the morning of 16 March, the first contingents of the 1st Battalion, 12th Infantry, encountered small-arms and automatic-weapons fire coming from a wood line surrounding the landing zone. Obviously, the North Vietnamese were ready. As the UH–1s landed, electronically detonated mines exploded, wrecking one helicopter and damaging seven others. Artillery and air strikes created enough of a distraction to enable the rest of the battalion to land, but the enemy held on, breaking contact the following day.

Late on the twenty-first Colonel Adamson's headquarters lost radio contact with a long-range reconnaissance patrol near the border, and the next morning he sent two of Granger's companies overland to find it. Each split into two columns, and all four soon met a battalion of the *95B*

---

[19] AAR, Opn SAM HOUSTON, 4th Inf Div, pp. 9–10; Intel Sum 3–183, 4th Inf Div, 15 Mar 67, Historians files, CMH; Msgs, Peers PKU 230 to Larsen, 12 Mar 67, sub: Action: 2/35—12 Mar 67, and Peers PKU 233 to Larsen, 13 Mar 67, sub: Results of 12 Mar 67 Action, both in Westmoreland Message files, CMH; Interv, author with Granger, 15 Nov 85.

[20] AAR, Opn SAM HOUSTON, 4th Inf Div, Incl 9; Critique, Opn SAM HOUSTON, 4th Inf Div, pp. 4, 41; Interv, author with Peers, 21 Oct 75.

[21] AAR, Opn SAM HOUSTON, 4th Inf Div, pp. 17–18 and Incl 10; Interv, author with Maj Gen James B. Adamson, Comdr, 2d Bde, 4th Inf Div, 4 Apr 79, Historians files, CMH.

Regiment. The four withstood repeated assaults until the North Vietnamese slipped across the border. So hastily did the enemy pull out that he left behind 136 dead. American losses were 27 killed and 48 wounded in addition to the long-range patrol, which was never found.[22]

Shortly after the 2d Brigade moved into the Plei Doc, the 1st Brigade began withdrawing from the Plei Trap in the belief that no major enemy forces remained. Late on the afternoon of the twenty-first, however, a North Vietnamese force waiting in ambush west of the Se San caught a company in a murderous crossfire. Within an hour, 22 Americans were dead and 53 wounded. The arrival of reinforcements before dark saved the remnant. A sweep of the battle area yielded only 18 enemy dead.

Although the *B3 Front* obviously still had troops in the Plei Trap Valley, General Peers saw no point in trying to root them out. With the oncoming rainy season about to turn the mountains and valleys into quagmires, prudence dictated a pullback to await the enemy's next move. By 28 March all major American units had left the valley. The next morning American engineers removed the bridge spanning the Se San.

Soon afterward Peers replaced the 2d Brigade with the 1st in the Plei Doc and continued to screen the border. Since the former had experienced most of the heavy fighting, it was ready for rest and refitting, although while in reserve he gave it the additional mission of assisting the South Vietnamese in moving some 2,500 Montagnard families from the border regions west of Pleiku into a resettlement area not far from Duc Co.[23]

At the same time the 4th Division began to dismantle its huge base at 3 TANGO. The installation was overstocked with supplies and equipment that had accumulated since October. Anxious to maintain stockage levels as required for a forward facility, logisticians at Camp Holloway had insisted on keeping three days of supplies at the base. Despite repeated division requests to end the requirement in anticipation of the shift to the Plei Doc, the stockage level remained unchanged until 29 March. Only after that date did it gradually decline by attrition. Consequently, General Peers had to employ an average equivalent of two rifle companies to secure 3 TANGO for the next ten days until the base could be closed. During that period supplies clogged the roads and placed a heavy burden on helicopters. The lesson sank in, for shortly afterward Peers was allowed to set his division's stockage levels rather than having them determined by a logistics officer two headquarters removed.[24]

---

[22] AAR, Opn SAM HOUSTON, 4th Inf Div, Incl 10; Intel Sums 3–272, 4th Inf Div, 23 Mar 67, and 3–282, 4th Inf Div, 24 Mar 67, both in Historians files, CMH; Intervs, author with Adamson, 4 Apr 79, and with Granger, 15 Nov 85.

[23] AAR, Opn SAM HOUSTON, 4th Inf Div, p. 18, and Incl 10; Interv, author with Peers, 21 Oct 75; MFR, MACCORDS-RE, 22 Jul 67, sub: Edap Enang Resettlement Project, Historians files, CMH.

[24] AAR, Opn SAM HOUSTON, 4th Inf Div, p. 18; Critique, Opn SAM HOUSTON, 4th Inf Div, pp. 5, 33, 41, 54; Interv, author with Peers, 21 Oct 75.

Cases of ammunition and "C" rations are stockpiled at Camp Holloway. A CH–47 Chinook stands ready for loading.

SAM HOUSTON ended on 5 April. In a number of ways it resembled the 4th Division's previous campaign, PAUL REVERE IV. Fought mainly in the Plei Trap during the dry season, both operations seemed to blunt an impending *B3 Front* offensive and drove the North Vietnamese regulars back into Cambodia. General Peers called SAM HOUSTON "eminently successful," and Colonel Adamson, the 2d Brigade commander, pointed out that "we sought the contact and every battle was the direct result of our tactical movements. At no time was the NVA the aggressor."[25]

It was true that the North Vietnamese took fairly heavy casualties—as they always did when the Americans called in air and artillery strikes. But in reality the enemy controlled the fighting, able to choose when he would stand and fight and when he would flee across the border. Combat in the highlands consisted of a series of sharp border fights waged under a jungle canopy that minimized American firepower while maximizing enemy opportunities for ambush.

American casualties verified this disadvantage. SAM HOUSTON cost the 4th Division dearly, over 200 more killed and wounded in ten fewer days of operations than during PAUL REVERE IV, with enemy losses in killed

[25] Critique, Opn SAM HOUSTON, 4th Inf Div, pp. 1, 14.

175

A battery of 105-mm. howitzers uses high-angle fire in the western highlands.

and captured at nearly 200 fewer. A change in North Vietnamese tactics made the difference. Earlier, the North Vietnamese had habitually attacked prepared defenses, as Viet Cong troops had often done in III Corps. In SAM HOUSTON they avoided set-piece ground assaults and relied instead on ambush. Patiently watching while American units cut noisily through the thick undergrowth, they struck again and again from ground of their own choosing, often close to the safety of Cambodia. Nine of the eleven major engagements during SAM HOUSTON occurred within five kilometers of the border.[26]

The North Vietnamese also learned that the best way to save themselves from B–52s was to move close to the Americans. Flying in groups of three, the bombers usually targeted a "box," 1 by 3 kilometers; but the bombs often strayed, necessitating a 3-kilometer safety zone outside each target box. All major fights west of the Nam Sathay during SAM HOUSTON took place within 3 kilometers of U.S. firebases, the safety margin established for B–52s.[27]

As enemy tactics became more discerning, the Americans continued to rely on massed firepower. During SAM HOUSTON the 4th Division fired over 230,000 rounds of artillery and employed 2,500 tactical air sorties and thirty-one B–52 ARC LIGHT strikes. The figures represented an increase over PAUL REVERE IV of about 100,000 artillery rounds, but a

---

[26] AAR, Opn SAM HOUSTON, 4th Inf Div, pp. 19, 22, 50. Reported enemy losses for SAM HOUSTON were 733 killed and 17 captured. U.S. losses were 169 dead and 720 wounded.

[27] Ibid., p. 43.

decrease of 200 tactical air sorties and one B–52 mission. Most of the increased artillery fire was against suspected rather than specifically identified targets.

The decrease in fighter-bomber sorties was due to the difficulty forward air controllers had in locating friendly forces under the jungle canopy. Colored marking smoke would frequently dissipate before reaching the tops of trees; hotter burning white phosphorous grenades drove the smoke through the canopy faster but still took up to thirty seconds to penetrate and were also subject to wind and weather. Artillery had its own problems, not just the delays in bringing it to bear with any accuracy during ambushes, but, as Peers remarked, the tendency of too many infantry and artillery commanders to skimp during actual firefights. For his part, Peers wanted the jungle to explode.[28]

Ultimately, the campaign drove three enemy regiments from the Plei Trap Valley and a fourth from the Plei Doc, frustrating any plans the *B3 Front* may have had to launch more ambitious ventures. But in the end SAM HOUSTON was simply another—and this time, more expensive—exercise in hide-and-seek with the North Vietnamese. It was becoming clear that the enemy really controlled the fighting near the border, making it a costly proposition to send American units there.[29]

Shortly after SAM HOUSTON ended, General Peers sent long-range reconnaissance patrols to screen the border, leaving his maneuver battalions to regroup west of Pleiku, but at a considerable distance from the Cambodian frontier. It seemed to make more sense to stand back and force the enemy to commit troops away from his sanctuaries before striking at them. Peers pointed out that "there was little to be gained" from stationing forces permanently in the Plei Trap, but old habits were hard to break. Instead of standing back from the border, the 4th Division commander made it clear that despite the many disadvantages of fighting there he would return to the region to "engage the NVA whenever he sallies forth in strength."[30] For Peers, containing the enemy's conventional units on the border would remain the objective throughout his stay in the 4th Division.

---

[28] Critique, Opn SAM HOUSTON, 4th Inf Div, p. 47.

[29] AAR, Opn PAUL REVERE IV, 4th Inf Div, pp. 12–13; AAR, Opn SAM HOUSTON, 4th Inf Div, pp. 4–6.

[30] AAR, Opn SAM HOUSTON, 4th Inf Div, p. 49.

The Lowlands: Signs of Success

At the close of 1966 American operations in Binh Dinh had turned a once-secure enemy stronghold into a dangerous place where Viet Cong and North Vietnamese units operated only at great peril. "The northeast Binh Dinh Province campaign succeeded in virtually eliminating enemy control over the lowland population south of the Lai Giang River," declared one official report.[1] Although the province was a traditional stronghold of Communist support, its distance from the supply lines of the Ho Chi Minh Trail made it one of the most difficult for enemy forces to exploit.

As the year turned, the time seemed right for more big operations to harass and hopefully destroy the enemy in coastal II Corps. February and March saw a gradual weakening of the northeast monsoon in eastern Binh Dinh, with the rains turning into little more than light showers. At the same time, American troop strength was climbing. With operations in the western highlands winding down, I Field Force could afford to augment the ongoing operations of General Norton's 1st Cavalry Division, which was still in the process of cleaning out eastern Binh Dinh. In January 1967 the 3d Brigade, 25th Division, arrived from Pleiku, and Norton looked forward to launching Operation PERSHING, a major offensive in the northern marches of Binh Dinh, scheduled to begin in February. This transfer would allow the Americans to put three brigades between the Siem Giang and Lai Giang Rivers to wind up Operation THAYER II and to strengthen their overall position for PERSHING the next month.

Previously, the 1st Cavalry Division had conducted only limited raids north of the Lai Giang. During Operation PERSHING, Norton planned to put two full brigades across the river. His first objective was to clear the entire Bong Son Plain of enemy forces; his second was the north-south An Lao Valley that paralleled the plain to the west.

The Bong Son Plain seemed like a vulnerable target. Enclosed on three sides by mountains and bordered on a fourth by the South China Sea, this rich agrarian flatland supported a population of nearly 100,000, mostly farmers and fishermen. It extended north twenty-five kilometers from the Lai

---

[1] CHECO Rpt, Opns THAYER/IRVING, PACAF, 12 May 67, p. 77, Historians files, CMH.

Giang to the Binh Dinh–Quang Ngai border but was only ten kilometers at its widest point. The An Lao Valley, whose entrance lay at the southern edge of the Bong Son, was separated from the plain by the Hon Go Mountains. Longer than the plain but much narrower, it supported perhaps 6,000 people.

Gearing Up for Operation PERSHING

To prepare for the move into northern Binh Dinh, General Norton continued to consolidate his position farther south during THAYER II. He assigned Colonel Shanahan's 3d Brigade of the 25th to the Suoi Ca and Vinh Thanh Valleys, regions known to contain an important enemy trail complex. Norton retained his 1st Brigade in the Kim Son Valley and assigned his 2d Brigade responsibility for the Cay Giep and Mieu Mountains in the northern sector. To improve control of these forces, on 9 January he established a forward division command post at HAMMOND, forty kilometers northwest of Qui Nhon.[2]

Ten days later, in the Suoi Ca Valley, patrols from one of Shanahan's units, the 1st Battalion, 14th Infantry, discovered a series of caves among large granite boulders. Erosion had caused the boulders to tumble into a steep draw, and they now "rested against each other like marbles in a jar." Double- and triple-canopied vegetation hid the caves from aerial observation. They turned out to be the insurgent political headquarters for Binh Dinh Province.[3]

The Americans heard the voices of women and children coming from one cave and ordered them out. When there was no response, a company commander and one of his sergeants crept in and found themselves in a large cavern. Suddenly, a shot rang out, and the company commander was killed; the sergeant dragged the body out. Immediately, the battalion commander, Lt. Col. William H. Miller, had his men surround the area and used tear gas and smoke grenades to flush out the cave. As the smoke swirled, the desperate Viet Cong fired rifles and lobbed grenades out of the entrance. Only after flamethrowers depleted the oxygen and suffocated those within did the resistance end.

Miller's men cautiously entered the cave and discovered many connecting tunnels that led to exits and storage areas for food, equipment, and ammunition. They found an unusual collection of records, including a complete local insurgent order of battle; personnel rosters; weapons and equipment lists; ammunition supply status reports; and a map showing the locations of caches throughout the province. The Americans also

---

[2] Msgs, Larsen A–2037 to Westmoreland, 21 Dec 66, sub: Visit of COMUSMACV, 21 December 1966, and Larsen A–0019 to Westmoreland, 2 Jan 67, sub: Visit of COMUS-MACV, 2 January 1967, both in Westmoreland History files, 12–A–5 and 12–B–3, CMH; AAR, Opn THAYER II, 1st Cav Div, pp. 38–43.

[3] AAR, Opn THAYER II, 3d Bde, 25th Inf Div, 25 Feb 67, pp. 34–40, Historians files, CMH.

General Norton (right) *and Army Vice Chief of Staff General Creighton W. Abrams*

uncovered several South Vietnamese Army documents, some classified and many uncomfortably accurate, containing information about allied installations. Two documents revealed the sophistication of the enemy's intelligence-gathering capability. One, classified "Top Secret" by the South Vietnamese, listed all radio frequencies and call signs for the province's paramilitary forces. The other was a lengthy study on military operations written in Vietnamese.

After the caves were thoroughly searched, engineers detonated charges in one cave, causing massive secondary explosions that blew a gap 100 meters long in the side of a hill. Over the next several days, repeated attempts to destroy the rest of the complex were only partially successful, so the engineers finally settled for sealing the entrances. In all, eight major complexes were either closed or destroyed.[4] (*Map 20*)

The brigade also assisted in removing over 2,600 civilians from the Suoi Ca Valley in early February. This effort, the second "area denial" operation that the South Vietnamese government had conducted in Binh Dinh Province within two months, was of questionable success. Although execution was relatively well organized, South Vietnamese officials failed to consider their limited capability to care for the displaced persons. Nearby refugee camps, already overcrowded from earlier operations, absorbed the new arrivals with great difficulty. Confronted with unsanitary facilities, unemployment, and a callous government attitude, many peasants quietly returned to their Suoi Ca homes over the next several months.

As usual, bad weather hindered both combat and logistical operations. The main supply route for the 1st Cavalry Division during THAYER II had extended north from Qui Nhon over Highway 1 to HAMMOND. In December a second supply base was built at Firebase ENGLISH, on the southern Bong Son Plain, just five kilometers north of the Lai Giang, to support the 2d Brigade. Washouts along Highway 1 between HAMMOND

---

[4] Ibid.; ORLL, 1 Nov 66–31 Jan 67, IFFV, p. 6; Intervs, author with Shanahan, 13 Aug and 4 Sep 81, and with Moore, 4 Aug 81.

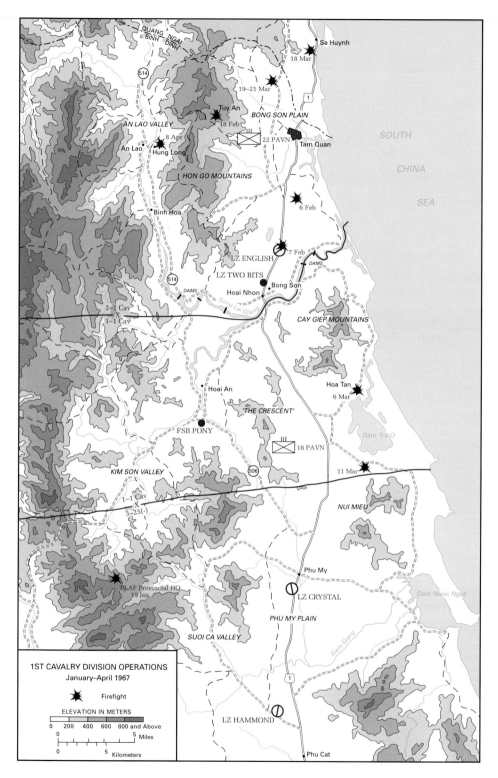

SOUTH

CHINA

SEA

Sa Huynh
18 Mar

19–21 Mar

QUANG NGAI
BINH DINH

514

Tuy An
18 Feb

AN LAO VALLEY

BONG SON PLAIN

8 Apr

An Lao

Hung Long

22 PAVN

Tam Quan

HON GO MOUNTAINS

Binh Hoa

6 Feb

7 Feb

LZ ENGLISH

DAMS

LZ TWO BITS

514

Bong Son

DAMS

Hoai Nhon

Song Lai Giang

2–1 Cav

1–1 Cav

CAY GIEP MOUNTAINS

Hoai An

Hoa Tan
6 Mar

'THE CRESCENT'

Dam Tra O

FSB PONY

18 PAVN

KIM SON VALLEY

506

11 Mar

NUI MIEU

1–1 Cav

3–25 (–)

PLAF Provincial HQ
19 Jan

Phu My

LZ CRYSTAL

Dam Nuoc Ngot

PHU MY PLAIN

SUOI CA VALLEY

Siem Giang

1ST CAVALRY DIVISION OPERATIONS
January–April 1967

Firefight

ELEVATION IN METERS

0 200 400 600 800 and Above

0   5   Miles

0   5   Kilometers

LZ HAMMOND

1

Phu Cat

MAP 20

and ENGLISH late in December, however, made the road impassable until 10 January, forcing the 2d Brigade to depend on aerial delivery at ENGLISH's hastily constructed runway. A combination of heavy rain and air traffic soon reduced the top layer of earth under the airstrip's steel matting to a thin mud that squirted up through the mesh and obscured the pilots' vision and made the runway extremely slippery. Deep ruts quickly developed underneath the steel surface, forcing the partial closure of the aerial supply terminal throughout January. Because of ENGLISH's unreliability as a fixed-wing supply base, the 1st Cavalry Division increased its normal three-day stockage level at HAMMOND to five days as insurance against heavy rains washing out the roads. It also stationed CH–47 Chinooks at HAMMOND to transport any logistical shortfall forward to ENGLISH.[5]

Norton decided against moving farther north until ENGLISH became fully operational and had a dependable runway. Instead, while waiting for resolution of his logistical challenges, he directed his 2d Brigade to support South Vietnamese 22d Division operations around ENGLISH. During the last two weeks of January the South Vietnamese fought two major battles against the *7th* and *8th Battalions* of the *22d PAVN Regiment* and, with timely American assistance, claimed to have killed or captured over 250 enemy soldiers.

Then, on 2 February Norton received an agent report indicating that two enemy battalions would attack PONY, an American firebase in the northern Kim Son Valley, sometime during the next seven days. In view of what had happened at BIRD in the same general area, Norton reacted quickly and airlifted the 3d Brigade headquarters with one battalion from Camp Radcliff to PONY. No longer could he afford to have a brigade defend his division base at An Khe. A reinforced battalion would have to suffice.

Another intelligence source, a defector from the *9th Battalion* of the *22d Regiment*, revealed that his unit was understrength but had plenty of ammunition and was planning to attack ENGLISH after the Tet truce, between 8 and 12 February. Norton strengthened the base's defenses and deployed additional 2d Brigade units around it.

A third piece of information, this provided by U.S. signal intelligence, pinpointed the command post of the *3d PAVN Division* in the An Lao Valley. Capturing such an important target would be a significant coup, and Norton sent an entire battalion to locate and destroy it. Although unable to find the actual headquarters, the American force came upon a major enemy supply base containing several tons of food and supplies.

On 6 February the South Vietnamese 40th Regiment, 22d Division, met an enemy battalion four kilometers north of ENGLISH and routed it in a short, violent fight. Accompanying U.S. advisers reported counting over 100 enemy dead. Still able to strike back, however, early the next morning

---

[5] AAR, Opn THAYER II, 1st Cav Div, pp. 8, 34–44, 50–52.

the enemy mortared ENGLISH, killing or wounding 52 soldiers and damaging 5 helicopters. Although the enemy probed the perimeter, he did not follow up with a ground assault.[6]

An uneasy, five-day Tet truce began at 0800 on 8 February. Unconfirmed reports still predicted a North Vietnamese attack against ENGLISH, during or immediately after the truce. Meanwhile, U.S. reconnaissance units, both ground and air, venturing near the base, continued to draw fire. That afternoon an enemy force of unknown size attacked an American unit in the Mieu Mountains between ENGLISH and HAMMOND. The 2d Brigade pursued with two battalions but failed to make contact.

Throughout these inconclusive engagements, General Norton impatiently waited at his new command post at TWO BITS, three kilometers south of ENGLISH, for the truce to end. During THAYER II, which now had lasted about two and a half months before officially ending on 12 February 1967, he had steadily worn down the *3d Division*, driving its *2d PLAF Regiment* out of Binh Dinh Province and severely damaging its *18th* and *22d PAVN Regiments*. Altogether, his troops had reported killing or capturing well over 2,000 enemy soldiers. Now they found themselves sitting idle, while the rest of the North Vietnamese division either fled from their grasp or, more ominously, seemed prepared to strike back.[7]

Operation PERSHING—The Bong Son Offensive

Realizing that ENGLISH, crammed full of supplies, presented an inviting target and that its loss or even partial destruction would seriously delay the pacification of northern Binh Dinh Province, Norton wanted to begin Operation PERSHING earlier than planned, before the truce ended. While awaiting permission for the move, he revised his operational concept. Instead of placing his forces on the high ground west and north of the plain and then sweeping north from the Lai Giang River with other units, a rather ambitious undertaking, he decided to limit his objective to trapping and eventually destroying the *22d Regiment*, thought to be located within a five to ten kilometer radius north of ENGLISH.

Norton chose to air-assault Colonel Casey's 2d Brigade into landing sites nine kilometers north of ENGLISH. Once on the ground, three battalions would move south, pushing the *22d Regiment* into an anvil formed by Casey's fourth battalion augmented by two battalions from the South Vietnamese 40th Regiment. At the same time Col. James S. Smith's 1st Brigade would fly one battalion north of Casey's attacking units to trap any enemy units in that direction. Probing northward, Smith would send two companies into the foothills of the Hon Go Mountains, cutting

---

[6] Periodic Intel Rpts 4, IFFV, n.d., pp. 1–9; 5, IFFV, n.d., pp. 2, 5–8; and 6, IFFV, n.d., pp. 5, 7–9, an. A. All in Historians files, CMH. Intervs, author with Norton, 1–2 Sep 83.

[7] AAR, Opn THAYER II, 1st Cav Div, pp. 49, 57; Intervs, author with Norton, 1–2 Sep 83, 2 Dec 83.

Men of the 1st Cavalry Division on a landing zone during Operation PERSHING

off any escape west into the An Lao Valley. The rest of the battalion would remain in reserve.

Norton's remaining two brigades would stay on the defensive. The 3d Brigade, under a new commander, Col. Jonathan R. Burton, used its single remaining battalion to hold the Highway 1 bridge over the Lai Giang just south of ENGLISH. Colonel Shanahan's 3d Brigade, 25th Division, was to hold the Kim Son and Suoi Ca Valleys south of the river.

Norton intended to smash the *22d Regiment*. When he did, he would shift the bulk of his forces north of ENGLISH to clear the enemy out of the Bong Son Plain and the An Lao. From there he could sweep into southern Quang Ngai Province and go after both the *3d Division* headquarters and the *2d Regiment*.[8]

Late on the afternoon of 10 February Westmoreland approved the plan. PERSHING was to begin at 1100 on 11 February, nineteen hours before the end of the Tet truce. Norton immediately ordered his troops to move out.[9] At 1100 gunships and troop-filled helicopters flew toward their assigned objectives. The final phase of the 1st Cavalry Division's Binh Dinh pacification campaign had begun.

[8] AAR, Opn PERSHING, 1st Cav Div, 29 Jun 68, p. 7, Historians files, CMH; Intervs, author with Norton, 1–2 Sep 83, 2 Dec 83.

[9] AAR, Opn PERSHING, 1st Cav Div, pp. 1–7; Intervs, author with Norton, 1–2 Sep 83, 2 Dec 83.

As the waves of helicopters flying north of ENGLISH signaled an abrupt end to the Tet truce, many enemy soldiers caught without weapons rushed from hamlets to seek safety in the jungle. Gunships hovering overhead cut many of them down; others waited until after dark to slip away.

Farther north, cavalrymen from the 2d Brigade leaped from their Hueys and began to search the hamlets to the south. Bulldozers moved forward from ENGLISH along Highway 1 to assist in collapsing bunkers and tunnels. Although a few captured North Vietnamese soldiers indicated that large numbers of their comrades were hiding nearby, the cavalrymen could not find them. As groups of refugees began clogging the roads and slowing the U.S. advance, local Viet Cong forces skillfully covered the withdrawal of their North Vietnamese comrades.

After the first day the tactical momentum gained by Colonel Casey's 2d Brigade melted away. Known enemy losses on 11 February were about 50 dead, but as the week proceeded the daily count dropped markedly. By 17 February the Americans were losing at least one soldier for every dead enemy claimed. Booby traps and mines along trails on the fringes of the hamlets accounted for most U.S. casualties. As the number of contacts with enemy units diminished, PERSHING appeared to be turning into another arduous, drawn-out sweep.[10]

Not until the second week of PERSHING did the 1st Cavalry Division engage a major enemy unit. The action began late on the afternoon of 18 February, when a rifle company from Smith's 1st Brigade found the *22d Regiment's 9th Battalion* in a fortified hamlet, Tuy An, at the base of the mountains west of Tam Quan. The normal confusion of combat combined with approaching darkness made it impossible for reinforcing units to encircle the enemy, and the Americans lost contact before midnight. Artillery fire on Tuy An produced the only results. When infantrymen entered the hamlet the following morning, they found 6 bodies in the rubble. Documents seized included sketches of ENGLISH and the Lai Giang bridge. Nine days later Smith's men attacked an element of the *9th Battalion*, two kilometers from Tuy An, and killed another 19 of the enemy.

While 1st Cavalry Division operations throughout January and February focused on destroying the *22d*, its sister regiment, the *18th PAVN*, located somewhere south of the Lai Giang, enjoyed a respite. During December Norton's men had severely mauled the unit, its discipline and morale broken to the extent that the *3d Division* considered the *18th* the least reliable of its three regiments. But after receiving replacements and undergoing extensive retraining, the *18th* was again prepared to fight.

On 6 March an air cavalry pilot on a routine dawn patrol north of the Tra O Marsh, sixteen kilometers southeast of ENGLISH, spotted a man disappearing into a foxhole outside a hamlet, Hoa Tan. While one helicopter

---

[10] AAR, Opn PERSHING, 1st Cav Div, pp. 7–8; ORLL, 1 Feb–30 Apr 67, 1st Cav Div, 23 May 67, pp. 18–19, 28–29, Historians files, CMH.

orbited above, a second landed within ten meters of the foxhole in a bold, perhaps foolhardy, attempt to capture the man for questioning. Rifle fire erupted from a nearby hedgerow and pierced the idling helicopter's hydraulic system. Although the pilot was able to coax his ship off the ground to land among sand dunes 800 meters away, a door gunner, who had leaped from the helicopter, was left behind. The second helicopter radioed for help and dropped to tree level to keep the enemy busy.

The commander of the 1st Squadron, 9th Cavalry, Lt. Col. A. I. T. Pumphrey, quickly ordered one of his aero-rifle "blue team" platoons stationed at Two Bits to rescue the abandoned door gunner and then investigate the situation around Hoa Tan. Gunships holding over the hamlet met the team, led the way to the stranded door gunner, and soon rescued him. Moments later the platoon moved on the hamlet and ran into heavy enemy fire.

Using the traditional airmobile "piling on" tactic, Colonel Shanahan's 3d Brigade sent units into the area. During the day five rifle companies formed a loose cordon around the hamlet, while a mixture of artillery, gunships, and fighter-bombers kept the enemy under fire.

Early the next morning, following a lengthy artillery bombardment, the Americans moved into Hoa Tan and met only feeble resistance. A lone North Vietnamese survivor revealed that the headquarters and two rifle companies from the *9th Battalion, 18th Regiment*, had been there at the beginning of the fight but had escaped during the night. North Vietnamese losses were 82 known dead, while 7 Americans were killed.[11]

On 8 March, concluding that the remainder of the *18th Regiment* might be in the Cay Giep Mountains northwest of Hoa Tan, General Norton sent his 2d Brigade on the heels of a B–52 strike. The search proved futile, and after three unproductive days he shifted operations farther south.

The enemy, as one rifle company soon discovered, could be found and engaged, but often only on his own terms. Shortly before noon on 11 March Company C of the 2d Battalion, 5th Cavalry, conducted an uncontested air assault south of the Tra O Marsh. As the last Huey departed and the men were organizing their sweep, a North Vietnamese company concealed in foliage around the landing zone sprang a trap. Within seconds hostile fire had cut down several Americans, and enemy soldiers had charged into Company C. So closely intermingled were the two forces that artillery and gunships were useless. For a time the outcome was in doubt, until two other companies arrived and forced the enemy to withdraw. American losses were 19 killed and 25 wounded, while the North Vietnamese left 10 dead soldiers behind.[12]

[11] AAR, Opn PERSHING, 3d Bde, 25th Inf Div, 1 May 67, Incl 1, and Unit Historical Rpt 9, Office of Information and History, 1st Cav Div, 7 Aug 67, sub: The Battle for Hoa Tan (1), both in Historians files, CMH; Intervs, author with Shanahan, 13 Aug 81, 4 Sep 81, and with Moore, 4 Aug 81.

[12] Interv, author with Moore, 4 Aug 81; ORLL, 1 Feb–30 Apr 67, 1st Cav Div, p. 28.

For another week Colonel Casey's 2d Brigade continued its fruitless searches. Only after the brigade had returned north to the Bong Son on 20 March did the South Vietnamese 41st Regiment, 22d Division, find the other two battalions of the *18th Regiment*—the *8th Battalion* southeast of Phu My and the *7th Battalion* west of HAMMOND. In two firefights the government troops netted some 50 enemy dead and 3 prisoners, but thereafter the enemy unit again dropped out of sight.[13]

Meanwhile, to the north of the Lai Giang, the *22d Regiment* continued to avoid battle. While its *8th Battalion* fled across the Hon Go Mountains into the An Lao, the rest of the regiment moved north into the upper reaches of the Bong Son Plain. The North Vietnamese hid themselves so well during the first half of March that neither Burton's 3d Brigade in the An Lao nor Smith's 1st Brigade in the Bong Son could find any trace of them.

This frustrating situation changed shortly after midnight on 18 March, when a Popular Forces outpost at Sa Huynh, a small port north of the Binh Dinh–Quang Ngai border, reported human-wave attacks by an estimated two battalions that threatened to overrun its position. Believing that the attackers were from the *22d Regiment*, Norton shifted Smith's brigade into the hills west of Sa Huynh to intercept. Captured documents later revealed that the attackers were actually the *3d Division*'s sapper battalion. Although the sappers escaped, the Americans were primed for an encounter with their real target, the *22d PAVN*.

The following evening, 19 March, while looking for a place to settle in after a hot, unproductive day in the jungle, one of Smith's rifle companies stumbled upon an enemy unit in Truong Son hamlet, eighteen kilometers north of ENGLISH. Since the size of the enemy force was unknown, the company formed a perimeter as a firefight erupted. Within a half hour its commander realized he had uncovered a major element, and he radioed for help.

Colonel Smith responded by dispatching four companies overland through the darkness toward Truong Son in an attempt to seal the enemy inside the hamlet. At the same time a helicopter hovered overhead, illuminating the enemy's positions with flares, while gunships raced in to add rockets and machine guns to the incoming artillery fire.

Back at TWO BITS, General Norton decided to reinforce before the enemy could escape north into Quang Ngai Province. Time was critical. The only way to keep the enemy in place was by blocking his exits with a night air assault—a risky business that was rarely attempted. After Norton transferred a battalion from the 3d to the 1st Brigade, Smith dispatched the better part of the unit to the battle area just after midnight.

Four hours later a prisoner from the *22d Regiment*'s reconnaissance company revealed that his mission had been to find escape routes for the North Vietnamese regimental headquarters, its signal and support companies, and its *9th Battalion*. The information made the size of the enemy force known to Norton for the first time.

[13] ORLL, 1 Feb–30 Apr 67, IFFV, 30 May 67, Historians files, CMH.

At dawn Colonel Smith sent additional units to seal off the area. One started a fight with the *22d's 7th Battalion* south of Truong Son. The new action prompted Norton to shift units from his 2d Brigade northward across the Lai Giang with bulldozers to help destroy enemy bunkers. In all, the 1st Cavalry Division had now committed thirteen rifle companies from five different battalions.

Yet, for all Norton's efforts to entrap the North Vietnamese, the *22d* escaped once more. The force surrounded at Truong Son succeeded in breaking off during the evening of 20 March, and the *7th Battalion* did the same twenty-four hours later. Subsequent sweeps through both areas produced a count of over 120 enemy dead for the three-day struggle, compared to 34 Americans killed. Nevertheless, by early April it was evident that the *22d* had slipped north into the mountains of southern Quang Ngai with only its *8th Battalion* remaining in Binh Dinh, shunning combat and well hidden in the An Lao Valley.[14]

Late in March a battalion from the 3d Brigade moved into the northern end of the An Lao in an attempt to find a North Vietnamese unit reported lurking there. As the Americans probed southward they encountered small groups of enemy soldiers attempting to escape, but not until 8 April did they come upon the main body of the *22d Regiment's 8th Battalion* in the recently abandoned hamlet of Hung Long. The 3d Brigade commander, Colonel Burton, quickly fed four additional companies and a tank platoon into the area.

The tanks were a temporary addition to the 1st Cavalry Division. Received on 30 March from the 4th Division, they required careful route reconnaissance and shallow stream fords but succeeded in holding down U.S. losses at Hung Long. Catching the enemy unprepared to cope with armor, they spearheaded the attack and contributed to a body count of 78, before the remaining enemy soldiers fled north into Quang Ngai Province.

The Refugee Issue

American and South Vietnamese forces in the Bong Son and An Lao had intended to keep the local population in place throughout PERSHING. That proved difficult. By mid-March over 12,000 of the area's inhabitants had left their homes voluntarily to seek the safety of government-secured areas south of ENGLISH and around Tam Quan City, where the Americans had provided food and shelter for refugees.

Compounding the problem, on 15 March the South Vietnamese 22d Division decided to launch a third and final area denial operation in Binh Dinh, this time in the An Lao Valley. For four days the South Vietnamese

---

[14] AAR, Opn PERSHING, 1st Cav Div, tab 6; CDEC, no. 06–3390–67, 18 Jun 67, sub: Combat Journal of 9th Bn, 22d NVA Regt, 3d Div, Historians files, CMH.

Army warned the people through leaflets and loudspeakers. Then, while units of Norton's 3d Brigade screened the high ground on either side of the valley, two Vietnamese marine battalions, chosen because they had no home ties in the region, moved north up the defile. Trailed by a long convoy of empty trucks, the marines loaded people and their possessions and sent them south. Reaching the north end of the valley within a week, they turned back south and swept stragglers and resisters into the waiting camps while destroying everything of value. In spite of those efforts, only 3,800 of an estimated 6,000 valley residents were found and evacuated.

Denial operations continued for the next three months in both the An Lao and Kim Son Valleys, resulting in the removal of 12,000 more civilians. In addition, the South Vietnamese reported killing 182 Viet Cong, capturing 152, and convincing another 399 to rally. By July there were close to 140,000 refugees in Binh Dinh Province, so stretching the government's ability to care for them that further population relocations had to be discontinued.[15]

Area denial operations were actually an essential part of Norton's campaign against the *3d Division*, particularly since he had the battered force in full retreat. With the civilians gone from the An Lao, Kim Son, and Suoi Ca Valleys, he could place unrestricted fire into those areas if the enemy ever returned. In addition, the *3d Division* would not have a ready source of food and laborers from which to draw. Using a minimum force to screen the valleys, Norton could continue pressing north to complete the destruction of the *3d Division* in southern Quang Ngai Province. But the ugly process of evacuation and destruction obviously made few friends for the Americans and the South Vietnamese government among the peasantry.

Success at Last

By the end of the 1966–1967 rainy season, the *3d Division* seemed on the verge of collapse. MACV estimates during 1966 had placed the division's strength at over 11,000, nearly twice the size of most enemy divisions in South Vietnam. By April 1967, however, despite the cannibalization of many of its support elements to fill the infantry units and the arrival of large numbers of replacements from North Vietnam, the division would remain ineffective for most of the year.

The departure of the *3d Division* from the Binh Dinh plain, the heartland of the Communist movement in central Vietnam, clearly represented a major setback for the revolutionary movement. The unwillingness of the division to stand and fight may have surprised the local inhabitants, but taking on the Americans was now recognized as suicidal. During THAYER II alone, of the 194 enemy soldiers captured, 70 had been North

---

[15] AAR, Opn PERSHING, 1st Cav Div, tab 30; ORLL, 1 Feb–30 Apr 67, 1st Cav Div, pp. 29, 49–51; RD Rpt, Binh Dinh Province, Jul 67, n.d., Historians files, CMH.

Engineers clear a stretch of Highway 1 in Binh Dinh Province.

Vietnamese.[16] Most of those who surrendered reported low morale in their units, acute shortages of food and medicines, and a lack of confidence in their leaders.

As General Norton became more aware of the North Vietnamese plight, so too had the commander of the *3d Division*, Col. Le Truc. In a message to his subordinate commanders in December 1966, he noted that "new difficulties have beset us" including "continuing attacks, serious casualties, and attacks upon our rear bases." He complained of a "considerable increase" in the number of "shirkers," many of whom "surrender and betray us." Discipline had to be restored immediately, even if it became necessary to "purge the ranks of undesirables."[17] As Norton's men persisted in grinding down the *3d PAVN* still further during the next three months, Truc's superiors decided to replace him.

Local Viet Cong forces in Binh Dinh were also in disarray. Having been firmly entrenched throughout the province for a generation, they were quickly losing their traditional areas of support. Of particular concern to the Communist province chief was the loss of the Siem Giang Valley and the Bong Son Plain. In the 1st Cavalry Division operational

---

[16] AAR, Opn THAYER II, 1st Cav Div, p. 49.

[17] Rpt, MACV J–2 Log 06–2289–67, 25 Jun 67, sub: TRANSLATION REPORT; Title: Objectives and Requirements for Security Mission in 1967—[3d NVA Div], Historians files, CMH.

area, General Norton estimated that 80 percent of the people had been removed from insurgent influence, at least temporarily, although they were not necessarily under the control of the South Vietnamese government. The enemy's military forces had been defeated, Norton correctly noted, but the political battle was still being fought.

Cautious optimism on the part of the U.S. advisers in Binh Dinh was evident in the province's Hamlet Evaluation System, or HES, report for April 1967. The HES reports estimated that 68 percent (660,000) of the people of Binh Dinh lived in areas under government control; another 14 percent resided in contested areas; while the remaining 18 percent still lived in regions under Communist domination. Six months earlier, in October 1966, General Westmoreland had reported that "only 22 percent of the population of Binh Dinh Province is considered secure." Whatever the long-term prospect, this apparent success was considered the most important turnaround in any province.[18]

The Expanding Korean Tactical Area

Part of the success achieved in Binh Dinh Province was due to forces that the Republic of Korea had sent. The combined campaign plan for 1967 had designated Qui Nhon, Binh Dinh's capital and major port, and the surrounding territory as II Corps' top priority. Along with the other coastal provinces—Phu Yen, Khanh Hoa, Ninh Thuan, and Binh Thuan—Qui Nhon was to be the focus of allied operations. Although not formally specified in the plan, the Koreans had primary responsibility for keeping the enemy main forces away from the lowlands and for rooting out the Viet Cong from Qui Nhon south to Cam Ranh Bay.[19]

Although both the South Korean Army's Capital and 9th Divisions were at full strength by November 1966, only the Capital Division had waged a major campaign, and then with only two of its regiments. Beginning in January the two divisions launched separate operations, the forerunners of a joint campaign that by June would extend the South Korean Army's responsibility from the Phu Cat area in Binh Dinh Province south to the Ninh Thuan–Binh Thuan border, a distance of nearly three hundred kilometers. Veering inland from the coast to depths varying from ten to fifty kilometers, this area contained 80 percent of the II Corps National Priority Area and the bulk of the region's population. (*Map 21*)

---

[18] HES Data Book, 1967, p. II–20. Quote from MACV Briefing Bk for Sec Def, J–3 Briefing, tab 4. The *3d PAVN Division*'s official history covering January–April 1967 notes that "hunger, raggedness, sickness, bombs, and bullets dogged the footsteps of every soldier." See *3d Division*, p. 67.

[19] CCP 1967, Incls 4, 5. For a general account of South Korean forces in South Vietnam, see Lt. Gen. Stanley R. Larsen and Brig. Gen. James L. Collins, Jr., *Allied Participation in Vietnam*, Vietnam Studies (Washington, D.C.: Department of the Army, 1975), pp. 120–57.

The Capital Division moved first. Operation MAENG HO ("Fierce Tiger") 8 began on 5 January, when the untested 26th Regiment pushed south from Qui Nhon toward Phu Yen. As the Koreans slowly advanced, enemy main force units, including the *5th PAVN's 95th Regiment*, refused to risk battle; they retreated inland followed by many civilians.

Wanting to keep the people in place, the Koreans sent troops ahead by helicopter to stop the refugees. The move yielded an unexpected dividend: while containing the civilians, it also trapped many North Vietnamese and Viet Cong soldiers trying to escape disguised as peasants.

Unsuccessful in enticing the enemy into combat, the Koreans spent two months in population control and conducted a series of cordon and search operations, a technique at which they excelled. Unlike the Americans, who were always anxious to move on, the Koreans went about their business meticulously. With field manual precision the Koreans moved quietly by night into preselected positions around a targeted hamlet and blocked its exits by placing concertina wire across paths and streambeds, which they then manned with fire teams and squads. At first light they would enter the hamlet, collect all the inhabitants in a safe central location, and segregate them according to age and sex. Then, using Vietnamese interpreters, they would question the women and children usually in two separate groups, offering inducements of food, medicine, money, candy, and cigarettes to elicit information. The Koreans habitually interrogated the men individually, using threats as well as bribes.

Other soldiers, meanwhile, systematically searched each structure in the hamlet. They took special care in examining straw piles, wells, attics, storehouses, and air-raid shelters. Normally, the Koreans would use different men to conduct a second or third search of an entire hamlet.

The Koreans did not rush to release the inhabitants, believing that if detained long enough they would provide the desired information. Only when satisfied that each household member was telling the truth would the commander allow the families to reunite. This process took hours, even days, but the Koreans were patient and usually able to persuade the inhabitants to point out Viet Cong dwellings and the location of weapons, booby traps, and equipment.

During MAENG HO 8 this tactic contributed to the elimination of over 600 enemy soldiers, 400 of whom became prisoners. The Communist "shadow government," active in the area for decades, also suffered. The Koreans seized many of its key members and kept others away from their homes. When notified of their return, the units reestablished the cordon and began the entire process anew.[20]

Equally impressive was the performance of the Korean 9th Division in northern Khanh Hoa. PENG MA ("White Horse") 1, beginning on 26 January, was the division's first major operation in Vietnam and

---

[20] ORLL, 1 Feb–30 Apr 67, IFFV, Incl 11; Op Sum, Opn MAENG HO 8, MACV–Military History Branch (MHB), 12 Feb 67, Historians files, CMH.

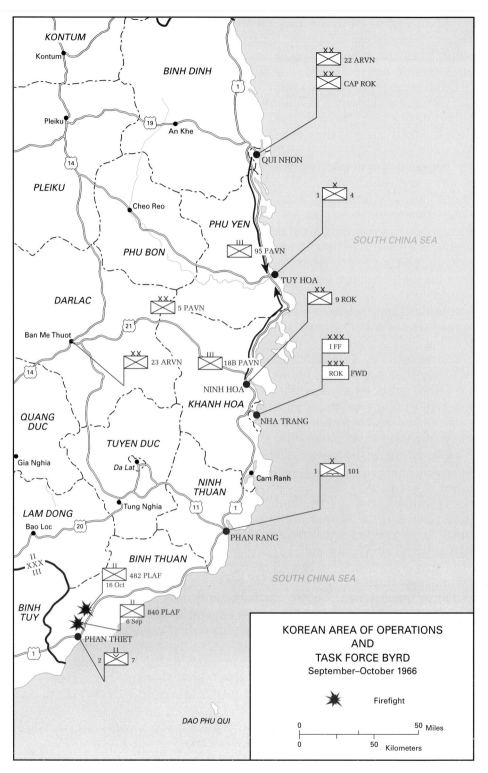

KONTUM

Kontum

BINH DINH

XX 22 ARVN

XX CAP ROK

Pleiku

19

An Khe

QUI NHON

PLEIKU

Cheo Reo

PHU YEN

X 1 4

SOUTH CHINA SEA

14

PHU BON

95 PAVN

TUY HOA

DARLAC

XX 5 PAVN

XX 9 ROK

21

Ban Me Thuot

XX 23 ARVN

18B PAVN

XXX I FF

XXX ROK FWD

14

NINH HOA

KHANH HOA

NHA TRANG

QUANG
DUC

TUYEN DUC

Gia Nghia

Da Lat

NINH
THUAN

Cam Ranh

X 1 101

Tung Nghia

11

1

LAM DONG

Bao Loc

20

PHAN RANG

II
XXX
III

BINH THUAN

482 PLAF

16 Oct

SOUTH CHINA SEA

BINH
TUY

840 PLAF

6 Sep

1

PHAN THIET

2 7

DAO PHU QUI

KOREAN AREA OF OPERATIONS
AND
TASK FORCE BYRD
September–October 1966

✴ Firefight

0   50 Miles

0   50 Kilometers

MAP 21

Korean troops near Cam Ranh Bay

involved four battalions that air-assaulted into the Hon Ba Mountains northwest of Nha Trang to destroy two battalions of the *18B Regiment* of the *5th Division*, as well as the Viet Cong provincial headquarters. Employing classic airmobile tactics, the South Koreans achieved surprise and encircled three objectives. Rather than limit their attacks to daylight, the battalions continued into the night, moving with multiple company-size columns through some of the most difficult terrain in Vietnam. When PENG MA 1 ended, thirty-six days later, the 9th Division had killed or captured over 400 enemy soldiers while losing but 19 of its own men. The operation destroyed the Viet Cong headquarters and rendered the *18B Regiment*'s *8th Battalion* combat ineffective. Only the *7th Battalion* escaped unscathed.[21]

Meanwhile, the U.S. 1st Brigade, 4th Division, sandwiched between the two Korean divisions in Phu Yen Province, conducted rice denial operations in ADAMS, an area extending fifty kilometers along the coast and twenty kilometers inland. Firefights with the enemy during January were so infrequent that late in the month General Larsen sent one of the brigade's battalions to the western highlands, followed by the brigade headquarters and a second battalion three weeks later. The force that remained—a reinforced battalion called Task Force IVY—assumed control of the entire ADAMS area and was directly responsible to I Field Force at Nha Trang.

On 8 March five Capital Division battalions moved into ADAMS from the north and were joined one week later by three battalions of the 9th Division from the south to begin the long-awaited Korean operation, OH JAC KYO. Lt. Gen. Chae Myung Shin, the commander of Korean forces in Vietnam, personally directed the linkup between the two units.

Impressed by the extremely favorable kill ratio that the South Koreans had previously reported, Larsen arranged with General Chae for thirty-two U.S. Army observers to accompany his forces to monitor the operation and check the accuracy of their statistics. Anxious to demonstrate to the Americans their tactical prowess, the South Koreans acted like a force being graded on a field maneuver. As a result, the two-pronged advance moved forward at a painfully slow and deliberate pace, much to the dismay of the Americans.

[21] MFR, 10 Apr 67, sub: MACV Commanders' Conference, 2 April 1967, pp. 14–15, Westmoreland History files, 15–A–5, CMH.

Caught between the Korean divisions, the enemy hastily retreated into mountain base camps. In the process one unit came upon an isolated American platoon on a hilltop overlooking the junction of Highway 1 and Route 6B. Shortly after midnight on 9 March the Viet Cong attacked, overran the American position, killed or wounded 28 of the defenders, and fled before Task Force Ivy could send reinforcements. A week later the Americans avenged the defeat when a rifle company killed 40 members of an enemy unit near the same road junction.

Disturbed by the leisure of the Korean advance, General Larsen decided on 14 March to reinforce Task Force Ivy with a battalion from the 1st of the 101st Airborne Division. Although the battalion strengthened the American position, it encountered only a few of the enemy before it was returned to its brigade in Khanh Hoa Province two weeks later.

The South Koreans, meanwhile, had assumed control over the Adams operational area, and I Field Force disbanded Task Force Ivy on 2 April, sending its units to the western highlands to rejoin the 4th Division.[22] During the next two months, the South Koreans consolidated their gains and pushed into the hills. Only once did the enemy attempt to contest the advance, attacking a company in night laager on 10 April and losing over 50 men. Between mid-March and the end of May, the Capital and 9th Divisions reported killing 940 of the enemy while suffering only 54 dead. This twenty-one to one kill ratio was a remarkable statistic, considering that fighting throughout the operation was characterized as light and sporadic against relatively small enemy forces. Even more impressive, and perhaps suspect, was the report of 681 individual and 90 crew-served weapons captured, figures the American observers were unable to confirm.[23]

In addition to the statistics, the pace of the South Koreans also left something to be desired. Units often refused to move without the guarantee of massive amounts of support from I Field Force. According to Lt. Gen. Arthur S. Collins, the Koreans often "made excessive demands for choppers and support" and then "stood down for too long after an operation." Collins equated the total effort from two Korean divisions to "what one can expect from one good U.S. Brigade."[24]

A Microcosm—Task Force Byrd

In Binh Thuan, the southernmost province in II Corps, a small operation code-named Byrd began in August 1966. Planned as a short-term,

---

[22] ORLL, 1 Feb–30 Apr 67, IFFV, pp. 15–16. Enemy losses reported by the 1st Brigade, 4th Division, during Adams (26 October 1966–2 April 1967) were 491 enemy killed and 160 weapons captured. U.S. losses were 46 killed and 491 wounded.

[23] Ibid.; MACV History 1967, vol. 1, pp. 380–81, CMH; Op Sum, Opn Oh Jac Kyo I and II, MACV-MHB, n.d., Historians files, CMH.

[24] Collins is quoted in Larsen and Collins, *Allied Participation*, p. 152.

economy-of-force measure, BYRD became a continuous offensive—a mini-campaign—that would last several years. As such, it was a microcosm displaying the types of problems that would remain even when the larger Viet Cong and North Vietnamese units were destroyed or driven away from the population. For, in Binh Thuan, as elsewhere in the region, the enemy and the civilians were identical, presenting U.S. commanders with a daunting task.

Binh Thuan, which means "peaceful order," was a province in flux. Intensely nationalistic since the 1930s, its people had accepted French rule grudgingly. The Viet Minh had gained control of the province during World War II, but the French reoccupied it in 1947. Early in 1950 the Communists reasserted their authority, forced the French to leave, and provided the region's sole governing force until 1956, when South Vietnamese government forces arrived.[25]

Much of Binh Thuan's history was influenced by a topography that insulated the province from national politics. Situated midway between Nha Trang and Saigon and shielded landward by the heavily forested mountains of the Truong Son Range, the region's coastal plains resembled the dry flatlands of New Mexico. Neither the northeast nor the southwest monsoons penetrated the province's mountain shield. The 250,000 people of the area grew little rice and subsisted mainly by fishing. They marketed their catches and pungent *nuoc mam* fish sauce in Saigon; this commerce constituted just about their only connection with the capital.

Almost three-quarters of Binh Thuan's population lived in and around Phan Thiet, the provincial capital. The area also contained the bulk of the province's rice farms and the site of a small schoolhouse where Ho Chi Minh had once taught. It was also the site of the National Liberation Front's regional government.[26]

By March 1966 the enemy had closed all the roads leading to Binh Thuan and dominated the Phan Thiet area. When the 1st Brigade, 101st Airborne Division, arrived a month later, local Viet Cong forces withdrew to the mountains and waited until the paratroopers left. The situation around Phan Thiet again became critical that August, when the *482d PLAF Battalion*, some four hundred men strong, ambushed and almost annihilated a Regional Forces company near Phan Thiet, leading the South Vietnamese again to request American assistance.

With the airborne brigade occupied in Phu Yen Province and the 1st Cavalry Division about to launch a campaign in Binh Dinh, General Larsen decided he could spare only a battalion task force from the 1st Cavalry Division. That would be enough, he reasoned, to secure the area and stabilize conditions in Binh Thuan during the national constitutional elections scheduled for 11 September. The 1st Cavalry Division

---

[25] CICV Study, ST 71–02, 6 Jul 71, sub: The Enemy System, Binh Thuan Province, and Briefing, OCO, Region II, Nov 66, Binh Thuan Province, both in Historians files, CMH.

[26] Rpt, DEPCORDS, 11 Dec 67, sub: Evaluation of Task Force BYRD, Historians files, CMH.

could provide more helicopters than the airborne brigade, allowing the task force to move at will through the province for what seemed to be a minor, temporary mission.

On 25 August 1966, the 2d Battalion, 7th Cavalry (Airmobile), arrived at Phan Thiet to form the nucleus of Task Force BYRD. Lt. Col. Billy M. Vaughn, the task force commander, immediately deployed his units in a show of force, along with two South Vietnamese battalions from the 23d Division. Believing the Americans would soon leave, the Viet Cong withdrew to the mountains as Vaughn's and the South Vietnamese units confiscated about sixty tons of rice. Vaughn then turned his attention to the local Viet Cong, estimated at two regular battalions and ten local force companies, prodding the territorial forces to return to the surrounding hamlets to provide security for newly arrived pacification teams.

At the time, I Field Force had operational control of Task Force BYRD, with the 1st Cavalry Division taking responsibility for administrative and logistical support. The system would have worked where shorter distances allowed for easy relationships, but Task Force BYRD was 350 kilometers away from its division headquarters at An Khe and 150 kilometers from the area support command up at Cam Ranh. Smooth coordination was impossible: the logistical units supporting BYRD often had to send four or five messages back to their superiors to clear the simplest decision. As Colonel Vaughn's task force grew, the number of support elements required to sustain it mushroomed into a top-heavy organization employing 950 men at Phan Thiet to support 650 fighters. General Larsen tried to remedy the problem by placing all of the local support units under Vaughn. Although the ratio of "support to supported" troops remained the same, the new arrangement had the virtue of reducing the logistical response time to the forces in the field.[27]

Meanwhile, Vaughn began having more serious trouble with the South Vietnamese and their U.S. advisers. Vaughn considered Binh Thuan's province chief, Lt. Col. Tran Dinh De, a capable administrator but a cautious military commander, whose help he nonetheless needed for his operations. Two problems immediately arose. The U.S. province adviser, who had long provided counsel to Colonel De on military matters, resented Vaughn's attempt to deal directly with the province chief. In addition, the two Americans seldom agreed on how best to employ the Regional and Popular Forces. Disagreements among the South Vietnamese were even more exacting. Although charged with providing security for the Binh Thuan population, De had no control over the two South Vietnamese battalions in his area. Once the enemy threat subsided, Regional Forces units returned and took up their normal area security

[27] AAR, Opn BYRD, 2d Bn, 7th Cav, 10 May 68, p. 34; Lt Col Joseph T. Griffin, Jr., Operation BYRD, A Model for U.S. Forces During Vietnamization, U.S. Army War College Case Study, 5 Mar 70; Order of Battle Book, G–2, IFFV, 1 Aug 70, pp. 136–60. All in Historians files, CMH. Intervs, author with Adamson, 4 Apr 79, and with Norton, 1–2 Sep 83, 2 Dec 83.

functions, leaving the Vietnamese regulars who had performed these chores since August with little to do. When Colonel De prodded the two battalion commanders to begin search and clear missions outside Phan Thiet, they declined, pointing out that all orders had to come from their regimental commander at Phan Rang, a hundred kilometers away. He in turn was awaiting guidance from his superior, the 23d Division commander, at Ban Me Thuot in the western highlands. When Vaughn attempted to intercede with the battalion advisers, they also hesitated. They were responsible to their own regimental and division advisers and in any case had little control over their Vietnamese counterparts.[28]

In November General Larsen informed Westmoreland of the impasse. Aside from providing security during the September elections, he pointed out, the Vietnamese regulars in Binh Thuan had been ineffective. Both agreed that the province chief, Colonel De, should have control over all Vietnamese forces in the province. Westmoreland threatened to withdraw American units immediately if Vinh Loc, the II Corps commander, failed to resolve the matter satisfactorily.[29] Subsequently, Vinh Loc persuaded the reluctant division commander to yield operational control of the battalions to De. Westmoreland then appointed Vaughn as Colonel De's senior adviser.[30]

While the allies floundered, the Viet Cong quietly filtered back into Phan Thiet and prepared for an attack on the Thien Giao District headquarters, eighteen kilometers north. Units of the *482d Battalion* struck on the evening of 16 October. The attackers penetrated the compound's outer defenses and destroyed three of four bunkers. Their failure to seize the entire complex was due only to the arrival of 1st Cavalry Division gunships. Unaccustomed to dealing with gunships, especially at night, the Viet Cong became confused, and their commander ordered a withdrawal. But with flares illuminating the battlefield, the Hueys spotted the fleeing enemy and exacted a heavy toll.

Task Force BYRD had its first major firefight one week later, when one of its companies came upon an entrenched Viet Cong force. The encounter was brief and its results inconclusive, for the enemy escaped in the darkness.

Throughout the remainder of October and November 1966 the American forces conducted air assaults in the area on an almost daily basis and honeycombed the region at night with ambushes. The Viet Cong in turn failed to mass in any formation larger than a platoon and spent most of their time trying to avoid the marauding Americans.

Particularly effective against the insurgents were BYRD's "night hunter" teams. Three helicopters participated in each mission. A "hunt"

[28] Griffin, Operation BYRD, p. 40; Interv, author with Adamson, 4 Apr 79.

[29] COMUSMACV Diary, Gen Westmoreland's Historical Briefing, 25 Nov 66, pp. 4–5, Sanitized Version of Historical Briefings, CMH.

[30] AAR, Opn BYRD, 2d Bn, 7th Cav, p. 26; Interv, John M. Carland, CMH, with Lt Gen John Norton, 16 Feb 96, Historians files, CMH.

ship carrying two to four infantrymen would fly at altitudes between fifty and four hundred feet. Equipped with Starlight night-imaging scopes mounted on M16 rifles fastened to the ceilings of the Hueys, the infantrymen would search possible targets with tracer fire. The second helicopter would then drop flares so the third, a gunship, flying at higher altitudes, could take targets under rocket and machine-gun fire. By the end of nine weeks these airborne teams, together with ground patrols, had claimed 250 enemy dead with few American losses. Impressed by the task force's success, Larsen decided to keep it in Binh Thuan indefinitely, an unusual arrangement for the Vietnam War.

Meanwhile, having gained operational control over South Vietnamese forces in Binh Thuan, Colonel De threw the two regular battalions into the fray. By December U.S. and South Vietnamese infantry were conducting combined operations on a regular basis, with U.S. helicopters providing fire support, medical evacuation, and resupply.[31]

In spite of the various efforts, the allies had yet to make serious inroads against the underground or to penetrate far outside Phan Thiet. Many farmers resided in homes scattered among the rice fields rather than in compact hamlet clusters. That made control difficult and forced the Americans and South Vietnamese to saturate the entire area with patrols, always maintaining a mobile reserve as a reaction force. There were too few allied soldiers to provide complete security.

The level of peasant cooperation with the authorities was also tenuous, as many people had relatives serving with the Viet Cong and could hardly be expected to support the South Vietnamese government. As long as the Americans remained, government authority was secure, but no one on either side expected the American troops to remain forever. Indeed, surveys revealed that most peasants believed the government would eventually crumble and the Communists would quickly fill the vacuum. Yet in January 1967 American security advisers held that 82 percent of the population in Binh Thuan Province lived in "secure" hamlets, while the remainder, 18 percent, lived in contested areas. Local Vietnamese officials were less optimistic, admitting to having only 25 percent of the population firmly under their control, conceding 15 percent to the Communists, and placing the remaining 60 percent in contested areas where the security campaign had hardly begun.[32]

Task Force BYRD remained in Binh Thuan throughout 1967 and during the first six months claimed steady progress in providing security. By May the *482d Battalion* appeared to have withdrawn completely from the Phan Thiet area, remaining active only along the region's fringe for much

[31] AAR, Opn BYRD, 2d Bn, 7th Cav, pp. 6–7, 21–24, 34–35; Rpt, DEPCORDS, 11 Dec 67, sub: Evaluation of Task Force BYRD.

[32] Province Study, Vietnam Studies Group, National Security Council, Feb 70, sub: Binh Thuan Province 1967–1969, Historians files, CMH; HES Data Book, 1967, p. II–25; RD Rpt, Binh Thuan Province, Apr 67, 15 May 67.

of the summer dry season. The *840th PLAF Battalion,* which normally operated in the northern part of the province, departed for Cambodia to receive new weapons and replacements, leaving the *482d* with temporary responsibility for the entire province.[33]

With the *482d* stretched thin and less of a threat, southern Binh Thuan gradually became a thriving community where farmers harvested their crops, sent their produce to market over government-protected roads, and prepared their fields and planted new crops. Although the people expected the enemy to return, many believed that the government, with the help of the Americans, could protect them.

After the national elections, the *840th* returned and attempted to reestablish Communist authority just north of Phan Thiet, attacking a South Vietnamese base on 6 September. The attack failed, and with the prompt arrival of units from Task Force Byrd the battalion was routed. It would again try to overrun another South Vietnamese base in the same area two months later, again unsuccessfully.

Although the underground throughout Binh Thuan remained intact, South Vietnamese officials in October 1967 believed that they would be able to hold the built-up areas indefinitely if Task Force Byrd remained. They reasoned that since August 1966 Byrd alone had killed or captured 850 of the enemy, seized nearly 300 weapons and over 400 tons of supplies, and suffered only 23 killed and 278 wounded. If the momentum continued, the strong possibility existed that the government could attain its goals. But the province chief had little confidence that his own forces could do the job alone.[34]

[33] AAR, Opn Byrd, 2d Bn, 7th Cav, pp. 29–30.

[34] Ibid., pp. 4, 11–15, 31–33. RD Rpts, Binh Thuan Province, May 67, n.d., pp. 1–4; Jul 67, n.d., pp. 1–7; Aug 67, n.d., pp. 1–7; and Nov 67, n.d., pp. 1–10; ORLL, 1 Aug–31 Oct 67, 1st Cav Div, 15 Nov 67, p. 9. Last five in Historians files, CMH.

12

A Looming Threat in the North

Saigon and the III Corps area remained Westmoreland's first priority, but trouble was also brewing in the north. The I Corps area was a constant threat, with the Marine forces stationed there insufficient for its protection. In early 1967 the MACV commander was once again forced to deploy more forces to the northern provinces of South Vietnam.

Westmoreland's target was I Corps' two southern provinces, Quang Tin and Quang Ngai. They were home to the *2d PAVN Division* as well as the *3d PAVN Division*, which, although badly bloodied from its encounters with American forces in Binh Dinh Province, was still formidable. Both divisions fell under the command of the *B1 Front*, which also controlled some six local force battalions as well as separate companies in every district.

MACV's planning for operations against these forces went back several months. Even as the 1st Cavalry Division was clearing the enemy out of northeastern Binh Dinh in the fall of 1966, Westmoreland had planned to connect those operations with his coming campaign in I Corps. In September he ordered the I Field Force commander, General Larsen, to ready the 1st Cavalry Division for a move north into Quang Ngai Province as early as March of the next year. This was the heart of Westmoreland's 1967–1968 dry season campaign for the northern sectors. Named Operation YORK, it would begin in April, last about three months, and involve up to twenty-five U.S. Army, Marine Corps, and South Vietnamese battalions. Larsen at I Field Force, rather than Walt's III Marine Amphibious Force, would control the operation. YORK would include a sweep into the Do Xa, the reported enemy supply base and suspected headquarters of the *B1 Front*, located in the mountainous tri-border area of Quang Ngai, Quang Tin, and Kontum Provinces. Upon YORK's completion, the I Field Force units would withdraw, and III Marine Amphibious Force would again assume responsibility for Quang Ngai Province.[1] (*Map 22*)

Quang Tin and Quang Ngai had been under nearly complete enemy domination for over two decades. Southern Quang Ngai had served as a

---

[1] Msg, CG, IFFV, A–0212 to COMUSMACV, 16 Jan 67, sub: Visit of COMUSMACV, 16 January 1967, Westmoreland History files, 12–D–3, CMH.

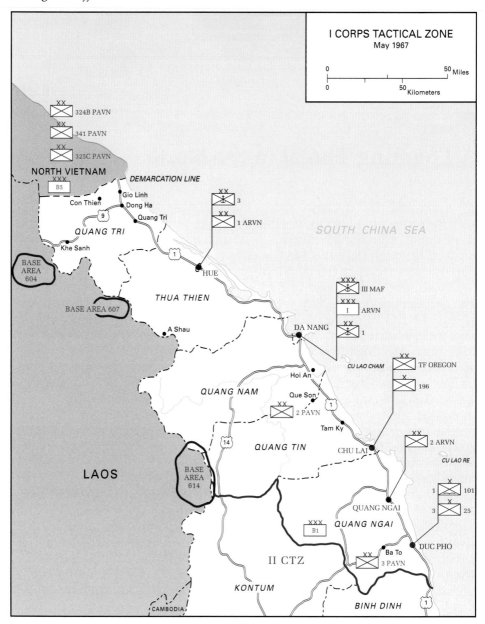

MAP 22

rest and recuperation area for battle-weary regiments of the *3d Division*. The province had also provided the enemy with an abundance of rice, salt, and fish products, as well as weapons and ammunition brought in by trawlers from the North. A favorite insurgent receiving area was the Batangan Peninsula, a broad, swampy region just northeast of Quang

Ngai City, the provincial capital. Even though this traffic decreased sharply after mid-1966, as more U.S. Navy ships patrolled the coastal waters, as late as March 1967 the *B1 Front* continued to bring in some 10 percent of its military stores by sea.[2]

As American planning for the pacification of Quang Ngai progressed, enemy activity in the province increased. After taking heavy losses in Binh Dinh at the end of 1966, the *2d PLAF Regiment* of the *3d Division* had moved into southern Quang Ngai to rest and regroup, moving west again in mid-December to the Annamite Mountains, thirty kilometers from the coast. At the time the only allied forces in the region were located at an isolated Special Forces camp at Ba To. Alerted to the move, American intelligence traced the regiment's progress and by mid-January 1967 reported that it had arrived in the vicinity of the Special Forces camp. Later that month intelligence also reported that the *2d Division*, with two of its regiments, had also entered Quang Ngai from the north.[3]

While I Field Force headquarters was alerting a brigade in late January to prepare to reinforce Ba To, III Marine Amphibious Force, in an unrelated operation, sent a battalion to Duc Pho, a district headquarters on Highway 1, twenty-five kilometers east of the Special Forces camp. The marines remained for ten weeks, encountering stiff resistance from local force units and guerrillas. Also during that time, a Marine Corps battalion landing team conducted a two-week operation east of Duc Pho along the coast. Both efforts sought to keep the insurgents away from populated areas and to sever the reported enemy supply route leading from the coast to Ba To and on to the *B1 Front* headquarters in the Do Xa.[4]

While this ominous activity around Ba To continued, another, far more serious threat began to emerge farther north in the A Shau Valley, a region the allies had abandoned after the enemy had overrun the Special Forces camp there nearly a year before. Marine observation flights had revealed no significant evidence of enemy activity in the valley. Yet when Special Forces long-range reconnaissance patrols entered in February 1967 they met heavy resistance and noted that the enemy was improving the roads and trails, perhaps to accommodate rapid movement of troops and supplies for a major offensive. Possibly more important, an intelligence report indicated that two North Vietnamese regiments were already gathering in Base Area 607 inside Laos, within a few hours' march of the A Shau. MACV immediately sent B–52s to strike the suspected locations of the two units, hoping that an air attack could blunt this looming threat.

---

[2] Evaluation Rpt, MACCORDS-RE, 13 Sep 67, Task Force OREGON Operations, Historians files, CMH; Intel Sum 114, IFFV, 23 Apr 67; Periodic Intel Rpt 17, IFFV, n.d., an. E. Both in Historians files, CMH.

[3] Evaluation Rpt, MACCORDS-RE, 13 Sep 67, Task Force OREGON Operations.

[4] For additional details, see Maj. Gary L. Telfer, Lt. Col. Lane Rogers, and V. Keith Fleming, Jr., *U.S. Marines in Vietnam: Fighting the North Vietnamese, 1967* (Washington, D.C.: HQ, USMC, History and Museums Division, 1984), ch. 5.

This increased enemy activity around Ba To and in the A Shau, together with growing trail activity during the 8–12 February Tet cease-fire, came as an unexpected and quite unpleasant surprise to Westmoreland and demanded his immediate attention and response, if not a major change in his campaign plan for 1967. The MACV commander remained convinced that sooner or later Hanoi would launch a conventional offensive across the Demilitarized Zone, supported by attacks from Laos. Now worried that a major enemy threat already existed in I Corps, where American manpower was already stretched to its limit, Westmoreland postponed Operation YORK, scheduled for April, and ordered that a division-size unit be sent to reinforce the marines as soon as possible. Westmoreland, however, was rapidly running out of uncommitted battalions. As a stopgap measure he created an entirely new force from existing formations then scattered throughout South Vietnam.[5]

The Provisional Division

The makeshift division was to have a small headquarters and four self-sufficient brigades. The 1st Brigade, 101st Airborne Division, would be the unit's mainstay, while the I Field Force commander would nominate a second brigade from his command. The II Field Force commander would nominate the other two brigades. Westmoreland gave command of the unit to his own chief of staff, Maj. Gen. William B. Rosson, and, in deference to Rosson's home state, named it Task Force OREGON. Upon activation the force would deploy in southern I Corps to free U.S. marines for use farther north. Although Westmoreland gave General Walt the option of placing Rosson's command either north or south of Chu Lai, southern Quang Ngai Province was the obvious choice for deployment. There, Task Force OREGON would undertake offensive operations in conjunction with the 1st Cavalry Division, which in turn would extend its tactical boundary northward into Quang Ngai from Binh Dinh Province. Contingency Plans NORTH CAROLINA and SOUTH CAROLINA—created in late 1966 and calling for the deployment of brigade-size units into I Corps—were to be used to develop logistical support and movement plans.[6]

On 28 February Westmoreland approved Rosson's organizational plan for Task Force OREGON, which included a headquarters, supporting units, and three infantry brigades. The MACV commander further directed that selected units would continue to perform their current missions elsewhere in South Vietnam. Only after the activation of the

---

[5] Msg, CG, III MAF, 121 to COMUSMACV, 2 Feb 67, sub: Visit of COMUSMACV to III MAF, 1130–1400H02 Feb 67, Westmoreland History files, 13–A–5; Westmoreland Jnl, 25 Feb 67, p. 26, Westmoreland History files, 13–B, CMH.

[6] ORLL, 18 Feb–30 Apr 67, Task Force OREGON, 6 Aug 67, pp. 2–3, and Interv, author with Gen William B. Rosson, CG, Task Force OREGON, and CG, IFFV, 13 Sep 77, both in Historians files, CMH.

General Rosson

provisional division headquarters would a final unit selection be made, based on the tactical situation in II and III Corps.[7]

Meanwhile, the pace of action quickened in southern I Corps. In mid-February South Korean marines and South Vietnamese forces fought the *21st PAVN*, one of the two regiments of the *2d Division* that had entered Quang Ngai from the north. In two separate battles northwest of Quang Ngai City, they reported killing over 1,000 of the enemy. To the south, in Binh Dinh Province, the 1st Cavalry Division had driven the *3d Division* and its *22d Regiment* toward southeastern Quang Ngai Province, an action that evidently prompted the enemy to postpone plans to overrun the Ba To Special Forces camp and to move the *2d PLAF Regiment* eastward to cover the retreat of the *3d Division*'s other units. Caught off balance, enemy main force units in and around Quang Ngai sought to avoid combat throughout March, which, from Westmoreland's viewpoint, lessened the need to activate Task Force OREGON immediately.[8]

More troubling was enemy activity directly south of the Demilitarized Zone in Quang Tri Province. Here, as Westmoreland feared, North Vietnamese leaders planned a major offensive as soon as the monsoon rains dissipated. In February an American patrol discovered an enemy regiment north of Camp Carroll, a Marine artillery base twenty kilometers inland. While a Marine sweep preempted a ground assault on the camp, the North Vietnamese did bombard the base on 7 March with nearly five hundred mortar and artillery rocket rounds. A week later South Vietnamese forces fought a second enemy regiment near Con Thien, a Marine base ten kilometers north of Camp Carroll. On 20 March the enemy attacked a Marine outpost at Gio Linh, ten kilometers east of Con Thien, with an estimated six hundred rockets and artillery rounds, the enemy's first major use of conventional artillery against American positions. Harassing fire continued to strike Gio Linh almost daily for the next two weeks.

---

[7] ORLL, 18 Feb–30 Apr 67, Task Force OREGON, pp. 10–11.
[8] MFR, 10 Apr 67, sub: MACV Commanders' Conference, 2 April 1967.

The Rockpile, a landmark just west of Camp Carroll on the rugged Demilitarized Zone

Despite over one hundred-fifty B–52 strikes in Quang Tri and Thua Thien Provinces during the first three months of 1967—40 percent of all such raids conducted in South Vietnam during that period—enemy attacks continued. As General Walt shifted battalions north to confront the offensive, Hanoi sent the *325C PAVN Division* south to join the *B5 Front*, the command responsible for operations in the Demilitarized Zone. Two of the division's regiments deployed from Dong Hoi in North Vietnam, moving into the mountains directly north of Khe Sanh, while the *325C*'s third regiment moved to a staging area in the eastern portion of the Demilitarized Zone. American intelligence now counted eight enemy regiments in the vicinity of the Demilitarized Zone, another regiment in Thua Thien Province, and two others in Laos.[9]

On 6 April North Vietnamese elements launched mortar attacks against the U.S. advisory compound in the provincial capital of Quang Tri, as well as at two nearby South Vietnamese district headquarters. Other enemy forces broke into the Quang Tri City jail and freed 220 imprisoned Viet Cong cadre and guerrillas. The extent and diversity of

[9] Ibid.; Monthly OB Sum, CICV, 1 Apr–31 May 67.

these actions, no more than thirty kilometers south of the Demilitarized Zone, indicated that the enemy was probing and testing American strength there. These events also suggested that additional enemy forces, possibly another regiment, had infiltrated Quang Tri Province and were poised for further, perhaps larger, offensive operations. This was all the proof Westmoreland needed of the imminent danger.[10]

That evening, 6 April, the MACV commander announced that the worsening crisis in I Corps demanded "immediate reinforcement" and that U.S. Army units would move to southern I Corps "on an urgent basis" so Walt could speed marines northward.[11] With this announcement, which served as the implementing order for Task Force OREGON, the troop units fell into place. In addition to the independent brigade of the 101st Airborne Division, the 3d Brigade, 25th Division, then operating with the 1st Cavalry Division in Binh Dinh Province, would be added to the task force, along with the 196th Brigade, the veteran of ATTLEBORO, CEDAR FALLS, and JUNCTION CITY. This was the II Field Force unit that the Army had designated a mobile reaction force in case the enemy reappeared in War Zone C. Westmoreland directed that the 3d of the 25th move to Duc Pho no later than 1 May, and that other elements move to Chu Lai. At that time the provisional division would be officially activated, with headquarters at Chu Lai.[12]

As MACV now fully realized, the North Vietnamese buildup along the Demilitarized Zone was no longer confined to the coastal plain, but now included major deployments all the way west to the Laotian border, threatening the exposed allied flank.[13] Westmoreland, therefore, took steps to speed up the northward movement of the marines, but only encountered further difficulties. Lacking sufficient troops, helicopters, and logistical bases in the two northern provinces of I Corps, General Walt could not hope to mount the kind of mobile defense that Army leaders favored to cope with the growing threat. In addition, in case the North Vietnamese planned to strike before the end of the monsoon, Westmoreland was pressing Walt to place a major Marine force to the west at Khe Sanh as soon as possible, further stretching already scarce Marine resources.[14]

Realizing Walt's dilemma, Westmoreland approved an immediate withdrawal of the marines from Duc Pho to reinforce the north on 6 April. To fill the gap, he instructed General Larsen to send an Army

---

[10] MACV History 1967, vol. 1, pp. 335–36.

[11] Msg, Westmoreland MAC 11468 to CG, IFFV, 6 Apr 67, sub: OPLAN NORTH CAROLINA, Westmoreland Message files, CMH.

[12] Msgs, Larsen A–0987 to Westmoreland, 15 Mar 67, sub: Visit of COMUSMACV, and Larsen A–1158 to Westmoreland, 30 Mar 67, sub: Visit of COMUSMACV, both in Historians files, CMH.

[13] Msg, Westmoreland MAC 3474 to Sharp and Wheeler, 12 Apr 67, sub: Situation in I Corps, Westmoreland History files, 15–B–3, CMH.

[14] Capt. Moyers S. Shore II, *The Battle for Khe Sanh* (Washington, D.C.: HQ, USMC, Historical Branch, G–3 Division, 1969), pp. 5–11.

battalion task force to Duc Pho on 7 April and to have a two-battalion brigade in position by the evening of the following day. Larsen was also ordered to begin building a supply base at Duc Pho, with an airfield capable of receiving C–130s, and to establish a port operation east of the district town to serve as a primary supply conduit. Finally, the northern boundary of I Field Force was extended to include Duc Pho and Ba To, the two southernmost districts of Quang Ngai Province. At some future date the brigade at Duc Pho would become part of Task Force OREGON, the task force would be placed under III Marine Amphibious Force, and the I Field Force boundary would revert to the Binh Dinh–Quang Ngai border.[15]

LE JEUNE

General Larsen immediately instructed Maj. Gen. John J. Tolson, who had succeeded General Norton as commander of the 1st Cavalry Division, to provide the brigade for Duc Pho. The attached 3d Brigade, 25th Division, had expected the move to come in May and was still so dispersed south of the Lai Giang that it could not comply with Westmoreland's schedule. As an interim measure, Tolson called on the 2d Battalion, 5th Cavalry, in reserve at Camp Radcliff. The 5th Cavalry commander, Lt. Col. Robert D. Stevenson, was to locate all available Caribous and Chinooks and move his battalion to Landing Zone ENGLISH in the southern Bong Son Plain at first light on 7 April, there to transfer to Hueys for the journey to Duc Pho. Another cavalry battalion and the headquarters of the 2d Brigade, 1st Cavalry Division, now commanded by Lt. Col. Fred E. Karhohs, were to follow, with Karhohs serving as the overall tactical commander until relieved in mid-April by Colonel Shanahan of the 3d of the 25th.

The movements into Duc Pho went smoothly. Before nightfall on 7 April Colonel Stevenson's battalion relieved the marines outside the village, while the headquarters of the 2d Brigade flew in the next morning and assumed control of all Army and Marine forces in the combat zone designated LE JEUNE. Only one hitch developed during the deployment. Short of helicopters, particularly those needed to lift trucks and artillery pieces, the last of the marines did not depart until 21 April.[16]

Anticipating problems in developing a logistical base at Duc Pho, General Tolson sent his assistant division commander, Brig. Gen. George S. Blanchard, to supervise the effort. Despite Blanchard's status as the

---

[15] Unit Historical Rpt 10, Office of Information and History, 1st Cav Div, 7 Aug 67, Opn LE JEUNE, Historians files, CMH; AAR, Opn PERSHING, 1st Cav Div, p. 9; Intervs, author with Shanahan, 13 Aug and 4 Sep 81; Joseph W. A. Whitehorne with Maj Gen John J. Tolson, CG, 1st Cav Div, 28 Jun 68, Historians files, CMH.

[16] AAR, Opn PERSHING, 1st Cav Div, p. 9; Op Sum, Opn LE JEUNE, MACV-MHB, n.d., Historians files, CMH.

General Tolson

senior commander on the ground, he confined himself to logistical matters, while Colonel Karhohs received his tactical guidance from Tolson. Blanchard's first task was to establish a landing zone for follow-on troops and supplies. He chose an open area east of the village at the base of Dang Mountain, naming it Landing Zone MONTEZUMA. During the next two days helicopters brought in over 200 tons of heavy engineer equipment, some of which had to be partially disassembled to meet lift capabilities. Meanwhile, working at times under floodlights, the 1st Cavalry Division's 8th Engineer Battalion carved out a rough but serviceable runway for Caribous in a little over twenty-four hours and by 12 April had lengthened the strip to accommodate C–130s. A second Caribou strip opened parallel to the first, and still later the 39th Engineer Battalion (Combat), an I Field Force unit sent to Duc Pho by ship on 10 April, began improving and paving the longer landing strip to give it an all-weather capability.[17]

Although clear skies prevailed throughout Operation LE JEUNE, other conditions made flying hazardous. Helicopter blades stirred up sand, but spreading peneprime, an oil-based dust suppressant, on helipads and refueling sites somewhat alleviated the problem. More serious was the congestion produced by the large numbers of helicopter and fixed-wing flights in and out of MONTEZUMA. A minimum of 240 tons of supplies had to be flown in daily to sustain the ground troops and maintain a three-day stock of 720 tons. On 9 April, the first day the strip was in full operation, over one thousand landings and departures occurred. So great was the aircraft density that air traffic controllers for a time lost their grasp on the situation. Anxious to move in and out quickly, some helicopter pilots failed to request landing and departure instructions and instead radioed directly to units on the ground, darted across the unit's air space to deliver their loads, and on occasion narrowly avoided midair collisions.[18]

---

[17] Unit Historical Rpt 10, Office of Information and History, 1st Cav Div, 7 Aug 67, Opn LE JEUNE, pp. 1–28; Interv, Whitehorne with Tolson, 28 Jun 68; AAR, Opn LE JEUNE, 3d Bde, 4th Inf Div, 1 May 67, pp. 5–6, Historians files, CMH.

[18] Unit Historical Rpt 10, Office of Information and History, 1st Cav Div, 7 Aug 67, Opn LE JEUNE, pp. 1–28; Interv, Whitehorne with Tolson, 28 Jun 68; AAR, Opn LE JEUNE, 3d Bde, 4th Inf Div, pp. 5–6.

LSTs at RAZORBACK Beach. In the foreground, 500-gallon rubber fuel bladders are lined up on the sand.

The delayed departure of the marines added to the difficulty. Marine helicopter pilots, according to the Army, were unfamiliar with the 1st Cavalry Division's air traffic control procedures and unaccustomed to flying in closely packed, blade-to-blade formations. The Marine pilots responded that the difficulties arose not because of their unfamiliarity with 1st Cavalry Division procedures, but because the division had no air control procedures. General Blanchard solved the problem by assigning the marines a separate air corridor and collocating their controllers with those of the division. With General Tolson's support, he notified all aircraft unit commanders in the division to adhere to the Duc Pho air traffic control plan, even if it meant slowing the delivery rate. Once the rush into Duc Pho was over, resupply by sea eliminated the difficulties.

So essential was the sea route for sustaining U.S. forces around Duc Pho that General Larsen formed a special group, Task Force GALLAGHER, to manage supply. Drawn from 5th Transportation Command port units at Qui Nhon, Tuy Hoa, and Cam Ranh Bay, the task force selected a site four kilometers east of Duc Pho, dubbed RAZORBACK Beach, for the shore operation. At first, RAZORBACK appeared an excellent choice, because a sharp shore gradient—hence the name—allowed cargo ships to anchor close in. Yet when the first of the LSTs (landing ships, tank) attempted to beach at high tide on 9 April, they ran aground a kilometer offshore, and their crews had to transfer cargo to smaller, shallow-draft vessels. More problems awaited on land. Not until 25 April did the 39th Engineer Battalion com-

Troops of Task Force OREGON in action near Chu Lai

plete a corduroy road from RAZORBACK to Landing Zone MONTEZUMA. In the interim, cargo had to be flown in by helicopter.

When the sea supply route became fully operational on 15 April, Tolson ordered the 3d Brigade of the 25th Division to relieve the 2d Brigade, 1st Cavalry Division, officially ending Operation LE JEUNE. At the same time the 1st Cavalry Division relinquished control of the 3d Brigade to Task Force OREGON, then operating under the III Marine Amphibious Force, and the I Field Force northern boundary reverted to its previous position. There had been no discernible enemy opposition to the move, and the problems had been largely administrative and logistical. Nevertheless, during the two weeks' worth of combat operations the Americans claimed over 300 enemy killed or captured in Quang Ngai Province.[19]

On 12 April 1967, Task Force OREGON was officially activated, and a day later the 196th Brigade reached Chu Lai, having been withdrawn a few days earlier from the final phase of JUNCTION CITY. On the fifteenth the 196th received operational control of a battalion of the 3d Brigade, 25th Division, sent from Binh Dinh, and four days later the rest of the 3d Brigade left the province for Duc Pho to relieve the 2d Brigade, 1st Cavalry Division.

---

[19] Unit Historical Rpt 10, Office of Information and History, 1st Cav Div, 6 Aug 67, Opn LE JEUNE; AAR, Opn PERSHING, 1st Cav Div, p. 9; Intervs, Whitehorne with Tolson, 28 Jun 68, and author with Shanahan, 13 Aug 81, 4 Sep 81.

On 20 April the headquarters of Task Force OREGON at Chu Lai assumed control of all U.S. Army forces in southern I Corps except those at Duc Pho. Upon the departure of the 2d Brigade, 1st Cavalry Division, two days later, General Rosson gained control of the 3d Brigade, 25th Division, at which time MACV readjusted the I Field Force area of responsibility southward to its former boundary. Thus, within sixteen days of Westmoreland's decision to activate Task Force OREGON, General Rosson's new command of two brigades had begun operations in southern I Corps under the operational control of Walt's command.[20]

General Westmoreland still believed that the approaching dry season campaign in I Corps could well decide the outcome of the war. He also felt that by stripping units from I and II Field Forces to form a provisional division for southern I Corps, he had gone as far as he could in reinforcing Walt's command. He conveyed these feelings to Admiral Sharp and General Wheeler on 12 April 1967, indicating that Rosson's force would free two U.S. Marine regiments, a total of five battalions, for operations farther north. But he still was uncertain whether the marines would have enough units to deal with the impending threat. For that reason, the MACV commander formally requested that the 9th Marine Amphibious Brigade on Okinawa, the Pacific reserve, be released for Walt's use. With support from Sharp and Wheeler, the secretary of defense approved partial commitment: two of the brigade's special landing forces were to be stationed on ships off the coast of northern I Corps, remaining available should Westmoreland need them. The rest of the brigade, still on Okinawa, would be placed on fifteen-day alert.[21]

With reinforcements on hand, Westmoreland told Walt to devote his full attention to meeting the threat in the north. If General Rosson needed more troops, Westmoreland promised to provide them from Army units. The stage was thus set for confronting what Westmoreland believed would be a major enemy effort during the dry season in the northern provinces. Only after that offensive had spent its fury would the MACV commander put his own offensive plans into action.

---

[20] ORLL, 18 Feb–30 Apr 67, Task Force OREGON, pp. 24–25.

[21] Msg, Westmoreland MAC 3474 to Sharp and Wheeler, 12 Apr 67, sub: Situation in I Corps; MACV History 1967, vol. 1, p. 368.

13

Taking Stock

As the dominant wind currents over Southeast Asia shifted during March and April, reversing the weather pattern, campaign emphases shifted in South Vietnam. Operations like FAIRFAX near Saigon might continue, but for the next six months of 1967 the northernmost provinces of I Corps, drying out as the rains moved south, would see the biggest battles. Those battles would be important, because thus far at least the year of the offensive had not gone as Westmoreland would have liked. He had launched a multitude of attacks in II and III Corps and had driven six enemy divisions deeper into the hinterlands or across the border. Still, he could not yet say that he was close to winning the war in the standard sense or that the gains on the battlefield were translating into anything permanent. Most of the categories used to analyze progress—tempo of operations, road and river security, the out-of-country air and naval effort, and pacification support—were showing only limited headway or inconclusive results at best. In one revealing category, strength of opposing forces, the trends were downright bleak.

Opposing Forces

Although they were only estimates, the strength figures told a disquieting story. Despite heavy enemy losses during the last six months of operations, some 72,000 men since October 1966, analysts believed that Viet Cong and North Vietnamese strength in the South had remained constant at 285,000. Early in 1967 MACV had increased its estimate of the monthly rate of recruitment and infiltration from 13,300 to a minimum of 14,000, or 168,000 annually. Subtracting projected enemy losses of 140,000 for 1967, theater analysts concluded that Communist military strength would actually have increased by 28,000 when 1968 began.[1]

It was against this backdrop, with no sign of the enemy weakening, that Westmoreland renewed negotiations with the White House for a new

---

[1] SEA Mil Fact Bk, Jan 68, pp. A–95, A–97, A–108; MACV Force Requirements FY 1968, 5 Apr 67, an. A.

MACV headquarters, with Tan Son Nhut in the background

package of combat and support forces. On paper, he had not done badly in filling out his army since meeting with the president in February 1966. Believing with MACV that 1967 could well be the war's decisive year, the Johnson administration had accelerated deployments, putting enough troops in the pipeline to approach the approved ceiling for 1967—470,000 men from all the services—as much as six months early. Even then, however, in spite of the patch of optimism that had accompanied the deployments, the ceiling was 85,000 short of the figure that Westmoreland had originally requested. He had accepted that decision and all it implied with his usual good-natured forbearance. It was clear by March, however, with the enemy avoiding contact during JUNCTION CITY and at the same time threatening in northern I Corps, that the theater would need another infusion of soldiers if the allies were to maintain momentum.[2]

On 5 April 1967, Westmoreland formally submitted his new troop requirements for fiscal year 1968, offering the Johnson administration a choice of two options: a "minimum essential force" of two and one-third divisions and five tactical squadrons, about 100,000 men; and an "optimum force" approximately double that, raising the troop ceiling for

[2] MACV Briefing Bk for Sec Def, 10–14 Oct 66, J–3 Briefing, tab 4; MACV History 1967, vol. 3, p. 1263; Msg, COMUSMACV 09101 to CINCPAC, 18 Mar 67, sub: Force Requirements, Westmoreland History files, 15–A–8, CMH.

Vietnam to 670,000. According to Westmoreland, he needed the minimum force chiefly to bolster I Corps—one full division and an armored cavalry regiment below the Demilitarized Zone to serve as a containment force and the second division for the Quang Ngai foothills and plains, still hotly contested territory. He required these additional forces "as soon as possible, but no later than 1 July 1968."[3]

Looking beyond mid-1968, Westmoreland also remarked that "it was entirely possible" that still another two and one-third divisions would be needed—four brigades for II Corps and an additional three-brigade division, preferably airmobile, for III Corps—to allow the entire 9th Division to move into the Mekong Delta. The only way to avoid "an unreasonably protracted war," said Westmoreland, was to deploy this optimum force with all due haste.[4]

In Washington, the Joint Chiefs' reaction was predictably rapid, with General Wheeler commissioning a study to determine whether the requested forces could be provided and supported. On 13 April the study concluded that for the United States to meet its worldwide commitments, the only practical solution was to mobilize the reserves for a minimum of twenty-four months and to extend involuntary tours of service of active forces for twelve months. Then MACV's minimum essential force could be in place by June 1968 and the optimum force by July 1969. If the president declined to mobilize or extend the duty tour, the minimum essential force could not deploy before November 1969, nor the optimum contingent before July 1972.[5]

Before authorizing a troop increase that would require a reserve call-up and would almost certainly touch off congressional debate, Johnson summoned his field commander to Washington and asked for an assessment of the war. On 27 April Westmoreland met twice with the president and his advisers and stated that the United States could not lose in Vietnam, but that it had become "a matter of action and reaction—an action by us to which the enemy had reacted or an action by the enemy to which we had reacted."[6] For the allies to sustain the offensive and inflict more casualties than the enemy could replace, Westmoreland would need a lot more soldiers, and he would need them fast.

At one point President Johnson asked what was to prevent the enemy from matching any increase in U.S. forces with one of his own. "If so, where does it all end?" Westmoreland replied that he was fighting a war of attrition and that in all likelihood the Communists would indeed

---

[3] Ltr, COMUSMACV to JCS, 5 Apr 67, sub: MACV Force Requirements FY 1968, and an. C, Westmoreland History files, 15–A, Incl 3, CMH. See also *The Senator Gravel Edition of the Pentagon Papers*, 4:427–31.

[4] Msg, COMUSMACV 09101 to CINCPAC, 18 Mar 67, sub: Force Requirements.

[5] The History of the Joint Chiefs of Staff and the War in Vietnam, 1960–1968; Part III (1967–1968) [Historical Division, Joint Secretariat, Joint Chiefs of Staff, 1 July 1970], ch. 43, p. 2.

[6] Westmoreland Jnl, 27 Apr 67, p. 15, Westmoreland History files, 15–B, CMH.

General Westmoreland presents his troop request to the president.

expand their forces, but that Hanoi would find it difficult to support its divisions beyond the summer of 1968. He went on to explain that according to his analysts a casualty crossover point had taken place in the South except in the two northern provinces. With this exception, the enemy in Vietnam was now suffering heavier losses than he could replace by infiltration and recruitment.[7]

There was one way out of the attrition morass, he said, taking dramatic military action to seal off South Vietnam from the source of the aggression. Marines already occupied a strongpoint defensive system, making unlikely a full-blown enemy invasion across the Demilitarized Zone. The next logical step, if the political risks were acceptable, was an amphibious hook into the North or a push into Laos. For two years plans had been sitting on the shelves at MACV headquarters, detailing several routes of advance into Laos to sever the Ho Chi Minh Trail. The preferred solution was to attack west along Highway 9, using the Marine base at Khe Sanh as a launch point for U.S. forces. A more politically acceptable scenario, code-named RAINBOW, would send a South Vietnamese division from II Corps into the tri-border area with American fire support. He could execute RAINBOW as early as the first of January.[8]

[7] *The Senator Gravel Edition of the Pentagon Papers*, 4:442.

[8] MFRs, 1 Apr 67, sub: CIIC Meeting, 31 March 1967, Westmoreland History files, 15–A–3, CMH, and 8 Apr 67, sub: CIIC Meeting, 8 April 1967, Westmoreland History files, 15–A–7, CMH; Westmoreland Jnl, 27 Apr 67.

General Vien (right) with Lt. Gen. Hoang Xuan Lam, commander of I Corps

Westmoreland left the meeting optimistic, believing that the president, noncommittal so far, would take decisive action on the war. As soon as the general returned to Saigon, he met with General Vien to lay the organizational spadework for the RAINBOW division. Unhappily for Westmoreland, it was one of those moments, so common during Vietnam, when the field command operated with assumptions different from the president and his advisers. The most the president offered was a vague willingness to consider reinforcing the theater if the Americans could squeeze more mileage out of the South Vietnamese. These were in fact his explicit marching orders to Westmoreland. They turned out to be easier said than done.[9]

The Question of the South Vietnamese Army

Marching orders of this kind had been aired in any number of mission council and MACV planning sessions as far back as Westmoreland could remember. Only the details had changed: expand the Regional and Popular Forces by a hundred thousand men by mid-1968; improve South Vietnamese morale through better pay, housing, and rations; enlarge the U.S. advisory structure, assigning more advisers to the territorial forces; and somehow put more South Vietnamese battalions in the field. Over the next six months Westmoreland attempted to do many of these things, both for their own sakes and to keep the door open for a U.S. troop increase. But other than on the advisory front, he made very little progress. Because of the murky political situation in Vietnam—both Nguyen Cao Ky and Lt. Gen. Nguyen Van Thieu, the chief of state, were running for the presidency of the republic—the leadership in Saigon would not even consider partially mobilizing the nation, which included lowering the draft age and extending terms of service, until after the elections in September. Despite Washington's avowed willingness to finance

---

[9] Westmoreland Jnl, 27 Apr 67; MFR, 6 May 67, sub: CIIC Meeting, 6 May 1967, Westmoreland History files, 17–A–3, CMH.

an expansion in the republic's forces, the manpower situation would show little improvement until 1968.

Nor was there tangible improvement in the politicized officer corps. The political and financial interests of the generals might be old news to MACV intelligence, but knowledge was not power in this case, especially with the electoral climate heating up. Other than Operation FAIRFAX, which offered a glimmer of hope, most South Vietnamese infantry battalions showed no signs of increasing the days they spent in combat. The closer the elections came, moreover, the more time commanders spent tending to their alliances. Attempts to encourage more battlefield promotions and a centralized career management program, the keys to MACV's officer-reform package for 1967, ran up against the entrenched interests in the South Vietnamese forces and secrecy in the Joint General Staff.[10]

On the other hand, Westmoreland did have some success in strengthening the area-security advisory program. With the exception of the Marine Corps' Combined Action Program in I Corps, which put Marine squads to work in the villages with the Popular Forces, there had been no American advisers formally assigned to the territorials. As a first step in the right direction the two field forces formed ad hoc teams in the spring and summer, although their training visits to Regional and Popular Forces units rarely maintained a consistent schedule. Finally, in October MACV established mobile advisory teams, formally assigning combat officers to work directly with the territorials in the field. Under the direction of the province senior advisers, each team consisted of two junior officers and three or four enlisted men. By year's end several hundred teams had been sent into the countryside to assist over a thousand territorial units. Whether this would translate into early improvement in territorial performance remained to be seen.[11]

Pacification Developments

Pacification was likewise a question mark for Westmoreland when he returned to Saigon in April. Vien had promised during the winter that he would assign at least half of his army's battalions to support pacification, and that all battalions would receive two weeks of counterinsurgency and nation building instruction sometime in 1967.[12] The reality was far different than Vien had promised. For one thing, the regulars received perfunctory training at best, with division commanders taking little interest in the program. In addition, although only about a quarter of the South

[10] Jeffrey J. Clarke, *Advice and Support: The Final Years, 1965–1973*, United States Army in Vietnam (Washington, D.C.: U.S. Army Center of Military History, Government Printing Office, 1988), pp. 218–19.

[11] Ibid., p. 236.

[12] MFR, 10 Apr 67, MACV Commanders' Conference, 2 April 1967, Westmoreland History files, 15–A–4 and 5, CMH.

Vietnamese battalions were conducting offensive operations (and averaging no more than six days per month in the field), few of the remainder rallied to the pacification banner, and not just because their commanders considered security duty demeaning.

The underlying issue was political. Division commanders had no intention of attaching their battalions to the province chiefs, who had primary responsibility for pacification. Even temporary loss of control over battalions reduced not only the military but also the economic and political powers of the division commanders. There were also divided loyalties: many division commanders supported Thieu, but Ky had appointed many of the province chiefs. For the rest of the year, pacification found little support among the South Vietnamese officer corps.[13]

Still, Westmoreland continued to try, and in this he had timely backing from President Johnson. In April the president selected General Creighton W. Abrams, the Army vice chief of staff, to serve as Westmoreland's deputy and specifically charged him to improve South Vietnam's armed forces and to get them in step on pacification. Johnson also took a more radical step, perhaps the most important realignment of the entire war, restructuring the U.S. mission in Saigon and giving MACV full responsibility for pacification support.

This move ended years of fragmented control of the security program and frustration at the highest U.S. mission level. Ambassador Lodge had taken a step in the right direction the previous November, when he established the Office of Civil Operations to coordinate the actions of all U.S. civilian agencies in Vietnam supporting revolutionary development. Westmoreland had also acted, upgrading to a directorate MACV's pacification advisory staff section and agreeing that both the directorate and the Office of Civil Operations would report directly to the deputy ambassador. But the dual reporting system was cumbersome at best, and the Office of Civil Operations was little better than a loose and sometimes quarrelsome confederation of competing theater agencies. In April, after a year of often heated controversy over whether the military or civil side could do the job best, President Johnson settled the issue. The Office of Civil Operations became part of MACV headquarters, and its new director, presidential adviser Robert Komer, became deputy commander for Civil Operations and Revolutionary Development Support (CORDS), under Westmoreland. This unified U.S. support of pacification for the rest of the war.

Anything but reticent, Komer moved quickly on the organizational front. At the corps level, he established CORDS advisory groups composed of both civilian and military personnel under the senior military adviser. At the province level, he merged the civilian and military advisory staffs, making the senior military adviser the team commander and the senior civilian his deputy. Finally, inheriting the Hamlet Evaluation System from the Office of Civil Operations, Komer made it work. By July

---

[13] Clarke, *Final Years*, pp. 234–35.

Komer reviews a self-help project in Bac Lieu Province, IV Corps.

the computer-compatible reporting system was operational in almost every district. By August the White House was using the data to publicize security developments in the countryside.[14]

Looking Ahead

If there was cautious hope on the pacification front, arising perhaps from the sense of doing something different, it was harder to see where the ground war was going, unless Westmoreland received the reinforcements he requested. For two years his plans for the theater had been founded on a rising tide of infantry, artillery, and air power, and it was only the surge of forces in the summer and fall of 1966 that had allowed him to dream of bringing the war in Vietnam to an acceptable end. Whatever the clouds of dissent gathering on the home front, tugging the White House this way and that, Westmoreland drew assurance from the president's avowal in early 1966 that the field commander would consistently get the troops in the numbers he requested, if not perhaps as quick-

[14] Hunt, *Pacification*, pp. 82–96; Clarke, *Final Years*, pp. 211–12.

222

ly as he desired them. Now, in the summer of 1967, another eighteen months into the conflict, a weary President Johnson changed his mind.[15]

At the time the White House described the new troop limit as a compromise, and in a sense it was. But from the standpoint of the Joint Chiefs of Staff and Westmoreland, who as late as July regarded the figure as still negotiable, the new troop ceiling, precisely because it came in at so much less than requested, represented a divergence from past policy and a defeat. Instead of the minimum essential force of 80,000, Westmoreland was granted about 55,000, taking the ceiling to 525,000. Included in that number were thirteen battalions of infantry, all scheduled to arrive in early 1968.

No sooner had the ink dried on the agreement than the military began urging the acceleration of these deployments, chiefly because of the threat along the Demilitarized Zone. Especially needed, according to Westmoreland, were the six battalions in the rest of the 101st Airborne Division, which would allow him to shift more units to hold in the north. The war in the highlands and around Saigon still had its share of tactical uncertainties, but he knew that nothing would unravel the allied cause of defending the Republic of Vietnam more quickly than North Vietnamese divisions streaming onto the plains of I Corps.[16]

---

[15] Hugh Sidey, *A Very Personal Presidency: Lyndon Johnson in the White House* (New York: Atheneum, 1968), p. 82.

[16] *The Senator Gravel Edition of the Pentagon Papers*, 4:510–33.

PART FOUR

Looking for Momentum
in I Corps

14

Task Force OREGON on the Offensive

A s the dry season deepened in the northern provinces, Westmoreland continued to worry about the enemy's ability to take the initiative there. Task Force OREGON had freed the marines to deal with threats along the Demilitarized Zone, but there was still a real possibility that the Viet Cong and North Vietnamese might strike back in southern I Corps. The next few months would tell.

The Task Force OREGON commander, General Rosson, reported directly to III Marine Amphibious Force, the primary American combat command in I Corps. As a rule, the Marine commander, General Walt, granted Rosson free reign to maneuver his brigades as he saw fit. The only exception was the requirement to protect the Marine Corps air base at Chu Lai, the most vital I Corps installation south of Da Nang.[1]

Rosson's command was divided into the Chu Lai enclave of southeastern Quang Tin Province and, sixty kilometers south, the Duc Pho quarter of southeastern Quang Ngai. Posted between the two were the South Korean 2d Marine Brigade in northeastern Quang Ngai and, south of the Koreans, elements of the South Vietnamese 2d Division. Six U.S. Army Special Forces camps were scattered throughout the mountainous interior, while South Vietnamese territorial forces guarded towns and installations along the coast.[2]

Technically, the South Vietnamese 2d Division was responsible for security in all of Quang Tin and Quang Ngai Provinces, but in the past Saigon's troops had performed inconsistently at best. (*Map 23*) American units would have to do the job. Eventually, Rosson expected to gain two more brigades if Operation YORK, the planned sweep of the Quang Ngai interior, took place. For the time being, his two brigades—the 196th and the 3d Brigade of the 25th Division—could do little more than attend to local security, patrolling the coastal plains and foothills as the marines

---

[1] Interv, author with Rosson, 13 Sep 77; Periodic Intel Rpt 7–67, 1st Marine Div, 18 Apr 67, an. B, pp. 2–3, and CICV Study, ST 67–080, 1 Sep 67, sub: NVA Rocket Artillery Units, p. 4, both in Historians files, CMH; Telfer, Rogers, and Fleming, *U.S. Marines in Vietnam, 1967*, ch. 6.

[2] From north to south, the Special Forces camps were at Tien Phuoc, Tra Bong, Ha Thanh, Minh Long, Ba To, and Gia Vuc.

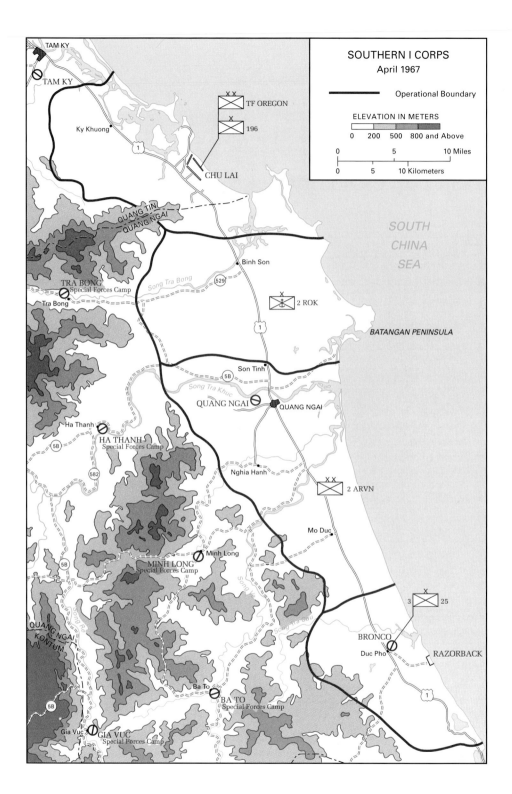

SOUTHERN I CORPS
April 1967

Operational Boundary

ELEVATION IN METERS
0 200 500 800 and Above

0   5   10 Miles
0   5   10 Kilometers

TAM KY

TAM KY

Ky Khuong

XX TF OREGON
X 196

CHU LAI

QUANG TIN
QUANG NGAI

SOUTH
CHINA
SEA

Binh Son

TRA BONG
Special Forces Camp

Tra Bong

Song Tra Bong

(529)

X 2 ROK

BATANGAN PENINSULA

Son Tinh

(5B)

Song Tra Khuc

QUANG NGAI

QUANG NGAI

Ha Thanh

HA THANH
Special Forces Camp

(5B)

(582)

Nghia Hanh

XX 2 ARVN

Mo Duc

Minh Long

MINH LONG
Special Forces Camp

(5B)

Song Ve

X
3   25

QUANG NGAI
KONTUM

BRONCO

Duc Pho

RAZORBACK

Ba To

BA TO
Special Forces Camp

(5B)

Gia Vuc GIA VUC
Special Forces Camp

1

had done before them. Thus, the Americans were facing yet another frustrating situation in which they had too many vital tasks to perform for the limited resources at their disposal.

Chu Lai

Until Rosson arrived in April 1967 the U.S. 1st Marine Division defended Chu Lai and had formed a provisional headquarters, the Chu Lai Defense Command, to guard the immediate approaches. The main line of defense was a series of bunkers stretching along a 23-kilometer trace manned by a company from each of four Marine battalions. Rosson discontinued this practice, which he considered a waste of good infantry, but he agreed to retain the Chu Lai Defense Command while insisting that troops for bunker duty come exclusively from Army or Marine support units.

The responsibility for the outer defense of Chu Lai went to Brig. Gen. Richard T. Knowles and his 196th Brigade. In addition to the brigade's three battalions, Knowles had an additional battalion from the 3d of the 25th and one squadron from the 11th Armored Cavalry Regiment, giving him a total force of just over 6,000 men. Unlike the marines, who usually returned at night to semipermanent camps around Chu Lai, Rosson wanted Knowles to maintain constant pressure on the enemy by keeping his troops in the field around the clock. He ordered several camps demolished, a job the marines undertook reluctantly since they expected to return to Chu Lai as soon as the crisis along the Demilitarized Zone had ended.[3]

Knowles' area of responsibility included Tinh Ly District in Quang Tin Province and the northern portion of Binh Son District in Quang Ngai. The area had about 90,000 civilians, most of whom lived close to Highway 1. With the exception of the beach at Chu Lai, the Viet Cong controlled the coastline and most of the inland plains. Like Binh Dinh to the south, Quang Tin and Quang Ngai were Communist territory. In the mountains, the *2d PAVN Division* presented the greatest threat to Chu Lai and its air base, yet the North Vietnamese seldom came down to the plains except for supplies. Knowles' primary enemy was a local Viet Cong battalion, four separate companies, and an underground supported by about 3,000 guerrillas.[4]

[3] ORLL, 18 Feb–30 Apr 67, Task Force OREGON, p. 15; Intervs, author with Rosson, 13 Sep 77, and with Col Oliver M. Whipple (USMC), Comdr, Co F, 2d Bn, 7th Marines, 1st Marine Div, 1 Dec 81, Historians files, CMH; ORLL, 1 Feb–30 Apr 67, 196th Light Inf Bde, pp. 8–9, 16.

[4] ORLL, 1 May–31 Jul 67, 196th Light Inf Bde, 22 Sep 67, p. 9; Intervs, author with Brig Gen Frank H. Linnell, CG, 196th Light Inf Bde, 6 Oct 81, and with Col Charles R. Smith, Comdr, Co A, 4th Bn, 31st Inf, 196th Light Inf Bde, 13 Aug 81; MFR, Maj Gen George I. Forsythe, Military Assistant to Deputy, CORDS, MACJOIR, 10 Oct 67, sub: Trip Report to Quang Ngai Province, 3–4 October 1967, MG George I. Forsythe, LTC Paul E. Suplizio, and Dr. Philip Worchel. All in Historians files, CMH. Evaluation Rpt, MACCORDS-RE, 13 Sep 67, Task Force OREGON Operations, pp. 4–5, 7, and Incl 2.

Chu Lai Air Base

Knowles' hunt for the insurgents around Chu Lai started off well. During the first six weeks the Americans averaged five firefights a day, which forced the Viet Cong to change tactics. The 196th, enemy commanders discovered, had far greater mobility than the marines, moving rapidly with its fleet of helicopters and tracked armor to cut off escape routes. Almost overnight the insurgents began to avoid battle, but the Americans' advantage would not last.

The normal cycle of troop rotation began to drain the 196th of combat-experienced men. The unit had deployed to Vietnam the previous July. In an attempt to avoid a one-year "rotation hump," II Field Force had instituted an infusion program in March, exchanging 642 men—16 percent of the brigade's strength—for a like number of men from other units in III Corps who had rotation dates after July 1967. Plans called for infusion to accelerate over the next three months, but when the brigade joined Task Force OREGON, the program had to be scrapped.

Significant manpower losses began in May and accelerated in June and July. During this brief period the 196th lost 184 officers (66 percent of its total strength) and 2,166 enlisted men (58 percent). The brigade also lost 15 of 18 key officers, including General Knowles and all 3 battalion commanders. Their replacements were fresh arrivals from the United States. This "revolving door policy," which guaranteed the rapid rotation of officers in combat commands, was later criticized as representing careerism at its worst. It destroyed any prospect for continuity of com-

230

*Newly arrived in Vietnam, troops at Duc Pho receive training in
Viet Cong booby traps.*

mand, it hurt field morale among the enlisted ranks, and it ultimately lessened the effectiveness of U.S. forces.[5]

To remedy the problem, the new 196th Brigade commander, Brig. Gen. Frank H. Linnell, set up a special training program for his officers and men, most of whom were serving together for the first time. In addition, he told his battalion commanders to abandon their productive small-unit operations for safer company-size actions until the new troops gained experience. Inevitably, brigade results slipped sharply in May and June, although casualties from mines, booby traps, and sniper fire remained steady.

Mines were the worst, wounding and killing American soldiers when they least expected it. One of the most common enemy mines, the "butterfly," got its name from two small wires extending like wings from the top of the mine that could be detonated by pressure or electricity. The enemy buried them with only the wings exposed. Step on one of the wings, as one mine disposal expert noted, and "farewell." Chinese claymores, grenades with trip wires, various antipersonnel mines, and rigged artillery shells and mortar rounds comprised the other explosive devices with which the 196th, and indeed all American units, had to contend.

---

[5] ORLL, 1 Feb–30 Apr 67, 196th Light Inf Bde, p. 1; ORLL, 1 May–31 Jul 67, 196th Light Inf Bde, pp. 1–3, 28; Interv, author with Linnell, 6 Oct 81.

231

A favorite Viet Cong tactic was to booby-trap rice or weapons caches, which they knew American soldiers would probably search. They also wired jungle trails, anticipating that American patrols would take the easy route rather than hacking their way through the thick underbrush. Another enemy tactic was to fire automatic weapons at long range into a night defensive position with the almost certain knowledge that the Americans would search the surrounding jungle the next morning and then stumble upon mines and booby traps. When one of the devices went off, soldiers rushing in to help the wounded became perfect targets for snipers. Eventually, Linnell's men became more experienced. During June they detected twice as many unexploded mines and booby traps as they had the month before. By mid-July casualties from such devices had dropped sharply.[6]

Duc Pho

In the other sector of Task Force OREGON the fighting was harder. When Colonel Shanahan's 3d Brigade of the 25th Division reached Duc Pho in April, government officials informed him that 80 percent of the district's 94,000 people were either Viet Cong or Communist sympathizers. The South Vietnamese exercised authority, they conceded, only in a few villages on Highway 1 near district headquarters. Traditionally, Duc Pho had served as a rest area for the *3d PAVN Division*, providing both replacements and food. Military stores came from trawlers off the coast, while other key items, such as medical supplies and batteries, were typically purchased in Saigon and shipped to Sa Huynh, the small port in the southern part of the district.

In March U.S. intelligence learned from a defecting North Vietnamese officer that the *3d Division* was scheduled to spearhead the *B1 Front*'s dry season offensive. According to the officer, a trawler was to deliver a shipment of arms and ammunition from North Vietnam to the mouth of the Tra Cau River, but it had run aground on the Batangan Peninsula. He went on to say that as part of the new offensive, the *2d PLAF Regiment*, which had been inactive in western Duc Pho since November, was to hit the Ba To Special Forces camp, thirty kilometers from the coast. The attack would begin in late April or early May.[7]

The information was welcome, but Colonel Shanahan, with two battalions, was already on the move. He gave the 2d Battalion, 35th Infantry, still commanded by Lt. Col. Clinton E. Granger, the job of securing the Duc Pho airfield, now renamed BRONCO, and the road extending east to

    [6] Interv, author with Linnell, 6 Oct 81; ORLL, 1 May–31 Jul 67, 196th Light Inf Bde, pp. 6, 9–20, 30–31; Interv, author with Smith, 13 Aug 81.

    [7] ORLL, 1 Feb–30 Apr 67, 3d Bde, 25th Inf Div, 10 May 67, pp. 3–4, Historians files, CMH; Evaluation Rpt, MACCORDS-RE, 13 Sep 67, Task Force OREGON Operations, pp. 2–4; Intervs, author with Shanahan, 13 Aug 81, 4 Sep 81.

RAZORBACK. Granger was also to work the coastal side of Highway 1, concentrating on the Tra Cau corridor, where the enemy received supplies by sea. Shanahan's other unit, the 1st Battalion, 35th Infantry, under Maj. James E. Moore, would operate on the inland side of the highway to screen the brigade's flank.

At first, Moore's units saw most of the action. The fighting was difficult, because the enemy was hiding among civilians. On the morning of 22 April, for example, Moore's men took fire from a hamlet six kilometers northwest of BRONCO. Hoping to cut off the enemy, he brought up most of his battalion and by early afternoon had encircled the village. Air strikes drove several civilians out in front of the waiting Americans, who held their fire. When the fighting resumed, Moore's men squeezed the Viet Cong into a corner of the hamlet, but before they could finish them off, darkness ended the battle. At first light the Americans attacked, overrunning the dazed Viet Cong and taking several prisoners. A sweep through the entire hamlet revealed a sophisticated, fortified complex containing bunkers connected by trenches and tunnels. Amid the rubble, the men counted thirty-three enemy bodies.

Through the next week Moore's troops pushed on, fighting small groups of Viet Cong almost every day. Twice they ran into fortified villages and fought running battles before pushing out the defenders. At the same time, Granger's battalion saw action east of Highway 1. By the end of April the two battalions accounted for over two hundred Viet Cong killed or captured. Most of the enemy casualties were guerrillas, but several prisoners claimed to be *2d Regiment* soldiers who had been detailed to train guerrillas and to handle logistical matters for their regiment bivouacked in the mountains west of BRONCO.[8]

Meanwhile, in late April Task Force OREGON received information that the *3d Division* headquarters had moved north out of Binh Dinh Province into Quang Ngai to join its *22d Regiment*. In addition, the *1st PLAF Regiment*, a *2d Division* unit, was now said to be twenty-five kilometers north of Ba To. The news prompted Rosson to request immediate deployment of the 1st Brigade, 101st Airborne Division. Although this unit was the I Field Force reserve, both Larsen and Westmoreland agreed to its early release and movement by sea from Nha Trang to RAZORBACK. From there, the brigade was to air-assault inland.

At the same time, Westmoreland shifted the I Field Force boundary northward so Larsen could use the 1st Cavalry Division against the headquarters of the *3d Division* and the *22d Regiment* in southern Quang Ngai. Rosson established a forward command post near BRONCO and directed the 196th at Chu Lai to place a battalion on two-hour alert.[9]

As these deployments were in progress, Shanahan's battalions prepared

---

[8] ORLL, 1 Feb–30 Apr 67, 3d Bde, 25th Inf Div, pp. 6–10, 12, and Incl 5; Intervs, author with Shanahan, 13 Aug 81, 4 Sep 81, and with Moore, 4 Aug 81.

[9] AAR, Opn MALHEUR, 1st Bde, 101st Abn Div, 2 Sep 67, p. 4, Historians files, CMH; AAR, Opn PERSHING, 1st Cav Div, p. 9; Interv, author with Rosson, 13 Sep 77.

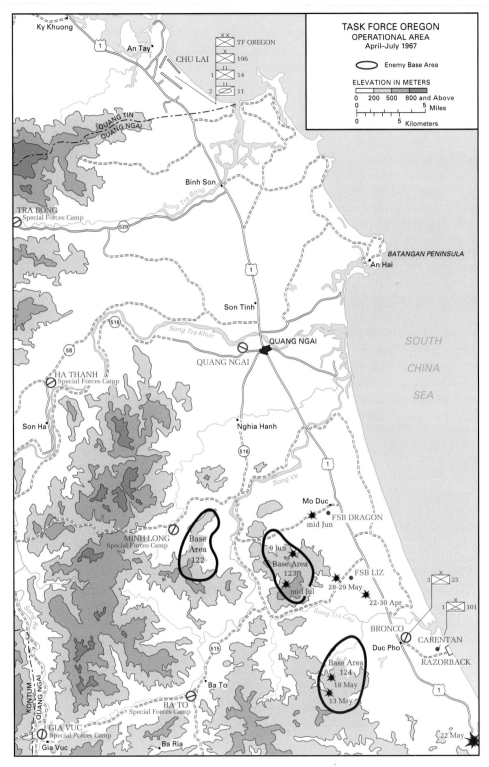

MAP 24

for action against the *22d Regiment*. Working from OLIVE DRAB, a firebase four kilometers west of BRONCO, Moore assumed control of the southern portion of the brigade sector, while Granger, reinforced with the brigade's cavalry troop and an attached tank company, took over the northern part, an area expanded to include southern Mo Duc District. Here Granger established Firebase LIZ, nine kilometers northwest of Duc Pho.

There would be no knockout blow here. U.S. commanders knew their actions would be little more than harassment of the enemy to keep him away from the populated areas. Over the next week, Granger's 2d of the 35th Infantry fought Viet Cong units daily. On 11 May Granger trapped an enemy unit six kilometers northeast of LIZ, overrunning its fortified hamlet as darkness fell. During the next night the Viet Cong retaliated with mortars, striking a battery position at LIZ. (*Map 24*) But when they shifted their fire to support a ground attack, rounds landed among their own men, and the assault ended before it began.

Isolated actions continued. On 19 May intelligence reported that an enemy battalion had just occupied a camp in a heavily wooded area, eight kilometers south of BRONCO. Although Moore's troops had searched the area a day before without making contact, they found the camp that afternoon, though they failed to encircle it before dark. Moore called in artillery and air strikes throughout the night, and when the Americans moved in the next morning they met only light resistance. Hastily laid communications wire and captured documents indicated a major command post, presumably that of the *22d Regiment*.

Two days later, on 22 May, Moore's troops ran into part of the *7th Battalion, 22d Regiment*, in a fortified hamlet along Highway 1, thirteen kilometers southeast of BRONCO. In a fight lasting over twenty-four hours, they killed more than seventy Viet Cong and found a cache of more than a hundred mortar rounds. The battle devastated the enemy: the Americans would not encounter the *7th Battalion* for another six months.[10]

By the end of May Shanahan was satisfied with the performance of his two battalions. They had taken the battle to an enemy who seemed incapable of putting up effective resistance. During the past thirty days, moreover, the Americans had counted 159 Viet Cong defectors in the Duc Pho area, whereas in the three months prior to the brigade's arrival there had been 3. In a small but encouraging way, the Americans had gained momentum on the coast. The question was whether they could duplicate that success in the interior.

[10] ORLL, 1 May–31 Jul 67, 3d Bde, 25th Inf Div, 10 Aug 67, pp. 4, 7, and ORLL, 1 May–31 Jul 67, 1st Cav Div, 15 Aug 67, pp. 12–18, both in Historians files, CMH; AAR, Opn PERSHING, 1st Cav Div, tab 6; Intervs, author with Shanahan, 13 Aug 81, 4 Sep 81; with Moore, 4 Aug 81; with Granger, 15 Nov 85.

Inland Sweeps

After leaving Kontum Province in January, the 1st Brigade, 101st Airborne Division, returned to its Phan Rang base in II Corps, having been in continuous combat for a year. After a week's respite it reentered the field on 26 January in Operation FARRAGUT, now under a new commander, Brig. Gen. Salve H. Matheson. FARRAGUT involved sweeps west and south of Phan Rang in suspected enemy staging areas.[11] The results were disappointing, however, and follow-on operations in search of an enemy headquarters north of Bao Loc, some one hundred kilometers west of Phan Rang, were equally dismal. Except for seizing some rice and killing some one hundred fifty Viet Cong, the brigade realized few successes in nearly two months of campaigning.[12]

Then, on 28 March Matheson launched Operation SUMMERALL to intercept enemy replacements reportedly moving east through Darlac Province to join the *18B PAVN Regiment* somewhere in the Hon Ba Mountains in Khanh Hoa Province. But the enemy learned of the operation and fled. When intelligence reached I Field Force on 17 April that the *18B* was in fact in the Hon Ba, Larsen extended the SUMMERALL area of operations, though the pursuit halted on 29 April, when Westmoreland ordered the brigade to leave immediately to join Task Force OREGON in I Corps.[13]

In early May Matheson's brigade put ashore at RAZORBACK Beach in southern Quang Ngai, established a base named CARENTAN, and prepared for action against the enemy's inland base areas—numbered 122, 123, and 124—which ran from north to south through the mountainous jungle overlooking the Ve and Tra Cau River Valleys. Although not the massive force that Westmoreland had envisioned for Operation YORK, the airborne brigade would have to do until more units became available.

On 11 May, while Shanahan's two battalions patrolled the coast, Matheson's brigade moved into the interior looking for a fight with the *1st* and *2d PLAF Regiments*, both of which were thought to lurk there. Two of his three battalions conducted air assaults into the western part of Base Area 124, a tangle of tree-clad low hills overlooking the coastal plain. Resistance was light. The next morning Matheson committed his remaining battalion to a blocking position on high ground in the eastern part of the base area and ordered the other two battalions to sweep toward it. Encountering little opposition in the days that followed, the brigade commander decentralized his operations and conducted a more rigorous search.

The major strength of Matheson's brigade lay in the experience of the junior leaders. All the battle-tested company commanders were captains,

---

[11] AAR, Opn FARRAGUT, 1st Bde, 101st Abn Div, n.d., p. 2, and Incls 1, 3, Historians files, CMH.

[12] ORLL, 1 Feb–30 Apr 67, 1st Bde, 101st Abn Div, 15 May 67, Incls 1, 2, Historians files, CMH.

[13] Ibid., pp. 2–3; AAR, Opn SUMMERALL, 1st Bde, 101st Abn Div, 21 May 67, pp. 2–8, Historians files, CMH.

A soldier of the 101st Airborne Division searches a North Vietnamese Army hospital.

and many had served as lieutenants with the brigade. In addition, the 1st of the 101st did not experience the shortages of noncommissioned officers that most units did in 1967. In fact, many of the brigade's noncommissioned officers had volunteered to remain for extended tours, and in many cases others, upon returning to the United States, had asked to return to Vietnam to rejoin their unit. Although the brigade had been in Vietnam for nearly two years, morale was still high.

Because Matheson had complete confidence in his troops, he allowed each battalion commander to work his operational area as he saw fit, insisting only that companies operate within a two-hour march of each other. Most units kept constantly on the move and traveled with three to five days' worth of supplies, so the enemy would be less likely to pinpoint their location by observing resupply helicopters. Companies split into platoons for wider coverage of a search area, but remained close enough to reassemble quickly if they ran into a sizable force.

These tactics often paid off. On 13 May, near the Tra Cau's headwaters, twelve separate firefights occurred, the largest against an entrenched

237

Viet Cong company. By nightfall, the Americans had killed 29 Viet Cong at a cost of 1 American killed and 7 wounded.

But the outcome was not always so one-sided. On 18 May Company B of the 2d Battalion, 502d Infantry, moved well inside a large enemy camp before realizing that the occupants had not yet fled. Confusion reigned during the furious firefight, and the Americans realized they were too close to their enemy to call in artillery or helicopter gunships. For six hours they fought, sometimes hand to hand, until reinforcements arrived and the enemy pulled back. Left on the battlefield were 31 Viet Cong dead, while American casualties were 12 killed and 41 wounded.

Matheson's men completed their scouring of Base Area 124 in early June, reporting that they had killed or captured over 400 Viet Cong, seized 125 enemy weapons, and razed several base camps.[14] General Rosson then ordered Matheson to shift his attention slightly north, to Base Areas 123 and 122. Both were more mountainous than 124 and were often drenched by cloudbursts leftover from storms brewing around the inland peaks near the Laotian border. If Matheson failed to find Viet Cong there, he was to assist the Quang Ngai province chief with the evacuation of all civilians from the Ve and Tra Cau Valleys. Whatever their political loyalties, these civilians had provided food and recruits for the enemy.

Matheson sent two battalions into Base Area 123 on 8 June and another into 122 the following day. While the first day's fighting ended with 22 enemy killed, it was apparent to the Americans that the Viet Cong were trying to avoid contact.

With few enemy units to be found, Matheson turned to evacuating civilians. For two weeks trucks and helicopters moved over 7,000 people and 1,200 head of cattle to refugee centers in Duc Pho and Nghia Hanh Districts. When the operation ended in late June, the valleys had been laid waste by combat and herbicides, while several hundred tons of rice and salt were either destroyed or airlifted to refugee centers.

In July, believing that the Viet Cong were re-forming in Base Area 124, the airborne brigade returned south. A week of searching, however, uncovered only small enemy units. Documents and prisoners revealed that both the *1st* and *2d Regiments* had lost several commanders and that illness, desertions, and heavy casualties had greatly diminished their effectiveness. When Matheson received a report in mid-July that the two units were converging on Base Area 123 to form a single combat-effective regiment, he called in B–52s. On the heels of the bombing, all three of his battalions air-assaulted back into the region, which they again swept clean through the rest of the month. Yet, once again, the Viet Cong evad-

---

[14] AAR, Opn MALHEUR, 1st Bde, 101st Abn Div, pp. 1–7, 13, and Incl 1; Interv, author with Col Howard H. Danford, Comdr, 2d Bn, 502d Inf, 101st Abn Div, 21 Sep 81, and Senior Officer Debriefing Program, DA, 2 Mar 68, sub: Brig Gen Salve H. Matheson [CG, 1st Bde, 101st Abn Div], pp. 17–18 (hereafter cited as Matheson Debriefing), both in Historians files, CMH.

ed, though American sweeps killed over 100 enemy soldiers, including a Viet Cong district chief and his aides.[15]

Back to the Coast

As the search of Base Area 124 neared completion, activity in the 3d of the 25th's coastal haunt began to rise. At noon on 27 May Shanahan received an electronic report indicating that a major enemy unit had established a command post at Tan Phong Hamlet in the Tra Cau Valley, two kilometers west of LIZ. Shanahan passed the information to Granger and, since the 2d Battalion, 35th Infantry, was fully occupied either in defending LIZ or in conducting sweeps to the east, provided him with the blue team platoon of Troop A, 1st Squadron, 9th Cavalry, to investigate.

The blue team landed in a rice paddy south of Tan Phong. As the helicopters flew away, gunfire crackled from the hamlet, and within minutes the enemy had pinned down the Americans. Before artillery and air support arrived, the enemy tried to flank the blue team, prompting Granger to send his reconnaissance platoon from LIZ, followed by an armored cavalry troop, to attack the hamlet from another direction. Sensing that he lacked the manpower to seal off the target, Granger decided to air-assault Company A, which was holding LIZ, into a clearing near the action, a risky move since it left LIZ virtually unguarded.

All three units arrived within the hour. They worked around the north, south, and east sides of the hamlet, asking for helicopter gunships to close the hole on the west. Worried about the vulnerability of LIZ, Granger wanted to complete the encirclement before dark, or at least to get some new troops into the firebase. LIZ waited tensely well into the night before the brigade sent helicopters carrying Company B from the coast. The next morning the Americans moved in and found that the Viet Cong had fled, leaving behind 81 dead.

That night Company B and the reconnaissance platoon established four platoon-size ambushes across the entrance to the Tra Cau Valley. Before daylight on 29 May a Viet Cong company attacked one of the positions. Although the defenders were hard pressed, they repulsed the assault, and the enemy fled before first light.

Timely intelligence and a prompt response had allowed the Americans to catch and destroy a large Viet Cong force as it prepared for an attack on LIZ. From captured documents and from prisoners Granger learned that his men had met the *60th Battalion*, the *1st PLAF Regiment's* best unit.

Especially valuable was a captured document containing the strengths of American units operating in Quang Ngai Province, together

---

[15] AAR, Opn MALHEUR, 1st Bde, 101st Abn Div, pp. 2–13, and Incls 1, 3; Matheson Debriefing, pp. 7–8, 13–14; Intervs, author with Rosson, 13 Sep 77; with Danford, 21 Sep 81.

Infantry and armor in action in coastal Quang Ngai

with their designations, tactics, and plans. The document also provided a critique of American tactics and instructions on how to exploit weaknesses. Copies were soon on the way to all U.S. commanders in the area.[16]

In early June intelligence reports indicated that the enemy intended to attack the headquarters of Mo Duc District, ten kilometers north of LIZ. Shanahan reacted by extending Granger's operational area north to include the entire Mo Duc Plain. A new firebase, DRAGON, was built next to the district headquarters and manned by an artillery battery provided by Task Force OREGON and an infantry company. The additional soldiers gave Granger the equivalent of six company-size maneuver units.

The timeliness and value of the reinforcements became clear in mid-June, when the Americans fought a series of battles within a few kilometers of DRAGON. These actions cost the enemy, thought to be of the *1st Regiment* from Base Area 123, more than 50 dead.

The fights near LIZ and DRAGON in May and June had confirmed the location of the *1st Regiment*, but the whereabouts of the *2d PLAF* and the *22d PAVN Regiments* remained less certain. Analysts reasoned that one or

[16] Rpt, 2d Bn, 35th Inf, n.d., Operational Report for Quarterly Period Ending 31 July 1967, pp. 10–14, Historians files, CMH; Intervs, author with Shanahan, 13 Aug 81, 4 Sep 81; with Granger, 15 Nov 85; Intel Sums 16, 3d Bde, 25th Inf Div, 27 May 67; 19, 3d Bde, 25th Inf Div, 30 May 67; and 20, 3d Bde, 25th Inf Div, 31 May 67. All in Historians files, CMH.

both regiments had to take some action in Duc Pho to reestablish local authority and concluded that BRONCO was the most likely objective.

The enemy struck on 23 June. Shortly past midnight twelve minutes of mortar and recoilless rifle fire hit the base, killing 3 Americans, wounding 51, and knocking out an 8-inch howitzer.[17]

Once again the enemy had picked the time and the place to attack, leaving the Americans guessing what would come next. Then in late June intelligence pinpointed a battalion of the *2d Regiment* and two local force battalions around the beaches near the mouth of the Tra Cau. Eager to bring the Viet Cong to battle, the new 3d Brigade commander, Col. George E. Wear, sent the 2d Battalion, 35th Infantry, after them. For two weeks, Granger's replacement, Lt. Col. Norman L. Tiller, searched hamlets and set night ambushes, killing some 30 Viet Cong. Once again, the Viet Cong were nowhere to be seen during the day.

Finally, on 10 July, a Viet Cong prisoner led his captors to a complex of underground hiding places, giving the Americans a lesson in concealment. The skillfully camouflaged positions had eluded detection even when Tiller's men were within feet of them. The Viet Cong often hid their positions with wooden trays of vegetation that fit snugly into rectangular wooden frames around the openings of the shelters. When the guerrillas climbed into the dugouts, which accommodated three to five men, villagers put the lids in place and blended the vegetation with plants growing nearby. Almost all the shelters were under clumps of bamboo, whose roots provided ceiling reinforcement, while hollow bamboo poles provided ventilation.

Tiller's men again searched the hamlets. Finding the dugouts required patience and persistence as soldiers gently probed the ground with bayonets or sharp bamboo stakes. For the most part, however, the Americans simply staked out a suspected area, knowing that in a few days the Viet Cong would have to come out to look for food and water. Once the men found a dugout opening, a soldier would fire a few rifle rounds into the entrance and, after checking for mines and booby traps, remove the trap door. When given the choice of surrendering or being killed, many hastened to surrender. If all else failed, the soldier tossed grenades into the opening. As Tiller's men became more adept at locating the dugouts, results improved markedly. During the last three weeks of July, at the cost of 9 American lives, Tiller claimed 260 Viet Cong dead, 47 captured, and 108 weapons seized.[18]

[17] ORLL, 1 May–31 Jul 67, 3d Bde, 25th Inf Div, pp. 3–5, 7–12, Incls 4, 5, 6; Intervs, author with Shanahan, 13 Aug 81, 4 Sep 81; with Danford, 21 Sep 81; AAR, Opn MALHEUR, 1st Bde, 101st Abn Div, p. 9.

[18] Rpt, 2d Bn, 35th Inf, n.d., Operational Report for Quarterly Period Ending 31 July 1967, pp. 18, 24–25; Rpt, 2d Bn, 35th Inf, n.d., Operational Report for Quarterly Period Ending 31 October 1967, Incls 1, 2, Historians files, CMH; MFR, 18 Sep 67, sub: MACV Commanders' Conference, 27 August 1967, pp. 14–17, Westmoreland History files, 21–14, CMH.

TABLE 1

Task Force OREGON Brigade Statistics
(1 May–31 July 1967)

Description	3d Bde, 25th Div	1st Bde, 101st Abn Div*	196th Bde
Enemy killed (body count)	1,339	869	448
Favorable kill ratio	13.7:1	10.7:1	11.2:1
Enemy weapons captured**	410	314	61

*1st Brigade, 101st Airborne Division, totals are from 11 May–2 August 1967.
**Includes weapons found in caches.

Source: ORLL, 1 May–31 Jul 67, 3d Bde, 25th Inf Div, pp. 8, 18, 20; AAR, Opn MALHEUR, 1st Bde, 101st Abn Div, p. 13; ORLL, 1 May–31 Jul 67, 196th Light Inf Bde, pp. 2, 20–22.

Summing Up

By MACV's standards of measurement, Task Force OREGON was winning in southern I Corps. The body count, now supplemented by the somewhat more meaningful "kill ratio" of enemy to friendly deaths, showed that more than half the enemy losses were Viet Cong local forces and guerrillas who could not be replaced as easily as main force recruits from North Vietnam.[19] (*Table 1*)

Whether a greater scouring of the key base areas or an even deeper probe into the interior would have produced fundamentally different results, no one could tell. Operations both in the interior and closer to the coast netted a relatively small number of weapons compared to the number of enemy dead, again posing the question of who was being killed, especially after subtracting weapons located in hidden caches from those taken from known enemy casualties on the battlefield.

The fact was that American operations in southern I Corps during the late spring and early summer of 1967 were less favorable than the kill ratios suggested. Operating in the coastal plains of southern Quang Ngai, the 3d Brigade, 25th Division, for the most part had confronted local force units and village guerrillas rather than the main forces. So, rather than fighting any decisive battles, the brigade measured much of its success by what in Vietnam passed for taking territory—keeping the roads open. By July

[19] ORLL, 1 May–31 Jul 67, 3d Bde, 25th Inf Div, pp. 8, 18, 20; AAR, Opn MALHEUR, 1st Bde, 101st Abn Div, p. 13; ORLL, 1 May–31 Jul 67, 196th Light Inf Bde, pp. 2, 20–22.

Highway 1 was open throughout the 3d Brigade sector during daylight, and South Vietnamese officials claimed that the government controlled over half of the Duc Pho District's population, a 100 percent increase since February. On the other hand, over 70 percent of that increase, some 19,000 people, consisted of refugees—people who either had been forced out of their homes by the allies or had fled the fighting around their hamlets. Except those located near Highway 1, few hamlets remained intact.[20]

With twice the number of men available to the 3d of the 25th, the 196th Brigade had kept Chu Lai free from attack and Highway 1 open during the day. Away from the road, many hamlets had been damaged by the fighting, but not on the scale of the destruction in Duc Pho District. The 196th's presence ensured that the South Vietnamese government dominated populated areas, but elsewhere the Viet Cong still prevailed.

The 1st Brigade of the 101st Airborne Division had taken on better armed units, and during the first two and a half months with Task Force OREGON had suffered more casualties, 81 killed and 594 wounded, than in any comparable period since reaching Vietnam. Though the inland mountain bases had been sanctuaries for many years, the paratroopers had entered them without difficulty. Once the Americans had "neutralized" them and evacuated the people in the valleys, the enemy's big units retreated deeper into the interior. It was a great boon to security along the coast.[21]

---

[20] Evaluation Rpt, MACCORDS-RE, 13 Sep 67, Task Force OREGON Operations, pp. 3, 5.
[21] AAR, Opn MALHEUR, 1st Bde, 101st Abn Div, pp. 13, 15, Incl 4, pp. 3–4.

15

Weary Battles of Summer

By the end of July 1967 enemy activity had declined in I Corps as the Communists regrouped for attacks around the September elections. Their plans called for assaults in each of the five northern provinces, together with a demonstration along the Demilitarized Zone intended to attract large numbers of U.S. forces to its defense. During the summer lull, the *1st* and *2d PLAF Regiments*, both weakened, departed from Quang Ngai Province. The former rejoined the *2d Division* up in Quang Tin, while the latter traveled south to rejoin the *3d Division* in Binh Dinh. The Americans detected neither redeployment for several weeks, a failure that would have Task Force OREGON commanders looking for units that were no longer there.

General Situation

Task Force OREGON's dispositions had not changed since early summer. While the 1st of the 101st Airborne Division worked the interior of Quang Ngai Province, the 3d of the 4th Infantry Division stayed busy in the southern districts, leaving the 196th to hold Chu Lai and the nearby villages.[1] Between Chu Lai and Duc Pho, Brig. Gen. Nguyen Van Toan's South Vietnamese 2d Division and Brig. Gen. Yun Sang Kim's South Korean 2d Marine Brigade occupied the populated areas. From his headquarters in Quang Ngai City, Toan deployed five battalions to guard the urban environs, commonly known as the central pacified core. Although these areas had remained free from enemy attack, U.S. advisers complained bitterly of Toan's refusal to expand security into the surrounding countryside.[2]

---

[1] On 1 August 1967, the 3d Brigade of the 25th Infantry Division was redesignated the 3d Brigade of the 4th Infantry Division. The 4th Division's original 3d Brigade, which had been operating with the 25th Division in III Corps since entering Vietnam, was simultaneously redesignated the 3d Brigade of the 25th Division.

[2] MACV History 1967, vol. 3, p. 1273; Evaluation Rpt, MACCORDS-RE, 13 Sep 67, Task Force OREGON Operations, p. 4; RD Rpt, Quang Ngai Province, May 67, 2 Jun 67, and Interv, author with Col Carl C. Ulsaker, Senior Adviser, 2d ARVN Div, 30 Aug 82, both in Historians files, CMH.

The Americans knew much less about the Korean area of operations. North of Quang Ngai City, Korean units had refused to have U.S. advisers join them in the field, leaving MACV in doubt as to what the Koreans were accomplishing. Moreover, Kim vetoed proposals to put South Vietnamese troops in his sector and took pains to control the movement of all South Vietnamese officials. Believing, as did the Americans, that Communists had penetrated the government, he rarely informed the South Vietnamese of pending operations, nor did he bother to obtain clearance to fire his artillery. If anything, the Americans and South Vietnamese assumed that, because of the no-nonsense manner of the Korean officers, they must have been dealing effectively with the Viet Cong. On the other hand, they knew that the Koreans avoided the Batangan Peninsula, long dominated by the enemy, and had heard rumors that Seoul had instructed Kim to keep casualties low.[3]

HOOD RIVER

In late July an opportunity arose for the Vietnamese, Koreans, and Americans to act in concert. Task Force OREGON received word from Toan's headquarters that the *1st PLAF Regiment* was regrouping in Base Area 121, twenty kilometers west of Quang Ngai City, and would soon be joined by the *21st PAVN Regiment*, also of the *2d Division*. From there, the enemy apparently planned to attack Quang Ngai City before the elections on 3 September.[4] Since the *2d Division* had attempted a similar operation the previous February, Maj. Gen. Richard T. Knowles, the new Task Force OREGON commander, was convinced that an attack was in the offing and sought to take advantage of the opportunity to trap the two regiments as they massed.

Knowles called the new operation HOOD RIVER. Two airborne battalions would encircle the target area on the west, while a similar-size force of Korean marines moved in from the north and two South Vietnamese ranger battalions closed the gap on the south. North of the Koreans, an infantry-armored task force of the 196th would reinforce the cordon by patrolling Route 529, an east-west road connecting the Tra Bong Special Forces camp to Highway 1. To the south, another airborne battalion, staging from the Minh Long Special Forces camp, would back up the ranger force. Once the cordon was in place, two of Toan's infantry battalions and a South Vietnamese mechanized troop would move overland and attack from the east, while the other units pushed to the center. (*Map 25*)

Surprise was key. The 1st Battalion, 327th Infantry, was already in place at the Minh Long Special Forces camp, while the 196th had been

---

[3] Evaluation Rpt, MACCORDS-RE, 13 Sep 67, Task Force OREGON Operations, pp. 2, 8; MFR, Forsythe, 10 Oct 67, sub: Trip Report to Quang Ngai Province, 3–4 October 1967, p. 3, and Incl 2; Intervs, author with Linnell, 6 Oct 81, and with Ulsaker, 30 Aug 82.

[4] AAR, Opn HOOD RIVER, 1st Bde, 101st Abn Div, 11 Sep 67, pp. 1–2 and an. A, Historians files, CMH.

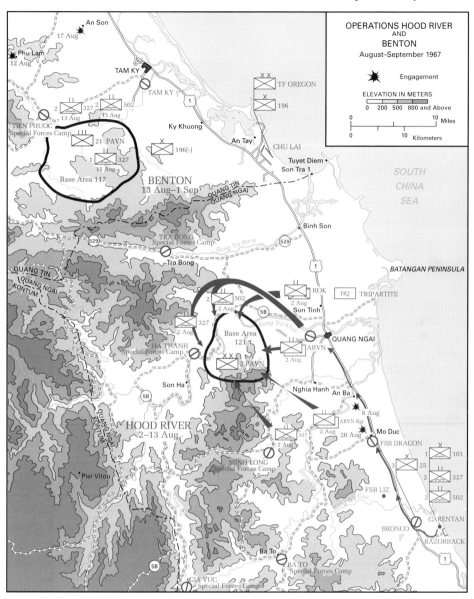

MAP 25

sweeping Route 529 since 21 July. To disguise the objective of the other paratroopers, they marched to Quang Ngai City to make it look as if they were clearing Highway 1. Not until the last moment would the paratroopers and rangers air-assault into position.

Despite the planning and coordination, HOOD RIVER fell short of expectations. Involving more than five thousand allied soldiers, the oper-

247

Men of the 196th Brigade return from a patrol along the Tra Bong River.

ation stepped off on 2 August. Supported by artillery and air strikes, the troops moved toward their initial objectives, which they reached by nightfall. Caught partly by surprise, small groups of enemy soldiers fought back at first, but as the cordon tightened over the next several days, resistance dropped off. Between 2 and 13 August, allied forces reportedly killed 166 of the enemy, captured 63 weapons, and evacuated about 500 civilians. Allied losses were 21 killed and 133 wounded.[5]

Commanders later speculated that the operation must have been compromised, perhaps by Communist agents among the South Vietnamese or perhaps by the movement of allied forces to their attack positions. Or maybe the enemy had fooled allied intelligence. Attacks on government outposts in the areas vacated by HOOD RIVER forces raised the real possibility that General Toan's information had been planted. Whatever the case, security quickly deteriorated, particularly around Quang Ngai City. Combined operations would continue to prove dissatisfying, especially when based, as they often were, on unconfirmed intelligence.[6]

BENTON

As the Americans continued the search for the enemy regiments, new intelligence placed the *21st Regiment* in southern Quang Tin Province, either west of Chu Lai in Base Area 117, or west of Tam Ky, fifteen kilometers farther north. Knowles reasoned that the unit might be protecting elements of the *368th PAVN Artillery Regiment*, thought to be preparing to rocket coastal installations. Although the information was founded on rumor and low-level reports, he ordered Linnell's 196th to sweep the eastern portion of 117.[7]

[5] ORLL, 1 Aug–31 Oct 67, Americal Div, 26 Nov 67, p. 18, Historians files, CMH; AAR, Opn HOOD RIVER, 1st Bde, 101st Abn Div, pp. 1–5, and an. A; Op Sum, Opn HOOD RIVER/DRAGON HEAD/LIEN KET 110, MACV-MHB, n.d.

[6] RD Rpt, Quang Ngai Province, Aug 67, 31 Aug 67, pp. 1–5, Historians files, CMH; Intervs, author with Danford, 21 Sep 81; with Granger, 15 Nov 85; with Ulsaker, 30 Aug 82; with Lt Gen Robert G. Yerks, Comdr, 2d Bn, 327th Inf, 101st Abn Div, 16 Sep 82, Historians files, CMH.

[7] CICV Study, ST 67–080, 1 Sep 67, sub: NVA Rocket Artillery Units, pp. 6, 8, and an. A; Interv, author with Linnell, 6 Oct 81; AAR, Opn BENTON, 196th Light Inf Bde, 24 Sep 67,

Linnell's planning was still under way on 10 August, when an eighty-year-old Catholic priest, a reliable informant in the past, reported that the *21st Regiment* headquarters had moved into the portion of his parish that extended into the base area. Since the search of Base Area 121 west of Quang Ngai was proving fruitless, Knowles reinforced Linnell with the airborne brigade, turning the sweep into a two-brigade operation code-named BENTON. The plan was simple: on 13 August Matheson would air-lift two battalions of the 101st to the western border of 117; Linnell would follow the next day with two battalions to the eastern trace; and the third airborne battalion would remain in reserve at Chu Lai. Because of the approaching elections, BENTON was to last no more than a few weeks, giving Linnell and Matheson time to redeploy around Chu Lai and Quang Ngai City in case the Viet Cong chose to launch election-eve attacks.[8]

An unexpected incident on 12 August prompted Knowles to change his orders. That afternoon a large enemy force assaulted a South Vietnamese ranger battalion about ten kilometers north of 117. Knowles anticipated that the attackers, thought to be from the *21st Regiment*, would withdraw south after the fight, back into the base area. Hoping to cut them off, he ordered Matheson to use his two battalions to intercept.

On the morning of 13 August the 2d Battalion, 502d Infantry, under Lt. Col. Ralph Puckett, and the 2d Battalion, 327th Infantry, led by Lt. Col. Robert G. Yerks, completed air assaults without opposition. Both battalions promptly turned north, with Puckett on the right and Yerks on the left. Yerks, with a 105-mm. battery in support, soon ran into trouble. That afternoon a fire broke out in the tall grass and threatened to engulf his position. The artillery ammunition was danger enough, but even more so was an unexploded "Daisy Cutter" somewhere in the area. Daisy Cutters were 1,000-pound bombs with fuzes designed to detonate above ground, clearing vegetation for helicopter landing zones. One had failed to go off just prior to the insertion of Yerks' battalion and had been lost. Fearing a huge explosion if the flames reached the bomb, Yerks ordered his men to abandon the howitzers and leave the base.

The North Vietnamese watched as the Americans took up new positions on a nearby hill. Shortly after dark they mortared the battalion. As the Americans hunkered down under the explosions, enemy soldiers moved in close enough to hurl grenades and fire automatic weapons. But there was no ground assault. One American was killed and four were wounded. The next morning a company from the brigade reserve secured the scorched firebase. Yerks evacuated his casualties, together with the fire-blackened howitzers.[9]

---

ans. A, B, and AAR, Opn BENTON, 1st Bde, 101st Abn Div, 28 Sep 67, Incl 1, both in Historians files, CMH.

[8] AAR, Opn BENTON, 1st Bde, 101st Abn Div, pp. 1–4, and an. B; ORLL, 1 Aug–31 Oct 67, Americal Div, pp. 11, 18; Interv, author with Danford, 21 Sep 81; Ltr, Maj Gen Salve H. Matheson to author, 3 Oct 82, Historians files, CMH.

[9] AAR, Opn BENTON, 1st Bde, 101st Abn Div, pp. 3, 5, and Incl 10; Interv, author with Yerks, 16 Sep 82.

Task Force OREGON troops examine the document pouch of a dead North Vietnamese soldier.

Meanwhile, on Yerks' right, Puckett found no enemy soldiers, at least not at first. But during the afternoon of 13 August he sent one company south toward the reported headquarters of the *21st Regiment*. As his men dug in for the night, the enemy opened fire. U.S. artillery responded, pounding the North Vietnamese, and an AC–47 Spooky gunship added its quick-firing miniguns to the barrage. Still the enemy held and at midnight assaulted behind a curtain of heavy mortar fire. For two hours the fight raged at close quarters. At last the North Vietnamese withdrew, leaving behind 35 dead and 18 weapons. The Americans lost 5 men killed and 15 wounded.[10]

On 15 August Matheson committed his reserve, Lt. Col. Gerald E. Morse's 1st Battalion, 327th Infantry, to the southern BENTON sector. The terrain there ranged from dense, jungle-covered mountains, to rolling hills covered with tall grass, to flat, cultivated valleys dotted with rice paddies. As the operation wore on, Morse's troops encountered mostly small groups of North Vietnamese support troops and replacements. They found that enemy units of platoon size or larger almost always waited until late afternoon before fighting, making it more difficult to use artillery and air support against them. If the fight went badly, the

---

[10] AAR, Opn BENTON, 1st Bde, 101st Abn Div, p. 3, and an. A; Sitrep 116, HQ, Task Force OREGON, 14 Aug 67, Historians files, CMH.

An F–100 Super Sabre in action during the summer

enemy simply withdrew under cover of darkness. Toward the end of August, however, these firefights became less frequent, and the enemy appeared to be breaking down into smaller, squad-size units of a few soldiers each. Throughout the operation, however, the enemy made good use of antiaircraft guns: twenty UH–1 Hueys were hit in Matheson's sector; five were destroyed.[11]

Knowles and Matheson could not have been pleased with BENTON. By the time the operation ended on 29 August, Base Area 117, an expanse of some two hundred square kilometers, had been combed by five battalions and subjected to heavy bombardment, including more than 500 tons of bombs, 300 tons of napalm, and 22,000 artillery shells. Yet hardly a trace was found of the *21st Regiment*. Between 12 and 29 August, the 1st of the 101st had killed 303 of the enemy and captured 132 weapons, a third of which were new and had been stored in a cave. The paratroopers also seized two large ammunition caches containing mortar and recoilless rifle rounds still in their original shipping containers. And they destroyed a large training facility that included several barracks, a hospital, and small-arms ranges, complete with target silhouettes and mock-ups of American planes, helicopters, and armor. In the process the brigade lost 41 killed and 286 wounded, a relatively high proportion for an operation

[11] AAR, Opn BENTON, 1st Bde, 101st Abn Div, p. 2; ORLL, 1 Aug–31 Oct 67, Americal Div, p. 1; Interv, author with Danford, 21 Sep 81.

lasting just two weeks, while to the east the 196th lost 4 men killed and 40 wounded. The 196th killed about 100 of the enemy, mostly guerrillas.[12]

The operation illustrated some typical anomalies of the war. North of Base Area 117, for example, was a six-kilometer east-west valley corridor that neither American nor South Vietnamese units were permitted to enter. To protect several villages in the area, the Quang Tin province chief had simply declared the region a government-controlled enclave. When Knowles requested a northward extension of the BENTON boundary, the province chief refused, declaring that if the Americans entered the area, damage and refugees would result. The Americans were convinced that the enemy was using the corridor as a sanctuary and escape route, but without the province chief's agreement, they could do nothing.[13]

Another issue was the disposition of the civilian population in Base Area 117. Although the Americans had made no plans to evacuate anyone, many people pleaded to be taken out. Helicopters removed more than 1,200 residents during BENTON, while some 300 others fled on their own. The Americans also detained some 200 villagers whom they suspected of actively supporting the enemy, but identifying sympathizers with certainty was problematic.[14] In many of the villages the people were using North Vietnamese currency, and most of the inhabitants had joined Communist support organizations. The Americans detained many simply because they lacked proper identification or appeared suspicious, despite the fact that they may have had no enemy affiliation. Others went free merely because they possessed the required documentation, difficult to procure legally in remote rural areas, or because they appeared to cooperate with the Americans. But U.S. commanders, even those with interpreters, had few reliable clues as to peasant sympathies.[15]

Hole Hunting

While Task Force OREGON concentrated on the area between Quang Ngai City and Chu Lai, two battalions of the 3d Brigade, 4th Division, still commanded by Colonel Wear, continued to work Duc Pho and Mo Duc Districts, farther south. Major Moore's 1st Battalion, 35th Infantry, patrolled the southern portion of the sector, which included the bases of the 3d Brigade and the 101st Airborne Division, as well as RAZORBACK Beach.

---

[12] AAR, Opn BENTON, 1st Bde, 101st Abn Div, pp. 3–6 and an. A; AAR, Opn Benton, 196th Light Inf Bde, pp. 6–24.

[13] ORLL, 1 Aug–31 Oct 67, Americal Div, p. 11; AAR, Opn BENTON, 1st Bde, 101st Abn Div, Incl 11; AAR, Opn BENTON, 196th Light Inf Bde, pp. 7–9; Op Sum, Opn COCHISE/LIEN KET 112, MACV-MHB, n.d.; Ltr, Matheson to author, 3 Oct 82; Interv, author with Yerks, 16 Sep 82.

[14] AAR, Opn BENTON, 1st Bde, 101st Abn Div, p. 2, Incls 6, 10; AAR, Opn BENTON, 196th Light Inf Bde, pp. 3–4.

[15] Intervs, author with Linnell, 6 Oct 81; with Danford, 21 Sep 81; with Yerks, 16 Sep 82.

Hole hunting by the 196th Brigade during August

Colonel Tiller's 2d Battalion, 35th Infantry, reinforced with a cavalry troop and tanks, deployed from two firebases farther north.

Tiller in southern Mo Duc District saw the heaviest action, as he played a deadly game of hide-and-seek with the Viet Cong. On 8 August a helicopter pilot reported columns of enemy troops moving north toward An Ba, a hamlet on the Ve River. Tiller set off in pursuit, and by noon the battalion had surrounded the hamlet on three sides, while gunships covered the river. As Tiller's men moved in, the enemy opened fire. The Americans struck back with artillery and air strikes before overrunning the hamlet and killing or capturing 60 Viet Cong. Judging from a unit-strength report found on one of the dead soldiers, almost none of the Viet Cong had escaped.

Not quite two weeks later, on 20 August, a helicopter pilot reported receiving fire from a hamlet a little farther south. Guided by the pilot, a column of tanks approached, only to find themselves the new center of attention for Viet Cong gunners holding a fortified position.

Tiller placed two infantry companies in blocking positions, and, as the tanks approached, some of the Viet Cong panicked. Several vainly charged the M48s, while others tried fleeing through the paddies and became ready targets for the infantry. Still others retreated to underground shelters, where half of the 53 Viet Cong killed or captured that day were found.

All told, during August Tiller's men discovered several hundred underground shelters containing enemy troops and supply caches. Of more than 300 enemy soldiers killed or captured, Tiller estimated that two-thirds resulted from "hole hunting," a South Vietnamese task that the Americans now performed. Tiller's losses were 6 killed and 41 wounded, mostly from mines and booby traps, which took a steady toll.[16]

In Binh Son District of northern Quang Ngai, Tiller's techniques were put to good use by another unit, the 4th Battalion, 31st Infantry, of the 196th, commanded by Lt. Col. Charles R. Smith. Initially, the unit had concentrated on road clearing, but had taken casualties with few results.

[16] Rpt, 2d Bn, 35th Inf, n.d., Operational Report for Quarterly Period Ending 31 October 1967, pp. 1–6, 13, and Incls 1, 2; Ltr, Lt Col Ben G. Crosby to author, 15 Oct 75, Historians files, CMH.

Once Smith started looking underground, enemy harassment declined, along with American casualties. Base areas that had once appeared unoccupied began yielding treasures, and before long villagers began cooperating with the Americans. The people of one farming village, Tuyet Diem, volunteered to abandon their homes to escape the grasp of the Viet Cong. To placate the province chief, who was appalled at the prospect of more refugees, Smith promised to provide security and materials to build new homes at Son Tra 1. The project began on 21 August, and in four days the Americans resettled 2,300 people, followed by 1,600 more after the September elections. A U.S. infantry platoon was soon working with the Popular Forces to improve the defenses.[17]

Again, Refugees

Could the Americans provide permanent security to the Vietnamese peasantry? This was the central question, yet there were precious few Son Tra 1s in 1967. In most cases American commanders, who often could not clearly distinguish between friend and foe, had two choices concerning the people in their operating areas. They could remove the entire population to the dubious control and sometimes horrendous conditions of government refugee centers, turning the vacated areas into free-fire zones, or they could do nothing, realizing that once American soldiers departed the villages the enemy would probably return. This would require another sweep of the area that would again raise the question of population control.

In an attempt to reduce civilian casualties and to deny peasant support of the Viet Cong, allied troops relocated more than 30,000 people from rural Quang Ngai between June and September, swelling the refugee lists to over 168,000, or some 20 percent of the provincial population. Although many of these people had relocated willingly to escape the fighting and Viet Cong harassment, their vast numbers created enormous social, political, and economic pressures, not to mention a public relations nightmare. If the government could effectively meet this test by providing adequate food, shelter, employment, and security, then perhaps the refugees could be converted from a liability into an asset. Unfortunately, Saigon's overburdened, inefficient, and often corrupt administration lacked the ability, and at times the will, to improve the refugees' condition. One official, senior province adviser James A. May, wondered if an effective pacification program would ever be possible.[18] If the struggle for Vietnam depended in important measure on gaining the "hearts and minds" of the Vietnamese people, the allies were a long way from winning in Quang Ngai Province.

---

[17] ORLL, 1 Aug–31 Oct 67, Americal Div, p. 38; Evaluation Rpt, MACCORDS-RE, 13 Sep 67, Task Force Oregon Operations, pp. 8–9, and Incl 2; Intervs, author with Linnell, 6 Oct 81; with Smith, 13 Aug 81, Historians files, CMH.

[18] Evaluation Rpt, MACCORDS-RE, 13 Sep 67, Task Force Oregon Operations, pp. 7–9, and Incl 1; RD Rpt, Quang Ngai Province, Aug 67, 31 Aug 67, an. C.

16

On the Demilitarized Zone

In most of South Vietnam, American soldiers confronted two kinds of fighting—guerrilla war and big unit war—and the enemy usually determined the type. But in northern I Corps, the thin neck of land between Laos and the South China Sea that bordered North Vietnam, the fighting was purely conventional. Heavily equipped enemy regiments sallied forth from the Demilitarized Zone and the base areas in southeastern Laos, threatening to spill onto the populated coast of South Vietnam.

The situation in northern I Corps during the summer of 1967 typified the emerging stalemate on South Vietnam's battlefields. While the North Vietnamese were being bloodied in nearly every engagement with U.S. forces, Westmoreland had failed to reach that point where losses would force Hanoi to cease its attacks in the South. By putting pressure on northern I Corps, Hanoi forced Westmoreland to move troops away from populated regions to deal with the threat on the Demilitarized Zone.

Here, in Quang Tri and Thua Thien Provinces, U.S. marines provided the defense. It was not an easy task. The limited logistical and helicopter support available to III Marine Amphibious Force discouraged forays into the mountains where the enemy big units lurked. So did General Walt's personal belief that his troops were better employed in providing direct support to pacification along the coast. More important, the ease with which North Vietnam could marshal large conventional forces on its southern border made the Demilitarized Zone especially dangerous. Task Force OREGON was already a big commitment to I Corps, but even before then Westmoreland had dispatched one battalion of the 173d Airborne Brigade to Da Nang in October 1966 and in October and November three U.S. Army artillery battalions to Dong Ha, still farther north.[1]

Guns Along the Demilitarized Zone

The enemy had always put heavy pressure on northern I Corps, but during April 1967 evidence mounted that North Vietnam intended some-

---

[1] Westmoreland Jnl, 8 Oct 66, Westmoreland History files, 9–C, CMH.

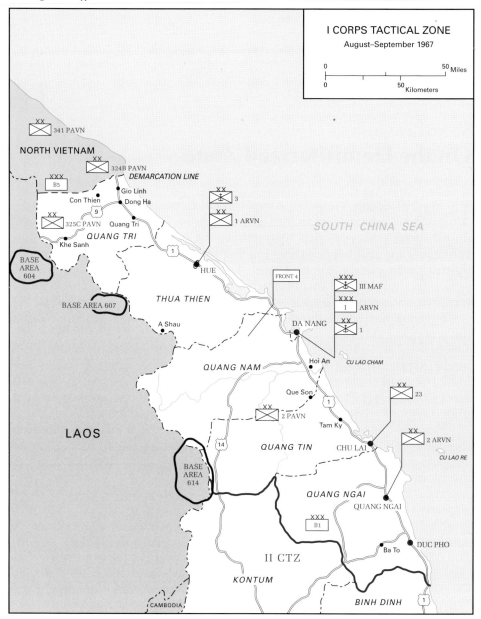

I CORPS TACTICAL ZONE

August–September 1967

MAP 26

thing big. (*Map 26*) The *B5 Front*, the North Vietnamese command for troops in and around the Demilitarized Zone, was moving units south—including some normally held in reserve to defend the North. In April intelligence discovered a regiment from the *325C PAVN Division* in the rugged hills north of Khe Sanh, prompting Walt to send two battalions from the 1st Marine Division to reinforce 3d Marine Division forces already there. The marines scaled the jungled mountains and, in bitter fighting reminiscent of the bloody ridge battles in Korea, pushed back the North Vietnamese and killed more than 900 before the enemy melted back into North Vietnam.[2]

Not to be deterred, the *B5 Front* followed up with an offensive across the Demilitarized Zone into eastern Quang Tri Province. On 8 May, the thirteenth anniversary of the fall of Dien Bien Phu, the *B5 Front* sent a multibattalion force against Con Thien. A combined American and South Vietnamese defensive effort pushed the North Vietnamese back over the Demilitarized Zone.

After regrouping, the *B5 Front* launched still another offensive in early July, this time with fewer men but with sharply increased fire from 122-mm. and 130-mm. artillery located north of the Ben Hai River running through the Demilitarized Zone. The main target was again Con Thien. During a two-week period the defenders endured an almost daily hail of rockets and artillery, but the base held fast. Once again the enemy retreated north, leaving behind nearly 1,300 dead.

The bombardment was the beginning of a new North Vietnamese tactic. Previously limited to heavy mortars and rockets, the enemy now had heavy artillery in position. By late August at least six North Vietnamese artillery battalions were inside the Demilitarized Zone, and an infantry regiment was operating against the marines between Khe Sanh and Con Thien. Westmoreland was not certain of North Vietnamese intentions, but an aborted ambush of a Marine convoy on Highway 9 on 21 August was a sign that the North Vietnamese had returned in strength.

The North Vietnamese kept almost constant pressure on the marines all along the Demilitarized Zone. On 28 August enemy artillery and rocket fire struck Dong Ha. The attack against this Marine Corps base destroyed most of the fuel storage area and damaged several helicopters. Six marines were killed and twenty-seven wounded. Casualties would have been greater had the marines not intercepted enemy gunners that afternoon and seized a rocket-launching site. Over the next week Marine bases along the Demilitarized Zone came under increasingly heavy fire.[3]

Second Front in Southern I Corps

As enemy units attacked in the far north, they also struck Quang Nam, Quang Tin, and Quang Ngai Provinces, opening a second front. The attacks were directed by a new North Vietnamese headquarters

---

[2] Telfer, Rogers, and Fleming, *U.S. Marines in Vietnam, 1967*, pp. 35–45.

[3] Msg, CG, III MAF, 1295 to COMUSMACV, 14 Sep 67, sub: Report of Gen Westmoreland Visit to III MAF on 13 Sep 67, Westmoreland History files, 22–1, CMH; Periodic Intel Rpts, MACV, Aug 67, n.d., p. 2, and Sep 67, n.d., pp. 5–6, both in Historians files, CMH. See also Telfer, Rogers, and Fleming, *U.S. Marines in Vietnam, 1967*, ch. 10.

A 175-mm. gun from the 2d Battalion, 94th Artillery, supports marines in the A Shau Valley.

called *Front 4*, established during the summer of 1967 to coordinate operations in Quang Nam and Quang Tin and the city of Da Nang. Although *Front 4* was composed of units from the *B1 Front*, it took orders directly from Hanoi. *Front 4* also directed the *368B PAVN Artillery Regiment*, a unit that had launched a destructive rocket attack against Da Nang Air Base in July.[4]

Arms, ammunition, and North Vietnamese replacements for *Front 4* came from bases in the A Shau Valley, a slash between two cloud-shrouded mountain ranges near the Laotian border. The A Shau ran roughly parallel to the coast, and its southern mouth opened only some forty kilometers southwest of Hue, South Vietnam's fourth largest city. The Americans had periodically tried to tame the A Shau, sending troops and air strikes to harass the North Vietnamese there. In June, for instance, they established a base at the valley's northern entrance,

---

[4] Periodic Intel Rpt, MACV, Mar 68, n.d., p. 2; Monthly OB Sum, MACV, 30 Apr 68. Both in Historians files, CMH.

258

pounding suspected enemy redoubts with 175-mm. guns, but three months later the monsoon rains closed in, making resupply impossible. The marines abandoned the base in September, again leaving the enemy unmolested in his A Shau redoubt.

The southern portion of the enemy offensive opened in Quang Nam Province. North Vietnamese and Viet Cong troops partially overran the provincial capital and two district headquarters, assassinating or abducting government officials and many of their known supporters. In Quang Ngai, an enemy force slipped undetected into the provincial capital on the night of 30 August, freeing 1,200 Communists from the city jail (about 800 of whom were quickly recaptured). Another enemy force struck east of Quang Ngai City, forcing pacification teams to abandon several partially completed hamlets for better than a week.[5]

Early in September the *B1 Front* ordered the *2d PAVN Division* into the Que Son Valley, a populated, fertile area extending inland from Highway 1 along the Quang Nam–Quang Tin boundary. It apparently hoped to lure American or South Vietnamese units into the valley.

Shortly before first light on 4 September, a U.S. Marine company searching the central part of the valley came under heavy fire from the *1st PLAF Regiment*. Machine-gun fire from hidden emplacements cut the marines down, but the company held its own until four other companies arrived later that afternoon. The battle continued intermittently for several days, ending on the morning of the seventh. When it was over, the marines estimated they had killed nearly 400 Viet Cong but at a cost in killed of almost 100 of their own.[6]

Farther south, three local force battalions converged on Quang Tin's capital, Tam Ky. During the first few hours of 6 September a patrol spotted the Viet Cong approaching from the north and called in an AC–47 Spooky gunship. South Vietnamese outposts also reported enemy troops moving in from the south and west, and the gunship went after them as well.

When the surviving Viet Cong reached Tam Ky at daybreak they were no match for the defending South Vietnamese Army units supported by American fighter-bombers and gunships. The Viet Cong fell back in disorder. A search of the battlefield turned up over 200 enemy dead and nearly 100 weapons, including a number of machine guns and rocket launchers. The South Vietnamese lost 21 killed and 54 wounded.[7]

---

[5] RD Rpts, Quang Nam Province, Aug 67, 1 Sep 67, pp. 1–4, and Sep 67, 1 Oct 67, pp. 1–19, both in Historians files, CMH; RD Rpts, Quang Ngai Province, Aug 67, 31 Aug 67, pp. 1–4, and Sep 67, 30 Sep 67, pp. 1–6, both in Historians files, CMH; Periodic Intel Rpt, MACV, Sep 67, n.d., p. 12.

[6] Op Sum, Opn Swift, MACV-MHB, n.d.

[7] RD Rpt, Quang Tin Province, Sep 67, 1 Oct 67, pp. 1–5, Historians files, CMH; Periodic Intel Rpt, MACV, Sep 67, n.d., pp. 3, 12; Westmoreland Jnl, 7 Sep 67, pp. 20–21; Westmoreland History Notes, 21 Aug–26 Dec 67, VIII, CMH; Interv, author with Ulsaker, 30 Aug 82.

The American Response

On 7 September General Westmoreland flew to Da Nang to discuss the worsening situation in I Corps. This was a difficult moment for the MACV commander. An attack in either the northern or southern parts of I Corps was bad enough, but to have them threatened at the same time stretched his troop commitment to the utmost. The marines had their hands full along the Demilitarized Zone and his Army units were busy enough with the insurgency in southern I Corps, but a two-front enemy attack demanded new solutions. During a briefing with Lt. Gen. Robert E. Cushman, Walt's replacement as commander of III Marine Amphibious Force, Westmoreland pointed out that intelligence placed all three regiments of the *2d Division* in or near the Que Son Valley and that the marines had committed only five companies to the sector.[8] General Cushman replied that the 1st Marine Division had the situation well in hand and was activating Task Force X-Ray, a separate tactical headquarters, to direct operations in the valley. If required, the task force could draw from two Marine regiments.

Westmoreland was not convinced that the marines had sufficient strength to take on the entire enemy division, so he sent north Task Force Oregon's most mobile unit, the 1st Brigade, 101st Airborne Division. He was also prepared to send a brigade of the 1st Cavalry Division should the enemy reemerge in Quang Ngai Province.

General Cushman placed the airborne brigade under Army control west of Tam Ky, the presumed location of the *21st PAVN Regiment*. But Westmoreland believed that Cushman was ignoring the Que Son Valley, so he convinced the I Corps commander, Lt. Gen. Hoang Xuan Lam, to send in some South Vietnamese ranger units.[9]

The main concern of both Cushman and Westmoreland was the continuing buildup of enemy troops and heavy weapons along the eastern portion of the Demilitarized Zone. The increased shelling of Con Thien endangered the construction of the inland flank of the Strong Point–Obstacle System, a part of the electronic anti-infiltration barrier, the "McNamara Line," which Secretary McNamara had ordered built from the coast to the Laotian border. There were to be two parts to this barrier: one parallel to the Demilitarized Zone to locate enemy units coming south; the other to unmask the movement of vehicles in Laos, where the North Vietnamese were upgrading their roads. When sensors registered movement, artillery and aircraft would respond. Plans called for the first part of the system, which extended ten kilometers west from Gio Linh to Con Thien, to be operational by 1 November 1967.[10] Although Cushman and Westmoreland had grave doubts

---

[8] Westmoreland Jnl, 7 Sep 67, pp. 20–22; Msg, CG, III MAF, to COMUSMACV, 8 Sep 67, sub: Visit of COMUSMACV on 7 Sep 67, Westmoreland History files, 21–27, CMH.

[9] Ibid.

[10] Telfer, Rogers, and Fleming, *U.S. Marines in Vietnam, 1967*, pp. 86–94; MACV History 1967, vol. 3, an. A.

Generals Westmoreland (right) *and Cushman in Da Nang. General Wallace M. Greene, commandant of the Marine Corps, is on the left.*

whether the system would work, even building it proved difficult. Both the existing static positions and the engineer construction sites were attracting enemy fire, while the main enemy infiltration routes into the area had merely shifted elsewhere. The Marine commander estimated that if he kept to the established construction schedule, he expected to have at least 450 men killed and 3,020 wounded by 1 November.

Westmoreland agreed that the undertaking was dangerous, so he called a temporary halt in construction to allow Cushman to turn his attention toward improving existing strongpoints and combat bases along the Demilitarized Zone. The MACV commander also promised that the III Marine Amphibious Force would continue to receive at least 50 percent of B–52 strikes in I Corps.[11]

---

[11] Interv, author with Gen Robert E. Cushman (USMC), CG, III MAF, 9 Nov 82, Historians files, CMH; MFR, 12 Oct 67, sub: MACV Commanders' Conference, 24 September 1967, Westmoreland History files, 22–12, CMH; MACV History 1967, vol. 3, an. A; Msg, CG, III MAF, to COMUSMACV, 8 Sep 67, sub: Visit of COMUSMACV on 7 Sep 67.

Marines dig in deep at Con Thien.

Even as the two commanders met at Da Nang on 7 September, they learned of heavy fighting south of the Demilitarized Zone. That morning a North Vietnamese battalion ambushed a Marine convoy moving on Highway 9 twenty kilometers west of Con Thien, and at noon another enemy force battered a Marine company a few kilometers south of the base. Both fights lasted until nightfall, with heavy losses on both sides. The marines claimed 103 enemy dead but lost 20 killed and 114 wounded.

Two days later the North Vietnamese attacked in regimental strength, striking a Marine battalion south of Con Thien. For over an hour the two sides fought, then just before midnight the enemy broke away and fled, leaving behind 140 dead. The marines lost 34 killed and 185 wounded.

On 12 September another Marine battalion working south of Con Thien ran into heavy mortar and possibly artillery fire that killed 4 men and wounded 93. Early the next morning enemy artillery pounded Con Thien, followed by a company-size ground assault. Four other Marine positions along the Demilitarized Zone were also hit by artillery and rocket attacks.[12]

It was more of the same in southern I Corps, with the action picking up sharply in Quang Nam and Quang Tin Provinces. The 1st Brigade, 101st Airborne Division, operated north and west of Tam Ky, while Task

---

[12] MACV Communique 270–67, MACV Office of Information, 27 Sep 67, Historians files, CMH.

262

Force X-RAY chased the *1st PLAF Regiment* in the northern Que Son Valley. General Lam's South Vietnamese ranger battalions took some of the pressure off the Americans by hounding the *3d PAVN Regiment*. But the enemy had plenty of strength left to strike elsewhere. A Viet Cong battalion overran and destroyed the Hieu Nhon District headquarters in southern Quang Nam, no more than a kilometer from Hoi An, the provincial capital, while another Viet Cong battalion attacked several government outposts along Highway 1 west of Hoi An, temporarily cutting the road between the provincial capital and Da Nang.[13] It seemed that just as the Americans began putting more combat power along the Demilitarized Zone and into the dense interior, the security of the heavily populated coastal plains threatened to evaporate.

Despite the deteriorating situation on the coast, the focus had to remain on the northern front. For even though Westmoreland had amassed the largest concentration of American air, naval gunfire, and artillery support yet to be used during the war in a single sector, the enemy shelling against Marine positions along the Demilitarized Zone continued, especially against Con Thien. On 25 September more than a thousand rounds of artillery, rockets, and mortar fire rained down upon the base, the most intense enemy shelling to occur during a single day. During a six-day span, 20–25 September, American casualties near the Demilitarized Zone totaled 26 killed and 677 wounded, which raised losses since the start of September to 198 killed and 2,119 wounded, with 884 of the wounds serious enough to require evacuation.[14] In contrast, during the first twenty-five days of September the defending 3d Marine Division reportedly killed 430 of the enemy, mostly during the first two weeks of the month. Actual enemy casualties were hard to estimate, because fog, clouds, and rain made aerial observation difficult.[15]

The weather provided the enemy a major advantage. He already knew the location of the Marine positions, while the marines had to search for the enemy's guns, which, even when found, were difficult to destroy. The North Vietnamese positioned many of their artillery pieces near the entrances to caves at the foot of steep hills north of the Ben Hai, and, after firing, pulled the guns into the caves for protection and concealment. Even a direct hit on a cave by a 1,000-pound bomb did not guarantee the destruction of the gun inside. In addition, enemy gunners could fire long-range rockets by remote control while remaining safe in deep bunkers, and individual firing positions were mobile and almost impossible to detect. Mortar crews could fire several rounds in less than a minute and then escape before American counterfire zeroed in on them.

[13] Op Sum, Opn SWIFT, MACV-MHB; Interv, author with Ulsaker, 30 Aug 82.
[14] Op Sum, Opn KINGFISHER, MACV-MHB, n.d.
[15] MFR, 12 Oct 67, sub: MACV Commanders' Conference, 24 September 1967; Op Sum, Opn KINGFISHER, MACV-MHB, n.d.; Periodic Intel Rpt, MACV, Sep 67, n.d., p. 2.

The huge effort to knock out the enemy's mortars, rockets, and artillery was obviously failing. The Americans needed a ground offensive north of the Ben Hai, which Westmoreland favored but had never initiated because of constraints Washington had imposed. In any case, the MACV commander saw no possibility of launching such an attack during the rainy season, but he made up his mind that if the enemy persisted when the dry season arrived the following May, he would again try to persuade Washington to authorize a drive into the lower North Vietnamese panhandle.[16]

"Our fundamental problem is that our posture south of the DMZ is defensive," said Westmoreland, and around Con Thien "relatively static."[17] Although convinced that American firepower would soon end the shelling along the Demilitarized Zone, he still believed that the III Marine Amphibious Force would have to be reinforced before the arrival of the monsoon rains. On 26 September Westmoreland directed General Rosson, who had taken command of I Field Force on 1 August, to prepare to send part of the 1st Cavalry Division, MACV's strategic reserve, either into Quang Ngai to preserve the recent gains in that province, or directly to Da Nang to free a Marine regiment for duty north.

In addition, Westmoreland gave Task Force OREGON, at that point renamed the 23d Infantry Division (American), responsibility for all of Quang Ngai and Quang Tin Provinces and part of Quang Nam. In conjunction with the increased responsibility of the Army division, General Cushman was to shift additional Marine forces north of the Hai Van Pass in Thua Thien Province to take the pressure off units of the 3d Marine and the South Vietnamese 1st Divisions operating farther north in Quang Tri Province.

The 3d Marine Division was to defend in strength along Highway 9 between Dong Ha and Khe Sanh, the length of the Demilitarized Zone, and Westmoreland recommended that Cushman consider thinning Marine forces north of the road to reduce casualties from enemy shelling. To improve support of American and South Vietnamese forces operating just south of the Demilitarized Zone, he told Cushman to give priority to constructing an airstrip and logistical base near Quang Tri City, out of range of enemy artillery from across the Ben Hai, and to enlarging port facilities near Hue to supplement those at Cua Viet, a small inland port near Dong Ha.[18]

At a briefing at Da Nang on 28 September, which both Westmoreland and Cushman attended, III Marine Amphibious Force intelligence report-

[16] Msgs, Westmoreland MAC 8095 to Wheeler, 26 Aug 67, and Westmoreland MAC 9616 to Sharp, 13 Oct 67, sub: Operations North of the DMZ, both in Westmoreland Message files, CMH; Msg, Westmoreland MAC 9056 to Gen Harold K. Johnson, Chief of Staff, Army, 27 Sep 67, sub: Situation Near DMZ, Westmoreland History files, 22–33, CMH.

[17] Msg, Westmoreland MAC 9056 to H. K. Johnson, 27 Sep 67, sub: Situation Near DMZ.

[18] Ibid.; Msg, Westmoreland MAC 9616 to Sharp, 13 Oct 67, sub: Operations North of the DMZ.

ed that although hostile fire along the Demilitarized Zone had decreased, the enemy still had large maneuver forces in the area, as well as in western Quang Tri Province and probably in western Thua Thien Province. In addition, over the past few days, the 1st Brigade, 101st Airborne Division, had made heavy contact with the *2d PAVN Division* in western Quang Tin, and unconfirmed reports held that an unidentified enemy regiment had recently moved into western Quang Ngai.

The information convinced Westmoreland to proceed with his plan to send the 1st Cavalry Division north. He told General Cushman that he would get a brigade of the 1st Cavalry Division in the "next several days" and the remainder of the division "over the next several weeks." Westmoreland wanted the lead brigade to come under the operational control of the Americal Division until the 1st Cavalry Division headquarters completed its move.[19]

Two days later the 3d Brigade moved north. Westmoreland watched it go with some reluctance. Since arriving in Vietnam, the division had taken great strides toward destroying the insurgency's main force units that continually impeded security for the coastal pacification effort. Ideally, the American forces would then have worked northward into the A Shau Valley, uprooting supply lines and base areas. However, instead of keeping the enemy out of the populated areas, the 1st Cavalry Division was being forced north in a defensive move that would keep it pinned down at least through the rainy season. Westmoreland found himself devoting two and perhaps three full divisions, about one-third of his combat strength in Vietnam, to northern I Corps. He would have to put on hold any ambitious plans to take the offensive elsewhere.

---

[19] Westmoreland Jnl, 28 Sep 67, p. 15, Westmoreland History files, 22, CMH.

17

The Americal Continues the Attack

Westmoreland resigned himself to the fact that Army troops would have to remain in the north indefinitely, and on 25 September 1967, he converted Task Force OREGON into a full-fledged infantry division. He called it the 23d Infantry Division (Americal) after a unit that had been formed in the Pacific during World War II. But rather than completely restructuring the task force, Westmoreland allowed its three brigades to retain their organizations.[1] The new division consisted of the 196th Light Infantry Brigade; the 3d Brigade, 4th Infantry Division; and the 1st Brigade, 101st Airborne Division. A fourth brigade, from the 1st Cavalry Division, soon was also attached. Three days prior to the activation date, Brig. Gen. Samuel W. Koster, a veteran of World War II combat in the Pacific, landed at Chu Lai to serve as division commander.

With the formation of the Americal Division, Westmoreland shifted everything northward. The attached 3d Brigade, 1st Cavalry Division, commanded by Col. James O. McKenna, replaced the 5th Marines in the Que Son Valley. The 5th Marines moved to Da Nang, which in turn freed the 1st Marines to reinforce Quang Tri Province near the Demilitarized Zone.

The change was driven by Westmoreland's perception of events in northern I Corps. By late September enemy attacks against Con Thien dropped sharply as the three North Vietnamese regiments on that front withdrew into North Vietnam, possibly to wait out the rainy season. Convinced that the effort against Con Thien had utterly misfired and that the enemy had taken heavy losses, Westmoreland predicted that the *B5 Front* would be unable to fight through the bad weather, which would allow him some breathing room to reorient the marines up north and to have them dig in a little deeper.[2]

But the coastal piedmont south of Da Nang, in Quang Nam and Quang Tin Provinces, also concerned Westmoreland, especially the Que Son Valley, home of the *2d PAVN Division*. Unhindered possession of the

---

[1] Msg, Westmoreland MAC 9056 to H. K. Johnson, 27 Sep 67, sub: Situation Near DMZ; Interv, author with Rosson, 13 Sep 77. The term "Americal" derived from "Americans in New Caledonia," the South Pacific island used as a staging base in World War II.

[2] Msg, Westmoreland MAC 9261 to H. K. Johnson, 3 Oct 67, sub: Force Deployments, Westmoreland History files, 23–5, CMH.

General Koster (right) *greets Vietnamese Vice President Nguyen Cao Ky at Chu Lai. Generals Lam and Cushman look on.*

valley had allowed the enemy to threaten the coastal plains for the last two years. Now, with the activation of the Americal Division and with one airmobile and one airborne brigade working the valley and the immediate interior, Koster's two infantry brigades, together with the South Vietnamese and Koreans, would, Westmoreland hoped, have an easier time managing the coast.

By the end of September Koster's division was almost combat ready. To accommodate the cavalry brigade's helicopters, he established an aviation base at Ky Hoa, an island north of Chu Lai, defended by Linnell's 196th Brigade. On 30 October, however, enemy sappers attacked the installation, destroying or damaging eleven helicopters and again illustrating the perennial problem of defending dispersed support bases.[3]

Providing fuel and ammunition to the Americal also proved troublesome. Most of the needs of Army units in southern I Corps had originally

---

[3] ORLL, 1 Aug–31 Oct 67, Americal Div, 26 Nov 67, pp. 1, 4, 31, and Incls 1, 2; and Interv, author with Brig Gen Samuel W. Koster, CG, 23d Inf Div, 26 Aug 82, both in Historians files, CMH.

The harbor at Sa Huynh, a month before the monsoon. A U.S. Army amphibious lighter is on the right.

arrived by water from Cam Ranh Bay, either at Chu Lai or at RAZORBACK Beach near Duc Pho. In early September resupply shifted from Cam Ranh Bay to Qui Nhon, 200 kilometers closer to the battle area. It proved too much for the smaller port to bear, particularly after the rains closed RAZORBACK on 1 October. The situation became critical one week later, when a tropical storm struck southern I Corps, dumping seventeen inches of rain within twenty-four hours. Flooding washed out portions of the main supply route, Highway 1, and in the week that it took engineers to repair the damage the troops in the field could receive supplies only by air.

In a race against the oncoming monsoons, Koster put his engineers to work repairing roads and opening a limited over-the-beach facility at Sa Huynh, twenty kilometers southeast of Duc Pho. At Duc Pho itself, logistical troops improved the airstrip and prepared additional ammunition and fuel storage sites.[4] Nevertheless, when the northeast monsoon began

---

[4] ORLL, 1 Aug–31 Oct 67, Americal Div, pp. 30, 33, 35; Intervs, author with Koster, 26 Aug 82, and with Col James O. McKenna, Comdr, 3d Bde, 1st Cav Div, 16, 22–23 Jun 82, Historians files, CMH.

in earnest at the end of October, the division's scattered elements would depend increasingly on Highway 1. Maintenance of the highway placed an enormous burden on the engineers, causing delays in almost all other construction projects in southern I Corps.[5]

WHEELER

Westmoreland's chief target in southern I Corps remained the *2d Division*, which in the summer of 1967 was being harried by the III Marine Amphibious Force. At least along the coast that was true. In the interior, away from the marines' logistical lines, the North Vietnamese had two base areas, 116 and 117, both located west of Tam Ky in Quang Tin Province. They were swaths of rolling jungle-covered hills and strips of flat lowlands cultivated with rice paddies. From Base Area 116 in particular, the enemy could stage attacks both north toward Da Nang and south toward Chu Lai. This had been Task Force OREGON territory, and starting in early September the 1st Brigade, 101st Airborne Division, and the 1st Battalion, 14th Infantry, 4th Division, both coming off of Operation BEN-TON, had been sent north from Quang Ngai specifically to clean out 116. Code-named WHEELER, the offensive had two objectives: find and destroy the *2d Division's 1st PLAF* and *3d PAVN Regiments*, thought to be withdrawing south from the Que Son Valley, and locate the third regiment, the *21st PAVN*, believed to be regrouping west of Tam Ky.

At first the Americans found few main force units, so they dispersed to widen their search. Soon enough, the sweeps started producing contacts, with the airborne claiming over 200 Viet Cong killed during the first two weeks of the operation, 11–25 September.[6]

General Matheson, commanding the 1st of the 101st Airborne Division, knew from intelligence reports that during earlier operations of the marines and South Vietnamese the *2d Division* routinely pulled back into the mountains to regroup near Hiep Duc, an abandoned district capital forty kilometers west of Tam Ky. By the end of the third week of September, Matheson felt certain that the *2d Division* was there once again. Radio intercepts seemed to bear out his suspicions, pinpointing a division headquarters on a hill three kilometers east of Hiep Duc and indicating that the *1st* and *21st Regiments* were also in the area.[7] (*Map 27*)

In another attempt to trap the enemy, Matheson planned a multibattalion encirclement of Hiep Duc. Using the Tranh and Chang Rivers as boundary lines, Colonel Yerks' 2d Battalion, 327th Infantry, was to establish blocking positions to the west of the village, while two companies of

---

[5] Ibid.

[6] AAR, Opn WHEELER, 1st Bde, 101st Abn Div, 11 Dec 67, pp. 4–5, Historians files, CMH; Interv, author with Danford, 21 Sep 81.

[7] Matheson Debriefing, pp. B–1, B–2; AAR, Opn WHEELER, 1st Bde, 101st Abn Div, p. 5; Interv, author with Danford, 21 Sep 81; Ltr, Matheson to author, 3 Oct 82.

A paratrooper of the 101st Airborne Division takes aim at an enemy position with an M72 LAW (light antitank weapon) during WHEELER.

Colonel Morse's 1st Battalion, 327th Infantry, did the same in the south. U.S. Marine and South Vietnamese reconnaissance units would occupy the high ground to the north overlooking Route 534. Once the three sides of the encirclement were in place, Colonel Puckett's 2d Battalion, 502d Infantry, would drive into Hiep Duc from the east.[8]

Although ARC LIGHT strikes were justified, no B–52s were available, because III Marine Amphibious Force was still using its entire allocation up at Con Thien. Preparatory fires would therefore be limited to fighter-bomber strikes and artillery fire from two batteries with Puckett's battalion and at Tien Phuoc, a Special Forces camp just south of Base Area 116. Two other firebases were to be established on ridges midway between the Special Forces camp and Hiep Duc.

On the morning of 26 September troops from the blocking units landed unopposed, while Puckett's battalion began its ground advance. During the course of the day the other battalions advanced as well, tightening the noose around the suspected enemy position. The operation generated small contacts but failed to uncover large units. Tired and frustrated, the Americans settled down for the night. Their peace was shattered shortly after midnight, when elements of the *1st Regiment* attacked Puckett's command post. But the attack was short-lived, and in a few minutes all was quiet again. A defector later revealed that the Viet Cong commander had called off the attack after his mortar crews had mistakenly fired on his assault troops.

Fighting continued over the next week, with the Americans slowly closing the ring around Hiep Duc. Low clouds and rain limited aerial observation and support. Nevertheless, as Matheson's men neared the suspected headquarters, the number of enemy sightings and skirmishes, together with an unusually heavy volume of mortar, recoilless rifle, and antiaircraft fire, indicated that at least some large units remained in place.[9]

[8] AAR, Opn WHEELER, 1st Bde, 101st Abn Div, pp. 5–6, and Incl 2, tab B; Interv, author with Danford, 21 Sep 81.

[9] AAR, Opn WHEELER, 1st Bde, 101st Abn Div, p. 6, and Incls 2, 10.

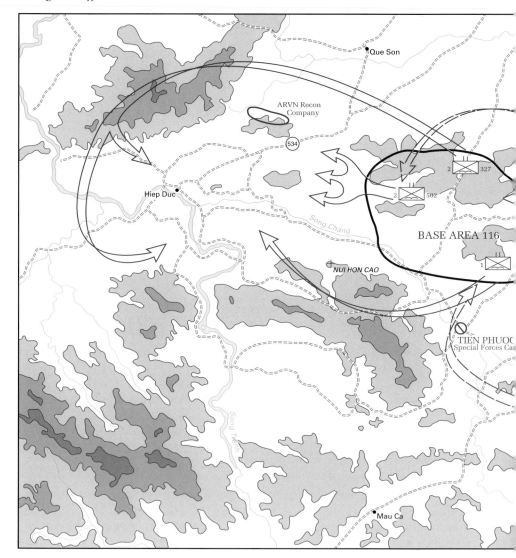

MAP 27

Around 3 October, amid increasingly heavier downpours, the situation started to turn murky. The *21st Regiment* eluded the Americans and crept back into Base Area 116 behind the 2d of the 502d. Matters became further confused when one of Colonel Yerks' companies ran into a battalion of the *21st* a few kilometers west of Hiep Duc. The North Vietnamese disengaged at nightfall, but not before shooting down three helicopters.[10]

[10] Ibid., p. 6, and Incl 1; Interv, author with Yerks, 16 Sep 82.

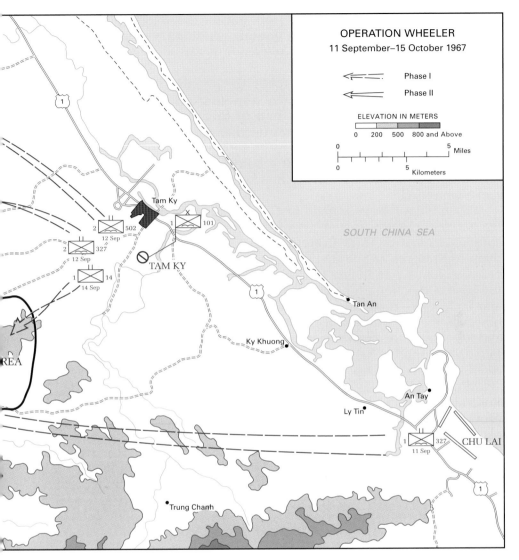

Worried about this infiltration, Matheson requested assistance from Koster, who sent a battalion from the 3d Brigade of the 4th Division. Arriving on 4 October, the 1st Battalion, 35th Infantry, under Lt. Col. Robert G. Kimmel, landed to the southeast of the 2d Battalion, 502d Infantry, now commanded by General Matheson's operations officer, Lt. Col. Howard H. Danford, who had replaced the wounded Puckett.

For about a week Danford's battalion had bumped into more and more enemy units and had taken many casualties. Company A was in particularly bad shape. In addition to the fighting, some of the soldiers came down with food poisoning from hot meals brought by helicopter. Down to fewer than forty men in fighting condition, Company A pulled back to a previously occupied defensive position to recover, absorb replacements, and await resupply.

Just after midnight on 5 October the enemy struck Company A. Grenades showered in, followed by a ground assault that overran the 2d Platoon. But the Americans, half of them green troops, steadied, helped by a .50-caliber machine gun that the company commander, who had expected trouble, had just brought in. Within half an hour, the enemy began to fall back, leaving behind 18 dead and 16 weapons, including a flamethrower. Company A, stunned but intact, lost 7 killed and 6 wounded.[11]

When the airborne brigade first deployed into Hiep Duc in late September, its logistical system was functioning smoothly. The bulk of its supplies moved by truck from Chu Lai to Tam Ky, where Hueys ferried them to firebases and troops in the field. To cut the thirty-minute flight between Tam Ky and Hiep Duc, support troops constructed another supply base at the Tien Phuoc Special Forces camp, where Air Force C–123s and C–7s were maintaining several days of supply. By early October, however, the dirt runway had deteriorated due to afternoon downpours and was thereafter limited to emergency missions. Thickening clouds and rain also grounded helicopters. By the end of the first week of October, consistent logistical support had become doubtful.

More trouble followed. On 8 October, when Yerks learned that the tropical storm would halt resupply, he decided to distribute the on-hand provisions among his widely separated companies. In the process, one platoon came under heavy fire, again from a unit of the *21st Regiment*. A final transmission from the platoon leader indicated that the unit was fighting hand-to-hand and was about to be overrun. In the downpour, a relief force could not find the platoon, and a forward air controller reported no survivors. The controller then directed an air strike on a nearby grove of trees where he suspected the enemy might be hiding. A later sweep revealed that he had guessed correctly—some 60 North Vietnamese bodies littered the area. American casualties totaled 17 killed and 3 wounded. Almost all of the dead came from the missing platoon, of which there were no survivors.[12]

Although the encirclement of Hiep Duc had failed to locate either the *2d Division* headquarters or the *1st Regiment*, the operation had cost the enemy more than 500 killed. American losses for the two-week period were also high, nearly 100 dead and more than 300 wounded.[13] And the

---

[11] AAR, Opn WHEELER, 1st Bde, 101st Abn Div, p. 7; Intervs, author with Danford, 21 Sep 81, 20 Aug 97, and with Lt Gen Charles P. Otstott, Comdr, Co A, 2d Bn, 502d Inf, 101st Abn Div, 19 Aug 97, Historians files, CMH. Otstott commanded Company A.

[12] AAR, Opn WHEELER, 1st Bde, 101st Abn Div, p. 7; Intervs, author with Danford, 21 Sep 81, and with Yerks, 16 Sep 82.

[13] AAR, Opn WHEELER, 1st Bde, 101st Abn Div, p. 7, and Incl 1.

withdrawal to the coast would not be easy. Intermittent rainstorms hampered troop movements, while on 15 October the enemy took a parting shot at the brigade's firebase on Hon Cao Mountain.

Located on a narrow ridge midway between Tien Phuoc and Hiep Duc, the Hon Cao was garrisoned by Battery A, 2d Battalion, 320th Artillery (Airborne), and a lone CIDG militia company. Their precarious position came under attack at 0315, when the first of over sixty mortar rounds fell on the defenders. As they tried to take cover from the shelling, enemy sappers sneaked through the defensive wire and stormed the fighting positions. Demoralized by the sudden attack, the militia company hardly fired a shot, allowing the sappers to knock out the fire-direction center with grenades and satchel charges. In the smoke and confusion, the sappers moved on to the battery's 105-mm. howitzers, but they were thwarted by the gun crew's desperate fighting. Though wounded, S. Sgt. Webster Anderson, the artillery section chief, rallied his men and saved the guns.[14]

The defense had to do without air support. Low-hanging clouds and drizzle kept all but medevac helicopters grounded. Guided into the firebase by the artillery's AN/MPQ–4 countermortar radar, three Hueys landed to pick up the most critically wounded. Other helicopters brought in a fresh team the next morning to replace Battery A, which during the previous night's battle lost 6 men killed and 29 wounded. The CIDG suffered 6 killed and 4 wounded, while the enemy left behind 6 bodies. Persistent rain kept the ridgelines socked in, and both the artillerymen and the CIDG company would have to wait five more days for an extraction. Although they feared an attack before the weather improved, the enemy never mounted one.[15]

WALLOWA

Directly north of WHEELER, in the Que Son Valley, Operation WALLOWA was in progress. On 4 October, as the 5th Marines left for Da Nang, Colonel McKenna's 3d Brigade, 1st Cavalry Division, pushed into the Que Son. It was familiar territory, with both the terrain and the enemy practically identical to those the air cavalry had faced in Binh Dinh Province. But, unlike the departing marines, the 3d Brigade had an abundance of helicopters, and this gave it an advantage—at least in the beginning. Against the marines, the insurgents had moved at will during daylight, sometimes virtually within sight of the firebases. Now they became easy prey for the cavalry's gunships that with unlimited

[14] Sergeant Anderson received the Medal of Honor for his actions on 15 October. See U.S. Congress, Senate, Committee on Veterans' Affairs, *Medal of Honor Recipients, 1863–1973*, 93d Cong., 1st sess., 1973, p. 809.

[15] AAR, Opn WHEELER, 1st Bde, 101st Abn Div, p. 7, and Incl 10; Ott, *Field Artillery*, pp. 121–24.

access to the terrain accounted for 210 enemy kills during the first two weeks of the offensive.[16]

McKenna blanketed the valley with his battalions. He set up his command post on Hill 63, the headquarters of the departing 5th Marines. Dubbed BALDY by the troops, Hill 63 lay thirty kilometers northwest of Tam Ky at the broad base of the Que Son Valley and was also home to the 1st Battalion, 7th Cavalry, commanded by Lt. Col. Edward M. Pierce. The 2d Battalion, 12th Cavalry (Airmobile), led by Lt. Col. Marion C. Ross, occupied a former Marine outpost on another hill near Que Son, the only area in the upper valley remotely under South Vietnamese control. South of BALDY, in an area inundated by recent flooding, McKenna sent the 5th Battalion, 7th Cavalry, under Lt. Col. John A. Wickham, to establish a firebase on Hill 23, later named Landing Zone COLT. (*Map 28*)

Now on the ground, the cavalry's airmobility was no longer a prime factor. The enemy knew this well from past experience, and he challenged the 3d Brigade almost immediately. The first target was Wickham's outpost, which mortar, rocket, and automatic weapons fire probed at 0400 on 10 October, before the Americans had completed even basic defenses. Infiltrating enemy soldiers with American uniforms headed straight for Wickham's operations center in a cave formed by large boulders. Grenades and rifle fire peppered the command post, killing everyone inside within minutes and leaving the radios in shambles. Wickham, who was not in the cave at the time, was wounded by a rocket and took cover in a foxhole as the enemy withdrew. Only when communication was restored an hour later was the brigade able to call in artillery fire around the perimeter.

At first light, helicopters evacuated 17 wounded and 7 dead Americans. Later in the day a gunship fired on an enemy squad moving away from the base. A follow-up patrol found several enemy bodies, one of which had a detailed map of Landing Zone COLT.

Later, McKenna attributed the enemy's success to the medical aid station Wickham had established inside the perimeter to treat civilians affected by the floods. Some peasant, McKenna believed, had entered the compound ostensibly to receive aid and had mapped the location of the bunkers and operations center for the local Viet Cong. McKenna decided that in the future he would not allow civilians inside bases under his command.[17]

Intelligence was also in need of improvement. McKenna later learned that the Americal Division headquarters had received intelligence placing the *3d PAVN Regiment* near Landing Zone COLT prior to the attack but had

---

[16] ORLL, 1 Aug–31 Oct 67, Americal Div, pp. 11, 20; ORLL, 1 Aug–31 Oct 67, 1st Cav Div, 15 Nov 67, pp. 21, 28, Historians files, CMH; Intervs, author with McKenna, 16, 22–23 Jun 82; with Col Edward M. Pierce, Comdr, 1st Bn, 7th Cav, 1st Cav Div, 14 Apr 82, 12 Aug 82; and with Col Alfred E. Spry, S–2, 3d Bde, 1st Cav Div, 11 Apr 83, both in Historians files, CMH. No records of the 3d Brigade, 1st Cavalry Division, in Operation WALLOWA could be found.

[17] Intervs, author with McKenna, 16, 22–23 Jun 82.

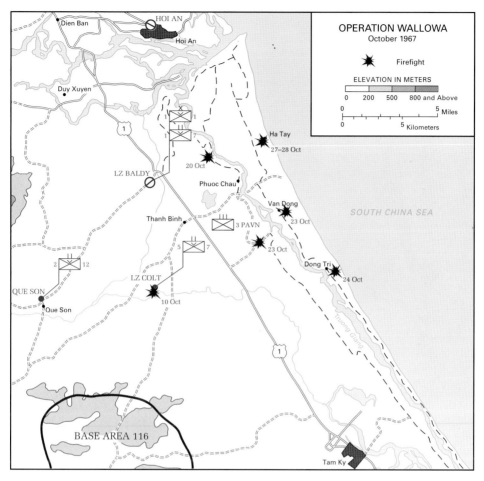

MAP 28

delayed passing down the information. So, he established a direct link between the aircraft that monitored enemy communications and his brigade intelligence staff.[18]

His staff also studied the code names collected by the 5th Marines, which the enemy used to identify havens in the sector. The Americans' work paid off on 19 October, when a twelve-year-old boy told a local district chief that a hundred North Vietnamese soldiers had passed through his hamlet the night before, saying they were moving to a rest area near the coast. McKenna's intelligence staff knew from its list of enemy code words that the rest area was a cluster of coastal hamlets a few kilometers due east of BALDY, between Highway 1 and the Truong Giang estuary. Since elements of the elusive *3d Regiment* might have left the valley to

---

[18] Intervs, author with Spry, 11 Apr 83, and with Pierce, 14 Apr and 12 Aug 82.

277

Troops of the 1st Cavalry Division question suspected Viet Cong during WALLOWA.

obtain supplies at the coast, McKenna sent Pierce's 1st of the 7th Cavalry to sweep the area.

On the morning of 20 October, as preparatory fire struck a wooded area adjacent to a proposed landing site south of the hamlets, a radio operator monitoring enemy communications heard a Vietnamese voice announce that his unit was receiving fire. Passing the information to McKenna's intelligence unit at BALDY, the operator added, "Whatever you're doing, keep it up."[19]

McKenna immediately increased the artillery fire, while Huey gunships converged to blast the enemy troops as they broke from the woods. The combined air and artillery barrage killed 64 North Vietnamese of the *3d Regiment.*

After dark on the twentieth American intelligence detected an enemy radio operating east of the Truong Giang estuary, which led Pierce to insert two companies the following morning. Finding no trace of the enemy, they swept south to search between the Truong Giang and the

---

[19] Intervs, author with Pierce, 14 Apr and 12 Aug 82.

coast. Meanwhile, the 1st Squadron, 1st Armored Cavalry, just in from the United States, drove north toward Pierce. Early that afternoon recoilless rifle, mortar, and automatic weapons fire hit a cavalry troop as it approached the hamlet of Van Dong. Pierce quickly reinforced, and by nightfall the Americans had surrounded the hamlet on three sides.

Artillery rained in during the night, while illumination rounds guided gunships crisscrossing the hamlet. At first light the infantry stormed the hamlet and easily overran the handful of enemy defenders. American casualties were 2 killed and 4 wounded, while the enemy lost 42 dead. According to captured documents and prisoners, the hamlet had been the headquarters of a sapper company charged with mining Highway 1 between Tam Ky and BALDY.

The next day, 22 October, McKenna's aerial scouts failed to detect any enemy activity east of Van Dong. But since one of his cavalry troops had killed 11 Viet Cong there a week before, McKenna decided to send the better part of the 5th Battalion, 7th Cavalry, to investigate.

The following morning two companies of the 5th Battalion, now commanded by Lt. Col. Herlihy T. Long, moved from COLT to the vicinity of Van Dong. When one unit became heavily engaged around noon, Long surrounded the position with a second company, then a third, and then a troop from the 1st Armored Cavalry Regiment. To prevent escape after nightfall, McKenna ordered Long to press the attack. Just before dark his men moved in, smashed through the defenses, and killed 98 of the enemy, mostly from the *3d Battalion, 3d Regiment*, whose assignment was to protect the regimental headquarters. But there was no sign of the headquarters itself.

McKenna was determined to sweep along the coast as long as possible. Late on the evening of the twenty-third intelligence told him that an enemy radio was transmitting from near Dong Tri, a coastal hamlet seven kilometers southeast of the scene of that day's fight. McKenna also learned that Dong Tri was one of three fishing hamlets suspected of being ports of entry for supplies arriving by sea from North Vietnam and that the enemy had dug storage tunnels under nearby Hill 21. He ordered Pierce to conduct an air assault with three companies the following morning.

Pierce's initial search of Dong Tri on 24 October came up empty. However, when Pierce learned from a helicopter pilot of fortified positions to the northwest, he sent a company to investigate. As predicted, the Americans found the enemy concealed in hedgerows. Though Pierce reinforced with his other two companies, they were unable to encircle before dark, and by daylight on the twenty-fifth the enemy had vanished.

Over the next two days, 25–26 October, Pierce's 1st of the 7th Cavalry moved north from Dong Tri, from time to time meeting snipers. Searching a small village, the Americans learned from the inhabitants that North Vietnamese soldiers had recently passed through, traveling at night in small groups. That information, coupled with a report that another enemy radio, possibly of the type a regiment would use, had been detect-

Soldiers of the 1st Cavalry Division search a well for enemy supplies.

ed in Ha Tay, a coastal hamlet twelve kilometers north of Dong Tri, determined the brigade's objective for the next day.

Again, Pierce planned to surround the hamlet during the morning hours. McKenna wanted two troops of the 1st Armored Cavalry to ford the Truong Giang south of Van Dong, advance north, bypass the hamlet, and assume blocking positions on the north and west. Meanwhile, Pierce was to conduct an air assault with three companies south of Ha Tay, after which his men were to move to a dike on the southern edge of the hamlet and await the arrival of the armor. If it appeared that the enemy had departed, Pierce planned to enter the hamlet without supporting fire, as he had entered Dong Tri, to prevent its destruction.

Pierce's men landed unopposed on the morning of 27 October. As they began moving toward the dike, a helicopter pilot saw occupied positions in a hedgerow farther on. Moments later the enemy opened fire, and the fight for Ha Tay commenced. Rushing for cover along the dike, Pierce's men lay low until artillery, gunships, and armor could be called in to cover the escape routes.

With two companies providing a base of fire, Pierce maneuvered a third to a position west of the hamlet, joined by the lead armored cavalry unit. Together they swept into Ha Tay and took it by midafternoon. Although the enemy commander and his staff had apparently escaped the night before, they left behind a trove of records belonging to the *3d Regiment* headquarters. The Americans also found 48 bodies and 17 weapons.

But the battle was not yet over. That afternoon Huey pilots spotted fortified positions north of Ha Tay, and elements of Pierce's battalion and the cavalry squadron renewed the attack, recording more kills. That evening, as the Americans began digging in for the night, a North Vietnamese force counterattacked but was quickly beaten back. Assuming that it was an attempt to cover the regiment's withdrawal, McKenna committed portions of his other two battalions on the next day, 28 October, to prevent the regulars from reaching the Cau Dai corridor, a populated area that led from the coast into the mountains. But his soldiers found little, and McKenna abandoned the effort three days later.

From captured documents and prisoner interrogations, McKenna discovered that his troops had fought part of the *3d PAVN Regiment* in what had become a familiar, deadly game of cat and mouse. But enemy losses had been high, with the brigade estimating that it had killed 465, of which 70 percent were North Vietnamese regulars. American losses during that eleven-day period were 34 dead and 125 wounded. Much of the brigade's success, McKenna believed, resulted from unseasonably good flying conditions and timely intelligence.[20]

Enclave Security

To the south, Colonel Wear and his 3d Brigade, 4th Division, still in Duc Pho and Mo Duc Districts, faced the same situation as McKenna. All through September Wear's men noted more and more enemy foraging parties coming down from the hills toward Highway 1. Intelligence reports indicated that defoliants and population resettlement over the summer had drastically curtailed food production in the inland valleys, making these forays a logistical necessity. Huey pilots saw convoys of oxcarts, bicycles, and motor scooters active at dusk and dawn, when normal commercial activity was light. But with only two battalions, Wear could do little. Initially, he tried putting men in the foothills, but that meant reducing the number of troops protecting the rice harvest near Highway 1.

To assist Wear, General Koster returned the 1st Battalion, 14th Infantry, in late September. But the reinforcement was short-lived. In early October Koster was forced to send another of Wear's units, the 1st Battalion, 35th Infantry, to reinforce Matheson's airborne in Quang Tin Province. Once again, the 3d Brigade and Quang Ngai Province had to make do with just two U.S. battalions.

---

[20] Rpt, 1st Bn, 7th Cav, n.d., Operations Summary for 1/7 Cav During the Period 1–31 Oct 1967, Historians files, CMH; Intervs, author with Pierce, 14 Apr and 12 Aug 82; with Spry, 11 Apr 83; and with McKenna, 16, 22–23 Jun 82.

281

The impact of this economy on Quang Ngai was soon apparent. In October Wear learned from captured documents and interrogations that at least three North Vietnamese battalion-size units had arrived in the mountains to the west, either passing through to join the *3d Division* or to fill a void created by the August departure of several main force units from southern Quang Ngai. But without enough soldiers to track down these units and still hold the plain, Wear had no choice but to remain in place, particularly since the Viet Cong in his sector had converted many of their local units to sappers who harassed his bases and supply routes with mines, booby traps, and small assaults.

Although the brigade reported killing 415 and capturing 112 of the enemy during September and October, those figures had little consequence for control of the territory. In October government officials estimated that in addition to organized Viet Cong units in Duc Pho and Mo Duc, the equivalent of three battalions or 1,000 men, there were over 1,200 political cadre in the villages, about 1,800 guerrillas, and 400 members of various youth associations. Officials believed that any positive shift in popular sentiment toward the government had been minimal at best.[21]

To the north, in the enclave around Chu Lai, Linnell's 196th Brigade could not find the enemy said to be threatening the base. In August the 1st Squadron, 1st Armored Cavalry, had been assigned to the 196th, freeing the attached 2d Squadron, 11th Armored Cavalry, for operations north to Tam Ky. Working with South Vietnamese territorials, 2d Squadron armor swept into several small base camps over the next two months and reported killing over 100 Viet Cong, a total that equaled the number claimed by the rest of the 196th during the same two months.

Immediately south of Linnell, the effectiveness of the Korean 2d Marine Brigade remained a question mark. Since arriving in Vietnam, the Koreans had stayed near their bases. When they did venture out, it was rarely for more than ten days at a time. On 5 September, however, learning that the *48th PLAF Battalion* had slipped onto the Batangan Peninsula for recruits and supplies, the marine commander, General Kim, attacked with three battalions, one of them conducting an amphibious assault from U.S. Navy vessels. In Operation DRAGON FIRE, the brigade's first sustained offensive in over a year, Kim intended not only to sweep the peninsula clean but also to establish a permanent presence by constructing a tactical base at the southern tip for his fourth marine battalion. By the end of September Kim reported killing 404 Viet Cong, capturing 14, and finding 28 weapons, for a remarkably high ratio of kills to weapons captured. Korean losses were 39 killed and 166 wounded.

At the same time Operation DRAGON FIRE generated many refugees. Some 2,100 congregated near Son Hai, the new Korean base on the peninsula. Government officials and U.S. advisers later learned that six insur-

---

[21] ORLL, 1 Aug–31 Oct 67, Americal Div, pp. 5–6, 12–13; ORLL, 1 Aug–31 Oct 67, 2d Bn, 35th Inf, pp. 2–8, Historians files, CMH.

gent-dominated hamlets on the peninsula had been "abandoned," in the term used by an American officer, but they had little other information on the matter, including the whereabouts of the people. Since General Kim had prohibited the South Vietnamese and Americans from entering the sector, they supported the refugees as best they could.

DRAGON FIRE continued for another month. While Kim reported no major encounters during that interval, he claimed another 137 Viet Cong killed and 17 more weapons confiscated. His own losses were 7 killed and 34 wounded.[22]

When it was all over, these summer, dry season operations in southern I Corps were not the ambitious sweeps into the interior that Westmoreland had envisioned. At best the airborne brigade's Operation WHEELER was inconclusive, while the other American units seemed to do better along the coast, where the flatlands were conducive to mechanized and airmobile warfare.

By the end of October the total tally of enemy killed during the Americal's two major operations, WHEELER (fifty days) and WALLOWA (twenty-seven days), was 1,415, almost equally divided between the airborne and airmobile brigades. If estimates were right, if half the enemy killed were soldiers of the *2d Division* and the rest local forces and guerrillas, then the probable strength of the division had been reduced by about 12 percent. While some of the *2d Division*'s five battalions were more badly hurt than others, the division remained an effective fighting unit.

[22] Op Sum, Opn DRAGON FIRE, ROK 2d Marine Bde, MACV, n.d., Historians files, CMH; RD Rpts, Quang Ngai Province, Sep 67, 30 Sep 67, and Oct 67, 31 Oct 67, Historians files, CMH. For the abandoned hamlets, see MFR, Forsythe, 10 Oct 67, sub: Trip Report to Quang Ngai Province, 3–4 October 1967, Incl 2.

PART FIVE

Trouble in Mid-Country

18

The Highlands Again

The annual rains of the southwest monsoon usually slowed the tempo of operations in the western highlands. But in the spring of 1967 the soggy weather was not enough to stop the enemy command. Beginning in May the *B3 Front* began a buildup aimed at drawing the Americans back into the border areas, where prowling North Vietnamese forces could attack them at will. Even after three U.S. campaigns in the highlands in two years, the North Vietnamese presence in the region was as strong as ever. In addition to sapper, artillery, and several independent North Vietnamese and Viet Cong battalions, the *B3 Front* had no fewer than six main force regiments at its disposal. Three of those, the *32d*, *66th*, and *88th*, all familiar to American veterans of Operation SAM HOUSTON and quickly back up to strength, belonged to the *1st PAVN Division* and were deployed in Cambodian Base Areas 701 and 702. The remaining regiments were operating independently—the *24th* in northern Kontum Province, the *95B* in Pleiku Province, and the *33d* in northern Darlac. In midsummer a seventh regular regiment, the *174th*, joined the *24th* in Kontum. Hanoi expected the *B3 Front* to use those assets as it always had—to draw the Americans away from the populated coast and into the rugged border regions where it could inflict heavy casualties.[1]

The U.S. 4th Division remained in the highlands to respond to any enemy incursion. It had just completed SAM HOUSTON in early April—just as the dry season ended—when intelligence got an inkling of the North Vietnamese buildup. Since the Americans knew that all *B3 Front* units were still active, it was clear that SAM HOUSTON had not caused the enemy too much pain.

Rain or shine, the border was a dangerous place, so General Peers, the 4th Division commander, decided to roll straight into a new border campaign, for all practical purposes a continuation of SAM HOUSTON. He called it Operation FRANCIS MARION, and it kicked off on 6 April.

Peers was acutely aware of the danger he faced. For the third time since its arrival in Vietnam the previous year, the 4th Division was guard-

[1] Order of Battle Book, G–2, IFFV, 1 Aug 70, pp. 64–94, 173–77; *Western Highlands*, pp. 43–44.

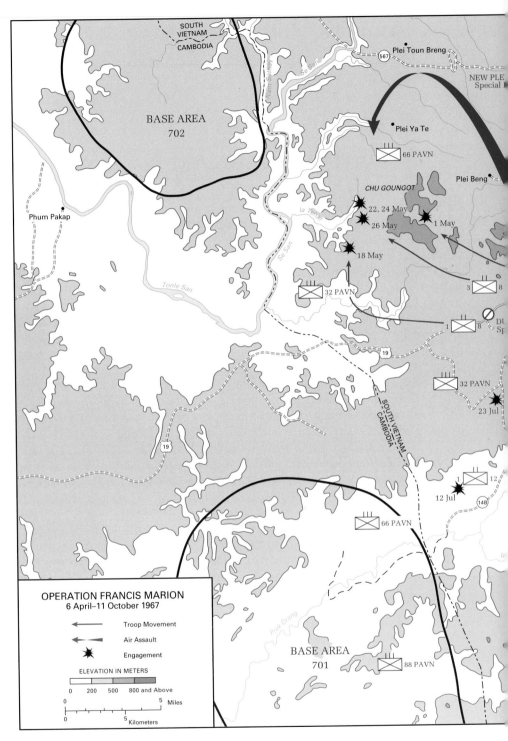

Plei Toun Breng
567
NEW PLE
Special

BASE AREA
702

Plei Ya Te

66 PAVN

Plei Beng

CHU GOUNGOT

22, 24 May

1 May

26 May

18 May

Phum Pakap

Se San

32 PAVN

3   8

1   8   DU
           Sp

Tonle San

19

32 PAVN

23 Jul

SOUTH VIETNAM
CAMBODIA

19

1   12

12 Jul   14B

66 PAVN

Prek Drang

BASE AREA
701

88 PAVN

OPERATION FRANCIS MARION
6 April–11 October 1967

⟵ Troop Movement

◀⟵ Air Assault

✦ Engagement

ELEVATION IN METERS

0   200   500   800 and Above

0   5   Miles

0   5   Kilometers

MAP 29

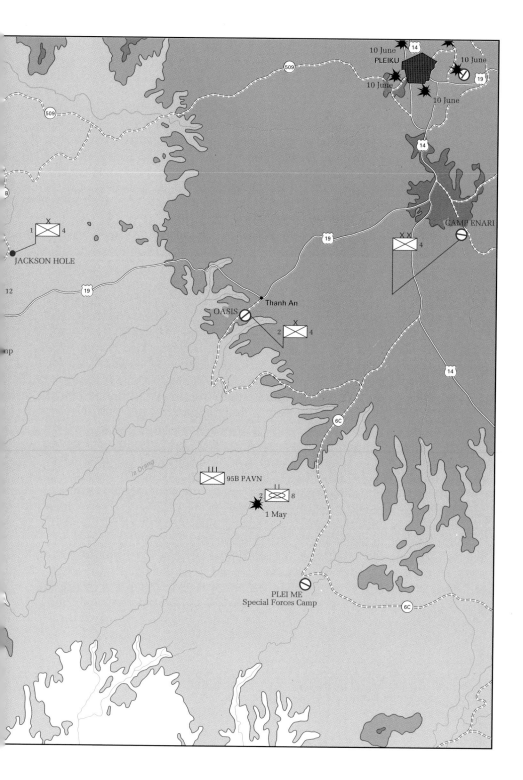

ing the border against North Vietnamese forays that seemed to grow more dangerous each time. So, rather than simply run operations along the border hoping to catch and bloody some hapless main force unit, Peers decided to make FRANCIS MARION a defense in depth.

He arrayed his 1st Brigade in an arc twenty kilometers east of the Cambodian border along Route 14B and the north-south line of Special Forces camps running from New Plei Djereng to Duc Co and down to Plei Me. Between this line and the border, Special Forces, CIDG units, and the division's own long-range reconnaissance teams searched for signs of the enemy. Behind the line, the 2d Brigade acted as a general reserve, ready to respond to reports of significant North Vietnamese activity.[2]

South Vietnamese Army units extended the screen, with units of the 23d Division to the south in Darlac Province and a nondivisional South Vietnamese regiment, the 42d, to the north in Kontum Province. The 42d Regiment was split between Kontum City, forty kilometers north of Pleiku City, and Tan Canh, a village another forty kilometers farther north. Several U.S. armor units backed the operation, as did the guns of I Field Force's 52d Artillery Group at Pleiku, strengthened in March by the newly arrived 1st Battalion, 92d Artillery (155-mm. towed).

The *B3 Front* wasted no time in implementing its plan. North Vietnamese activity increased sharply in western Pleiku and northern Darlac Provinces within days after Peers had initiated FRANCIS MARION. Most of these contacts were small, fleeting affairs. Then, in mid-April Special Forces teams reported engaging a North Vietnamese battalion in northern Darlac. A few days later, near the Buon Blech Special Forces camp, some seventy kilometers south of Plei Me, Special Forces reported the presence of two Viet Cong companies. Peers responded to this rash of sightings by sending a battalion task force from the 1st Brigade into northern Darlac Province on 24 April.[3] He then realigned his remaining forces—the 1st Brigade with two battalions stayed along Route 14B, while the 2d Brigade with three battalions moved on line with the 1st Brigade into positions south of Highway 19 and west of Plei Me in the Ia Drang Valley.[4] (See *Map 29.*)

As the 2d Brigade relocated, a company from the 2d Battalion, 8th Infantry, a unit undergoing conversion from straight-leg infantry to mechanized, began a sweep north of Plei Me on 28 April. When the armored vehicles ran into difficult terrain, the company commander returned them to the battalion firebase. The company continued the sweep for two days, ambushing a group of North Vietnamese and killing thirteen. The rest

---

[2] ORLL, 1 Feb–30 Apr 67, 4th Inf Div, pp. 2–10, Incls 1, 3, Historians files, CMH; Interv, author with Peers, 21 Oct 75; ORLL, 1 May–31 Jul 67, 4th Inf Div, 20 Aug 67, pp. 2–7, Incl 3, and AAR, Opn FRANCIS MARION, 4th Inf Div, 25 Nov 67, p. 11, both in Historians files, CMH.

[3] Intel Sum 112, IFFV, 20 Apr 67, p. 7; FRAGO 3–2, Opn FRANCIS MARION, 4th Inf Div, 25 Apr 67; AAR, Opn HANCOCK, 3d Bn, 8th Inf, 7 Jun 67, pp. 1, 3, all in Historians files, CMH.

[4] Intel Sum 115, 4th Inf Div, 25 Apr 67, Historians files, CMH.

fled, taking up positions in a partially fortified camp. Unable to break through the defenses, the Americans called for artillery and air strikes and, later in the day, an M113 scout platoon. All failed to dislodge what now appeared to be a full enemy company. The next morning the attackers recalled the rest of their armored personnel carriers and were joined by two tanks from the division cavalry squadron. But when they stormed the defenses, the enemy was gone.

Pushing on, the column ran into another part of the enemy's base. When the armor attacked, the North Vietnamese charged from their bunkers, hurling grenades in a desperate attempt to stop the oncoming tracks. It was a forlorn hope. Canister rounds and machine-gun fire raked the North Vietnamese, and those who came too close were crushed beneath the tracks. By late afternoon the killing was over. One hundred thirty-eight North Vietnamese soldiers of the *95B Regiment* lay dead, while one American had lost his life. The base yielded forty-two weapons and large amounts of ammunition and equipment.[5]

Afterward there was little further evidence of enemy activity around Plei Me. But just to the north, near Duc Co, an American company repulsed a battalion-size attack on 1 May. A prisoner captured during the action revealed that two of the *66th Regiment*'s battalions had recently entered South Vietnam and were building base camps northwest of Duc Co. He also said that the *66th* planned to attack the Special Forces camp at Duc Co on 6 June, before moving against Plei Me.[6]

In the debris of its skirmish with the *95B* a few days earlier, the 2d of the 8th Infantry found a notebook listing North Vietnamese objectives for the rainy season offensive. The list included a South Vietnamese district headquarters at Thanh An, the 2d Brigade base at Oasis, and the Special Forces camps at New Plei Djereng, Plei Me, and Duc Co.[7] A series of firefights south of Duc Co, the discovery of a complex containing a radio that a North Vietnamese battalion headquarters would use, and the interrogation of a prisoner from the *1st PAVN Division* provided further evidence of a likely strike against the Special Forces camp.[8]

Border Battles Begin Anew

Convinced that an attack was imminent, Peers made a preemptive strike. After launching four B–52 raids southwest of the camp, he twice sent the 1st Battalion, 8th Infantry, a 2d Brigade unit commanded by Lt. Col. Timothy G. Gannon, into the area. Neither foray found evidence of

[5] AAR, Opn Francis Marion, 4th Inf Div, Incl 7; Interv, author with Adamson, 4 Apr 79.
[6] Periodic Intel Rpt 18, IFFV, 8 May 67, an. D, Historians files, CMH.
[7] MACV Intel Bulletin 4594, 13 May 67, and Intel Sum 133, IFFV, 13 May 67, both in Historians files, CMH; AAR, Opn Francis Marion, 4th Inf Div, pp. 1–2; Interv, author with Adamson, 4 Apr 79.
[8] Periodic Intel Rpt 21, IFFV, 30 May 67, p. 4.

A self-propelled 155-mm. howitzer leads a convoy toward the Cambodian border as the battles of May begin.

enemy activity. On the thirteenth the 1st Brigade commander, Col. Charles A. Jackson, instructed Gannon, whose battalion had now been placed under Jackson's control, to conduct a two-company probe of the site of a fifth B–52 strike fifteen kilometers northwest of Duc Co. The companies were then to move east away from Cambodia and end the operation at JACKSON HOLE, the 1st Brigade base on Route 14B. At the same time another 1st Brigade unit, the 3d Battalion, 12th Infantry, was to move to within supporting range of Gannon's column.[9]

Despite its proximity to the border, Gannon's force saw no sign of the enemy until the morning of 18 May, when Company B spotted a lone North Vietnamese soldier. He fled with the Americans in hot pursuit. This seemingly insignificant event marked the beginning of what the 4th Division would soon call the "nine days in May border battles."

The acting company commander, 1st Lt. Cary D. Allen, ordered his 4th Platoon to follow the soldier for up to 200 meters, while the rest of Company B executed cloverleaf patrols and cut a hole in the jungle canopy so a helicopter could evacuate some captured rucksacks. As the 4th Platoon neared the 200-meter limit, it again saw an enemy soldier, gave chase, and soon became embroiled in a firefight with a large Communist force. Realizing that the 4th Platoon had been lured into a trap, Allen tried to rescue it, but intense fire all around forced him to form a perimeter and call for artillery support.

Allen was learning what other American officers in earlier encounters along this section of the border already knew: the terrain was as much an enemy as the North Vietnamese. This sliver of relatively flat—though heavily jungled—ground was wedged between the Chu Goungot Mountains and the Se San River, which marked the Cambodian border. Known as the Ia Tchar Valley, it was lined by a series of narrow ridges separated

---

[9] AAR, Opn FRANCIS MARION, 4th Inf Div, Incl 7; Interv, author with Col Timothy G. Gannon, Comdr, 1st Bn, 8th Inf, 4th Inf Div, 31 Aug 78, Historians files, CMH.

by steep-sided gorges covered with double-canopy jungle. Trees with trunks the diameter of 55-gallon drums reached fifty meters tall, and the foliage was so dense that aerial observers could not see the impact of shells exploding on the jungle floor.

Allen called in artillery, but as the first marking rounds thudded through the treetops they were swallowed by the foliage. Hardly a wisp of smoke rose skyward to tell observers how close they were to the target. Not until Colonel Gannon arrived overhead in his helicopter could they adjust the incoming artillery rounds to within fifty meters of the 4th Platoon. The besieged Americans also fired tracer rounds into the canopy to help pinpoint their location for circling gunships. Intense enemy fire, however, soon drove the Hueys off.

Meanwhile, Gannon ordered Company A to reinforce the embattled unit. Slowed by difficult terrain and sniper fire, Company A was still a kilometer away when a voice crackled over the radio to say that the 4th Platoon was being overrun and to call for an artillery strike directly on his position. This was the last communication from the stricken platoon.[10]

Alarmed by the apparent loss of the platoon, Gannon sought to speed Company A's arrival before the rest of Company B was overrun. He directed Company A to move to a small grove to await helicopter extraction, a process that took several hours to complete. Not until sunset did Company A arrive at the battlefield, at which point it joined Company B to search for the missing unit. When the men of Company A finally located the 4th Platoon the next morning, they found the worst. Only 1 soldier had escaped unscathed; 19 men were dead, 1 was missing, and 7 were wounded but alive.

The survivors told a terrible tale. When the enemy overran the position, those still alive played dead. For half an hour the enemy kicked at the American bodies and executed those who stirred. The rest of Company B lost 10 dead and 24 wounded, while sweeps turned up 119 enemy dead but only 4 weapons. The fallen enemy soldiers were from a battalion of the *1st Division's 32d Regiment*, last seen in March 1967. They wore clean khaki uniforms, had fresh haircuts, and seemed well nourished, unmistakable evidence of the advantages of the Cambodian sanctuary.[11]

After this clash the *32d Regiment* hastened to renew the fight. When the Americans selected one of the regiment's base camps as a night defensive position on the eighteenth, they triggered the enemy attack. Just after dark the Americans saw lights and at once requested artillery support. Almost immediately the North Vietnamese opened fire with mortars and launched a three-wave ground assault that swept to within five meters of

---

[10] Ibid.; Interv, author with Lt Col Robert H. Sholly, Comdr, Co B, 1st Bn, 8th Inf, 4th Inf Div, 25 Oct 78, Historians files, CMH; U.S. Congress, Senate, Committee on Veterans' Affairs, *Medal of Honor Recipients, 1863–1973*, 93d Cong., 1st sess., 1973, pp. 850–51.

[11] AAR, Opn Francis Marion, 4th Inf Div, Incl 7; Intervs, author with Gannon, 31 Aug 78, and with Sholly, 25 Oct 78.

the perimeter before being stopped. For two hours the battle raged, then at midnight the enemy withdrew, leaving behind 38 dead and 8 weapons. Ten Americans were killed and 65 were wounded. Although the North Vietnamese stayed quiet after that, B–52s struck the area four times over the next twenty-four hours.[12]

Meanwhile, General Peers reacted to Gannon's debacle by returning the battalion task force in northern Darlac Province to the 1st Brigade. He also ordered a battalion working in the upper Ia Tchar Valley, the 3d of the 12th Infantry, to move south to join Gannon's unit, while sending the brigade's reserve battalion to Duc Co, where it would revert to 2d Brigade control. Peers then shifted the boundary between the brigades north of Highway 19 to the Chu Goungot Mountains. The 2d Brigade was to commit two battalions north of the road, leaving its remaining battalion to protect Plei Me. Finally, General Larsen arranged for the 173d Airborne Brigade to fly from III Corps to the western highlands as reinforcement.[13]

By nightfall on the twenty-first the 3d of the 12th Infantry under Lt. Col. David M. Peters had formed a two-company perimeter five kilometers north of Gannon. After an uneventful night, Peters' men were just about to break camp when mortar shells rained down on them. A North Vietnamese battalion swept in behind the barrage. Despite artillery support, the outcome remained in doubt for two hours, until low-hanging clouds lifted, allowing fighter-bombers and helicopter gunships to sweep through and force the enemy to withdraw.

After evacuating 10 American dead and 77 wounded and after receiving a third company that afternoon, Peters established a new position on commanding terrain farther west. The Americans also counted 79 enemy dead, found 20 weapons, and captured 4 wounded soldiers who admitted coming from the same battalion of the *66th Regiment* that had attacked a company of the 3d of the 12th Infantry north of Duc Co on 1 May.[14]

A break in the fighting came on 23 May as units of the 4th Division observed a truce honoring Buddha's birthday. Colonel Jackson decided that evening to pull Colonel Gannon's unit back to JACKSON HOLE, replacing it with the 3d Battalion, 8th Infantry, the unit returning from Darlac Province, led by Lt. Col. Thomas P. Lynch. After making the switch, Jackson planned to have two battalions in the Ia Tchar Valley sweep east to search the lower ridges of the Chu Goungot Mountains.

On the afternoon of the twenty-fourth helicopters shuttled a company from Peters' battalion back to protect his firebase. As one company

---

[12] Periodic Intel Rpts 20, IFFV, n.d., an. A, and 23, IFFV, n.d., an. C, both in Historians files, CMH; AAR, Opn FRANCIS MARION, 4th Inf Div, Incl 7; Interv, author with Sholly, 25 Oct 78.

[13] FRAGO 10–2, Opn FRANCIS MARION, 4th Inf Div, 21 May 67; Msg, Larsen A–1495 to Westmoreland, 3 May 67, sub: Guidance Issued by COMUSMACV, Westmoreland History files, 17–A–1, CMH.

[14] AAR, Opn FRANCIS MARION, 4th Inf Div, Incl 7.

secured the pickup site for the departing company, the battalion's third company, considerably understrength from the fight on the twenty-second, began preparing a defensive position on nearby high ground.

The Hueys had hardly departed when the North Vietnamese hit the company as it was digging in. Colonel Peters called in artillery, then ordered the company still waiting at the extraction point to race back to help the besieged unit. The relief column arrived within a half hour, and although the fight lasted another sixty minutes, the North Vietnamese tired on the steep slopes leading up to the perimeter. Late that afternoon they abruptly broke off the attack. Left behind were 37 dead from the *32d Regiment*. American losses were 4 killed and 17 wounded.[15]

In the meantime, two companies of Colonel Lynch's 3d of the 8th Infantry operating in the lower Ia Tchar probed eastward, moving from one prominent terrain feature to another. On the twenty-sixth Company C broke camp and moved through the fog-shrouded jungle to link up with Company B on Hill 521, no more than a kilometer away. At 0855, as the men of Company C took a break before climbing the hill, snipers in nearby trees killed the company commander. An attack quickly followed. After repulsing the assault, the Americans concentrated on the snipers, blowing most of them out of the trees with M79 grenade launchers. But the snipers had taken their toll—accurate shooting had killed or wounded every officer in the company. M. Sgt. Richard L. Childers, the first sergeant, assumed command, rallying the company around a small knoll to the rear.

Colonel Lynch had ordered Company B to send three of its platoons to join the besieged force. The North Vietnamese stopped two of Company B's platoons with heavy fire, but the third managed to reach Childers' position by marching blindly through the dense jungle, guiding on the sounds of battle.

As the fighting raged, the foliage that had originally concealed the enemy now became an ally to the Americans. The canopy over Childers' position was so thick that it detonated most of the enemy's mortar rounds prematurely, showering the defenders with bark and twigs but sparing them from the more lethal metal shards. Then, midway through the three-hour fight, Sgt. Michael J. Scott and his men defending a portion of the knoll "stared in disbelief as fifty North Vietnamese armed with AK–47 assault rifles and sporting red berets walked casually up the slope toward them." Apparently the enemy soldiers did not know that the Americans were above them. Scott and the others held their fire, letting the North Vietnamese approach to within point-blank range before springing a devastating ambush.[16]

[15] Ibid.

[16] Quote from John T. Wheeler, "Company C Fought for Freedom Too . . . In a Nothing Place Called Hill 571 [521]," *Staten Island Sunday Advance*, 2 Jul 67.

Still the enemy pressed, launching several more assaults. At times the North Vietnamese closed to within ten meters of the American lines, only to be repulsed. When artillery and gunships finally broke the enemy's embrace, Colonel Lynch pulled everyone back to Hill 521. Late that afternoon, after helicopters had brought in reinforcements, the troops returned to the scene of the fight. There they found 96 enemy bodies, 32 weapons, and 2 enemy wounded. The prisoners revealed that their unit was the *6th Battalion*, the reserve for the *32d Regiment*.[17]

As the last big fight ended, the 173d Airborne Brigade arrived to reinforce the 4th Division. Apparently convinced that the 1st Brigade had the situation well in hand, Peers sent the 173d into the Ia Drang Valley and Chu Pong Mountains west of Plei Me. Now he would have three brigades operating near the border: the 1st Brigade to the north, the 2d Brigade in the center around Duc Co, and the 173d to the south.[18]

The enemy's tactics in this first phase of the monsoon offensive were fully apparent. The North Vietnamese had sent tracking parties to determine the location and approximate strength of the American units and had then sent units of at least battalion strength to strike them while on the move or in hastily prepared field positions—all in an attempt to annihilate them before help could arrive. To that end the enemy used an unusually large number of RPG2 rocket and 82-mm. mortar rounds to support his ground attacks. When unsuccessful, the North Vietnamese quickly withdrew, knowing the Americans would not pursue across the border.

During the five major engagements that occurred within a nine-day span in late May, the Americans had fought well, killing at least 367 of the enemy, a ratio of six to one, with enemy losses probably much greater than accounted for. After action reports indicated that in almost every fight the enemy evacuated at least some of his killed and wounded, which agents and prisoners confirmed.

Most of the enemy dead left on the battlefields had been killed by small-arms fire. Rather than performing a normal close-in support role, most of the 31,304 artillery rounds and the 219 tactical air strikes had been used to contain the battle area and hit enemy escape routes. In addition, B–52s had made fourteen strikes against suspected enemy troop concentrations and base camps with unknown results.[19]

Not that the seemingly large number of enemy dead meant that he was losing. As in earlier border battles, the North Vietnamese preferred this kind of fighting—drawing the Americans close to the border near their sanctuaries. Once again, almost every engagement was at a time and place

---

[17] AAR, Opn FRANCIS MARION, 4th Inf Div, Incl 7; Periodic Intel Rpt 21, IFFV, 30 May 67, p. 3.

[18] AAR, Opn FRANCIS MARION, 4th Inf Div, Incl 2; AAR, Opn GREELEY, 173d Abn Bde, 24 Oct 67, Incl 1, Historians files, CMH. See also Edward Hymoff, *Fourth Infantry Division, Vietnam* (New York: M. W. Ladds Publishing Co.), pp. 96–107.

[19] AAR, Opn FRANCIS MARION, 4th Inf Div, pp. 15, 36, 75–76, and Overlay 6.

of the enemy's choosing. The casualties may have been lopsided, but they always were. Hanoi had proved long ago that it was more than willing to exchange heavy losses for keeping steady pressure on the Americans.

Despite what appeared to be heavy losses, enemy activity began anew after a two-week lull. On the night of 10 June local Viet Cong units shelled five allied military installations around Pleiku City, a region that had been free of enemy activity for about six months. Then, on 19 and 23 June, the North Vietnamese shelled the Duc Co Special Forces camp. Although the damage from these attacks was slight, South Vietnamese casualties at one compound, a Montagnard training center, exceeded fifty.[20]

To the north, in Kontum Province, activity also increased. Early in June, Communist harassment along Highway 14 in the Tan Canh area caused the inhabitants of eight government hamlets to abandon their homes and move south. Then, on 13 June a company of the *K101D PAVN Battalion*, operating under the control of the *B3 Front*'s forward echelon in Base Area 609 opposite Kontum, battered a CIDG company twenty kilometers southwest of Tan Canh; two days later the entire North Vietnamese battalion ambushed and overwhelmed a Special Forces mobile guerrilla force in the same area. This prompted General Peers to order a battalion of the 173d Airborne Brigade to reinforce the Dak To Special Forces camp, five kilometers west of Tan Canh, on 17 June. Peers now expected the battle for the highlands to shift north to Kontum Province.[21]

Kontum

Kontum Province was to become the center of some of the fiercest fighting in the Central Highlands. Nestled in the northwest corner of II Corps, Kontum stretched over almost ten thousand square kilometers of the roughest terrain in South Vietnam. Although it was one of the largest provinces in the country, only about 100,000 people lived there, most of them Montagnards.

The North Vietnamese put Kontum's isolation to good use. One spur of the Ho Chi Minh Trail emptied into Base Area 609, a supply depot near the junction of South Vietnam, Laos, and Cambodia, the so-called tri-border area. In 1967 Base Area 609 grew into a major *binh tram*, or military way station, on the Ho Chi MinhTrail.

In the earliest days of American involvement, combat had centered on the string of Special Forces camps arrayed along the Laotian border. In mid-1966 the 1st Brigade of the 101st Airborne Division had battled the *24th PAVN Regiment* and had bloodied it but had done no permanent damage. The *24th* simply melted back into Laos to regroup.

---

[20] Intel Sum 163, IFFV, 11 Jun 67.
[21] Periodic Intel Rpt 24, IFFV, n.d., p. 1, Historians files, CMH; AAR, Opn FRANCIS MARION, 4th Inf Div, 15 Jun 67, Change 1 to OPLAN 24–67.

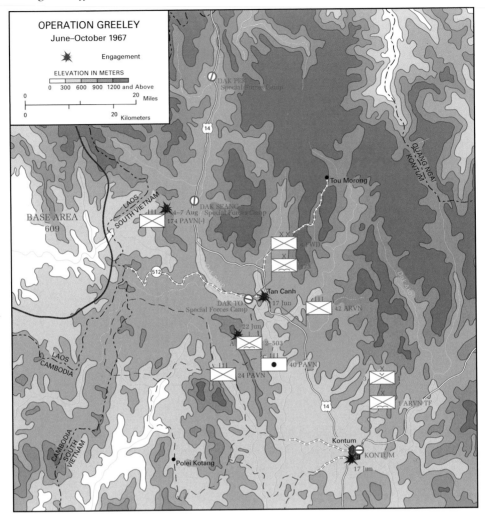

MAP 30

In May, as the rainy season began, intelligence believed that North Vietnamese forces in the base area were growing in strength, hoping to draw the Americans back into the highlands and to establish new infiltration routes to the coast.

By June it appeared that the intelligence was correct. Early on the seventeenth a battalion of the *24th Regiment* attacked the compound of the 24th Special Tactical Zone at Kontum City with fifty rounds of mortar fire. Three hours later another battalion of the *24th*, reinforced with a battalion of the *40th PAVN Artillery Regiment*, struck the headquarters of the South Vietnamese 42d Regiment at Tan Canh and the Special Forces camp at Dak To with mortars and rockets. Four of the one hundred rounds that fell on Tan Canh were long-range 122-mm. rockets, and ten of the sixty rounds that hit Dak To were 120-mm. mortar rounds, marking the first time the enemy had employed such large caliber weapons in II Corps.[22]

With one battalion of the 173d Airborne Brigade, along with armor and plenty of artillery, already on the way to Dak To, Peers instructed General Deane, the brigade commander, to follow with his headquarters and a second battalion. As those forces landed, Deane sent one battalion to search for two American advisers and several CIDG soldiers missing since 15 June. The other battalion scoured the jungle for the mortar and rocket positions used to shell Dak To and Tan Canh.[23]

Thus began the 173d Airborne Brigade's Operation GREELEY, which would be fought in some of the most difficult terrain in Kontum Province. Mahogany and other hardwood trees grew to sixty meters in height in the region south of Dak To, forming a thick canopy that limited the effectiveness of air support and artillery fire. Below the canopy was a dense secondary growth of bamboo, vines, small trees, and scrub that reduced visibility on the ground and made movement through the highland forests a grueling task. Those few areas that appeared as clearings on military maps were often choked with bamboo, and in the jungle proper the air was still, the wildlife often watchful and mute, and nature's ability to regenerate astounding. Decay hastened by the constant moisture made the jungle floor an endlessly fermenting compost. In only a day savanna grass could sprout in fresh bomb craters, within a week new scrub would spring forth, and one month later the crater scar would be nearly erased and the jungle whole again.

Weather and topography had an impact as well. Steep and slippery spiny spurs, many uncharted, radiated downward from the high ridges into the narrow valleys, and movement through the higher, steeper elevations was always difficult. Mountains, ridges, and high hills also interfered with radio communications and aerial resupply, as did the weather. Regularly during the rainy season the region was beset by low-hanging clouds and fog that obscured the tops of ridges until late morning, while heavy showers often continued throughout the day. (*Map 30*)

Such was the environment on 22 June, when a violent fight took place between a battalion of the *24th Regiment* and Company A of the 2d Battalion, 503d Infantry, on a search and destroy mission five kilometers south of Dak To. On the previous evening the Americans had been instructed to return to Dak To no later than 1500 the following day. Because of the difficult terrain, the company commander, Capt. Frederick J. Milton, decided to begin moving his 141 men at 0625 on the twenty-second. Unknown to Milton, a North Vietnamese battalion of 300 to 400 men was encamped behind a ridgeline just a few hundred meters east of the American position.[24]

---

[22] Intel Sum 170, IFFV, 18 Jun 67, Historians files, CMH; Periodic Intel Rpt 24, IFFV, n.d., p. 5.

[23] AAR, Opn GREELEY, 173d Abn Bde, pp. 1, 16–19.

[24] AAR, Opn GREELEY, 4th Inf Div, 16 Dec 67, pp. 6–7, Historians files, CMH; AAR,

Troops of the 173d Airborne Brigade prepare to evacuate wounded during GREELEY.

The enemy battalion also got an early start that morning, apparently intent on returning to Laos after its 17 June attack against Tan Canh. At 0658 the lead squad of the American company, proceeding north down a ridgeline under a canopy pierced by little sunlight, spotted several khaki-clad North Vietnamese soldiers. The Americans opened fire, then withdrew up the ridge toward their parent platoon. When informed of the encounter, Milton's battalion commander, Lt. Col. Edward A. Partain, directed him to reestablish contact and press the enemy.

Before Milton could act, his lead platoon was raked by automatic weapons and small-arms fire along its front and on both flanks. Calling for artillery support, the company commander sent another platoon to reinforce. As the platoons moved, shell fragments from the incoming artillery rained down on them, forcing a check-fire until the reinforcements were in place. About an hour later the reinforcing platoon broke through to the point unit, just as the first air strikes and helicopter gunships arrived. Because of the thick canopy, neither was very effective.

The first enemy ground assault came at 0810 in platoon strength, followed forty minutes later by a larger attack. Captain Milton tried to move

Opn GREELEY, 173d Abn Bde, Incl 1; Periodic Intel Rpt 26, IFFV, n.d., an. A, Historians files, CMH; Westmoreland Jnl, 25 Jun 67, Westmoreland History files, 18, pp. 18–19, CMH.

up the rest of his company and clear a landing zone at the same time. Only the 1st Platoon made it through. The other platoon was forced back to Milton's position, leaving the Americans divided into two pockets.

Meanwhile, Colonel Partain had ordered one of his other companies located about one and a half kilometers south of the firefight to assist Milton. He also prepared to air-assault another unit, then in reserve at Dak To, into a one-ship landing zone approximately eight hundred meters north of the besieged platoons. Back at Tan Canh, General Deane, the brigade commander, began putting together another reserve force consisting of the 1st Battalion, 503d Infantry (Airborne), then fully committed east of Highway 14. Before any of these forces could arrive, however, the enemy launched an all-out assault. Already, all three platoon leaders of the trapped element had been killed and all of the platoon sergeants critically wounded; judging the situation hopeless, the senior surviving noncommissioned officer ordered the few able-bodied men and those less seriously wounded to make their way up the ridge to Milton's position. Only a few survivors reached the Company A command post.

Shortly after noon the North Vietnamese, continuing up the ridgeline, hit Milton's position, then held by some thirty men forming a perimeter around thirty-five wounded. To the north, enemy fire forced the soldiers from the air-assaulted company back down the ridge, and it was not until midafternoon, with the arrival of reinforcements, that the enemy finally withdrew. Intermittent sniper fire continued into the late evening, when the Americans were able to clear a landing zone to evacuate the surviving members of Milton's command. That night a muster at Dak To revealed that seventy-five men were missing.[25]

Concerned about the size of the battle and the U.S. losses, General Larsen flew from I Field Force headquarters to meet with Peers at Dak To. Although the 4th Division commander had already approved reinforcing Deane with the 4th Battalion, 503d Infantry, the 173d's remaining battalion still operating in Pleiku Province, none of the senior commanders could say for certain that it would be enough. Based on conversations with the returning troops and air observers, Deane's staff believed that the Americans had bumped into the better part of a regiment. From other intelligence, the generals concluded that the airborne brigade might soon face up to three North Vietnamese regiments in a region that greatly restricted air and artillery support.

Returning to Nha Trang, Larsen briefed General Westmoreland. At the time reinforcing with units of the 4th Division seemed like a bad idea, because Peers expected that such a move would only encourage a *1st PAVN Division* offensive in Pleiku. Instead, Larsen proposed sending a brigade of the 1st Cavalry Division to Kontum Province: one battalion to reinforce Dak To and the others to positions just north of Kontum City, where the *24th Regiment* was thought to be lurking. Aerial resupply would be necessary at

---

[25] AAR, Opn Greeley, 173d Abn Bde, Incl 1.

first, but the I Field Force commander asked the South Vietnamese II Corps command to secure the road from Pleiku to Tan Canh.[26]

On 23 June Westmoreland approved Larsen's plan and arranged to have a two-battalion airborne task force, part of the South Vietnamese general reserve, fly to Kontum City, where it would join forces with the reinforcing cavalry brigade. He also gave the Kontum battle area priority for tactical air support and placed the 1st Brigade, 101st Airborne Division, then with Task Force OREGON, on alert.[27]

Meanwhile, Partain's companies returned to the battlefield where his platoons had been overrun. Scouring the brush, they found the missing American soldiers. Only four were still alive, and over half of the dead had head wounds inflicted at close range, which indicated that the North Vietnamese had systematically executed the wounded. The losses in the 2d Battalion, 503d Infantry's Company A totaled 79 dead and 23 wounded. Eighteen enemy bodies were located during the following days, with the final total 106 dead and 45 weapons captured.[28]

The arrival of a 1st Cavalry Division contingent at Dak To on 23 June gave General Deane four infantry battalions. Two of these units, the 2d Battalion, 12th Cavalry, under Lt. Col. William J. Buchanan, and the 4th Battalion, 503d Infantry, under Lt. Col. Lawrence W. Jackley, were sent to block the enemy's withdrawal routes into Laos. Five days later, on 28 June, Buchanan's battalion fought a North Vietnamese company, many of whose soldiers were sporting American uniforms, M16 rifles, and M79 grenade launchers. After the enemy fled that afternoon, the Americans found 6 dead and 1 wounded North Vietnamese, who told them that the *K–101D Battalion* had obtained the equipment when it overran a CIDG unit earlier that month. Encouraged, Deane committed the 1st Battalion, 503d Infantry, commanded by Lt. Col. William H. Sachs, west and southwest of Dak To.

One week later allied signal intelligence pinpointed an enemy regimental headquarters twenty miles southwest of Dak To. On 10 July Colonel Jackley's 4th Battalion was moving in column within a few kilometers of the reported position when machine guns opened up on the lead company. As the pointmen scrambled for cover, they saw that the fire was coming from concealed bunkers on a hilltop thirty-five meters away.

While American artillery rounds rained down on the North Vietnamese positions, a second company moved to outflank the enemy, only to be halted by small-arms fire. The third company went after the

---

[26] Msg, Larsen NHT 0713 to Westmoreland, 22 Jun 67, sub: Operation in Kontum Province, Westmoreland Message files, CMH; Intel Sum 175, IFFV, 23 Jun 67.

[27] Msgs, Westmoreland MAC 5910 to Sharp, 23 Jun 67, sub: Developments in Kontum Province, Westmoreland History files, 18–18, CMH, and Westmoreland MAC 5995 to Sharp, 24 Jun 67, Westmoreland Message files, CMH.

[28] Intel Sums 175, IFFV, 23 Jun 67; 177, IFFV, 25 Jun 67; and 180, IFFV, 28 Jun 67. All in Historians files, CMH. AAR, Opn GREELEY, 173d Abn Bde, p. 13, and Incl 1. See also MFR, National Military Command Center, Washington, D.C., 25 Jun 67, sub: Operation GREELEY Casualty Report, Historians files, CMH.

opposite flank, and it was also brought up short by the determined machine gunners. The fight dragged on for several hours, until the enemy withdrew during an afternoon storm. American losses were heavy—22 dead and 62 wounded. When the airborne troops entered the enemy position the next day, they found an abandoned complex of mutually supporting bunkers, many with two feet of overhead cover, and 9 enemy bodies.[29]

During the next two weeks the sweeps continued, but with few results. Deane's men ran into one North Vietnamese platoon, killing 13, and found recently used trails and abandoned base camps, but conducted no major actions. According to one prisoner, the *Doc Lop Regiment*, an ad hoc unit composed of independent battalions, was operating against the Dak To–Tan Canh area, but apparently had either departed or had simply found the noisy American troops easy to evade.[30]

Other American operations stepped off north of Kontum City on 24 June. There, Brig. Gen. Glenn D. Walker, the senior assistant commander of the 4th Division, set up an advanced headquarters as the 3d Brigade of the 1st Cavalry Division and the South Vietnamese 1st Airborne Task Force arrived to conduct combined operations against the *24th PAVN Regiment*, still thought to be somewhere in the Dak Akoi River Valley, thirty-five kilometers east of Dak To.

On 26 June, in the wake of three B–52 raids, the South Vietnamese moved up Highway 14 for a drive east toward the valley. That same day the air cavalry brigade under Colonel McKenna was ordered to conduct airmobile assaults into the valley proper and to serve as a blocking force. Although bad weather delayed the attack, the effort was in full swing by early July. As always, finding the enemy proved difficult. On 5 July a captured North Vietnamese soldier claimed that the headquarters of the *24th* was nearby, and General Walker immediately reinforced McKenna's battalions with Buchanan's 2d Battalion, 12th Cavalry. But they found no trace of the enemy, and on 25 July the cavalry brigade returned to the coast, while the Vietnamese task force stood down at Kontum, serving as a mobile reaction force.[31]

The last major action of Operation GREELEY happened in early August near the Dak Seang Special Forces camp. Prisoner interrogations indicated that Hanoi had recently moved a new unit, the *174th PAVN Regiment*, into the Dak Poko Valley with the intent of overrunning the Special Forces camps at Dak Pek and Dak Seang. Both camps had endured harassing fire over the past few weeks, and when the North Vietnamese

---

[29] AAR, Opn GREELEY, 173d Abn Bde, Incl 2; AAR, Opn GREELEY, 4th Inf Div, p. 8, and Incl 4; Periodic Intel Rpt 28, IFFV, n.d., p. 3, both in Historians files, CMH.

[30] AAR, Opn GREELEY, 173d Abn Bde, pp. 14, 29–35; Periodic Intel Rpt 29, IFFV, 25 Jul 67, an. D, and ORLL, 1 May–31 Jul 67, 173d Abn Bde, 15 Aug 67, p. 7, both in Historians files, CMH.

[31] AAR, Opn GREELEY, 4th Inf Div, pp. 7–9; Intervs, author with Walker, 3 Apr 79; with McKenna, 22 Jun 82.

ambushed a CIDG patrol within a kilometer of Dak Seang on 3 August it seemed clear that the predicted offensive was imminent.

The South Vietnamese 24th Special Zone immediately airlifted a battalion of the 42d Regiment and the entire 1st Airborne Task Force to the camp, adding a third airborne battalion soon after. As these forces pushed westward into the rugged hills overlooking Dak Seang, they met a strongly entrenched and reinforced battalion of the *174th Regiment*. After a fight lasting four days, with heavy air support called in by U.S. advisers, the South Vietnamese seized the position and drove the enemy into Laos. The South Vietnamese found 189 enemy bodies, large quantities of ammunition and equipment, and a sophisticated regimental command post with training areas and an elaborate mock-up of the Dak Seang camp. The Vietnamese speculated that the regiment had probably planned to attack Dak Seang on the moonless night of 6 August.[32]

Pleiku Again

With the threat to Kontum gradually diminishing, Peers' attention returned to Pleiku and FRANCIS MARION. Although the *1st PAVN Division* had been quiet throughout June, American electronic intelligence had noted an increase in enemy activity between the Ia Drang Valley and Duc Co in the 2d Brigade sector. In response the 4th Division arranged for two B–52 strikes on 10 July and asked the commander of the 1st Battalion, 12th Infantry, Lt. Col. Corey J. Wright, to investigate the results.[33]

Wright approached his mission with caution. The enemy often set ambushes in the wake of bombing strikes, hoping to catch American units sent to verify their results. Moreover, the field strength of his companies had shrunk to well under one hundred men because so many of the soldiers were rotating back to the United States after completing their one-year tours. Rotation policies had also brought in large numbers of inexperienced company grade and noncommissioned officers. Above all, poor weather reduced the effectiveness of air support, making operations close to the border especially risky.

Setting off on 11 July, Companies B and C of Wright's battalion arrived at the strike zone by noon and found little but bomb craters. Both then moved east and established separate perimeters about a kilometer apart amid wooded, rocky hills within five kilometers of the Cambodian border. In keeping with brigade policy, they began work on defensive positions in midafternoon so they could construct covered bunkers and clear a helicopter landing site by nightfall.

[32] Periodic Intel Rpt 30, IFFV, n.d., pp. 1–4 and an. C, Historians files, CMH; AAR, Opn GREELEY, 4th Inf Div, pp. 2–3, 9–11, 20; Interv, author with Walker, 3 Apr 79.

[33] AAR, Opn FRANCIS MARION, 4th Inf Div, pp. 3, 26, and tabs G, H; Intervs, author with Brig Gen Corey J. Wright, Comdr, 1st Bn, 12th Inf, 4th Inf Div, 26 Feb 79, Historians files, CMH; with Walker, 3 Apr 79; and with Adamson, 4 Apr 79.

The night passed without incident, but at dawn Colonel Wright was anxious to move away from the border as quickly as possible. Dense fog prevented the men from moving for a couple of hours. About 0830, as the men sat nervously in their positions, a patrol from Company C ran into a small North Vietnamese force, killing three of the enemy and driving off the rest. It was only a prelude. About thirty minutes later Company C spotted thirty enemy soldiers northeast of its perimeter and called in artillery and mortar fire. When Colonel Wright ordered Company C's scouting platoon to head for Company B's position to avoid being hit by the incoming fire, it bumped into yet another North Vietnamese force and by midafternoon found itself surrounded. Company B sent out a platoon to guide Company C's patrol to safety, and it was also hit.

The weather also played against Wright. Low clouds and rain prevented him from reaching his beleaguered platoons and effectively cut off any air support. He knew the location of the two company perimeters but had only a vague idea of where the two embattled platoons were. Despite the risk, Wright called in artillery fire, hoping the platoon leaders could keep their heads down and adjust it by sound. At the same time he prepared to move his reserve company to the battle as soon as weather permitted. But not until about 1100 was Wright able to board a command helicopter and direct the action from the air.

Once above the battle, Wright ordered both companies to move out to support their isolated platoons, promising to guide them with smoke grenades while coordinating artillery and mortar support. But no sooner had the companies set out than Company B's command group was struck by mortar fire, and the company commander was mortally wounded. An attempt to insert a new commander by helicopter failed when enemy fire wounded the pilot.

Aware of the inexperience of all the unit's platoon leaders, Wright radioed the company's forward artillery observer, 1st Lt. Fred G. Bragg, an officer with several months of combat duty, instructing him to take command. Bragg told Wright that Company B was pinned down and had lost radio contact with its isolated platoon. Before Wright could respond, his helicopter had to return to Duc Co to refuel.

Meanwhile, fighter-bombers had arrived and were awaiting an opportunity to strike. Rather than abort the mission, the forward air controller requested that the artillery fire supporting Bragg's unit be shifted so the planes could attack. The 2d Brigade approved the check-fire despite strong objections from Bragg.

As it turned out, Bragg was right. The air strikes accomplished little— except to halt all artillery support to the embattled American infantrymen for half an hour. Fortunately, the check-fire had not prevented Company C from rescuing its isolated platoon before withdrawing to its original defensive position.

Upon returning, Colonel Wright canceled the artillery check-fire and ordered Company C to move to B's assistance. As it set out under intermittent fire, helicopters bearing Wright's reserve company arrived, depositing the reinforcements at 1335 in a large clearing a few kilometers south of Bragg. Seeing that the battle was about to shift, the North Vietnamese broke away and withdrew into Cambodia.

The investigation of an ineffectual B–52 strike cost the 1st Battalion, 12th Infantry, 31 dead, 34 wounded, and 7 missing, with most of the dead and all of the missing from Company B's ill-fated platoon. Searches failed to locate the missing soldiers; 6 would be repatriated when the war ended, but 1 man would never be found. Wright's men reported killing 142 regulars from the *66th PAVN Regiment*. In many ways the fighting resembled the battles of the 173d Airborne Brigade in Kontum Province, where American advantages in technology and firepower were largely nullified by the terrain, weather, and, in this case, inexperience.

Meanwhile, north of the 2d Brigade and the Ia Drang Valley, the units of the 4th Division's 1st Brigade had fewer problems with rotations. Despite hard fighting, the rifle companies of its three battalions had a field strength of over one hundred men each, most seasoned veterans.

On the unseasonably pleasant morning of 23 July the 3d Battalion, 8th Infantry, the 1st Brigade's southernmost unit, under Colonel Lynch, was manning two company patrol bases four hundred meters apart, north to south, about ten kilometers from the Cambodian border.[34] Both were located on open savanna with reasonably good visibility. The battalion headquarters and its third company were located at Duc Co, about six kilometers farther north. Based on reports that the enemy might be operating south or west of the two advance camps, Lynch instructed the company commanders to send their three platoons on independent scouting missions. Company C was perhaps the less cohesive of the two, having lost most of its experienced officers, including the company commander, in a battle on 26 May; the replacements were untested.

Shortly before noon one of Company C's platoons spotted two North Vietnamese and fired at them. Within minutes the enemy hit back from all sides. Soon a second platoon, ordered to assist the first, was also pinned down by enemy fire. Lynch's first reaction was to order Company B to recall its platoons and prepare to join the battle. But even as Company B began to regroup, another enemy force hit Company C's patrol bases with mortar and rocket fire followed by a ground attack. Assisted by helicopter gunships, the Company C command group repelled the initial attack and with the arrival of Company B defeated a second assault at about 1245. But the fate of Company C's isolated platoons was still in doubt.

With favorable weather, Colonel Lynch ordered Company B to join up with Company C's missing forces while he airlifted his reserve company to the latter's patrol base. Other reinforcements included a mechanized company and a cavalry troop from Duc Co, although by the time they

---

[34] The following account is based on AAR, Opn FRANCIS MARION, 4th Inf Div, p. 16, and tab H.

arrived the enemy was in full retreat, hastened by heavy supporting fires from eight batteries of artillery, Huey gunships, and an almost continuous flow of F–100 Super Sabres. During the five-hour fight Lynch's battalion had lost 18 killed and 37 wounded. A hasty search of the battlefield turned up 184 enemy dead from all three battalions of the *32d Regiment*, with one-third of the deaths attributed to air strikes. Large quantities of ammunition and equipment, as well as 63 weapons, were also found. This time victory, although costly, had gone to the Americans.

Pacification in the Western Highlands

While the border battles raged, a second struggle took place to the rear. Both the North and South Vietnamese governments had had problems dealing with the Montagnard minorities living in the Annamite Mountains. Some 800,000 made their homes in South Vietnam, with a majority residing on the western plateau, loyal neither to Saigon nor to the Communists.[35]

Although Peers and Larsen considered the political disagreements between the Montagnards and the Vietnamese internal matters, most of the American-led Special Forces programs, including the CIDGs, recruited heavily from these ethnic minorities, as did the Viet Cong. Moreover, Montagnard tribes often provided supplies and information to North Vietnamese regulars on both sides of the border, while their villages inhibited the free use of American firepower. The 4th Division therefore developed a plan to relocate forty-eight Montagnard villages away from the border area west of Pleiku and Kontum Cities.[36]

By July the 4th Division had evacuated about 8,000 Montagnards to South Vietnamese resettlement centers. There, the displaced tribesmen, mostly farmers, were to receive land and construction materials while local officials provided food and social services. The reality was different. Although Americans believed that General Vinh Loc, the Vietnamese corps commander, fully supported the effort, financial backing from Saigon was weak. The truth was that many Vietnamese officials saw no value in supplying amenities to people they considered savages. For their part, the Montagnards often wanted nothing more than to return to their ancestral lands. They found the confines of the overcrowded resettlement areas little better than prisons, made worse by the fact that there had been little provision for planting crops. Finally, the depredations of some of the South Vietnamese troops supposedly guarding the resettlement areas led many families to flee and in general made a mockery of the entire effort.

[35] MACV History 1967, vol. 3, an. C.

[36] AAR, Opn FRANCIS MARION, 4th Inf Div, pp. 30–32; MFR, Jerry D. Dodson, CORDS Field Evaluator, 22 Jul 67, sub: Edap Enang Resettlement Program, Historians files, CMH; Sharp and Westmoreland, *Report*, pp. 148–49; Intervs, author with Adamson, 4 Apr 79, and with Walker, 3 Apr 79; RD Rpt, Pleiku Province, 1–28 Oct 67, 28 Oct 67, pp. 1–16, Historians files, CMH.

Special Forces troops in the highlands

By October Vinh Loc and Peers, responding to Montagnard complaints, had corrected some of the worst abuses, but by the end of the year the program was again close to collapse because of a lack of support from Saigon. Worse, those who had fled were forced to return, while the camps themselves were placed under heavier internal security. Feeling betrayed, the Montagnards began a mass exodus in December. By March 1968 only about 2,200 Montagnards remained in the camps.

While Montagnards from the border regions suffered, those who lived within a ten-kilometer radius of Camp Enari, the 4th Division's base camp at Pleiku, were more fortunate. Here, the 4th Division worked closely with village chiefs to provide short-term civic action services for a population of around 15,000. Special Forces soldiers at the various CIDG bases throughout the region performed similar services on a smaller scale. But nothing permanent could be done by either the division's brigades or the cavalry and airborne units that reinforced the highlands. These units moved too frequently to have a positive, long-term impact on the people, though they often stayed just long enough to disrupt the land and villages over which they moved and fought. With little to endear them to the allied cause, only the hostility the Montagnards held for all ethnic Vietnamese kept them from providing outright, wholehearted assistance to the enemy.

Final Days

Between 24 September and 10 October General Peers launched the final segment of FRANCIS MARION. While the 1st Brigade took responsibility for the border surveillance line in western Pleiku Province, 2d Brigade units attempted to interdict an enemy infiltration route in the Dak Payau Valley, southeast of Pleiku City. The operation generated only one major contact. That took place on 1 October, when tactical air and helicopter gunships engaged a group of North Vietnamese troops moving along a trail. Afterward, American troops counted forty-nine enemy dead and captured two prisoners from the *95B Regiment*.[37]

On 11 October Rosson declared both operations, FRANCIS MARION and GREELEY, officially over. He completed the deployment of the 173d to coastal Phu Yen and ordered the 4th Division's 2d Brigade to continue east into Phu Bon Province in search of enemy infiltration routes. About that time the South Vietnamese Airborne Task Force returned to its home base near Saigon.

Taking advantage of the lull in activity along the border, Peers sent his mechanized element, the 2d Battalion, 8th Infantry, north into Kontum to assist engineer troops repairing Highway 14 and Route 512, opening the latter west to a proposed Special Forces camp, later named Ben Het. The camp, within fifteen kilometers of the Laotian border, would enable U.S. heavy artillery to fire across the frontier. Westmoreland still had not given up hope that Washington would approve some sort of cross-border land strike during the approaching 1967–1968 dry season.

During its monsoon campaign, the 4th Division claimed to have killed or captured over 1,600 enemy soldiers, at a cost of about 300 American and 100 South Vietnamese dead. But the *B3 Front* had also accomplished much. It had tied down and dispersed large allied forces and had repeatedly required the allies to dispatch reinforcements from the coast. Kontum Province alone had soaked up the 3d Brigade, 1st Cavalry, for one month and the 173d Airborne Brigade for nearly four, not to mention a large slice of the South Vietnamese general reserve, at little cost to the enemy.

Over and over, the North Vietnamese had lured the allies into the border wilderness. Seven of the eight major engagements during Operations FRANCIS MARION and GREELEY took place within ten kilometers of Cambodia or Laos, close to the enemy's bases. Although 4th Division policy would continue to dictate prompt action against all major enemy forces found entering the South, General Peers had grown increasingly wary of fighting on the border. General Larsen, on the other hand, still supported the border engagement policy, and it remained in place until his midsummer departure from I Field Force.[38]

---

[37] AAR, Opn FRANCIS MARION, 4th Inf Div, pp. 17–18, 30–31, and Incl 6; Interv, author with Adamson, 4 Apr 79.

[38] Intervs, author with Rosson, 20 Sep 77; with Peers, 21 Oct 75; with Walker, 3 Aug 79; and with Adamson, 4 Apr 79.

Replacing Larsen on 1 August, General Rosson was more circumspect about the border, and Peers may have welcomed the change for several reasons. Between August and October, the 4th Division would lose almost 10,000 experienced officers and men to the one-year rotation policy, representing three-fourths of the division's authorized strength. As elsewhere, their replacements were mostly untested soldiers. So Rosson's conservatism, as well as slackening enemy activity, gave the division time to assimilate the thousands of new soldiers and prepare them for the rigors of combat.[39]

Nevertheless, the large personnel turnover reduced the division's effectiveness, as it had other units in South Vietnam. By November the division's tactical area of operations had increased significantly, encompassing Kontum and Pleiku Provinces in their entirety, as well as parts of Phu Bon and Darlac. Yet the experienced men Peers needed to control this region were gone. He could still use the thirteen Special Forces camps for news of enemy operations, but his best source of information had always been his own soldiers. Since February 1967 his men had volunteered for over five hundred long-range reconnaissance patrols into enemy territory. Two-thirds of those missions had produced sightings, with one-fourth of those leading to firefights. The enemy had lost 88 dead at a cost of 1 American. By November those volunteers were gone, along with their experience.[40]

By mid-October the western highlands had eased into its semiannual change in seasons. With the Annamite Mountains shielding the interior from the northeast monsoon, the thick, moisture-filled clouds from the South China Sea remained trapped in the coastal lowlands, allowing rays of sunshine to begin drying out and warming the central plateau. Highland farmers made plans to reap harvests of vegetables and mountain rice early in November, hoping that the war would go away. That did not happen. Already in August, the *B3 Front* had received its marching orders from Hanoi.[41] The *32d* and *66th Regiments* slipped into Kontum Province via the Plei Trap, joining two other veteran regiments, the *24th* and *174th*. Their target was Dak To, but this time the battle would be different.

---

[39] ORLL, 1 May–31 Jul 67, 4th Inf Div, p. 26; ORLL, 1 Aug–31 Oct 67, 4th Inf Div, 26 Dec 67, pp. 24, 41, Historians files, CMH.

[40] MFR, 12 Oct 67, sub: MACV Commanders' Conference, 24 September 1967, Incl 9, Westmoreland History files, 22–12, CMH; AAR, Opn FRANCIS MARION, 4th Inf Div, pp. 9–10.

[41] Msg, Abrams MAC 10931 to Westmoreland, 15 Nov 67, sub: 67–68 B3 Front Winter Campaign, Westmoreland Message files, CMH.

19

Old Coastal Haunts

As in the highlands, the war for coastal II Corps dragged through a bloody summer, neither side having much to show for its swelling losses, other than the certainty that the fighting in the villages and piedmont would invariably continue. If Larsen had been guardedly optimistic earlier in the year, he now knew that recent changes in the balance of forces—the loss of the 1st Brigade, 101st Airborne Division, to Task Force OREGON and the rejuvenation of the two enemy divisions, the *3d* and *5th PAVN*—spelled harder times ahead. And there was little likelihood that the Korean and South Vietnamese units on the coast would lighten the load of his main attack force, the 1st Cavalry Division.

The Korean Factor

The Koreans as always were puzzling. Westmoreland had emphasized to the Korean commander, General Chae, the importance of continuing the offensive through the summer. Larsen had weighed in as well, offering any number of inducements, from daily intelligence briefings and suggestions of inland base areas as lucrative targets to forming a battalion task force for combined operations, if only the Koreans would start fighting. General Chae was not enthusiastic. He continued to favor the deliberate approach, arguing that the security of the population in the Korean sector was more important than beating the jungle for enemy regulars. Once his forces had taken an area, he assured MACV and the South Vietnamese, it would stay clear of the main forces and guerrillas. By and large, he had remained true to his word.[1] (*Map 31*)

Circumstances did, however, force Chae onto the offensive in mid-1967, if only for a brief time. In June a rested and refitted *95th Regiment* of the *5th Division* left its base area for the coast, attacking South Viet-

---

[1] Msg, Westmoreland MAC 5978 to Sharp, 25 Jun 67, sub: ROK Operations in South Vietnam, Westmoreland Message files, CMH.

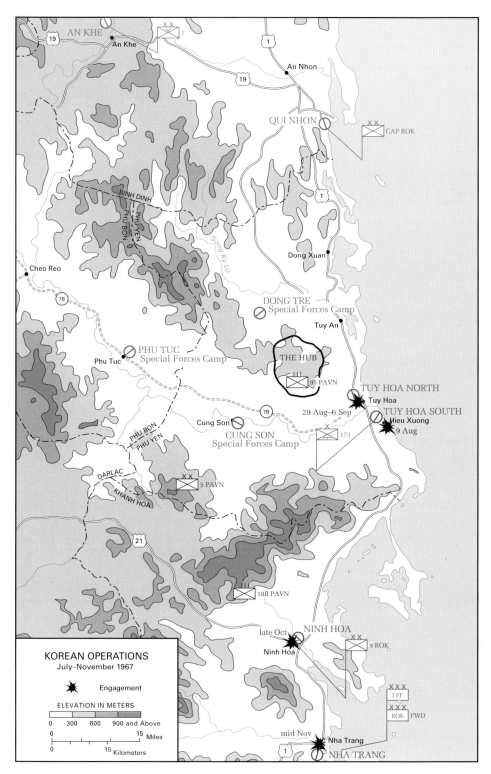

KOREAN OPERATIONS
July–November 1967

✴ Engagement

ELEVATION IN METERS

0   300   600   900 and Above

0   15 Miles

0   15 Kilometers

MAP 31

namese and Korean forces not far from Tuy Hoa in Phu Yen Province. Chae vacillated before deciding to strike back. Leaving some 60 percent of his forces on the plains for security, he sent the rest of the Capital and 9th Divisions into the Hub, the *95th Regiment*'s traditional redoubt northwest of Tuy Hoa.[2] During the previous November U.S. forces had attacked this same area in Operation GERONIMO with good results. Chae was going over old ground.

Operation HONG KIL DONG, named for a legendary Korean folk hero, began on 9 July when four battalions of the Capital Division deployed south of Dong Tre to attack southeast, and three battalions of the 9th Division staged at Cung Son to assault northeast.[3] While the Korean troops moved out, B–52s blanketed the target, and two battalions from the South Vietnamese 47th Regiment, 22d Division, manned blocking positions to the east, on the fringes of the populated coast. On the first day the Koreans encountered a few of the enemy, but resistance was slight and easily handled. Pressing forward methodically, no more than one or two kilometers a day, the Koreans trapped several enemy companies in small base camps and caves, claiming over 500 North Vietnamese dead by 25 July.

All seven battalions then swept east through the Hub, meeting strong resistance at first and then almost nothing in the two weeks that followed. The first phase of the offensive ended with the troops eliminating bypassed pockets of North Vietnamese.

On 12 August the second phase of HONG KIL DONG began with the two divisions conducting separate offensives. In the north, the four battalions of the Capital Division moved northwest into the Ky Lo Valley, searching for the headquarters of the *5th Division*. The drive ended on the morning of the twenty-fifth, when the Koreans reached the Phu Yen–Phu Bon provincial border without locating either the headquarters or any of the division's rear service units and installations.

Meanwhile, the 9th Division sent three battalions into a base area along the Phu Yen–Khanh Hoa border. But they too were unsuccessful, finding no trace of their target, the *18B PAVN Regiment*. When Chae returned his men to their coastal bases in late August, he nonetheless reported that they had eliminated over 700 of the enemy, mostly from the *95th Regiment*, and had captured over 450 weapons, at a cost of 27 soldiers.[4]

But while Chae received messages of congratulation all around, survivors of the resilient *95th* were escaping into the hills west of Tuy Hoa. Unobserved, the North Vietnamese regrouped and were replenished by

---

[2] U.S. intelligence believed 1,300 North Vietnamese replacements went to the *95th Regiment* between April and July 1967; 925 more went to the *18B Regiment* and *30th Main Force Battalion* between March and September; and another 3,100 went directly to the *5th PAVN Division* between July and August. See Order of Battle Book, G–2, IFFV, 1 Aug 70, pp. 174–76.

[3] MFR, 12 Oct 67, sub: MACV Commanders' Conference, 24 September 1967.

[4] Op Sum, Opn HONG KIL DONG, MACV-MHB, Sep 67, Historians files, CMH; MFR, 12 Oct 67, sub: MACV Commanders' Conference, 24 September 1967.

313

the Viet Cong. On 9 August they attacked, this time at Hieu Xuong, a district capital adjacent to the U.S. air base south of Tuy Hoa. After overrunning a revolutionary development headquarters and killing 13 defenders, the enemy quickly withdrew, taking 57 weapons and large amounts of radio equipment.[5]

For the next three weeks everything was quiet in Tuy Hoa. Then, on the evening of 29 August the *95th* attacked again and, occupying hamlets west of the city, dared the Koreans and South Vietnamese to respond in force. Unaccustomed to fighting in built-up areas, the allies reacted slowly. When they did, they chose to risk taking casualties over using firepower indiscriminately. It took a week to regain the lost hamlets. For the Korean and South Vietnamese forces the cost was high.

Eight days later, on 6 September, the enemy returned to the same hamlets. This time the Koreans and South Vietnamese reacted differently. Unwilling to take heavy losses, they brought in artillery and air strikes, destroying both the enemy and the hamlets. Overall results were predictable. Although the North Vietnamese lost over 400 men during the three-week offensive, the fragile pacification program suffered from the attacks. The fighting destroyed 9 hamlets and 3,700 dwellings. Over 20,000 people lost their homes, while civilian casualties, although unrecorded, reportedly were high.

The struggle was so intense that the new I Field Force commander, Lt. Gen. William B. Rosson, believed that the enemy might attempt to take Tuy Hoa Air Base. To reinforce, he brought in two battalions of the 173d Airborne Brigade from the western highlands, adding a battalion from the 1st Cavalry Division on the eighteenth. By that time the threat had subsided.

The following day, 19 September, the 173d began Operation BOLLING, moving into the hills west of Tuy Hoa to intercept retreating enemy forces. The results were meager. Meanwhile, the Vietnamese and Korean units provided a security ring around the city, allowing the burned-out civilian farmers to return, harvest their crops, and begin rebuilding their homes with materials diverted from other projects.[6]

As the fighting flared around Tuy Hoa, the *18B Regiment* began to come back to life. For the past several months the regiment had been inactive in Khanh Hoa Province, plagued by allied harassment, a high malaria rate, low morale, and a dearth of replacements. But when allied attention turned to Phu Yen Province and the Hub, the *18B*'s fortunes changed. No longer compelled to keep moving to survive, the unit

[5] RD Rpt, Phu Yen Province, Aug 67, 31 Aug 67, Historians files, CMH.

[6] Ltr, CG, IFFV, to COMUSMACV, 14 Sep 67, sub: Joint CORDS/MACV Region/Corps Revolutionary Development Overview; Ltr, CG, IFFV, to COMUSMACV, 16 Oct 67, sub: Joint CORDS/MACV Region/Corps Revolutionary Development Overview; AAR, Opn BOLLING, 173d Abn Bde, 2 Mar 68, pp. 1–4; RD Rpt, Phu Yen Province, Sep 67, 30 Sep 67. All in Historians files, CMH. Interv, author with Rosson, 29 Sep 77.

began to receive replacements, food, and medical supplies. Late in October the *18B* left its mountain bases for the coast to launch its first offensive campaign in over a year.[7]

Employing the same tactics as the *95th*, the *18B* sent two battalions to seize hamlets around Ninh Hoa, a district capital twenty-five kilometers north of Nha Trang. When the Koreans reacted, they found the North Vietnamese using the inhabitants as human shields. Unwilling to slaughter people who had relied on him for protection, the South Korean commander attempted to separate the noncombatants from the enemy troops. After three days of bitter small unit fighting, the Koreans regained control of the area but took heavy casualties. A week later the enemy returned and reoccupied two of the hamlets. The Koreans had had enough. As at Tuy Hoa, they sat back and watched as artillery and air strikes obliterated the hamlets.

Three weeks later the *18B*'s uncommitted battalion mortared the American air base at Nha Trang, seized two hamlets west of the city, and sent six sapper teams to destroy military facilities within the city limits. Prompt reaction by the allies forced the enemy to retreat, but the psychological impact was severe. No insurgent force had directly threatened Nha Trang in two years. The fact that the enemy could still penetrate the city's defenses immediately lowered confidence in the central government.[8]

The 1st Cavalry Division in Binh Dinh and Quang Ngai

North of the Korean sector, the 1st Cavalry Division continued to hound the *3d Division* in Binh Dinh Province. Although the *3d* was supposed to lead off the *B1 Front*'s spring-summer offensive, the front commander, Lt. Gen. Nguyen Chanh Thai, was unhappy with the division's performance. Its *18th* and *22d Regiments* had done little since April, while its third regiment, the *2d PLAF*, had been inactive since October. Consequently, he relieved the division commander and replaced him with his own chief of staff, Col. Vo Thu. He admonished the new commander to push his units into the field and take on the Americans as soon as possible.[9]

Thai's orders had the unintended effect of helping the 1st Cavalry Division locate the *3d* during the middle stages of Operation PERSHING. Capitalizing on excellent flying weather, the division's 1st and 2d Brigades massed against battalion-size formations from two of the regi-

---

[7] U.S. intelligence estimated that between January and October 1967, the *18B Regiment* received some 2,440 replacements from North Vietnam. See Order of Battle Book, G–2, IFFV, 1 Aug 70, pp. 174–76.

[8] Msgs, CG, IFFV, NHT 1397 to COMUSMACV, 9 Nov 67, sub: Evaluation and Assessment of Situation in II CTZ October 1967, and CG, IFFV, NHT 1536 to COMUSMACV, 10 Dec 67, sub: Evaluation and Assessment of Situation in II CTZ November 1967, both in Westmoreland Message files, CMH.

[9] Periodic Intel Rpts 20, IFFV, n.d., an. A, app. 2, and 23, IFFV, n.d., an. C.

*An enemy hut burns while reconnaissance troops from the
1st Cavalry Division look on.*

ments, fought five separate battles over a six-week period beginning in May, and put both units briefly out of action.[10]

In the meantime, the 3d Brigade had completed a sweep of the An Lao Valley in April and then, extending PERSHING north into the lower reaches of Quang Ngai Province, had air-assaulted into two areas the allies had not previously entered—the Sang Mountains and the Nuoc Dinh Valley. There, the brigade found caretaker units, ammunition and weapons caches, and several sophisticated base camps, but failed to locate its major objective, the headquarters of the *3d Division. (Map 32)* As June opened, the 3d Brigade raided the western fringes of the PERSHING area and the lowlands along the South China Sea, but again the enemy evaded. The brigade then flew off to the western highlands.[11]

By late June the 1st Cavalry Division had but four battalions to continue the hunt for the North Vietnamese division: two with Col. Donald V. Rattan's 1st Brigade north of the Lai Giang and two south of the river with Col. Fred E. Karhohs' 2d Brigade, ensconced on the Phu My Plain.

[10] AAR, Opn PERSHING, 1st Cav Div, tabs 6, 21.
[11] Ibid.; ORLL, 1 May–31 Jul 67, 1st Cav Div, pp. 18–19.

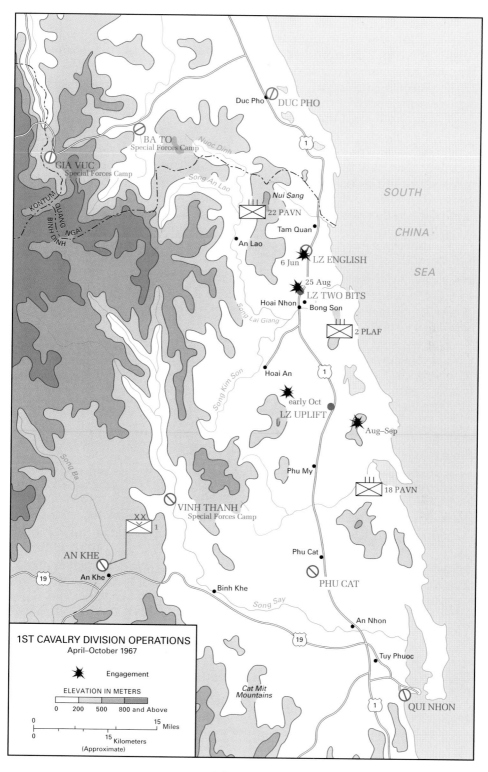

DUC PHO
Duc Pho

BA TO
Special Forces Camp

Nuoc Dinh

GIA VUC
Special Forces Camp

Song An Lao

KONTUM
QUANG
BINH DINH
NGAI

Nui Sang

22 PAVN

Tam Quan

An Lao

SOUTH

CHINA

SEA

6 Jun LZ ENGLISH

25 Aug

LZ TWO BITS

Hoai Nhon Bong Son

Song Lai Giang

2 PLAF

Song Kim Son

Hoai An

early Oct

LZ UPLIFT

Aug–Sep

Phu My

18 PAVN

Song Ba

VINH THANH
Special Forces Camp

XX
1

AN KHE

19   An Khe

Binh Khe

Phu Cat

PHU CAT

Song Say

An Nhon

19

Tuy Phuoc

Cat Mit
Mountains

1

QUI NHON

1ST CAVALRY DIVISION OPERATIONS
April–October 1967

✷   Engagement

ELEVATION IN METERS

0	200	500	800 and Above

0   15
                                         Miles
0   15
                            Kilometers
(Approximate)

MAP 32

Meanwhile, the number of enemy troops was on the rise. During May, June, and July—the opening months of the northern dry season—a steady stream of North Vietnamese replacements flowed into Binh Dinh. Colonel Thu, the *3d Division* commander, soon set his units into motion, with the *22d Regiment* resuming attacks north of the Lai Giang, the *2d Regiment* maneuvering south of the river, and the *18th* deploying still farther south for operations against the Koreans.[12]

As the *18th* displaced south, in mid-August the 2d Brigade happened upon a replacement group that had recently joined the North Vietnamese regiment. The new troops, presumably still in training, were in a series of caves south of the Lai Giang and east of Highway 1 in the Mieu Mountains. After surrounding the caves, Karhohs' men killed thirty-three and captured another forty-one. Then the cavalry division lost contact with the *18th Regiment*.[13]

By this time the 3d Brigade was back on the coast, and on 7 August General Tolson sent Colonel McKenna's troops into the Song Re Valley in Quang Ngai Province, twenty kilometers west of Ba To. Stretching some forty kilometers north to south, the narrow valley was laced with carefully cultivated rice paddies and well-fed livestock, but seemed devoid of people.

McKenna advanced cautiously from Gia Vuc, leapfrogging battalions and establishing intermediate firebases. Although the troopers encountered no one in the first two days, they had a feeling they were being watched. On the morning of the ninth, one cavalry company conducted an air assault onto three small hills, an objective called Landing Zone PAT, fifteen kilometers north of Gia Vuc. As the last six Hueys lifted off, the enemy opened fire with heavy machine guns. Bullets riddled all of the helicopters, bringing three to the ground. The other three limped back to Gia Vuc.

On the ground, the North Vietnamese swarmed the lone company. One group, hidden at the base of the hill area, surged out of its trenches and bunkers, while another unit, hidden midway up the western slope of the valley, fired down on the isolated American soldiers.

While the cavalry troopers sought cover and returned fire, their company commander, Capt. Raymond K. Bluhm, called in artillery and air strikes. They rained down quickly on the attackers, saving the American company from certain extinction. When the fight ended four hours later, a third of the company were casualties, some eleven killed and twenty-seven wounded, while only a few enemy dead and some weapons were found. The North Vietnamese had vanished. Over the next several days McKenna's troops continued northward, but there was little evidence of the enemy.

When the operation finally ended on 21 August the Americans had learned little more about the region than they knew before entering it.

[12] ORLL, 1 Feb–30 Apr 67, 1st Cav Div, p. 30; ORLL, 1 May–31 Jul 67, 1st Cav Div, p. 19; ORLL, 1 Aug–31 Oct 67, 1st Cav Div, p. 14; AAR, Opn PERSHING, 1st Cav Div, tab 24.

[13] ORLL, 1 Aug–31 Oct 67, 1st Cav Div, pp. 14, 22; AAR, Opn PERSHING, 1st Cav Div, tab 21.

*A CH–54 Flying Crane brings in a 155-mm. howitzer as artillerymen of the
173d Airborne Brigade establish a firebase in Phu Yen Province.*

Because of the heavy antiaircraft fire at Landing Zone PAT on the ninth,
they speculated that they had been near a major headquarters, but more
than that they could not say.[14]

After the operation was completed, Tolson returned the 3d Brigade to
the An Lao Valley, detaching two of its battalions to reinforce the other
two brigades on the coastal plain. Intelligence indicated that the enemy
planned to launch attacks from there against 1st Cavalry Division installations before the September elections. Mentioned frequently in the reports
was Landing Zone ENGLISH, the division's large logistical base on the
southern Bong Son Plain just north of the Lai Giang. On 6 June a fire, presumably set by enemy sappers, had nearly destroyed ENGLISH, and it was
still vulnerable to attack.

This time the advance information proved reasonably accurate. The
first sign of the predicted offensive came after dark on 22 August, when

[14] AAR, Opn PERSHING, 1st Cav Div, p. 10; ORLL, 1 Aug–31 Oct 67, 1st Cav Div, p. 20;
Tolson, *Airmobility*, pp. 139–41; Interv, author with McKenna, 16, 22–23 Jun 82; Ltr, Capt
Raymond K. Bluhm, to CG, 1st Cav Div, 17 Jan 69, sub: Recommendation for Unit Award
to Co A, 2d Bn, 8th Cav, and HQ, USARV, General Orders (GO) 841, 8 Apr 70, sub: Award
of the Valorous Unit Award, both in Historians files, CMH.

an enemy force assaulted a company of the 1st Brigade just east of ENG-LISH. Although the attack failed, American intelligence still believed that the *22d Regiment* would soon attack ENGLISH itself. Instead, the enemy chose to strike Tolson's forward command post, Landing Zone TWO BITS, a few kilometers south.

Shortly before midnight on the twenty-fifth, the troops defending TWO BITS conducted a Mad Minute. The enemy reciprocated with recoilless rifle and mortar fire that continued for fifteen minutes. American artillery responded immediately, followed later by gunships. The concentrated fire may have upset the enemy's plans, and there was no ground attack that night.[15]

Other than these two attacks, enemy attempts to interfere with the presidential elections in Binh Dinh were minimal. Ultimately, over 95 percent of the registered voters in the province voted, giving it one of the highest percentages of any province in South Vietnam (with a national average of 83.8 percent). In hindsight, however, the turnout may have been cosmetic. As American advisers pointed out, the Saigon-appointed province and district chiefs could threaten anyone who failed to vote. More revealing, the strong showing of peace candidates in the election indicated that many preferred a cessation of hostilities rather than a continuation of the Thieu regime.[16]

Shortly after the election, one of Tolson's battalions left to reinforce the 173d Airborne Brigade in Phu Yen for a month, and activity generally dropped off in Binh Dinh Province. For the remainder of the northern dry season, Tolson kept the 1st and 2d Brigades on the coastal plain, protecting the rice harvest and working with local troops and officials against low-level guerrillas, leaving the 3d Brigade to probe the mountains and valleys for larger prey. On 14 September this force, now operating with two battalions, found the headquarters of the *22d Regiment* in a narrow draw that led into the An Lao Valley, about fifteen kilometers northwest of ENGLISH. Although the base had been abandoned, McKenna's men discovered large ammunition stores and a cache containing forty-one weapons, over half of which were crew-served. Also captured was a large radio, the *22d Regiment's* code books, and most of its administrative records. In October American intelligence detected a reconstituted headquarters of the *22d* operating from the Cat Mit Mountains in Quang Ngai Province, far removed from its three battalions presumably still hiding in the Binh Dinh interior.[17]

As the 3d Brigade continued to search for the enemy battalions in September, I Field Force again tasked the division to provide a brigade for

[15] ORLL, 1 Aug–31 Oct 67, 1st Cav Div, pp. 22–23.

[16] Ibid., p. 35; Rpt, DEPCORDS, Pacification Studies Group (PSG), 12 Jun 71, Binh Dinh Province—The Challenge—1971, pp. 4–5, and Msg, CG, IFFV, to COMUSMACV, 10 Jan 68, sub: I FFORCEV Annual Assessment CY 1967, p. 16, both in Historians files, CMH.

[17] ORLL, 1 Aug–31 Oct 67, 1st Cav Div, pp. 14, 20; ORLL, 1 Aug–31 Oct 67, IFFV, 15 Nov 67, p. 9, Historians files, CMH; Intervs, author with McKenna, 16, 22–23 Jun 82; with Pierce, 14 Apr 82; with Spry, 11 Apr 83.

UH–1D Hueys pick up troops during an October search and destroy mission near Landing Zone UPLIFT.

operations elsewhere, this time for the Americal Division in southern I Corps. Again Tolson nominated the 3d Brigade, and the unit left Binh Dinh, this time for good, on 1 October, leaving only four cavalry battalions in the coastal province once deemed critical. A further reduction came in November, when the 1st Brigade left for the western highlands with two battalions. Binh Dinh, once the focus of U.S. activity in II Corps, was becoming a sideshow.

General Rosson, however, still had unfinished business in Binh Dinh Province. To maintain some muscle there, he attached the 1st Battalion, 50th Infantry (Mechanized), a 2d Armored Division unit that had arrived in September from Fort Hood, to the cavalry for service along the coast. Tolson partially converted the mechanized battalion into an airmobile force, concentrating its armored personnel carriers at the 2d Brigade's base camp, Landing Zone UPLIFT. Since the approaching monsoon season would bog down the armor, the battalion was to rely on whatever helicopters the division could spare. In an emergency, assuming the ground was dry enough, the infantry could always fly back to UPLIFT, climb into its armor, and move overland.

Operating in its airmobile mode in early October, the battalion came upon an enemy force in bunkers west of Highway 1 in the 506 Valley (named for the road running through it). The enemy was subsequently

321

identified as the *93d Battalion*, a unit of the *2d PLAF Regiment* that had left Quang Ngai earlier in the month. When the fight ended, the Americans counted 58 enemy dead and 48 captured weapons. Two months later the mechanized battalion would also trounce a unit of the *22d Regiment*, this time a few kilometers north of ENGLISH, near Tam Quan.

Since 11 February, when Operation PERSHING had begun, the 1st Cavalry Division had killed over 3,900 enemy soldiers and captured more than 2,100 prisoners and 1,100 weapons. The cost had been high, however—498 troopers killed and 2,361 wounded. But the successes also showed that the enemy was still trying to contest Binh Dinh Province, albeit with only poorly trained troops and recent replacements. His basic strategic mission remained the same: divert the attention of the allied regulars to ensure the survival of his local organizations.[18]

The Security Campaign

As was true elsewhere in Vietnam, the insurgency had continued apace along the coast, independent of the main force war that attracted U.S. attention. But in May, I Field Force had extended the 1st Cavalry Division's mission in Binh Dinh to include the destruction of the Viet Cong underground. To assist, the cavalry was reinforced by the South Vietnamese 816th National Police Field Force Battalion, a paramilitary unit trained to interrogate civilians and track down Communist cadre and sympathizers. General Tolson welcomed the police unit, collocated its headquarters with his own at TWO BITS, and encouraged his commanders to work closely with its members.

On 26 May the division began Operation DRAGNET, actually a series of ventures pairing cavalry and police units. While the former provided armed escort, police teams entered hamlets with "black lists" and attempted to locate and arrest suspected members of the revolutionary apparatus. This resulted in the voluntary surrender of many Viet Cong and a slow growth of intelligence files pinpointing others. Even after the 222d National Police Field Force Battalion replaced the 816th in September, Operation DRAGNET continued to produce results. When it ended on 27 January 1968, 323,261 interrogations had led to the capture of 944 members of the underground, including 191 leaders. In the process American and South Vietnamese forces had conducted over nine hundred small security operations and revisited some hamlets twenty or thirty times, with each new sweep netting one or two more suspects. During these operations, cavalry troopers also claimed to have killed 223 enemy soldiers and to have captured another 625, while losing 12 of their own.[19]

---

[18] AAR, Opn PERSHING, 1st Cav Div, tabs 6, 7, 9; ORLL, 1 Aug–31 Oct 67, 1st Cav Div, pp. 14, 24; Interv, Whitehorne with Tolson, 28 Jun 68.
[19] ORLL, 1 May–31 Jul 67, 1st Cav Div, pp. 17, 31; ORLL, 1 Aug–31 Oct 67, 1st Cav

Vietnamese study a handbill on the eve of the September elections.

But despite the umbrella of the 1st Cavalry Division, the government's hold on rural Binh Dinh remained tenuous. Although the revolutionary development program had taken root in the southern reaches of the province, no active initiatives were under way north of the Lai Giang, and the demands of the September elections soon diverted the attention of pacification officials in the south. Advisers reported that the gradual reduction in American strength during the fall had generated widespread anxiety, with many civilians doubtful that the South Vietnamese 22d Division and the territorials could protect them. Without the powerful opposition of the U.S. Army, many civilians were convinced that the Communists would take outright control of Binh Dinh Province.[20]

Neighboring Phu Yen also saw a reduction in American forces when three of four battalions of the 173d Airborne Brigade returned to the western highlands in early November. With all the Korean forces in Phu Yen committed to security missions, the lone American battalion, the 3d of the 503d Infantry (Airborne), having just arrived in country from Fort Bragg, was the only unit available to deal with the *95th Regiment*, which reports now had at full strength. Although the North Vietnamese continued to avoid combat, U.S. advisers deemed local security "inadequate," noting that the enemy still could "move in small groups and concentrate at will."[21]

The dry season results in coastal II Corps were thus uncertain, despite the concerted efforts of the Americans and the South Koreans. True, sustained regiment-size enemy offensives were no longer possible, and even battalion-level operations were fraught with danger. Nevertheless,

Div, pp. 16, 34; ORLL, 1 Nov 67–31 Jan 68, 1st Cav Div, 17 Mar 68, Incl 10, Historians files, CMH. RD Rpts, Binh Dinh Province, May 67, Sep 67, and Oct 67. Last three citations in Historians files, CMH. AAR, Opn PERSHING, 1st Cav Div, p. 8; Intervs, Whitehorne with Tolson, 28 Jun 68; author with Lt Gen John J. Tolson, 24 Jun 76, Historians files, CMH.

[20] Rpt, DEPCORDS, PSG, 12 Jun 71, Binh Dinh Province—The Challenge—1971, pp. 1–6.

[21] RD Rpt, Phu Yen Province, Nov 67, 30 Nov 67, pp. 1–6, Historians files, CMH.

Hanoi's ability to provide a stream of combat replacements continued to offset the allies' battlefield successes, while the enemy's underground cadre, though damaged, remained entrenched. Although the individual quality of the North Vietnamese replacements may have been increasingly marginal, the replenished main forces, given relief from allied pressure, were fully capable of regaining their offensive punch. At the very least, until their command and control apparatus was finally destroyed, they appeared able to fight small unit actions indefinitely.

PART SIX

Protracted War in III Corps

20

Counterstrike

To the tired, jungle-thrashing American infantrymen, "grunts" as they called themselves, MACV's "year of the offensive" had not brought them or their generals the victory they sought. No territory had been won; no enemy armies had been vanquished. Instead, a thousand fire-fights had worn down both sides in a hot, rain-sodden land that neither side could really claim to dominate unless physically entrenched there. The optimistic statistical reports emanating from MACV headquarters could never disguise the fact that the allies would not have victory until they had broken the enemy's will. That seemed unlikely as long as the cross-border sanctuaries remained inviolate.

A Matter of Logistics

Since Westmoreland could not take the war across the border, he concentrated on destroying what he could inside South Vietnam. The large offensives in 1966 and 1967 had indeed made it more difficult for *COSVN* to recruit soldiers and gather food from inside South Vietnam, but they had only a marginal impact on the steady flow of men and materiel from outside. As early as June 1967 half of *COSVN's* regular units, including the *5th* and *9th PLAF Divisions*, were composed of North Vietnamese–born "volunteers," a statistic that revealed Hanoi's continuing ability to keep its war effort alive regardless of American and South Vietnamese success against the Viet Cong. Meanwhile, the flow of supplies for *COSVN's* divisions steadily increased from Cambodia, whose government had acquiesced for years in the sale of rice, vegetables, and other foodstuffs to the Communists. Initially, military stores had only trickled across the border, most coming instead down the Ho Chi Minh Trail or by trawler along the coast. Once the U.S. Navy closed the coastal route, however, Cambodia was the only solution, and by December 1966 the essential agreements with the Phnom Penh government were firmly in place. On the twenty-third the first large shipment of military stores arrived at Sihanoukville aboard a Chinese ship,

A U.S. Coast Guard cutter stands off from an enemy trawler forced aground.

and two more shipments arrived in February and March 1967. In all, the three contained over 6,200 tons of weapons, munitions, and other cargo, sufficient to equip and sustain *COSVN*'s three divisions—the *5th* and *9th PLAF* and *7th PAVN*—at their existing level of combat, one day out of every thirty, for the next three years.[1]

After the supplies were unloaded, trucks transported them inland to a Phnom Penh depot for distribution. There, the Cambodian government siphoned off about 10 percent for the Cambodian Army in exchange for the use of the port and Cambodian territory. The rest passed on to Communist forces in South Vietnam. Those supplies earmarked for *COSVN*'s divisions in III Corps moved from Phnom Penh to Kampong Cham, a Communist regional distribution center, and then on to forward depots located in the Mimot-Snuol-Fishhook area and to Base Area 351 farther east.

Local force units also received supplies from Cambodia. Communist-hired trucks transported supplies and ammunition southeastward from Phnom Penh over Highway 1 into the Cambodian city of Svay Rieng and the adjacent Base Area 703, which served as another regional distribution center. These supplies then flowed north from Svay Rieng

[1] Brig. Gen. Tran Dinh Tho, *The Cambodian Incursion*, Indochina Monographs (Washington, D.C.: U.S. Army Center of Military History, 1979), pp. 18–27; Assistant Chief of Staff for Intelligence (ACSI) Study, 13 Apr 71, sub: The Role of Cambodia in the NVN-VC War Effort, 1964–1970, pp. 242, 327–41, and Logistics Fact Bk, MACV J–2, 1 Jun 67, pp. 49, 51, both in Historians files, CMH.

along Route 24, paralleling the Cambodian–South Vietnamese border, until they arrived at Lo Go, Base Area 354. Other stores moved eastward from Svay Rieng along Highway 1 and then southward to Ba Thu, Base Area 367, in the Parrot's Beak. Porters with bicycles, oxcarts, and sampans could move at will across the 120 kilometers of international boundary between Ba Thu and Lo Go. (*Map 33*)

While the Svay Rieng center provided some supplies for the northern delta, most stores for IV Corps left Phnom Penh by boat moving down the Mekong River to Base Area 704, located at Kas Kok on the border. From Kas Kok, sampans delivered the supplies at night into South Vietnam using the Bassac and Mekong Rivers and their tributaries. Still another supply corridor extended south from Phnom Penh along Route 2 to a regional distribution point at Takeo, still in Cambodia and about forty kilometers west of Kas Kok. From Takeo, supplies moved farther south on Route 2 to the Seven Mountains region, a base area that straddled the border. Those stores earmarked for the extreme south normally came directly from Sihanoukville by truck via Route 3 to a small inland port, Kampot. From Kampot, junks and sampans traveled south after dark to resupply those units working out of the Three Sisters Mountain and U Minh Forest.

In addition to large seaborne deliveries of military cargo to the port of Sihanoukville, North Vietnamese agents had made arrangements with the Cambodian government to have locally purchased rice shipped north on the Mekong and Tonle Kong Rivers to the Laotian border. At the border, the rice moved eastward on Route 110, a dirt road that the North Vietnamese had built in Laos, to Base Area 609, the southernmost terminus of the Ho Chi Minh Trail. From that point, the North Vietnamese distributed the rice to units operating in the southern Laotian panhandle and in the western highlands of South Vietnam's II Corps. If Sihanoukville closed, plans called for resupplying *COSVN* directly from North Vietnam by way of the Ho Chi Minh Trail and Route 110 in Laos and the Tonle Kong and Mekong Rivers in Cambodia.

The first important use of this alternate land route occurred in December 1966, when North Vietnam moved approximately 273 tons of small arms and ammunition south to *COSVN* bases. Three months later, in March, a second shipment arrived with 100 tons of large Soviet-type rockets, followed a month later by another 165 tons of similar munitions. Once inside Cambodia, the rockets moved downstream on the Tonle Kong and Mekong to a distribution point at Kratie and then overland through Snuol to Base Area 351.[2]

MACV intelligence presented persuasive evidence of a dramatic increase in enemy use of Cambodia. But while Westmoreland was convinced, the White House rejected his argument that Washington should publicly expose the enemy's support from Phnom Penh. President

[2] ACSI Study, 13 Apr 71, sub: The Role of Cambodia in the NVN-VC War Effort, 1964–1970, pp. 327–41.

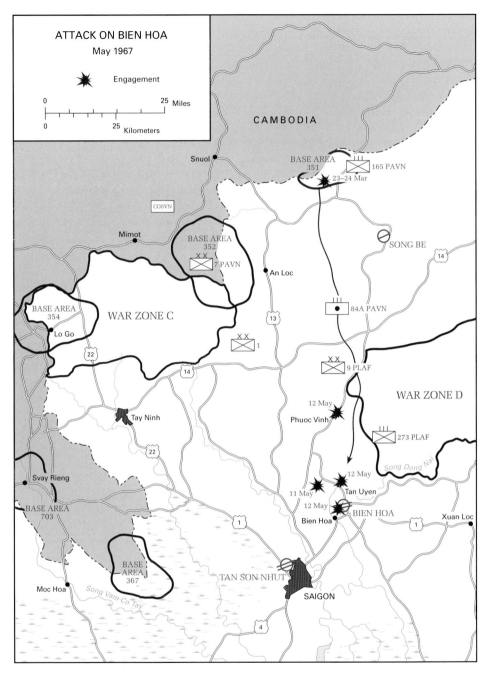

ATTACK ON BIEN HOA
May 1967

Engagement

0   25 Miles

0   25 Kilometers

CAMBODIA

Snuol

BASE AREA
351

165 PAVN

23–24 Mar

COSVN

Mimot

BASE AREA
352

7 PAVN

An Loc

SONG BE

14

BASE AREA
354

WAR ZONE C

84A PAVN

Lo Go

13

22

1

9 PLAF

14

WAR ZONE D

Tay Ninh

12 May

Phuoc Vinh

273 PLAF

22

Song Dong Na

Svay Rieng

12 May

BASE AREA
703

11 May

Tan Uyen

12 May

BIEN HOA

Xuan Loc

Bien Hoa

1

1

BASE
AREA
367

TAN SON NHUT

Moc Hoa

Song Vam Co Tay

SAIGON

4

MAP 33

Johnson feared a domestic and international political reaction, and he would not change his policy of pretending that the enemy sanctuaries were unimportant.[3]

This failure to close down the cross-border bases seriously undermined Westmoreland's accomplishments during the southern dry season. By the spring of 1967, despite some serious setbacks, General Thanh's COSVN forces were still amply supplied. In fact, despite the losses he had suffered since ATTLEBORO, he was ready with new replacements and new weapons to renew the offensive. It was no small stroke of luck for him that the Americans at that moment were ending their big unit sweeps just north of Saigon and turning their attention to I Corps.

The Opposing Forces

By April Thanh had begun moving his forces out of War Zone C into the relatively untouched forests of War Zone D. The *9th Division's 273d Regiment* was already in the big redoubt, soon to be joined by the *271st Regiment* with portions of the *9th Division* headquarters and COSVN staff. Also arriving was the *84A PAVN Artillery Regiment*, a new unit that was to spearhead Thanh's rainy season drive.[4]

For the Americans, a major enemy offensive in III Corps seemed a remote possibility because of the losses Thanh had recently suffered. On instructions from General Westmoreland, General Palmer at II Field Force had pulled the 1st and 25th Divisions tighter around Saigon. Although retaining the option of rapid offensive maneuver, Palmer's main task was to support pacification by grinding down local insurgent forces, low-level guerrillas, and political operatives. Additional combat forces such as the U.S. 9th Infantry Division were becoming operational in III Corps, but they were being echeloned west and southwest of the capital, where the government had been unable to make progress against the enemy underground.

Target: Bien Hoa

As the war progressed, American troops increasingly relied on air and artillery support and consequently on the huge bases that housed their airfields and depots. Like anchored aircraft carriers and ammunition ships, these bases, because of their size, were difficult to defend and always vulnerable to attack and sabotage. For many years the insurgents had depended on carefully trained sappers to strike these targets directly or more commonly had used mortar and recoilless rifle fire. But this had involved getting close to the allied bases, increasing the likelihood of discovery and

[3] Ibid., pp. 345–48, 354–56; *The Senator Gravel Edition of the Pentagon Papers*, 4:443–45.
[4] Periodic Intel Rpts 15, IIFFV, 18 Apr 67, pp. 1–2, 8, and an. G, and 17, IIFFV, 2 May 67, p. 1.

Viet Cong, with a simple but effective means to transport supplies

retaliation. Nevertheless, the threat of these attacks had kept many troops tied down in base defense, a concern that had been the immediate cause of the first deployment of U.S. ground combat troops in 1965.

In 1967 North Vietnam came up with a new answer to an old problem. In February North Vietnamese forces had attacked Da Nang Air Base with the 140-mm. rocket, a new weapon with a range of 10 kilometers. Subsequently, Hanoi added to its weapons inventory a second version, the 122-mm. rocket, with a slightly smaller explosive charge but with a range of 11 kilometers. In fact, the lighter 122-mm. rocket had four times the range and six times the lethal effect of the standard North Vietnamese 82-mm. mortar round. For ease of carrying, the 2-meter-long weapon could be broken down into three components: a fuze (2 pounds), a warhead (41 pounds), and a rocket motor (59 pounds). Movement of these weapons south along the Ho Chi Minh Trail had begun in 1966, and by mid-1967 they were beginning to reach the *COSVN* area in quantity.[5]

[5] Periodic Intel Rpt 13, IIFFV, 4 Apr 67, p. 4; CICV Study, ST 67–080, 1 Sep 67, sub: NVA Rocket Artillery Units, pp. 9–11; Periodic Intel Rpt 20, IIFFV, 23 May 67, an. I, Historians files, CMH; SEA Mil Fact Bk, pp. A–84 to A–88.

Compared with targets in I Corps, those in III Corps were much more vulnerable and lucrative.

The *84A PAVN Artillery Regiment* had left North Vietnam in March 1966, over a year before, moving south through the Laotian and Cambodian border regions with its full complement of 1,500 men. As the regiment marched south, one of its battalions dropped off in the highlands to support the *B3 Front*, while sickness, malaria, and American air strikes cut further into the regiment's strength. When it arrived six months later in *COSVN*'s Base Area 351, only half of the original contingent remained.[6]

Although rocket units working in I Corps had typically infiltrated with launchers and rockets, the *84A Regiment* had come south with neither because of the distance involved. One rallier later revealed that the regiment initially had mortars, recoilless rifles, and antiaircraft guns. But when trucks finally delivered the regiment's rockets in March 1967, preparations had already begun for an attack on a large U.S. installation.[7]

The target was Bien Hoa Air Base, the huge air and logistical complex some twenty-five kilometers northeast of Saigon. With a perimeter of about ten kilometers, the base was difficult to defend, and approaching it undetected within ten to twelve kilometers a relatively easy task. The allies had cleared its perimeter of vegetation, but only to about fifty meters, and it was impossible to patrol regularly to any distance. In this respect Bien Hoa was no different than any other American installation in Vietnam, large or small. Only its vastness gave its occupants a degree of passive protection, since the space occupied by its expensive and vulnerable fuel and bomb dumps, repair and communications facilities, and air crew and maintenance quarters—not to mention the aircraft themselves—represented a relatively small portion of the base's total area.

From March to May, even as his forces were fighting in Junction City, Thanh began preparing for the attack. Security and secrecy were vital. When porters from the *86th Rear Service Group*, assisted by small vehicles and oxcarts, began hauling the rockets to a storage area in central War Zone D, special guards accompanied the transfer. The rockets themselves were swathed in black plastic to conceal their identity from all observers, hostile or otherwise.

Complications arose in late March. At the time, the bulk of the *84A Artillery Regiment* had assembled in Base Area 351, while the *165th Regiment* took up positions along a road leading south into War Zone D, presumably to screen movement of the artillery. On 23 March an American-advised South Vietnamese Special Forces unit on routine reconnaissance began probing the road and was attacked by the *165th*. During a two-day fight the Special Forces unit held its ground, while air strikes pounded

[6] CICV Study, ST 67–080, 1 Sep 67, sub: NVA Rocket Artillery Units, pp. 6–7; Periodic Intel Rpts 6, IIFFV, 14 Feb 67, an. F, and 18, IIFFV, 8 May 67, an. F. The *84A Artillery Regiment* was one of two rocket regiments of the *351st PAVN Artillery Command* in South Vietnam by May 1967; the other was the *368B* in I Corps.

[7] Periodic Intel Rpt 19, IIFFV, 15 May 67, p. 8, Historians files, CMH.

A Soviet-made 122-mm. rocket launcher and rocket

the regiment and forced it from the field with heavy losses. That chance encounter may have left the *84A* without the infantry protection it needed and apparently contributed to a month's delay in its movement south.[8]

Another reason for the delay was *COSVN*'s fear that the U.S. 1st Division, which had moved two brigades close to the Cambodian border, might launch a raid into the sanctuaries as an extension of JUNCTION CITY. Only after the Americans began pulling back in mid-April did *COSVN* order the artillery regiment to proceed to War Zone D.

In the meantime, preparations continued for the attack on Bien Hoa Air Base. Using sampans, porters had begun moving a few rockets at a time from the storage site in War Zone D south on the Song Be River and then west on the Dong Nai to a previously selected launching site nine kilometers north of the target. South Vietnamese agents reported during April that they had seen North Vietnamese troops in that area, with carrying parties moving from the river with heavy loads in wicker baskets covered with black plastic. But there were no clues as to what they concealed.[9]

American intelligence also knew something was afoot. Documents captured during JUNCTION CITY indicated that the artillery unit was nearby, was equipped with rockets, and was urgently seeking two men who had deserted in March, concerned that they might reveal sensitive information. But lacking further data, the analysts had no way of tying the regiment to the reports of porter sightings.

In April, seeking to develop new information, the unit responsible for southern War Zone D, the 173d Airborne Brigade, sent a battalion to search the vicinity of the reported activity. The investigation turned up little. Later, the brigade left its base at Bien Hoa to participate in an operation many kilometers to the east. Its deployment eliminated a threat to the Bien Hoa strike.[10]

To disguise his intentions, Thanh ordered diversionary efforts by two of his regiments, the *101st* and *272d*. In early April the 1st Division had captured a document that discussed plans for an attack by the *101st* against An Loc sometime after 30 March. Believing that an assault was

---

[8] Periodic Intel Rpt 12, IIFFV, 28 Mar 67, p. 1, Historians files, CMH.
[9] Periodic Intel Rpt 20, IIFFV, 23 May 67, an. I.
[10] Ibid.

imminent, General Hay on 1 May sent his only uncommitted brigade, the 1st, to defend the town.[11]

Hay's decision seemed timely, for the following day an enemy force equipped with mortars shelled the Tong Le Chon Special Forces camp just west of An Loc. Nearby French plantation operators immediately began evacuating planeloads of employees. Quan Loi Village, adjacent to the airstrip, was soon in turmoil as many inhabitants fled their homes. American military police noted that about 40 percent of the bar girls had vanished, usually a sign of impending enemy action. In addition, the An Loc police chief relayed agent reports that prior to 19 May, Ho Chi Minh's birthday, the enemy would attack An Loc and Quan Loi with two battalions, while a full regiment would hit the Loc Ninh Special Forces camp, twenty kilometers north on Highway 13. Rumors persisted until May, sufficient indication of danger for General Hay to keep the 1st Brigade on station—and out of the way of the enemy troops moving on Bien Hoa.[12]

All through April radar and emissions-sensitive aircraft had detected increased activity in the Song Be corridor east of An Loc. Particularly significant readings occurred on the twenty-seventh and twenty-eighth. North of Phuoc Vinh, reconnaissance flights discovered a recently constructed road under the jungle canopy extending east of the Song Be into central War Zone D, and then south toward the Dong Nai, bypassing Phuoc Vinh. American intelligence also located the *271st Regiment* northwest of the Song Be's juncture with the new road. Accompanying that force, according to a rallier, was an unknown North Vietnamese regiment.[13]

Looking for confirmation, on 3 May a South Vietnamese Special Forces company conducted an air assault near the junction of the road and the river corridor. Twenty minutes after landing the soldiers ran into an enemy platoon, soon reinforced by what were reported to be two companies. The Special Forces troops reported that the reinforcements, clad in dark blue uniforms, spoke Chinese. They were probably North Vietnamese speaking a dialect different from that spoken in the South, and North Vietnamese troops frequently wore dark blue uniforms.

Late that day two additional enemy companies wearing black uniforms, which Viet Cong units normally wore, joined the fight. As the blue-clad soldiers disengaged, those in black made five separate attempts to overrun the Special Forces unit before air strikes forced their withdrawal. When the fight ended late that afternoon, helicopters removed the entire Special Forces element, including 15 dead and 55 wounded; no one attempted to count enemy bodies. The Special Forces commander estimated that his men had killed 100 of the enemy and that air strikes had killed

[11] Periodic Intel Rpt 18, IIFFV, 8 May 67, p. 1; Daily Jnls, G–2, 1st Inf Div, 3 May 67, and 8 May 67, both in Historians files, CMH; Periodic Intel Rpt 13, IIFFV, 4 Apr 67, p. 1.

[12] Daily Jnls, G–2, 1st Inf Div, 11 May 67, and 15 May 67, both in Historians files, CMH.

[13] Periodic Intel Rpts 16, IIFFV, 25 Apr 67, p. 2, Historians files, CMH, and 17, IIFFV, 2 May 67, pp. 1, 3.

another 150. But, as was often the case, the precise size and identity of the units and the true extent of their losses remained unknown.[14]

Meanwhile, east of the battle area arrangements for the big attack continued. *Headquarters, 9th Division*, coordinating the assault, moved into central War Zone D to join its regiment, the *273d*. The *84A Artillery Regiment*, with about 450 men, also joined the *273d*. The division commander, Colonel Cam, planned to send the *84A* to the rocket-launching sites north of the Dong Ngai, with the *273d*'s antiaircraft company and one infantry battalion providing protection. The remainder of the *273d*'s heavy weapons battalion, with mortar and recoilless rifle companies, and another infantry battalion deployed south of the river to positions east of the air base. Between those forces, the regiment would insert its remaining battalion north of the river to cover the withdrawal following the attack. Once the *273d*, reinforced by the *84A Artillery*, departed War Zone D, there would be no turning back. If discovered, the attacking forces were to fight to reach their firing positions.

Although unaware of the enemy's plan, on 8 May U.S. Air Force police captured a member of an enemy reconnaissance team attempting to breach the Bien Hoa perimeter. The prisoner revealed that he had left War Zone D to confirm information about aircraft parking areas to prepare for a future attack, details of which he had no knowledge. If successful on the eighth, he was to infiltrate the base one more time, on either the ninth or the tenth.[15]

Little concerned with the fate of the lone scout, the *9th Division* ordered the move to begin on the afternoon of 10 May. Traveling south from War Zone D in battalion columns, the troops crossed the Song Be in the middle of the night, rested for five hours, then pushed on. Two hours past sunrise on the eleventh, an American forward air controller spotted the force five kilometers southwest of the river, called in air strikes, and dispersed it. A Special Forces team landing in the strike area counted fifty-two enemy bodies and captured three wounded soldiers.

Interrogation of the prisoners that afternoon revealed that they were from the *273d* and that many North Vietnamese had joined their unit to attack sometime on or before Ho Chi Minh's birthday, 19 May. One reported seeing "4 DKZs." Although the interrogator apparently did not know that "DKZ" denoted a large Soviet-type rocket launcher, he mentioned "4 DKZs" in the summary report sent to 1st Division headquarters late that evening, 11 May. But the recipient failed to recognize the significance of the acronym, for he stated in the intelligence journal that no further action was necessary.[16]

---

[14] Daily Jnl, G–2, 1st Inf Div, 4 May 67.

[15] Periodic Intel Rpt 20, IIFFV, 23 May 67, an. I.

[16] Ibid.; Daily Jnl, G–2, 1st Inf Div, 11 May 67; Intel Sum 133, 1st Inf Div, 11 May 67, Historians files, CMH. The *273d*'s *2d Battalion* and *23d Medical Company* suffered 20 killed and 70 seriously wounded during the 11 May engagement, and "almost everyone had minor injuries; some vomited blood for the next month." See Rpt, USARV, 5 Feb 70, History of the 273d VC Regiment July 1964–December 1969, p. 12.

A South Vietnamese Air Force A–1H Skyraider destroyed in the 12 May attack

That evening troops of the North Vietnamese artillery unit moved into the rocket site north of the Dong Nai. East of Bien Hoa Air Base, the other attacking force crossed the river after dark. Guerrillas guided the troops between American and South Vietnamese outposts to prepare mortar and recoilless rifle positions within a few thousand meters of the edge of the runway. At 2215 an American outpost reported movement west along a trail and alerted another outpost, which at 2320 reported ambushing a small enemy force and killing three. Newly arrived in South Vietnam as replacements and undergoing training at the 173d Airborne Brigade's jungle school, the troops staging the ambush were inexperienced and took no further action. At daybreak they would find twenty-one unexpended 82-mm. mortar rounds.[17]

Midnight found the area around the giant air base once again quiet. Along the Dong Nai, North Vietnamese crews at the previously surveyed rocket site set up a total of eighteen launchers at three separate positions. To each launcher, they brought three rockets and placed one in the tube, the other two close at hand. Then they waited. One hour past midnight, 12 May, they let loose the first salvo of rockets. They streaked toward their target, followed five minutes later by a second, and after another five minutes by a final salvo. Knowing that air strikes would soon be on the way, the rocket crews quickly took down the launchers and faded away to the north.

East of the base, the assault by mortars and recoilless rifles also went off on schedule. This fire ceased as the last rocket salvo left its launchers. The crews dismantled their guns and fled northeast. Before sunrise they had crossed the Dong Nai.

[17] Periodic Intel Rpt 20, IIFFV, 23 May 67, an. I.

Meanwhile, as Bien Hoa was being hit, planned mortar diversionary attacks struck Phuoc Vinh and Tan Uyen. By first light these attackers also had vanished.[18]

The Americans were caught by surprise. Within the closely timed fifteen-minute attack, fifty-three rockets and over one hundred fifty mortar and recoilless rifle rounds exploded at Bien Hoa. Although many of the mortar rounds failed to detonate, the net result was forty-nine American and South Vietnamese aircraft destroyed or damaged. Clearly, the attackers knew where the aircraft were parked and aimed accordingly. Although only briefly affecting the tempo of air operations, the attack vividly underlined the vulnerability of the American base system in South Vietnam.[19]

Aftermath

Throughout the early morning of the twelfth, artillery and air strikes pounded likely enemy firing positions, but to no avail. By the time ground troops found the sites later in the day, pursuit was useless. Admitting that the enemy had mounted a well-executed attack, U.S. commanders moved immediately to prevent a recurrence, building higher revetments around their aircraft and extending Bien Hoa's defenses deeper into the countryside. Both tasks would take troops and time. The attack had deeper implications, impressing American commanders with the vulnerability of the Saigon area and serving notice that the enemy would not be content to leave his conventional units in Cambodia during the monsoon season.[20]

As for Thanh, who had experienced so many setbacks in the past six months, the success against Bien Hoa Air Base was welcome succor indeed. Though a limited victory, it established a blueprint for the future. Despite the Americans' ravaging of War Zone C, *COSVN*'s future seemed a good deal brighter. The Americans would not enter Cambodia, nor could they be everywhere at once. At the same time Thanh's logistical system appeared healthy. More than 80 percent of his military needs for 1967 had arrived from the port of Sihanoukville, and the remainder had come down the Ho Chi Minh Trail. Most, having reached his border depots before the rainy season, waited deep in underground bunkers, immune from ground and air attacks. When II Field Force deferred an assault on War Zone D until 1968 and virtually abandoned War Zone C, Thanh began moving supplies out of these depots to forward bases, certain that an even greater opportunity lay ahead. In comparison, the strike against Bien Hoa would look paltry indeed.

---

[18] Ibid.

[19] Ibid. American and South Vietnamese aircraft losses were as follows: 3 destroyed, 10 heavily damaged, and 22 lightly damaged. Another 14 South Vietnamese aircraft received unspecified damage.

[20] Ibid.; MFR, 12 May 67, sub: CIIC Meeting, 12 May 1967, Westmoreland History files, CMH.

21

The Ordeal of the Big Red One

With his *7th* and *9th Divisions* largely replenished in Cambodia, General Thanh determined to make the rainy season as unpleasant as possible for the U.S. 1st Division. Thanh's objective differed little from that of his opponent: fight a big unit war of attrition aimed at killing as many soldiers as possible. The question in mid-1967, after two full years of combat, was: who could best absorb the losses?

The 1st Division's area of operations had not shifted during the past year. Headquartered at Di An, just fifteen kilometers northeast of Saigon, the division maintained brigades at Lai Khe and Phuoc Vinh, as well as a forward base at Quan Loi, thirty kilometers south of the Cambodian border.

Nor had the division's mission changed: keep the marauding enemy away from the III Corps population. The Americans had basically accomplished this during the first five months of 1967, but as the southwest monsoon season approached, General Palmer, the II Field Force commander, knew full well that the North Vietnamese would use the rain and mud to cover their offensive plans. Palmer's own wet season agenda called for the 1st Division's 2d Brigade to continue to support pacification around Di An, while the 1st and 3d Brigades to the north provided a shield against a detected enemy buildup in War Zone D. The news of that buildup, as well as a report that the *271st Regiment* of the *9th Division* was about to take the offensive north of Phuoc Vinh, prompted General Hay to launch a strong preemptive assault of his own.[1] (*Map 34*)

Landing Zone X-RAY

The spoiling attack, code-named BILLINGS, soon to encompass eight battalions, began on 12 June as 1st Division troops moved at first ten, then

---

[1] Periodic Intel Rpt 19, IIFFV, 15 May 67, p. 1; ORLL, 1 May–31 Jul 67, 1st Inf Div, 25 Aug 67, p. 9, and AAR, Opn BILLINGS, 1st Inf Div, 26 Jul 67, an. B, both in Historians files, CMH; Interv, author with Hay, 29 Apr 80.

MAP 34

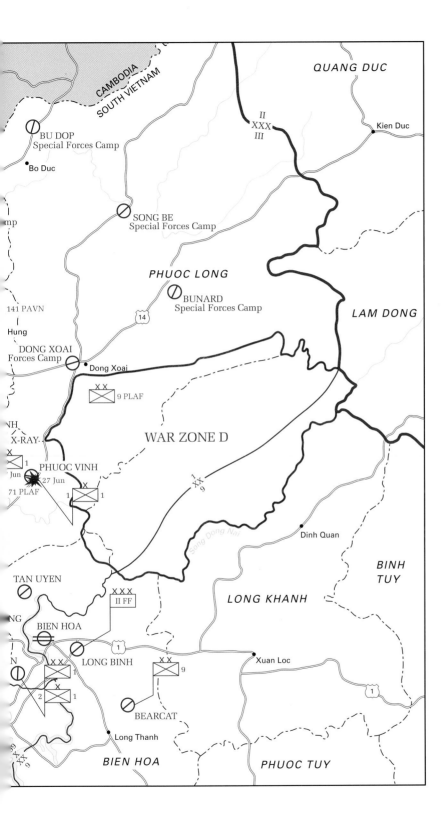

QUANG DUC

CAMBODIA
SOUTH VIETNAM

II
XXX
III

Kien Duc

BU DOP
Special Forces Camp

Bo Duc

mp

SONG BE
Special Forces Camp

PHUOC LONG

LAM DONG

BUNARD
Special Forces Camp

141 PAVN

14

Hung

DONG XOAI
Forces Camp

Dong Xoai

XX
9 PLAF

WAR ZONE D

NH
X-RAY

X   1

Jun   27 Jun

PHUOC VINH

71 PLAF

X
1   1

XX
9

Dinh Quan

BINH
TUY

LONG KHANH

TAN UYEN

XXX
II FF

NG

BIEN HOA

Xuan Loc

1

N

XXX   1

LONG BINH

XX
9

1

X
2   1

BEARCAT

Long Thanh

XXX
9

BIEN HOA

PHUOC TUY

Song Dong Nai

Troops of the 1st Division north of Phuoc Vinh during BILLINGS

thirty, kilometers north of Phuoc Vinh searching for the enemy. The absence of resistance led Hay to conclude that the *271st* had moved even farther north, most likely to a large, bean-shaped clearing designated Landing Zone X-RAY. Hay had a hunch that the Viet Cong would be lying in wait for an airmobile insertion, so he sent Col. Sidney M. Marks' 3d Brigade overland from Landing Zone RUFE.

On the morning of 17 June Lt. Col. Rufus C. Lazzell's 1st Battalion, 16th Infantry, led the way to X-RAY, preceded by a walking artillery barrage. After positioning his men thirty to fifty meters into the tree line around the clearing, Lazzell awaited the arrival of Lt. Col. Jerry S. Edwards' 2d Battalion, 28th Infantry, which was to close RUFE and follow in Lazzell's footsteps.

No sooner had Edwards' first elements reached X-RAY than a patrol reported a group of Viet Cong approaching from the northwest. About 1300 the enemy attacked, punching through the northern and northwestern perimeters. Only prompt artillery and gunship support and the commitment of a reserve platoon prevented the attackers from reaching the central clearing.

Hardly had the Americans beaten back these assaults when the Viet Cong launched a second attack, this time from the southeast. The defenders met the onslaught with determined fire, and at first it looked as though the enemy would falter. "We were stacking them up like cordwood," one platoon leader later said, but it was not enough to turn back the attack. The enemy soon overran the position, and Lazzell lost radio contact with the platoon. The few survivors withdrew into a clearing to join adjacent units, forming a defensive line to halt the assault.[2]

What at first had appeared a chance engagement soon proved to be the well-executed, possibly rehearsed, attack of a force estimated at two battalions. Alerted by the marching artillery fire and further informed by scouts with telephones positioned around the clearing, the Viet Cong commander had ample time to prepare. His men, wearing khaki uniforms and steel helmets and armed with recently acquired Soviet-type AK47s and RPG2s, had been well rested and well trained. When told to move out, they traveled over carefully marked trails under the jungle canopy to their assault positions, attacking the Americans before they had a chance to fortify their perimeter.

The arrival of the first air strikes at 1345 stabilized the situation, and soon after the Viet Cong began to withdraw, covered by a twenty-minute mortar barrage. By the time the division's reaction force, the 1st Battalion, 18th Infantry, under Lt. Col. Richard E. Cavazos, had air-assaulted into a nearby clearing, the battle was already over. Lazzell's battalion had been mauled, with 35 dead and 150 wounded. (*Map 35*)

Marks evacuated Lazzell's casualties and placed Cavazos in overall command. A hasty search of the battle area on the late afternoon of 17 June produced 72 enemy bodies. When the 1st Division asked for a body count later that night, the 3d Brigade reported 135; shortly past midnight the total increased to 196. The next morning sweeps conducted deeper into the jungle resulted in the discovery of an additional 26 bodies.

On succeeding days the Americans found more enemy dead a few kilometers away. In one Viet Cong camp, which a prisoner captured on the seventeenth identified as his assembly area, were 35 dead, apparently killed by artillery fire and air strikes, an indication of the haste with which the enemy had withdrawn.

In an attempt to mete out more punishment, General Hay placed heavy fire, including B–52 strikes, on likely withdrawal routes. Assuming that the *271st Regiment* would head deeper into War Zone D, he also established blocking positions east and northeast of X-RAY, but the insurgents stayed out of the way. When the operation ended on 26 June, the 1st Division claimed to have killed 347 Viet Cong and captured 1 prisoner. Yet, during the two-week effort, the division also reported that it had found only 6 enemy weapons, casting suspicion on the high body count claim. Overall American losses were 57 killed and 196 wounded.[3]

---

[2] Quote from Rpt, Capt George E. Creighton, 17th MHD, 1 Aug 67, Battle of Xom Bo II, 17 Jun 67, VNI 125, CMH.

[3] AAR, Opn BILLINGS, 1st Inf Div, pp. 3–7, tabs B, H, I, K; ORLL, 1 May–31 Jul 67, 1st Inf Div, pp. 1–9, and Incls 3, 5, 18; Interv, author with Hay, 29 Apr 80; Periodic Intel Rpt 24, IIFFV, 17 Jun 67, pp. 1–2, 5, and an. B; Daily Jnl, 1st Bn, 16th Inf, 17 Jun 67, Historians files, CMH.

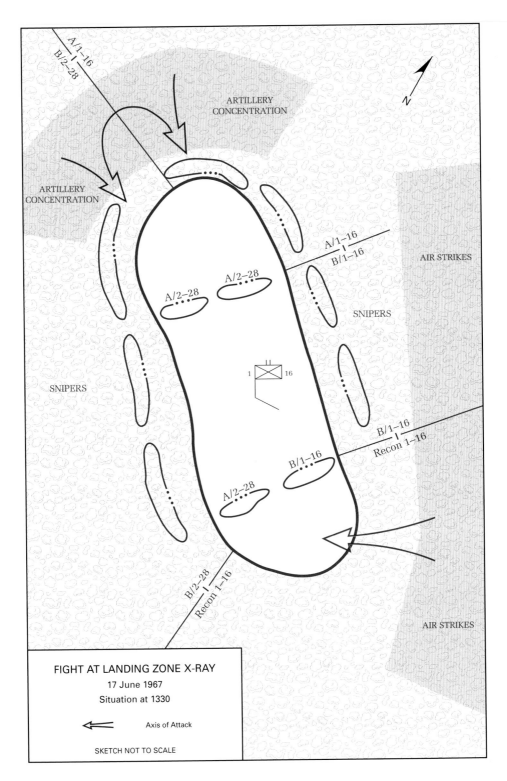

ARTILLERY
CONCENTRATION

A/1–16
B/2–28

ARTILLERY
CONCENTRATION

A/1–16
B/1–16

AIR STRIKES

SNIPERS

A/2–28

A/2–28

SNIPERS

1 [XX] 16

B/1–16
Recon 1–16

B/1–16

A/2–28

B/2–28
Recon 1–16

AIR STRIKES

FIGHT AT LANDING ZONE X-RAY
17 June 1967
Situation at 1330

⟵   Axis of Attack

SKETCH NOT TO SCALE

MAP 35

Xa Tan Hung

To help the *271st* slip away from the Big Red One, General Thanh ordered the *7th Division* to take the offensive. While elements of the division attacked An Loc, the capital of Binh Long Province, and the 1st Division's forward base at Quan Loi, the *141st PAVN Regiment* was to seize the hamlet of Xa Tan Hung, five kilometers southeast of Quan Loi.[4] For some unknown reason, the *141st* left its assembly area after dark on 10 July without the type of thorough reconnaissance typical of enemy operations. It was to pay dearly for this oversight.

Shortly past midnight Americans manning the perimeter at Quan Loi spotted movement to their front and opened fire. The *7th Division* had lost the element of surprise but pressed on. The assault upon An Loc was perfunctory, but that against Quan Loi was quite deliberate. Enemy sappers slipped undetected into the base before the attack, then struck an artillery position on the northern side and tried to cut paths through the perimeter wire to allow their comrades to reinforce them. After two hours of confused fighting, the Americans ejected the sappers.

When the diversionary attack on Quan Loi began, the *141st Regiment* was still several kilometers from Xa Tan Hung. Illuminating shells fired from Quan Loi revealed that the regiment's lead unit, the *2d Battalion*, was on the move through rubber trees a few kilometers northeast of Xa Tan Hung. Informed of a possible attack, the defenders of the hamlet, a company from the South Vietnamese 9th Regiment, 5th Division, went on full alert.

Earlier that night the *2d Battalion* commander had lost contact with the other battalion slated to participate in the assault. Realizing that his unit had been discovered and would likely come under artillery fire, he decided to push on without waiting. An initial mortar barrage missed the South Vietnamese Army compound and landed instead on a nearby settlement, wounding fifty civilians. The assault began just as the diversionary attack upon Quan Loi ended. Although hard pressed, the South Vietnamese regulars held fast with help from American artillery and gunships. Not until three hours later did the other North Vietnamese battalion arrive, committed piecemeal with disastrous results. At dawn the North Vietnamese fled in disorder, leaving behind 144 dead and 67 weapons, 20 of them crew served. In addition, the South Vietnamese captured 10 North Vietnamese, including 2 officers. But the defenders paid for the rout of the enemy battalions with 15 killed and 46 wounded.[5]

The success at Xa Tan Hung enhanced the image of the South Vietnamese Army in Binh Long Province. So did reports of atrocities commit-

[4] Periodic Intel Rpts 27, IIFFV, 11 Jul 67, an. B; 28, IIFFV, 18 Jul 67, pp. 1–2, 5–6; 32, IIFFV, 15 Aug 67, an. G; 49, IIFFV, 9 Dec 67, an. F. All in Historians files, CMH. Rpt, USARV, 5 Feb 70, History of the 273d VC Regiment July 1964–December 1969.

[5] ORLL, 1 May–31 Jul 67, 1st Inf Div, Incl 20. RD Rpt, Binh Long Province, Jul 67, n.d., pp. 2–6; Daily Jnls, G–2, 1st Inf Div, 11 Jul 67, 12 Jul 67, 13 Jul 67, and 14 Jul 67. Last five in Historians files, CMH. Periodic Intel Rpt 28, IIFFV, 18 Jul 67, pp. 1–6.

Soldiers of the 1st Division search the sky for a medical evacuation helicopter.

ted by North Vietnamese stragglers in nearby hamlets. Many civilians who had secretly sided with the Viet Cong or had remained noncommittal were now openly hostile to the "foreigners from the North." Yet neither they nor their defenders could do much to eliminate these cross-border excursions by enemy regulars.

Similar attacks continued throughout the summer. Shortly past midnight on 27 June a North Vietnamese artillery battalion fired eighty 122-mm. rockets and over sixty mortar rounds against the 1st Division base at Phuoc Vinh, causing heavy damage and 84 casualties. Two days later the enemy launched artillery raids against 1st Division installations at Phu Loi and Lai Khe. These attacks caused another 59 casualties and considerable damage to aircraft, buildings, and equipment.[6]

An investigation of the effectiveness of counterbattery radar at Phu Loi revealed that readings of the enemy launch sites were off by several kilometers. Of 2,744 American artillery rounds fired during the attack, only one exploded near a launch point. There, a single enemy body was found, and a wounded enemy soldier was captured nearby.

Sporadic attacks continued, culminating in an attempt to overrun the Tong Le Chon Special Forces camp. Shortly after midnight on 7 August the *7th Division's 165th Regiment* struck the camp, which sat on a strategic hill deep in Communist-held territory ten kilometers south of the Fishhook. Gunships guided by illuminating shells stopped the first wave of sappers, but a second assault penetrated the southern perimeter. Many of the defenders in that sector surrendered, only to be executed by their captors. A similar fate might have befallen the others had the camp's ammunition bunker not detonated. The explosion caused heavy casualties on both sides and forced most of the enemy to flee. Although the North Vietnamese assaulted the camp twice more

---

[6] CICV Study, ST 67–080, 1 Sep 67, sub: NVA Rocket Artillery Units, pp. 5, 8, and an. A; Periodic Intel Rpts 28, IIFFV, 18 Jul 67, p. 2; 29, IIFFV, 25 Jul 67, p. 2; and 30, IIFFV, 1 Aug 67, pp. 1–2, 5–6; ORLL, 1 May–31 Jul 67, 1st Inf Div, Incls 3, 4; Intervs, author with Hay, 29 Apr 80; with Col Paul B. Malone, Comdr, 1st Avn Bn, 1st Inf Div, 27 Feb 80, Historians files, CMH.

that night, they had lost their momentum, and the defenders held. In the end the garrison lost 26 men killed and 87 wounded. A search of the area around the camp turned up 152 enemy dead and 60 weapons.[7]

September Uncertainty

The variety of enemy initiatives perplexed the U.S. command, which could see no discernable pattern in *COSVN*'s actions. Agents of varying reliability spoke of an enemy buildup of division size around Dong Xoai, a Special Forces camp thirty kilometers northeast of the 1st Brigade's base at Phuoc Vinh, but no one could be sure whether this was real or another false alarm. At the time II Field Force intelligence placed the headquarters of the *9th Division* and the *271st* and *273d Regiments* near Dong Xoai, possibly to prepare for another strike on Bien Hoa Air Base, and the *272d* north of Dong Xoai to threaten Quan Loi and An Loc. But all this was no more than conjecture.[8]

Until Hay knew the enemy's intentions, he put a stop to large unit operations, which had thus far proved unproductive. The 1st Brigade returned to Phuoc Vinh to operate locally and to prepare to reinforce Dong Xoai in case of an attack. The 2d Brigade continued to support pacification in southern Binh Duong, while the 3d Brigade worked out of a series of firebases north of Lai Khe along Highway 13 to protect engineers clearing jungle astride the road.

On 1 September the U.S. 9th Division assumed responsibility for STRIKE, the operational area north and west of Bien Hoa Air Base, allowing Hay to devote his full attention to the region north of Saigon. To improve coordination in that area, he permanently relocated his headquarters from Di An to Lai Khe. During September he placed massive fires on reported enemy troop concentrations, but refrained from sending his troops out to "beat the bush."[9]

Behind Hay's caution was a familiar personnel problem. In the course of the summer, he had lost his three brigade commanders and all but one of his nine infantry battalion commanders either to tour rotations or to MACV's policy of limiting field grade officers to six months of command duty. Since few of the new battalion commanders had prior battle experience, Hay personally monitored their performance in a series of local operations. After an air assault, for example, he would meet with them to critique the action in detail. If their performance seemed marginal, Hay

[7] Rpt, Detachment B–33, 5th SF Gp, 1st SF, 14 Aug 67, 165th NVA Regiment Attack on Tong Le Chon, 7 Aug 67, VNIT 225, CMH; Periodic Intel Rpt 32, IIFFV, 15 Aug 67, pp. 1, 5, and an. B.

[8] Periodic Intel Rpts 33, IIFFV, 21 Aug 67, p. 12, Historians files, CMH; 34, IIFFV, 28 Aug 67, pp. 1–2; and 35, IIFFV, 4 Sep 67, pp. 1–2, and an. B.

[9] ORLL, 1 Aug–31 Oct 67, 1st Inf Div, n.d., pp. 7–9, Incls 3, 4, 5, Historians files, CMH; Interv, author with Hay, 29 Apr 80.

arranged for another test. If there was no marked improvement, he arranged for replacements.[10]

The division also instituted a program to indoctrinate incoming junior officers and noncommissioned officers in small unit tactics. By the end of October some nine hundred junior leaders had received training from roving teams of combat-experienced professionals. Still, everyone knew that there was no substitute for practical experience in the field.

The division also revamped its seven infantry battalions, adding a fourth rifle company to each. Like all American divisions, the 1st Division's rifle battalions had deployed to Vietnam with the standard three-company establishment. Such an organization well suited the needs of linear warfare, in which a battalion typically deployed two companies on the battle line and kept the third in reserve. The conventional three-company structure, however, had proved inadequate for the demands of Vietnam, where widely dispersed battalions had to search and control large areas, block and surround elusive enemy units, and maintain their own base security. A four-company establishment significantly increased the reach, resiliency, and combat power of American rifle battalions by allowing battalion commanders to employ three maneuver elements in active operations while holding the fourth for reserve, reaction, and base defense.

Westmoreland had expressed interest in the four-company structure as early as 1965, but the matter quickly became embroiled in manpower issues back in Washington.[11] To provide the five thousand soldiers needed to man the extra companies, Secretary McNamara would have to exceed the administration's self-imposed troop ceiling in Vietnam, and this he was loath to do. Accordingly, many division commanders took the initiative in 1966 to form ad hoc fourth companies for their rifle battalions by pulling together soldiers from organic elements like reconnaissance, anti-tank, and mortar platoons; ground surveillance sections; and headquarters elements. However, it was not until mid-1967—two years after Westmoreland had first made his request—that Washington formally authorized the four-company structure and began sending each rifle battalion in Vietnam a full company trained in the United States.

Like other commanders in theater, Hay chose to break up the newly arrived units, known as D Company Packets. He assigned most of their members to Companies A, B, and C of each battalion and infused combat-experienced men from those companies into the new ones. The shuffling produced four companies of relatively equal size and combat experience. The new Company Ds then received intensified training, culminating in a 48-hour combat reaction test administered by the division.[12] The new companies proved a welcome, if belated, addition to the combat comman-

---

[10] ORLL, 1 Aug–31 Oct 67, 1st Inf Div, pp. 12–14, and Incl 1; Interv, author with Hay, 29 Apr 80.

[11] Rpt, Army Study Group, Jul 65, Organization and Equipment of U.S. Army Units, box 6, 68A/3306, RG 319, NARA.

[12] ORLL, 1 Aug–31 Oct 67, 1st Inf Div, pp. 12–13; Interv, author with Hay, 29 Apr 80.

der's arsenal. That it had taken two years to obtain them did not bode well in a war in which time was fast becoming an enemy.

The Long Nguyen Secret Zone

The Communists did not trouble themselves with artificial troop ceilings but made every effort to mobilize the human resources under their control. Given the high casualties they usually suffered at the hands of the Americans, however, they were forced to suspend operations periodically and regroup at one of their clandestine base areas or cross-border sanctuaries. September and October were the traditional months in which the *9th Division* prepared itself for the next winter-spring offensive, and 1967 was no exception. While the bulk of the division moved into northern Binh Long Province, the division sent its badly damaged *271st Regiment* to Base Area 255, the Long Nguyen Secret Zone, between Highway 13 and the Michelin Rubber Plantation. Located along the Binh Duong–Binh Long provincial boundary near the Saigon River corridor, the zone's nearly road-less jungles and marshes made for a perfect staging area. There, the regiment was to receive replacements and food. Allied search and destroy and food control measures had created a significant food shortage for the Communists in War Zone D, and by early September the men of the *271st* received only enough rice each day to make soup. After recuperating for a few weeks in the Long Nguyen, the regiment was to rejoin the *9th Division* in northern Binh Long for a multiregiment attack against Loc Ninh.[13]

Hay was determined to disrupt the enemy's rest period, and on 29 September he sent the 1st Brigade, commanded by his former division support commander, Col. George E. Newman, into the northern portion of the Long Nguyen. The following day he launched the 3d Brigade, under Col. Frank E. Blazey, toward the southern half. To provide artillery support for the two forces, Hay established a series of firebases along Highway 13, the eastern edge of the redoubt, between Chon Thanh, the headquarters of the South Vietnamese 5th Division's 9th Regiment, and Ben Cat, a village forty kilometers to the south. Resupply of the 1st Brigade units was to be mainly by helicopter, while logistical support of the 3d Brigade was to be almost entirely over Route 240. This road extended northwest from Ben Cat, and the 3d Brigade was to use it to attack into the heart of the Long Nguyen. Initially, both brigades would employ two battalions: in the north, the 1st Brigade would have the 1st Battalion, 2d Infantry, and the 1st Battalion, 28th Infantry; in the south, the 3d Brigade would have the 2d Battalion, 2d Infantry (Mechanized), and the 2d Battalion, 28th Infantry. Whereas 1st Division operations there

[13] AAR, Opn SHENANDOAH II, 1st Inf Div, 12 Apr 68, an. G; RD Rpt, Long Khanh Province, Oct 67, 31 Oct 67, both in Historians files, CMH; Periodic Intel Rpts 28, IIFFV, 18 Jul 67, an. F, and 39, IIFFV, 1 Oct 67, an. G; Daily Jnl, G–2, 1st Inf Div, 14 Oct 67, Historians files, CMH.

had been brief in the past, Hay planned to remain indefinitely, or at least until the brigades could make a thorough search.[14]

During the early stages of the operation, SHENANDOAH II, the Americans found few enemy. The first important contact took place on 2 October, not in the Long Nguyen but east of Highway 13 near Chon Thanh, when a South Vietnamese unit came upon a large enemy force and took heavy casualties. Documents found on the body of an enemy soldier seemed to indicate that the allies had found the *271st*. But the South Vietnamese later learned that the bulk of the force they had fought had most likely been from a battalion of the *272d*, sent south to attack Chon Thanh and divert attention away from the movement of the *271st* across the highway into the Long Nguyen.[15]

Two days later the 1st Battalion, 2d Infantry, commanded by Lt. Col. Richard R. Stauffer, came upon an enemy company nine kilometers southwest of Chon Thanh and killed twelve Viet Cong. At the time the 1st Brigade's other unit, the 1st of the 28th Infantry, under Lt. Col. James F. Cochran, was operating four kilometers north of the battle area. There were no American forces to the west, the apparent direction in which the enemy withdrew.

To pursue, Colonel Newman was given the 1st Battalion, 18th Infantry, still under the experienced leadership of Colonel Cavazos and constituting the division's reaction force at Phuoc Vinh. Newman directed Cavazos to conduct an air assault into a clearing two kilometers west of Stauffer. The battalion landed unopposed. Later it came upon partially destroyed enemy camps near the landing area and found thirty enemy dead, apparently killed by artillery fire and air strikes.[16]

After landing, Cavazos' men immediately began constructing the 1st Division's standard battalion field position, a circular base composed of mutually supporting timbered bunkers with overhead cover around a perimeter enclosed by wire entanglements. Two days later, on 6 October, five enemy mortar rounds struck the base. Although the shells caused little damage, Cavazos guessed that the enemy was attempting to register his mortars for an attack that night.

At 1800 rain began falling. Within an hour an ambush patrol spotted several Viet Cong north of the base and opened fire before pulling back. Shortly after dark the insurgents launched a mortar attack against the American position, hurling seventy-five rounds in twenty minutes. After artillery and mortar fire silenced the Viet Cong pieces, the south side of the perimeter began receiving heavy automatic weapons fire. Then, at

[14] AAR, Opn SHENANDOAH II, 1st Inf Div, p. 5, ans. C, H; Interv, author with Hay, 29 Apr 80.

[15] Periodic Intel Rpts 40, IIFFV, 7 Oct 67, pp. 7–8, and 41, IIFFV, 15 Oct 67, p. 1, both in Historians files, CMH.

[16] AAR, Opn SHENANDOAH II, 1st Bn, 18th Inf, 30 Nov 67, pp. 4–5, Historians files, CMH; AAR, Opn SHENANDOAH II, 1st Inf Div, pp. 6–7; Daily Jnl, G–2, 1st Inf Div, 4 Oct 67, Historians files, CMH.

Gunners of the 1st Division in action

2114, the enemy renewed the attack. Shooting from the wood line, the Communists would fire for five to seven minutes, then pause for a similar amount of time, apparently to entice the Americans to expend their ammunition and reveal their precise positions.

Because the rain made aerial resupply for both the battalion and the supporting artillery impossible, Cavazos' men relied on their rifles. They fired sparingly, zeroing in on the staccato flashes of automatic weapons firing from behind cover. They used artillery and mortars only against known enemy positions. Fire discipline would be a critical factor in determining the outcome of the fight.

At 2317 the Viet Cong launched a final, violent attack, striking the southern portion of the perimeter with mortar and automatic weapons fire followed by a ground assault. Although some reached the wire entanglements, none broke through. The attackers soon withdrew, leaving behind 24 dead. A member of the attacking force, the *2d Battalion, 271st Regiment*, captured three weeks later, reported that the action had cost his battalion 59 killed and 56 wounded. American losses were 5 killed and 4 wounded.[17]

[17] AAR, Opn SHENANDOAH II, 1st Inf Div, p. 9, and ans. B, L; Daily Jnls, G–2, 1st Inf Div, 6 Oct 67, and 27 Oct 67, both in Historians files, CMH; AAR, Opn SHENANDOAH II, 1st Bn, 18th Inf, p. 5; Rpt, Maj William E. Daniel, 17th MHD, n.d., Combat After Action Interview Report: Sp5 Stephen C. Williams with Lt Col Richard E. Cavazos, Comdr, 1st Bn, 18th Inf, 1st Inf Div, VNI 132, CMH.

On 8 October General Hay pulled Stauffer's battalion back to Phuoc Vinh to become the division's reaction force and replaced it with the 2d Battalion, 28th Infantry, now under the command of Lt. Col. Terry D. Allen. Newman immediately inserted Allen's battalion into a clearing three kilometers northwest of Cavazos. Two days later Cochran's 1st Battalion, 28th Infantry, replaced Stauffer's rested unit at Phuoc Vinh, allowing Newman to put Stauffer's battalion into position to block enemy forces thought to be moving west toward the Michelin Plantation. Although Stauffer's troops made no contact with the enemy, they found documents showing that the *1st Battalion, 271st Regiment,* had recently evacuated the area. In the meantime, Cavazos' men, while patrolling north of their base, found hastily vacated camps and had several brief firefights with small enemy units.

The 1st Brigade now had three battalions in the eastern and northern sections of the Long Nguyen Secret Zone. Operating roughly east to west were Allen's 2d Battalion, 28th Infantry, Stauffer's 1st Battalion, 2d Infantry, and Cavazos' 1st Battalion, 18th Infantry.

On the morning of 11 October Cavazos accompanied two of his companies on a northward probe. Moving about sixteen hundred meters from the base camp, they broke down into cloverleaf patrols along the flanks.

Suddenly, the point man spotted movement to his front and opened fire. As the fighting escalated, Cavazos ordered the lead company to fall back under cover of an artillery barrage into a perimeter formed by the second company. As the lead company fell back, the Viet Cong edged around the flank, trying to cut it off from safety.

Above the battlefield, a supporting Huey gunship spotted the enemy force massing for an assault and opened fire with rockets. Goaded by the streaking missiles, enemy troops rushed the beleaguered company in a human-wave attack. They were cut down before they reached the defenders. Within twenty minutes the enemy was in full retreat, pursued for the next two hours by artillery fire and fighter-bombers.

After making a hasty search of the battle area and finding 21 enemy dead, Cavazos decided to continue moving north. About four hundred meters into the march, the lead platoon in the column heard movement and began a reconnaissance by fire, triggering a second firefight. Rather than forming a perimeter and risking a fight that might continue after dark, Cavazos reversed the column and returned to his battalion base, at that time protected by a single company. As the column neared the base, a squad remained in the bush to set an ambush, into which 5 pursuing Viet Cong stumbled. The squad killed 4 before falling back to the battalion's perimeter. American casualties for the day were 1 killed and 4 wounded.[18] Thereafter, encounters with the enemy became less frequent, and on the thirteenth General Hay returned Cavazos' battalion to Phuoc Vinh for rest and refitting.

---

[18] AAR, Opn SHENANDOAH II, 1st Bn, 18th Inf, p. 6; Rpt, Daniel, 17th MHD, n.d., Combat After Action Interview Report: Sp5 Stephen C. Williams with Lt Col Richard E. Cavazos, VNI 132; Daily Jnl, G–2, 1st Inf Div, 11 Oct 67, Historians files, CMH.

On the morning of 17 October Hay left to attend a MACV conference in Saigon. At the time he noted that his forces had accounted for about one hundred fifty enemy dead in the Long Nguyen, had found and destroyed many base camps, and had captured over sixty tons of rice. Although some Viet Cong obviously remained in the base area, many signs suggested that the *271st* had suffered a major defeat and was in the process of attempting to leave the Long Nguyen. Assuming the enemy would move west into the Michelin Plantation, blocking forces of the 25th Division had already deployed there to prevent his escape.

Ong Thanh

General Hay appeared ready to end his campaign in the Long Nguyen, but increased enemy activity in the area of the Ong Thanh Stream caused him to reconsider. The stream flowed near the Binh Duong–Binh Long provincial boundary, where the 1st Brigade had made all its major contacts. The enemy's continued presence there suggested that the Viet Cong were determined to defend their jungle bases.[19]

On the morning of 16 October Colonel Allen had moved out from his temporary base along the Ong Thanh with two companies to patrol to the southeast. After traveling two kilometers, the point of his column spotted a fortified enemy camp. Allen pulled his men back and placed air strikes on the area in accordance with 1st Division policy.

After the bombing runs, the Americans entered the camp. Suddenly, an enemy mine exploded, and sniper fire erupted from the surrounding trees. Several soldiers went down in the hail of bullets. Allen ordered a quick withdrawal and formed a two-company perimeter around his casualties. Meanwhile, several batteries of artillery rained shells into the camp from firebases along Highway 13, and within an hour enemy fire had ceased. Allen's men returned to the area and counted seventeen enemy dead.

While probing the western edge of the camp, the Americans saw and fired on two Viet Cong. That set off a second firefight against an estimated sixty enemy soldiers hiding in the jungle. Again, Allen formed a perimeter and called in air strikes, but late that afternoon, to avoid committing to a fight that might continue into the night, he broke contact and returned to his base. Allen's mission for 17 October was to reenter the area of the previous day's encounter to determine if the enemy was still there.[20]

At the time Colonel Newman, who had commanded the brigade for only a month, believed that battalion commanders should accompany their men in the jungle. Allen, also in command of his unit for a month,

[19] The following account is based on Rpt, Daniel and Capt John A. Cash, n.d., Combat After Action Interview Report: The Battle of Ong Thanh, 17 Oct 67, VNIs 133, 134, CMH.

[20] Daily Jnl, 2d Bn, 28th Inf, 16 Oct 67, Historians files, CMH; DF, Daniel to G–3, 1st Inf Div, DAUNTLESS ENCOUNTER, VNI 133, CMH; Interv, author with Hay, 29 Apr 80; Intel Sum 289, 1st Inf Div, 16 Oct 67, and Incl 1, Historians files, CMH.

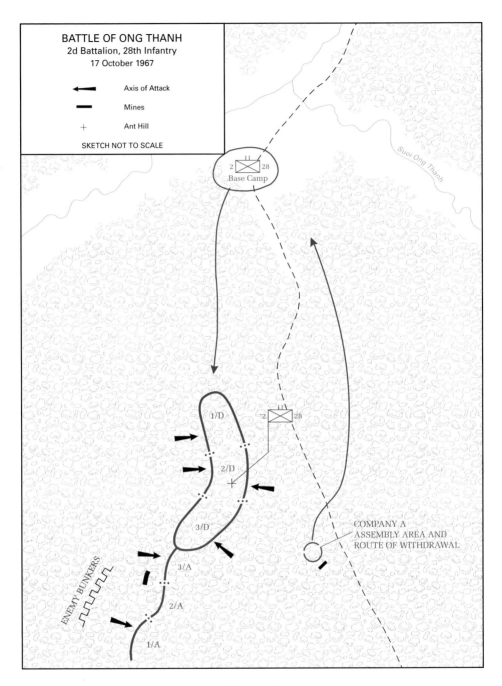

2 ⊠ 28
Base Camp

1/D

2 ⊠ 28

2/D
+

3/D

3/A

2/A

1/A

ENEMY BUNKERS

COMPANY A
ASSEMBLY AREA AND
ROUTE OF WITHDRAWAL

Suoi Ong Thanh

MAP 36

preferred supervising the action from a helicopter. Although that practice was normal in the 3d Brigade, as long as Allen was serving under 1st Brigade control he followed Newman's policy. (*Map 36*)

At 0800 on 17 October, a bright, sunny morning, Allen's unit struck out, with Company A in the lead followed by Company D. He intended to move directly south for 1,500 meters and then to head east to reenter the enemy camp from a slightly different direction. The column would then continue farther east to assess the damage in an area that B–52s had hit on the fourteenth. Allen and a command group of six went with Company D.

Both companies were far below their normal combat field strength of 100 to 120 men, and some of their leaders had left for training or other temporary duty. Each company had left behind its mortar sections, a division policy, to help guard the battalion base along with Company B and the men from the battalion headquarters company. Allen's fourth rifle company was under the direct control of the 1st Brigade, protecting another supporting firebase, CAISSON V. Because of the reduced strength—Company A had only sixty-five men and Company D seventy-three—each unit had reorganized two of its three rifle platoons into two-squad platoons. Allen could count on artillery support from four batteries of 105-mm. howitzers and one battery of 155-mm. howitzers located at CAISSON V and two other firebases, CAISSON III–S and LORRAINE III. The men of both companies carried extra ammunition.

Preceded by marching artillery fire, Allen's men entered the jungle with flank security extending twenty to thirty-five meters. During the first forty-five minutes, they traveled no more than five hundred meters, periodically halting to conduct cloverleaf patrols to the front, rear, and flanks. At 0956, after continuing in the same manner for another five hundred meters, the point squad of the column from the 1st Platoon, Company A, came upon a well-traveled northeast-southwest trail that had been used within the hour. The acting platoon leader, sensing that another enemy camp was close by, obtained permission to make cloverleaf patrols east and west of the trail. The rest of the column halted, placed flank security out at a greater distance, and awaited the findings of the patrols.

At that time most of Allen's men were in moderate jungle that did not form a complete canopy. The vegetation did not obstruct movement by foot, but it obscured ground visibility beyond fifteen to twenty meters. At a greater distance to the flanks and to the south, where the lead unit of Company A was moving, the jungle was more dense, with some trees as high as forty meters.

Almost immediately, the men of the 1st Platoon, scouting west of the trail, sighted a Viet Cong soldier. Moments later a group of enemy troops appeared on the trail just ahead. The commander of Company A, Capt. James E. George, told the patrol to form a hasty ambush, but by the time his men were in position the enemy had disappeared and all was quiet.

As they lay silent on the jungle floor, the 1st Platoon leader heard movement in the trees, the clicking of rifle bolts, and the rattle of metal.

George told him to reinforce the ambush patrol at once. Moving out, the rest of the men of the platoon immediately ran into sniper fire. They pressed on until a machine-gun burst from a well-camouflaged bunker killed one man and wounded two others. Then heavy fire poured into both flanks and the platoon was pinned down.

The next platoon in the column, the 2d, tried to reinforce but was brought up short by the same hidden machine-gun nest. As the bullets flew, the radio went dead and the company commander could no longer communicate with either platoon.

Captain George had few options. His trail unit, the 3d Platoon, had only eleven men, and since he needed to maintain a link with Company D, George decided to move his own command group forward to join his beleaguered platoons. Maneuvering to a position some fifteen meters in front of the enemy bunker, he tossed in a flurry of grenades and temporarily silenced the troublesome machine gun.

But the enemy was still in the fight. Perhaps an alert Viet Cong soldier spotted the antennas on the radios carried by members of George's command group and realized the importance of what he had found. Whatever the case, one soldier dashed forward with a claymore-type mine and set off the explosive before the Americans could cut him down. The blast killed a radio operator and wounded Captain George and most of the rest of the command group.

As Company A battled on, Company D began drawing sniper fire from trees west of its position. The shooters wounded two men before return fire silenced them. Colonel Allen directed his command group to remain in place beside a prominent ant hill and told the Company D commander, 1st Lt. Albert C. Welch, to form a two-platoon perimeter around the command group. Welch's leading platoon, the 3d, was to stay in contact with Company A's rear. Since he needed to call in artillery and air strikes, Allen radioed George to break contact and withdraw into Company D's perimeter, the same kind of maneuver the battalion had conducted successfully the day before.

Captain George, blind and deaf from the explosion of the claymore, gave the order to pull back. But all three of his platoons were under heavy fire, and all three platoon leaders were wounded. With his officers out of action, George radioed Allen that he was placing his senior noncommissioned officer, M. Sgt. Jose B. Valdez, in command of the company.

Company A's plight was serious. The fight had unfolded so quickly, and it was so difficult to see through the underbrush, that few survivors would remember seeing the enemy. Despite heavy return fire by the Americans, enemy fire continued undiminished. And with most of the company's officers wounded early in the action, communication within the unit broke down almost immediately.

As the firefight degenerated into a general melee, withdrawing to safety became a matter of individual initiative. Pfc. James C. Jones, the artillery forward observer's radio operator, found himself with two jobs—calling in artillery and fighting off the enemy closing in around him. After emptying his .45-caliber pistol at his attackers, he snatched up a wounded soldier's M16 and kept firing. As the bullets flew, Jones stayed on the radio, walking in the artillery fire so close that shell fragments spattered all around him. When the enemy fire lessened, Jones, believing himself to be the sole survivor in the area, crawled to the rear, eventually rejoining Company A's command group.

Meanwhile, many of the men from Company A's 2d and 3d Platoons were able to join Company D. Some reached the perimeter around Colonel Allen and his command group, while others joined a second perimeter that Company D's 3d Platoon had set up some fifty meters away. Having no contact with Company A's platoons, Sergeant Valdez and Company A's surviving command group formed their own perimeter a hundred meters or more east of where the fight had started. In an effort to assemble all survivors, Valdez repeatedly fired shots into the air, shouting, "Come to the shot in the air! Come to us! Be calm!" Individuals and small groups gradually filtered into Valdez's position, most of them from the 1st Platoon.[21]

The use—or possibly misuse—of air strikes influenced how the battle would play out. Earlier that morning F–100s and B–57 Canberras had flown preplanned air strikes against known and suspected enemy base camps within the 1st Brigade's sector, but none were in direct support of Allen's advance. The last was completed at 1012, only minutes before Company A ran into the enemy and Colonel Newman, flying overhead at 1020, called for close air support for Allen's battalion. Even so, apparently no planes were immediately available to answer Newman's request. Thirty minutes would pass before A–37 Dragonflies on strip alert at Bien Hoa Air Base, nearly sixty kilometers from the fight, could arrive. Another ten minutes would elapse before a forward air controller could brief the pilots on the target. By then, about 1100, only sporadic fire threatened Allen's men.

Believing that the Viet Cong were withdrawing south, Newman directed the air strikes to two hundred meters south of the southernmost point where he had seen smoke, which Company A had used to mark its position. Before the first of what would eventually total sixteen strikes went in, Newman agreed to halt the supporting artillery fire coming from CAISSON III–S and CAISSON V; during the partial check-fire only the two artillery batteries at LORRAINE III continued to fire, striking an area west of Company A's initial contact. According to Colonel Allen's operations officer, Maj. John F. Sloan, the check-fire was against Allen's wishes, but he deferred to the judgment of his brigade commander.

The target that Colonel Newman had indicated was in dense jungle, and the forward air controller who was to vector in the fighter-bombers

---

[21] Interv, Daniel with Capt James D. George, Comdr, Co A, 2d Bn, 28th Inf, 1st Inf Div, 20 Oct 67, with comments by 1st Lt Paul R. Kay, Arty Fwd Observer, Co A, p. 3, VNI 134, CMH. Lieutenant Kay is the source of the Valdez quote.

A–37 Dragonflies head for a target.

had no direct communication with the troops on the ground. For these reasons, the air controller had the attacking aircraft make several passes over the designated target to ensure that the pilots knew exactly where to deliver their bombs. After obtaining final clearances, the first of two aircraft attacked at 1110. The second began its run ten minutes later, at which time Allen informed Newman that all enemy fire had ceased.

The duration of the check-fire was difficult to reconstruct. Conflicting reports ranged from fifteen to forty-five minutes. Whatever its length, the enemy, far from withdrawing, used the respite to redeploy into a horseshoe with troops west, south, and east of Company D.

Starting at 1135 enemy fire against Company D began to intensify. Lieutenant Welch had chosen his position around a prominent ant hill, and the small landmark may have made it easier for the Viet Cong to pinpoint his location. Because the men could make out few targets in the underbrush, Welch told them to hold their fire until they either had the enemy in their sights or could pick out muzzle flashes. As the enemy fire grew in volume, the men could make out the distinctive sound of an American-made M60 machine gun firing at them from the south.

When Sergeant Valdez had assumed command of Company A, Colonel Allen had instructed him to move on an azimuth of 360 degrees (due north) to join him. When Allen heard the machine-gun fire, he assumed that it indicated Company A's approach and that Valdez's men were mistakenly firing into Company D. He yelled for Company A to cease fire, but the word also passed down the line of Company D. With American fire slacking, the volume of enemy fire grew, forcing Allen's troops to hug the ground and making it impossible for them to challenge enemy fire superiority.

Colonel Newman later recalled that as soon as the new enemy attack began at 1135, Allen contacted him by radio, saying, "Sir, I can use my artillery now." Newman halted all further air strikes and ordered the artillery to resume firing. Newman later noted that the switch took about two minutes, but explained that "it was never made known to me that he, Allen, was experiencing difficulty with artillery fire support."[22]

Meanwhile, Sergeant Valdez and the twenty-four men with him, many of them wounded, stumbled through the jungle, dodging not only enemy fire, but also friendly artillery rounds. Although they had hoped to link up with Company D, they never found it and eventually arrived instead at the battalion base.

Within Company D's perimeter, the situation was also deteriorating. Allen himself had been wounded, and enemy snipers in trees and machine gunners firing low grazing fire six to twelve inches off the ground were pounding the trapped Company D from three sides. Any American who tried to move instantly became a target. Many of the company's leaders were now casualties, including the company commander, Lieutenant Welch.

Shortly before noon Allen ordered the wounded Welch to pull the unit back to the battalion base and Company B to come forward to cover the withdrawal. Refusing assistance from those men about to leave, the battalion commander elected to remain with those wounded who were immobile.

The withdrawal proved costly. As the troops began to move back, enemy fire cut down several of them, and the movement north quickly turned into a disorganized scramble. A platoon sergeant moving to the rear was the last to see Allen alive. With the help of the sergeant, Allen had begun removing a radio from the back of a dead operator to call in more artillery fire. Moments later a short burst of machine-gun fire grazed Allen's helmet, knocking him down. Allen told the sergeant to forget the artillery and get his people "the hell out of there."[23] Shortly after leaving, the sergeant looked back and saw either an RPG round or a claymore mine explode near Allen, followed quickly by a burst of machine-gun fire, which killed him.

As the withdrawal proceeded, the brigade commander, Colonel Newman, headed for the battalion base to assume command of the unit. An assistant division commander, Brig. Gen. William S. Coleman, in his helicopter above the battlefield, took control of the brigade. Soldiers arriving at the base said that many of the wounded had been left behind, so the

[22] Interv, Cash with Col George E. Newman, Comdr, 1st Bde, 1st Inf Div, 22 Oct 67, VNI 134, CMH.

[23] Statement by Sfc George A. Smith, Platoon Sgt, 3d Platoon, Co D, 2d Bn, 28th Inf, 1st Inf Div, VNI 134, CMH.

brigade operations officer, Maj. Donald W. Holleder, who had landed with Newman, organized a small group of men to attempt to reach Company D's old position. Holleder himself took the lead and soon outdistanced the other men by fifty meters. Suddenly, an enemy sniper in a tree fired and Holleder fell mortally wounded.

Meanwhile, Colonel Newman obtained helicopters to evacuate the casualties and to bring Allen's Company C from CAISSON V. Newman planned to lead Company C and the battalion's reconnaissance platoon to Company D's former position while Company B kept a corridor open to the base. Expecting to find many wounded, he instructed the battalion surgeon and medical aid men, augmented from division by another physician and other aid men, to accompany him. Unsure as to where the wounded were, he intended to advance without artillery support for fear of hitting them.

While Newman gathered the relief force, a wounded grenadier from Company A, Pfc. Joseph J. Costello, managed to locate a radio near Allen's last position and about 1330 sent a message over the battalion command net: "This is Costello, please help, we need help."[24] Overhead, General Coleman heard his call and told him to mark his position with a smoke grenade.

Seeing the smoke rise from the trees, Coleman told Costello that help would soon arrive. Instructing those stations on the battalion command net to switch to an alternate frequency so he and Colonel Newman could remain in continuous contact with Costello, Coleman planned to vector Newman's relief to Costello's position. Meanwhile, he encouraged Costello to set up a perimeter defense with the surviving troops and gave him advice for treating the wounded. When the enemy fire around Costello's position finally ended at 1430, a helicopter dropped bags of smoke grenades and medical supplies.

By that time Newman's relief force, with the reconnaissance platoon in the lead, was on the move with volunteers from Companies A and D to assist in the search for their comrades. The relief force arrived at Costello's location at 1515, reporting that it had found 30 to 40 dead or wounded Americans. As Company C passed through the reconnaissance platoon and began to form a perimeter, the company came upon another group of Americans, raising its estimate to 50 killed and wounded. On a sweep around the area, the reconnaissance platoon found 3 enemy weapons, several blood-covered trails leading away from the area, and 22 enemy bodies.

While air and artillery struck likely routes of withdrawal, Colonel Newman's most pressing problem was how to evacuate the large number of American casualties from the area. There were no clearings for Hueys to land, and moving the dead and wounded overland would take too much time. Flying above the battlefield, General Coleman found the solution. Within a short distance from where Colonel Allen's body had been

---

[24] Quote from Memo, Brig Gen William S. Coleman, Asst Div Comdr, 1st Inf Div, for CG, 1st Inf Div, 21 Oct 67, sub: DAUNTLESS After Action Report. Interv, Daniel with Pfc Joseph J. Costello, Co A, 2d Bn, 28th Inf, 20 Oct 67. Both in VNI 134, CMH.

found, he spotted a deadfall that could be made into a helicopter landing zone. While troops cut down the vegetation with machetes and chain saws, a helicopter lowered a jungle penetrator rig to take out the most critically wounded. Not until late that afternoon was "the hole," as the men called it, large enough for a helicopter to land, and not until 1810 was the last of the wounded finally evacuated. Because of the presence of enemy snipers and the lateness of the day, Newman decided to leave the American dead near the hole until the next morning.

Throughout the night, to keep the enemy away from the bodies, "skyspots" (radar-directed air strikes) and artillery fire boxed the area. The next morning, when Newman's men returned to remove the dead, they found no evidence that the enemy had tampered with the bodies, and none were booby trapped, a common enemy practice. A further search turned up 17 more American dead, none of whom showed evidence of having been hit by artillery fire or air strikes. That accounted for all who had participated in the fight except for two soldiers. American losses came to 56 killed, 75 wounded, and 2 missing—totaling almost the entire complement of Allen's original force.

Viet Cong losses were unknown. Based on an estimate from each of the companies, the 1st Brigade reported an enemy body count of 101, but the relief force that removed the American dead on the following morning found only 2 enemy bodies.

Looking back, General Coleman felt that when Company A had first become embroiled in heavy combat at 1020 and had taken casualties, Allen should have instructed the unit to form a perimeter and then reinforced it with Company D. Yet 1st Division policy stated otherwise, supporting Allen's action. The same maneuver had been successfully executed by Colonel Cavazos' men on the eleventh and by Colonel Allen's men on the sixteenth. The error, if there was one, may have been using the same tactic repeatedly and automatically, without considering alternatives.

On the afternoon after the dead had been removed from the battlefield, General Westmoreland met with General Hay to determine why the engagement had been fought on the enemy's terms. Hay made no attempt to gloss over the calamity. Allen's men had been ambushed. Although they had apparently fought well under extreme circumstances, they had been dealt a terrible blow, taking more casualties in a single action than any other battalion under Hay's command.

Early in November the 2d Battalion, 28th Infantry, would again join the 1st Brigade to participate in a fight against two enemy regiments of the *9th Division* at Loc Ninh. Missing at Loc Ninh was the *9th Division's* remaining regiment, the *271st*. According to prisoners captured later, members of the *271st* who had fought in the Long Nguyen during October, their regiment had taken heavy casualties there and for months was in no condition to fight. But such news was no consolation to Americans mourning the loss of their own.

22

The 25th Division's Search for Progress

Unlike the 1st Division's battles with its big unit nemesis, the Viet Cong *9th*, General Tillson's 25th Division off to the west spent the rest of the year in a low-end but still lethal guerrilla war. Seldom did his troops meet enemy units larger than company size. Yet the short, painful firefights with the local forces and guerrillas testified to the insurrection's resiliency and renewed the old question about which side had the staying power to see the war for Vietnam through to the end.

The Base

In April, as the rainy season descended on III Corps, making large maneuvers hard to plan for and to execute, Tillson decentralized operations, allowing his brigades new autonomy to fight the local war as they saw fit. He required only that each brigade have a company ready within two hours and a battalion within four to commit to combat outside the brigade's tactical sector. Otherwise, he expected his commanders to harry the insurgents and the underground, protect the villages in their assigned territory, keep the main roads open, and defend the division's bases: Cu Chi, Tay Ninh West, and Dau Tieng. Whether they had enough troops to accomplish all these goals effectively remained an open question, as did whether they could count on the government's forces, the regulars and territorials, to carry part of the load.[1]

The 25th Division's main base at Cu Chi epitomized the dilemmas Tillson faced in trying to multiply his combat power. By mid-1967 Cu Chi was in many ways similar to the bases back home, providing comforts and conveniences for his soldiers. No longer were the camp's main roads covered with foot-deep dust or soft, unnavigable mud; most were paved and usable in any weather. The tent cities had disappeared, replaced by

---

[1] ORLL, 1 May–31 Jul 67, 25th Inf Div, 15 Aug 67, p. 1, and Interv, author with Maj Gen John C. F. Tillson, CG, 25th Inf Div, 28 May 76, both in Historians files, CMH.

Cu Chi base camp, October 1967

semipermanent "Southeast Asia huts" with wooden floors, screened walls, and corrugated metal roofs. Almost all units operated modern, half-brick, cement-floored mess halls that served hot meals three times a day, and there were clubs for officers and enlisted men to attend after duty hours. Tillson, as commanding general, lived in a two-room cottage, and several of his senior assistants and staff officers enjoyed the comforts of air-conditioned house trailers.

The base also housed a post exchange that grossed over a million dollars each month, a swimming pool, and a miniature golf course. On any given night a soldier could watch feature films at more than twenty different locations, with live shows at the base's "Lightning Bowl" theater twice monthly. Over the course of each month the division would send more than a thousand men for "R&R," MACV's five-day rest and recuperation program in Hawaii; Hong Kong; Bangkok, Thailand; or Sydney, Australia. The division also sent more than a hundred men each week, mainly combat troops, for an additional two-day rest at Vung Tau on the South China Sea.[2]

Cu Chi was also similar to other established U.S. bases in South Vietnam. The longer the life of a base, the more comfortable it became,

[2] Interv, author with Col Thomas A. Ware, Comdr, 1st Bde, 25th Inf Div, 26 Jan 81, Historians files, CMH; *"Tropic Lightning" in Vietnam*, secs. IX, X; Hay, *Tactical and Materiel Innovations*, pp. 148–51.

requiring more and more soldiers to support and maintain it. Many officers and enlisted men spent their entire tours in Vietnam at these installations, putting in a normal workday and having Sunday mornings free. It was sometimes galling to field commanders that combat units had to provide men to support and protect the base complexes, leaving units with little more than two-thirds of their assigned strength for operations. Between casualties, illnesses, troop rotations, and rear area duties, rifle companies sometimes took the field with less than half of their men present for duty.[3] Yet, without facilities to house the Army's administrative and logistical overhead—the maintenance, communications, supply, and command and control staffs and organizations—the fighting power of the forces would have been greatly reduced. Besides, rear-echelon duty gave the infantry and others a respite from the trials of combat. In Vietnam, R&R took many forms.

The 3d Brigade

Aside from Cu Chi, the larger of the two other division bases was Tay Ninh West. The base contained the Philippine Civic Action Group, Vietnam, a force of two thousand men committed solely to the nonmilitary aspects of pacification; a forward supply point for Saigon Support Command; and a rear detachment of the 196th Brigade, which had just joined Task Force OREGON. With the departure of the 196th for I Corps, the area of responsibility of the 3d Brigade, 25th Division, expanded from its old base at Dau Tieng to encompass Tay Ninh West. The shift made the brigade commander, Col. Kenneth E. Buell, responsible for a huge tactical area that included western Binh Duong and almost all of Tay Ninh Province.[4]

Although the rainy season favored enemy forces, by May they were still lying low. The primary enemy battle group in the area, the *7th PAVN Division*, had yet to take the field as a complete entity, used instead to provide replacements for other units. But by the summer of 1967 the *7th Division* was in better shape, with two veteran regiments, the *101st* and possibly the *141st*, just north of Dau Tieng and Tay Ninh in War Zone C. Both regiments were apparently ready for action. (*Map 37*)

Buell's men shed some light on enemy intentions. On 4 June they discovered a large rice cache west of Dau Tieng, the enemy base area where ATTLEBORO had unfolded the previous November. American troops also captured a guard who claimed that the rice was for a North Vietnamese battalion due to arrive later in the month.

Staking out ambush positions throughout the redoubt, the Americans waited and four days later ambushed and killed seven North Vietnamese.

---

[3] Bergerud, *The Dynamics of Defeat*, p. 131.

[4] Periodic Intel Rpt 22, IIFFV, 5 Jun 67, pp. 4–5, an. B, Historians files, CMH; Intervs, author with Garth, 26 May 76, and with Lt Gen R. Dean Tice, Comdr, 2d Bn, 12th Inf, 25th Inf Div, 3 Feb 81, Historians files, CMH.

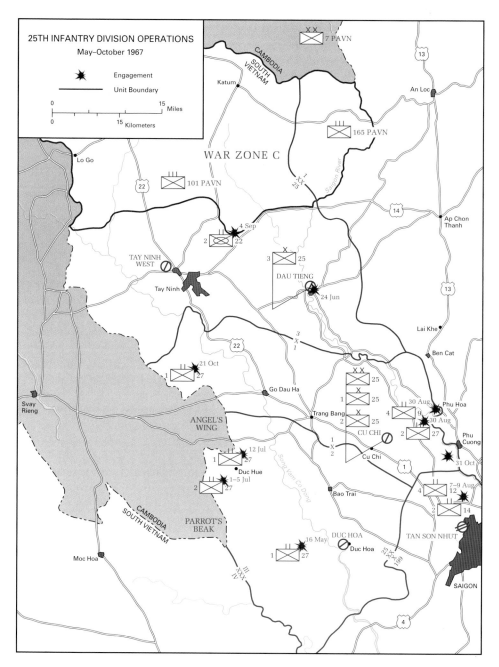

MAP 37

Documents found on the bodies revealed that the soldiers were from the *2d Battalion, 101st Regiment*. Their mission had been to reconnoiter six nearby installations for possible attack. The documents specifically targeted the 3d Brigade's base at Dau Tieng.

Over the next two weeks the only enemy forces to be found were in the Michelin Plantation east of Dau Tieng. On the night of 24 June an unidentified unit hiding in the rubber trees fired over eighty mortar rounds into Dau Tieng. The shelling lasted only five minutes, but twenty-seven helicopters were damaged and forty-nine Americans wounded.[5]

Within a week Tillson instructed Buell to plan a major operation in southern Tay Ninh Province. Although this part of Tay Ninh was one of the most secure areas in III Corps thanks to the strong presence of the Cao Dai, an anti-Communist religious sect, illegal trade had long thrived between Tay Ninh and the Cambodian province of Svay Rieng. In May American intelligence pinpointed a supply base in eastern Svay Rieng, in an area known as the Angel's Wing, and learned that *COSVN's Military Region 2* was about to launch at least two battalions from the Angel's Wing into Tay Ninh Province sometime in July. Buell's job was to stop them.[6]

The 3d Brigade effort, code-named Diamond Head, began on 11 July and initially focused on locating the enemy's supply routes from Svay Rieng into Vietnam. Using his mechanized 2d Battalion, 22d Infantry, to protect his two bases, Buell sent his other maneuver units, the 2d Battalion, 12th Infantry, and the 3d Battalion, 22d Infantry, south from Tay Ninh to begin a sweep, along with eight Regional Forces companies, between the Vam Co Dong River and the Cambodian border. But the searchers found no trace of the enemy or his supplies.

On 14 July Colonel Buell received two agent reports suggesting an early enemy offensive near Tay Ninh, South Vietnam's third largest city.[7] That very night contingents of the *101st Regiment* and possibly of the *165th*, the *7th Division's* third regiment, attacked government outposts between Tay Ninh West and Dau Tieng and overran one of them.

Tillson immediately ordered Buell to cancel operations along the border and turn his attention eastward. While his two rifle battalions were returning on the fifteenth, Buell committed his mechanized battalion, reinforced by the division's cavalry squadron, to the threatened area. That afternoon the American armor caught company-size enemy units at two locations between Tay Ninh City and Dau Tieng, but in both cases the enemy fled. Three days later in the same area, an American patrol ambushed and killed several enemy soldiers, later identified as members of the *165th*. Other

---

[5] Periodic Intel Rpt 24, IIFFV, 17 Jun 67, pp. 1, 6–7; AAR, Opn Diamond Head, 3d Bde, 25th Inf Div, 25 Dec 67, p. 6, Historians files, CMH.

[6] Periodic Intel Rpt 27, IIFFV, 11 Jul 67, pp. 2, 5, 10; AAR, Opn Diamond Head, 3d Bde, 25th Inf Div, pp. 6–7; Interv, author with Tice, 3 Feb 81.

[7] Periodic Intel Rpt 28, IIFFV, 18 Jul 67, pp. 1, 6, 10–11, and an. B; CDEC, no. 6–028–1131–67, 11 Jul 67, sub: TRANSLATION REPORT; Title: Possible Attack on TAY NINH WEST, Historians files, CMH.

intelligence suggested that the *101st Regiment* had moved to within striking distance of Tay Ninh West. Yet, once again, no attack occurred. Just as suddenly as it had begun, enemy activity dropped sharply.[8]

The pattern of events, if there was one, remained a mystery. Whether the prompt return of Buell's battalions from the Cambodian border caused *COSVN* to call off the attack against Tay Ninh West was impossible to determine. The repeated false alarms only renewed speculation that the enemy was merely feinting to keep the 3d Brigade away from the border, so supplies could flow unhindered to enemy units in the Saigon corridor.[9]

Whatever the case, since the beginning of DIAMOND HEAD the men of the 3d Brigade seemed to be chasing a will-o'-the-wisp bent on keeping them constantly on the move. Although they had killed 61 of the enemy by the end of August, after more than three and a half months of campaigning the effort had cost 32 American lives. September would prove equally frustrating.[10]

On the night of 2 September an enemy force equipped with rocket-propelled grenades struck the perimeter of one of Buell's mechanized companies. During the half-hour fight the attackers knocked out 2 armored personnel carriers and wounded 10 Americans. Enemy losses were unknown. Two days later the same mechanized company came upon an estimated enemy battalion at the base of Nui Ba Den. During the fighting, 4 Americans died and 51 were wounded, with enemy losses again unknown.

When the second fight ended at dark, Colonel Buell directed his mechanized battalion commander to assemble his entire force for an attack the next day. He may have acted more out of exasperation than sound judgment, but the possibility existed, however remotely, that the enemy remained pinned to the side of the mountain.

The attack was slow in developing. Preceded by a lengthy artillery barrage and nineteen air strikes, the troops finally moved out at 1530, only to be halted by what was reported as enemy fire but was more likely ricochets from American rounds striking the rocky slope of the mountain. Two soldiers were wounded. After pulling his men back, the battalion commander called for additional artillery and air strikes, which were not carried out until evening. Supporting artillery hit the suspected enemy position throughout the night. When the Americans finally entered the area the next morning, they met no opposition and found no enemy bodies.[11]

---

[8] RD Rpt, Tay Ninh Province, Jul 67, n.d., Historians files, CMH; AAR, Opn DIAMOND HEAD, 3d Bde, 25th Inf Div, p. 7; Periodic Intel Rpt 29, IIFFV, 25 Jul 67, pp. 1–2, and ans. B, C; Periodic Intel Rpt 30, IIFFV, 1 Aug 67, p. 3, an. C; Interv, author with Tice, 3 Feb 81.

[9] Intervs, author with Tice, 3 Feb 81, and with Col Robert M. Ward, G–3, 25th Inf Div, 8 Feb 81; CDEC, no. 6–028-3239–67, 22 Aug 67, sub: TRANSLATION REPORT; Title: Possible Attack on TAY NINH CITY. All in Historians files, CMH.

[10] Monthly Evaluation Rpt, IIFFV, Aug 67, n.d., Historians files, CMH.

[11] AAR, Opn DIAMOND HEAD, 3d Bde, 25th Inf Div, pp. 7, 35–37; Interv, author with Tice, 3 Feb 81.

In late September the 3d Brigade received a fourth maneuver unit, the 2d Battalion, 34th Armor. Colonel Buell assigned it to the least active area at the time, Tay Ninh West, so the crewmen could perform long overdue maintenance on their M48A3s while protecting the base. Throughout October Buell's other battalions operated from Dau Tieng, assisting in the relocation of villagers from the Michelin Plantation to camps closer to the brigade base and conducting sweeps into nearby base areas. In the process they counted seventy-five enemy dead, seized several supply caches, and razed a number of fortified positions. They encountered only local forces in small, scattered groups.

During the third week of October Buell's men manned blocking positions in the eastern Michelin, while the U.S. 1st Division swept westward through the Long Nguyen Secret Zone in Operation SHENANDOAH II. Although a tentative plan called for the 3d Brigade to join 1st Division forces in a more complete cleansing of the Long Nguyen, the proposal was discarded on 29 October after a major assault on the Loc Ninh Special Forces camp in Binh Long Province. The 1st Division moved to Loc Ninh, and in early November two battalions of the 3d Brigade followed as reinforcements. Until those battalions returned, Colonel Buell concentrated on protecting his own bases. Operation DIAMOND HEAD had begun with the promise of thwarting an enemy offensive but had ended with a whimper.[12]

The 1st Brigade

At the start of rainy season Tillson's 1st Brigade had three maneuver units: the 4th Battalion, 9th Infantry; the 2d Battalion, 14th Infantry; and the 4th Battalion, 23d Infantry (Mechanized). These forces were concentrated in Tay Ninh, Hau Nghia, and Binh Duong Provinces. Most of the men worked north of Highway 1 in the Cu Chi and Trang Bang Districts of Hau Nghia, where they contended more with mines, booby traps, and sniper fire than with organized units. The insurgent units they did find were usually in or around populated areas, making it difficult to use artillery and air strikes because of the high concentration of civilians. Having little advantage over the enemy, the brigade commander, Col. Doniphan Carter, claimed 34 enemy dead during one six-week period but suffered losses of 25 killed and 157 wounded.[13]

In addition to pacification security, Carter was responsible for the outer defenses of the division base at Cu Chi and was required to provide troops for at least a portion of the base's perimeter. Division intelligence

---

[12] AAR, Opn DIAMOND HEAD, 3d Bde, 25th Inf Div, pp. 43–55; ORLL, 1 Aug–31 Oct 67, 25th Inf Div, 14 Nov 67, p. 14, Historians files, CMH; Intervs, author with Tice, 3 Feb 81, and with Ward, 8 Feb 81.

[13] Monthly Evaluation Rpt, IIFFV, Jun 67, n.d., Historians files, CMH; Intervs, author with Col Doniphan Carter, Comdr, 1st Bde, 25th Inf Div, 16 Jan 81, Historians files, CMH; with Ware, 26 Jan 81; with Tillson, 28 May 76.

still placed three Viet Cong battalions in the Boi Loi and Ho Bo Woods and the Filhol Plantation north and northeast of Cu Chi, despite recent American sweeps through those areas. The threat was enough to keep a portion of at least one infantry battalion at the base camp throughout the summer and fall.

Carter soon received a task in Binh Duong Province. Fifteen kilometers northeast of Cu Chi was the large Saigon River village of Phu Hoa. During CEDAR FALLS the Saigon government had reestablished a district capital there, but by February the insurgents had returned, leaving the government in control of little more than the district headquarters compound. Helicopters provided the only safe way to reach the compound from Cu Chi. The security situation was obviously embarrassing to both the government and the Americans. Carter's mission, together with the South Vietnamese 7th Regiment of the 5th Division, was to "recapture" Phu Hoa.

On 8 July parts of all three battalions of the 1st Brigade sealed the land approaches to Phu Hoa, while South Vietnamese troops entered the village to conduct a search. Those people living in the western part of the village were to be resettled in a more open and more easily secured area to the southwest. The cordon and search operation lasted seventeen days. In the early stages some Viet Cong escaped through tunnels that extended outward and under the American positions into the Filhol Plantation, but South Vietnamese troops soon found the entrances inside several huts and collapsed the underground pathways, forcing several Viet Cong to surrender.

Once the people had been removed from western Phu Hoa, American engineers bulldozed the area of all structures and vegetation to make passage between the village and the Filhol easier to detect. In the meantime, sweeps conducted in the plantation brought on several firefights and, with no restriction on American firepower, the brigade killed seventy-five Viet Cong and had a favorable kill ratio of six to one for July.[14]

At the time the enemy's recent rocket attacks against Phuoc Vinh, Lai Khe, and Phu Loi, the 1st Division bases north of Saigon, and the May attack on Bien Hoa prompted concern for all the major bases in III Corps, including Tan Son Nhut and the recently built MACV headquarters just outside the air base. Although Tan Son Nhut lay in the 199th Brigade sector, the 25th Division shared a boundary with the brigade within ten kilometers of the air base, the maximum effective range of enemy long-range rockets. Astride that boundary was the Rach Tra, a small Communist base area frequented by the *2d Battalion*, a local force unit of *Military Region 4*. According to unconfirmed reports the *2d Battalion* had recently received some of the long-range rockets.[15]

---

[14] AAR, Opn BARKING SANDS, 1st Bde, 25th Inf Div, 28 Dec 67, pp. 6–7, 21; RD Rpt, Binh Duong Province, Jul 67, 31 Jul 67, pp. 1–6; Monthly Evaluation Rpt, IIFFV, Jul 67, n.d. All in Historians files, CMH. Intervs, author with Carter, 16 Jan 81, and with Ware, 26 Jan 81.

[15] Periodic Intel Rpt 32, IIFFV, 15 Aug 67, pp. 5–6.

General Mearns

On 7 August troops of the 199th, searching the Rach Tra, bumped into the *2d Battalion*. In the ensuing fight the new 25th Division commander, Maj. Gen. Fillmore K. Mearns, ordered Colonel Carter to block the area to the north with one battalion. On the following day men from the 2d of the 14th Infantry landed, only to find themselves in waist-deep water and under fire. All day long they held, repelling three attacks but taking heavy casualties, six dead and thirty-four wounded. Despite twenty-two air strikes and a continuous artillery pounding, the fight lasted until the next morning. When the Americans entered the Rach Tra, they found only abandoned bunkers—and not a single enemy body.[16]

Two weeks later, reacting to information that the *2d Battalion* had reoccupied the base area, Carter again sent in a battalion, this time with the assistance of a battalion from the 199th and two South Vietnamese ranger battalions. Once the base was surrounded, thirteen American artillery batteries were to pummel it before the infantry swept through.

The operation, WAIMEA, began on 22 August with the artillerymen setting their point-detonating fuzes on delay in hopes of destroying the underground enemy bunkers and exploding enemy mines and booby traps. The method may have worked, for when the troops entered the Rach Tra they were not opposed and took no casualties. On the other hand, the three-day operation accomplished little; the troops found only five Viet Cong bodies.[17]

Throughout most of August, because of washed-out roads and trails, Colonel Carter's mechanized battalion operated dismounted from patrol bases around Cu Chi. At the same time the 4th Battalion, 9th Infantry, worked in Trang Bang District, meeting little opposition. Blaming the lack of statistical results on passive field grade leadership, General Mearns told Carter to air-assault that same unit east of Phu Hoa Village, an area that when entered almost always produced a fight.

[16] Monthly Evaluation Rpt, IIFFV, Aug 67.

[17] AAR, Opn WAIMEA, 1st Bde, 25th Inf Div, 23 Sep 67, pp. 1–9, and Interv, author with Lt Gen David E. Ott, Comdr, 25th Inf Div Arty, 18 Aug 80, both in Historians files, CMH; ORLL, 1 Aug–31 Oct 67, 25th Inf Div, pp. 5–6; Periodic Intel Rpt 32, IIFFV, 15 Aug 67, pp. 5–6.

Shortly afterward, on 30 August, part of the 4th of the 9th Infantry landed east of Phu Hoa in open terrain. Almost immediately, enemy fire erupted from bunkers along the Saigon River, forcing the men to dive into flooded paddies. There they spent the rest of the day, unable to move or evacuate the wounded due to the intense fire. Efforts to relieve the element by landing the rest of the battalion on the enemy's flank stalled when the reinforcements found themselves out of range of supporting artillery. The battle raged until nightfall, when the Viet Cong withdrew shortly before the arrival of the 2d Brigade's 2d Battalion, 27th Infantry, which Mearns sent by truck. A search the following day uncovered 4 dead enemy soldiers. The Americans lost 11 killed and 43 wounded.[18]

Later, General Weyand, who had replaced General Palmer at II Field Force in July, met with Mearns to review the battle action. In January, Weyand recalled, a battalion of the 25th Division had landed in the same area and had met a similar fate; since then the division had apparently learned little. To Mearns, who had commanded an infantry battalion in World War II but had spent most of his career in artillery, the key failing had been an absence of adequate artillery support. He directed that in the future no maneuver unit of the 25th Division, platoon-size or larger, was to operate beyond the range of the equivalent of an artillery battalion.[19]

During the month of August the 1st Brigade reported killing 50 Viet Cong at a cost to the brigade of 30 dead and 195 wounded. During firefights on 8 and 30 August each of the brigade's rifle battalions took heavy losses without hurting the enemy. Early in September General Mearns and the deputy MACV commander, General Abrams, arrived unannounced at 1st Brigade headquarters and requested a briefing from Colonel Carter on brigade operations. Although Mearns and Abrams made few comments, Carter knew they had not been impressed. A few days later Col. Edwin H. Marks, who had recently commanded a brigade in Germany, arrived to take over the 1st Brigade.[20]

Under Colonel Marks, the brigade received an additional mission, the destruction of enemy base areas, a task now given precedence over pacification security and one that would permit the unrestricted use of artillery. As the first target, Mearns assigned the brigade the Ho Bo Woods, the familiar sixty square kilometers north of Cu Chi containing dense jungle and abandoned rice paddies and rubber plantations. Last entered by the

---

[18] Periodic Intel Rpt 35, IIFFV, 4 Sep 67, n.d., an. F; ORLL, 1 Aug–31 Oct 67, 25th Inf Div, p. 3; Intervs, author with Carter, 16 Jan 81, and with Maj Gen Edward C. Peter, Comdr, 2d Bn, 27th Inf, 25th Inf Div, 12 Feb 81, Historians files, CMH.

[19] ORLL, 1 Nov 66–31 Jan 67, 25th Inf Div, 20 Feb 67, p. 4, and Interv, author with Lt Gen John R. Thurman, Comdr, 25th Inf Div Arty, 23 Feb 81, both in Historians files, CMH; Interv, author with Ward, 8 Feb 81.

[20] Monthly Evaluation Rpt, IIFFV, Aug 67; ORLL, 1 Aug–31 Oct 67, 25th Inf Div, p. 3; Interv, author with Carter, 16 Jan 81.

Tanks of the 1st Brigade bog down in mud in the Ho Bo Woods.

Americans in January, the Ho Bo Woods supported the *1st* and *7th Battalions* of *Military Region 4*. Both units had apparently returned to rebuild their fortifications and storage depots, careful not to give away their presence by disturbing the vegetation, already liberally pockmarked by bomb craters and collapsed trench lines.

Marks' plan, Operation KUNIA, called for four artillery battalions to fire in support of the attack. Two were to move north from Highway 1 over Route 6A, a dirt road west of the Ho Bo Woods, and to establish firebases near the Saigon River. On 15 September, when all four were in position, and a battalion screening force provided by the 3d Brigade had deployed along the river opposite the base area, the 1st Brigade was to sweep into the Ho Bo Woods with its three battalions. After they had eliminated any insurgents in the area, a land-clearing team equipped with Rome plows from the 168th Engineer Battalion would flatten the woods, clearing away all vegetation. The operation was to be completed by the end of October.[21]

At first little went according to plan. On 14 September two artillery battalions moving up Route 6A during a heavy downpour became mired in deep mud several kilometers from their destination. Unable to free the vehicles, Marks rushed elements of the 4th of the 23d Infantry to guard the stranded column through the night. Two more days were required before engineers using tactical bridging equipment and corduroy surfaces could reopen the route and allow the column to proceed.

When the attack finally got under way it met little resistance other than the usual mines, booby traps, and an occasional sniper.[22] On the twentieth Rome plows began clearing the woods. For that phase of the operation Lt. Col. Thomas A. Ware, the commander of the mechanized 4th of the 23d, formed three teams, each consisting of a mechanized company, a tank platoon, and a section of plows. Aircraft and artillery preceded the plows, blasting sectors to be cleared that day—driving off snipers and detonating mines. Meanwhile, Colonel Marks swept other areas of the woods with his two rifle battalions.

[21] AAR, Opn KUNIA, 1st Bde, 25th Inf Div, 26 Nov 67, pp. 2–5, Historians files, CMH.
[22] Ibid.; Intervs, author with Thurman, 23 Feb 81, and with Ware, 26 Jan 81.

Enemy resistance was minimal, although occasionally a few Viet Cong would emerge from underground fortifications to replace the mines and booby traps destroyed by the preliminary artillery barrage. Others conducted hit-and-run assaults with rocket-propelled grenades and mortars. Not until mid-October did the harassment end, by which point Ware had cleared the northern and western portions of the woods and turned his plows toward the less heavily vegetated southern sector. Before the operation ended on 10 November, the bulldozers had also partially cleared the Filhol Plantation to the southeast.

Whenever tunnels were found, engineers pumped water from the Saigon River into their entrances; after waiting a few days for the water to weaken the structures, they collapsed them with demolitions. When the troops left, artillery and fighter-bombers finished the job.

During the eight-week operation, in addition to stripping the land of foliage and destroying tunnel complexes and bunkers, the brigade killed 105 Viet Cong and captured several tons of munitions and other supplies. In the process the Americans expended 826 tons of ammunition, not including the tonnage delivered by fighter-bombers on 601 sorties, had 33 vehicles destroyed, and lost 40 men killed and 412 wounded. Some began to question the point of it all. Within two months the Viet Cong would return and use the Ho Bo Woods and Filhol Plantation as staging areas for a major offensive in early 1968.[23]

The 2d Brigade

The 2d Brigade began the wet season with the 1st Battalion, 5th Infantry (Mechanized), and the 1st and 2d Battalions, 27th Infantry. At the time the brigade's operations were concentrated on southern Hau Nghia Province, a delta region inundated with marshlands and rice paddies. The Vam Co Dong divided the area into two distinct zones: west of the river was the Plain of Reeds, the wasteland that the Viet Cong controlled; east of the river, Duc Hoa and northeastern Duc Hue Districts were farming areas for which Saigon and the insurgents wrestled. Operations of the U.S. 9th Division in Long An Province by this time relieved the brigade of responsibilities farther south.

Two Viet Cong battalions, the *269th* and the *506th*, operated in the Vam Co Dong corridor to ensure the continued flow of supplies from Cambodia. A third battalion, the *276th*, secured Communist installations in Cambodia and recruited and trained replacements.[24] Unconfirmed reports had still another battalion, the *267th*, guarding two other major supply bases, one in the Parrot's Beak and the other ten kilometers north in the Angel's Wing.

[23] AAR, Opn Kunia, 1st Bde, 25th Inf Div, pp. 2–9; Interv, author with Ware, 26 Jan 81.
[24] AAR, Opn Kole Kole, 2d Bde, 25th Inf Div, 29 Dec 67, pp. 3–4, Historians files, CMH; Periodic Intel Rpt 24, IIFFV, 17 Jun 67, an. B.

During the summer the 2d Brigade commander, Col. Marvin D. Fuller, was to assist the South Vietnamese in pacifying Duc Hoa District, a national priority area, and to halt the eastward movement of supplies from Cambodia. The brigade's first major contact took place on 16 May, not in Duc Hoa, but to the west in Duc Hue District, when the *269th Battalion* struck a CIDG unit west of the Vam Co Dong. Although out of range of American artillery, Colonel Fuller reinforced with two battalions and pursued the enemy until after midnight. The combined South Vietnamese–American effort tallied 33 enemy dead.[25]

The Duc Hue action reflected the different operating techniques of the 2d Brigade. Unlike the other two brigades of the division, the 2d continued to use eagle flights, as it had since before ATTLEBORO, to seek out and destroy the insurgents. These operations were particularly suited to the region's flat, open terrain that offered the enemy relatively few places to hide. Throughout the spring and summer 90 percent of brigade kills were a result of these energetic eagle flights.[26]

During the first five days of July units of the brigade operating west of the Vam Co Dong tangled with both the *269th* and *506th Battalions* in actions that produced 63 enemy kills. On 6 July, as Colonel Fuller left to become operations officer of II Field Force, he could note with satisfaction that since the spring his troops had eliminated more than two hundred of the enemy on both sides of the Vam Co Dong, effectively shielding Duc Hoa District. According to a captured document, Fuller had cut in half insurgent "combat potential" in the district.[27]

Considering the South Vietnamese capable of holding Duc Hoa District, the new brigade commander, Col. Edwin W. Emerson, began shifting his forces north to pacify eastern Duc Hue District. On 12 July one of Emerson's rifle battalions conducted an air assault along a canal that served as the provincial boundary between Hau Nghia and Tay Ninh. As the troops landed, circling gunships spotted two Viet Cong and gave chase. The sudden appearance of the helicopters apparently either spooked or angered a unit of the *269th* into attacking. During the sharp firefight three Americans were killed and 34 wounded before the enemy was driven off.

By the time Emerson reinforced with his other rifle battalion, darkness had fallen and the enemy slipped away, hounded by American fighter-bombers. Although no enemy bodies were found the next day, a prisoner taken a short time later admitted that the planes had inflicted heavy casualties on his unit.[28]

---

[25] AAR, Opn KOLE KOLE, 2d Bde, 25th Inf Div, p. 9; Intervs, author with Peter, 12 Feb 81, and with Thurman, 23 Feb 81.

[26] AAR, Opn KOLE KOLE, 2d Bde, 25th Inf Div, p. 2; Interv, author with Peter, 12 Feb 81.

[27] AAR, Opn KOLE KOLE, 2d Bde, 25th Inf Div, pp. 24–26; Periodic Intel Rpt 27, IIFFV, 11 Jul 67, p. 9.

[28] AAR, Opn KOLE KOLE, 2d Bde, 25th Inf Div, p. 29; Periodic Intel Rpt 28, IIFFV, 18 Jul 67, p. 7; Interv, author with Peter, 12 Feb 81.

Throughout the rest of the month the brigade operated with two battalions in Duc Hue; the third returned to Duc Hoa, where the insurgents had again become active. Over a period of five days the battalion fought small enemy units along a canal south of Duc Hoa Village, which the Viet Cong habitually used to move supplies. Using assault boats and helicopter insertions, the battalion killed or captured 38 enemy soldiers.

Although for most of August the brigade lacked a rifle battalion, which was sent to help protect the U.S. logistical complex at Long Binh, the other two battalions continued their counterguerrilla campaign. While upgrading the road between Bao Trai and Trang Bang, the mechanized 1st of the 5th discovered several rudimentary ammunition factories near the Vam Co Dong. The men found a metal lathe, several hundred pounds of tools, a thousand unfinished mines, and enough material to produce five hundred grenades. Much of the equipment was discovered at low tide in large earthenware crocks buried in the mud along the riverbank. Elsewhere during August Emerson's men captured 61 enemy weapons and claimed 121 Viet Cong dead with few friendly casualties.[29]

By September the 2d Brigade had outperformed the other two brigades combined, at least statistically. Whereas the 2d Brigade reported killing 430 Viet Cong and capturing 162 weapons since the start of the summer campaign, the 1st Brigade's cumulative totals were 162 enemy killed and 54 weapons seized and, for the 3d Brigade, 63 enemy killed and 37 weapons captured. In terms of kill ratios, one of the preferred indicators of progress, the 2d Brigade boasted a nine to one ratio; the 1st Brigade less than three to one; and the 3d Brigade barely two to one.[30]

The 2d Brigade's statistical advantage would not last. In September its units began to operate in unfamiliar and more difficult terrain. While the mechanized element, the 1st of the 5th Infantry, remained in Duc Hue District through November, the rifle units, the 1st and 2d Battalions of the 27th, left to work the forested territory of southeastern Tay Ninh and northwestern Hau Nghia. In Tay Ninh, the troops conducted sweeps on the border to prevent supplies amassed in the Angel's Wing from entering Vietnam. In Trang Bang District of Hau Nghia, they replaced units of the 1st Brigade in the Ho Bo Woods. In both areas Emerson's men fought a series of battles and casualties rose—17 killed and 168 wounded during September. They claimed 75 enemy dead, less than half the total for August.[31]

More sharp fighting erupted in October, also outside the original 2d Brigade sector. The first clash happened on the twenty-first against an enemy platoon caught in the open north of the Angel's Wing. Before the guerrillas could slip away, the Americans pinned them in place and anni-

[29] AAR, Opn KOLE KOLE, 2d Bde, 25th Inf Div, pp. 36–48; RD Rpt, Hau Nghia Province, Aug 67, 31 Aug 67, pp. 1–6, Historians files, CMH; Monthly Evaluation Rpt, IIFFV, Aug 67.

[30] Monthly Evaluation Rpt, IIFFV, Aug 67.

[31] AAR, Opn KOLE KOLE, 2d Bde, 25th Inf Div, pp. 47–65; Monthly Evaluation Rpt, IIFFV, Sep 67, n.d., Historians files, CMH.

Near Dau Tieng, a Chinook moves Vietnamese families to a secure area.

hilated them. A week later the infantrymen came upon a Viet Cong company near the Saigon River but were unable to engage it decisively. A final fight took place on the thirty-first in southern Binh Duong Province, and here the enemy was routed. During the three contests Emerson's men killed 52 while losing 14 of their own.[32]

An Overview

Although base defense requirements, particularly for the 3d Brigade, had detracted from the overall mission of area security, the statistical results—when viewed at division level—were encouraging. Between mid-May and November, the 25th Division claimed to have killed or captured over 1,400 of the enemy, destroyed over 10,000 emplacements, and seized 400 weapons, 200 tons of rice, and huge amounts of ammunition and other supplies. Although the *7th Division* sustained some of these losses, most were from the ranks of local force and guerrilla units. During the campaign, South Vietnamese units claimed to have killed an additional 600 insurgents, while twice that number had opted to defect. Almost all major roads were open during

[32] AAR, Opn KOLE KOLE, 2d Bde, 25th Inf Div, pp. 66–84.

daylight hours, and prospects of the rice harvest reaching market later in the year were rated as good or better.

On the surface, the situation looked good. According to the Hamlet Evaluation System, some 550,000 people lived in the 25th Division's territory. Almost all those in Tay Ninh Province, about 300,000 Vietnamese, lived in hamlets considered "secure." Hau Nghia Province did even better. In May 42 percent of the people in Hau Nghia were judged to be protected; by November the figure increased to 45 percent, or 7,500 more villagers. An additional 30,000 inhabitants lived in areas that moved up in the ratings from "Viet Cong controlled hamlets" to "contested hamlets."

But problems lay beneath the surface of the encouraging picture. The figures did not indicate the actual security of the population, because the HES categories were skewed in such a way that any government presence—no matter how insignificant—warranted some sort of favorable rating. Furthermore, west of Saigon, improvements were due almost exclusively to the 25th Division's combat operations, rather than Saigon's pacification effort. One 25th Division program, the Combined Reconnaissance and Intelligence Platoon, brought together American soldiers and South Vietnamese territorials to hunt down small insurgent groups. Its success prompted other American divisions to copy it. Another 25th Division experiment, the Combined Lightning Initial Project, linked American, South Vietnamese Army, and militiamen into a single combined platoon. This also showed promise but was eventually abandoned in favor of the more conventional mobile advisory teams detailed to improve the performance of the territorials.

While American soldiers harried the Viet Cong, keeping them away from the villages, the pacification program itself was not producing much. The government's pacification vanguard, the revolutionary development cadre, was simply not getting the job done. In Hau Nghia Province, not a single revolutionary development team was credited with enhancing village security or otherwise improving the government's tenuous hold over the countryside during 1967.

Stagnation, rather than improvement, was the real picture in western III Corps. The old adage that the government controlled the countryside by day, but the Viet Cong ruled at night remained true. And west of Saigon, the situation might have been even worse. The fact that enemy sanctuaries in Cambodia were actually larger than before, and that the 25th Division would eventually depart, made a decline in security appear almost inevitable.[33]

---

[33] ORLL, 1 Aug–31 Oct 67, 25th Inf Div, pp. 1–5; HES Data Book, 1967, pp. II–28/II–29.

23

East of Saigon

As the rainy season enveloped III Corps, American and South Vietnamese forces renewed the offensive east of Saigon. This was familiar territory to the 9th Division and the 11th Armored Cavalry Regiment, both of which had been fighting here since the end of 1966. Indeed, having weakened the *5th PLAF Division* during the winter and spring campaign, the 9th Division now sought to finish the job under the leadership of Maj. Gen. George G. O'Connor, who assumed command from General Eckhardt on 1 June 1967. Available for operations east of the capital were the 9th Division's 1st Brigade, based at Bearcat, plus the 1st and 3d Squadrons of the 11th Armored Cavalry, based at Blackhorse, just south of Xuan Loc, the capital of Long Khanh Province. The 11th's 2d Squadron was detached to Task Force OREGON, while the 9th Division's 2d and 3d Brigades were south of Saigon in Dinh Tuong and Long An, respectively. For additional support O'Connor could call on the South Vietnamese 18th Division based at Xuan Loc and the 1st Australian Task Force at Nui Dat.

The Hat Dich

The traditional staging area for Senior Col. Nguyen The Truyen's *5th Division* was the Hat Dich—Base Area 301 in the MACV intelligence atlas. Although American operations had pushed the *5th* farther east into the more remote May Tao Mountains, O'Connor believed that the Hat Dich remained the key to regional security. From there the insurgents could still harass Highway 1, the east-west lifeline between Xuan Loc, Blackhorse, and the Saigon depots, as well as Highway 15 to Vung Tau and Route 2 into Phuoc Tuy Province. They could also close down Highway 20, which led to an important rock quarry at Gia Ray, before the road turned northeast to the truck farms of Da Lat and southern II Corps. Keeping the *5th Division* out of the Hat Dich and bottled up in the May Tao would best achieve allied security goals east of Saigon. But because the Hat Dich was so close to enemy supply lines from the delta, O'Connor

General O'Connor

predicted an early return of its traditional occupant, the *5th Division's 274th Regiment*, as soon as the rains arrived.

He was not disappointed. Early in June American patrols in "Slope 30," fifteen kilometers south of Blackhorse, spotted groups of ten to twenty men with full rucksacks crossing into the base area. Although reliable intelligence placed the *274th* somewhere south of the May Tao, O'Connor concluded that the sightings indicated that the regiment was about to move.

Rather than attempting to intercept the *274th*, O'Connor chose a bolder plan—a huge clearing operation against the Hat Dich itself, all 250 square kilometers of its jungle and rubber plantations. The scheme called for his 1st Brigade to drive east from Highway 15 accompanied by an engineer task force with Rome plows. While the infantry conducted searches and provided protection, the engineers were to enlarge two parallel trails that eventually met just east of Route 2 near Slope 30 and a third that joined the two in the Hat Dich's center, tracing out a giant letter "H." At the same time, the 11th Armored Cavalry was to provide a squadron to work with a South Vietnamese ranger battalion in the eastern Hat Dich. When the Rome plows reached their operating area, the troopers would protect the engineers until the operation ended.[1] (*Map 38*)

Operation AKRON began on 9 June and at first met only token resistance from caretaker units. Nine days later, however, the 3d of the 11th Armored Cavalry entered an empty battalion-size campsite near Slope 30. Unknown at the time, a battalion of the *274th* had briefly occupied the camp before slipping across Route 2 into the Hat Dich. The rest of the regiment was apparently between Xuyen Moc and May Tao Mountain, restoring base areas lost in April.

As the 3d Squadron pulled back from the jungle on the afternoon of 18 June, the enemy battalion commander watched the Americans preparing night laagers in four separate clearings at least a kilometer apart from

---

[1] ORLL, 1 May–31 Jul 67, 9th Inf Div, 7 Nov 67, pp. 1–2; AAR, Opn AKRON, 1st Bde, 9th Inf Div, 7 Jul 67, pp. 1, 5, Historians files, CMH.

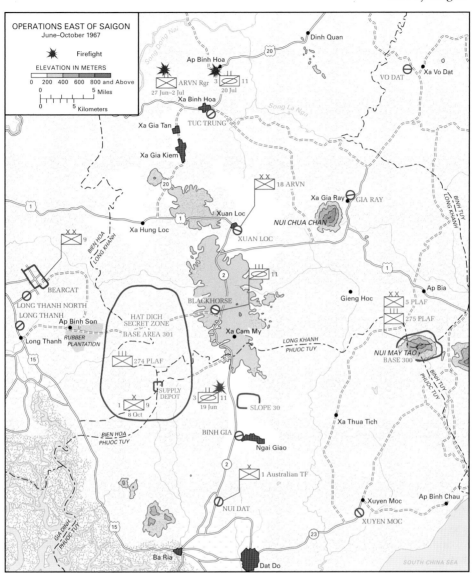

MAP 38

each other. He planned to strike the northeasternmost position, which contained the majority of vehicles, and to do most of his damage by fire. The attack was to begin sometime after midnight.

The target laager contained the squadron command post, commanded by Lt. Col. Arthur F. Cochran, a battery of self-propelled 155-mm. howitzers, and engineer vehicles, all protected by a cavalry troop. Altogether, Cochran had about two hundred soldiers. Outside the perimeter he placed ambushes and listening posts in the rubber trees and jungle, while

381

Men of the 3d Squadron, 11th Armored Cavalry, receive a briefing before a night patrol during Akron.

between the two lines of defense, the men put in trip flares and booby traps. The defensive preparations were routine, and no one anticipated an attack. Indeed, no 11th Armored Cavalry unit had ever been challenged in the field at night.

Though the outposts reported movement early in the evening, soon all became quiet. Then, after 0100 on 19 June, mortar rounds began exploding on the position. Intense fire ensued from recoilless rifles, machine guns, and small arms. The Americans responded in kind, with mortar crews lofting illumination over the defenses. The attack persisted for an hour, despite the arrival of Huey gunships and fire from heavy batteries at Nui Dat. Then, as suddenly as it had begun, the violence stopped. Although Cochran pursued north, he learned from a prisoner at daybreak that the attackers had withdrawn to the east. By then they had vanished.

In the morning Cochran's men found 56 enemy dead. American losses were 9 killed and 32 wounded. Although several vehicles had been hit, none were destroyed. Agent reports later revealed that the enemy battalion had carried away many dead and wounded and that several wounded had died en route. The attacking unit, the *1st Battalion, 274th Regiment,* would not be identified in another action for several months.[2]

---

[2] AAR, Opn Akron, 1st Bde, 9th Inf Div, pp. 1, 5, 7–15; AAR, Opn Akron, 11th Armd Cav Rgt, n.d., pp. 8–9, 11, and an. H; Periodic Intel Rpts 23, IIFFV, 12 Jun 67, an. B; 25, IIFFV, 27 Jun 67, pp. 6–7; and 46, IIFFV, 19 Nov 67, an. F. All in Historians files, CMH.

When AKRON ended on 29 June, overall enemy losses included over 80 dead or captured, 70 weapons and nearly 20 tons of rice seized, and 24 base camps destroyed, 5 of which were battalion size or larger. Since the engineers had completed their clearing mission, O'Connor intended to continue the operation into July to allow for a more thorough search of the Hat Dich. That would not happen.[3]

The Fight at Tuc Trung

On 26 June, three days before AKRON ended, a Viet Cong enlisted soldier named Trang Hoai Thanh rallied to the government at Tuc Trung, an outpost astride Highway 20, some forty kilometers northeast of Bearcat. Thanh claimed to be a member of the *3d Battalion, 275th Regiment*. He told interrogators that one month earlier his regiment had left for War Zone D. While traveling north, his battalion was split off and ordered to remain south of the Dong Nai to reconnoiter South Vietnamese outposts along Highway 20 near Tuc Trung. His regiment's *1st Battalion*, he said, had already left War Zone D to join the *274th* for an offensive farther south in Phuoc Tuy Province. The *275th's 2d Battalion* would soon follow, crossing south over the Dong Nai and joining his own unit. When shown a map the defector pointed out his battalion's campsite ten kilometers northwest of Tuc Trung.[4]

Other defectors had already revealed much of this information, but the location of his unit, the *3d Battalion*, and word that another battalion would soon join it, were fresh intelligence. The news prompted the South Vietnamese 18th Division commander, Brig. Gen. Do Ke Giai, to send a ranger battalion to find the camp on the next day, 27 June. Late that afternoon the rangers discovered a recently vacated laager.

It turned out to be a trap. Moments later the Viet Cong unleashed an ambush, inflicting heavy casualties and scattering the South Vietnamese. The commander lost contact with many of his men.

Learning of the fight, the 11th Armored Cavalry commander, Col. Roy W. Farley, sent a 1st Squadron task force, consisting of two cavalry troops and two howitzer batteries, to reinforce. That evening the squadron established a firebase near Tuc Trung and dispatched a cavalry troop into the camp the next morning. Meeting no resistance, the troops were suddenly overcome by the stench of dead bodies. Corpses lay everywhere—enemy and ally alike—some clothed in light blue and khaki uniforms, others in South Vietnamese fatigues, clear evidence of an intense fight at close quarters. A wounded enemy soldier stumbling around the killing ground identified his unit as the *3d Battalion, 275th Regiment*.

---

[3] AAR, Opn AKRON, 1st Bde, 9th Inf Div, p. 23; AAR, Opn AKRON-PLOW, 15th Engr Bn, 9th Inf Div, 5 Jul 67, pp. 1–5, Historians files, CMH.

[4] Periodic Intel Rpt 26, IIFFV, 4 Jul 67, p. 5, Historians files, CMH.

ACAVs pull back for an air strike near Blackhorse.

In the meantime, a South Vietnamese Army battalion sent to reinforce the rangers had found the bulk of them off to the east, the rangers having escaped the trap during the night. But hardly had the two forces linked up early on the twenty-eighth when the enemy renewed the fight.

O'Connor sent artillery and an additional infantry battalion to the rescue. All would come under Farley's direction. It would be his job to block enemy escape routes to the east and south, while gunships and artillery plugged the exits across the Dong Nai. Farley was to reinforce the South Vietnamese only if the situation grew critical; the fight was to be decided by Giai's men, who, in O'Connor's judgment, had by that time gained the edge.

The fight ended abruptly that evening, when the enemy withdrew. The next day the South Vietnamese met a dug-in Viet Cong company and, after reinforcing with a third battalion, overran the position. But searches conducted over the next three days turned up only occasional stragglers. Overall, the government forces lost 51 men but claimed 167 of the enemy. The Americans, who had taken few casualties, claimed 49 more, mainly from air strikes, gunships, and artillery fire. Learning of the battle, South Vietnamese Premier Nguyen Cao Ky flew in to congratulate his soldiers. The government forces had won a tough battle, proving they could fight effectively.[5]

[5] AAR, Opn AKRON, 11th Armd Cav Rgt, p. 13; ORLL, 1 May–31 Jul 67, 9th Inf Div, p.

Eager to reinforce success, O'Connor launched a week-long combined operation in eastern Phuoc Tuy, bringing together nine battalion equivalents of American, South Vietnamese, and Australian units. Bad weather and the enemy's skill in avoiding combat tempered the results. In one action, nevertheless, a South Vietnamese battalion came upon an enemy force and killed 40, refusing an offer of U.S. assistance. When the operation ended, enemy losses exceeded 100 men.

Unsure of O'Connor's next move, the enemy commander, Colonel Truyen, retained only the *1st Battalion* of the *275th* in the May Tao and kept the *274th* dispersed east of Route 2 for the rest of July. Not until August would he return the *274th* to the Hat Dich, and then to resupply and reorganize rather than for offensive operations.[6]

Ambush on Highway 20

At the beginning of July the 11th Armored Cavalry Regiment began a major personnel reorganization. Having been in South Vietnam for nearly a year, almost 75 percent of its men were about to return to the United States. Over the next six weeks a mass exodus stripped the regiment of the majority of its veteran soldiers. This was especially true of the 3d Squadron, whose new commander, Lt. Col. Hillman Dickinson, was left with a virtually green unit.

Colonel Dickinson's first operation was to clear Highway 20, which branched northeast from Highway 1 toward II Corps and ultimately to Da Lat, where most of the vegetables for the Saigon market were grown. As enemy food problems had worsened, the Viet Cong had become more active along the road, stopping trucks at remote, heavily wooded defiles to confiscate some of their cargo. Dickinson's job was to provide security for an engineer task force that was to remove vegetation from both sides of the road in III Corps, a distance of ninety kilometers. Intelligence indicated that the *D800 Battalion*, a local force unit, normally operated along Highway 20 and that the *275th Regiment*, although thought to be recovering in War Zone D from its defeat at Tuc Trung, might also be met.

Because of washouts along the road, Colonel Farley directed Dickinson to move with the lighter track vehicles of his three cavalry troops at the head of the column, followed by the heavier Rome plows and tanks. On the morning of 21 July the squadron left Blackhorse in that formation to open an operating base for the plows, thirty kilometers north of the

21; ORLL, 1 May–31 Jul 67, 11th Armd Cav Rgt, n.d., p. 7; Msg, Saigon 10573 to State, 7 Nov 67, sub: Measurements of Progress, Westmoreland History files, 24–24, CMH; Interv, author, with Lt Col Martin D. Howell, Comdr, 1st Sqdn, 11th Armd Cav Rgt, 26 Aug 80, Historians files, CMH.

6 ORLL, 1 May–31 Jul 67, 9th Inf Div, pp. 30–31; Interv, author with Howell, 26 Aug 80; Periodic Intel Rpts 27, IIFFV, 11 Jul 67, p. 4; 28, IIFFV, 18 Jul 67, p. 7; 29, IIFFV, 25 Jul 67, pp. 2, 5–7; and 46, IIFFV, 19 Nov 67, an. F.

juncture of Highways 20 and 1. The cavalry troops traveled three to five kilometers apart.

At 0940, as the lead unit, Troop L, neared the future location of the engineer camp, an enemy force some five hundred men strong opened fire from a rubber plantation on both sides of the road. The fire raked the entire column, spread out over 1,200 meters. Dickinson had no sooner learned of the action than the troop commander's radio fell silent. All attempts to regain contact failed.

Troop L was clearly up against a sizable force—one that had the upper hand. Dickinson immediately ordered the unit closest to the action, Troop K, to reinforce and edge around the ambushers' flank. Delayed as it moved through several villages, Troop K arrived thirty-five minutes later at the southern edge of the ambush. Dickinson's only experienced commander, Capt. Ronald A. Hoffman, was in charge of the fresh unit. His men had just arrived when Hoffman saw several enemy soldiers swarming over Troop L's vehicles, stripping them of machine guns and radios. Without radio contact with Troop L and concluding that the unit had been overrun, Hoffman pushed forward into the maelstrom to rescue any survivors and drive the enemy off.

At the time the decision seemed right. The Troop L commander was dead, and his disorganized soldiers were low on ammunition. Hoffman charged forward in his armored cavalry assault vehicles (ACAVs). Those of the enemy who escaped his bullets crossed a berm west of the road that extended the entire length of the ambush. When Troop K tried to pursue, the ACAVs came up short against the steep banks. An enemy officer, dressed in a starched khaki uniform with a pistol belt and holster, presumably the commander, stood on the berm urging his men to stand fast. When they realized that the armor could not close with them, the Viet Cong renewed the fight. As Hoffman wondered what to do next, an enemy rocket slammed into his vehicle in a fiery burst, blinding him.

One hour after the Viet Cong sprang their ambush, Dickinson arrived overhead in a helicopter. He saw immediately that his soldiers were too close to the enemy for him to risk using artillery. Immersed in the battle, they were also unable to fall back. Just as bad, the closely spaced rubber trees obscured aerial observation and made it difficult for helicopter gunships to add their firepower to the battle. Both cavalry troops had lost their commanders, no one appeared to be in charge, and the men in the vehicles seemed to be fighting for their lives. Dickinson's only hope of relief appeared to be with his remaining troop and tanks, still moving forward on Highway 20.

Dickinson ordered Troop I to continue north, clear the enemy on the opposite (eastern) side of the road, and then link up with Troops K and L. He told the commander of Company M, his tank unit, to move off the highway before reaching the enemy position and push through a series of trails leading into the enemy's southern flank.

Traveling with Company M was Dickinson's intelligence officer, Capt. William M. Boice, a recent replacement. When the M48s turned to flank, Boice left them and proceeded up the road on foot to the ambush. There, he learned that a combat-experienced lieutenant had assumed command of Troop L. Boice told him to gather his men in a nearby clearing so the wounded could be evacuated. Taking command of Troop K himself, he assembled the men and prepared to attack the northern flank. He reasoned that after Troop I had cleared the eastern side of the road, it would await instructions from Dickinson.

While the two troops were regrouping, the Company M tanks punched into the southern flank. Just the sight of the big Pattons was enough to panic the enemy soldiers, and the Viet Cong fled west through the rubber trees into jungle too dense for armor to follow.

By midafternoon all firing had ceased. The troopers found 96 enemy bodies and 29 weapons, along with an assortment of equipment and ammunition. Captured documents and a prisoner confirmed that the enemy force consisted of the *2d Battalion, 275th Regiment*, and a company from the *D800 Battalion*. Some speculated that the enemy regimental commander, later reported to have been killed in the action, had risked attacking the American armor because he knew the troops to be inexperienced. It was more likely, however, that the appearance of the Americans had come as a surprise. Earlier that morning, the rest of the *D800* had struck a government outpost twenty-five kilometers farther north and had ambushed a South Vietnamese relief force coming down from the north. The enemy commander was probably anticipating the approach of another South Vietnamese relief force from the south, but when Troop L showed up instead, he had little choice but to continue the fight.

During the battle 14 Americans died and 63 were wounded. Although several ACAVs suffered heavy damage, none were permanently disabled. Some American commanders believed that the lack of experienced soldiers had been a significant factor, and that with seasoned leaders and men, American casualties would have been fewer and those of the enemy much higher. Whatever the case, after this engagement II Field Force began a stringent infusion program, replacing some of the 11th Cavalry's new men with more experienced soldiers from other armored units in III Corps. Never again would more than 25 percent of an armored unit's troopers rotate in any given month.[7]

[7] Intervs, author with Lt Gen Hillman Dickinson, Comdr, 3d Sqdn, 11th Armd Cav Rgt, 12 and 25 Sep 80; with Col William M. Boice, Comdr, Troop K, 3d Sqdn, 11th Armd Cav Rgt, 25 and 29 Sep 80; ORLL, 1 Aug–31 Oct 67, 11th Armd Cav Rgt, 20 Nov 67, pp. 26–27. All in Historians files, CMH. ORLL, 1 May–31 Jul 67, 11th Armd Cav Rgt, n.d., pp. 1–7, and Incl 5; Periodic Intel Rpts 29, IIFFV, 25 Jul 67, pp. 2, 8–9, and 42, IIFFV, 22 Oct 67, pp. 5, 9, Historians files, CMH.

Back to the Hat Dich

While the 11th Armored Cavalry worked Highway 20 near War Zone D, the 1st Brigade, 9th Division, probed the Hat Dich for the *274th*, which reportedly had returned. Though initial sweeps were unrewarding, documents and prisoners captured in August revealed that all three battalions were now present in the redoubt, understrength and short of rations but still dangerous. The *84th Rear Service Group* and two local force battalions provided their support.[8]

Although the service group reportedly maintained a large underground ordnance depot in the Hat Dich sufficient to meet the needs of those forces, the critical problem of adequate food remained unsolved. O'Connor knew that his operations were hampering the *84th*'s supply lines, but in October he received more help with his interdiction effort when the Royal Thai Army Volunteer Regiment (the "Queen's Cobras") was placed under his operational control. O'Connor positioned the Thai unit in southwestern Bien Hoa Province, further cementing the ring around the Hat Dich.[9]

However, the problem of finding the wily *274th* and bringing it to battle remained. On 26 September O'Connor again sent the 1st Brigade into the Hat Dich with an engineer task force of Rome plows to continue the detailed searches and physical destruction begun in June. Although the men encountered only occasional enemy resistance, on 8 October they discovered a series of huge underground complexes in the heart of the redoubt along the Bien Hoa–Phuoc Tuy boundary. It turned out to be the ordnance depot that a rallier had described in late 1966.[10]

Within each complex, tunnels four to five feet high and three feet wide led to storage rooms on up to four separate levels. Vertical shafts forty feet deep provided a means for lowering and raising supplies and served as the main source of ventilation in the bottom levels, where ammunition was stored. Bamboo shoots and metal pipes aided in venting tunnels and sleeping quarters closer to the surface. While some of the rooms showed signs of having been hastily emptied, most were full of supplies.

Before destroying the complex the troops removed over 1,000 small arms and 124 crew-served weapons along with quantities of spare parts. Over half the weapons were of American, French, or German origin, left behind because they were obsolete. The search also uncovered over 200,000 rounds of small-arms ammunition and more than 7,000 explosives, including grenades, mines, and recoilless rifle and mortar rounds. The brigade

---

[8] AAR, Opn Akron II, 1st Bde, 9th Inf Div, 8 Sep 67, pp. 5–11, Historians files, CMH; Periodic Intel Rpt 46, IIFFV, 19 Nov 67, an. B.

[9] AAR, Opn Riley, 1st Bde, 9th Inf Div, 12 Oct 67, pp. 11–13; AAR, Opn Riley II, 3d Sqdn, 5th Cav, 9th Inf Div, 28 Sep 67, pp. 1–2; ORLL, 1 Aug–31 Oct 67, 9th Inf Div, 23 Dec 67, pp. 7–8. All in Historians files, CMH. Periodic Intel Rpt 46, IIFFV, 19 Nov 67, an. B.

[10] AAR, Opn Akron III, 1st Bde, 9th Inf Div, 23 Oct 67, pp. 3–7, 19, Historians files, CMH; AAR, Opn Riley, 1st Bde, 9th Inf Div, pp. 4, 13.

Rome plows level a former jungle haunt of the Viet Cong.

also discovered an underground field hospital containing 1,400 pounds of medical supplies, enough to care for 1,000 patients for over a month.[11]

In late October, with the return of the 2d Squadron, 11th Armored Cavalry, from Task Force OREGON and the deployment of the Royal Thai Regiment, allied strength east of Saigon reached a peak. On the whole, operations seemed to be progressing well, though many of the indicators were ambiguous. On the one hand, despite the mounting tempo of American operations, local force and guerrilla units had become more active, though main force units were idle. On the other hand, the increasing pressure kept the enemy chronically short of food and supplies.

Pacification indicators were also mixed. As elsewhere in III Corps, the figures were rising. According to the HES rating system, more than 80 percent of the people in the region lived in "secure" hamlets. But a more telling yardstick of the success of pacification was the state of the Viet Cong underground, which, despite the American operations, was still alive and well east of Saigon. On the positive side, however, virtually all major roads were open during daylight hours, a marked improvement over the situation only a few months earlier.

[11] AAR, Opn RILEY, 1st Bde, 9th Inf Div, pp. 3, 85–90, 94; Periodic Intel Rpt 42, IIFFV, 22 Oct 67, p. 3.

In the end, none of these operations produced significant contacts, though the allies uncovered and destroyed many base camps. As usual, the enemy chose the time and place to fight, and when he did, American and South Vietnamese soldiers died. However, III Corps considered the operations successful in the long run because the Viet Cong, always short of supplies in this area so far from their strongholds on the Cambodian border, now found themselves even more hard pressed. While this might be viewed as favorable in Saigon, the bottom line was that the territory east of the capital was not of great importance to the enemy.

PART SEVEN

Winding Up

24

Early Delta Battles

The Mekong Delta was South Vietnam's heart and soul. Forty thousand square kilometers of shimmering rice fields fed by the Mekong River provided South Vietnam with 75 percent of its food. More than a third of the country's seventeen million people lived in the region's sixteen provinces, cultivating their crops and using the vast network of rivers and canals to ship produce to Saigon.

The ancient way of life of the region's people was tied inexorably to the great Mekong. From its headwaters in southern China the river flows for nearly 4,200 kilometers before emptying into the South China Sea. Over the course of its journey the river collects rich alluvial soil that over the centuries created the Mekong Delta. On its journey south, the river splits into nine main arteries and countless smaller waterways before forming a triangular plain extending from Saigon to the South China Sea. The base of this wedge parallels the ocean, while the body tapers toward the northwest between broad marshes and coastal swamps. The center of the wedge was South Vietnam's rice basket, which the Vietnamese people called *Cuu Long Giang*, the River of the Nine Dragons.

The delta seldom reaches more than three meters above sea level, its endless flatness broken only by the Seven Mountains, an outcropping of rocky hills in the west along the Cambodian border. Roads were numerous, though narrow and poorly maintained. Highway 4, a blacktop road running from Saigon to the Ca Mau Peninsula in the far south, was the exception but was used sparingly because of enemy interdiction. Seasonal flooding further impeded cross-country movement.

Compared to the raging war in the rest of South Vietnam, the Mekong Delta was relatively peaceful. But beneath the veneer of quiet countryside and thriving economy lay a conundrum that confounded planners in Saigon and Washington. Predominantly rural, the delta was heavily populated; economically tied to the ruling regime, it boasted some of the most pro-Communist provinces in the country. By 1967 this riddle was nowhere near solution. (*Map 39*)

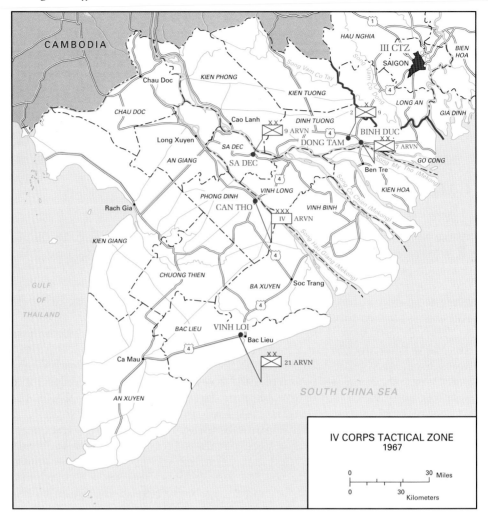

MAP 39

The Mekong Delta was the cradle of the Communist insurgency. An extensive revolutionary underground, the forerunner of the National Liberation Front, had been active there since the 1930s. By the beginning of 1967 American advisers estimated that the Viet Cong had about 50,000 guerrillas in IV Corps, 45 percent of the total insurgent strength in the entire country, supported by about 20,000 main force troops organized into twenty-one battalions and eighty-one separate companies or platoons.[1]

---

[1] Senior Officer Debriefing Program, DA, 1 Jan 68, sub: Brig Gen William R. Desobry, U.S. Advisory Gp, IV CTZ, pp. 1–8 (hereafter cited as Desobry Debriefing), Historians files, CMH; Monthly OB Sum, CICV, Dec 66, p. I–1.

In the years before 1967 the South Vietnamese Army did the fighting in the delta. Maj. Gen. Nguyen Van Manh, the IV Corps commander, had at his disposal 30,000 troops in three infantry divisions—the 7th and 9th in the eight central provinces and the 21st in the five southernmost provinces. General Manh also had five ranger battalions and three armored cavalry squadrons, which he normally parceled out to the divisions. Backing the regulars were about 100,000 Regional and Popular Forces militiamen and a smattering of Special Forces arrayed in camps along the Cambodian border and naval units patrolling the coastline and the Mekong River looking for enemy infiltrators. With this force, the South Vietnamese outnumbered the enemy by almost two to one.

Clearly, the delta was crucial to both sides, but Saigon intended to win there at all costs. According to the combined campaign plan for 1967, the heavily populated central delta—composed of An Giang, Sa Dec, and Vinh Long Provinces as well as portions of Phong Dinh and Vinh Binh—was IV Corps' National Priority Area. General Manh's task was to maintain and expand government control and to keep the overland link with Saigon, Highway 4, free of Viet Cong harassment. About two-thirds of his combat strength at any one time was devoted to offensive operations, while the remainder handled pacification security. Unfortunately, Manh was unable to take the initiative from the Viet Cong, and by 1967 the best Saigon could claim in the delta was a stalemate.

During the early years of the war, the Americans had only a small presence in IV Corps. Politically, no South Vietnamese government could tolerate the prospect of foreign soldiers operating among the delta's highly concentrated population. Nor were there any particularly pressing military reasons for the U.S. Army to do so. Despite its economic importance, the delta was a strategic backwater, far from the Demilitarized Zone and the major enemy base areas in Laos and northeastern Cambodia. The Viet Cong rarely operated in large units, and the North Vietnamese Army was virtually absent. Moreover, the delta's dense population, innumerable waterways, poor roads, and marshy ground made it an inhospitable environment for American formations with their heavy equipment, large logistical requirements, and firepower-intensive methods.

While the delta was destined to escape the brunt of the American war effort, it would not avoid an American presence altogether. Although U.S. military operations were out of the question for most of IV Corps, Westmoreland had always recognized the desirability of extending the ring of American troops defending Saigon to the delta areas south and west of the capital. Moreover, he believed that South Vietnamese military units operating in IV Corps would benefit from working alongside the aggressive and efficient American military. Perhaps, reasoned Westmoreland, a little demonstration of American prowess would inspire them to do better.

With these thoughts in mind, in 1965 Westmoreland directed his staff to prepare contingency plans for stationing a force, known for planning purposes as the Z Division, in an arc running through the

American troops file along a dike in the Mekong Delta.

northern delta just below Saigon. These plans envisioned that the head-quarters of the Z Division and one of its brigades would be located at the small port of Ba Ria near Vung Tau. A second brigade would take up station in the delta's Dinh Tuong Province, while a third would be placed aboard U.S. Navy ships for amphibious operations along the area's major inland waterways.[2]

The most novel aspect of the Z Division was its riverine component, designed to take advantage of the delta's 6,400 kilometers of navigable streams and canals. Convinced that the idea was workable, Westmoreland sought formal approval for the project. In July 1966 Secretary McNamara ordered the deployment of two U.S. Navy barracks ships, on which a reinforced infantry battalion could be billeted, with sufficient landing craft to transport the troops during operations and to provide fire support. Although Westmoreland pressed for additional vessels to support a brigade of three battalions, McNamara preferred to wait until the concept had been tested. Nevertheless, by then Westmoreland had designated the 9th Infantry Division, soon to arrive from Fort Riley, Kansas, as the Z

[2] MACV Conference Rpt, 7 Mar 67, sub: Mekong Delta Mobile Afloat Force (MDMAF) Concept and Requirements, and Fact Sheet, MACV J–3, 8 Apr 67, sub: Mobile Riverine Force, both in Historians files, CMH. See also Maj. Gen. William B. Fulton, *Riverine Operations, 1966–1969*, Vietnam Studies (Washington, D.C.: Department of the Army, 1973), pp. 42–67.

force, and many of its key commanders had begun to receive amphibious warfare training in the United States geared to the operation of land forces in a riverine environment.[3]

Events in South Vietnam soon altered the underlying premises of the Z Division. The force had been conceived at a time when American military leaders were still optimistic about the chances for an early victory in Vietnam and when American political leaders had indicated that additional troops would be readily forthcoming. Neither had proved to be true. Faced with a prolonged conflict with insufficient forces, Westmoreland began to have second thoughts about deploying the incoming division south of Saigon. Indeed, for a time the threat of a major North Vietnamese offensive in I Corps led him to consider sending the division north. In the end the division's headquarters and 1st Brigade went to Bearcat in Bien Hoa Province to protect Saigon's eastern approaches and to serve as a II Field Force reserve. And with the continuing stalemate in the nation's rice bowl too much to ignore, the other two brigades soon headed south.

War in Long An

By April 1967 the 3d Brigade of the 9th Division was operating in Long An Province between Highway 4 and Route 5A. Each battalion was assigned a district and worked in tandem with local South Vietnamese soldiers. Although all three of the battalions supported pacification, each operated differently.[4]

Rach Kien, a recently created district, bordered Gia Dinh Province. Because the government had declared Rach Kien a National Priority Area, the 3d Brigade placed its 3d Battalion, 39th Infantry, in the district seat, the village of Rach Kien, previously under Communist control. (*Map 40*) Working from the village, the Americans conducted patrols, eagle flights, and cordon and search operations with South Vietnamese forces in an attempt to pacify the surrounding hamlets. But at night the Viet Cong returned, moving easily in and out of the area to collect taxes, to hunt for recruits and information, and to search for those known to side with the government. No official dared to risk spending the night in an unsecured hamlet for fear of being kidnapped or assassinated. On the other hand, because of the security provided by the new American presence, the population of Rach Kien Village increased fivefold, to over a thousand, by May.

In the central district, Tan Tru, between the Vam Co Dong and Vam Co Tay Rivers, another 3d Brigade battalion, the 2d of the 60th Infantry,

---

[3] Msgs, COMUSMACV 00005 to CINCPAC, 1 Jan 66, sub: Deployment of U.S. Forces to Mekong Delta, and Commander in Chief, U.S. Army, Pacific, 6501 to CINCPAC, 28 Mar 66, sub: Mekong Delta Mobile Afloat Force, both in Historians files, CMH.

[4] AAR, Opn ENTERPRISE, 3d Bde, 9th Inf Div, pp. 1–3, Historians files, CMH.

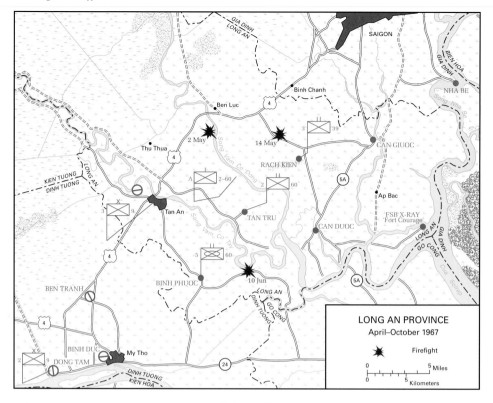

MAP 40

operated from two locations: the town of Tan Tru; and a company-size base at Ap Nhut Tang, a formerly Communist-controlled hamlet along the Vam Co Dong. Because of security requirements for the bases, normally only one company of the battalion was free to remain overnight elsewhere in the district. However, the main mission was to secure the Vam Co River corridor, operating at first with South Vietnamese riverine forces on the major waterways and then, in May, using smaller craft to patrol lesser streams and canals.

In the southern district, Binh Phuoc, the brigade stationed its one mechanized battalion, the 5th of the 60th Infantry, at the village of Binh Phuoc. A predominantly Catholic and anti-Communist community, Binh Phuoc was the most secure of the three district capitals. This allowed the battalion to work outside the district, escorting convoys along Highway 4 between Tan An and Saigon and reinforcing the U.S. riverine force in Dinh Tuong Province.[5]

During the 3d Brigade's first month in Long An, American operations dispersed the *2d Independent Battalion* and bloodied the *506th PLAF Battal-*

[5] Ibid., pp. 60–66.

ion near Rach Kien. Yet less than three weeks later, on 2 May, the same *506th* struck an American company in its night defensive position near Highway 4, killing 17 and wounding 48, the highest casualties any 3d Brigade unit had suffered in a single action since arriving in Vietnam. By the time reinforcements arrived, the enemy had vanished, and a search of the battle area failed to turn up any Viet Cong bodies.[6]

A week later the *2d Independent Battalion* took the offensive, launching a series of company-size attacks against South Vietnamese units in Rach Kien District. Three of the fights were standoffs, but the fourth resulted in an embarrassing South Vietnamese defeat.

During the early hours of 14 May the Viet Cong entered the compound of a South Vietnamese battalion, the 2d of the 50th Infantry, 25th Division, through two gates that someone from inside had opened. Possessing detailed information of the camp's defenses and troop quarters, the attackers quickly overran the compound and early in the fight jammed the American adviser's radio with voice transmissions, preventing him from calling for help. Within two hours, the insurgents had killed 31 and wounded 34 and then fled with 68 South Vietnamese weapons. Known enemy losses were 3 dead. Afterward the 3d Brigade conducted a two-day search for the attackers, but to no avail.[7]

What made the Viet Cong offensive all the more remarkable was that during the first five months of 1967, reported enemy losses (killed, captured, or rallied) in Long An had exceeded 2,400 men, 80 percent of the estimated total enemy strength in the province. Regardless of the accuracy of either figure, it was evident that the insurgents could move at will within the province without fear of betrayal and that they also commanded a seemingly inexhaustible supply of replacements.[8]

Throughout June, the men of the 3d Brigade worked in the Vam Co corridor, uncovering enemy caches and destroying Viet Cong base camps. With one exception, they met only small enemy patrols. Late in the afternoon of 10 June two mechanized companies returning to their base at Binh Phuoc came upon an occupied insurgent camp on a stream near the Vam Co Tay. As the companies maneuvered to encircle, the enemy scrambled aboard sampans and fled. Huey gunships pursued, pouring in rockets and gunfire, killing some 30 Viet Cong, and sinking 20 sampans. During the night, while Air Force Spooky gunships kept the battlefield illuminated, armor machine-gunned 10 Viet Cong trying to flee. The Americans detected no further movement and at daylight found the camp deserted.[9]

Over the next three months, as the Viet Cong became harder to find, the American battalions broke down into smaller units to conduct saturation

---

[6] Ibid., p. 23; Periodic Intel Rpt 16, IIFFV, 25 Apr 67, an. B, Historians files, CMH.

[7] RD Rpt, Long An Province, May 67, n.d., pp. 1–6; Periodic Intel Rpt 20, IIFFV, 23 May 67, p. 10; AAR, Opn ENTERPRISE, 3d Bde, 9th Inf Div, pp. 29–30; AAR, Opn KOLE KOLE, 2d Bde, 25th Inf Div, p. 8.

[8] RD Rpt, Long An Province, May 67, n.d., pp. 1–6.

[9] AAR, Opn ENTERPRISE, 3d Bde, 9th Inf Div, pp. 42–44.

A member of the 9th Infantry Division returns the fire of an enemy sniper during a Long An operation.

patrols and ambushes. Rainfall flooded the paddies, slowing movement by foot. To make matters worse, whenever units remained in the field for more than forty-eight hours, the men would suffer various nonbattle injuries, primarily "paddy foot," an infection caused by prolonged exposure to water. Weeks sometimes passed without a single firefight. When one did blaze up, the enemy usually started it, opening fire from concealed positions in tree lines, dikes, or hamlets, then often vanishing without a trace.

During July, August, and September artillery and gunship fire, along with air strikes, accounted for nearly half of the 185 Viet Cong claimed by the 3d Brigade in Long An Province, about 20 percent of the number slain during the previous three months. Whereas the brigade had obtained an impressive kill ratio of ten to one in the second quarter of 1967, that ratio dropped to less than five to one in the third quarter. The Viet Cong were becoming more adept at dealing with the Americans.[10]

In October the tempo of the war in Long An quickened as insurgent units equipped with new AK47s and RPG2s conducted harassing attacks against the government's "New Life" hamlets and attempted to cut Highway 4 and Route 5A. Although II Field Force intelligence had unconfirmed reports that the Viet Cong had upgraded several companies to small battalions, actual enemy strength in Long An was still unknown. Clearly, the insurgents had become more aggressive, yet rarely did they employ more than a platoon in any attack.

In addition to the high number of Viet Cong reported killed in 1967, the province recorded the largest number of ralliers of any province in III Corps. By the end of October intelligence analysts would continue to rate both the *2d Independent* and *506th Battalions* as "marginally effective" for combat and the *5th Battalion* in eastern Long An as "combat ineffective." But as elsewhere, such judgments were always open to question.[11]

---

[10] Ibid., pp. 29, 57–58.

[11] RD Rpts, Long An Province, Oct 67, n.d., pp. 1–6, and Dec 67, n.d., p. 1; Periodic Intel Rpt 44, IIFFV, 5 Nov 67, an. B. All in Historians files, CMH.

Perhaps the most revealing indicators were the Hamlet Evaluation System reports. Although they tended to be optimistic, HES data showed that in January 1967 only 23 percent of the people in Long An lived in areas rated secure and by November, only 32 percent. Of the province's estimated 377,000 people at the start of November, 92,500 lived in contested areas and 164,600 in the areas fully controlled by the insurgents—all in a region only fifteen kilometers from Saigon, virtually in the shadow of the allied center of power.[12]

Deeper Into the Delta

While the 3d Brigade chased Viet Cong shadows in Long An, General Eckhardt, the 9th Division commander, made plans to move the rest of his men farther into the delta. At Bearcat the 2d Brigade commander, Col. William B. Fulton, prepared his arriving men for their role as the Army component of the "Mekong Delta Mobile Afloat Force," later redesignated the "Mobile Riverine Force." In mid-February 1967 he sent the first of his units, the 3d Battalion, 47th Infantry, to the Rung Sat Special Zone south of Saigon for on-the-job training with the U.S. Navy.[13]

After becoming familiar with its new combat environment, the brigade moved to Dong Tam in Dinh Tuong Province, where American engineers were busy erecting a major new base south of Saigon. Situated at the confluence of the My Tho River and the Kinh Xang, a canal, the soggy marshland seemed an unlikely spot for a base. But in February dredges removed sand from the river bottom to create a landfill, and within a month the site was ready for partial occupation.[14]

Colonel Fulton's main focus was Dinh Tuong Province. Designated an operational priority area in the combined campaign plan, it was part of Saigon's lifeline to the delta. Highway 4 ran through the province from east to west, while enemy infiltration and supply routes ran not only east to west, but also north to south, connecting the northern delta with *COSVN* base areas in Cambodia. All of these lines of communication intersected in Dinh Tuong.

MACV intelligence estimated that 50 percent of Dinh Tuong's half-million inhabitants were under some sort of insurgent control. Analysts also knew that the province was the home of a long-established Viet Cong sanctuary, the 20/7 Heartland Zone, located west of Dong Tam between Highway 4 and the My Tho to the south. The zone was divided into two base

---

[12] HES Data Book, 1967, p. II–31.

[13] AAR, Opn RIVER RAIDER, 3d Bn, 47th Inf, 9th Inf Div, 31 Mar 67, pp. 12–14, Historians files, CMH; Fulton, *Riverine Operations*, pp. 60–63.

[14] ORLL, 1 Feb–30 Apr 67, 9th Inf Div, n.d., p. 10, Historians files, CMH; Westmoreland Jnl, 8 Oct 66, pp. 10–11, Westmoreland History files, 9–C, CMH; Msg, Westmoreland MAC 8211 to Sharp, 20 Sep 66, sub: U.S. Forces in the Delta, Westmoreland Message files, CMH; Westmoreland, *A Soldier Reports*, pp. 207–09; Fulton, *Riverine Operations*, pp. 55, 57.

Dong Tam, a few months after the 9th Division arrived

areas, the Cam Son Secret Zone in the west and the Ban Long Base Area in the east, separated by a meandering north-south stream, the Rach Tra Tan. Together, these bases provided an important source of manpower and supplies for *Military Region 2*, the Viet Cong headquarters responsible for the northern third of IV Corps and parts of III Corps. Through the 20/7 Heartland Zone passed the main corridor connecting *Military Region 3* in the southern part of the delta with *Military Regions 1* and *4* in III Corps.

The Viet Cong naturally viewed the new base at Dong Tam as a serious threat to the Heartland Zone, and *Military Region 2* hoped to overrun it before its defenses became too formidable. The first sign of the enemy's interest came on 7 March, when insurgents ambushed and nearly annihilated a 9th Division platoon patrolling outside the partially constructed installation. On the following night another enemy unit shelled the base with over eighty mortar rounds.[15]

But the Viet Cong never seriously threatened Dong Tam. By 10 March the 2d Brigade headquarters was at the new base, and by midmonth the 3d Battalion, 47th Infantry, had completed riverine training and had also moved there.

[15] David W. P. Elliot and W. A. Stewart, Pacification and the Viet Cong System in Dinh Tuong: 1966–1967, RAND Memo 5788, Jan 69, pp. 7–11; AAR, Opn NIGHT WALK, 3d Bn, 60th Inf, 9th Inf Div, 16 Mar 67; Periodic Intel Rpts 10, IIFFV, 14 Mar 67, pp. 2, 5, and an. B; 11, IIFFV, 21 Mar 67, an. B; and 21, IIFFV, 30 May 67, an. G. All in Historians files, CMH.

Late in April the South Vietnamese 7th Division commander, Brig. Gen. Nguyen Viet Thanh, told Fulton that the *514th Local Force Battalion* had moved into the Ap Bac Secret Zone, a base area north of Highway 4 that linked the Plain of Reeds with the 20/7 Heartland Zone. Nearly four and a half years earlier, that same Viet Cong battalion had humiliated a much larger South Vietnamese force at Ap Bac in a much publicized battle. Knowing that one of General Westmoreland's main reasons for sending American troops into the delta was "to set an example of tactical aggressiveness," Fulton decided to sweep the secret zone.[16]

Penetrating the target would prove difficult. The enemy's stronghold was a 100-square-kilometer area bounded by Highway 4 to the south and by the Kinh Xang to the east and north. Obstructions prevented river assault craft from using the canal, while a shortage of helicopters compelled Fulton to truck most of his troops to their start positions along Highway 4. On the morning of 2 May two battalion commands—the 3d Battalion, 47th Infantry, with three companies, and the 3d Battalion, 60th Infantry, with one company plus an attached company of mechanized infantry from the 5th Battalion, 60th Infantry—swept north toward the hamlet of Ap Bac 2 supported by 105-mm. howitzers from the 3d Battalion, 34th Artillery. A second company from the 3d Battalion, 60th Infantry, was scheduled to deploy by helicopter north of the hamlet as a blocking force, but just before the operation began Fulton learned that the assigned helicopters had been diverted for a tactical emergency elsewhere. (*Map 41*)

Unknown to Fulton, at least two companies of the *514th Battalion* lay in wait in an extensive bunker complex at Ap Bac 2 near the Suoi Sau, a steep-banked stream that ran roughly north to south through the center of the secret zone. As the men of the 47th Infantry approached Ap Bac 2, snipers opened fire. It was not enough to slow the advance, which continued until early afternoon when a squad that had crossed the Suoi Sau southwest of the hamlet was mowed down at point-blank range. Other Americans were killed and wounded trying to reach their fallen compatriots, and within a half-hour the enemy had pinned down the entire battalion south and east of the stream.

To the west, Fulton's other infantry battalion, the 3d of the 60th, had advanced without opposition. When Fulton heard that the 3d of the 47th was pinned down, he sent the 60th, reinforced now by the reserve company that it had initially left behind, to attack the hamlet from the west. One company would skirt north to seal off escape routes in that direction.

---

[16] Quote from Westmoreland, *A Soldier Reports*, p. 207. The following account of actions in the Ap Bac Secret Zone is based on AAR, Opn Hop Tac XVI, 2d Bde, 9th Inf Div, 16 Jun 67, and CHECO Rpt, Air Operations in the Delta, PACAF, 8 Dec 67, pp. 35–38, both in Historians files, CMH; Lt. Col. Edwin W. Chamberlain, Jr., "The Assault at Ap Bac," *Army* 18 (August 1968): 50–57; Interv, author with Lt Gen William B. Fulton, Comdr, 2d Bde, 9th Inf Div, and Asst Div Comdr, 9th Inf Div, 10, 22 Aug 79, Historians files, CMH; Fulton, *Riverine Operations*, pp. 77–79.

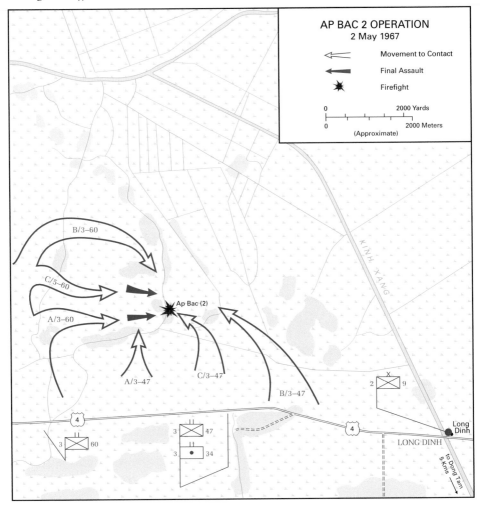

MAP 41

The Viet Cong saw the trap closing, and many tried to flee. An Air Force gunship circling overhead spotted the retreat and poured minigun fire on the Viet Cong (the crewmen would later estimate that they killed forty of the enemy, about half the number they saw). But most of the Viet Cong stood and fought, braving American artillery fire and air strikes throughout the day. After dark they would again try to escape.

Fulton knew this and tried hard to overrun the enemy before nightfall. But his mechanized forces needed time to find crossings over the canals and streams. Late in the afternoon they were ready, and the 60th Infantry attacked with tracked infantry from the north and the foot soldiers from the south.

Advancing behind an artillery smoke screen, the armored personnel carriers got within five hundred meters of Ap Bac 2 before they were stopped by recoilless rifle fire. As they slowed an American aircraft on a strafing run veered to avoid enemy antiaircraft fire and inadvertently sprayed the entire line of M113s with its 20-mm. miniguns, killing one soldier and wounding three others. Though stunned by the deadly accident, the mechanized company rallied and eleven armored personnel carriers swept forward with machine guns blazing, easily overrunning the dazed Viet Cong.

For the dismounted company farther south, which had no such supporting fire to keep enemy heads down, the going was slower. Plodding across paddies, the men were forced to hunker down at times until they regained fire superiority. As they neared the bunkers, four armored personnel carriers from the mechanized company joined them for the final thrust.

On the dismounted company's southern flank, one platoon executed a semi-independent mission, sweeping through underbrush alongside the Suoi Sau to the site where the squad had been ambushed earlier. Pausing only to remove ammunition from the American dead, the platoon pressed on and, with the help of flanking fire from a company deployed on the other side of the stream, cleared the southern defenses of the hamlet. Following the assault, the few remaining Viet Cong panicked and fled, only to be cut down. At twilight, the bone-tired Americans formed perimeters and the next day counted nearly 200 Viet Cong bodies. American losses were 15 dead and 27 wounded, most having occurred during the first half-hour of the fight.[17]

The Start of Riverine Operations

On 13 May the 4th Battalion of the 47th Infantry, which had completed its training in the Rung Sat, joined the 47th's 3d Battalion and the 3d Battalion, 60th Infantry, at Dong Tam. Already at the base were riverine elements of the U.S. Navy's River Assault Flotilla One (Task Force 117) with twenty-two recently reconfigured landing craft, mechanized (LCM)–6s, each capable of transporting up to forty infantrymen. The craft could operate in waters as shallow as a meter and could travel at a speed of about fifteen kilometers per hour. Above the deck of the armored troop carriers were three armor-plated turrets, one containing a 40-mm. cannon, each of the others a .50-caliber machine gun. Other armament consisted of four 7.62-mm. machine guns and two 40-mm. hand-cranked grenade launchers capable of firing 200 grenades per minute. For added protection above the waterline, the craft had bar-armor welded to their hulls. Two additional LCM–6s had been modified to serve as command and control

---

[17] AAR, Opn Hop Tac XVI, 2d Bde, 9th Inf Div, pp. 7–8; Fulton, *Riverine Operations*, pp. 80–81; AAR, Opn Palm Beach II–Coronado, 2d Bde, 9th Inf Div, 15 Aug 67, pp. 12–13; Sitreps 123–67, MACV, 2 May 67, and 124–67, MACV, 3 May 67. All in Historians files, CMH.

Vessels of the Mobile Riverine Force move in formation toward their objective.

ships, each capable of transporting an eleven-man command post, and two others served as fire support ships, called monitors, each equipped with an 81-mm. mortar.

With his full brigade now assembled at Dong Tam and with enough river transport to move almost two battalions, Fulton wanted to begin a sustained campaign against the 20/7 Heartland Zone. Highway 4 in the north and the My Tho in the south would serve as approach avenues and boundaries for the effort. His initial target was the western portion of the base area, the Cam Son Secret Zone. Intelligence identified remnants of the *514th Local Force Battalion* and possibly the *263d Main Force Battalion* as having recently moved there. Fulton wanted five companies from the 3d and 4th of the 47th Infantry to board river craft at Dong Tam and to move west on the My Tho to beaches along the zone's southern bank between two tributary streams, the Ba Rai and Tra Tan. Upon landing the troops were to sweep north, while elements of the South Vietnamese 7th Division held blocking positions along Route 212, an unimproved dirt road paralleling the My Tho four kilometers to the north. Company A of the 4th of the 47th at Dong Tam was to serve as a heliborne reaction force.

On 14 May, the day before the operation began, tugboats towed six artillery barges, each mounting two lightweight M102 105-mm. howitzers, along the My Tho to an island directly south of the brigade's objective. Moored to the riverbank and protected by troops drawn from the 3d Battalion, 60th Infantry, the platforms would provide close fire support for the operation.

With infantrymen aboard, the river assault craft pushed off shortly after daybreak on 15 May and soon put the men ashore unopposed, the 3d Battalion on the left, the 4th on the right. Throughout the morning the

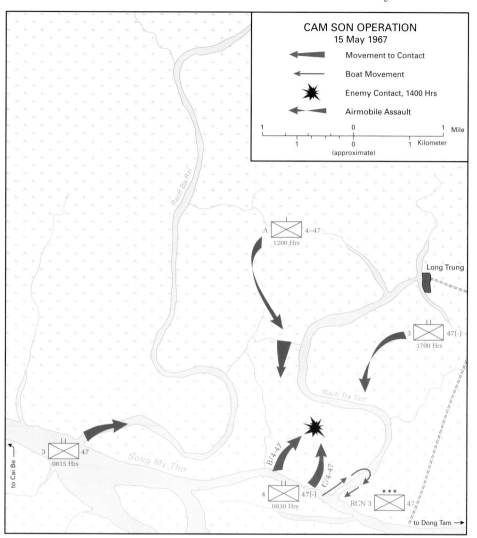

MAP 42

troops advanced northward over terrain similar to that of the Ap Bac Secret Zone but failed to find any sign of the enemy. Hoping to stir some reaction, at noon Fulton loaded his reserve company aboard helicopters and leapfrogged it to a spot ahead of the rest of the 4th Battalion, near a bend in the Tra Tan, where the company set up a blocking position.

To the south, one of the companies advancing overland ran into fire from a Viet Cong unit. Seeing their compatriots bog down, the blocking troops moved forward, striking the enemy from the rear. Surprised by the unexpected attack, the Viet Cong fled toward the Tra Tan, only to find themselves trapped in a loop of the river. (*Map 42*) Fulton called for

407

artillery fire and air strikes to hold the enemy soldiers in place, then sent a reconnaissance platoon aboard a landing craft up the Tra Tan to work in behind the Viet Cong. But the insurgents were far from helpless. They used machine guns to keep the boats at a distance; then the dropping tide forced the craft to pull back.

Since Fulton's 3d Battalion to the west had yet to make contact, he decided to airlift it into a blocking position on the far bank of the Tra Tan, but a rain squall delayed the move. As darkness fell, only one company was in position. Calling off the air movement for the rest of the battalion, Fulton kept the area illuminated throughout the night and continued to fire artillery and put in air strikes until first light.

At daybreak the Americans advanced. In the loop of the river, they found a large bunker complex and over 100 enemy dead. A prisoner revealed that he was from the *514th Battalion*, but the *263d Main Force Battalion* had not been involved in the fighting. Sweeps beyond the area during the day netted two defectors and twenty-nine males of military age who were turned over to the district chief for questioning. For the entire operation, American losses were 1 man killed and 25 wounded.[18] However, a similar operation on 18–19 May against Base Area 470 in western Dinh Tuong some thirty-six kilometers inland from the My Tho turned out to be a "dry hole," perhaps because it took so long to shuttle troops by helicopter from the beaches to the target area.[19]

Results

The 9th Division's operations in the delta, collectively code-named PALM BEACH, killed 570 enemy soldiers—11 for every fallen American. The division had seriously mauled the *514th Local Force Battalion*, forcing *Military Region 2* to dispatch the *263d Main Force Battalion* into the 20/7 Heartland Zone as a replacement.[20] Yet, in the broader scheme of things, the American war in the northern delta had only begun.

Elsewhere in IV Corps, combat was more intense during 1967.[21] In the central delta, a priority area for pacification, the pace of combat quickened for the South Vietnamese 9th Division as increased government efforts to gain control of contested and Viet Cong–held areas in Vinh Long Province produced strong enemy reactions. One pacification project in particular, the reopening of the Mang Thit River–Nicola Canal to provide

---

[18] AAR, Opn PALM BEACH II–CORONADO, 2d Bde, 9th Inf Div, p. 8; Fulton, *Riverine Operations*, pp. 81–83; Periodic Intel Rpt 21, IIFFV, 30 May 67, an. B; Interv, author with Fulton, 10, 22 Aug 79.

[19] AAR, Opn PALM BEACH II–CORONADO, 2d Bde, 9th Inf Div, pp. 9–13.

[20] MACV History 1967, vol. 3, p. 1248; AAR, Opn PALM BEACH II–CORONADO, 2d Bde, 9th Inf Div, p. 3.

[21] The following overview is based on Desobry Debriefing, pp. 3–5, and Harvey Meyerson, *Vinh Long* (Boston: Houghton Mifflin Co., 1970), pp. 8–66.

a direct water route for shipping rice to Saigon, was the cause of a violent three-day fight in March. Although the South Vietnamese 9th Division reported routing two enemy battalions and killing nearly 150 Viet Cong, control of the waterways remained in doubt. Despite assurances by government officials that the water route was safe, merchants were reluctant to use it because of Viet Cong threats to anyone using the route for commercial purposes. When the enemy demonstrated his strength by destroying one of the platoon-size outposts on the Mang Thit in early May, it was clear that he was alive and well in central IV Corps.

In the lower delta, the South Vietnamese 21st Division had won a series of fights in January and February 1967 against the *D2 PLAF Regiment*, a unit under *Military Region 3*, in Chuong Thien, a province virtually under Communist control. The division not only inflicted major casualties on the regiment but also bloodied a provincial local force battalion dispatched by *Military Region 3* to assist. Nevertheless, much of the lower delta remained an enemy preserve at the start of the wet season in May.

If American and South Vietnamese forces in the delta had taken the initiative in the winter and spring, the question remained whether they could continue to hold it when the rains began. In May the weather would turn from dry to wet, forcing a change in the way both sides fought. During the rainy season the Viet Cong would become more mobile, better able to use sampans on swollen streams and canals to move men and supplies. South Vietnamese forces, on the other hand, would be seriously hampered by the change in weather. Low clouds and frequent downpours limited helicopter and fixed-wing support, forcing them to move on the ground. And once on foot the South Vietnamese would be at a disadvantage, for they did not know the terrain as well as did the more lightly equipped insurgents. Yet for the American riverine force the wet season would promise greater mobility, allowing for deeper penetration into enemy base areas that once had been inaccessible.

The Riverine Balance Sheet

By June 1967 the growing American riverine base at Dong Tam occupied twelve square kilometers. In addition to the cantonment and storage facilities for the 9th Division's 2d Brigade, the installation had a 500-meter airstrip and a two-square-kilometer turning basin for shipping, with boat and barge landing sites. Located ninety kilometers from Bearcat, the division's main base camp in III Corps, Dong Tam received most of its supplies directly from the port of Vung Tau.

On 1 June the Mobile Riverine Force was officially activated with the arrival at Dong Tam of its full naval complement. Subsequently, Colonel Fulton placed his brigade headquarters, the 3d and 4th Battalions, 47th Infantry, and supporting units aboard ship, leaving only rear-area detachments and the 3d Battalion, 60th Infantry, ashore. Those units at Dong Tam were responsible for the operation and security of the base under the direct control of the 9th Division commander, General O'Connor.[1] (*Map 43*)

Capt. Wade C. Wells, U.S. Navy, commanded Task Force 117, the Navy component of the Mobile Riverine Force. His flotilla consisted of River Assault Squadrons Nine and Eleven and River Support Squadron Seven. Each assault squadron contained twenty-six assault troop carriers, three command and control boats, five "monitor" fire support ships, and a refueler. All were reconfigured LCM–6s. Shortly after the Mobile Riverine Force became operational, small flight decks for helicopters were added to the command and control boats, and two assault troop carriers were modified to serve as medical aid stations for each battalion. Later, between September and November, each squadron was strengthened

---

[1] AAR, Opn Palm Beach II–Coronado, 2d Bde, 9th Inf Div, p. 13; Rpt, 4th Bn, 47th Inf, 9th Inf Div, 2 Aug 67, Combat Operations After Action Report, 1 Jul–2 Aug 67, pp. 1–23, Historians files, CMH.

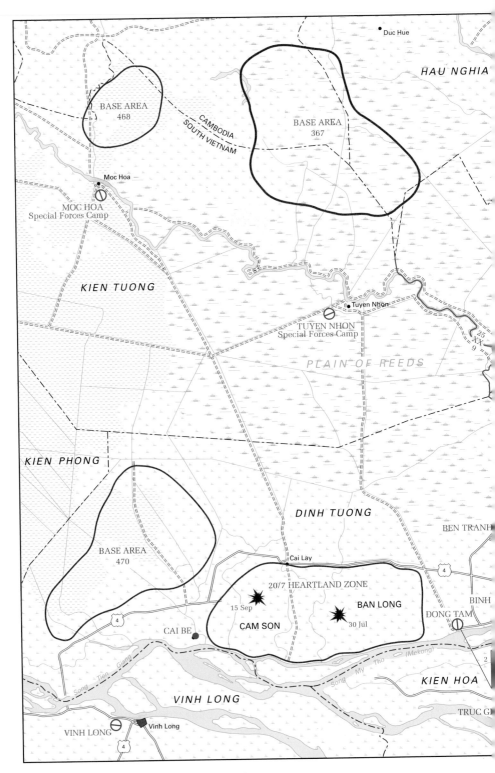

MAP 43

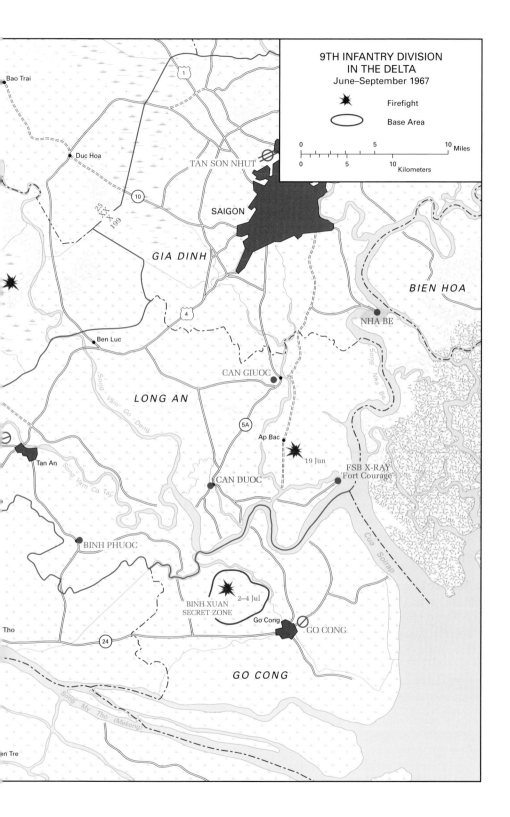

Bao Trai

Duc Hoa

TAN SON NHUT

SAIGON

GIA DINH

BIEN HOA

NHA BE

Ben Luc

CAN GIUOC

LONG AN

5A

Ap Bac

19 Jun

FSB X-RAY
'Fort Courage'

Tan An

CAN DUOC

BINH PHUOC

BINH XUAN
SECRET ZONE

2–4 Jul

Go Cong

GO CONG

Tho

24

GO CONG

n Tre

Song My Tho (Mekong)

Song Vam Co Dong

Song Vam Co Tay

Song Nha Be

Cua Soirap

1

10

4

25
XXX
199

with sixteen assault support patrol boats, lighter and faster craft built for use in South Vietnam as minesweepers and escorts. Until then, LCM–6s equipped with drag chains performed minesweeping chores for the flotilla.

River Support Squadron Seven consisted of four modified LSTs, a large barge, and two harbor tugboats. One LST, the USS *Benewah*, served as the flotilla flagship and carried the brigade headquarters, the supporting artillery troops, and a security detachment that normally operated on shore. The second landing ship, the USS *Colleton*, had quarters for an infantry battalion. The barge, APL–26, an auxiliary personnel lighter that the Navy normally used to house crews whose ships were being overhauled, carried quarters for the other battalion. The two remaining LSTs provided logistical support, one as a maintenance and repair ship, the other as a floating warehouse. Rotating weekly with the warehouse ship was another LST from the Mobile Riverine Force's supply base at Vung Tau.[2]

The security units aboard the *Benewah* had been created by reorganizing Fulton's brigade and battalion headquarters. Spaces not needed for riverine fighting, such as drivers and mechanics, were converted to combat positions, thereby providing an additional two platoons of men for each rifle battalion. Adding them to a battalion's combat support company created, in effect, a fourth rifle company. The new organizations, called reconnaissance and security companies, served as shore security forces for the main anchorage and for any associated command posts or firebases, thereby freeing the three assigned rifle companies of each battalion for combat operations.[3]

Compared to conditions in the field, life aboard the barracks ship was comfortable. Returning from the rigors of combat in the hot, humid delta, the troops looked forward to clean water, hot showers, and a change of uniforms, amenities that improved morale and guarded against skin infections. After cleaning and oiling their weapons and ammunition—often corroded from exposure to water—the men ate well-prepared meals and retired below deck to air-conditioned quarters with snack shops, movies, and other luxuries.[4]

As might be expected in a multiservice task force, command arrangements provoked much discussion. General Westmoreland first suggested that the Mobile Riverine Force be commanded by an assistant division commander of the 9th Division, a general officer, who would have a small Army-Navy staff to plan operations. The Navy objected. Viewing riverine and amphibious operations as one and the same, Navy officials pointed out that Joint Staff doctrine specified that command of an amphibious

---

[2] MFR, 12 Oct 67, sub: MACV Commanders' Conference, 24 September 1967, Incls 7, 8, Westmoreland History files, 22–12, CMH; MACV History 1968, vol. 1, p. 466, CMH. See also MACV History 1967, vol. 1, pp. 520–25.

[3] AAR, Opn PALM BEACH II–CORONADO, 2d Bde, 9th Inf Div, pp. 14–17; MFR, 12 Oct 67, sub: MACV Commanders' Conference, 24 September 1967, Incls 7, 8; Fulton, *Riverine Operations*, p. 76.

[4] Intervs, author with Fulton, 10 and 22 Aug 79.

USS Benewah

operation belonged to the Navy until the troops were ashore, at which time command passed to the ground commander.

Rather than risk losing Navy support, Westmoreland agreed not to have an overall commander. Instead, the force would conduct operations on the basis of coordination and cooperation. The senior Army commander had the responsibility for all Army and Navy riverine bases ashore and afloat. When the force weighed anchor, the senior Navy commander assumed control during the move until the element dropped anchor at a new location.

A similar arrangement governed combat. As soon as troops boarded landing craft, they came under the control of the Navy commander. Once the troops had landed, the Army commander regained control of his men while the Navy provided him with close support. Upon reembarking, the men reverted to Navy control until they arrived at a base, whether ashore or afloat.

Each commander had his own staff. Both staffs worked separately, but they were enjoined to produce plans acceptable to both commanders. If an impasse developed, Wells could appeal to the commander, U.S. Naval Forces, Vietnam, while on the Army side the issue would pass through 9th Division headquarters to II Field Force. If II Field Force and the commander, U.S. Naval Forces, Vietnam, were unable to reach an agreement, they would present the issue to General Westmoreland for final resolution. Wells and Fulton consistently ironed out their differences, however, and never had to resort to this procedure.[5]

The only real source of friction between them revolved around the role of the division commander, General O'Connor. Wells disliked the fact that O'Connor regularly assigned missions to the Mobile Riverine Force and wanted Fulton's infantry brigade divorced from the division. He believed that the force would work best as a separate organization reporting directly to the commander, U.S. Naval Forces, Vietnam. But with the 9th Division playing a major role in holding the outer ring around Saigon, Westmoreland insisted that the 2d Brigade remain under division control. This would make it readily available for use immediately south of the capital, particularly in Long An Province and the Rung Sat, areas of first priority for the 9th Division.[6]

CORONADO Operations Begin

After an initial shakedown around Dong Tam and in the Rung Sat in early June, the Mobile Riverine Force established an anchorage where the Soirap, Vam Co, and Rach Cat Rivers joined between the Rung Sat and Can Giuoc, the easternmost district of Long An Province. Just off the anchorage to the west stood an abandoned French fort, "Fort Courage" to the Americans, where Colonel Fulton established Firebase X-RAY. From there the force launched a series of operations code-named CORONADO.

Located over fifty kilometers northeast of Dong Tam, but only ten kilometers south of Saigon's city limits, Can Giuoc's waterways made it ideal for riverine warfare. Because few bridges still existed, the difficulty of overland travel left the area somewhat isolated. Although local government troops in the district outnumbered Communist forces three to one, they had done little more than defend their compounds. Since government officials seemed mainly concerned with personal gain, many of the district's 60,000 people followed a policy of noninvolvement or sided with the revolutionaries.[7]

The riverine force's general objective was a large enemy redoubt that began about two kilometers south of the district capital, also named Can Giuoc, and continued south for about eight kilometers to the Rach Cat. Reportedly, the base area provided local force units with rest and training camps.[8] (*Map 44*)

[5] Ibid.; Planning Directive 6–67, MACV, 20 Jun 67, sub: Command Relationships for Riverine Operations in SVN, Historians files, CMH.

[6] MACV History 1968, vol. 1, p. 466; Fulton, *Riverine Operations*, pp. 87–88; Intervs, author with Fulton, 10 and 22 Aug 79.

[7] RD Rpt, Long An Province, May 67, n.d., pp. 1–7; Operation Order (OPORD) 14–67, Opn CORONADO, HQ, Mobile Riverine Force (MRF), 26 Jun 67, an. A, Historians files, CMH.

[8] OPORD 12–67, Opn CORONADO, HQ, MRF, 21 Jun 67, Historians files, CMH; AAR, Opn PALM BEACH II–CORONADO, 2d Bde, 9th Inf Div, p. 18.

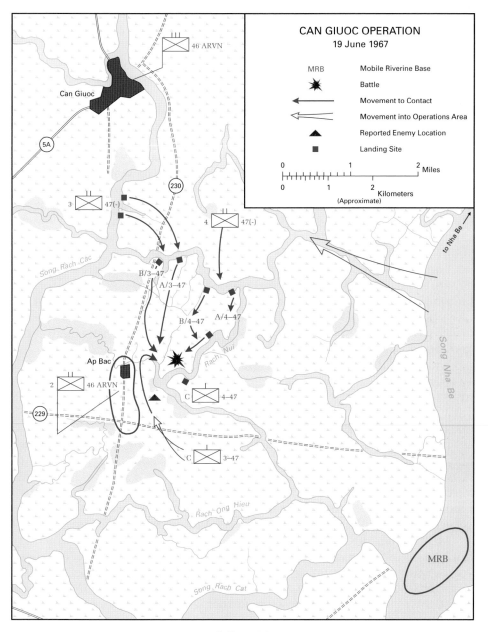

CAN GIUOC OPERATION
19 June 1967

MRB   Mobile Riverine Base

Battle

Movement to Contact

Movement into Operations Area

Reported Enemy Location

Landing Site

0   1   2 Miles

0   1   2 Kilometers
(Approximate)

MAP 44

On 18 June, the evening before the operation was to begin, nearly eighty LCM–6s and barges clustered offshore around the main ships of the flotilla. Blackout conditions prevailed, and the night was moonless. An hour before dawn the floating base came to life as troops began forming on barges moored to the barracks ships and then transferred to the

417

adjacent landing craft, a procedure that despite the darkness took a rifle company only twenty minutes to complete, a battalion, an hour. While the boarding took place, minesweepers, monitors, and command and control boats rendezvoused at two designated points to await the arrival of the troop carriers. When they arrived, the flotilla set out, minesweepers in the lead, toward the beaches.

Fulton planned for the 4th Battalion of the 47th Infantry to land north and east of the objective, while two companies of the 3d of the 47th debarked north and west of the target. After sweeping the northern portion of the base area, the two battalions were to assemble along an east-west stream that bisected the redoubt, ferry across the waterway, and continue southward. A South Vietnamese battalion would protect the brigade's west flank along Route 230, while river assault craft guarded the eastern flank on the Rach Nui. The 3d Battalion's remaining element, Company C, was to deploy by helicopter as a blocking force between the South Vietnamese and the Rach Nui.

Landing without opposition, the troops had assembled and had begun to sweep their assigned sectors when the district chief informed Fulton that a Viet Cong battalion occupied the southeastern section of the redoubt. Just three months earlier the 199th Brigade had mounted an airmobile operation in the same area in response to similar information but had found little.

Unwilling to abandon his original plan, Fulton decided to continue sweeping south. But, just in case they might be able to catch the Viet Cong unaware, he ordered his 4th Battalion commander, Lt. Col. Guy I. Tutwiler, to hit the reported enemy location, assisted by the brigade's reaction force, Company C from the 3d Battalion.

Helicopters shuttled the reaction force just south of the suspected hotspot, landing the soldiers about an hour before noon. At the same time Tutwiler's own Company C moved down the Rach Nui, going ashore north of the objective. With this company and the South Vietnamese battalion to the west taking up blocking positions, the reaction force converged on the suspected stronghold but found no trace of the enemy.

Meanwhile, the remainder of the 2d Brigade prepared to launch the final phase of the operation. First to move was Company A of Tutwiler's 4th Battalion. After traveling a short distance south on the Rach Nui, the men debarked on the west bank, intending to link up with their sister unit, Company C, still several kilometers farther south. But rather than trying to hack through the vegetation along the bank, the Company A commander headed south over the open paddies with his three platoons abreast. Worn down after several hours of plodding through foot-deep water and viscous mud, the men let down their guard and bunched together.

Unknown to the struggling soldiers, the *5th Battalion*, a local force unit from *Military Region 4's* Gia Dinh Province, lay in wait in a fortified position between Tutwiler's Companies A and C. Although local force battalions seldom crossed provincial and almost never crossed regional boundaries, the *5th Battalion* had been driven from Gia Dinh by the 199th Brigade and was in the process of rebuilding deep within Can Giuoc District. Tutwiler's Company C had actually passed the enemy earlier that morning, but the Viet Cong had remained hidden. Now, as Company A approached, enemy soldiers established an L-shaped ambush facing away from the stream, in the elbow of which was a cluster of thatched huts.

When the men of Company A neared the huts shortly before noon, the insurgents opened up and caught them in a deadly cross fire. Pinned to the ground, the company took heavy casualties. While artillery fire and gunships kept the Americans from being overrun, Fulton ordered the rest of the 2d Brigade to reinforce.

Execution proved difficult, however, especially for Company C of the 3d Battalion, which found a ten-meter-wide stream barring the path to its blocking position on the west. Although some soldiers found a ford, most swam across, while "requisitioned" sampans transported the nonswimmers and equipment.[9] Meanwhile, Tutwiler's Company B came up behind the embattled Company A to assist in evacuating the more seriously wounded. Heavy fire and lack of cover made the task costly. Before nightfall four medevac helicopters had been shot down.

To lessen the pressure, Tutwiler's Company C, by then southeast of the stronghold, attacked in midafternoon. It punched through the enemy's outer defenses, but with twenty men dead or wounded during the assault, it was forced to back off. When the remainder of the 4th Battalion arrived, Company C joined a two-company attack but again failed to carry the Viet Cong position. Company C made yet a third attempt after nightfall. Once again the attackers penetrated the complex, but pulled back exhausted and disoriented.

As darkness fell the 2d Brigade had troops on three sides of the enemy. Yet gaps still existed between Fulton's scattered units, and the Rach Nui, while unfordable, was left unguarded. By morning the enemy had gone. Navy patrols on the Rach Nui during the night might have prevented the escape, but the local Navy commander had pulled his boats back before nightfall. When Captain Wells learned of the withdrawal the next day, he assured Colonel Fulton that it would never happen again.[10]

During the early evening II Field Force headquarters, presumably at MACV's urging, had pressed for a body count. Although Fulton had lost 50 men killed and 150 wounded, he informed General O'Connor that he could not produce meaningful numbers, especially at night, as long as the fight continued. Undeterred, division headquarters informed II Field Force that 256 enemy bodies had been found and 50 weapons captured. However, an actual body count on the following day produced only 70 enemy dead and fewer than 10 weapons. Apparently, division headquar-

[9] AAR, Opn PALM BEACH II–CORONADO, 2d Bde, 9th Inf Div, p. 18; Intervs, author with Fulton, 10 and 22 Aug 79; Fulton, *Riverine Operations*, pp. 104–08.

[10] AAR, Opn PALM BEACH II–CORONADO, 2d Bde, 9th Inf Div, pp. 18–19; Intervs, author with Fulton, 10 and 22 Aug 79.

ters had created the spurious statistics out of concern that MACV might relieve Fulton if it believed that there had not been adequate compensation for the heavy U.S. losses. Captured documents and prisoners later revealed that the 2d Brigade had killed 170 Viet Cong, including the commander of the *5th Battalion*, in the fight on 19 June. The 9th Division's imaginary body count may not have been far off the mark after all.[11]

After Can Giuoc, the 9th Division assigned Fulton and Wells their next objective, the Binh Xuan Secret Zone. Located in north-central Go Cong Province, immediately south of their previous target, the Binh Xuan served as a replacement and training center for the *514th PLAF Battalion*, a local force unit. South Vietnamese forces had not entered the area since November 1966, and the Americans believed that an accommodation existed between government officials and the insurgents. Nevertheless, the extensive waterways in the redoubt and its close proximity to the capital made it a logical target for the riverine soldiers and sailors.

On the night of 3 July a territorial forces battalion took up blocking positions along the southwestern edge of the base area, a sector inaccessible to river assault craft. The next morning riverine forces established a series of platoon- and company-size patrol bases along two rivers that bordered the remainder of the enemy stronghold. Having sealed the objective, Colonel Fulton saturated it with eagle flights. Throughout the day company-size infantry units shuttled in and out of likely enemy haunts. Fulton also used a riverine variation, the "eagle float," which employed river craft rather than helicopters to insert and extract the infantry. At night the Americans established ambushes along the rivers, while boats patrolled between the ambush sites.

During the three-day operation the riverine force, without taking a single casualty, killed or captured over 100 Viet Cong, searched more than 700 sampans, and detained several hundred civilians for questioning by government officials. The Binh Xuan, it turned out, was more than an enemy base; it was also a haven for South Vietnamese draft dodgers and deserters, more than 100 of whom South Vietnamese officials apprehended. According to Fulton, most were sent to I Corps as their punishment.[12]

Returning to Can Giuoc District in Long An Province, the Mobile Riverine Force and several South Vietnamese units conducted a number of smaller operations that resulted in the seizure of arms and munitions caches. By 25 July the American–South Vietnamese effort had resulted in 250 enemy dead and 100 captured.[13] More significantly, the Americans had established a presence in areas once off limits to the government.

---

[11] ORLL, 1 May–31 Jul 67, 9th Inf Div, pp. 18, 29; Periodic Intel Rpt 25, IIFFV, 27 Jun 67, pp. 3, 6–7, and an. B; Sitrep 170–67, MACV, 18 Jun 67, Historians files, CMH; Periodic Intel Rpt 28, IIFFV, 18 Jul 67, pp. 2, 6; Intervs, author with Fulton, 10 and 22 Aug 79.

[12] OPORD 16–67, Opn CORONADO, HQ, MRF, 2 Jul 67, an. A, and RD Rpt, Go Cong Province, Jul 67, n.d., pp. 1–6, both in Historians files, CMH; AAR, Opn PALM BEACH II–CORONADO, 2d Bde, 9th Inf Div, pp. 22–23; Intervs, author with Fulton, 10 and 22 Aug 79.

[13] AAR, Opn PALM BEACH II–CORONADO, 2d Bde, 9th Inf Div, pp. 23–28.

Coronado II

In the meantime, intelligence officers had detected a major enemy buildup in Dinh Tuong Province. According to a captured directive from *Military Region 2*, the region's four main force battalions had been ordered to prepare for a coordinated monsoon season offensive to begin on 29 June. Although nothing unusual had taken place by early July, on the twelfth the *261st Main Force Battalion* left Kien Hoa Province moving north and crossed the My Tho west of Dong Tam, apparently to join the *263d Main Force Battalion* and the partially rebuilt *514th Local Force Battalion* hiding in the 20/7 Heartland Zone. About the same time the *267th Main Force Battalion* entered the Plain of Reeds to the north, a day's march away. Beginning in mid-July and for an entire week, enemy forces cut Highway 4, the lifeline between the delta and Saigon, at eleven separate points north of the Heartland Zone, halting traffic for periods of up to twenty-four hours. In addition, mortar fire struck Dong Tam on the nights of 22 and 23 July, and the second attack severely damaged the base hospital.[14]

General Westmoreland, believing that the enemy in the delta had yet to experience "the firepower, mobility, and flexibility of U.S. Forces and [did] not appreciate the threat this posed to his massed formations," decided to strike hard at the Viet Cong.[15] He assembled a formidable armada: not just the Mobile Riverine Force, but a second brigade of the 9th Division, brigade elements of the 25th Division, several South Vietnamese army and marine battalions, and three U.S. helicopter battalions.

The plan for Coronado II was simple. The riverine force would sweep from the south into the Cam Son Base Area, the western part of the Heartland Zone, while the mechanized 5th Battalion, 60th Infantry (detailed from the 3d Brigade, 9th Division), and the South Vietnamese 44th Ranger Battalion assumed blocking positions to the north. Once the Cam Son had been cleared, the riverine force would enter the Ban Long redoubt in the eastern part of the zone. A South Vietnamese marine brigade and the 1st Brigade, 25th Division, stood by to reinforce.

At dawn on 28 July the two battalions of the 47th Infantry went ashore at five beaches in the southern Cam Son and swept north toward blocking positions established during the morning. That afternoon the South Vietnamese marine brigade and the command post and supporting artillery of the 1st Brigade, 25th Division, arrived at Dong Tam. Yet, as night fell, there was little sign of the enemy, with the troops receiving only sporadic sniper fire. The operation's first kills, five Viet Cong, were made by gunships, not in the Cam Son but to the east in the Ban Long.

---

[14] OPORD 23–67, Opn Coronado, HQ, MRF, 27 Jul 67, an. A, Historians files, CMH; Periodic Intel Rpt 21, IIFFV, 30 May 67, p. 2; RD Rpt, Dinh Tuong Province, Jul 67, n.d., pp. 1–7; Msg, COMUSMACV 25690 to CJCS, 3 Aug 67, sub: Operation Coronado II Command Report, both in Historians files, CMH.

[15] Msg, CG, IIFFV, 70658 to COMUSMACV, 27 Jul 67, sub: Visit by COMUSMACV, 26 Jul 67, Westmoreland History files, 19–16, CMH.

Riverine soldiers fire 105-mm. artillery from well-anchored barges.

Operations the next day were almost as frustrating. Although Fulton's 3d Battalion bumped into small groups of Viet Cong, the enemy eluded the pursuers, whether they were on foot, in helicopters, or aboard river craft. When sharp fights erupted, first on the Ba Rai and then later about a kilometer east of the river, Fulton sent his 4th Battalion and the 5th of the 60th Infantry to encircle. Arriving shortly before dark, they found little.

General O'Connor concluded that the enemy was withdrawing eastward from the Cam Son toward new positions in the Ban Long. That evening the South Vietnamese marine commander, Col. Bui Yho Lan, volunteered to send his brigade after the main enemy force. Since American gunships had killed Viet Cong in the central Ban Long, that seemed the best place to start, and Lan proposed putting his battalions there.

O'Connor agreed, and the search of the Ban Long began the next day, 30 July. At first light helicopters began landing South Vietnamese marines just south of the Tra Tan, another northern tributary of the My Tho that actually curved around to bisect the Ban Long from east to west. Almost immediately the marines took heavy fire from a wooded area along the watercourse. Although the South Vietnamese counterattacked, they were unable to carry the position, despite five hours of intense fighting.

As O'Connor saw it, the enemy was in a bad spot: on two sides were wide expanses of flooded paddy, and downstream was the South Vietnamese ranger battalion reinforced by a mechanized cavalry troop.

The only withdrawal route left to the Viet Cong was upstream to the east. O'Connor asked that two battalions of the 1st Brigade, 25th Division, be airlifted from Hau Nghia Province to Dong Tam and then into blocking positions.

He also decided to remove both 47th Infantry battalions from the operation temporarily, because so many of their men had developed serious cases of paddy foot. He sent the 3d Battalion to a floating blocking position near the mouth of the Tra Tan with the stipulation that the troops remain aboard their river craft throughout the night; he returned the 4th Battalion to its barracks ship off Dong Tam. But he wanted both battalions ready for action the next morning, depending on what the South Vietnamese and the 25th Division found.

Back in the Ban Long, the Viet Cong held fast into late afternoon. With the arrival of the two battalions of the 25th Division, the principal withdrawal route appeared blocked. When O'Connor suggested to Colonel Lan that he disengage his marines and form a perimeter for the night, the South Vietnamese commander said he had other plans. The enemy expected him to dig in for the night, he said, so with assurances that the Americans would keep the battlefield illuminated, Lan ordered an attack to begin an hour after dark. Although the assault failed and resulted in heavy South Vietnamese casualties, it did hold the Viet Cong in place overnight and forced them to expend scarce ammunition.

Later, prisoner interrogations revealed that the enemy situation was indeed desperate. As a last resort, the Viet Cong commander had ordered a counterattack just before dawn. If the assault succeeded, the men were to take ammunition from the South Vietnamese marines and fight their way out; if not, they were to hide their weapons, head south in small groups, and conceal themselves among the people living along the My Tho. Later, sampans would take them across the river to reassemble in Kien Hoa Province.

The enemy assault began at 0430. Although both sides took heavy losses, the attack failed to dislodge the marines. Soon after daybreak South Vietnamese rangers to the west captured a few enemy soldiers trying to escape, while gunships began to report small groups of unarmed men moving away from the scene of the fighting and heading south toward the My Tho. They had adopted their commander's second option. The commander himself was unable to join them: South Vietnamese marines found his body near their position on the morning of 31 July.

O'Connor gave Fulton the job of organizing a pursuit. To prevent the Viet Cong from crossing the My Tho, Fulton arranged for all the riverine force's uncommitted assault craft, reinforced by GAME WARDEN boats diverted from patrolling the inland waterways, to blockade the river from its juncture with the Tra Tan east to Dong Tam. He sent the 5th Battalion, 60th Infantry, to reinforce the South Vietnamese ranger battalion, which was feeling some pressure from enemy troops trying to flee west. Simultaneously, he placed his own two battalions of the 47th Infantry just east of the juncture of the Tra Tan and My Tho with instructions to sweep east, while airlifting another 3d Brigade battalion, the 3d of the 39th Infantry, to the opposite end of the battle area with orders to sweep west. At that point, the three battalions would form a horseshoe-shaped cordon, with the open end along the My Tho and the village of Ap Binh Thoi in the center.

By late afternoon, with the cordon in place, Fulton sent troops into Ap Binh Thoi to assist South Vietnamese police in screening suspects. Of more than four hundred detained, eighty-three admitted being from the *263d Main Force Battalion.*

Although the operation ended the next day for the Mobile Riverine Force, mop-up actions continued until 4 August. The South Vietnamese 7th Division completed seven separate sweeps north of Highway 4, reporting 234 Viet Cong dead, some from the *261st Main Force Battalion.* South of the road in the 20/7 Heartland Zone, the Americans and South Vietnamese claimed to have killed over 200 of the enemy, the majority credited to the South Vietnamese marines. Throughout the operation the marines took the heaviest casualties, 44 killed and 115 wounded, most of them in night combat. American losses were 10 killed and 65 wounded during the five days in the field, but nonbattle losses were much higher. Over 50 percent of the 3d Battalion and 40 percent of the 4th Battalion, 47th Infantry, were incapacitated by various skin infections, most hospitalized for three to seven days and some for as long as fourteen. One company of the 3d Battalion, in the field for six consecutive days, had two-thirds of its men incapacitated.[16]

During 1967 the dry season in the delta had been unusually long, extending into July. Until then, commanders had kept skin problems within manageable limits by alternating two to three days in the field with at least a full day to recuperate and dry out. Forced to stay longer because of the action during CORONADO II, many more soldiers now fell prey to various skin infections, 90 percent of which doctors diagnosed as paddy foot. Treatment consisted mainly of bed rest and medicines for pain and fever. But, like frostbite and trench foot, once a soldier contracted the infection, he became very susceptible to recurrence.

The Americans seemed to have the monopoly on skin ailments. Clothed in loose-fitting shorts and either wearing sandals or going barefoot, the Viet Cong captured during CORONADO II had few of these infections. South Vietnamese troops, though they dressed like the Americans, were also rarely affected, perhaps because they seldom spent more than two days out of seven in the field. U.S. troops used silicone ointment in their socks and placed salve on those parts of their bodies exposed to the most friction from their uniforms. But the skin problem would never be

---

[16] MACV History 1967, vol. 3, pp. 1245, 1249; Msg, CG, IIFFV, 1173 to COMUSMACV, 6 Aug 67, sub: Results of CORONADO II, Westmoreland Message files, CMH; Periodic Intel Rpt 31, IIFFV, 8 Aug 67, p. 3, Historians files, CMH; AAR, Opn PALM BEACH II–CORONADO, 2d Bde, 9th Inf Div, pp. 28–30; RD Rpt, Dinh Tuong Province, Aug 67, n.d., pp. 1–9, Historians files, CMH; Intervs, author with Fulton, 10 and 22 Aug 79.

solved, even after the introduction of special "delta boots" made of loose-knit plastic mesh with leather reinforcements at heel, toe, and other points. Few Americans became acclimatized to the delta environment.[17]

CORONADO III Through V

With both riverine battalions suffering from paddy foot, the 3d Battalion, 60th Infantry, the security unit at Dong Tam, replaced the 4th Battalion, 47th Infantry, as a riverine unit. For the next six weeks the 4th Battalion remained at Dong Tam defending the base and recuperating. Meanwhile, on 4 August the Mobile Riverine Force sailed to Vung Tau for limited operations, called CORONADO III, in the Rung Sat. The exercise provided training for the 3d of the 60th in delta warfare, while the remaining battalion of the 47th Infantry performed refresher training on drier terrain east of the Rung Sat.[18]

As the health of the 2d Brigade improved, the riverine force resumed operations in Long An Province. For that purpose, the force reestablished its floating base off Fort Courage and at midnight on 19 August launched CORONADO IV. Ordered to mount a raid deep into the province, the riverine force sailed seventy kilometers up the Vam Co Dong. Nine hours later the 2d Brigade's battalions landed at an overgrown pineapple plantation and, while sweeping inland, flushed out a unit of the *506th Battalion*. As the Viet Cong attempted to flee across paddies, Huey gunships killed 45, and the riverine infantrymen struck down another 11 before reembarking the next day.

During the next three weeks the 2d Brigade conducted a series of operations with the 199th Brigade and South Vietnamese units in eastern Long An. Then, after relocating the riverine base to Vung Tau, the 2d Brigade operated with other units of the 9th Division in the Rung Sat. In addition to eliminating more than 100 Viet Cong, the series of raids turned up a number of caches containing nearly 200 enemy weapons and over 1,000 grenades.[19]

With the attention of the riverine forces directed elsewhere, the Viet Cong began to mass again in Dinh Tuong Province. American intelligence placed the *263d Battalion* back in the Cam Son Base Area in early September. Sources put two or three other main force battalions in the Plain of Reeds north of the Cam Son, but within a day's march.

---

[17] Senior Officer Debriefing Program, DA, 25 Feb 68, sub: Maj Gen George G. O'Connor, CG, 9th Inf Div, an. B (hereafter cited as O'Connor Debriefing), Historians files, CMH; Lt. Col. Alfred M. Allen, MC, USA, *Skin Diseases in Vietnam, 1965–72*, Internal Medicine in Vietnam (Washington, D.C.: Office of the Surgeon General and U.S. Army Center of Military History, 1977).

[18] ORLL, 1 Aug–31 Oct 67, 2d Bde, 9th Inf Div, 23 Dec 67, p. 1, Historians files, CMH; Intervs, author with Fulton, 10 and 22 Aug 79.

[19] ORLL, 1 Aug–31 Oct 67, 2d Bde, 9th Inf Div, pp. 1–5; Periodic Intel Rpt 34, IIFFV, 28 Aug 67, p. 2.

In response, General O'Connor ordered the riverine force back to Dong Tam on 11 September. By that time command of the 2d Brigade had passed to Col. Burt A. David. Fulton, promoted to brigadier general, became an assistant division commander in the 9th Division, with responsibility for both the 2d and 3d Brigades. Although General Fulton would maintain a small command post at Dong Tam, Colonel David would control CORONADO V, the new push into the Cam Son and the third since the riverine force had been constituted.

For the start of CORONADO V, the riverine force was again bolstered by the 3d Brigade's mechanized battalion, the 5th of the 60th Infantry. David's plan called for South Vietnamese forces and the mechanized unit to cordon off the northern and northeastern sections of the redoubt, while one of the riverine battalions, the 3d of the 47th, swept north from landing sites on the My Tho. Launched on the morning of 12 September, the effort turned up almost as empty-handed as the sweep during July.[20]

The next day, while the 3d of the 47th continued to scour the Cam Son, mounted troops of the 5th of the 60th Infantry prepared to push into the Ban Long from Route 20. Joining them were the men of the 3d Battalion, 60th Infantry. Earlier that morning they had debarked at Dong Tam and had been airlifted to positions immediately south of the mechanized battalion. By noon both battalions had entered the Ban Long and contacted what appeared to be a Viet Cong covering force. As the Americans pursued, resistance stiffened near the site of the South Vietnamese marines' difficult fight in July. Because the mechanized battalion had only two companies, and only one of them had armored personnel carriers, Colonel David reinforced with a company from the 3d of the 47th, still operating in the Cam Son. With gunships covering the enemy's open flanks and a battalion of Regional Forces blocking on the east the attack continued with heavy fire support until gathering darkness allowed the enemy to break contact. Even though many Viet Cong escaped during the night, the operation netted sixty-two enemy dead.[21]

As the Americans and South Vietnamese left the Ban Long the next afternoon, 14 September, the South Vietnamese 7th Division reported that a large force, presumably the *263d Battalion*, remained in the Cam Son. That force, analysts concluded, was most likely in a fortified salient along the east bank of the Rach Ba Rai, about ten kilometers upstream from the My Tho and a few kilometers farther north than the areas previously swept. (*Map 45*)

To encircle the enemy, two riverine battalions were to sail up the Ba Rai early the next day, one to land north of the salient, the other to the

[20] Rpt, 2d Bde, 9th Inf Div, 5 Nov 67, sub: Operation Report–Lessons Learned for August, September, and October 1967, p. 6, and Incls 1, 2, Historians files, CMH; ORLL, 1 Aug–31 Oct 67, 9th Inf Div, pp. 10, 16; Periodic Intel Rpt 37, IIFFV, 18 Sep 67, pp. 3, 8–9.

[21] Rpt, 2d Bde, 9th Inf Div, 5 Nov 67, sub: Operation Report–Lessons Learned for August, September, and October 1967, p. 6, and Incls 1, 2. American losses were nine killed and twenty-three wounded.

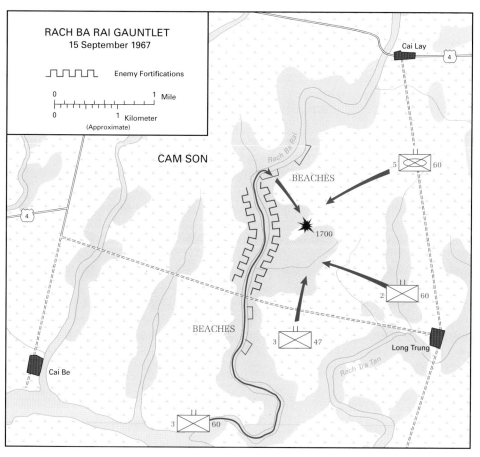

MAP 45

south. The mechanized battalion was to push west from Route 20 and pin the enemy against the Ba Rai. The 3d of the 60th Infantry would make the most dangerous movement. Reaching its assigned position north of the salient required that it first sail past the enemy fortifications at a point where the Ba Rai was only thirty meters wide. Surprise was crucial, so the ships would advance without the usual curtain of artillery fire.[22]

With minesweepers in the lead, two riverine squadrons left their floating base in darkness and entered the Ba Rai at sunrise on 15 September. The lead squadron, with the 3d Battalion, 60th Infantry, moved up the river in column, leaving an interval of fifteen meters between boats. After about an

---

[22] OPORD 24–67, Opn CORONADO V, 3d Bn, 60th Inf, 11 Sep 67, ans. A, B; Daily Jnls, 3d Bn, 60th Inf, 15 Sep 67, and 16 Sep 67. All in Historians files, CMH. Intervs, Maj John A. Cash with Col Burt A. David, Comdr, 2d Bde, 9th Inf Div, 6 Nov 67; with Lt Col Mercer M. Doty, Comdr, 3d Bn, 60th Inf, 9th Inf Div, 18 Sep 67; and with Maj Johnnie H. Corns, S–3, 2d Bde, 9th Inf Div, 18 Sep 67. All in box 1, 69A/4709, RG 319, NARA.

hour the column drew near the danger zone. But the ruse failed, and the Viet Cong immediately opened fire. Entrenched on either side of the river for a distance of 1,500 meters were two companies of the *263d Battalion*.

As the column tried to battle its way through, enemy fire intensified. Although rounds from recoilless rifles and rocket launchers did little damage to the armor-plated hulls, fragments wounded many sailors and troops below. Dense smoke soon cloaked the river, and boat captains worried that their assault craft might run aground. Unable to push through the hail of fire, most boats stopped within ten minutes of the start of the fight. Only one succeeded in passing the Viet Cong position, but when the rest of the column failed to follow, it had no choice but to turn around and run the gauntlet again. The heavy losses, particularly to the crews of the boats at the head of the column, forced the squadron commander to retreat downstream.[23]

After replacing the wounded crewmen with others from the uncommitted squadron, Captain Wells ordered a second try at running the gauntlet, this time preceded by a rolling artillery barrage. After an hour's fighting the boats broke through to land the troops.

With the northern beach secure, the 3d of the 47th landed south of the enemy salient as planned. In the meantime, out of concern that the second attempt to push past the ambush might fail, Colonel David had ordered the mechanized battalion to press toward the northern beaches, leaving a large gap between it and the slower moving 3d of the 47th Infantry. To fill the gap, he moved the 2d Battalion, 60th Infantry, a two-company outfit from the 3d Brigade in Long An Province, into position. By midafternoon it had air-assaulted into the gap.

Although artillery fire and air strikes hit the enemy hard, by noon the only ground unit fighting the Viet Cong was the riverine battalion, the 3d of the 60th, on the northern beach, its ranks sharply depleted by the casualties taken in the ambush. Of its three companies, only one had more than two effective platoons. Nevertheless, David ordered the battalion to attack south. Advancing three companies abreast, it progressed slowly against moderate resistance; but shortly before 1700 a company commander reported heavy contact. Aware that the company was badly understrength, David ordered the battalion commander to pull all three companies back to the northern beach and form a perimeter for the night.

Soon all contact was broken, and under cover of darkness the Viet Cong escaped, either by filtering through gaps between American units or by swimming the Ba Rai. Entering the base the next day, the Americans found abandoned bunkers and 24 Viet Cong dead. Adding those to the number reported killed on the fifteenth, the Mobile Riverine Force would list 79 enemy killed in the action. American casualties after five days in the field

---

[23] For additional details of the action, see John Albright, John A. Cash, and Allan W. Sandstrum, *Seven Firefights in Vietnam* (Washington, D.C.: U.S. Army Center of Military History, 1970), pp. 66–84.

Troops of the 9th Division waist-deep in the delta

were 7 killed and 123 wounded. Almost all the losses had occurred on the fifteenth and over 60 percent were Navy crewmen, with most of the wounded returning to duty within a week.[24]

As units of the 3d Brigade's 60th Infantry returned to Long An, David replaced the 3d Battalion, 47th Infantry, with the 4th Battalion, which supposedly had been resting at Dong Tam. However, while there the men had either stood guard or patrolled beyond the base perimeter. As a result, nearly half of the 4th Battalion's soldiers still had foot problems. During the first week more than one hundred were unavailable for field duty.[25]

To rebuild the field strength of the brigade, Colonel David continued to stagger battalion operations, limiting them to no more than two days' duration. He also rotated the reconnaissance and security companies of each riverine battalion with its three lettered rifle companies, so that every day at least one company from each would always be aboard ship drying out. Over the next month he was able to increase the number of men available for field duty in each battalion to about three hundred fifty.[26]

Later in the year, while preparations for enlarging the Mobile Riverine Force continued, a MACV study group recommended disbanding it, primarily because of the high number of noncombat casualties. Since the original concept of operating four to five consecutive days in the field had proved impractical during the wet season, the group concluded that the riverine brigade was "about one-third less cost-effective" than brigades fighting in other parts of South Vietnam.[27] Against these

---

[24] Rpt, 2d Bde, 9th Inf Div, 5 Nov 67, sub: Operation Report–Lessons Learned for August, September, and October 1967, pp. 7–8, and Incl 1; Intel Sums 221–67, 2d Bde, 9th Inf Div, 15 Sep 67, and 222–67, 2d Bde, 9th Inf Div, 16 Sep 67, both in Historians files, CMH; Daily Jnls, 3d Bn, 60th Inf, 15 Sep 67, and 16 Sep 67; Intervs, Cash with David, 6 Nov 67; with Doty, 18 Sep 67.

[25] O'Connor Debriefing, an. B.

[26] Rpt, 2d Bde, 9th Inf Div, 9 Dec 67, sub: Intensified MRF Operations, Incl 1, Historians files, CMH.

[27] Lt Col Thomas C. Loper, The Mobile Riverine Force or the Marriage of the Brown Water Navy and the Rice Paddy Army, U.S. Army War College Case Study, 9 Mar 70, pp. 66–67, Historians files, CMH.

arguments MACV had to weigh the value of employing at least some American troops in the delta. Moreover, since there were never enough helicopters in Vietnam to go around, the unique maneuverability of river craft was another factor that MACV could not ignore. In General Westmoreland's view these advantages constituted a strong case for retaining the force, which from June through November 1967 had reported a kill ratio of fifteen to one.[28] The riverine force gave the MACV commander some direct regional leverage in a war whose course was becoming increasingly difficult to chart.

[28] MACV History 1967, vol. 3, p. 1340.

26

Strains of an Open-Ended War

"Come see the light at the end of the tunnel," read the invitations to the U.S. embassy's New Year's Eve party.[1] The mood in Saigon was clearly upbeat as 1967 came to a close, bolstered by good results against the North Vietnamese and Viet Cong main forces and by mounting progress in pacifying the rural areas. General Westmoreland had promised that this would be the "year of the offensive," a time when the Americans and South Vietnamese would turn the tide. According to MACV's yardsticks he had been true to his word.

Westmoreland's assessment of the war drove his optimism. When he looked back on 1967, he saw success. Success tinged with disappointment to be sure, but he still believed that genuine progress had been made. "At the beginning of the year [1967] the enemy still enjoyed relative security in the huge War Zones in III Corps, and our use of roads was generally restricted to Saigon and the immediate vicinity. . . . With the exception of ATTLEBORO in late 1966, we had not yet entered these enemy areas on large-scale offensive operations, so that many of them were still largely untouched."[2] One year later, he noted optimistically, there had been progress toward his military goals and a decline in the enemy's combat effectiveness and control over the population.[3] By his own criteria, set out in the combined campaign plan for 1967, Westmoreland had accomplished what he set out to do and could move on. "I envisioned 1968 to be the year of the third phase, in which we would continue to help strengthen the Vietnamese Armed Forces—turning over more of the war effort to increasingly capable and better armed forces."[4]

This was possible because the American troops sent to Vietnam in 1966 had been able to make their presence felt in 1967. American military

---

[1] David Halberstam, *The Best and the Brightest* (New York: Random House, 1972), p. 647.
[2] Sharp and Westmoreland, *Report*, pp. 132–33.
[3] Msg, Westmoreland MAC 9514 to Lt Gen John A. Heintges, Dep CG, Seventh Army, 11 Oct 67, Historians files, CMH.
[4] Sharp and Westmoreland, *Report*, p. 136.

strength had increased from 313,100 at the start of October 1966 to 459,700 one year later. Westmoreland had used his soldiers to pursue the enemy aggressively, concentrating primarily on South Vietnam's heartland around Saigon, but also on the coastal plains and western highlands, and up along the Demilitarized Zone. Between October 1966 and October 1967, U.S. and allied forces were involved in scores of operations. Some two dozen of those operations each had a known body count of 500 or more enemy soldiers. MACV estimated that during the year more than 81,000 enemy soldiers had been killed in battle, a figure which heightened Westmoreland's confidence that the war was slowly being won.[5] He said during a visit to Washington in November 1967:

> I could quote you a number of meaningful statistics, such as roads that are being opened, the increasing number of enemy that are being killed, the number of defectors that are coming in from the Communist side to the government, the number of weapons being captured, and other statistical information that we are making progress and we are winning.[6]

There were problems, of course, but Westmoreland believed they lay in the political constraints on his ability to wage the war, not in strategy he had implemented. Without permission to strike the enemy in his sanctuaries in Laos and Cambodia, MACV could only react to enemy activity in South Vietnam. But Westmoreland believed he had adjusted to these handicaps and had gained the upper hand on the battlefield. Every Communist offensive had failed, often with enormous loss of enemy life, and American troops had made inroads in traditional enemy strongholds on the II Corps coast and all around Saigon. In the end, the Americans' operational mobility had permitted them to shift units throughout the country, dealing with crises as they arose.

Yet, despite the successes so far, Westmoreland realized they were not enough. The combination of inviolate enemy sanctuaries and the sheer size of the hostile areas along the border meant he could not go after the big units and still secure the countryside from the guerrillas. Even with the arrival of reinforcements in the summer and fall of 1966, Westmoreland could not be everywhere at once. Defending his bases and roads and supporting pacification ate into his strength, detracting from the big unit war. Hanoi saw this and used its sanctuaries to advantage. Enemy troops lurking over the border kept constant pressure on I Corps, forcing Westmoreland to reinforce there and thin out his troops elsewhere, including the corridor from Cambodia to the outskirts of Saigon. Whipsawed between the northern battlefront and the rest of the country, Westmoreland felt he had only one recourse—call for more troops.

---

[5] Ibid., pp. 282–85.
[6] Quoted in Michael Maclear, *The Ten Thousand Day War* (New York: St. Martin's Press, 1981), pp. 199–200.

They did not come, at least not in the numbers Westmoreland wanted. Washington allowed him only six brigades plus support troops in late 1967 and early 1968. This was far short of his requests, barely sufficient to continue his offensive plans.

So Westmoreland did what he could to enhance his combat power. In October 1966 he had twenty-five U.S. Army artillery battalions in Vietnam, just enough to support the Army's infantry. One year later the number of Army artillery battalions had climbed to forty-eight, almost doubling the number of guns, while at the same time the number of infantry battalions rose from thirty-nine to fifty-eight. By November 1967 there was almost one artillery battalion for every infantry battalion.[7]

Aircraft also played an important role. Air bases throughout the country provided tactical air support to troops on the ground within fifteen minutes. At the end of 1966 there were some 400 U.S. Air Force combat planes based in South Vietnam; one year later the figure was about the same, but the number of tactical air strikes had risen 40 percent. B–52 strikes had risen over 50 percent.[8]

Airmobility also increased. Helicopters made American troops far more mobile than their opponents, enabling them to leapfrog to hot spots within minutes. Westmoreland had been chronically short of helicopters in 1965 and 1966, but in 1967 the numbers looked better. In October 1966 the Army had 1,511 Hueys and Chinooks in country; one year later there were 2,288. The largest numerical increase was in the UH–1 Huey, the Army's workhorse helicopter. The inventory grew almost 50 percent, from 1,374 in October 1966 to 2,039 one year later. This unprecedented airmobility was reflected in the number of independent aviation companies available to Westmoreland: sixty-one in October 1966 and ninety-two at the end of October 1967.[9]

On the ground, Westmoreland tried to make up for his troop shortage by relying more on his allies. The South Vietnamese Army fought in the Mekong Delta, around Saigon, in the highlands, and up north, but its performance was mixed. By the fall of 1967 Westmoreland rated most South Vietnamese divisions as poor, noting that most were in the field no more than six days per month. The exceptions were the 1st Division in I Corps, considered the best in the South Vietnamese Army, and the 21st Division in the delta.

The South Koreans fought along the coast of I and II Corps, keeping their areas of operations under reasonable control during 1967. But questions were beginning to arise about their conduct in the villages, and their demands on American logistical and helicopter support were heavy.

Finally, intelligence gathering also grew more effective in 1967, though it had plenty of room for improvement. A fledgling organization

[7] Army Buildup Progress Rpt, 20 Dec 67, p. 5.
[8] Schlight, *Years of the Offensive*, pp. 159, 186–87, 257.
[9] Army Buildup Progress Rpts, 21 Dec 66, p. 51, and 29 Nov 67, pp. 7, 58.

during the previous two years, the MACV J–2 expanded during 1967, concentrating on identifying the enemy order of battle. Electronic eavesdropping became more sophisticated, allowing analysts to detect the infiltration and movement of enemy units more accurately. Rarely were American commanders surprised by the North Vietnamese, and in most instances MACV knew approximately where North Vietnamese and Viet Cong units were. But this knowledge was only general—it was still up to the infantry to find them and bring them to battle.

Situation on the Ground

What exactly had Westmoreland accomplished during the twelve months starting in October 1966? While Washington generally looked at the country as a whole, MACV tended to break it down by corps areas. For, as Westmoreland had learned, the situation on the ground varied greatly from region to region.

If an observer looked only at I Corps, especially the two northernmost provinces, the situation would have seemed bleak. In northern I Corps, the North Vietnamese held the advantage, and MACV intelligence predicted that they could launch large-scale attacks at any time. Despite the presence of III Marine Amphibious Force, Westmoreland had to reinforce with a U.S. Army division as a balance against three enemy divisions perched in or near the Demilitarized Zone, where they could strike quickly at Quang Tri and Thua Thien Provinces. North Vietnamese artillery was also a serious threat, more so than in any other part of South Vietnam. Marine units were constantly pounded by the big guns, hampering their operations and pinning them inside fortified bases. By October 1967 Westmoreland considered this to be the most sensitive area in the country.

To the south in II Corps, the situation was a little better, though still far from settled. Split between the rugged western highlands and the coastal lowlands, Westmoreland divided his time between fending off North Vietnamese encroachments across the border and pushing main force units out of their old haunts near the coast. On the coast, the Americans made inroads into the Communist-dominated countryside, but in the mountains, while casualties on both sides climbed, little else changed. Two enemy divisions lurked just over the border west of Kontum and Pleiku Provinces, forcing from one to three U.S. brigades to remain on guard. Westmoreland believed that the enemy wanted to control the western plateau, something he could not allow, so he reacted each and every time the enemy crossed the border. During PAUL REVERE IV and FRANCIS MARION, two operations in the highlands, American troops killed more than 2,000 enemy soldiers and halted what appeared to be the early stages of a North Vietnamese offensive. But, while the 4th Division inflicted heavy losses, the Americans never pinned down a major enemy unit. Nor did they hurt the North Vietnamese enough to force them onto the defensive. In November 1967 the North Vietnamese launched a violent division-size attack against Dak To. Obviously, they were far from beaten.

Westmoreland had more success in the II Corps lowlands. Despite having to divert troops to the highlands from time to time, he was still able to make important gains against the strongholds on the coast. Before mid-1966, he had exerted very little pressure on the Communist redoubts in Binh Dinh and Phu Yen. But after a year in the field, the 3d Brigade, 4th Division, grew skilled in hunting down guerrillas. Add to that the deployment of the airmobile 1st Cavalry Division to the Bong Son Plain late in the year, and the North Vietnamese found themselves on the defensive. The pressure clearly hurt. In March 1967 Hanoi reacted by deploying troops to coastal Quang Ngai in hopes of pinning down American and South Vietnamese units and diverting attention from the highlands. It failed. Despite pressure on his manpower, Westmoreland managed to fight on both fronts simultaneously.

MACV's main emphasis was on III Corps. Not only did the region contain the country's capital and command center of the war, but it was particularly vulnerable because of the relatively open terrain between Saigon and the enemy bases in Cambodia. In 1966 enemy troops could infiltrate into the plains north and west of Saigon with relative ease, and they maintained redoubts throughout III Corps, including east of the capital. In early 1967 Westmoreland launched two corps-size operations, the keystones of his new offensive strategy, aimed at the Iron Triangle and War Zone C. Operations CEDAR FALLS and JUNCTION CITY cleared out the enemy and allowed Westmoreland to move toward the border, stationing part of his troop strength in areas known to be prime infiltration routes. But, while successful in many ways, these operations never decisively defeated the enemy, nor did they prevent the enemy from returning to his in-country base areas in the summer and fall.

In the Mekong Delta, IV Corps, American troops found themselves fighting a new kind of war in the heartland of the insurgency. This was the birthplace of the Viet Cong: almost half of their total military strength was here. Before 1967 the South Vietnamese Army had done the fighting in the delta and tried to keep the roads open to Saigon. But when it came to wresting the initiative from the local forces, the best Saigon could claim in IV Corps was a stalemate.

Not until 1967 did Westmoreland have enough troops to deploy to the delta. Nor, because of the dense population and watery terrain, was he eager to send them there. On the other hand, once the 9th Division's riverine force entered IV Corps, it quickly penetrated previously inaccessible Communist strongholds. At first the introduction of assault boats and their firepower stunned the Viet Cong and forced them onto the defensive. By the fall of 1967, however, they had learned to cope with these new war machines in much the same way they had learned to fight helicopters. The Viet Cong prowled the riverbanks with rocket-propelled grenades waiting for the riverine force. In several instances they used this tactic with deadly effectiveness.

As with combat operations, the campaign to control the villages differed from region to region. In 1967 pacification had just been elevated to importance. The establishment of CORDS in March provided a much-needed chain of command for the many military and civilian agencies involved, but by the fall it was still too early to predict the organization's effectiveness. On the other hand, the emphasis on reestablishing Saigon's presence in the countryside led to an increase in government programs and saw more military operations aimed at rooting out the Viet Cong underground and severing its ties with the guerrillas.

One point was immediately clear: like much of the rest of the war, pacification became entangled in statistics. HES reports showed the rural population being slowly but surely wrested from the grip of the Viet Cong, leading Ambassador Ellsworth Bunker to announce in November 1967 that the population under Saigon's control was growing steadily.[10] But the statistics failed to show that while more of the countryside was indeed coming under government dominion as the year progressed, many of these villagers were in fact refugees uprooted by the war and placed in camps. According to Saigon's statistics, there were more than two million refugees in South Vietnam by the end of 1967. While they were theoretically out from under Communist domination, it was impossible to call them loyal to the Saigon government.[11]

Hanoi's Prospects

After a year of battling the Americans the North Vietnamese had been badly bloodied, and Westmoreland was convinced that they were nearing exhaustion. On 15 October 1967, he submitted to Admiral Sharp and the Joint Chiefs a study concluding that "the enemy is meeting increasing difficulty in maintaining the thrust of his effort, whereas the [United States/Free World/Republic of Vietnam] forces are increasing in size and are becoming more proficient and experienced in developing and executing operations against the enemy." Success was "demonstrated by the enemy's avoidance of contact, his failure to mount an offensive in the north and his increased terrorist activities." In Westmoreland's opinion, the enemy had settled for a protracted war of attrition in which "he seems to believe that his will, patience and resources will outlast those of the Free World. This strategy implies that his will and resources will sustain him for the time required, but present evidence indicates that his time may indeed be limited."[12]

---

[10] *New York Times*, 15 Nov 67.

[11] Louis A. Wiesner, *Victims and Survivors: Displaced Persons and Other War Victims in Viet-Nam, 1954–1975* (New York: Greenwood Press, 1988), pp. 79–100.

[12] The October 1967 study is quoted in U.S. Congress, Senate, Committee on Foreign Relations, *The U.S. Government and the Vietnam War: Executive and Legislative Roles and Relationships, Part IV, July 1965–January 1968* (Washington, D.C.: Government Printing Office, 1994), pp. 928–29.

In short, the North Vietnamese had paid a terrible price with little to show for the effort. In another report, Westmoreland pointed to the battles in the western highlands, which he considered a clear defeat for the enemy. He cited a "ranking Communist officer" who defected as saying the border battles were both "useless and bloody."[13]

Westmoreland also believed that Hanoi's increasing logistical problems were taking a toll on the enemy's war effort in the South. Most of the men and supplies leaving North Vietnam moved by way of the Ho Chi Minh Trail through Laos. The trail system had grown throughout 1967, but so had the American bombing campaign, forcing Hanoi to defend the route from air attack. By late 1967 American intelligence estimated that 175,000 North Vietnamese were being used for air defense, with another half million used for maintaining and repairing roads damaged by U.S. bombs. Men and supplies continued to move south, but only, according to the U.S. military, at heightened cost.

At the end of 1966 MACV had estimated enemy strength in South Vietnam at 278,000. One year later the figure was down to 220,000. Westmoreland interpreted the figures to show that Hanoi had to keep its manpower pipeline wide open to try to keep up with the losses.[14]

Infiltration was indeed declining. In late 1965 and the first half of 1966, more than 9,000 North Vietnamese soldiers entered the South each month; by the end of 1967 the number was thought to have decreased to under 6,000. Studies based on captured documents and prisoner interrogations also revealed that by October 1967 the average monthly Viet Cong recruitment rate in South Vietnam had dropped by at least 50 percent to 3,500. This significant decline, coupled with enemy losses during the summer monsoon period, which MACV estimated at more than 7,300 per month, indicated to analysts that the enemy was losing about 5,000 men per month more than it could replace. One MACV study conjectured that the long sought-after "crossover point" actually may have occurred back in November 1966.[15]

By October 1967 the North Vietnamese had 162 maneuver battalions inside South Vietnam, up from 158 one year earlier. But MACV intelligence considered only 87 of that total combat effective, in contrast with 132 in October 1966. Guerrilla strength, which served as a replacement pool for the maneuver battalions, dropped from 120,000 in 1966 to 80,000 in October 1967.[16] Westmoreland also pointed out that battle losses in South Vietnam were slowly diminishing the Viet Cong main force strength, forcing North Vietnam to assume an ever-increasing share of the war. In January 1967 intelligence estimated that North Vietnamese sol-

---

[13] Sharp and Westmoreland, *Report*, p. 139.

[14] Msg, Westmoreland MAC 10295 to Wheeler, 30 Oct 67, sub: Information for General Wheeler, 1 November Briefing, Westmoreland Message files, CMH.

[15] SEA Mil Fact Bk, Jan 68, pp. A–76, A–95, A–107, A–108.

[16] Msg, Westmoreland MAC 10295 to Wheeler, 30 Oct 67, sub: Information for General Wheeler, 1 November Briefing.

diers made up about 43 percent of enemy combat units; by December the figure was around 50 percent.[17]

MACV divided enemy strength into three broad categories: conventional forces, political cadre, and militia. In late 1966 MACV intelligence had placed conventional force strength at 118,600 and political cadre strength at 39,000.[18] The figure for militia was much more difficult to pin down, and during 1967 it became a bone of contention between those who saw progress in the war and those who saw the war as futile.

For the past year the Central Intelligence Agency had felt that MACV was underestimating enemy strength. The agency believed there were an additional 205,000 nonmilitary political cadre and self-defense forces not included in the MACV total. But Westmoreland insisted that only the enemy's actual military strength, not the nebulous self-defense forces, should be reported. Guerrillas, he argued, were full-time soldiers, but the self-defense forces were civilians, at best part-time combatants, poorly armed and trained. While they were not harmless, they posed no significant military threat and thus should not appear in the order of battle.

The standoff continued into November. Richard M. Helms, Director of Central Intelligence, soon realized that Westmoreland would never accept an enemy order of battle over 400,000, so he settled on MACV's terms. Militia forces were removed from the list, keeping the overall enemy strength between 223,000 and 248,000. Westmoreland cabled Admiral Sharp to say that the Central Intelligence Agency agreed with MACV and that "I am satisfied that this is a good estimate and the best that can be derived from available intelligence." Since the new figure was less than the 285,000 estimate of September 1966, Westmoreland concluded, "we believe that this represents a decline in total enemy order of battle."[19]

No matter whose numbers were correct, the question remained: Were enemy losses heavy enough to force Hanoi to cease and desist? General Nguyen Chi Thanh, the *COSVN* commander, believed they were not—nor would they ever be. "All the strategic objectives set forth and all methods used by the US aggressors have been frustrated," he wrote. "The US expeditionary troops are on the decline. The puppet troops are even worse. The US ruling clique is facing difficult, insoluble problems. When and how can the Viet Cong main force be destroyed? What is to be done to win a turning point on the battlefield?" Of course, Thanh thought he knew the answer—neither Washington nor Saigon would reach that point.[20]

---

[17] Sharp and Westmoreland, *Report*, p. 135.

[18] MACV Briefing Bk for Sec Def, J–2 Fact Sheet, tab 3A; MFR, 24 Jun 67, sub: MACV Commanders' Conference, 11 June 1967, an. A.

[19] For an excellent account of the order of battle controversy between MACV and the CIA, see Berman, *Lyndon Johnson's War*, pp. 81–83. The Westmoreland cable is quoted in Ibid., p. 82.

[20] Thanh wrote in *Quan Doi Nhan Dan*, the People's Army daily, 31 May 1967, and is quoted in Patrick J. McGarvey, comp., *Visions of Victory: Selected Vietnamese Communist Military Writings, 1964–1968* (Stanford, Calif.: Hoover Institution Publications, 1969), p. 116.

Indeed, if history was any indication, the North Vietnamese and Viet Cong could take a lot more punishment than the United States was prepared to mete out. Past American wars in Asia—against the Japanese during World War II and the Chinese and North Koreans during the Korean War—had shown that causing heavy casualties in itself was not enough to win. The French experience in Vietnam also showed starkly the Communists' will to fight against heavy odds. Westmoreland ignored the fact that an estimated 200,000 North Vietnamese males reached draft age each year, far more than the number killed on the battlefield, which enabled Hanoi to replace its losses and match each American escalation.

The leaders in Hanoi had little concern for numbers—they were in the war for the long run. And despite their losses, the North Vietnamese were pleased with their performance during 1967. Defense Minister Vo Nguyen Giap wrote that "the situation has never been as favorable as it is now [September 1967]. The armed forces and people have stood up to fight the enemy and are achieving one great victory after another."[21] Giap also forecast heavy fighting ahead for the United States. In particular, he touted his border strategy that drew American troops into the remote areas so guerrillas and local forces could press toward victory in the heavily populated areas.[22] Giap believed that American troops were stretched "taut as a bowstring" all across South Vietnam and predicted that the United States "lacked the patience" to continue the protracted war.[23]

And yet, regardless of any public pronouncements, Giap was never comfortable with the attrition strategy of his commander in the South, General Thanh. Until his death in July 1967, Thanh remained an advocate of the main force war despite defeats stretching back to the Ia Drang campaign of 1965. His critics in Hanoi pointed out that this strategy resulted in a weakening of the Viet Cong and a greater need to use North Vietnamese regulars on the battlefield. The increasing precariousness of the Viet Cong position in turn hurt recruiting in the South Vietnamese villages, which by the end of 1967 had declined to an all-time low. The Party in Hanoi complained of a weakening of the bond between cadre and the Southern peasantry, and feared that the sympathies of many Vietnamese in the South were about to shift.

Clearly, American pressure had hurt the Communists. In the short run, neither Viet Cong guerrillas nor North Vietnamese regulars could stand up to the weight of American firepower. They were often forced back into their base areas and separated from the population. But the Communists were nothing if not resourceful, and, as they had done in years past, they compensated for this American advantage. In addition to occasional pitched battles, the guerrillas also used a practice that had

[21] Vo Nguyen Giap, *Big Victory, Great Task* (New York: Frederick A. Praeger, 1968), pp. 18–19.

[22] Sharp and Westmoreland, *Report*, p. 135.

[23] William J. Duiker, *The Communist Road to Power in Vietnam* (Boulder, Colo.: Westview Press, 1981), p. 261.

served them well against the French: mines and booby traps supplement-ed by carefully rehearsed sapper assaults and quick hit-and-run mortar and rocket attacks. These tactics not only conserved manpower, but they also constituted an immense source of frustration for allied commanders and their soldiers.

Still, although they were in no danger of running out of troops, the Party leaders faced a dilemma. North Vietnamese units could always stay safe in their sanctuaries, but they could not force a military decision in the South as long as American troops remained. Instead, the Communists needed some sort of "decisive blow" to "force the U.S. to accept military defeat."[24] The Party leadership met in June and decided to launch a major offensive during the following dry season. Final approval came later in the year at the Party's Fourteenth Plenum. The decision sprang partly from the increasing effectiveness of American forces and partly because Hanoi saw a chance to break the stalemate. Whatever the case, it seems clear that while Westmoreland had hurt the enemy in 1967, he had not prevented him from massing for a large offensive. Hanoi may not have been able to stand toe-to-toe with the United States, but it could try again and again.

The Strains of War

Westmoreland also faced a dilemma as the war entered the fall—growing doubt on the American home front that the strategy in Vietnam was working as well as advertised. "We must somehow get hard evidence out of Saigon on steady if slow progress," Walt Rostow cabled Westmore-land on 27 September 1967. But statistics were not sufficient. In fact, the American public was fed up with statistics. "The data do not explain away dismay at our own casualty figures," argued Deputy Assistant Sec-retary of State Philip C. Habib. "They do not answer the question of how much longer we will be required to maintain our effort."[25]

Casualties were indeed beginning to "dismay" the American public. With both sides pursuing an attrition strategy, body counts mounted—and, given Hanoi's closed society and Washington's unfettered press interest, there was no question who would feel the pain first. The year 1967 was expensive in terms of American soldiers killed. Between 1961 and October 1966, 5,737 U.S. servicemen had been killed in Vietnam. Dur-ing the next twelve months, through September 1967, 8,237 Americans died. This was an average of 158 men per week, a statistic fed regularly to the American public on the evening news. With casualties mounting, Westmoreland's calls for more men and more time sounded all the more futile—not to mention costly. Time had become a critical factor.

[24] *The Anti-U.S. Resistance War of National Salvation, 1954–1975: Military Events*, trans. Foreign Broadcast Information Service, Joint Publications Research Service 80968 (Hanoi: People's Army Publishing House, 1980), pp. 100–101, copy in CMH.
[25] Berman, *Lyndon Johnson's War*, pp. 84–85.

For Washington, 1967 began with great expectations and ended in doubt. At the beginning of the year President Johnson basically shared MACV's feeling that the military was on the right track. In a meeting with key senators in January, Johnson had confided that the United States was "doing better now than we have ever done in Vietnam if we just don't blow it."[26]

Some of the president's advisers were even more confident. Walt Rostow argued that during 1967 it would become "patently clear to all that the war is demonstrably being won." Robert Komer, the administration's point man on pacification, wrote the president at the close of 1966 that "we're doing much better than we think" and predicted that 1967 would finish the job. By "properly orchestrating" the war effort, which including bombing the North as well as escalating the ground war, "we can achieve sufficient cumulative impact either to force the enemy to negotiate or cripple his ability to sustain the war." This "win strategy," Komer concluded, could be developed "without further major escalation against the North, or sizable US deployments beyond what you've already approved."[27]

But one year later few agreed. The president best summed up the nagging doubts in the summer of 1967, when he asked in frustration, "Are we going to be able to win this goddamn war?"[28] Even Komer began to temper his optimism. He now considered the war "slow, painful, and incredibly expensive," though he still felt the war could be won in the long run.[29]

Johnson's doubts were exacerbated by increasing pessimism on the part of the Central Intelligence Agency. An intelligence report in December 1967 noted that "no early turning point appears likely," because "the North Vietnamese remain confident that they can hold out, in a protracted war of attrition, longer than the U.S. They apparently remain willing and able to accept the high cost of U.S. attacks in the South and in the North, at least at present levels, in the hope that the American and South Vietnamese will to fight to the end eventually will weaken under the strain of military frustrations and domestic pressures."[30]

Johnson increasingly believed that while the war might indeed be "winnable" through Westmoreland's attrition strategy, victory would only come at some point far down the road. And during that time the generals would ask for a wider war, or at the very least, an increase in troops. Neither his domestic programs nor public opinion could abide either course for much longer. During Westmoreland's troop request in the spring of 1967, Johnson had wondered aloud if the enemy would not simply add new divisions of his own.

[26] *The U.S. Government and the Vietnam War*, p. 464.

[27] Ibid., pp. 464–65, 484.

[28] Harry Middleton, *LBJ: The White House Years* (New York: Harry N. Abrams, 1990), p. 178.

[29] *The U.S. Government and the Vietnam War*, p. 486.

[30] The CIA estimate is quoted in Ibid., pp. 942–43.

Westmoreland responded as he always did: the crossover point was very near and more troops would push it over the top. But even according to MACV's best-case scenario, the war would last until at least 1970—still too long, considering waning public support. None of the choices were palatable.

On 11 October McNamara asked the Joint Chiefs for their strategy recommendations for the coming year. Despite President Johnson's implacable opposition to allowing operations outside South Vietnam, one month later the chiefs again recommended "ground operations in Laos; ground operations in Cambodia; and possible ground operations against North Vietnam."[31] In spite of the clamor within the administration against any such move, General Wheeler maintained his position that it was the only way to win the war. "The real question we face is how long we can tolerate these people operating from a sanctuary," he said during a White House meeting.[32]

But Secretary of State Dean Rusk led the opposition to expanding ground operations, particularly in Cambodia: "This would change the entire character of the war. If Cambodia is attacked, they may ask the Chinese to side with them. Then we will really have a new war on our hands."[33]

Wheeler was correct about the need to eliminate the sanctuaries, but the opinions of military men were becoming less important to the president, who was fed up with suggestions that in effect only widened the war. He told the Joint Chiefs to "search for imaginative ideas to put pressure to bring this war to a conclusion." But he did not want to hear the same old military solutions—more men, more bombing.[34]

A high-level meeting on 1 November seemed to bring out all the factors: there had been great progress by the military since 1965, but it was not enough to cause North Vietnam to give up the fight in the foreseeable future. The Central Intelligence Agency's top Vietnam analyst, George A. Carver, asserted that Hanoi would end the war only when its leaders "had decided the U.S. would not behave like the French did in 1954 and when a viable state structure seemed on the way to emerging in Vietnam." Neither was going to happen any time soon; the United States was showing every sign of tiring, and South Vietnam showed no sign of turning into a strong state capable of standing alone. A special intelligence estimate put an even finer point on the debate. Entitled "Capabilities of the Vietnamese Communists for Fighting in South Vietnam," the report summed up the enemy's fighting abilities by remarking that manpower was indeed a problem for the enemy, although the "Communists still retain adequate capabilities to support this strategy for at least another year."[35]

---

[31] *The Senator Gravel Edition of the Pentagon Papers*, 4:536–37.
[32] *The U.S. Government and the Vietnam War*, p. 939.
[33] Ibid., p. 938.
[34] Quoted in Berman, *Lyndon Johnson's War*, p. 78.
[35] For the 1 November meeting, see Ibid., pp. 93–109. The Carver quote is in Ibid., p. 97. The CIA's special intelligence estimate, SNIE 14.3–67, is quoted in Ibid., p. 110.

While most agreed that the attrition strategy was not working, there was no consensus on how to replace it. Some favored bombing, others negotiating, but all seemed to agree that despite the fact that there was no end in sight, the United States should not cut and run. Former Ambassador Lodge told the president: "Unthinkable. We are trying to divert a change in the balance of power." "As impossible as it is undesirable," said McGeorge Bundy, Johnson's former national security adviser. Bundy also warned that both the military and the administration had overemphasized statistics as an indicator of success in Vietnam. "I think we have tried too hard to convert public opinion by statistics and spectacular visits of all sorts," he told Johnson. "I think people are getting fed up with the endlessness of the fighting. What really hurts, then, is not the arguments of the doves, but the cost of the war in lives and money, coupled with the lack of light at the end of the tunnel."[36]

The polls showed the frustration, but also that Americans disapproved of North Vietnamese actions as well. A Gallup poll in November 1967 illustrated that while only 58 percent of those polled supported the war in general—an all-time low—67 percent favored continuing to bomb North Vietnam because of its continuing assault on the South. This was not lost on the president. At the close of a meeting with his top advisers on 2 November he pointed out that while the administration could hold out for the long run against North Vietnam, he doubted "the resoluteness of the American people."[37]

Westmoreland was out of options. MACV's campaign plan for 1968 differed little from that of the previous year, calling for broad goals: "defeat the VC/NVA main forces," destroy the enemy's base areas and resources, and drive him "into sparsely populated food scarce areas so as to permit the GVN to protect the population." In other words, do to the enemy what had supposedly been done in 1967.[38]

It was ironic that one of the men most responsible for America's strategy in Vietnam, Robert McNamara, would best sum up America's predicament. "Nothing can be expected to break [the Communists'] will other than the conviction that they cannot succeed," he wrote to the president just before his resignation in November. "This conviction will not be created unless and until they come to the conclusion that the U.S. is prepared to remain in Vietnam for whatever period of time is necessary."[39] But the American public was no longer willing to wait for the light at the end of the tunnel—or even to believe that there was any such thing. The U.S. Army in Vietnam was running out of time.

---

[36] Ibid., pp. 101–03.

[37] Ibid., p. 100.

[38] JGS/MACV Combined Campaign Plan for Military Operations in the Republic of Vietnam, 1968 [11 Nov 67], AB 143, pp. 2, 11, Historians files, CMH.

[39] Berman, *Lyndon Johnson's War*, p. 94.

Bibliographical Note

Unpublished Sources

The volume of unit records for the Vietnam War surpasses that of any other conflict in American history. The advent of the computer and the photocopying machine during the war led to a proliferation of written materials in Vietnam and their duplication as they passed from one agency to the next. Those sources vary in quality from unit to unit and are sometimes so general and lacking in detail when viewed in isolation that they seem of little value to the historian. That they also have to be used with caution because far too many exaggerate successes while obscuring failures only makes matters worse. Despite their inadequacies, when used in combination with one another and supplemented with oral history interviews, those sources can fill in for one another to provide a framework for determining not only what happened in Vietnam but also, at times, why.

This book is thus built upon a broad range of materials generated by units involved in combat operations. Foremost among them are command reports, quarterly summaries entitled Operational Reports–Lessons Learned, unit journals, and unit after action reports. The after action reports are important because they often identify commanders and other key officers by name, allowing the historian to begin his search for interviewees.

Perhaps the most basic types of combat records are the daily journal files. These brief, round-the-clock logs record times and locations and at their best set down quick summaries of messages and reports. These journals were maintained by battalion, regiment, and brigade headquarters, but the staff components of higher headquarters kept comparable records. Those from the higher commands often summarized the reports of their component units, but a careful comparison of the two sets of records, where both exist, will show that important information at times has been lost or garbled in the process. In addition, enemy casualties and other measures of progress seemed to grow as they progressed up the chain of command.

The records of the various intelligence and operations staffs (G–2 and G–3) are particularly important to the historian. These were based on contributions from subordinate headquarters and included situation reports, which informed higher headquarters of significant incidents or new developments. The G–2 sections (J–2 at MACV) produced daily intelligence summaries and, at the field force and MACV level, periodic intelligence reports, weekly and monthly, respectively.

National Archives and Records Administration

Most source documentation for this volume is located in the Washington, D.C., area. The largest holding is at the National Archives and Records Administration, College Park, Maryland. The U.S. Forces in Southeast Asia, 1950–1975, file (Record Group [RG] 472) occupies some 30,000 linear feet of shelf space. Other important record groups deal with the Army Staff (RG 319); U.S. Army Commands (RG 338); Interservice Agencies such as MACV (RG 334); and documents collected during the Westmoreland-CBS libel trial (RG 407).

U.S. Army Center of Military History

The second most important record collection dealing with the U.S. Army's role in Vietnam is maintained by the U.S. Army Center of Military History in Washington, D.C. Upon completion of the U.S. Army in Vietnam series, the materials involved, including interviews conducted by historians, will be transferred to the National Archives.

The Center's largest and most important holding is a photocopied set of the papers of General William C. Westmoreland collected during his tour of duty as commander of the Military Assistance Command, Vietnam. The originals are in the possession of the Lyndon Baines Johnson Library in Austin, Texas. A second set of photocopies is on file at the U.S. Army Military History Institute, Carlisle Barracks, Pennsylvania.

Occupying about eighteen linear feet of space, the Westmoreland Papers are in two parts. The first contains a history that the general dictated at intervals, often daily, to members of his staff. It constitutes a detailed account of his activities, his decisions, and often the thinking behind those decisions. Attached are copies of relevant incoming and outgoing messages, memorandums, reports, staff studies, and other documents that the general considered important. The second is a virtually complete set of backchannel messages between Westmoreland and his superiors in Hawaii and Washington. It often sheds light on the political policies that affected Westmoreland's approach to the war and the problems that field commanders sometimes confronted.

The Center of Military History maintains another collection, which also has an important bearing upon the Vietnam period. It contains more than a thousand interviews conducted by members of military history detachments dispatched to South Vietnam during the war. In all, twenty-seven military history detachments served, most composed of one officer and one enlisted man, assigned to various U.S. Army units and commands in Vietnam. They produced eyewitness accounts of combat actions, studies in lessons learned, and end-of-tour interviews with important officers. Although the quality of the workmanship varied with the producer, the collection as a whole is valuable for the understanding of platoon- and company-level operations that it imparts.

Personal interviews conducted by the author are also on file at the Center. Most involve officers who served as commanders during the period covered by the book. This group consists of the MACV commander, as well as four field force, nine division, and a host of regiment, brigade, and battalion commanders. Filed chronologically within these interview files are folders pertaining to important commanders who could not be interviewed. Included in the folders are correspondence, Department of the Army debriefing reports that each senior officer compiled upon leaving Vietnam, and extracts of interviews that others conducted. The author conducted the following interviews:

Maj. Gen. James B. Adamson, commander, 2d Brigade, 4th Infantry Division (4 Apr 79); 1st Lt. John Albright, S–1, 1st Squadron, 11th Armored Cavalry Regiment (25 Mar 76); Maj. Gen. James G. Boatner, commander, 4th Battalion, 12th Infantry, 199th Light Infantry Brigade (22 May 80); Col. William M. Boice, commander, Troop K, 3d Squadron, 11th Armored Cavalry Regiment (25 and 29 Sep 80); Col. Doniphan Carter, commander, 1st Brigade, 25th Infantry Division (16 Jan 81); Maj. Gen. William W. Cobb, commander, 11th Armored Cavalry Regiment (26 May 76); Lt. Gen. Arthur S. Collins, commanding general, 4th Infantry Division (28 Feb 75); Col. Francis S. Conaty, commander, 196th Light Infantry Brigade, and commander, 1st Brigade, 25th Infantry Division (24 Sep 75 and 29 and 30 Jun 76); General Robert E. Cushman, commanding general, III Marine Amphibious Force (9 Nov 82); Col. Howard H. Danford, commander, 2d Battalion, 502d Infantry, 101st Airborne Division (21 Sep 81); General John R. Deane, assistant division commander, 1st Infantry Division, and commanding general, 173d Airborne Brigade (5 Jan 78); General William E. DePuy, commanding general, 1st Infantry Division (3 and 7 Oct 77); Lt. Gen. Hillman Dickinson, commander, 3d Squadron, 11th Armored Cavalry Regiment (12 and 25 Sep 80); Lt. Gen. William B. Fulton, commander, 2d Brigade, 9th Infantry Division, and assistant division commander, 9th Infantry Division (10 and 22 Aug 79); Col. Timothy G. Gannon, commander, 1st Battalion, 8th Infantry, 4th Infantry Division (31 Aug 78); Maj. Gen. Marshall B. Garth, commander, 3d Brigade, 4th Infantry Division (26 May 76); General Paul F. Gorman, G–3, 1st Infantry Division (22 Jun 95); Col. Clinton E. Granger, commander, 2d Battalion, 35th Infantry, 3d Brigade, 25th Infantry Division (15 Nov 85); Lt. Gen. John H. Hay, commanding general, 1st Infantry Division (29 Apr 80); Col. Martin D. Howell, commander, 1st Squadron, 11th Armored Cavalry Regiment (26 Aug 80); Col.

Ralph W. Julian, commander, 2d Battalion, 22d Infantry (Mech), 25th Infantry Division (15 Feb 96); Brig. Gen. Samuel W. Koster, commanding general, 23d Infantry Division (26 Aug 82); Col. William E. LeGro, G–2, 1st Infantry Division (15 and 20 Jan 76); Brig. Gen. Frank H. Linnell, commanding general, 196th Light Infantry Brigade (6 Oct 81); Col. Paul B. Malone, commander, 1st Aviation Battalion, 1st Infantry Division (27 Feb 80); Col. James O. McKenna, commander, 3d Brigade, 1st Cavalry Division (16 and 22–23 Jun 82); Brig. Gen. James E. Moore, S–3, 3d Brigade, 25th Infantry Division, and commander, 1st Battalion, 35th Infantry, 3d Brigade, 25th Infantry Division (4 Aug 81); Lt. Gen. John Norton, commanding general, 1st Cavalry Division (1–2 Sep and 2 Dec 83); Lt. Gen. Charles P. Otstott, commander, Company A, 2d Battalion, 502d Infantry, 101st Airborne Division (19 Aug 97); Lt. Gen. David E. Ott, commander, 25th Infantry Division Artillery (18 Aug 80); General Bruce Palmer, commanding general, II Field Force, Vietnam, and deputy commanding general, U.S. Army, Vietnam (2 May 78); Lt. Gen. William R. Peers, commanding general, 4th Infantry Division (21 Oct 75); Maj. Gen. Edward C. Peter, commander, 2d Battalion, 27th Infantry, 25th Infantry Division (12 Feb 81); Col. Edward M. Pierce, commander, 1st Battalion, 7th Cavalry, 1st Cavalry Division (14 Apr and 12 Aug 82); General William B. Rosson, commanding general, Task Force OREGON, and commanding general, I Field Force, Vietnam (13, 20, and 27 Sep 77); Lt. Gen. Jonathan O. Seaman, commanding general, II Field Force, Vietnam (25 May 76); Brig. Gen. James G. Shanahan, commander, 3d Brigade, 25th Infantry Division (13 and 21 Aug and 4 Sep 81); Col. Robert H. Sholly, commander, Company B, 1st Battalion, 8th Infantry, 4th Infantry Division (25 Oct 78); Col. Charles R. Smith, commander, Company A, 4th Battalion, 31st Infantry, 196th Light Infantry Brigade (13 Aug 81); Col. Alfred E. Spry, S–2, 3d Brigade, 1st Cavalry Division (11 Apr 83); Lt. Gen. John R. Thurman, commander, 25th Infantry Division Artillery (23 Feb 81); Lt. Gen. R. Dean Tice, commander, 2d Battalion, 12th Infantry, 25th Infantry Division (3 Feb 81); Maj. Gen. John C. F. Tillson, commanding general, 25th Infantry Division (28 May 76); Lt. Gen. John J. Tolson, commanding general, 1st Cavalry Division (24 Jun 76); Col. Carl C. Ulsaker, senior adviser, 2d ARVN Division (30 Aug 82); Lt. Gen. Glenn D. Walker, assistant division commander, 4th Infantry Division (3 Apr 79); Col. Robert M. Ward, G–3, 25th Infantry Division (8 Feb 81); Col. Thomas A. Ware, commander, 1st Brigade, 25th Infantry Division (26 Jan 81); General William C. Westmoreland, commander, MACV (6 Dec 89); Col. Oliver M. Whipple, commander, Company F, 2d Battalion, 7th Marines, 1st Marine Division (1 Dec 81); Col. Jack G. Whitted, commander, 1st Battalion, 28th Infantry, 1st Infantry Division (19 Jan 76); Brig. Gen. Corey J. Wright, commander, 1st Battalion, 12th Infantry, 4th Infantry Division (26 Feb 79); Lt. Gen. Robert G. Yerks, commander, 2d Battalion, 327th Infantry, 101st Airborne Division (16 Sep 82).

U.S. Army Military History Institute

The archives of the Military History Institute have 128 linear feet of special collections and documents regarding Vietnam, many of which are duplicated at the Center of Military History and the National Archives. In addition, during the past twenty years, under the sponsorship of the Military History Institute oral history office (as part of the larger Department of the Army Senior Officer Debriefing Program), students attending the Army War College have conducted extensive interviews with senior retired general officers, many of whom served in Vietnam. A large majority of those interviews are available to the public.

Published Sources

Socialist Republic of Vietnam Histories

The government of Vietnam has its own official history-writing program, and the effort has produced dozens of books and monographs over the past three decades. There are histories of each division (as well as of several regiments), campaign narratives, oral histories, and many specialized studies. Although often unreliable about casualty figures, they provide crucial information on North Vietnamese and Viet Cong battle plans and troop movements. By and large, these valuable sources are still unfamiliar to American scholars. The works cited in the text and noted below can be found at the Center.

The Anti-U.S. Resistance War of National Salvation, 1954–1975: Military Events. Translated by Foreign Broadcast Information Service. Joint Publications Research Service 80968. Hanoi: People's Army Publishing House, 1980.

Luc Luong Vu Trang Nhan Dan Tay Nguyen Trong Khang Chien Chong My Cuu Nuoc [The People's Armed Forces of the Western Highlands During the War of National Salvation Against the Americans]. Hanoi: People's Army Publishing House, 1980.

Su Doan Sao Vang (Su Dong 3) Binh Doan Chi Lang Quang Khu 1; Ky Su [Yellow Star Division (3d Division), Chi Lang Military Group, Military Region 1; Memoir]. Hanoi: People's Army Publishing House, 1984.

Su Dong 9 [The 9th Division]. Hanoi: People's Army Publishing House, 1990.

"Tay Ninh Battle." Annex to *South Vietnam: Initial Failure of the U.S. "Limited War,"* pp. 45–54. Hanoi: Foreign Languages Publishing House, 1967.

Thanh, Nguyen Chi. "Ideological Tasks of the Army and People in the South." *Hoc Tap* (July 1966).

Tra, Col. Gen. Tran Van. *Vietnam: History of the Bulwark B2 Theater*, vol. 5, *Concluding the 30-Years War*. Translated by Foreign Broadcast Information Service. Joint Publications Research Service 82783. Southeast Asia Report 1247. Ho Chi Minh City: Van Nghe Publishing House, March 1982.

U.S. Biggest Operation Foiled. Hanoi: Foreign Languages Publishing House, 1967.

Primary Publications

McGarvey, Patrick J., comp. *Visions of Victory: Selected Vietnamese Communist Military Writings, 1964–1968*. Stanford, Calif.: Hoover Institution Publications, 1969.

The Senator Gravel Edition of the Pentagon Papers: The Defense Department History of the United States Decisionmaking on Vietnam. 4 vols. Boston: Beacon Press, 1971.

U.S. Congress, Senate, Committee on Foreign Relations. *The U.S. Government and the Vietnam War: Executive and Legislative Roles and Relationships, Part IV, July 1965–January 1968*. Washington, D.C.: Government Printing Office, 1994.

U.S. Department of Defense Official Histories

Bowers, Ray L. *Tactical Airlift*. The United States Air Force in Southeast Asia. Washington, D.C.: Government Printing Office, 1983.

Clarke, Jeffrey J. *Advice and Support: The Final Years, 1965–1973*. United States Army in Vietnam. Washington, D.C.: U.S. Army Center of Military History, Government Printing Office, 1988.

Schlight, John. *The War in South Vietnam: The Years of the Offensive, 1965–1968*. The United States Air Force in Southeast Asia. Washington, D.C.: Government Printing Office, 1988.

Shore, Capt. Moyers S. II. *The Battle for Khe Sanh*. Washington, D.C.: Headquarters, United States Marine Corps, Historical Branch, G–3 Division, 1969.

Telfer, Maj. Gary L., Rogers, Lt. Col. Lane, and Fleming, V. Keith, Jr. *U.S. Marines in Vietnam: Fighting the North Vietnamese, 1967*. Washington, D.C.: Headquarters, United States Marine Corps, History and Museums Division, 1984.

Memoirs, Firsthand Accounts, and Special Studies

Adams, Sam. *War of Numbers: An Intelligence Memoir*. South Royalton, Vt.: Steerforth Press, 1994.

Albright, John, Cash, John A., and Sandstrum, Allan W. *Seven Firefights in Vietnam*. Washington, D.C.: U.S. Army Center of Military History, 1970.

Allen, Lt. Col. Alfred M. *Skin Diseases in Vietnam, 1965–72*. Internal Medicine in Vietnam. Washington, D.C.: Office of the Surgeon General and U.S. Army Center of Military History, 1977.

Eckhardt, Maj. Gen. George S. *Command and Control, 1950–1969*. Vietnam Studies. Washington, D.C.: Department of the Army, 1974.

Fulton, Maj. Gen. William B. *Riverine Operations, 1966–1969*. Vietnam Studies. Washington, D.C.: Department of the Army, 1973.

Giap, Vo Nguyen. *Big Victory, Great Task*. New York: Frederick A. Praeger, 1968.

Hay, Lt. Gen. John H., Jr. *Tactical and Materiel Innovations*. Vietnam Studies. Washington, D.C.: Department of the Army, 1974.

Larsen, Lt. Gen. Stanley R., and Collins, Brig. Gen. James L., Jr. *Allied Participation in Vietnam*. Vietnam Studies. Washington, D.C.: Department of the Army, 1975.

McChristian, Maj. Gen. Joseph A. *The Role of Military Intelligence, 1965–1967*. Vietnam Studies. Washington, D.C.: Department of the Army, 1974.

Ott, Maj. Gen. David E. *Field Artillery, 1954–1973*. Vietnam Studies. Washington, D.C.: Department of the Army, 1975.

Sharp, Admiral U. S. G., and Westmoreland, General William C. *Report on the War in Vietnam (As of 30 June 1968)*. Washington, D.C.: Government Printing Office, 1968.

Starry, General Donn A. *Mounted Combat in Vietnam*. Vietnam Studies. Washington, D.C.: Department of the Army, 1978.

Taking the Offensive

Tho, Brig. Gen. Tran Dinh. *The Cambodian Incursion*. Indochina Monographs. Washington, D.C.: U.S. Army Center of Military History, 1979.

Tolson, Lt. Gen. John J. *Airmobility, 1961–1971*. Vietnam Studies. Washington, D.C.: Department of the Army, 1973.

Vien, General Cao Van, and Khuyen, Lt. Gen. Dong Van. *Reflections on the Vietnam War*. Indochina Monographs. Washington, D.C.: U.S. Army Center of Military History, 1980.

Westmoreland, William C. *A Soldier Reports*. Garden City, N.Y.: Doubleday & Co., Inc., 1976.

Secondary Publications

Bergerud, Eric M. *The Dynamics of Defeat, The Vietnam War in Hau Nghia Province*. Boulder, Colo.: Westview Press, 1991.

Berman, Larry. *Planning a Tragedy: The Americanization of the War in Vietnam*. New York: W. W. Norton & Co., 1982.

———. *Lyndon Johnson's War*. New York: W. W. Norton & Co., 1989.

Boatner, James G. *American Tactical Units in Revolutionary Development Operations*. Air University Report 3570. Maxwell Air Force Base, Ala.: Air War College, August 1968.

Brewin, Bob, and Shaw, Sydney. *Vietnam on Trial: Westmoreland vs. CBS*. New York: Atheneum, 1987.

Chamberlain, Lt. Col. Edwin W., Jr. "The Assault at Ap Bac." *Army* 18 (August 1968):50–57.

Davidson, Phillip B. *Vietnam at War: The History, 1946–1975*. Novato, Calif.: Presidio Press, 1988.

Duiker, William J. *The Communist Road to Power in Vietnam*. Boulder, Colo.: Westview Press, 1981.

Ezell, Edward C. *Small Arms of the World*. Harrisburg, Pa.: Stackpole Books, 1983.

Fall, Bernard B. *The Two Vietnams: A Political and Military Analysis*. 2d ed. New York: Frederick A. Praeger, 1963.

Halberstam, David. *The Best and the Brightest*. New York: Random House, 1972.

Herring, George C. "The Vietnam War." In *Modern American Diplomacy*, edited by John M. Carroll and George C. Herring, pp. 161–81. Wilmington, Del.: Scholarly Resources, Inc., 1986.

Hunt, Richard A. *Pacification: The American Struggle for Vietnam's Hearts and Minds*. Boulder, Colo.: Westview Press, 1995.

Hymoff, Edward. *Fourth Infantry Division, Vietnam*. New York: M. W. Ladds Publishing Co.

Maclear, Michael. *The Ten Thousand Day War*. New York: St. Martin's Press, 1981.

Marshall, S. L. A. *Bird: The Christmastide Battle*. Nashville, Tenn.: Battery Press, 1968.

Meloy, Maj. Gen. Guy S. "Operation Attleboro: The Wolfhounds' Brave Stand." *Vietnam* 10 (October 1997):39–44.

Meyerson, Harvey. *Vinh Long*. Boston: Houghton Mifflin Co., 1970.

Middleton, Harry. *LBJ: The White House Years*. New York: Harry N. Abrams, 1990.

Murphy, Edward F. *Dak To*. Novato, Calif.: Presidio Press, 1993.

Sidey, Hugh. *A Very Personal Presidency: Lyndon Johnson in the White House*. New York: Atheneum, 1968.

Stanton, Shelby L. *Anatomy of a Division: The 1st Cav in Vietnam*. Novato, Calif.: Presidio Press, 1987.

Thayer, Thomas C. "How To Analyze a War Without Fronts: Vietnam 1965–72." *Journal of Defense Research, Series B: Tactical Warfare, Analysis of Vietnam Data* 7B (Fall 1975):767–943.

———., ed. *A Systems Analysis View of the Vietnam War: 1965–1972*, vol. 5, *The Air War*. Arlington, Va.: Defense Documentation Center, Defense Logistics Agency, c. 1975.

The 25th Infantry Division: "Tropic Lightning" in Vietnam, 1966–1967. Doraville, Ga.: Albert Love Enterprises, 1967.

U.S. Congress, Senate, Committee on Veterans' Affairs. *Medal of Honor Recipients, 1863–1973.* 93d Cong., 1st sess., 1973.

Wheeler, John T. "Company C Fought for Freedom Too . . . in a Nothing Place Called Hill 571 [521]." *Staten Island Sunday Advance,* 2 Jul 67.

Wiesner, Louis A. *Victims and Survivors: Displaced Persons and Other War Victims in Viet-Nam, 1954–1975.* New York: Greenwood Press, 1988.

Military Map Symbols

Military Units—Identification

Airborne Infantry . . . .

Airmobile Infantry . . . .

Armor . . . .

Armored Cavalry . . . .

Field Artillery . . . .

Infantry . . . .

Marines . . . .

Mechanized Infantry . . . .

Size Symbols

Platoon . . . .   •••

Company or Armored Cavalry Troop   I

Battalion or Armored Cavalry Squadron   II

Regiment   III

Brigade   X

Division   XX

Corps   XXX

Examples

Company C, 2d Battalion, 27th Infantry . . . . . .   C [⊠] 2-27

3d Brigade, 1st Cavalry Division (Airmobile) . . . .   3 [⊠] 1

Boundary between 1st and 25th Infantry Divisions . .   ——— XX ———

Headquarters, 1st Infantry Division . . . .   [⊠] 1

Cultural Feature

Airfield . . . . ⊘

Geographic Terms

Ap	Hamlet
Cua	Channel, river mouth
Dam	Lake, marsh
Ia	River
Kinh	Canal
Nui	Mountain
Prek	Stream
Rach	Stream
Song	River
Suoi	Stream
Xa	Village

Acronyms and Abbreviations

ARVN	Army of the Republic of Vietnam
COSVN	Central Office for South Vietnam
CTZ	Corps tactical zone
FF	Field Force
FSB	Fire support base, firebase
FWD	Forward
LZ	Landing zone
MAF	Marine Amphibious Force
PAVN	People's Army of Vietnam
PLAF	People's Liberation Armed Forces
RCN	Reconnaissance
RGR	Ranger
ROK	Republic of Korea
TF	Task force

Index

Giai, Brig. Gen. Do Ke: 383, 384
Giap, General Vo Nguyen: 17, 18, 439
Ginsburgh, Col. Robert N.: 26
Gio Linh. *See* Bases, U.S. Marine Corps.
Go Cong Province: 420
Granger, Lt. Col. Clinton E.: 172, 173–74,
    232–33, 235, 239, 240, 241
Green Berets. *See* Special Forces, U.S. Army.
Grenade launchers
    40-mm., ship-mounted: 405–06
    M79: 15, 295, 302
Grenades: 274, 275, 276, 356
    captured enemy: 50, 58, 132, 376, 388–89,
        425
    enemy use against tanks: 290–91
    fragmentation: 15
    RPG2 rocket-propelled: 21, 127–29, 131,
        132, 142–43, 296, 343, 368, 374, 400, 435
    smoke: 15, 16, 50, 180, 305, 360
    with trip wires: 231
    white phosphorous: 177
Grimsley, Col. James A.: 133, 135, 138, 139
Guam: 16
Gulf of Thailand: 62

Ha Tay: 279–81
Habib, Philip C.: 440
Hai Van Pass: 264
Haig, Lt. Col. Alexander M.: 100, 138–39
Hamlet Evaluation System (HES): 192,
    221–22, 378, 389, 401, 436
Hamlets
    destruction of: 96–97, 314–15, 370
    fortified by Viet Cong: 233, 235
    "New Life": 400
Hau Nghia Province: 31, 114, 145, 148–50,
    153, 369, 374–75, 376, 378, 423
Hay, Maj. Gen. John H.: 114–15, 117, 123,
    127, 133, 138, 145–46, 334–35, 339, 342,
    343, 347–48, 349–50, 352–53, 361
Heintges, Lt. Gen. John A.: 42
Helicopters
    CH–47 Chinook: 17, 37, 80, 85, 183, 210,
        433
    command: 305–06, 355, 359–60, 386
    damaged in enemy attacks on bases:
        183–84, 257, 268–69, 367
    damaged as they landed: 129, 169, 173
    flight decks for, on command and control
        boats: 411

Helicopters—*Continued*
    gunships: 9, 85, 90–91, 101, 102–03, 118,
        121, 157, 160–61, 172, 185–87, 188,
        199–200, 239, 250, 275–76, 278, 279, 280,
        294, 296, 300, 306–07, 309, 320, 342–43,
        345, 346, 352, 375, 382, 384, 386, 399,
        400, 404, 419, 421, 425, 426
    heavy-lift: 17
    light observation: 17
    limited availability of, to U.S. Marine
        Corps: 209, 255, 275
    maintenance for: 97
    night hunter teams: 199–200
    numbers of, in Vietnam: 17, 85, 433
    scout: 85, 167
    shortages of: 17, 37, 97–98, 209, 210, 403,
        430, 433
    shot down: 55, 73, 89, 186–87, 251, 272,
        318
    UH–1 Iroquois, or Huey: 17, 55, 73, 85,
        90–91, 100, 102–03, 118, 129, 169, 173,
        199, 210, 251, 295, 318, 360, 399, 425, 433
    use of, affected by weather: 87–88
    used for medical evacuation: 200, 275,
        276, 335–36, 360–61, 419
    used for resupply: 9, 85, 183, 212–13, 200,
        349
    used in support of South Vietnamese
        forces: 200
    used to transport engineer equipment: 211
    used to transport troops: 9, 44, 47, 55, 63,
        73, 80–81, 85, 100, 102–03, 115–16, 118,
        124, 129, 169, 172, 173, 185–87, 210, 239,
        293, 294–95, 296, 318, 335–36, 376, 403,
        406–08, 418, 422–23, 426, 433
    weaponry on: 85, 199–200
Helms, Richard M.: 438
Herbicides: 238, 281
Hiep Duc: 270–71, 272, 274–75
Hieu Nhon District: 263
Hieu Xuong: 313–14
Highways
    1: 52*n*, 77, 80, 83, 147–48, 181, 183, 185,
        186, 196, 205, 229, 232–33, 235, 242–43,
        246–47, 259, 263, 269–70, 276–77, 279,
        281, 318, 321–22, 328–29, 369, 373,
        379–80, 385–86
    4: 150, 393, 395, 397–400, 401–02, 403, 406,
        421, 424
    9: 19, 218, 257, 262, 264

ISBN 0-16-049540-7

9 780160 495403

90000

PIN : 076472-000